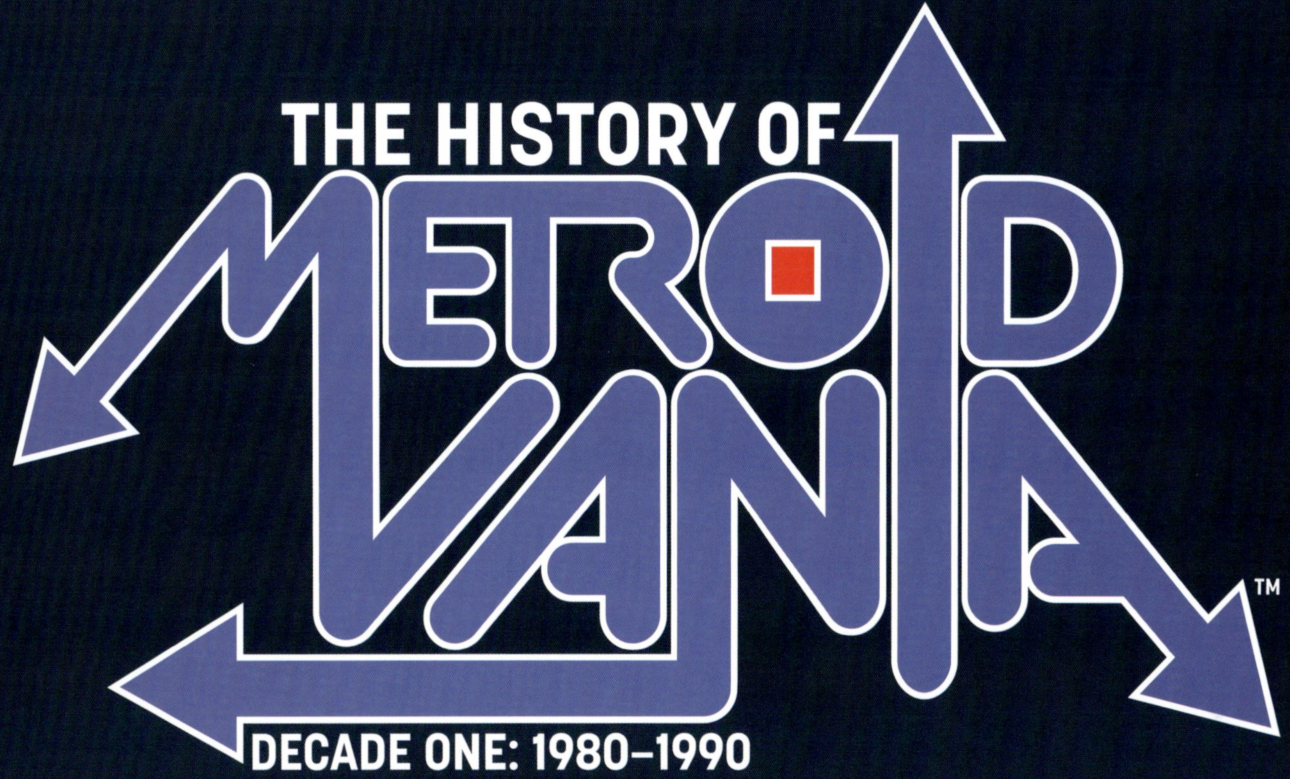

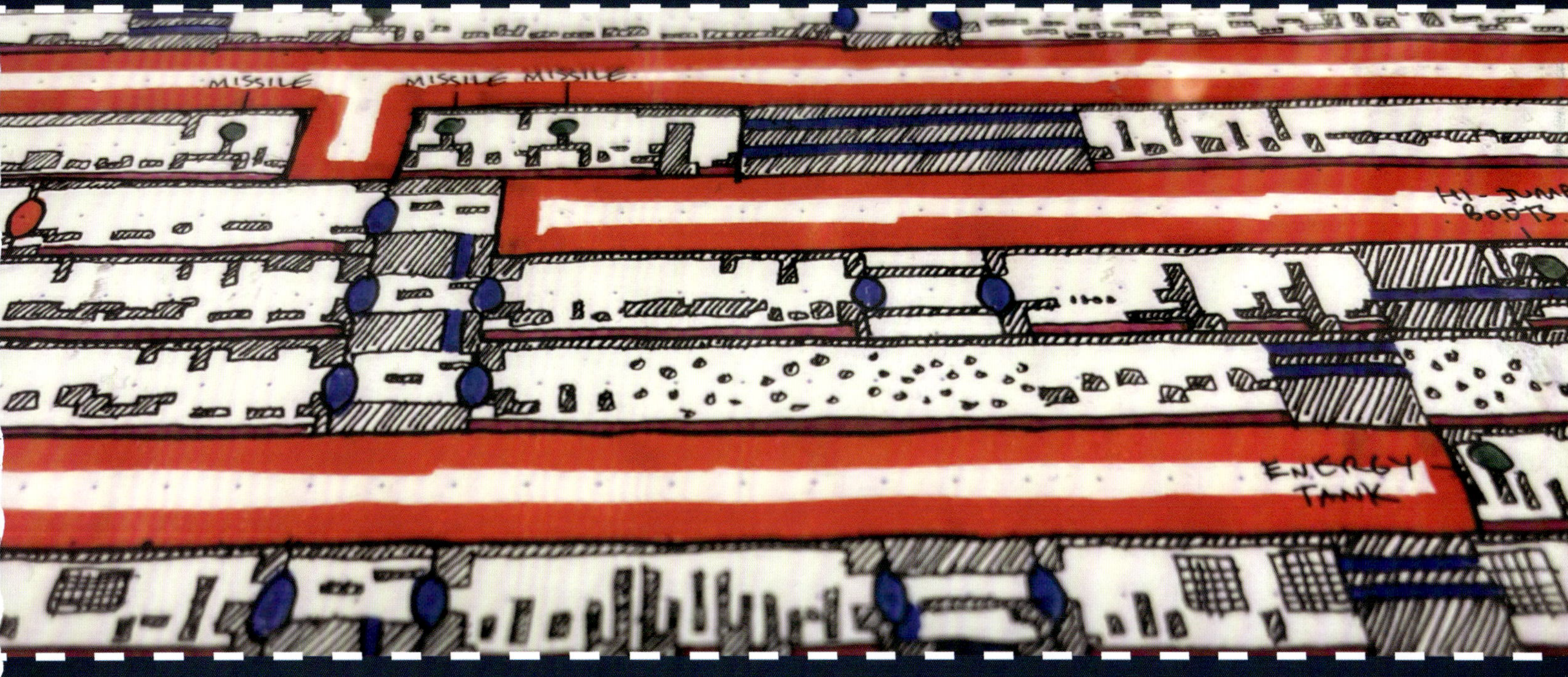

A chronological journey through gaming's least linear format: the action-RPG.

Exploring the first decade of inspirations and evolutions behind the metroidvania genre from Z to A (*Zork* to *A Boy and His Blob*).

By Jeremy Parish

LIMITED RUN

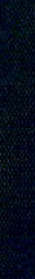

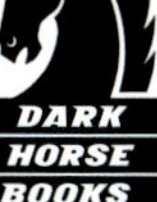

DARK HORSE BOOKS

THE HISTORY OF METROIDVANIA: DECADE ONE—1980-1990

By Jeremy Parish

DARK HORSE BOOKS

President and Publisher
Mike Richardson

Editor
Patrick Thorpe

Assistant Editor
Tara McCarron

Additional Design
Rex Xie and May Hijikuro

Digital Art Technician
AJ Newell

Prepress Technician
Maureen Heaster

Special thanks to Rachel Lapidow and all Video Works patrons

Text, layout, and images by Jeremy Parish

Based on the YouTube video series Metroidvania Works, née Metroidvania Chronicles

Published by Dark Horse Books
A division of Dark Horse Comics LLC
10956 SE Main Street, Milwaukie, OR 97222

Represented in the EU by Authorised Rep Compliance Ltd.
Ground Floor, 71 Lower Baggot Street
Dublin, D02 P593, Ireland
ARCCompliance.com

DarkHorse.com
To find a comics shop in your area, visit ComicShopLocator.com.

First edition: March 2026
Ebook ISBN: 978-1-50675-453-6
Hardcover ISBN: 978-1-50675-454-3

1 3 5 7 9 10 8 6 4 2
Printed in China

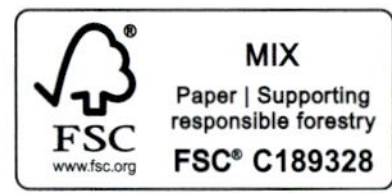

Previous page: A detail of a hand-drawn map of Nintendo's *Metroid*, illustrated by the author.

FOREWORD: IT'S NOT MY FAULT

Listen: I did not come up with the word "metroidvania." I accept no responsibility for the pervasive nature of the word in these modern times. Someone else made up the word, and I'm pretty sure I wasn't the first to start tossing it around to describe any and every nonlinear, exploration-based platform action-adventure game. It's just a coincidence that I happen to be the owner of the *metroidvania.com* domain name and that my name appears prominently in places like Wikipedia's Metroidvania entry or on Reddit's dedicated subreddit, *r/metroidvania*. Who can account for the myriad mysteries of the internet, really?

Rather than pointing fingers before we even get to the main text, we should begin by defining what "metroidvania" actually means. On one hand, the word practically belongs on a Rorschach test at this point. For some people, it exclusively means the games that originally summoned the word into existence more than two decades ago: Portable *Castlevania* games whose design and user interface call to mind Nintendo's *Metroid* series. *Et voila*: Metroidvania. For others, it has a more fluid definition. It may mean any 2D game that has a nonlinear structure. Maybe it needs to involve some sort of numeric statistics-oriented system derived from role-playing games. Maybe it has to feature some particular mechanical trait, such as a contiguous world design, which would rule out a game like *Clash at Demonhead*, whose fully interconnected world consists of a series of standalone "routes" rather than allowing players to roam from one end of the world to another without shifting visual format. Maybe it demands players empower their characters by collecting permanent upgrades and tools. Or maybe it's just a nebulous catch-all that can even encompass 3D games that involve some degree of backtracking, like *Batman: Arkham Asylum* or *Dark Souls II*. On the other hand, maybe it's just a stupid non-word whose only purpose is to send internet prescriptivists into an apoplectic tizzy and write embittered social media posts wishing ill on me for inventing it. (Did I mention that I did not come up with the word Metroidvania? I feel that point merits repeating.)

So, with that out of the way, let's talk about what the word Metroidvania means in the context of this particular book, *Metroidvania: The First Decade*. Well. Truth be told, the entire point of this book is about figuring that out. Or rather, it's about tracing the origins of the games that *do* fall under the term's umbrella, whether *Arkham Asylum* or *Castlevania: Aria of Sorrow*. I should stress here and now that none of those games actually appear in this volume. In fact, this book doesn't even cover the first games that could arguably qualify as proper takes on the broad definition of "Metroidvania," *Super Metroid* and *Castlevania: Symphony of the Night*.

No, those are for future volumes; I envision this *Metroidvania* book project as a three-volume series (assuming people choose to pick up this one to justify follow-ups). This trilogy will be a long, leisurely stroll through video game history, and this first volume encompasses the 1980s. Rather than documenting the robust, latter-day Metroidvania efforts in this first volume, I hope instead to touch on the seminal works that culminated in the Metroidvania genre (as it were). That includes creative dead-ends and forgotten efforts, and it also encompasses key adventure games and RPGs. After all, *Symphony of the Night* director Koji Igarashi has stated that he took more influence for the design and structure of that game from *The Legend of Zelda: A Link to the Past* then he did from the *Metroid* series. And that means you can't establish a proper understanding of what it means to be a Metroidvania without also dissecting the games that built up to that third entry in the *Zelda* franchise.

Again, the "decade" in question for *Metroidvania: The First Decade* is the 1980s, working from the technical definition of decade. Which is to say, 1981–1990. An era of rapid and radical video game hardware and software evolution, which you can see here as the chronology begins with *Zork* (a text-based adventure game) and wraps with *Metal Gear 2: Solid Snake* (arguably the most refined and sophisticated work ever to appear on an 8-bit gaming platform). In between, you'll find forgotten innovators like *Exile* (both of 'em), cult favorites like *The Guardian Legend*, and all-time classics like *Pitfall!* and *The Legend of Zelda*. Metroidvania—or at least this collection of proto-Metroidvania works—contains multitudes.

No, I did not invent the word Metroidvania. But I wish I had.

Jeremy Parish
March 2025

CONTENTS

PROLOGUE

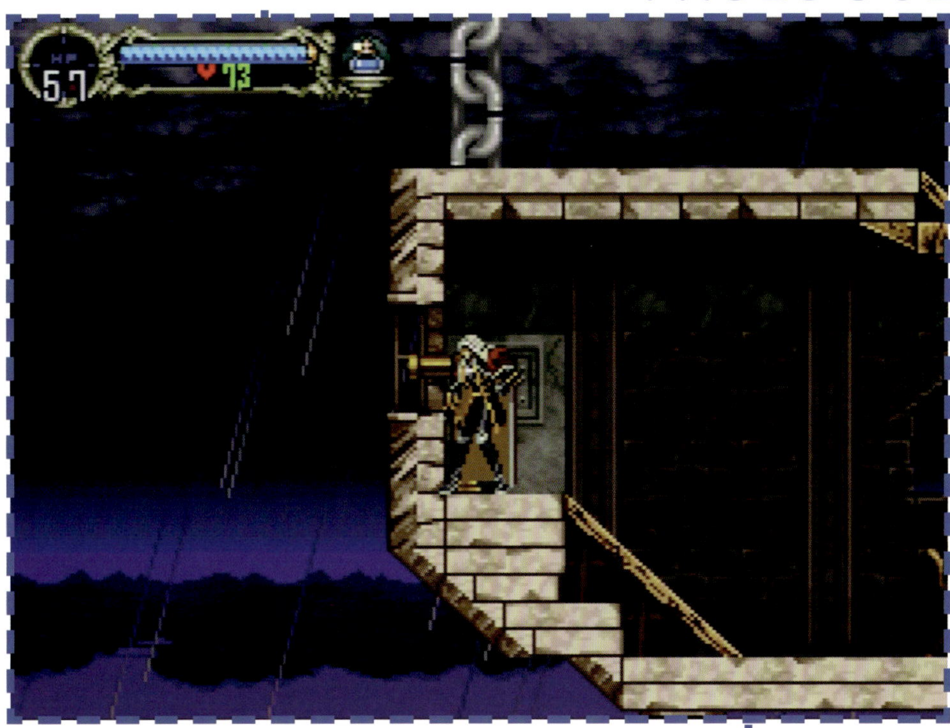

The game pictured above is *Castlevania: Symphony of the Night*. Many people consider it one of the greatest video games ever made. It is the definitive example of a metroidvania game. The player controls their character, Alucard, as if he were part of an action game, but he also benefits from permanent character upgrades—new skills, greater strength, improved weapons and armor—as he progresses through his adventure. And that progression doesn't happen in the traditional video game sense, where players complete one stage and move along to another, never looking back. Alucard has to traverse his father's castle methodically, combing its corridors in search of the tools he needs to open up new areas.

This is the heart of the metroidvania concept: traversing a virtual world while gathering the strength and items you need to further expand your ability to explore. Metroidvanias combine the essence of three different established video game genres:

- Adventure games
- Role-playing games
- Action games

How did these very different game styles come together to create the likes of *Symphony of the Night*? And how have other games built on *Symphony*'s concepts to further expand the definition of metroidvania? This is the question at the heart of this book and the (hopefully) two volumes due to follow in a few years. Evolution is always a messy process; that holds true for metroidvania evolution every bit as much as it did the sequence of events that turned tyrannosaurs into parrots (though, fingers crossed, with fewer extinction-level catastrophes). *The History of Metroidvania* doesn't only concern itself with side-scrolling action games that have role-playing hooks; it also dwells on role-playing, adventure, and action-RPG games and the way those formats developed over time and eventually converged to give us the metroidvania. Because this volume in particular addresses the metroidvania's "prehistory," there's a heavy focus on action games with RPG elements as well as action-RPGs. These are not the same thing, somehow.

In any case, it's curiously fitting that this text begins with a game consisting entirely of text.

METROIDVANIA TIMELINE

1980 AND BEFORE

By most measures, the world's first video game dates back to 1962. *Spacewar!* was created by a bunch of model railroad aficionados. Although this may not sound the most likely candidates to create an entire medium, bear in mind that these particular toy train fanatics belonged to a club at Massachusetts Institute of Technology dedicated to exploring the extremes of the hobby. They used their electric engineering know-how to build elaborate mechanical systems with which to control their miniature trains and the scale model environments that surrounded them. That is to say: they applied sophisticated engineering skills to the concept of play. If that's not a DNA-level description of video games, what is?

Spacewar! was very different from the commercial products it inspired. For one thing, it was created as a collaborative venture. Once it creators laid the foundation of the game—a pair of spaceships attempting to gun each other down in the inky void of the cosmos—fans of the game began contributing their own embellishments to the code. Most of these additions had little to do with the spaceships but rather the universe around them. Add-on *Spacewar!* modules incorporated highly accurate star fields and a central gravity well that affected the ships' movements to the screen.

In a way, this means that the spirit of the metroidvania genre defined gaming right from the start. Once *Spacewar!*'s contributors figured out the mechanics of shooting, they began thinking about the world in which the shooting took place. Then, they began to explore how the player's actions could interact with that world. The first "true" metroidvania—*Castlevania: Symphony of the Night*—made its debut in 1997, exactly 35 years after *Spacewar!* first distracted MIT grad students from their dissertations. And yet, the through line between tiny ships sniping at one another and the son of Dracula trying to put a stop to his father's ambitions is more direct than you might imagine. The ships in *Spacewar!* used the stars to track their movements as they maneuvered around the sun; Alucard unraveled the convolutions of his father's castle in order to face him down. Video games have *always* expected players to pay attention to virtual worlds. Metroidvania games simply make that their central hook.

Video games were slow to develop in the wake of *Spacewar!*, mainly because computers cost millions of dollars and only showed up in military labs and college campuses. But by the 1970s, video games began to enter the larger world via several vectors. Arcade games appeared, distributed through existing vending networks for location-based amusement like pinball and jukeboxes. Home games appeared through purpose-built devices that inexpensively recreated arcade experiences, first in dedicated machines and, later, through consoles that accepted interchangeable cartridges. And home computers made their first appearance, reaching millions of families and putting electronic games within reach of the average consumer. The big academic mainframes evolved, too, manifesting in networked systems like PLATO (Programmed Logic for Automatic Teaching Operations), which ended up serving as home to some of the most groundbreaking video games of all time—games that would go on to establish the baseline for numerous genres.

With so many different avenues becoming available, it didn't take long before the medium at large figured out the basics—how should video games play?—and began focusing on the player's relationship to the world. By 1980, the principles of exploration and survival that define metroidvanias and action-RPGs were set. *M*

TIMELINE OF EVENTS:

1962

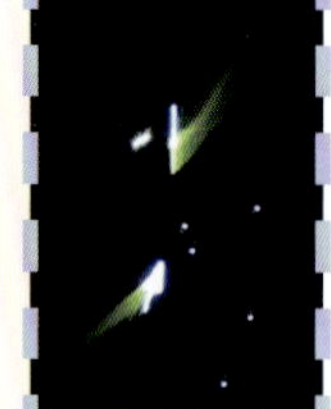

Spacewar!
The first video game, the point where it all began. *Spacewar!* didn't have much to do with metroidvanias and action-RPGs, but where would we be without it?

1972

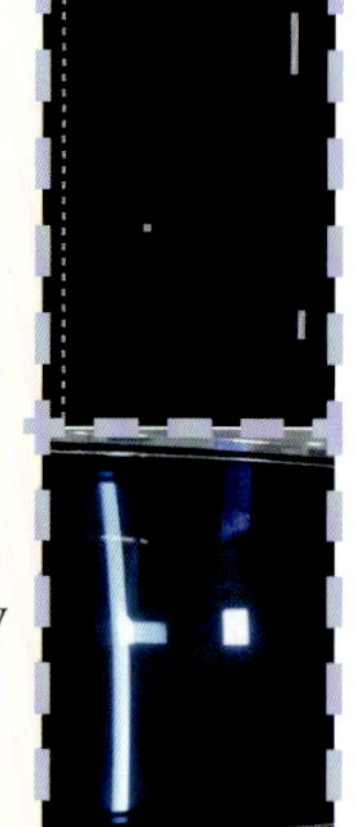

Pong
Gaming's first commercial hit, this simple, competitive coin-op take on table tennis introduced the public to the concept of computer gaming, and helped establish a new medium.

Magnavox Odyssey
The first home video game system, the Odyssey contained several rudimentary games that relied on screen overlays and circuit jumpers to operate. Clumsy, but a revolution all the same.

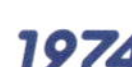

1974

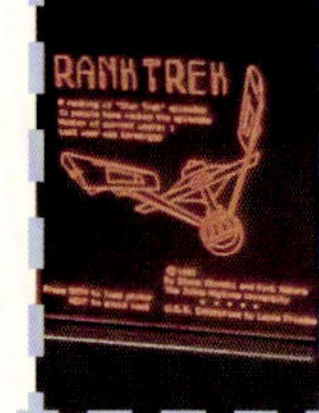

PLATO
This networked computer platform put mainframe power in the hands of students. Naturally, they used it to make games, inventing multiple genres (including RPGs) in the process.

1975

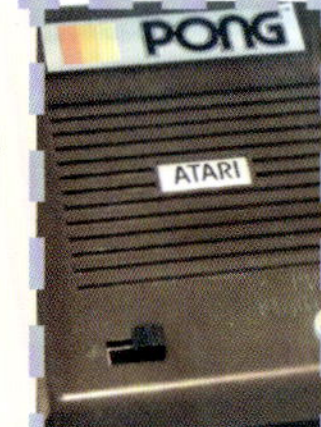

Home Pong
Atari brought home their arcade smash in the form of a low-cost TV-based device dedicated to playing *Pong* and nothing but *Pong*. Within a year, the market was flooded with knockoffs.

METROIDVANIA LANDMARKS AND GAME INDUSTRY MILESTONES

1976

Colossal Cave Adventure
Originally designed as an exercise in virtually mapping a real cave network, the gamification of this project laid the groundwork for exploratory games… metroidvanias, for example.

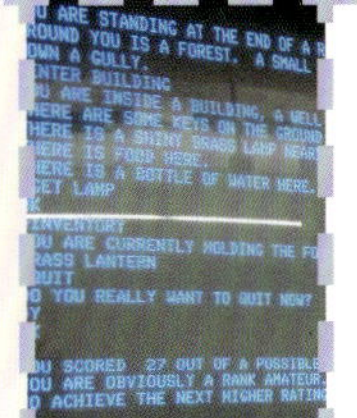

1977

Apple II
While not the first home computer, it was the first to have a meaningful impact. The massive reach of the Apple II made it a key platform for game design for more than a decade.

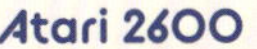

Atari 2600
Breaking from the *Pong*-style dedicated console in favor of interchangeable cartridges, this popular system became the foundation of an industry and the template for home games.

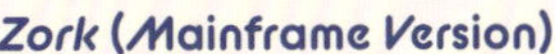

Zork (Mainframe Version)
The earliest version of *Zork* came into existence sometime in 1977 as a collaborative mainframe-based project. It would be broken into two parts for its commercial release.

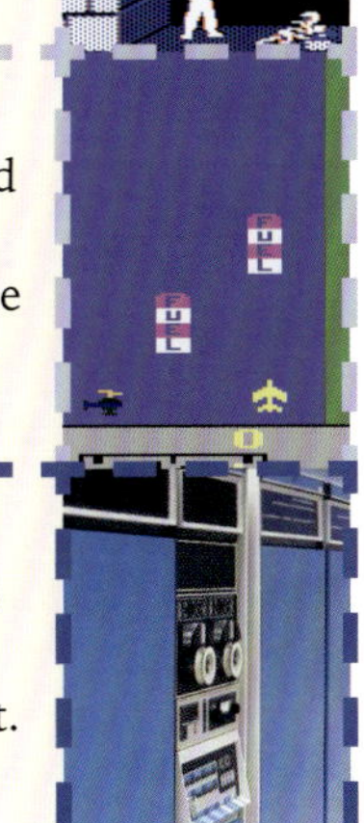

1978

Space Invaders
The tremendous success of Taito's coin-op shooter marks the point in time that the Japanese game industry heralds as its true beginning.

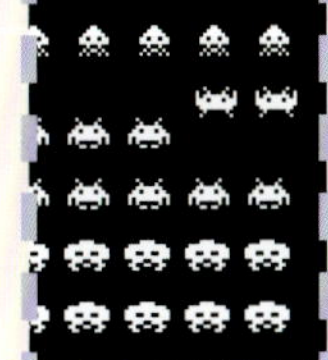

1979

Atari 8-Bit Computers
A low-cost alternative to the Apple II line, the family of Atari home computers had no relationship to the 2600 console but would prove every bit as fertile a ground for game design.

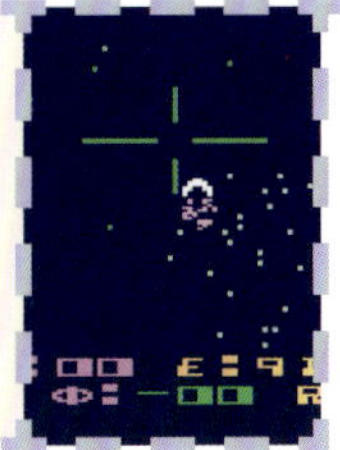

1980

Adventure
How do you make an RPG work on a console with a single-button joystick? You pare it down to the essentials: a hero, a maze, various monsters, some tokens, and a few simple objectives.

Mystery House
Developer Sierra On-Line added a graphical component to the text adventure, allowing players to parse the environment visually rather than merely imagining it.

Game & Watch
Nintendo enjoyed a global hit with this line of LCD devices that established the company's template for success: using cheap, common components in fun, inventive ways.

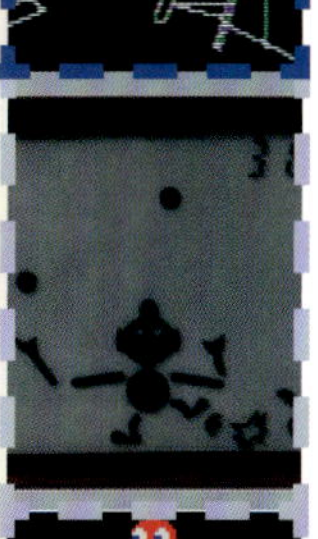

Pac-Man
This iconic maze-action hit became a global phenomenon, racking up earnings not only as a game but also through a cottage industry of licensed toys, foods, and media spin-offs.

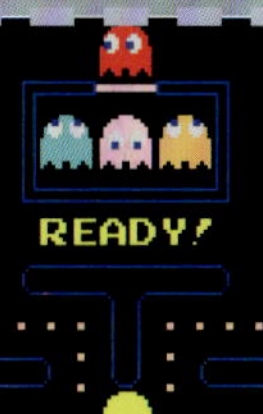

Rally-X
Pac-Man's sibling release combined maze-chasing action with race cars. It influenced metroidvania design with its real-time map that tracked the player, their enemies, and their objectives.

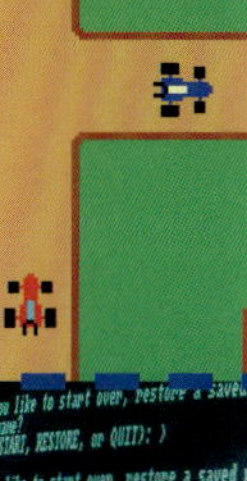

Zork I
The commercial release of *Zork* brought the adventure to the masses. Due to the limitations of home computers, it only contained half of the original mainframe release.

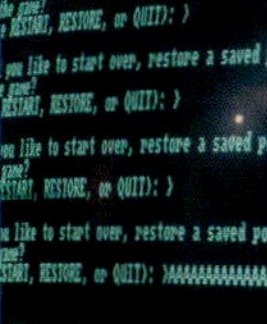

NOTABLE FOR: **CREATING A PERSISTENT SPACE THAT DEMANDED EXPLORATION AND MAPPING**

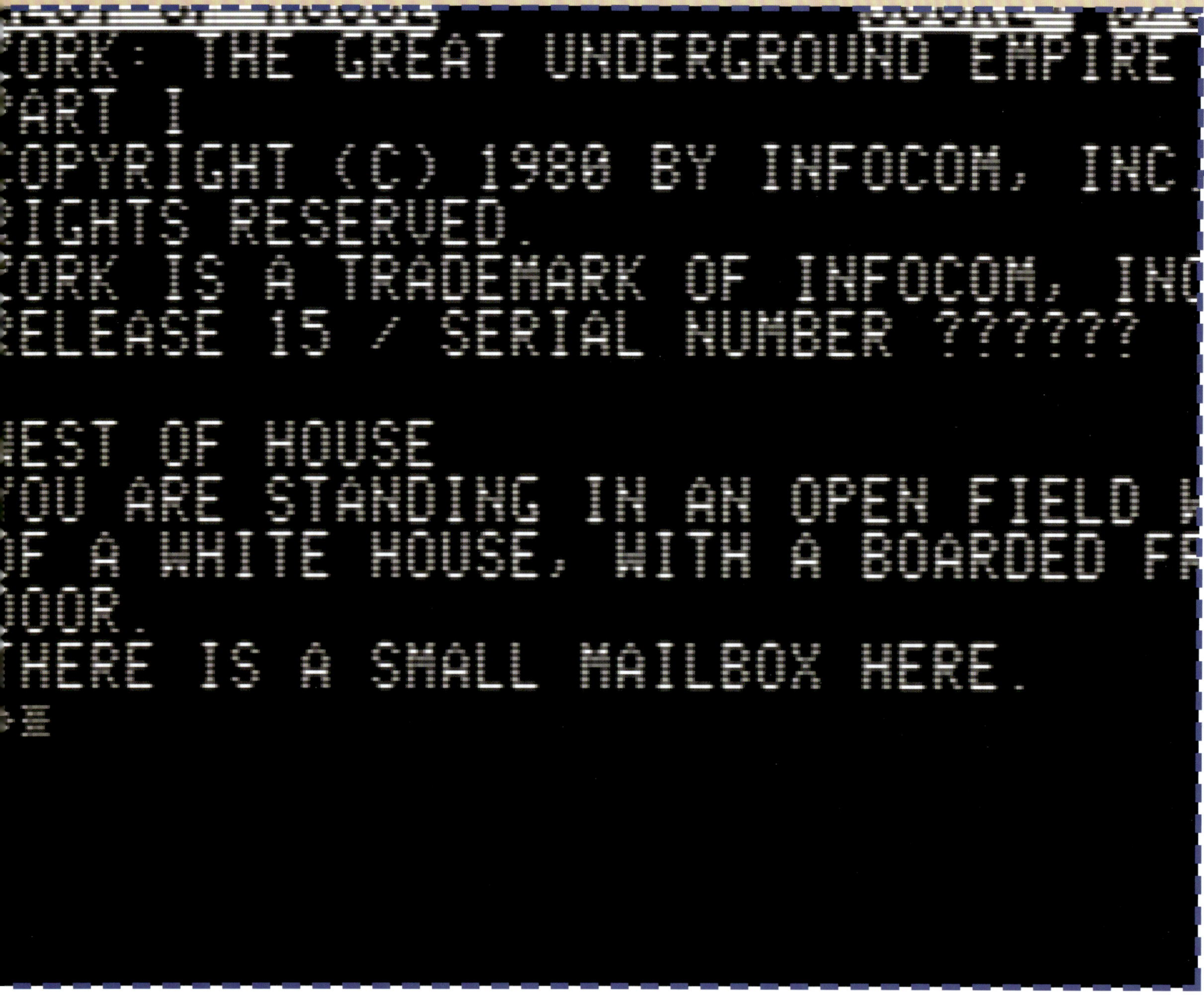

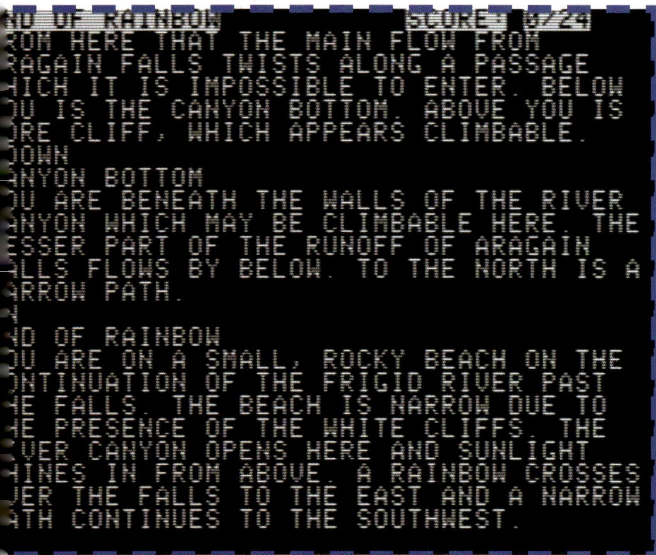

ZORK I:
THE GREAT UNDERGROUND EMPIRE

PLATFORM: **MAINFRAME AND PERSONAL COMPUTERS**
DEV: **INFOCOM** | PUB: **INFOCOM**
INITIAL RELEASE: **1977 / DEC. 1980**

GREAT UNDERGROUND IMPERIAL ORIGINS

Every story has a beginning, and every author has to drop a pin somewhere on the map of history and proclaim, "Here's where it all starts." For the story of the metroidvania subgenre, that map pin bears the name *Zork*. On its surface, *Zork* bears almost zero resemblance to the kind of game you usually find under the metroidvania header. It involves no platform jumping, no real combat—no action at all, in fact. You don't kill monsters to gain levels, and you don't equip progressively better gear to strengthen your protagonist. There's certainly no auto-map. Basically, none of the features that normally go to make up the word "metroidvania" have any place here.

That is, with one exception. A lone exception that sits at the very core of the metroidvania concept even more so than the 2D barrel-hopping of *Donkey Kong* or the shooting platform action of *Ghosts 'N Goblins*: the adventure game genre got its proper start here with this text-driven trip into an underground empire. *Zork* sends players wandering through caverns abandoned to time and forgotten by all but a handful of monsters (and one annoyingly persistent thief). At the time of *Zork*'s inception, no such designation or genre as "adventure games" even existed. The game's creators, a group of programmers from MIT, had originally set out to create a video role-playing game, not an adventure. In a sense, they succeeded.

Zork stands apart from other early computer RPGs due to its creators' focus. Most computerized takes on the RPG in the 1970s and '80s (and, for that matter, now) revolved around the statistical elements of role-playing: experience points; gear attributes; and random, abstracted dice roll values. The ur-RPG, *Dungeons & Dragons*, evolved from miniature war games along the lines of *Warhammer*. When the genre made the transition to computers… well, you know, computers can't tell stories, but they are really good at numbers. A random number generator works just as well as dice. And it's so much less trouble to program all those complex

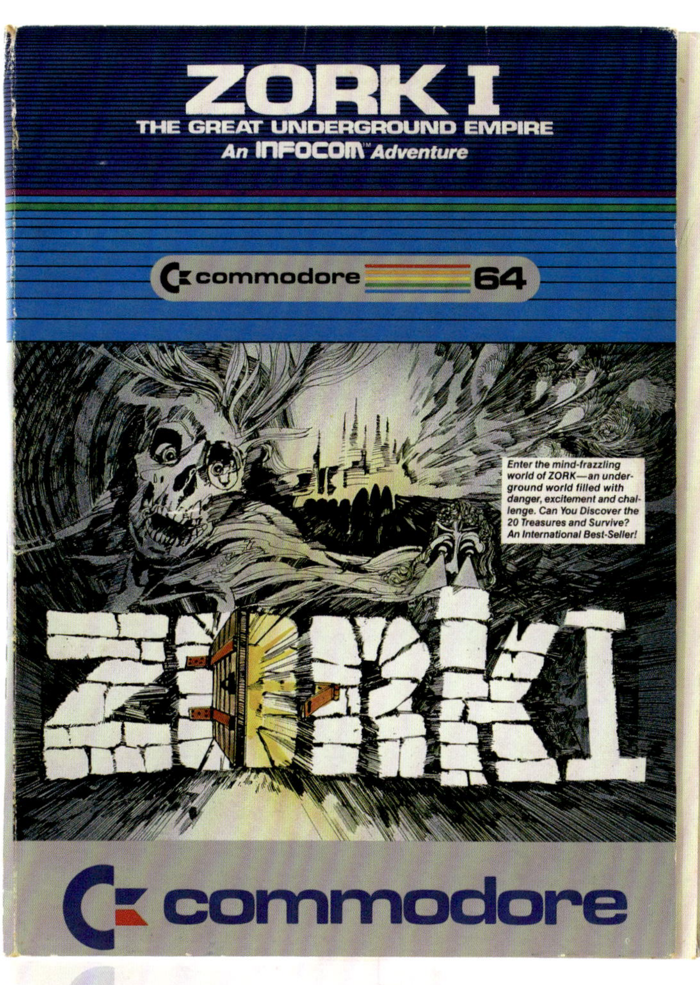

FOREST SCORE: 30/177
SCRATCHES (PERHAPS MADE BY AN AXE) MAR THE WALLS.
A NASTY-LOOKING TROLL, BRANDISHING A BLOODY AXE, BLOCKS ALL PASSAGES OUT OF THE ROOM.
YOUR SWORD HAS BEGUN TO GLOW VERY BRIGHTLY.
THE FLAT OF THE TROLL'S AXE HITS YOU DELICATELY ON THE HEAD, KNOCKING YOU OUT.
CONQUERING HIS FEARS, THE TROLL PUTS YOU TO DEATH.
IT APPEARS THAT THAT LAST BLOW WAS TOO MUCH FOR YOU. I'M AFRAID YOU ARE DEAD.

**** YOU HAVE DIED ****

NOW, LET'S TAKE A LOOK HERE... WELL, YOU PROBABLY DESERVE ANOTHER CHANCE. I CAN'T QUITE FIX YOU UP COMPLETELY, BUT YOU CAN'T HAVE EVERYTHING.
FOREST
>

STUDIO SCORE: 40/161
SOUTH END OF THE ROOM IS AN OPEN DOOR (ALSO COVERED WITH PAINT). AN EXTREMELY DARK AND NARROW CHIMNEY LEADS UP FROM A FIREPLACE; ALTHOUGH YOU MIGHT BE ABLE TO GET UP IT, IT SEEMS UNLIKELY YOU COULD GET BACK DOWN.
LOOSELY ATTACHED TO A WALL IS A SMALL PIECE OF PAPER.
>READ PAPER

CONGRATULATIONS!
YOU ARE THE PRIVILEGED OWNER OF A GENUINE ZORK GREAT UNDERGROUND EMPIRE (PART I), A SELF CONTAINED AND SELF MAINTAINING UNIVERSE. IF USED AND MAINTAINED IN ACCORDANCE WITH NORMAL OPERATING PRACTICES FOR SMALL UNIVERSES, ZORK WILL PROVIDE MANY MONTHS OF TROUBLE-FREE OPERATION. PLEASE CHECK WITH YOUR DEALER FOR PART II AND OTHER ALTERNATE UNIVERSES.
>

conditional rules and combat modifiers than it is to commit them to memory! Thus, the computer RPG became an exercise in designing systems and processes, an excuse for combat and stat growth. Yet numbers ultimately comprise only half of the full RPG experience—maybe less than that, really, if you really want to get to the heart of what role-playing truly means. A great RPG session turns on the art of storytelling; it lives and dies by the skills of its narrator. Will the game master send a group of friends through a combat meat grinder, or will they regale the party with an intricately constructed tale?

The problem with computers is that for all their skill with numbers, they're not very flexible and lack any real spark of invention. Even if you believe the present-day hype about artificial intelligence, computers ultimately can only recompile existing data or churn through the text it's fed. So, what happens when your party wanders off in a weird direction that the game master never accounted for? A talented GM will improvise and come up with something new, maybe something even better than what they'd originally intended. A computer will either churn out filler or simply give an error message before forcing you back on track.

Zork's authors—Bruce Daniels, Dave Lebling, Marc Blank, and Tim Anderson—aimed to solve that question by creating an interactive text parser that could divine a player's intent and respond with natural language. Of course, what they came up with was a matter of simple conditional statements, but it felt convincing enough to work. *Zork* was no match for ELIZA, the natural language processing computer from the '60s, but it was sarcastic, descriptive, and adaptive. It painted pictures with words, gave players enticing clues, and let them figure out the world around them. It could remember what players had acquired, what they had done in the world, and what challenges they'd overcome. And, if players said something improper, it would respond with a chiding or even mocking remark.

However, it's the world of *Zork* that matters most for our purposes. While *Zork* plays nothing at all like a metroidvania game in the "2D action platformer" sense, what those four geniuses at MIT created was, for all intents and purposes, gaming's first nonlinear, persistent world that gated player progression by means of exploration and the application of tools. The workings of *Zork* don't map directly onto something like *Castlevania: Symphony of the Night*; some obstacles in the underground empire work more as riddles than as tests of how effectively you've gathered and utilized equipment. For instance, no item will allow you to bypass the cyclops; instead, you simply need to figure out (somehow) that you need to speak the word "Ulysses" to get past him. In other areas, though, your advancement hinges upon determining how your collected items can be put to use to grant you access to new places. Need to descend a high, steep rise? Maybe that rope will do the trick. Need to get down a river? Well, you may have found a pump and a pile of plastic. What happens if you combine the two? And doesn't that shovel seem like it would be good for digging in the sand?

Zork works best when it combines puzzle-solving with your inventory—like any good adventure game, really. Can't figure out how to open the locked treasure egg without shattering it? Perhaps you should give it to someone whose vocation suggests they might be adept at picking locks.

Like most games of its vintage, *Zork* does occasionally rely on unintuitive solutions and sometimes even pure guesswork. Particularly annoying is the thief, whom you need for certain solutions (like opening the treasure egg) but who has the potential to completely ruin your game if he randomly steals the wrong item or lucks into surviving your confrontation with him.

But, you know, those are the breaks with pioneering works. *Zork*'s fundamental innovations made it one of the most influential games of all time; even people who have never even heard of it draw on the concepts and mechanics it inspired. Of course, *Zork* had its own predecessors. Besides *D&D*, its creators also looked for inspiration to earlier works like William Crowther's *Colossal Cave Adventure*, a.k.a. *ADVENT*. *Zork*'s creators drew heavily on that game's cavernous structures and text-based parser when building their own world.

Still, *Zork* is where I've chosen to draw a line in the sand as the starting point for this particular historiography, simply because the contiguous world contained in the ruins of its Great Underground Empire was so much more intricate and persistent than the real-world caves mimicked by *ADVENT*. Solving *Zork* relied far more on player ingenuity and the creative application of tools and equipment, as well. There was even that meager little bit of combat with the wandering thief, which involved knowing your opponent's weak point—namely, greed. While limited in many ways, and by no means an action-adventure game, *Zork* introduced a number of fundamental concepts that would become integral to the oddball little subgenre we call "metroidvania."

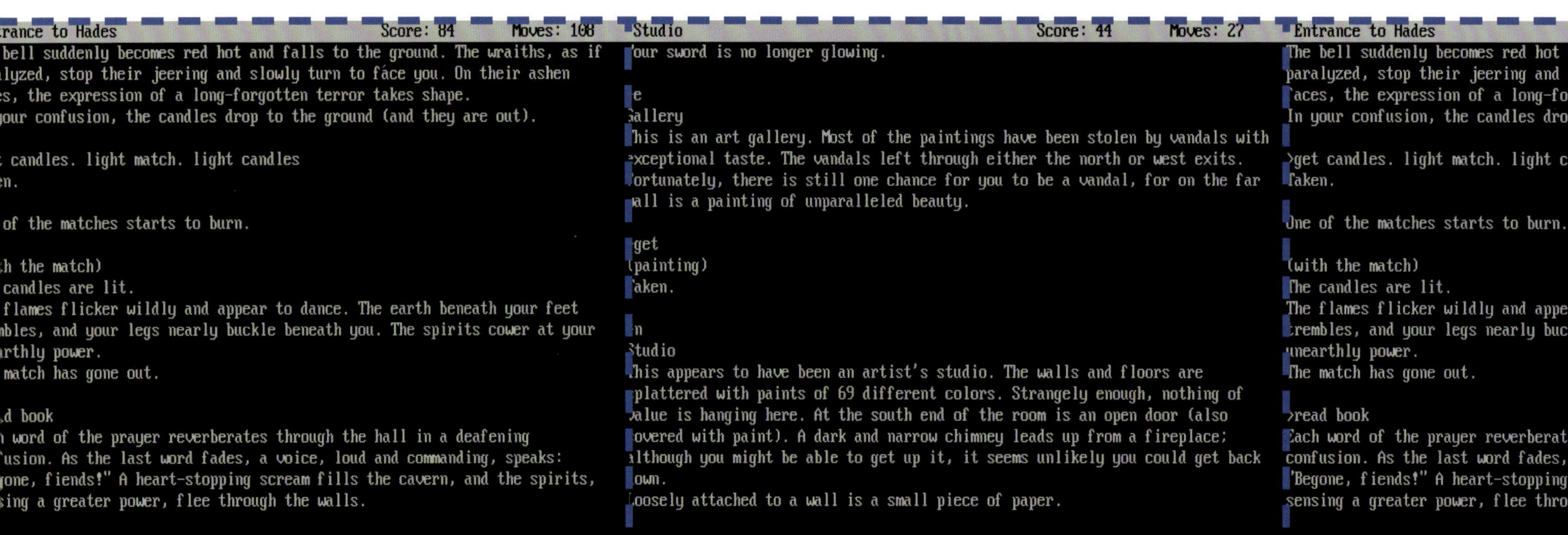

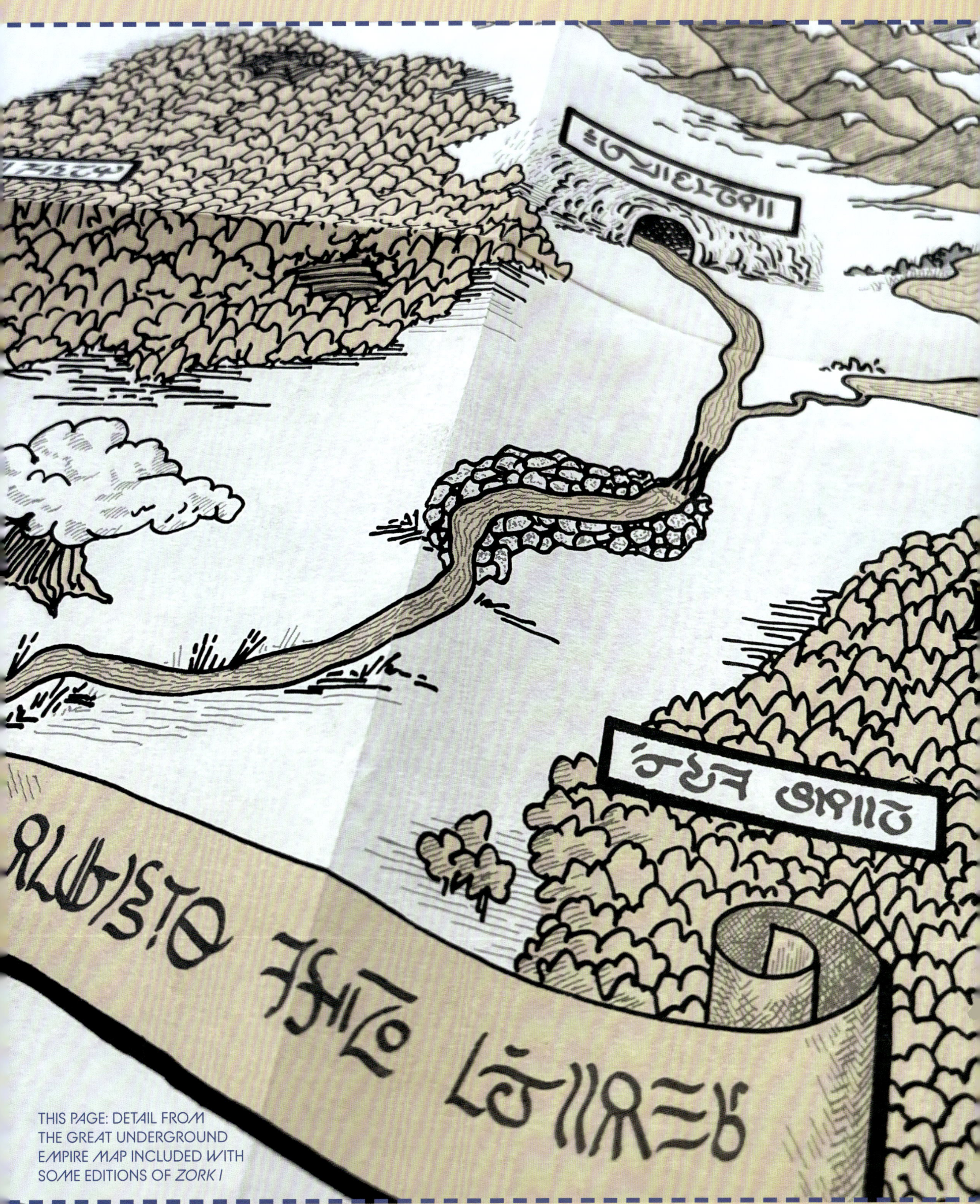

THIS PAGE: DETAIL FROM THE GREAT UNDERGROUND EMPIRE *MAP* INCLUDED WITH SOME EDITIONS OF *ZORK I*

NOTABLE FOR: **DISTILLING THE ADVENTURE GENRE INTO SIMPLE ACTION**

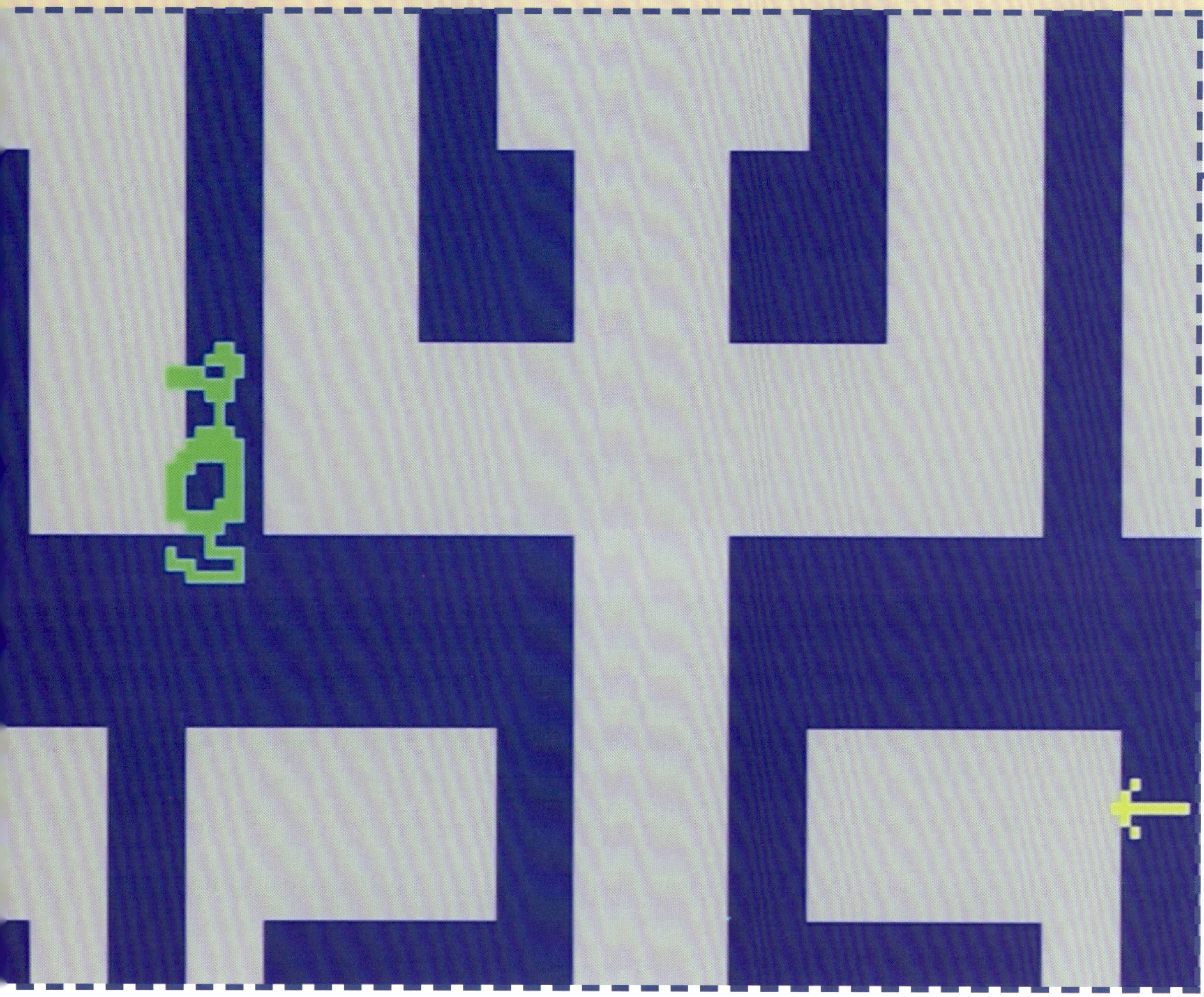

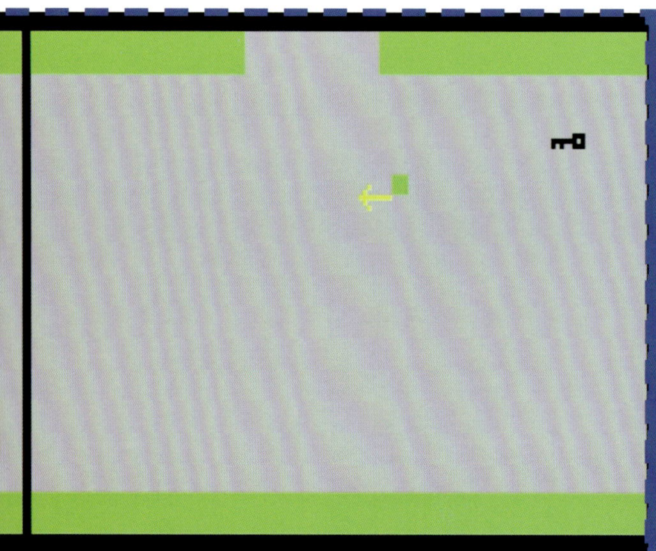

ADVENTURE

PLATFORM: **ATARI 2600**
DEV: **ATARI** | PUB: **ATARI**
INITIAL RELEASE: **JAN. 1980**

IF THERE'S A GRUNDLE IN YOUR HEDGEROW

You can't really talk about Zork—especially with regard to its influence over exploratory action games—without also discussing that game's flip side: Atari's Adventure for the 2600 console. If Zork resulted from game designers who made an early attempt at transforming a tabletop RPG experience along the lines of Dungeons & Dragons into electronic format, Adventure represented an effort to distill the concept even further. Not just into a video game, but more specifically into an action game.

The Implementers originally coded Zork for mainframe: that is, networked computers with vastly more computing and memory resources than personal computers of that era. Indeed, Zork's eventual home release had to be slimmed down significantly, and much of its 1981 sequel (Zork II) consisted of material that the Implementers incorporated into their original version of the game but had to trim in order to squeeze their adventure onto floppy disks. Adventure's designer Warren Robinett, however, had to deal with the consumer computing constraints of the 1970s from the very inception of his project. As an Atari employee in the company's console products division, he couldn't even take advantage of the relative luxuriousness offered by 8-bit microcomputers like the Apple II—or even Atari's own machines, the 400 and 800. As an Atari 2600 game, Adventure had to fit within a meager 4 KB of code, a vastly smaller space than the several hundred KB or floppy capacity that contained Zork's home incarnation. As such, Adventure was fundamentally constrained both in terms of scale and interface. Whereas players could interact with Zork by typing fragments of English grammar on a full computer keyboard, Adventure had to be controlled with a single one-button joystick.

Robinett chose to make the most of what the Atari did offer. Namely, colorful graphics and responsive controls. While these were no great shakes by today's standards, they got the job done.

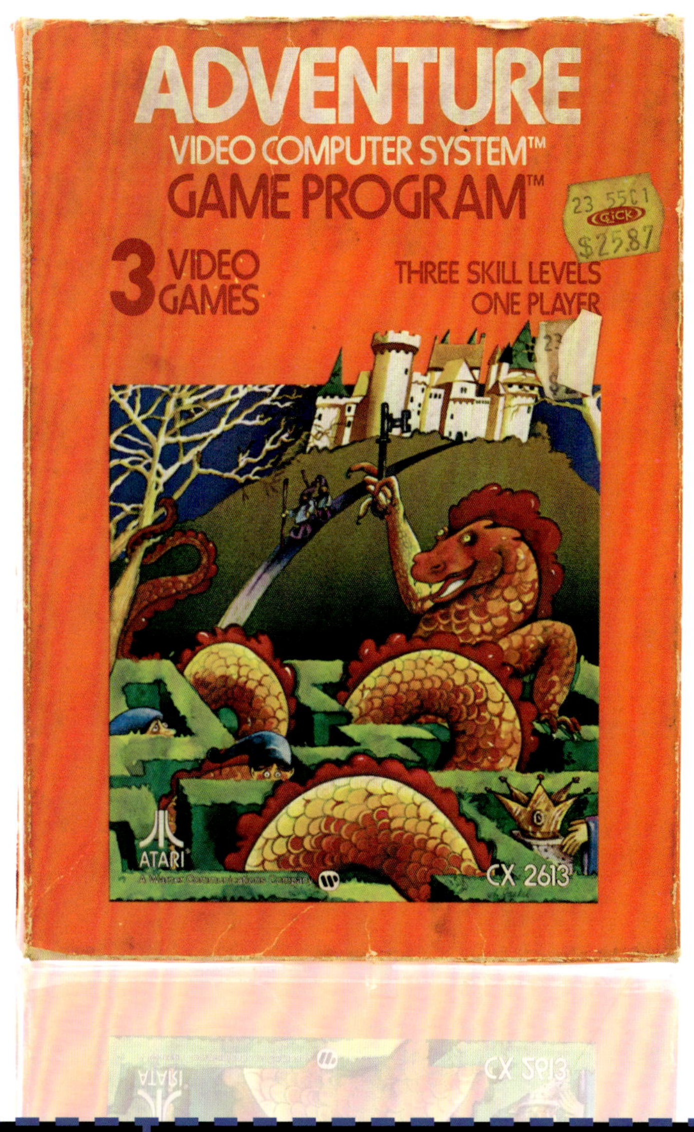

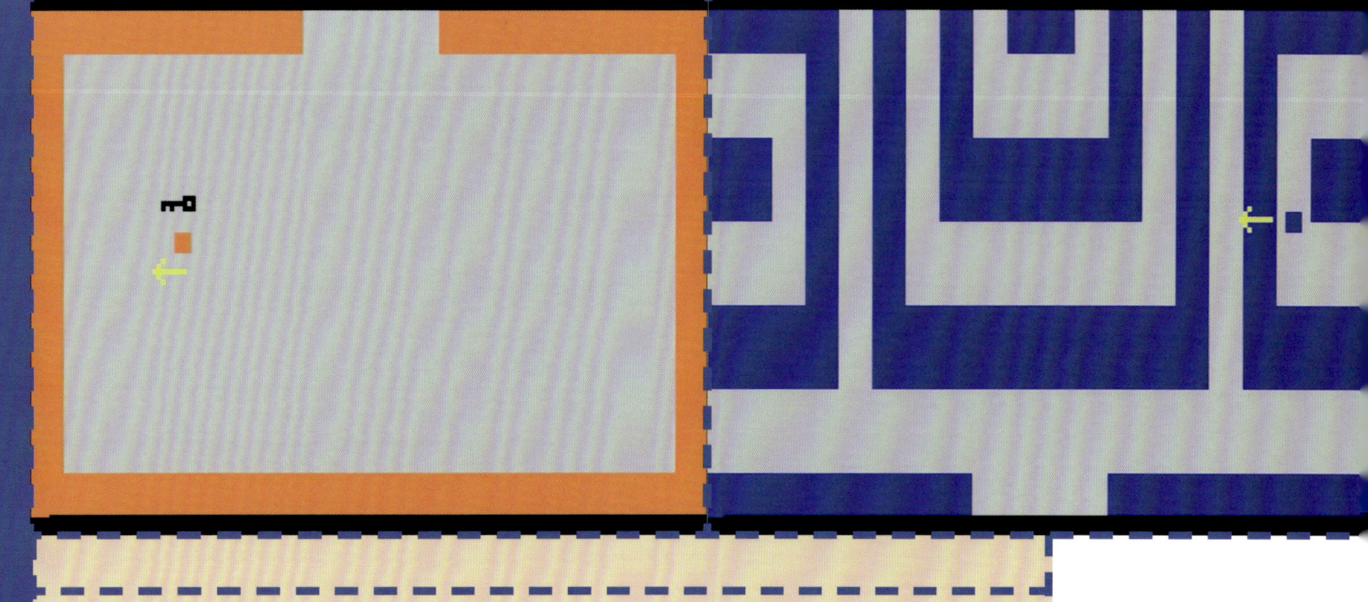

Adventure players didn't have to visualize Zork's maze of twisty passages, all alike; they could simply head north into the confusing multiscreen maze area and begin navigating their way around the game's maze. Nor did they need to figure out arcane tools and deliberately vague sequences of actions for killing foes; it seemed fairly obvious that you could use the sword to take care of most foes. The question, of course, was whether you could coax enemies into range while you actually had those lethal items in your possession…

Much of Adventure works similarly to Zork, albeit in simplified manner. For instance, it lacks Zork's inventory system; you can't type a simple command to take stock of your possessions. Nevertheless, Adventure still makes toting objects around with you one of the key components of your quest. In this case, though, you can only carry a single item at a time, requiring you to drop the item currently in your grasp to pick up another. This really isn't fundamentally different from the limited carrying capacity Zork's hero had to contend with; it's simply a more severe approach.

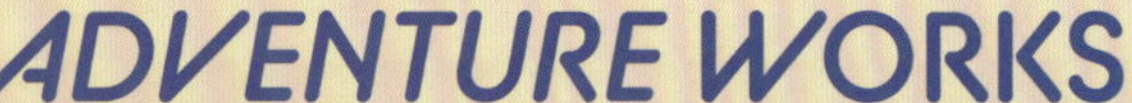

SIMILARLY TO *ZORK*, ALBEIT IN A SIMPLIFIED FORM. IT LACKS *ZORK*'S INVENTORY SYSTEM, AND YOU CAN'T TYPE A SIMPLE COMMAND TO TAKE STOCK OF YOUR POSSESSIONS, EVEN THOUGH TOTING OBJECTS IS A KEY COMPONENT OF THE QUEST.

Perhaps more importantly, despite its harsh limitations, *Adventure* nevertheless maintains *Zork*'s sense of persistence. Items remain in the spot where you dropped them during your current quest. This allows you to return to claim them as needed, turning micromanagement into a critical strategy. Which item do you need for the moment, and how quickly can you return to the location of another weapon or tool to affect a quick swap?

Adventure even incorporates randomness as a play factor, one that works similarly to *Zork*'s thief. A bat flutters around the game world, grabbing items without warning…including, at times, whatever the hero holds in his hands. If you're very unlucky, the bat will grab, say, the Enchanted Chalice, which it will then replace with, for example, a deadly dragon that will instantly slay your adventurer. It's possible to manipulate the bat, but its presence keeps players on their toes.

Like *Zork*, *Adventure* doesn't go out of its way to explain itself. The main objective of the game—retrieving the Enchanted Chalice and carrying it to the Golden Castle—is described in the instruction manual, but the actual process of making that happen is left charmingly enigmatic. Your hero, depicted onscreen as a small square block of color, begins south of the Golden Castle. It's on you to figure out what to do from there.

In the easiest game variant, the task is fairly self-explanatory. You can see a gold key beside the Golden Castle, and this tool unlocks the castle's door, which grants you access to an arrow—actually the sword—a weapon that can frighten away the dragons that lurk nearby. This play mode still takes a little effort to complete, but not so much that a modern player wouldn't be able to decrypt the process and master it within a few attempts.

It's really in the game's more difficult variants that you begin to see the interlocking map design that would come to define metroidvania games taking shape. Again, your goal remains simple: take the chalice to the Golden Castle. But in the harder mode, this is no easy task. The Gold Key no longer sits beside the Golden Castle; instead, you have to find it tucked away in a maze to the south. The chalice itself sits behind the gate of the Black Castle in both variants, but in the harder version you need to find the Black Key in a maze inside the White Castle, but you can't enter that structure until you traverse the main maze to find the White Key.

This sort of backtracking to unlock hidden areas is a mainstay of metroidvania games. While *Adventure* admittedly lacks the permanent power-ups of something like *Metroid*, the concept remains sound here even in this primal form. M

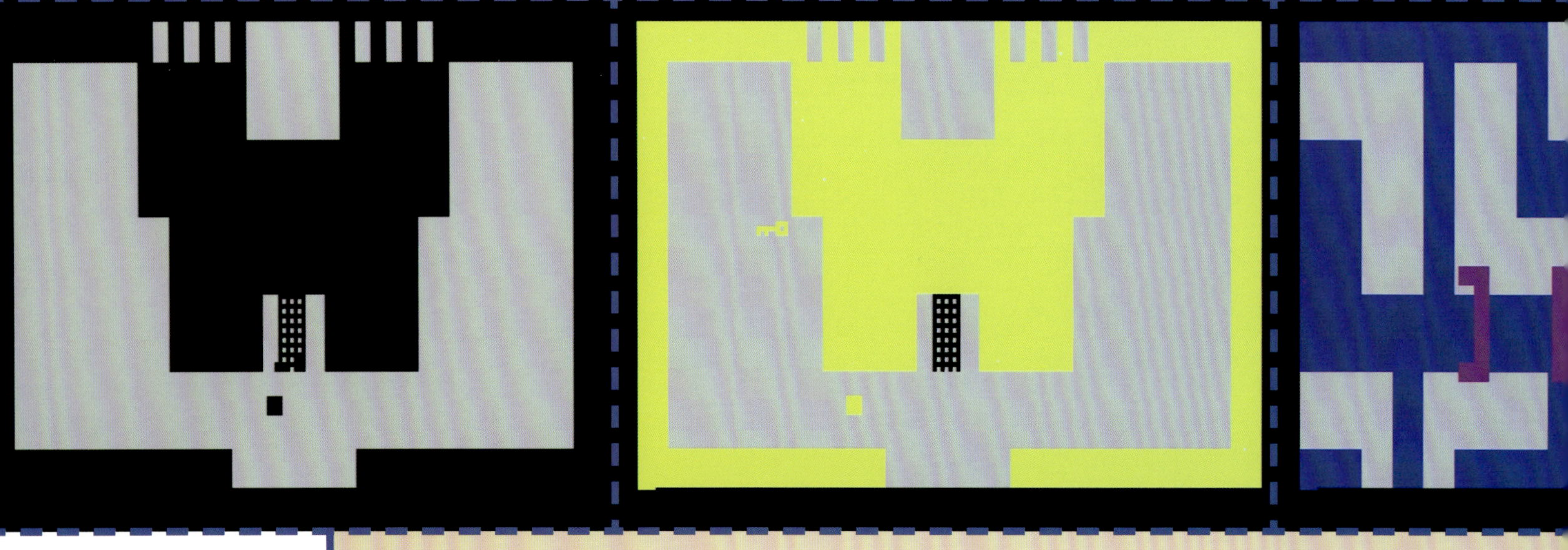

THE BEFORE TI/MES

M*The History of Metroidvania* does not specifically chronicle firsts in video gaming but rather looks at first influential works, rarely looking back further than 1980. When you venture into the video game history of the 1970s (and even earlier), "firsts" become difficult to pin down thanks to the largely non commercial and inconsistently documented nature of the medium in those days. Many of the games appearing in this book can trace the origins of their key design concepts back into the primal soup of 1970s computing. However, it's hard to know just how much sway those early efforts truly had. Many of the most groundbreaking works of the decade appeared on academic computing systems and never saw a commercial release—in fact, those games never made their way into the lives of anyone but a small community of people with access to an early networked computing service called PLATO at a handful of American universities.

PLATO, along with standalone mainframe computing platforms like Digital Equipment Corporation's PDP-10, attracted creative, technically minded types who saw the emergence of computing systems as an opportunity to push gaming pastimes in new directions. In just a few years, PLATO users created early iterations of the dungeon crawler role-playing game, massively multiplayer experiences (including a trade simulation capable of supporting two dozen people on a cross-country network), procedurally generated quests that predated the roguelike (and in fact predated *Rogue* itself), and more. But because users could only access PLATO by spending time at a select number of universities and libraries, most people who designed the games covered in this volume came to their ideas independently or else twigged to them based on secondhand references. There are exceptions, of course—notably *Wizardry* designers Robert Woodhead and Andrew Greenberg, who took direct inspiration from PLATO adventures when building their seminal adventure—but for the most part, PLATO amounted to a creative Galápagos where brilliant innovations evolved unseen by the larger world. Game designers eventually reinvented those radical wheels on their own throughout the latter '70s and '80s.

It was really the advent of consumer-oriented microcomputers in 1977—the Apple II and Commodore PET—along with the breakout success of the Atari 2600 console that enabled the proper evolution of the foundational concepts of the metroidvania format. And even then, those devices didn't reach critical mass until 1979 or '80; around the same time, the staggering success of arcade games like *Space Invaders*, *Pac-Man*, and *Asteroids* established video games as a whole as more than just a passing fad for playing increasingly elaborate takes on table tennis.

This is why I chose to begin this chronology with *Zork*. Thanks to its unique history, *Zork* serves as a bridge between the closed system, room-sized mainframes of the '70s and the home computing (and gaming) devices that exploded in popularity and reach through the '80s. *Zork* began its life on a shared-time academic system as a reinvention of 1977's *Adventure/ADVENT*, itself an expansion of William Crowther's 1976 *Colossal Cave Adventure*, which had begun life as a recreation of a real-world cave system for users to explore that had gradually taken on a more fanciful air. Like *Zork*, *Adventure* received commercial releases, though it never caught on to the same degree as Infocom's creation (which received half a dozen sequels over the space of nearly two decades). In fact, *Adventure* faded largely into the mists of time within the larger gaming community until the 2010 documentary *Get Lamp*, which foregrounded it. This documentary likely influenced a crucial plot point in AMC's cult 2014 premium cable drama *Halt and Catch Fire* that focused on the collective challenge of solving *Adventure*. All this is to say that *Zork*'s comparative reach and influence, along with its deliberately structured quest and objectives, make it a compelling embarkation point for the metroidvania genre. Even if it's not a first in any technical sense of the word, its success made it a breakout moment for key concepts like mapping and navigating a persistent world.

(For those interested in learning more about the embryonic years of the PLATO system, I highly recommend *The Friendly Orange Glow: The Untold Story of the PLATO System and the Dawn of Cyberculture* by Brian Dear.) M

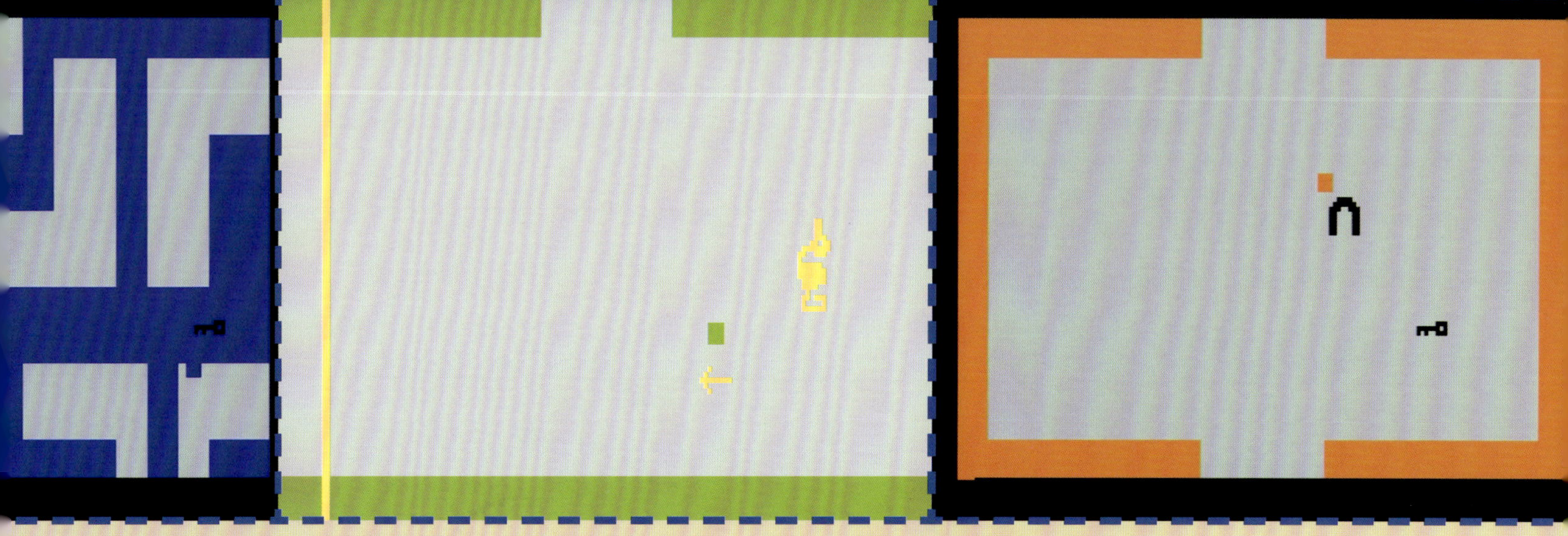

NOTABLE FOR: **BRINGING A VISUAL COMPONENT TO THE ADVENTURE GENRE**

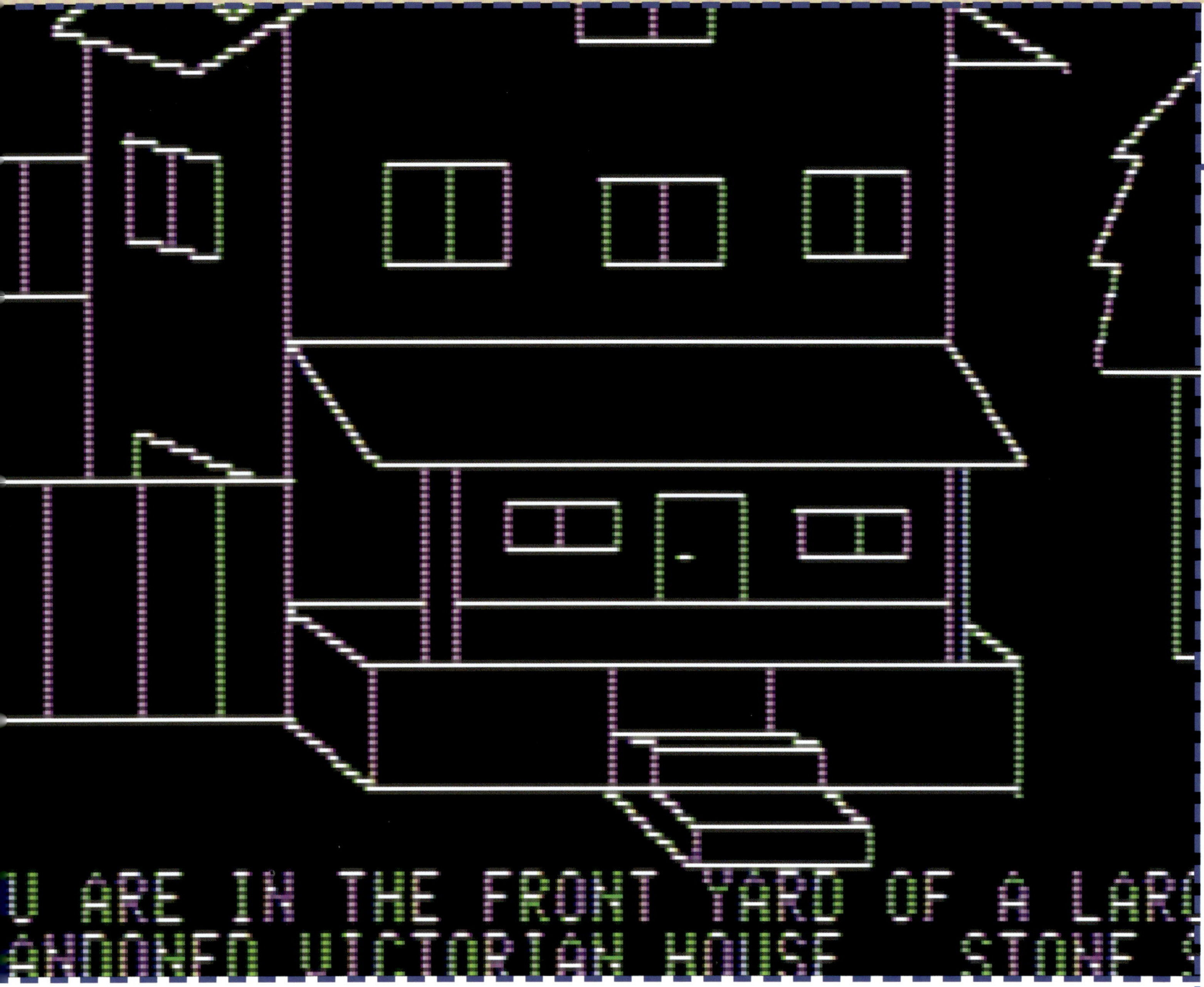

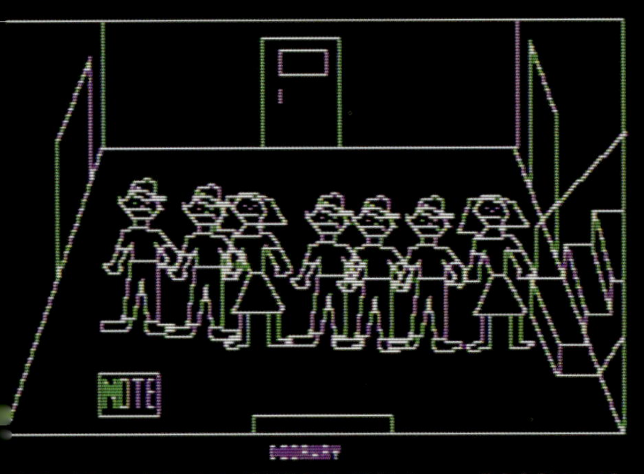

MYSTERY HOUSE

PLATFORM: **APPLE II / VARIOUS**
DEV: **SIERRA ON-LINE** | PUB: **SIERRA ON-LINE**
INITIAL RELEASE: **MAY 1980**

MYSTERIOUS VISIONS

With *Mystery House*, Sierra On-Line struck a midpoint between *Zork* and *Adventure*: a parser-based text adventure that incorporated graphical elements. In terms of gameplay, it skews decidedly in *Zork*'s direction—naturally, given its emphasis on text, an element completely lacking in the Atari 2600 game. *Mystery House* upholds the workings of the narrative adventure, requiring players to navigate its world through terse bursts of simple text and providing them feedback in kind.

However, it's difficult to overstate just how radically the addition of graphics changes the overall feel of the experience. *Mystery House* did not exactly set a new standard for comput- er graphics, even by the standards of 1980. Roberta Williams, the designer, built the game world with stark white outlines against a black background. Not even fluid, natural outlines at that. *Mystery House* depicts its environments with segments of straight lines, even when rendering organic objects like trees, with a sort of naïve quality that treats basic artistic principles (such as a common vanishing point) almost like alien concepts.

Nevertheless, it does the trick. *Mystery House*'s combination of barebone visuals and a story set almost entirely within a single self-contained locale (the mysterious house of the title) makes for a much less daunting style of adventure than the likes of *Zork* and *ADVENT*. Rather than delineating its world through prose, *Mystery House* provides a visual component alongside its descriptive text, giving players a clear sense of the creators' intent. Of course, this leaves less of the world open to the player's imagination—but given the complexity inherent to certain sections of *Zork*, not to mention how that ambiguity could bring the adventure to a temporary halt as players struggled to grasp the geography of the spaces in play, the additional helping hand is hardly a negative here. It's one thing to be told you've entered a room with a variety of topological features, but actually seeing those details rendered onscreen—however crudely!—makes the entire process of casing the joint and tracking your movements far more manageable.

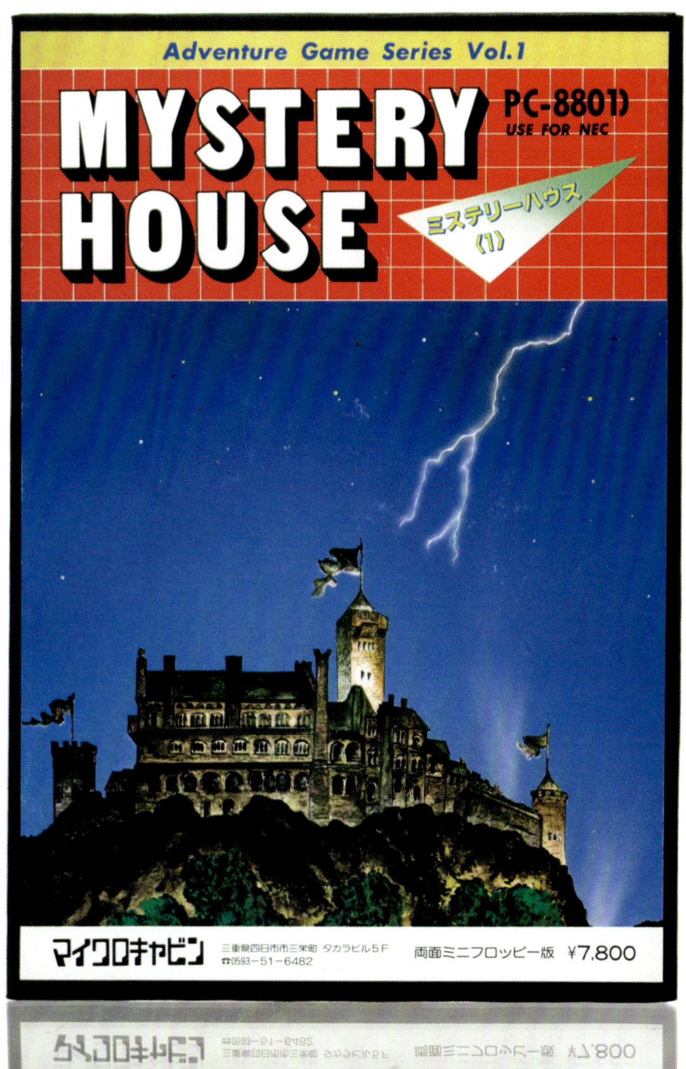

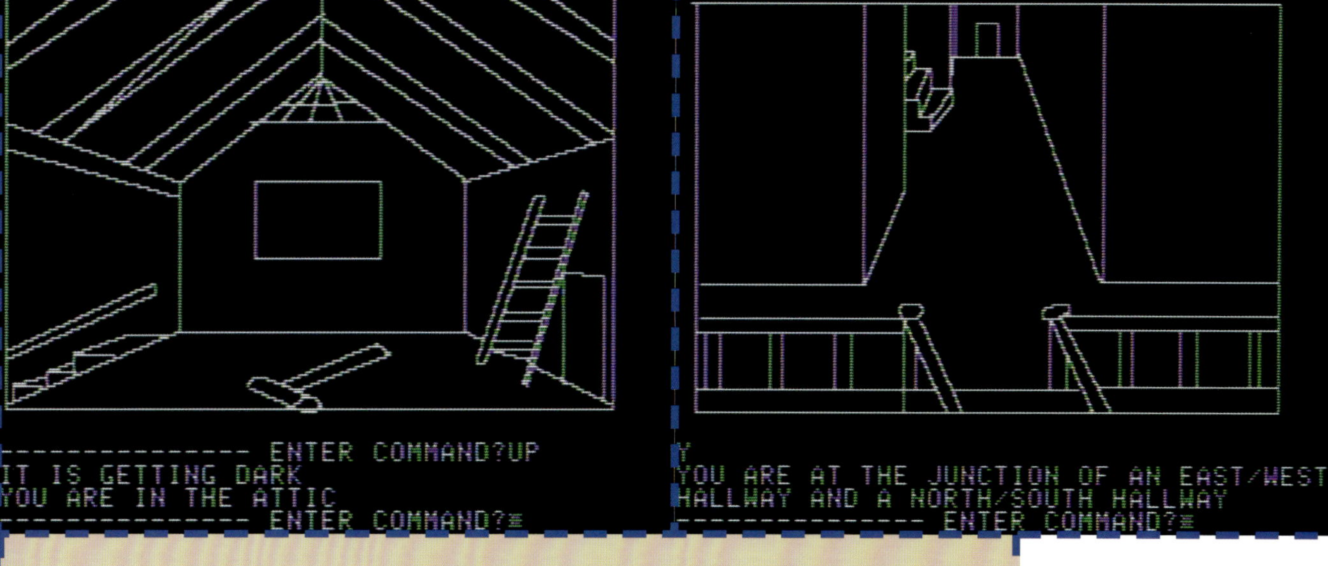

METROIDVANIA TIMELINE 1981

Space Invaders for Atari 2600. *Pac-Man* fever. The breakout popularity of Game & Watch. *Missile Command*'s addictive (albeit grim) distillation of Cold War–nuclear anxiety! Video games captured the zeitgeist of 1980 and wove themselves inextricably into popular culture. What could have been another short-lived 1970s fad like Pet Rocks and geodesic domes became a cultural fixture as gaming fanatics of all ages, genders, and races flocked to arcades; harnessed their home computers for purposes more entertaining than filing recipes; and bought millions of devices purpose-built for allowing them to play games on their televisions.

As the new decade began and a new American president took office amid promises to wipe away the doldrums of the '70s, video games and computers exploded into popularity. New, economical platforms shipped in the US and Europe, making that fabled technology affordable for the average household—and, with it, the ability to take advantage of this incoming tsunami of games. Admittedly, platforms like Commodore's VIC-20 and Texas Instruments' 99/4A offered rudimentary gaming capabilities compared to bespoke arcade machines and even systems like the Apple II, where medium-defining works *Ultima* and *Wizardry* made their debuts this year, but it was hard to argue with the price. At the higher end, IBM launched the "true" personal computer line—a platform targeted at business professionals, but whose popularity and easily reproducible design turned it into the de facto industry standard by decade's end, becoming the underpinning for modern Windows-based computers.

Japan, well into its postwar rehabilitation and rapidly growing into one of the most powerful economic forces on the planet, also saw its share of major innovations. The first Japan-centric computing systems debuted in 1981, offering support for higher-resolution graphics than those produced by Western PCs, necessitated by the intricate text glyphs of the Japanese language's three different forms of writing. While lacking in color depth, the dense graphic resolution and impressive audio capabilities of NEC's PC-8801 and its descendants made those systems into a lively incubator for video game innovation—not only in terms of design but music as well.

And, of course, the character-driven arcade-action trend cemented by *Pac-Man* continued with games like *Donkey Kong*. Working in collaboration with electronics firm Ikegami Tsushinki, Nintendo created a visually opulent and highly varied action game whose story played out across four distinct stages. The game's controls and physics defined the platform action format—an essential building block of the metroidvania. Although that genre was still a long way away in 1981, all the components that make up its DNA were brewing. M

TIMELINE OF EVENTS

January

VIC-20
Commodore designed this computer to be friendly to everyday household users in terms of simplicity and price. It paid off: the VIC-20 was the first PC to sell more than a million units.

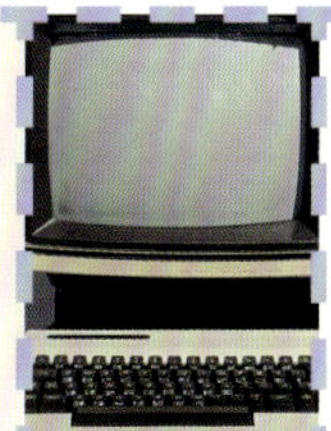

February

Defender
This blistering space shooter featured high-speed scrolling action that moved so quickly and aggressively that it needed to borrow *Rally-X*'s mini-map to keep players oriented.

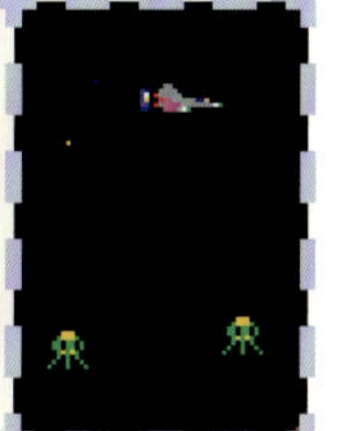

June

TI-99/4A
The consumer-friendly 99/4A sold at a competitive price but offered expansion options for those who craved more power. Its CPU and graphics chip became industry standards.

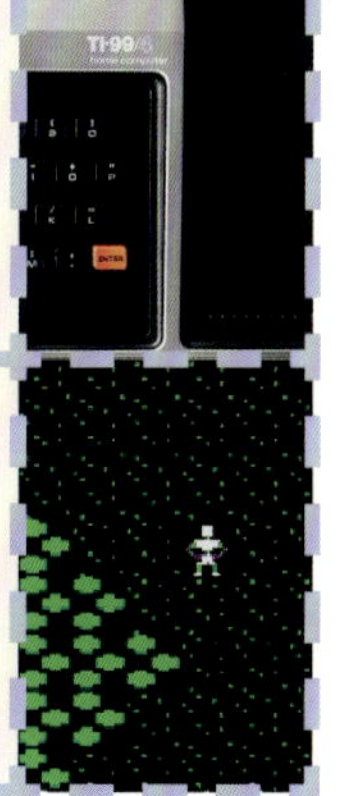

Ultima
While hardly the first-ever computer role-playing game, *Ultima* was the first to make any real headway at retail, kicking off a franchise that defined the genre for nearly two decades.

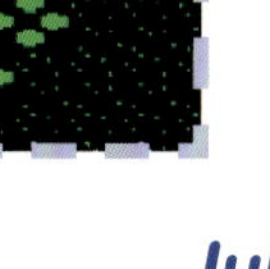

July

Venture
Refining the principles of *Adventure* into a form even better-suited to quick arcade sessions, Exidy's *Venture* turned the dungeon labyrinth into a large space containing smaller rooms.

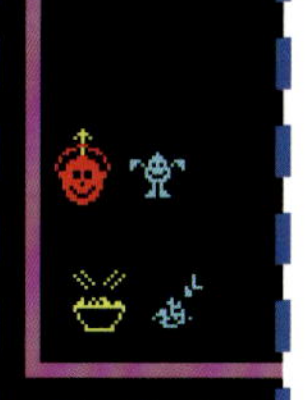

July, cont.

Donkey Kong
Nintendo's megahit perfected runand-jump play and applied a narrative framework to the action game (climb building, save girl), eventually leading the way to story-driven metroidvanias.

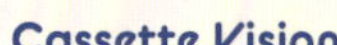

Cassette Vision
As Japan's first truly original home console of note, Epoch's machine repurposed standalone *Pong* clone tech into an affordable, interchangeable, cartridge-based device.

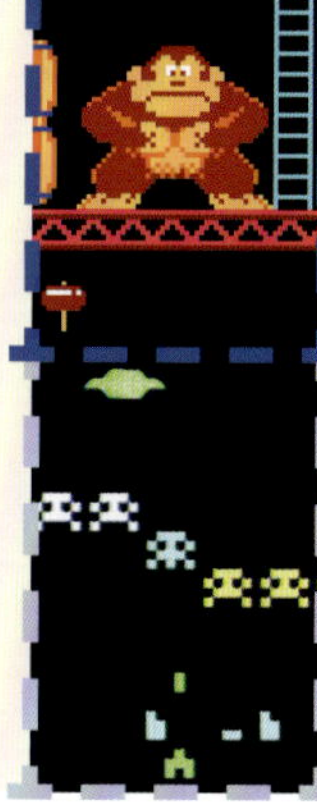

August

IBM Personal Computer
A high-end business machine, IBM's PC was soon cloned by competitors, who turned the format into an industry standard. Its descendants still define home computing decades later.

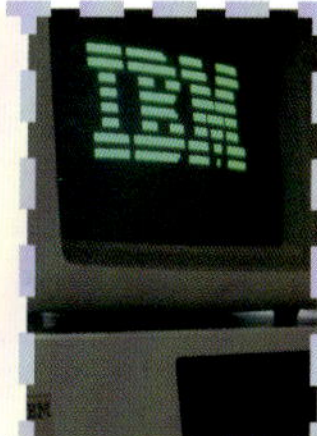

September

Wizardry
Playing like a *Dungeons & Dragons* treasure quest in computer form, *Wizardry*'s emphasis on mapping a single dungeon defined the workings of virtual game spaces.

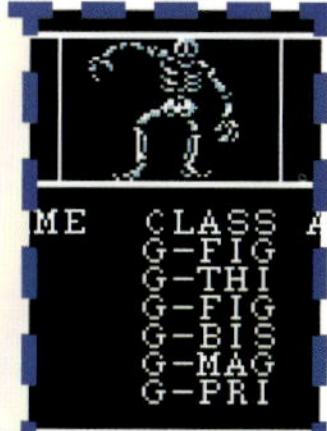

November

PC-8801
Designed around the specific needs of the Japanese language, NEC's computer platform featured high-resolution visuals that made it a compelling venue for video gaming.

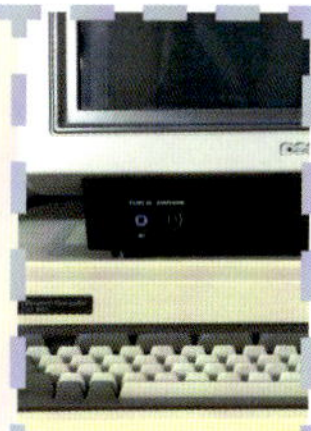

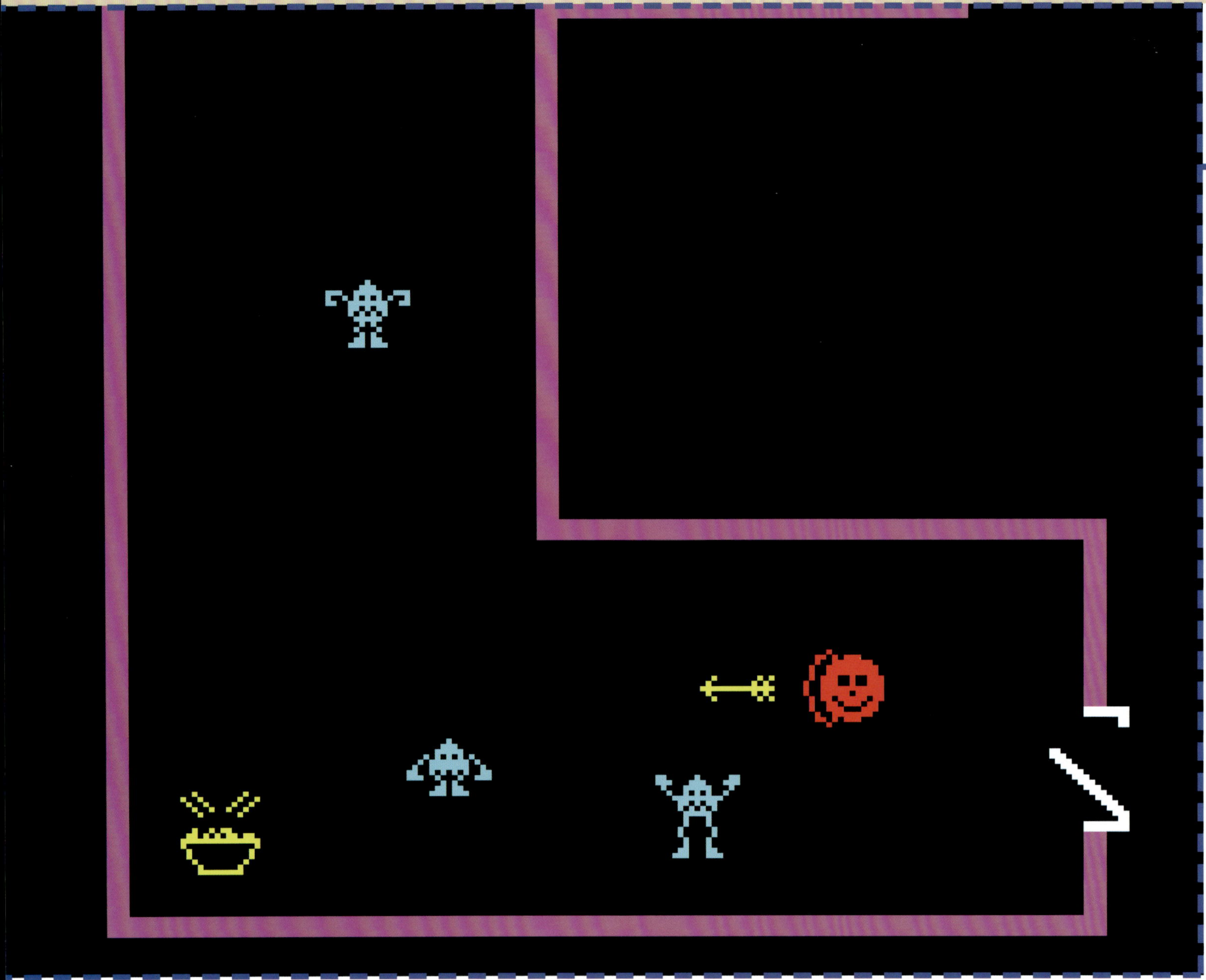

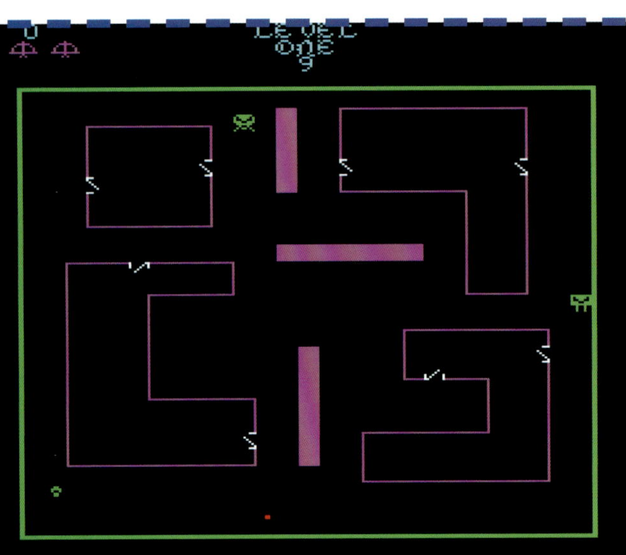

© Exidy

VENTURE

PLATFORM: **ARCADE/VARIOUS**
DEV: **EXIDY** | MFG: **EXIDY**
INITIAL RELEASE: **JULY 1981**

NOTABLE FOR: **REINVENTING *ADVENTURE* INTO AN ARCADE CORRIDOR SHOOTER**

A WINKY'S AS GOOD AS A NOD

Because metroidvania games combine both platforming and action/role-playing elements, you can't really gain a proper appreciation of the format without studying the evolution of both genres. So, while *Zork* and *Adventure* represent one side of the equation, Exidy's 1981 RPG-inspired arcade title *Venture* deserves notice for helping to define its action side. Although *Venture* features none of the platforming that typically forms the backbone of a metroidvania quest, it took an even more dramatic approach to reducing RPG concepts into action form than in Atari's *Adventure*.

The game's title leaves no question of its origins and intentions. "Venture" is obviously a truncated form of "Adventure," that hack-and-stab odyssey for the Atari 2600—or perhaps of *Adventure/ADVENT*, a.k.a. *Colossal Cave Adventure*, the text game that inspired *Zork*. *Venture, ADVENT, Adventure*: they're all cut from the same cloth, and they all aspire to achieve the same end. *Venture* simply takes the concept the furthest into a pure action structure suitable to early '80s arcades. It boils down the fundamental concept of role-playing rules into a form tailored for a coin-drop-driven reality.

Protagonist Winky journeys across a dungeon in search of treasure, fighting monsters with a bow and arrow through a string of multi-room spaces too simple to be called labyrinths. *Venture*'s platform—an arcade cabinet designed for quick, three-minute sessions—demanded a simple game design, so there's not really much to the game. Each level consists of a large space populated by four rooms, each containing a different treasure. Winky himself appears as a well-armed smiley face, a friendly version of the deadly Evil Otto from Stern's *Berzerk* or a slightly martial take on Pac-Man. Much like the space fighter in Namco's *Galaxian*, Winky can fire only a single arrow at once; his rate of fire is determined not by his reload speed but by how long it takes his projectile to strike something and vanish from play, be it a wall or a monster.

Venture moves a little too slowly to be deemed a shooter, yet its action is too zippy and shallow to qualify as a proper RPG. Of

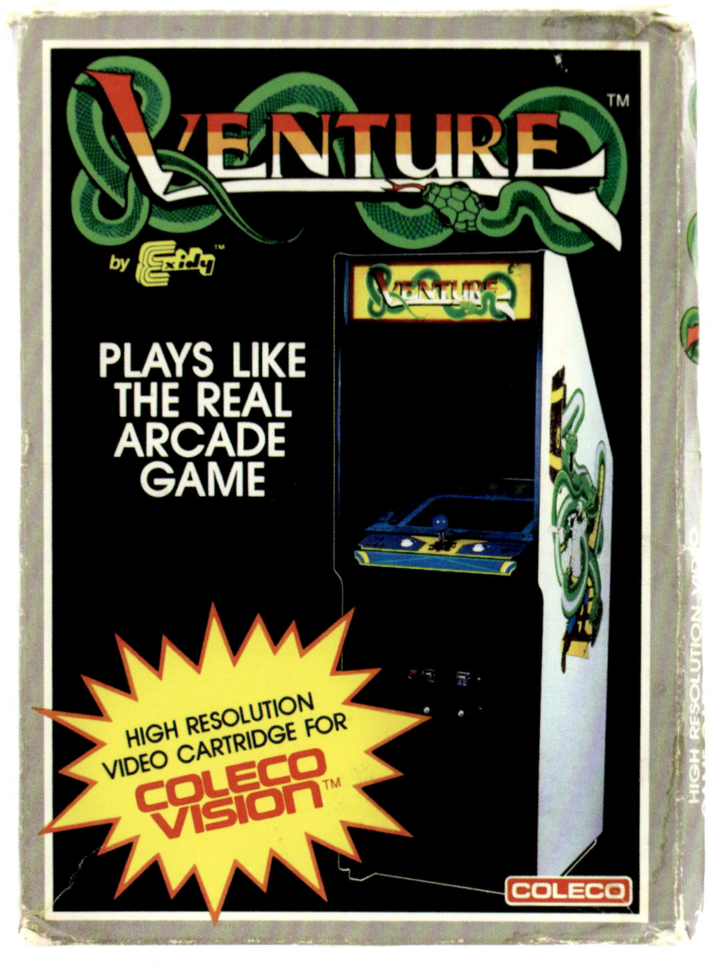

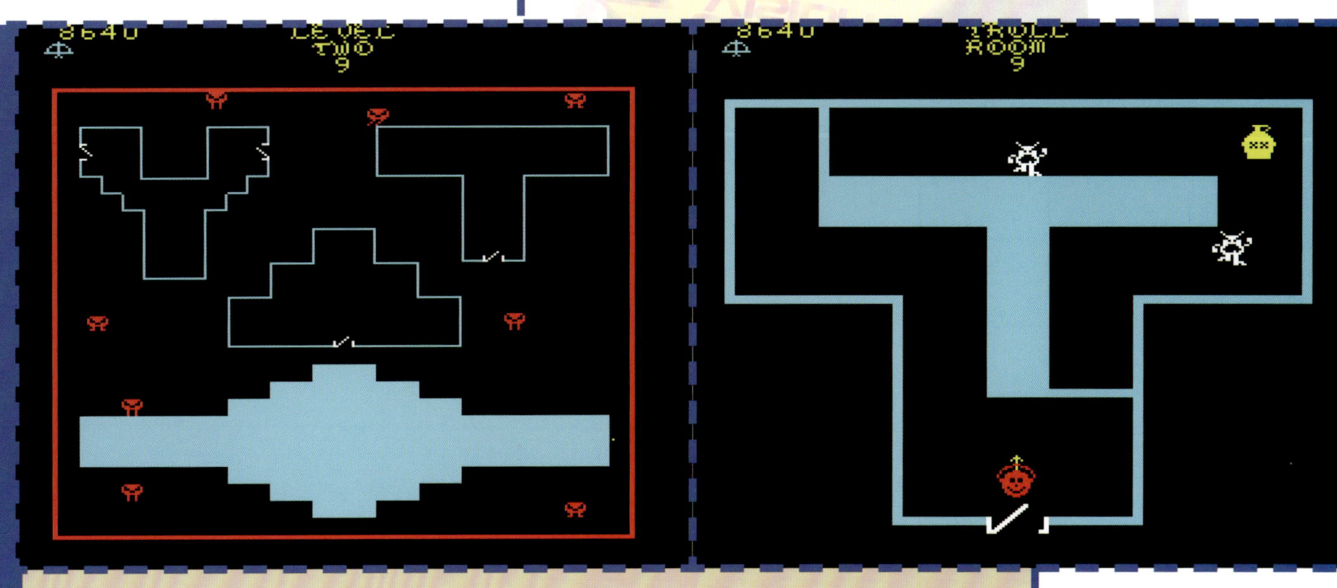

the two, it definitely favors the latter, albeit in a fairly naïve manner. Given its age, *Venture* impresses with the way it almost accidentally stumbled into the duality of overworld/underworld spaces that would become a mainstay of RPGs and adjacent games like *The Legend of Zelda*. Each level (or dungeon) contains exactly four rooms, each of which feature two entrances connecting their inner spaces to the dungeon exterior. While roaming the halls that surround the rooms, you'll encounter a legion of huge skull-like monsters that wander generally (if somewhat randomly) in Winky's direction. Winky can't destroy these beasts, since these exterior spaces appear with a pulled-back point of view in which Winky is reduced to a tiny dot—too small to make out details or fire arrows.

The hall monsters will kill Winky on contact, but you can evade them by ducking into treasure rooms. When you step into a room, the viewpoint zooms in to a closer perspective, in which Winky scales up to his proper size and gains the power to take out foes. Inside these enclosed spaces, you'll find a treasure protected by a handful of monsters that lurk nearby. You can shoot the monsters, which will collapse when struck by an arrow.

These sequences feel remarkably reminiscent—or rather, prescient—of *The Legend of Zelda*. Not only does the zoomed-in view bear a striking similarity to Nintendo's groundbreaking NES game, but so to do the creatures within. As you fight snakes, skeletons, and other *Zelda*-esque foes, you can't shake the sensation that this game had a huge influence on Nintendo (perhaps indirectly, through Nihon Falcom's *Xanadu* or Namco's *The Tower of Druaga*). This is especially true in some of the trap rooms, such as the one with moving walls that can crush Winky, or the one where grabbing the loot will cause the quartet of tiny, meandering spiders to turn into huge yellow spiders that make a deadly beeline for Winky.

When you capture a room's treasure, a hall monster will burst into the room. In the zoomed-in areas, these creatures look enormous, and they remain invulnerable to arrows—again, evocative of *Berzerk*'s Evil Otto. All you can do once confronted by these foes is escape, though you must proceed with caution. The world outside the treasure rooms maintains a certain element of persistence, which means it can be dangerous to exit a room through the door you originally entered, as you may find the monsters that were chasing you outside to be lurking where you left them.

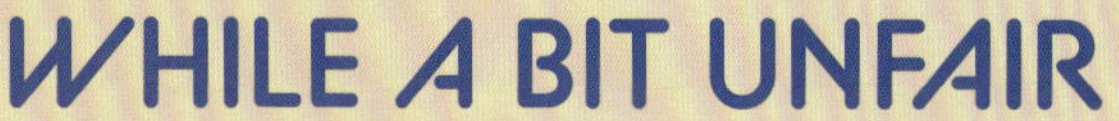

IN TERMS OF ITS DIFFICULTY LEVEL, ESPECIALLY IN ITS LATER STAGES, *VENTURE* OFFERED A REMARKABLE DEGREE OF COMPLEXITY AND SOPHISTICATION FOR A 1981 ARCADE GAME AND ESTABLISHED SOME CRUCIAL EARLY ACTION-RPG BASICS.

While a bit unfair in its difficulty level, especially in later stages, *Venture* offered a remarkable degree of complexity and sophistication for a 1981 arcade game. Still, it's a very simple game at heart. It lacks anything like an upgrade path; its treasures exist only to be added to the player's score. The entire dungeon consists of just a few stages, each with fixed layouts; once you beat them all, the game loops again at a torturous difficulty level. Plus, its graphics look barely a step above ASCII visuals. Add some randomness to the layout and this could easily have been acoin-op rendition of procedurally generated classic *Rogue* rather than a spin on *Adventure*. Nevertheless, with its free-roaming dungeon layouts and RPG trappings, you can see something great taking shape here.

Unfortunately, Exidy never credited *Venture*'s designers, only its composers, so it's impossible to know who actually came up with the game concept. Whoever it was, they did the world a solid by helping to establish some early basics for the action-RPG concept. That feat alone almost makes up for the sheer goofiness of naming your protagonist "Winky."" M

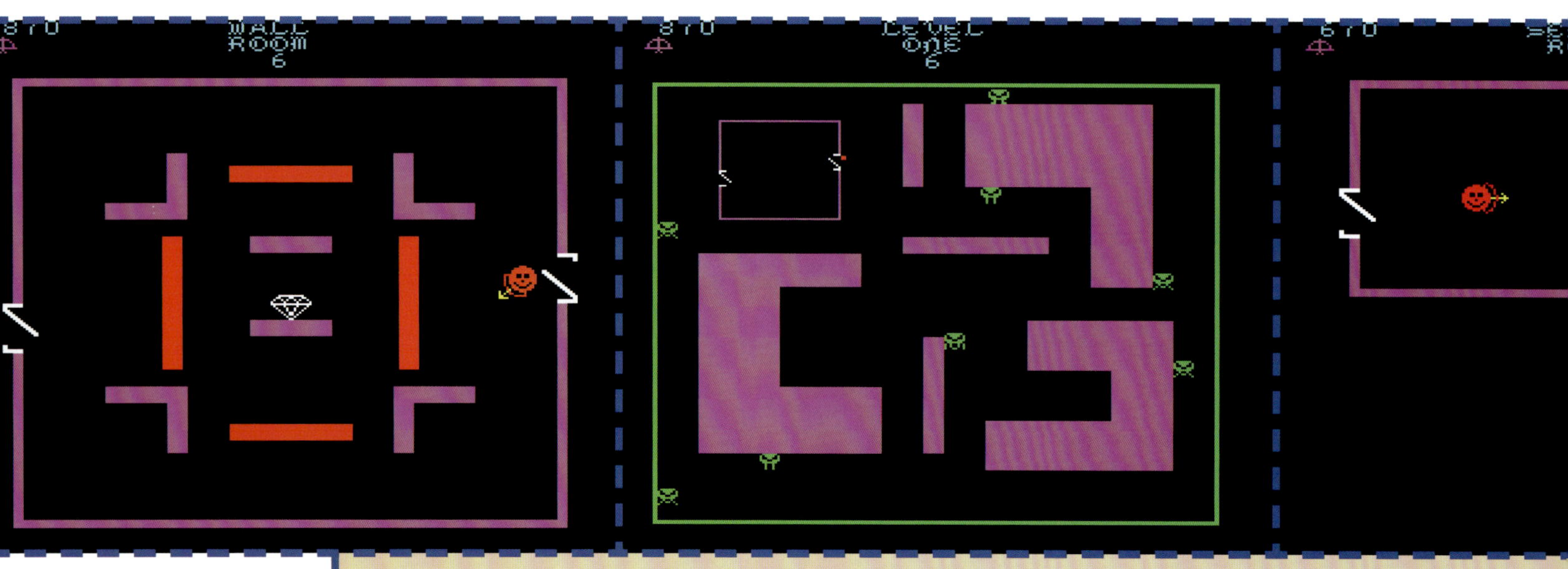

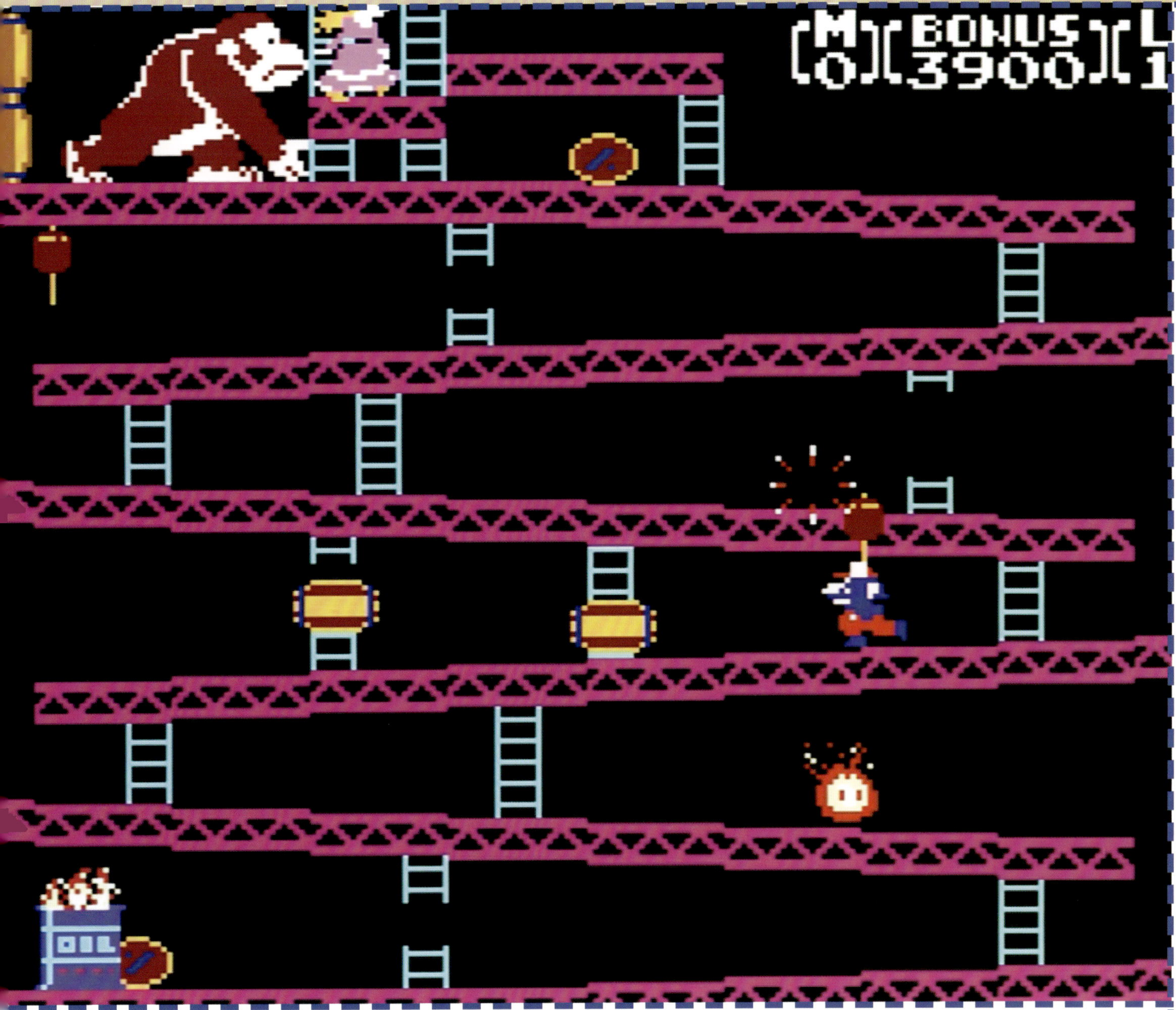

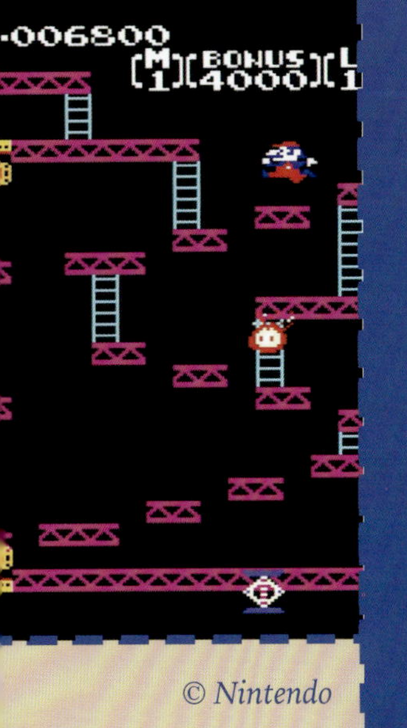

DONKEY KONG

PLATFORM: **ARCADE / VARIOUS**
DEV: **NINTENDO / IKEGAMI TSUSHINKI** | MFG: **NINTENDO**
INITIAL RELEASE: **JULY 1981**

NOTABLE FOR: **EFFECTIVELY INVENTING THE PLATFORM ACTION GENRE**

LEAPING INTO THE FUTURE

The metroidvania genre is more or less synonymous with action-RPGs, combining the moment-to-moment play mechanics of platform action games with the structure and expectations of role-playing games. Surprisingly, despite the relative simplicity of run-and-jump action compared to the workings of *Dungeons & Dragons* and its children, the RPG actually entered video game history many years before the platform genre's first true cornerstone appeared in the form of the 1981 arcade smash *Donkey Kong*.

Given that half of the word "metroidvania" comes from the *Metroid* series, perhaps it's only fitting that *Metroid* comes from the company that *Donkey Kong* put on the map in the first place: Nintendo. Although *Donkey Kong* may not have been the first game to incorporate platforming mechanics into its design, it was by far the most fully realized expression of the concept to that point in history. Following in its Mario-sized footsteps, 2D platforming would go on to become more or less the de facto basis of action gaming until the advent of proper 3D graphics and game cameras fifteen years later. Even so, it wasn't a given that the industry would arrive at that consensus. Just look at games before and immediately after *Donkey Kong*. Rather than accepting a side-view perspective, many action games on 8-bit computers and consoles attempted to emulate a three-dimensional viewpoint by placing the camera in a false overhead perspective. The UK collectively settled on isometric 3D as its go-to point of view; Sega even created their own answer to *Donkey Kong* in *Congo Bongo*, which transplanted the monkey-chasing action of Nintendo's hit into isometric 3D.

Compared to something like *Adventure* or *Berzerk*, where the forced top-down viewpoint gave players the ability to move freely along two axes, *Donkey Kong*'s point of view—in which players could move freely along the ground but could only venture momentarily into vertical space by leaping or climbing ladders—seemed almost unnaturally limiting.

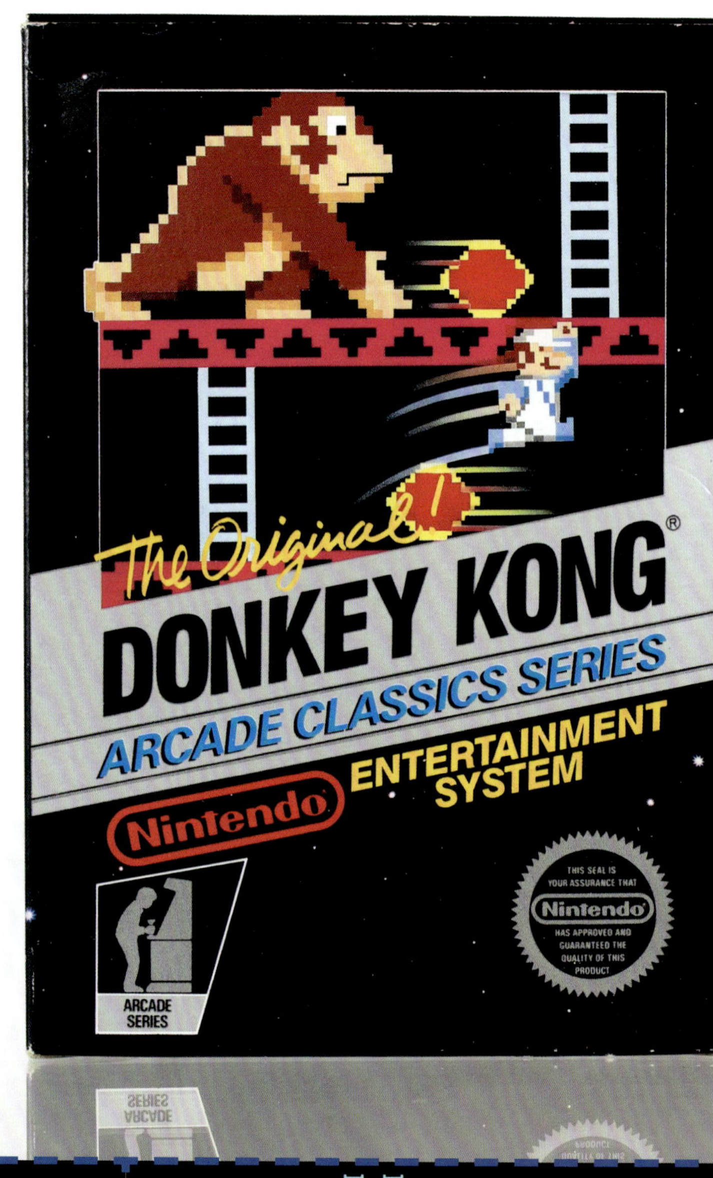

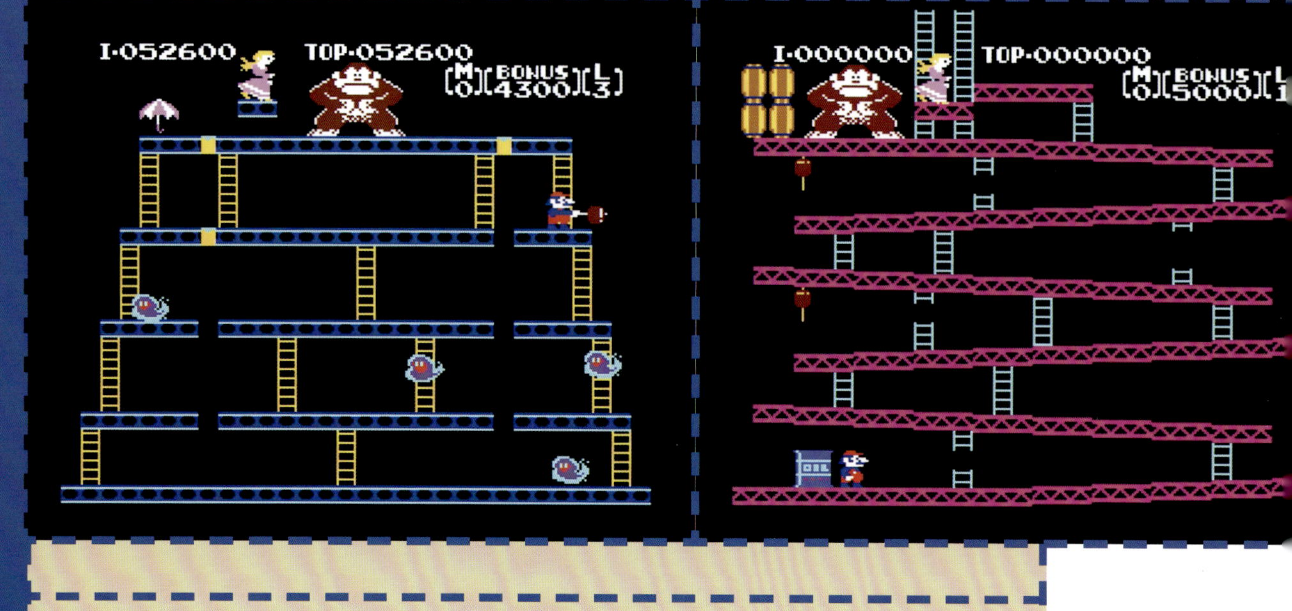

By committing to the side-on 2D perspective that Nintendo perfected here, game designers sacrificed a certain degree of freedom and potential. Rather than moving in 360 degrees as in a top-down game, *Donkey Kong* protagonist Mario became almost entirely restricted to lateral movement. The vertical axis became a challenge, a threat, something to be exploited in moderation for navigation or self-defense. Mario can run left and right to his heart's content, but to move vertically he must use a ladder or an elevator. If he attempts to move up and down on his own steam, he can only jump a short height—enough to sail over a single rolling barrel—before quickly dropping back to the ground. But what Mario lacks in range, he makes up with accessibility. The side-on 2D viewpoint came handin-hand with strict limitations, yes, but those boundaries also amounted to a certain ease of use. There was no mystery about how to manipulate Mario. The cartoonish perspective, akin to an ant farm cutaway, spoke for itself. Mario begins at the bottom of each stage and aims to reach the top, overcoming a variety of obstacles along the way. Power-ups and bonus collectibles litter the screen, enticing the player to leap. Ladders provide obvious conduits from one platform to the next. And, in case there was any doubt about Mario's need to move, the game goads the player into action by placing Mario directly beneath eponymous villain Donkey Kong's perch. Kong opens the game by dropping a barrel directly toward Mario. A player inclined to dawdle will quickly regret that lackadaisical impulse when the barrel comes crashing down and ends Mario's first life within a matter of seconds: to survive, you need to move.

> **THE SIDE-ON VIEW OF *DONKEY KONG* TURNS THE SIMPLE ACT OF MOVEMENT INTO A CHALLENGE IN ITSELF. SO MARIO FACES FEWER DYNAMIC HAZARDS THAN MANY OTHER GAME HEROES OF THE ERA HERE, AND HIS POWERS OF NAVIGATION DOUBLE AS OFFENSIVE AND DEFENSIVE OPTIONS.**

Donkey Kong subscribes to the philosophy perfected a year earlier by Namco's *Pac-Man*: the disempowered hero. The player finds Mario surrounded by hazards at all times, and their only recourse comes in dashing away from hazards, by leaping over them, or by plucking a hammer from midair and smashing them. However, these weapons only appear in two stages (the first and last), and operate for only a limited time. Worse, the hammers in the final stage are hindered by the mechanics of the level itself. Mario spends the level removing bolts from girders in order to cause the entire structure to collapse and send *Donkey Kong* crashing down to defeat. Once a bolt has been plucked, it leaves behind an empty space that dangerous fireballs can't cross…but neither can Mario, unless he jumps, which he can't do while holding a hammer.

The sideways perspective of *Donkey Kong* turns the simple act of movement into a challenge. Mario actually faces fewer dynamic or active hazards than protagonists of other games of the era, and those hazards are bound by the same rules as he is. Barrels can only roll downward, and fireballs drift erratically as they slowly pursue Mario. Their predictability doesn't make them any less dangerous to Mario, though.

It's incumbent on the player to respond to and avoid these perils by employing the core game mechanics of running and jumping. This fundamental facet of *Donkey Kong*—skills that double as navigational tools and offensive or defensive options for Mario—would eventually become an integral facet of the great metroidvania games. Nintendo would hone the concept with *Metroid*, where Samus Aran's combat upgrades like bombs and missiles also doubled as keys to allow for greater traversal of the world, and countless other games would further expand on it.

Donkey Kong codified the 2D platformer, but it also helped demonstrate that the most interesting skills in video games are those with multiple uses. In this sense, a simple girder-climbing action game provided an essential part of the metroidvania's DNA. *M*

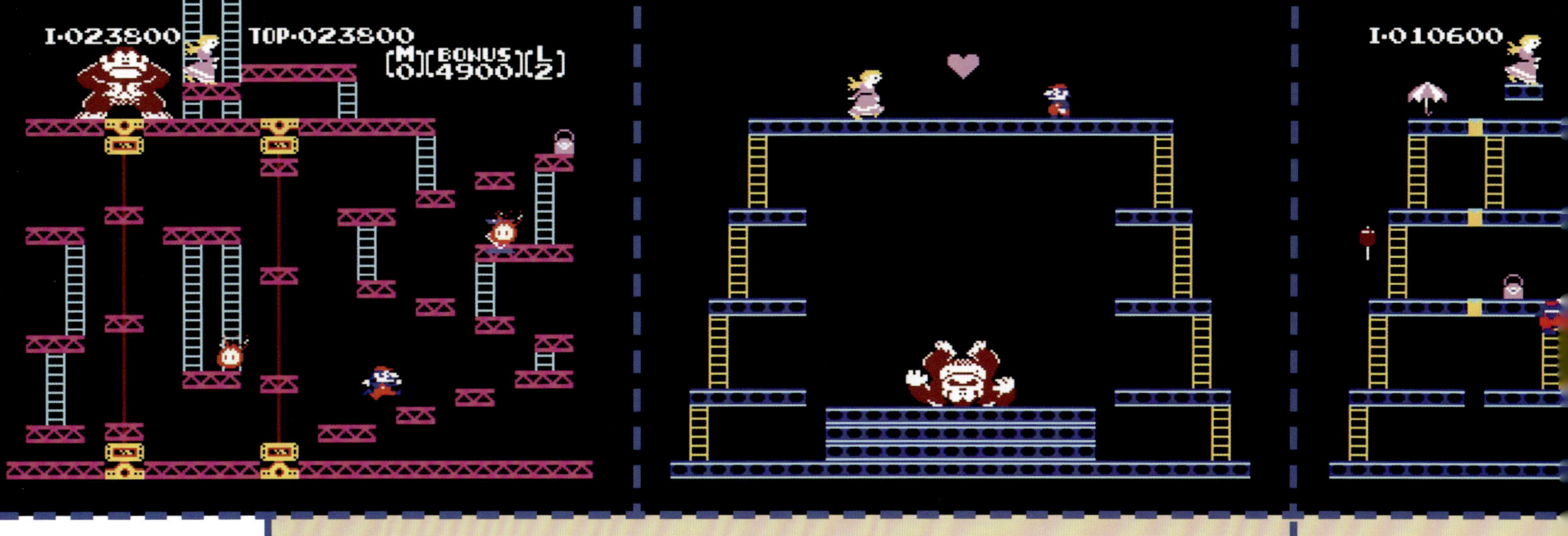

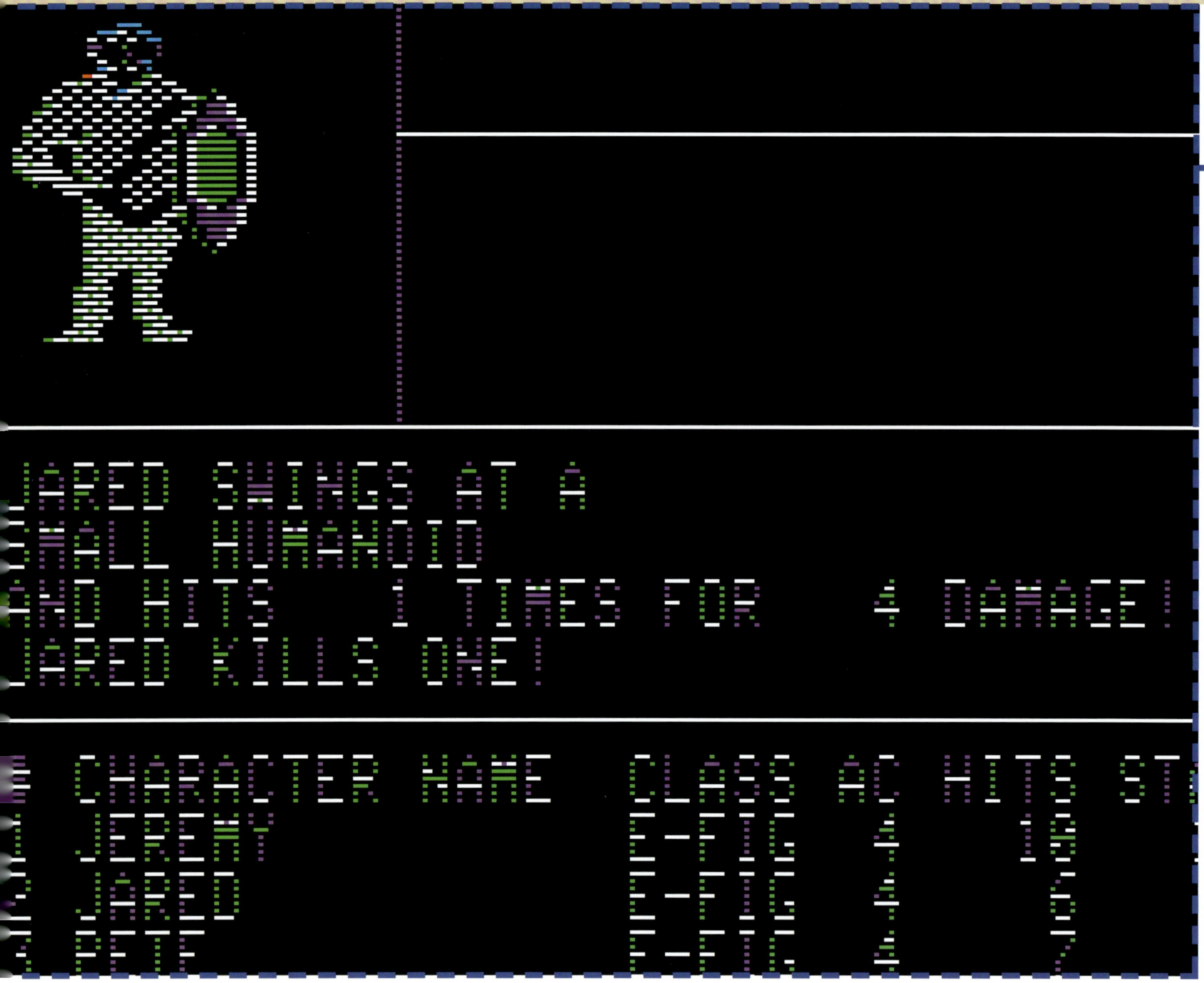

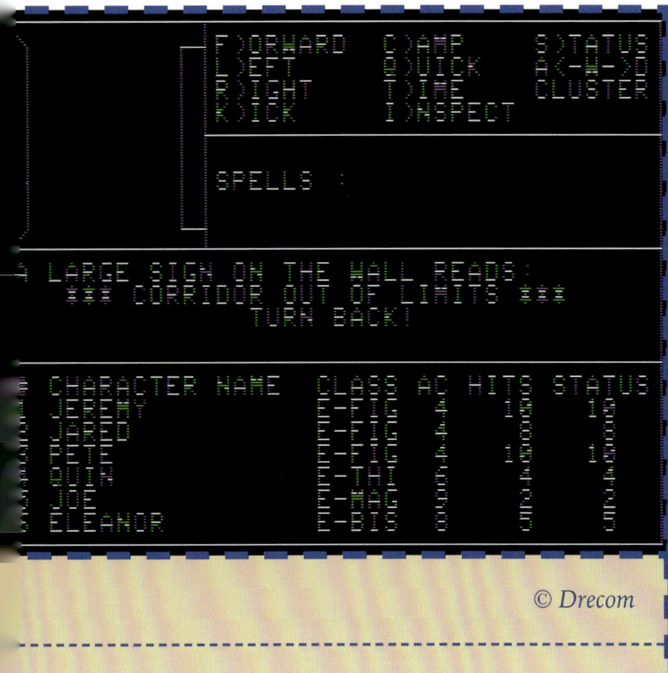

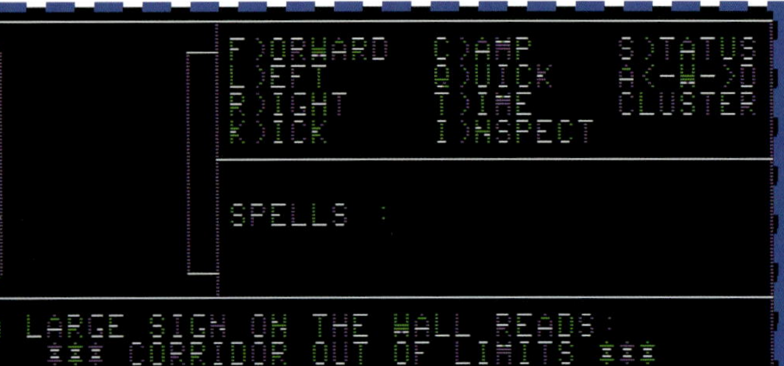

WIZARDRY:
PROVING GROUNDS OF THE MAD OVERLORD

PLATFORM: **APPLE II / VARIOUS**
DEV: **SIR-TECH** | PUB: **SIR-TECH**
INITIAL RELEASE: **SEPT. 1981**

CRAWL OF THE WILD

Wizardry, a 1981 role-playing game by Sir-Tech, sits at the midpoint between *Zork* and Atari's *Adventure*. Like the latter, *Wizardry* pares the role-playing concept down almost entirely to its combat and treasure-seeking components. What scant narrative exists largely unfolds within the confines of the game manual rather than over the course of the adventure itself; the moment-to-moment details of the quest and other story details (party banter, parlaying with merchants, that sort of thing) are left entirely to the player's imagination. On the other hand, Wizardry avoids boiling the mechanisms of adventure all the way down to a direct-action form, relying instead on a text parser interface that describes the player's actions and their outcomes.

But, like *Akalabeth* and a handful of PLATO-based RPG interpretations before it, *Wizardry* combines visual elements with its text. Rather than simply describe the monsters you encounter, *Wizardry* depicts them onscreen in varying levels of detail depending on the version of the game—the original Apple II game used crude outlines, while latter-day iterations like the NES and WonderSwan cartridges (not to mention 2023's elaborately overhauled Steam remake) rendered creatures in far greater detail. Most importantly, *Wizardry* depicted its environments visually as well. Using a windowed first-person perspective, the game didn't simply tell you that you had wandered into a maze of twisty passages (all alike). Rather, it dropped you into the thick of the maze, presenting you with a simplified view of the corridors and intersections ahead, and left you to sort your way through them. Eschewing the tool-based riddles of *Zork*, *Wizardry* instead turned its complex world into an ongoing puzzle for players to unravel through attentive exploration and manual mapping—sometimes as literal puzzles, as seen in the disorienting teleporter maze sequence. Between its emphasis on character experience growth and increasingly powerful weapons and armor, *Wizardry* neatly adapted the pen-and-paper RPG into digital form…provided all you wanted in an RPG was fighting and dungeon-crawling.

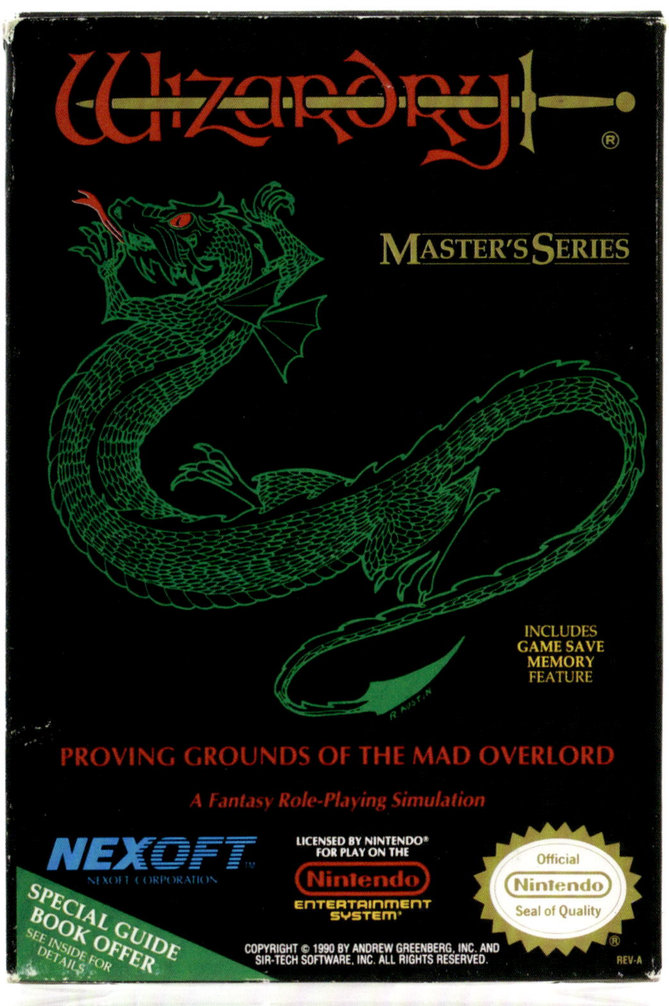

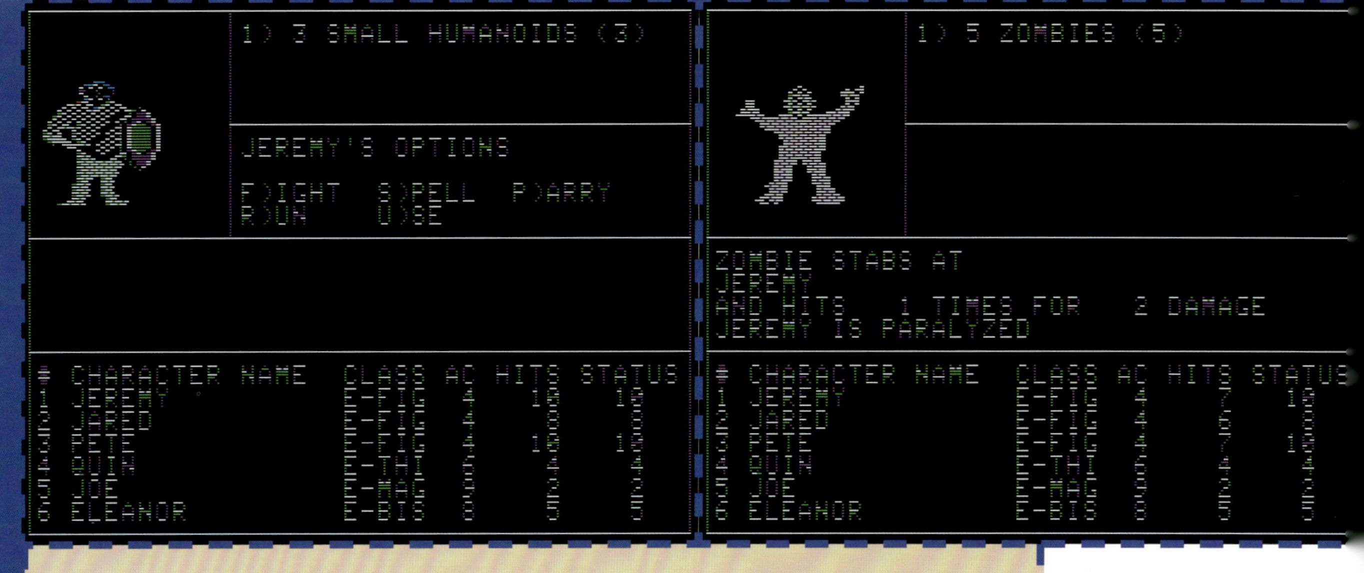

METROIDVANIA TIMELINE 1982-83

By 1982, the video game industry had entrenched itself as a going concern the world over. The Americas, Europe, and Japan all played host to a sparkling, seemingly ever-growing assortment of game creators and publishers across a widening spectrum of devices with increasing technical potential. Indeed, 1982 saw the advent of the first proper "next-generation" console and computer: the ColecoVision and the Commodore 64, respectively. Offering graphical and processing power well beyond previous consumer-level offerings, these machines promised to propel video gaming to new heights. Meanwhile, Cinematronics began showing off its upcoming LaserDisc-based *Dragon's Lair* arcade machine, a cabinet that incorporated high-fidelity film media into a game—the advent of interactive movies. Video games seemed to be downright unstoppable.

Looks can be deceptive. As 1982 drew to a close, Warner Communications—the conglomerate whose cash infusion had made possible true mass-market distribution for the 2600 console and 400/800 computer line—reported an unhappy fact. The very same Atari division that had propelled Warner's earnings to the greatest level of annual profits ever seen by a corporation only a couple of years earlier had missed its sales targets by a bafflingly wide margin, resulting in one of the greatest annual losses ever experienced by a corporation. This financial roller coaster spoke to the fact that the video games biz lacked stable foundations or long-term thinking. A quick rush to cash in had undermined the appeal of games for consumers, who lacked reliable means to judge whether they were about to spend $30 on a masterpiece or an absolute dud. Warner moved to divest itself of Atari the following year, and retailers backed away from gaming as a whole. Video games were dead.

...in America, at least for the moment. Meanwhile, Europe quickly cottoned to the new wave of affordable microcomputers—not only the C64 but also Sinclair's ZX Spectrum. And over in Japan, Sharp and NEC rolled out the first-ever computers designed for Japanese language support, which is to say they offered high-resolution graphical capabilities that translated neatly into games. At the same time, a number of different toy and electronics businesses took their earnings from LCD-based handheld game devices (the Game & Watch and its imitators) and launched a shocking number of game machines. Bandai, Casio, Gakken, Tomy, and Tsukuda Original all shipped game consoles toward the end of 1983...though none of these managed to make any headway against the systems that had launched that summer: The unstoppable trifecta of Nintendo Family Computer, Sega SG-1000, and the MSX computer standard. As the US console market collapsed in on itself, Japan saw its consoles come to life, buoyed by the uncoupling of the yen from its fixed postwar ties to the dollar and a new law that forbade children from hanging out in arcades on school nights.

As for the metroidvania, well, these new machines would become fertile soil for new concepts (especially the Famicom and PC- 9801). But even in America, new forms of gameplay continued percolating despite the industry's troubles. Atari's collapse didn't stop Activision from building on *Donkey Kong* with a technically intricate jungle adventure called *Pitfall!* Nor did it stop *Montezuma's Revenge* from transforming the puzzle exploration of the text adventure genre into a zippy platform action-adventure.

TIMELINE OF EVENTS

April 1982

ZX Spectrum

The most popular UK microcomputer of all time, the low-cost Spectrum offered low-level capabilities to match. That didn't keep it from being a hotbed of innovation for gaming.

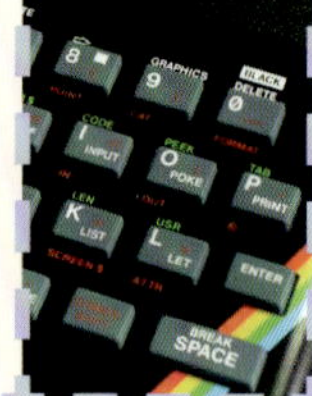

August 1982

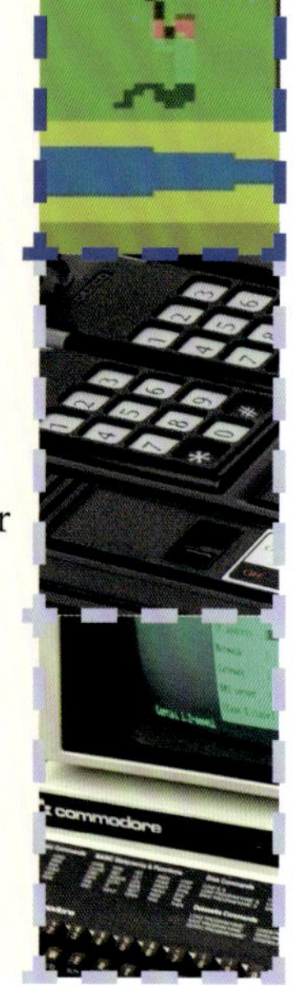

Pitfall!

Building on the run-and-jump action of Donkey Kong, Pitfall! spread its action across dozens of interconnected screens with a mazelike quality that demanded players map their progress.

ColecoVision

Built around the Z80 processor of the ZX Spectrum and a graphics processor derived from the TI99/4A, the ColecoVision console tapped the power of a computer—a next-gen machine.

Commodore 64

The follow-up to the VIC-20 offered even more power at an even better price, not to mention a robust audio chip. It became the bestselling 8-bit computer of all time.

October 1982

PC-9801
A more powerful computer than the 8801 (with which it offered backward compatibility), NEC's updated system become the de facto standard for Japanese computing in the '80s.

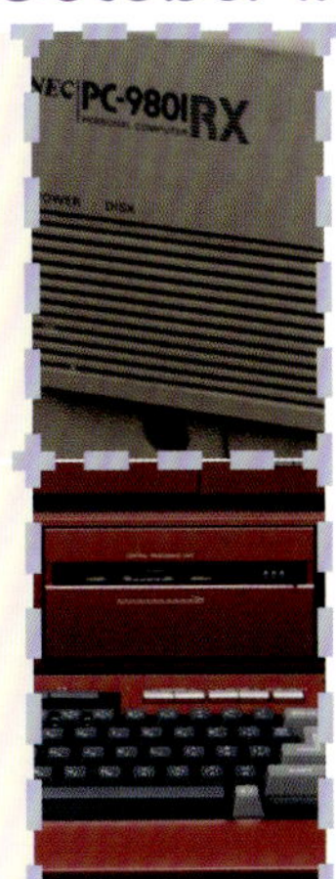

Sharp X1
While this Japan-only machine offered less computing power than rival machines from NEC, the X1 appealed to consumers for its attractive design and pioneering multimedia focus.

December 1982

The Dragon and the Princess
Often regarded as the first role-playing game created by Japanese developers for the Japanese market, this rough but interesting game hinted at the shape of things to come.

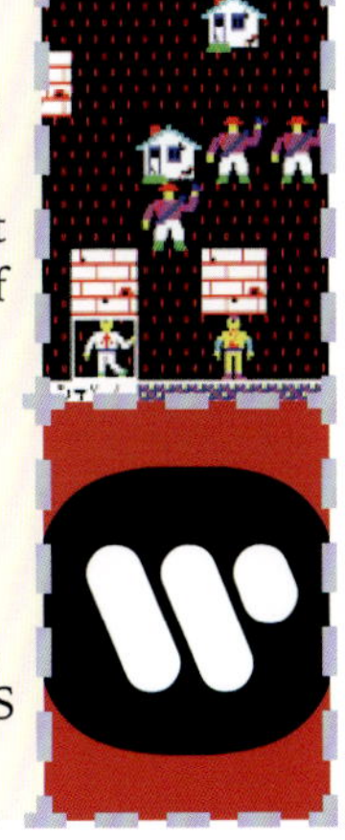

The Atari Crash Begins
Atari's parent corporation Warner announced a devastating profit shortfall for 1982 due to Atari's losses, initiating a crash that wiped out the US console industry by 1985.

June 1983

Portopia Renzoku Satsujin Jiken
An adventure game built in the *Mystery House* style, *Portopia* mixed things up by making its text parser diegetic, with commentary provided by the player's assistant Yasu.

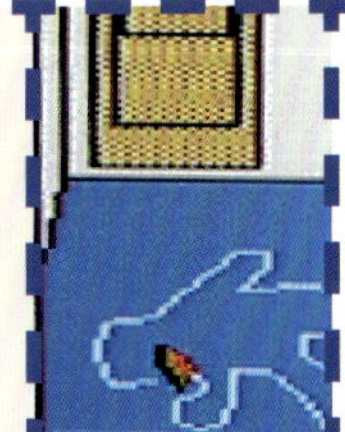

July 1983

Family Computer
Nintendo built its console with the goal of playing a mean game of *Donkey Kong*, but its expandability and vibrant third-party support made it the liveliest 8-bit system ever created.

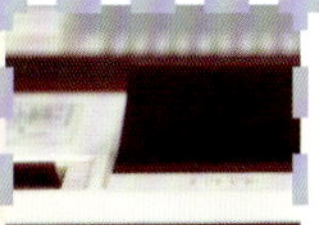

SG-1000 / SC-3000
Released day and date with the Famicom, Sega's console was almost identical to ColecoVision—and in time, it would evolve into the powerful Mark III (a.k.a. the Master System).

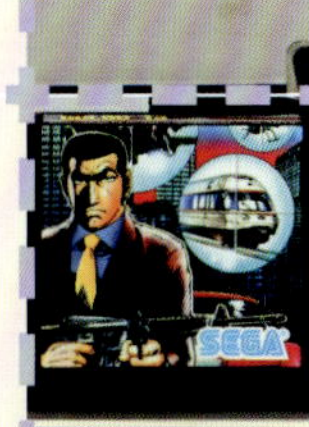

MSX
Also appearing alongside Famicom, the MSX was a computer/console hybrid standard rather than a product. Produced by multiple manufacturers, it turned into a favorite for game devs.

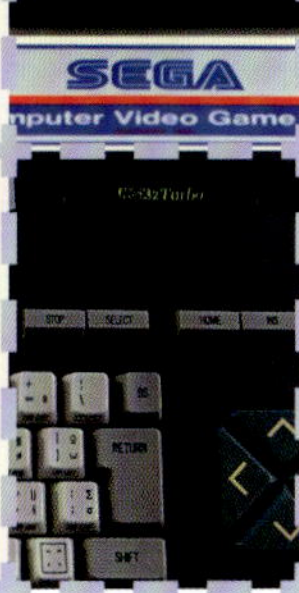

August 1983

Acorn Electron
Another low-cost UK computer built to compete with the Spectrum, the Electron didn't achieve the same degree of popularity as Sinclair's machine despite its superior features.

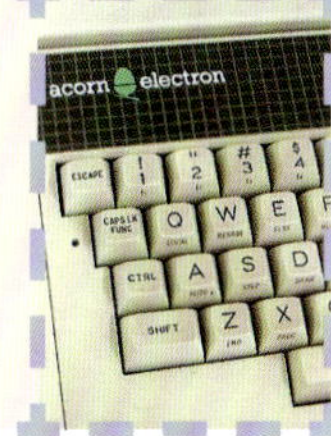

October 1983

Coleco ADAM
Coleco designed this computer to use the ColecoVision console as its heart; consumers could buy the ADAM as a standalone device or build one around an existing game console.

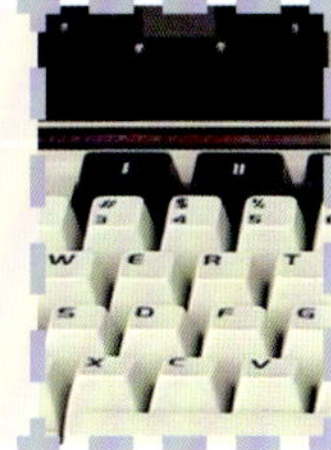

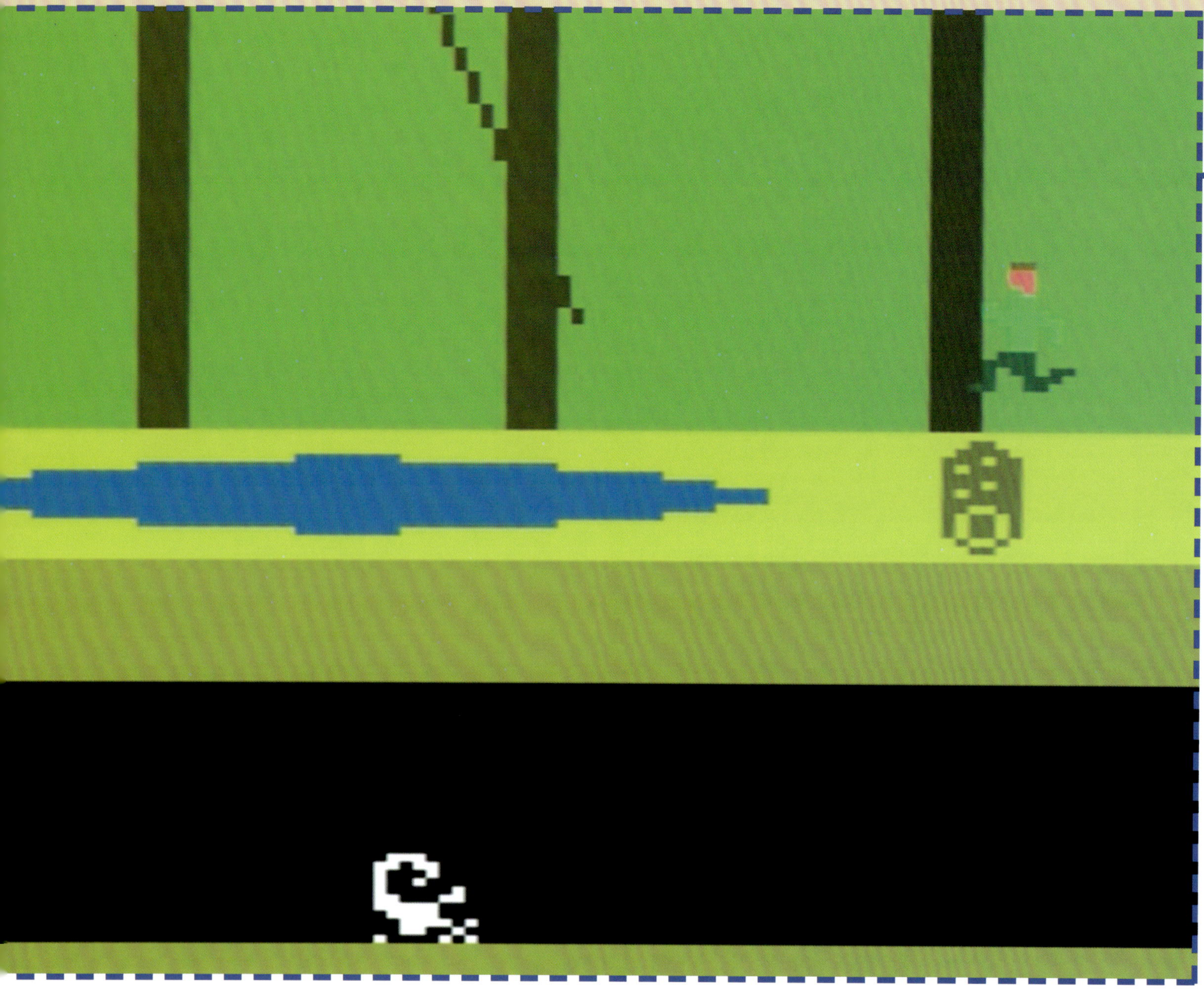

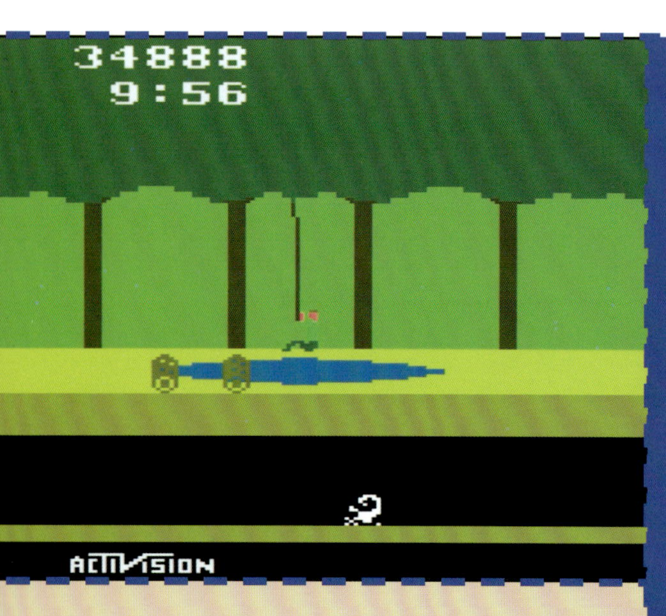

PITFALL!

PLATFORM: **ATARI 2600 / VARIOUS**
DEV: **ACTIVISION** | PUB: **ACTIVISION**
INITIAL RELEASE: **AUG. 1982**

NOTABLE FOR: **INTEGRATING EXPLORATION INTO THE PLATFORM ACTION FORMAT**

CONCRETE JUNGLE

Donkey Kong may have canonized the workings of platform action games, but it employed those mechanics in service of a simple, gymnastic obstacle-climbing challenge. Activision's *Pitfall!* expanded on *Donkey Kong*'s workings to combines platforming with exploration—the first hint of what we would eventually come to recognize as the metroidvania.

Of course, *Pitfall!* wasn't a "proper" metroidvania game as we think of them today, if such a thing could even be said to exist. But, as exploratory platformers and action-RPGs evolved throughout the 1980s, *Pitfall!* played a tremendous part in that process. Debuting in August 1982, it took the platforming mechanics laid down in *Donkey Kong* and applied them to something grander than a single-screen action game. Granted, *Pitfall!* lacks scrolling backgrounds. The action spans a series of individual, self-contained screens, but you'd never mistake this for a single-screen arcade title of that era. It has far less density to its design, and a laxer form of action than seen in its coin-op contemporaries. Early platform games like *Donkey Kong*, *Kangaroo*, *Roc 'N Rope*, and *BurgerTime* crammed their layouts full of hazards across multiple tiers. Their worlds felt tiny and compact. *Pitfall!*, on the other hand, sprawls. It lets its world unfurl more loosely, with only two tiers of action—above and below ground—which run in parallel.

This decompression of design had plenty of precedent by 1982, of course. We saw it in *Adventure*, where the game world spread across multiple screens, and in *Zork*, a minicomputer creation so vast it had to be broken into multiple chapters to fit within the bounds of a home computer. Those games may have used a text-based format to relay their worlds, yet the rooms you explored—equivalent to *Pitfall!*'s individual screens—possessed an incredibly dense design sensibility. Nearly every space contained multiple elements to consider, explore, and interact with, all connected by labyrinthine passages that required careful navigation.

You can arguably find a more direct predecessor to *Pitfall!*'s design in 1981's *Defender*, a blazing-fast shoot-'em-up manufactured by American coin-op powerhouse Williams Electronics. With *Defender*, designer Eugene Jarvis had taken the

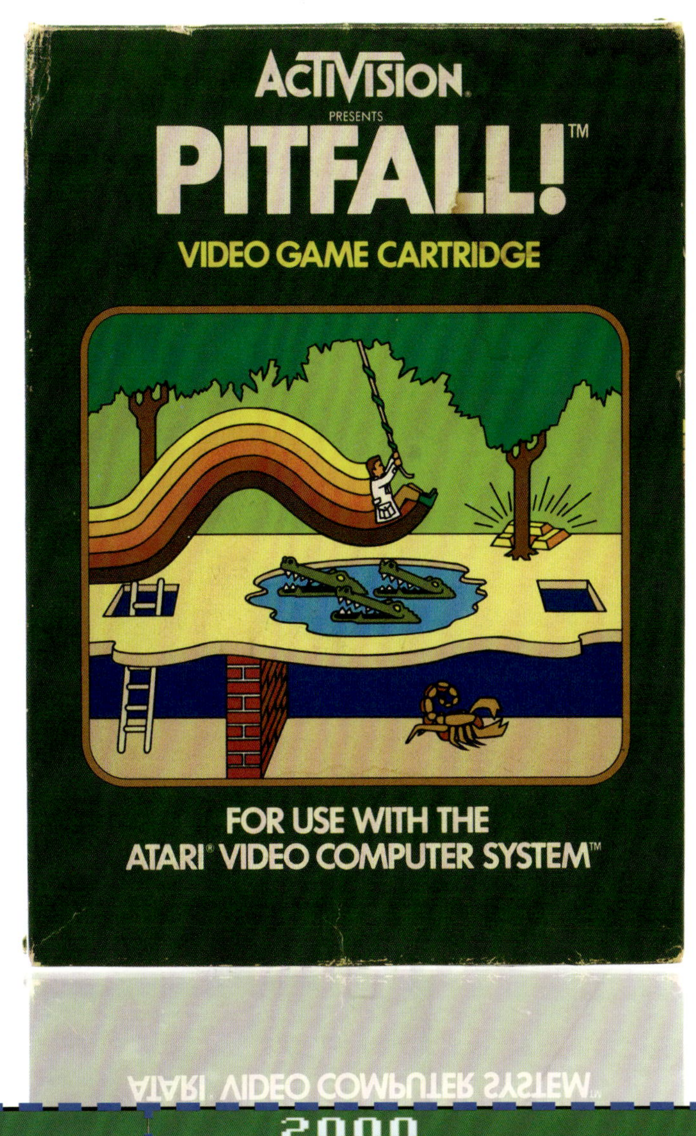

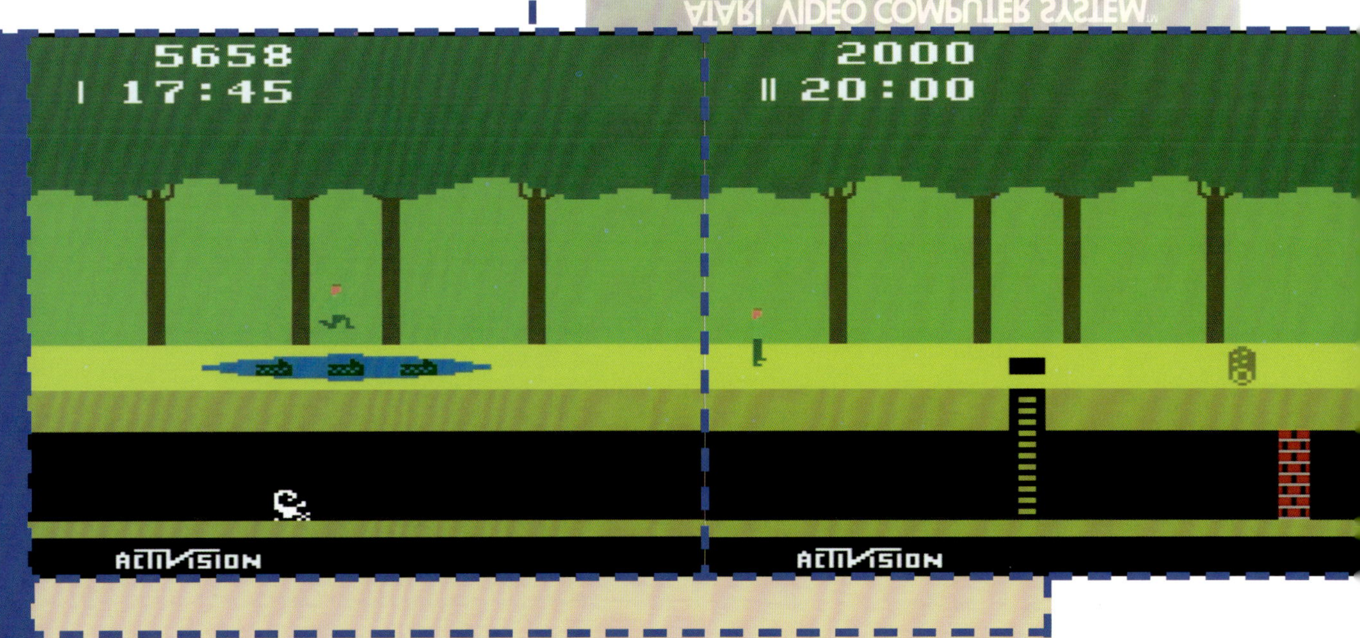

looping, all-directional screen-wrap of *Asteroids* and pushed it beyond its original single-screen format, creating a play space two screens high and several screens wide. *Defender*'s world only wrapped on the horizontal axis, it was hemmed in by hard boundaries along the top and bottom edges, working more like a torus than a sphere.

In creating a world that existed beyond the boundaries of what the player could see at a glance, *Defender* benefited in several ways. First, it created a sensation of persistence within action games, introducing the concept that things could exist beyond the player's current screen view and that they would continue to act even when they scrolled out of sight. *Defender* provided a radar mini-map along the upper edge of the screen that allowed players to take in events all across the game "world" at a glance. Namco had introduced that concept a few months before *Defender*'s release with their maze-race *Rally-X*, but Jarvis's implementation took the mechanic to the next level.

Second, *Defender*'s decompressed structure made for a blazingly fast game. Because the screen scrolled with the player, zipping around became less disorienting; the player's craft would always appear near the center of the screen. The linked screen spaces meant that hazards could appear farther apart from one another, too, allowing Jarvis to give players the ability to cover more pixel real estate with their movements without compromising the number of objects at play in the active game world. Pushing beyond the bounds of a single screen had a transformative effect, changing not only *Defender*, but countless games to follow.

That includes *Pitfall!* Granted, *Pitfall!* didn't (or couldn't) make use of scrolling graphics the way that *Defender* did, but designer David Crane did his best to incorporate its concept of a world that spanned far beyond what's currently visible to the player. At the same time, *Pitfall!* deliberately and actively worked to betray the player's perception. The game's jungle world consisted of a sort of Möbius strip of 256 screens arranged in a line, and any player who could survive long enough to make their way from screen 1 to screen 256 would loop back to screen 1. However, the path through the jungle sprawled out across two levels: along the surface of the ground and along a subterranean route that ran beneath the surface route. These tracks never crossed over, but occasionally players would have the opportunity to use a ladder to switch tracks. What isn't immediately apparent when you first begin playing *Pitfall!* is that the underground path operates under different rules than the jungle route. Whereas the overworld is strictly a linear march from screen 1 to 256, the dark spaces beneath the ground connect differently, almost like a warp, often skipping over multiple screens at a time.

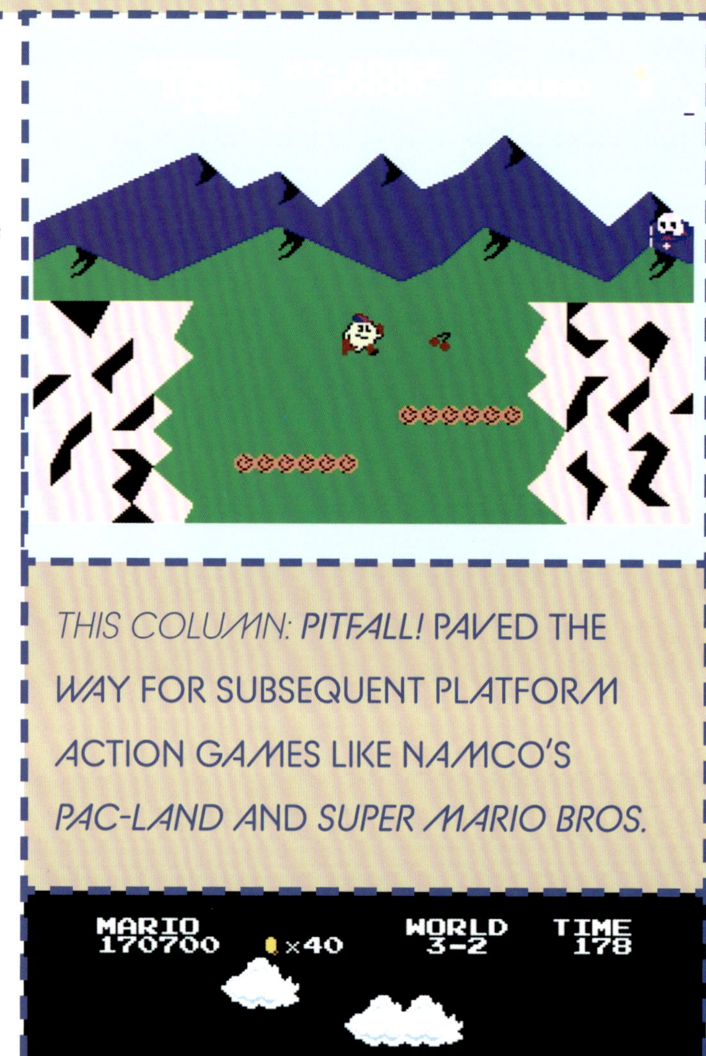

THIS COLUMN: **PITFALL! PAVED THE WAY FOR SUBSEQUENT PLATFORM ACTION GAMES LIKE NAMCO'S PAC-LAND AND SUPER MARIO BROS.**

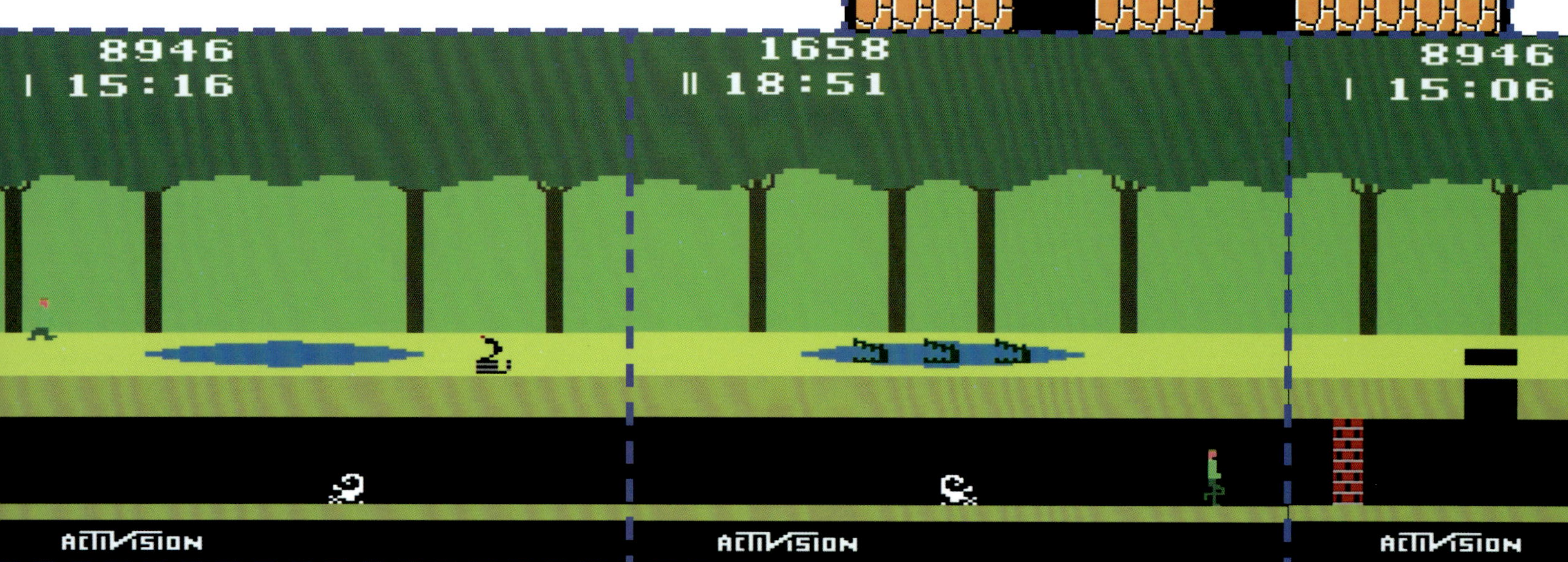

Pitfall! thus became the first action game that demanded its fans sit down and map out routes, breaking down the complex arrangement of what initially appears to be a simple linear path. The game presents players with a straightforward goal: collect a certain number of treasures within twenty minutes. This proves to be more difficult than it sounds, though. Many treasures appear in seemingly inaccessible underground spaces, meaning you can see them while tramping about overhead but have to figure out how to negotiate the quirks of the underground to reach them—a spiritual precursor to the metroidvania trademark of placing objects just out of reach and demanding you return upon expanding your skill set.

Pitfall! isn't a "true" metroidvania game given that its protagonist, Pitfall Harry, never acquires any sort of power-ups or skill upgrades. Nor do you need any tools to make your way through the world. But the concept of tantalizing players with seemingly unreachable riches and challenging them to figure out how to collect that loot? That is 100 percent metroidvania, and while we saw a little bit of it in *Adventure*, *Pitfall!* took the idea and literally ran with it. *Pitfall!* also introduced the idea of backtracking, in a sense. The optimal route through the game to collect all the jungle treasures demands you double back early on to take an underground shortcut from screen 12 to screen 246, emerging from the lower route from time to time to pick up treasures or change shortcut paths.

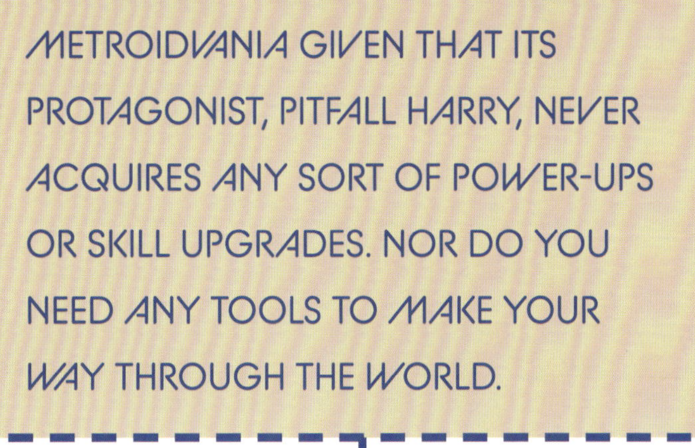

It's a tricky and devious game…and it's not an easy one. In addition to the pretzel-like map, *Pitfall!* also demands you deal with platforming hazards, such as scorpions, alligators, and, inevitably, pitfalls. Crane managed to squeeze all this into just a few kilobytes of storage space, meaning *Pitfall!* serves as much as a feat of creative programming as it does a pioneering work of design. Ultimately, though, *Pitfall!*'s gameplay innovations had the greater lasting impact, definitively establishing third-party Atari 2600 publisher Activision as a force to be reckoned with.

Pitfall! arrived about a year after *Donkey Kong*, and shortly after *Donkey Kong Jr.* Similarities between certain hazards in those games highlight what Crane brought to the platformer. One of the first dangers you have to deal with in *Pitfall!* are rolling logs that tumble across the jungle floor, and which look an awful lot like the barrels that Kong tosses. These logs appear more predictably than Kong's barrels, and they operate more simplistically due to simpler layout of *Pitfall!*'s platforming spaces. Rather than demanding quick reactions from players, avoiding the logs instead becomes a matter of timing and prediction. Likewise, the snapping alligator pools more than slightly resemble *Donkey Kong Jr.*'s Snapjaw traps. Where Snapjaws moved in randomized patterns along vines and flooring, *Pitfall!*'s gators sit in place and open their mouths cyclically.

In short, the *Donkey Kong* approach to platformers gave players a self-contained space whose dangers resulted from the chaotic, dynamic hazards within. *Pitfall!*, on the other hand, turns the environment itself into the enemy. You'll always encounter logs and scorpions in the same places, so the challenge isn't so much to outmaneuver them as it is to learn to navigate the mazelike paths while being mindful of the perils along the way. It's a subtle difference, but a meaningful one. *Pitfall!* belongs to the platformer genre, but athleticism and finger speed play less of a crucial role here than planning and exploration. *Pitfall!* is a game about seeking a high score, but the real challenge is simply to figure out how to complete the adventure. Needless to say, *Pitfall!* would have a huge influence on countless games to come. The UK would quickly see its own enormously successful variant on *Pitfall!* with games like *Manic Miner*, *Jet Set Willy*, and *Knight Lore*. Countless other "treasure hunting" adventures would pop up across PCs and consoles, including *Spelunker*, *The Pharaoh's Curse*, and *Montezuma's Revenge*. As quickly as it was conceived, the platformer genre began straining at the boundaries of arcade design to become a vessel for more demanding works of greater complexity. And *Pitfall!* led the charge.

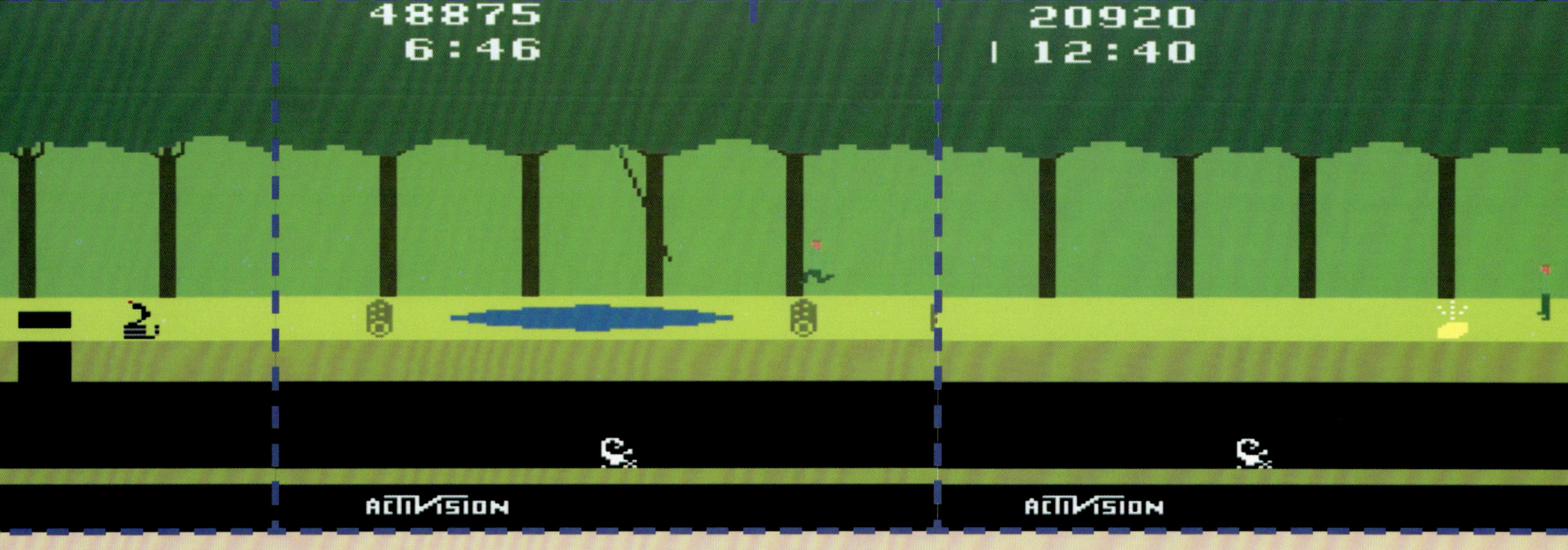

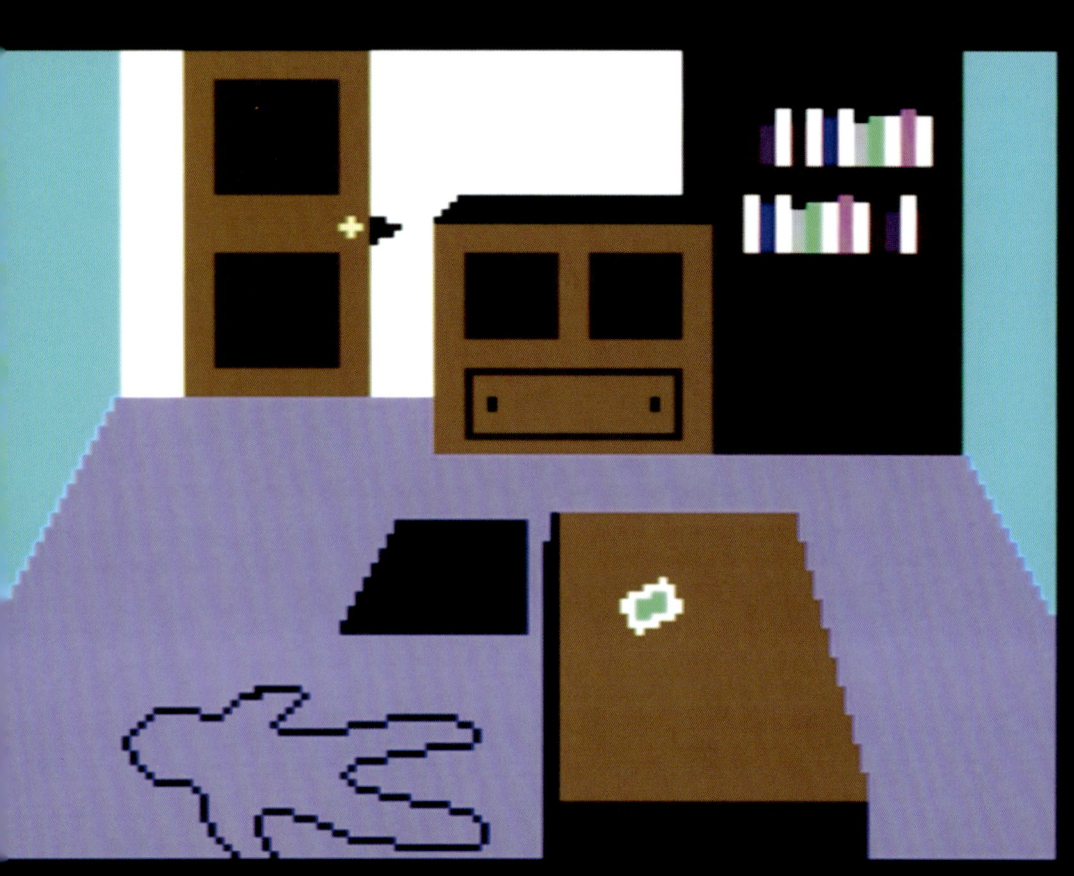

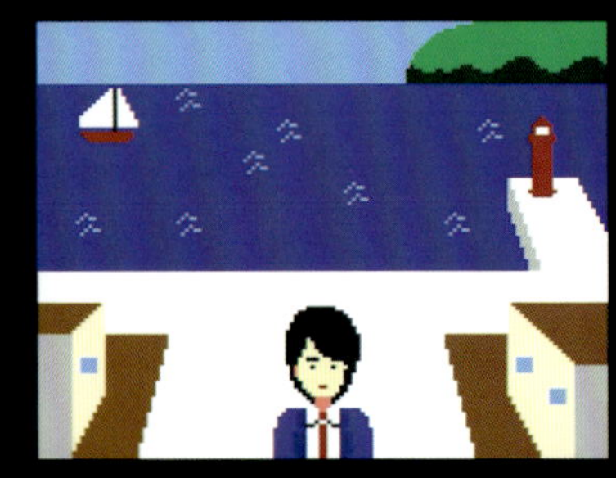

PORTOPIA RENZOKU SATSUJIN JIKEN

PLATFORM: PC-8801 / VARIOUS
DEV: CHUN SOFT | PUB: ENIX
INITIAL RELEASE: JUNE 1983
SHOWN HERE: NINTENDO FAMICOM VERSION, 1985
[UNOFFICIAL ENGLISH TRANSLATION]

NOTABLE FOR: **USING THE ADVENTURE GENRE TO LAY THE GROUNDWORK FOR CONSOLE RPGS**

MURDERVANIA MYSTERY

While something of a tangent to the central through line of metroidvania evolution, *Portopia Renzoku Satsujin Jiken* (or, if you prefer, *The Portopia Serial Murder Case*) nevertheless sits at an important junction in the genre's history. A graphical adventure, it distills the essence of computer games like *Zork* and *Mystery House* into a simple, digestible format that works neatly within the limitations of a console. In fact, *Portopia* began its life as a personal computer release that functioned similarly to the sort of game you saw from Sierra On-Line and Infocom.

Players navigate about the world—largely centered around several different neighborhoods of Kobe, Japan—and view the world from a first-person perspective. As in most *Zork*-derived games, backtracking played a huge part in *Portopia*, as did the need to collect and use items to advance past certain points in the story or the world. The player takes on the role of a police detective assigned to investigate the death of a wealthy businessman, inputting commands through a text parser and receiving information by way of a clever, immersive design element that led to a major a story twist. Rather than receive feedback from a disembodied narrator or terse text prompt, the player relays instructions to his assistant, a young junior detective named Yasu. Yasu will comment on your instructions, adding a touch of color, humor, and personal entanglement to the narrative.

In bringing *Portopia* to Nintendo's Famicom, developer Chunsoft had to account for the fact that the console only had two buttons rather than entire keyboard; could only store a fraction of the computer game's data; and had to work within Famicom's restrictive, tile-based graphical system. Somehow, programmer Koichi Nakamura and designer Yuji Horii made it work. The limitations of the system forced them to come up with a menu-driven interface that streamlined the process of investigating and exploring into a simple cursor-based setup. This would become the basis of more or less the entire console role-playing genre going forward: these same developers moved on to create *Dragon Quest* the following year, which then led to the likes of *Phantasy Star*, *Final Fantasy*, ports of *Wizardry* and *Ultima*, and many others.

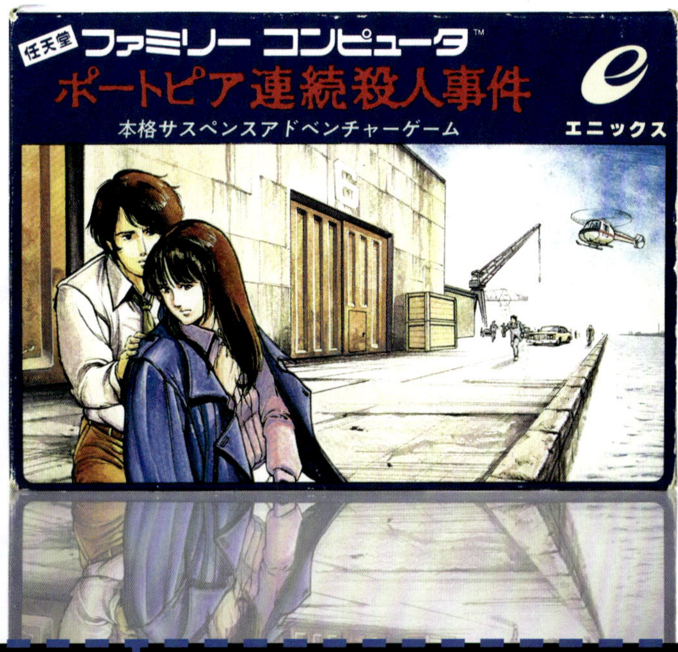

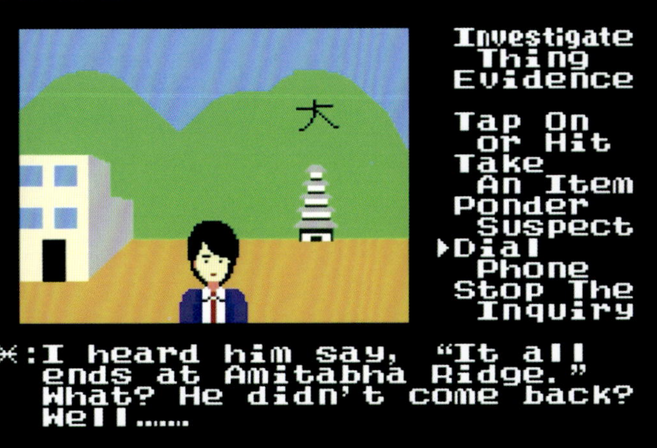

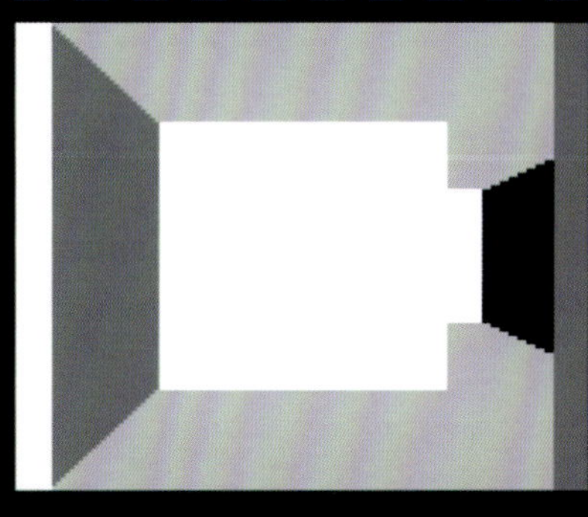

METROIDVANIA TIMELINE 1984

As American publications lamented the short life and pathetic death of video games—the Pet Rock fad of the '80s!—the rest of the world began to explore the potential of the medium in earnest. The quick, bite-sized, skill-based experiences that defined arcades remained popular, but developers began to dig deeper into what it meant to create a "home game"—adventures designed for players who purchased software to enjoy in the leisurely comfort of their own spaces. The pay-per-play nature of coin-op games, and the spectator-driven social environment of arcades, drove designers to create short-lived, flashy works that would draw in viewers and players and give them a few minutes of fun before demanding another quarter (or ¥100 coin, as the case may be). But those dynamics didn't make sense at home. There was no need to pump coins into a console, and the personal computer in your living room didn't draw crowds of strangers to celebrate your feats. Home games needed to be different.

And, in 1984, game developers truly began to embrace that reality. Enter games like *Pitfall II: Lost Caverns*, which abandoned the limited time (and limited lives) of its predecessor to present a game that anyone could complete but only the truly skilled could perfect. Enter *Dragon Slayer*, a slow-paced, methodical distillation of the role-playing genre into a one-button action game. Enter *Jet Set Willy* and *Knight Lore*, British computer adventure games that placed a heavy emphasis on finger skill, but which also demanded players to invest the time they needed to take each game at a measured pace and memorize the interconnected virtual worlds they spanned. Enter *Below the Root*, a young adult novel transformed into a platform adventure game set in a sprawling world among the treetops.

Even the arcades saw new innovations in this direction. The *Tower of Druaga* took the time-tested *Pac-Man* concept and turned into a sword-and-sorcery affair across a sixty-story tower packed with secrets. *Dragon Buster* did likewise for the *Donkey Kong* concept, not only equipping the hero with a sword and shield but also a life meter. And the influence of these games made itself apparent almost immediately. *Druaga* shipped to arcades in late spring, and in December T&E Soft launched their own homegrown take on the concept with *Hydlide* for Japanese personal computers. Despite the lacuna in the US market, where the video game ball had started rolling in the first place, the medium's maturation barreled full steam ahead, moving ever closer to the true metroidvania. M

TIMELINE OF EVENTS

January

The Black Onyx

Though not the first RPG developed in Japan, this dungeon crawler finally gave that country's aspiring RPG fanatics a Wizardry-style experience in their own native language.

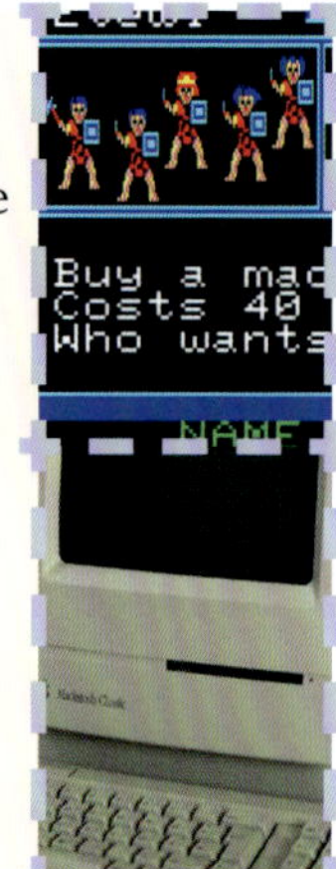

Macintosh

Apple's Mac centered the user experience around its mouse-driven controls and a high-resolution (though monochrome) graphical interface, making it a natural fit for video games.

February

Pitfall II: Lost Caverns

The follow-up to Pitfall! sent protagonist Harry beneath the jungle to rescue his niece and collect treasures in a huge, open cavern with no time limit and no lives.

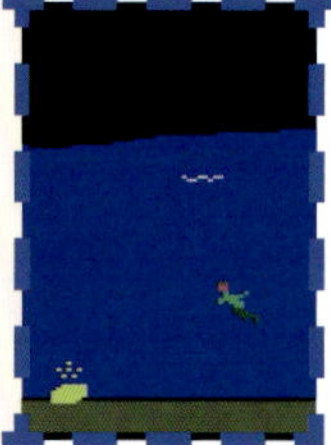

June

Jet Set Willy

Another treasure hunt in the Pitfall! mode, Jet Set Willy played down the puzzle elements in favor of a series of intensely difficult platforming challenges.

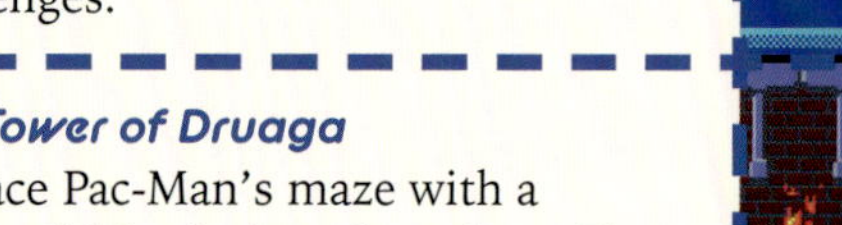

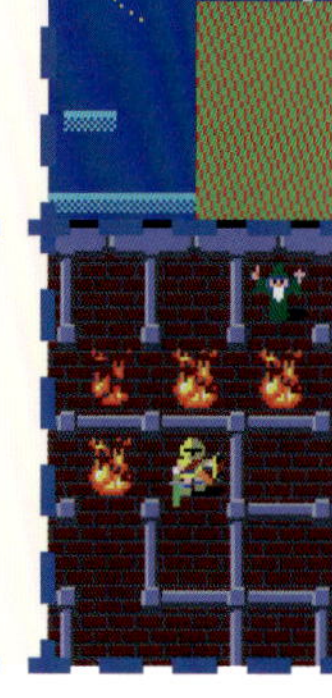

The Tower of Druaga

Replace Pac-Man's maze with a medieval labyrinth and you have The Tower of Druaga, a complex sword-and-sorcery adventure packed with secrets and escalating challenges.

July

Nuts & Milk

A simple arcade-style game, this Hudson classic has a place in history for opening the door to third-party publishers on Famicom—the petri dish for a decade of gaming innovation.

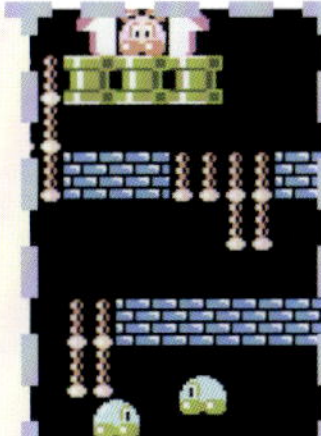

August

Below the Root

Based on a young adult novel from the 1970s, *Below the Root* presented players with a large, open quest in a fantastical world: a graphical adventure that played as a puzzle platformer.

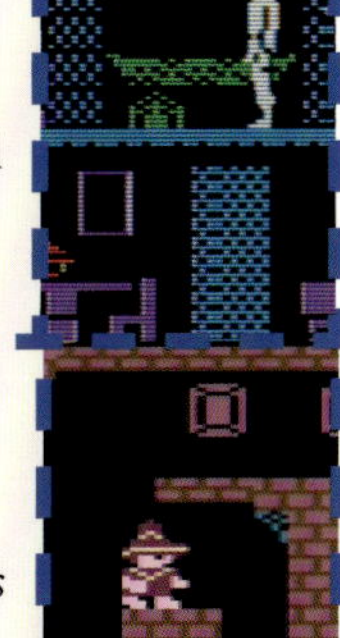

Montezuma's Revenge

Another *Donkey Kong* descendant, but rather than focusing on sheer sprawl and immensity like *Pitfall!*, *Montezuma's Revenge* asked players to explore compact, puzzle-like structures.

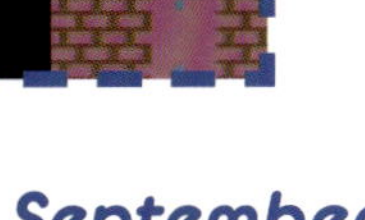

September

Impossible Mission

A wholly distinct take on the puzzle platformer from *Below the Root*, *Impossible Mission* was about survival and finger skill rather than narrative—but was no less influential for it.

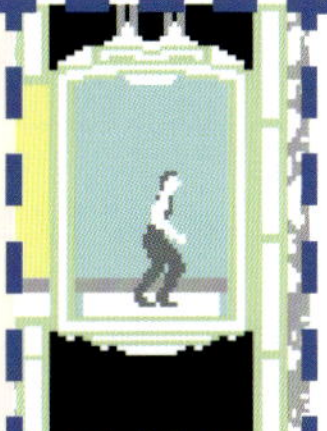

October

Dragon Slayer

Nihon Falcom dropped players into a labyrinth packed with treasures and monsters, challenging them to collect experience without causing the bad guys to grow too powerful.

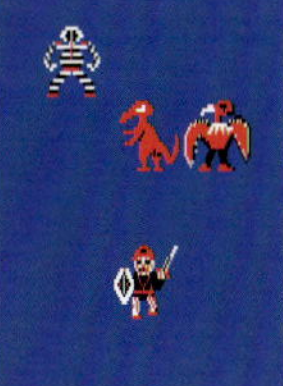

November

Knight Lore

A seek-and-collect treasure adventure in the spirit of *Dragon Slayer*, but centered around isometric platforming and randomized item placement—with a groundbreaking day/night cycle!

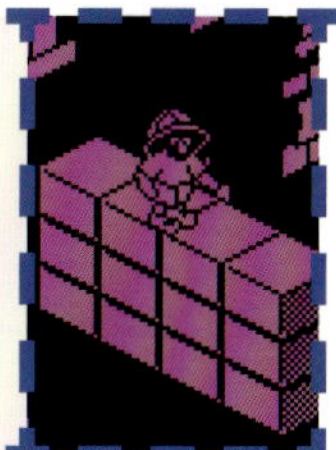

December

Hydlide

Built in the image of *Druaga*, *Hydlide* took the adventure out of the tower confines and into an open landscape dotted with caverns, castles, and oblique secrets to uncover.

Dragon Buster

Years before *The Legend of Zelda* became a side-scroller with *Zelda II*, Namco effectively did the same thing to *Druaga* and came up with this influential sword combat RPG for arcades.

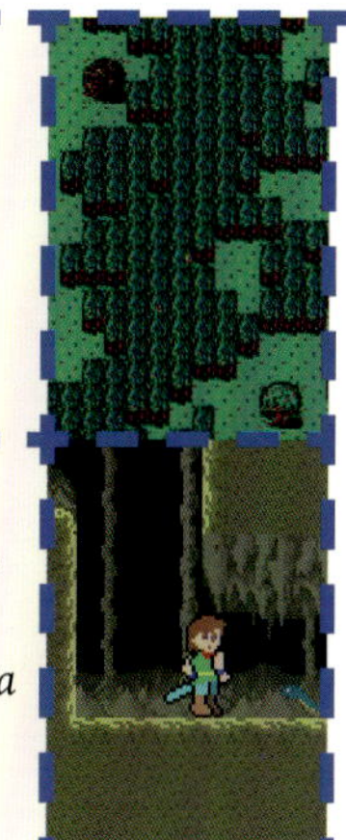

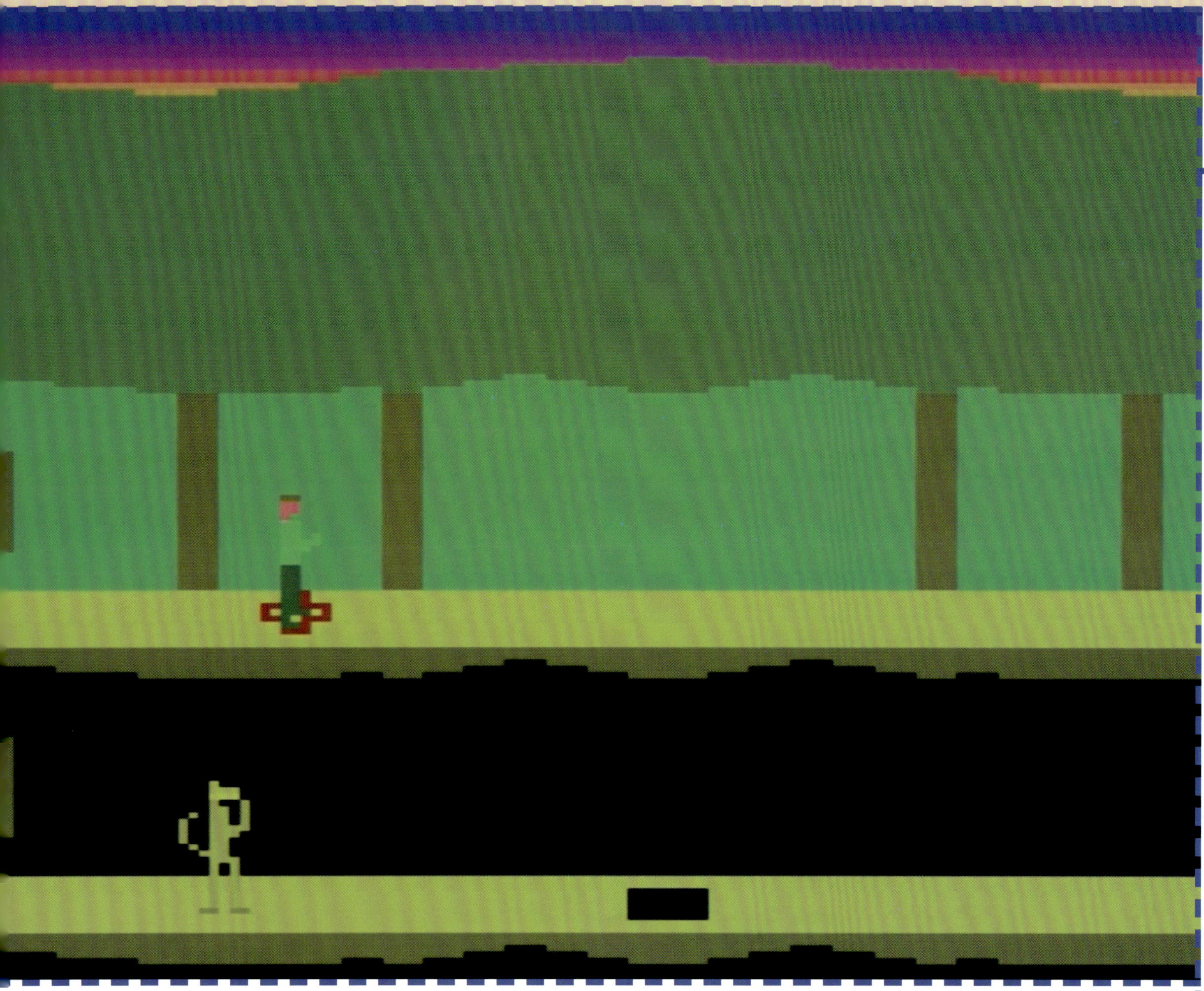

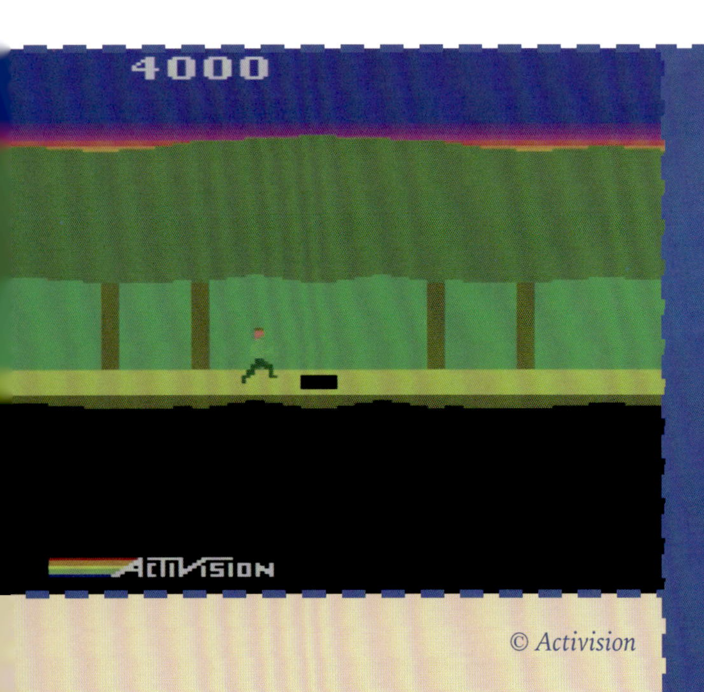

PITFALL II: LOST CAVERNS

PLATFORM: **ATARI 2600 / VARIOUS**
DEV: **ACTIVISION** | PUB: **ACTIVISION**
INITIAL RELEASE: **FEB. 1984**
SHOWN HERE: **ATARI 2600 VERSION, 1984**

NOTABLE FOR: **GIVING PLAYERS A WHOLLY OPEN WORLD IN AN ACTION GAME**

THE WORLD BELOW

Adding exploration to the run-and-jump platformer was a completely natural sequence of events. If you're moving a character around the screen, trying to lead them to a goal, the next step is to give that character a goal that took more than a single screen to complete. What if they could break out of their linear track? What if there were more to the world than simply the path between points A and B? *Pitfall!* took the first step in that journey, spreading the single-screen navigation of *Donkey Kong* across 256 different screens. While *Pitfall!*'s world existed as an infinite linear loop, that loop contained obstructions, detours, and secret passageways, making it a sort of environmental puzzle.

For its 1984 sequel, Crane expanded on this puzzle concept even further. One of the final major releases for Atari 2600, *Pitfall II: The Lost Caverns* turned out to so ambitious in scope that it exceeded the base capabilities of the console! As with next-generation exploratory Nintendo games like *Metroid* and *The Legend of Zelda*, *Pitfall II* wouldn't have been possible with the system's stock hardware. Publisher Activision stuffed the cartridge with extra memory to house the game's expansive world along with a special chip to enhance the 2600's audio, allowing *Pitfall II* to accompany its action with a rousing, dynamic ditty rather than the ear-splitting static and beeps for which the 2600 was known.

This makes it quite an innovative landmark game, especially in light of the fact that it abandons the concept of lives and timers altogether. *Pitfall II* feels more like a modern-era indie game with its generous design; although you need to avoid cave-dwelling critters, bumping into a bat or eel simply sends the player spinning back to the latest checkpoint they've crossed. You can fling yourself against *Pitfall II*'s underground caverns indefinitely until you win rather than having to start a fresh game after a few failures. The challenge comes not from a demand for nimble dexterity but rather for observation and thoroughness: The Lost Caverns are packed with treasure, just like the first game's jungle, and each treasure nets Pitfall Harry a certain number of points.

You lose points when you bump into a hazard, though, meaning the goal of *Pitfall II* is ultimately to find all 199,000 points' worth of treasure hidden throughout the caverns and reach the end

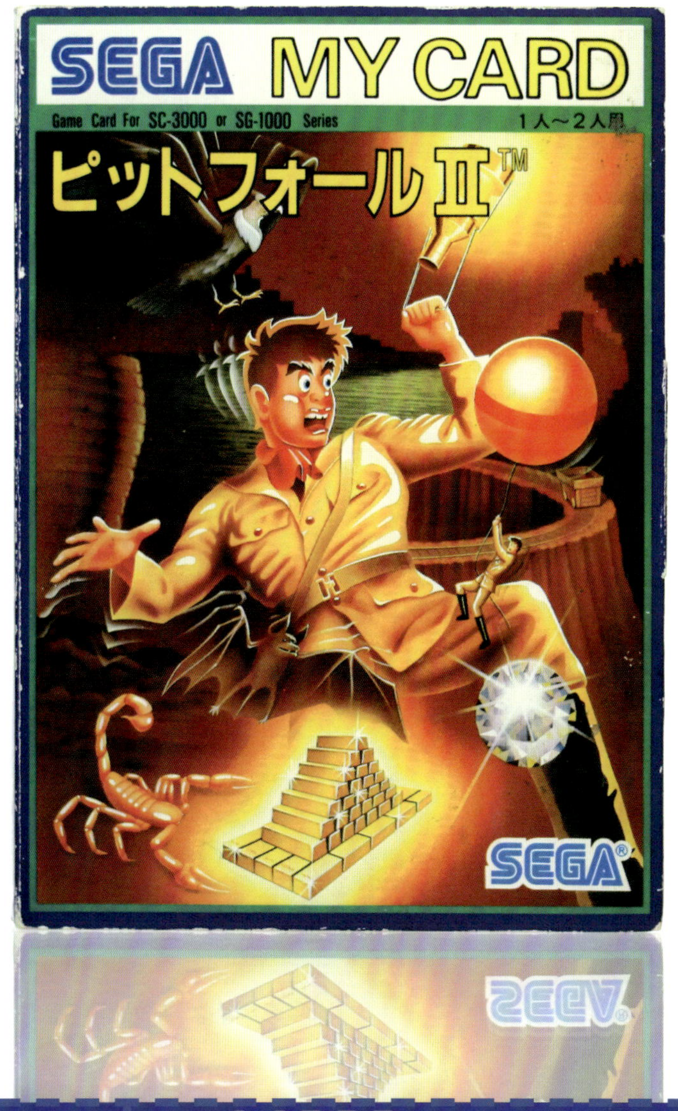

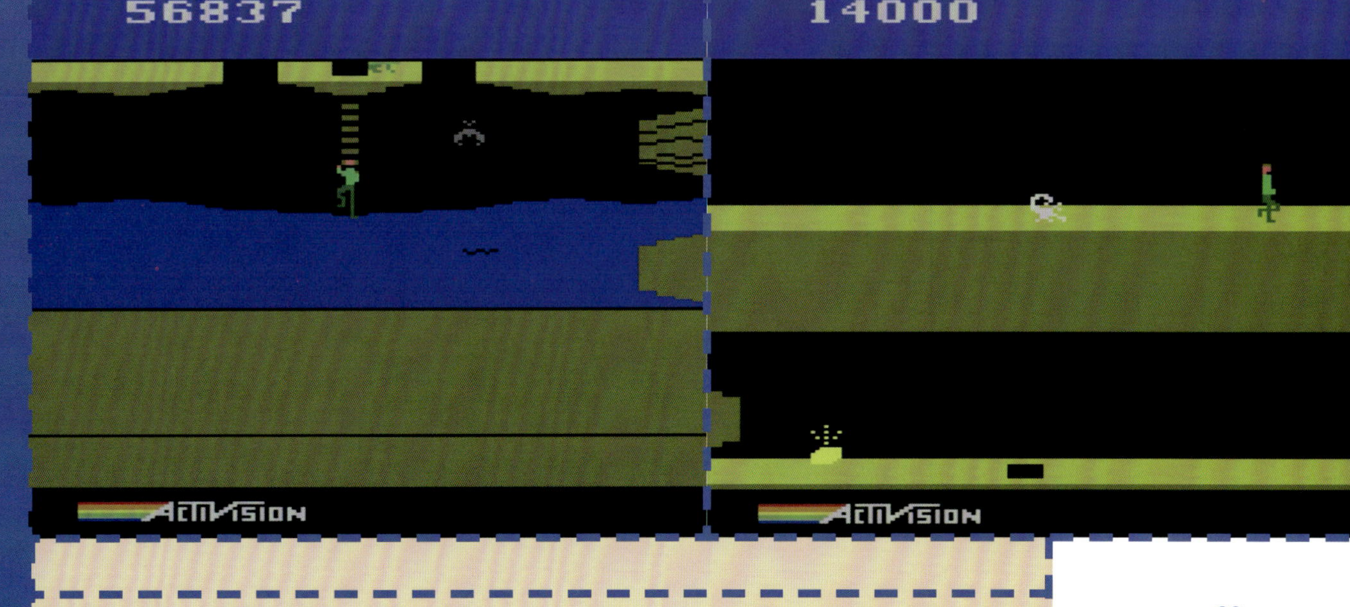

without a single point being docked. Despite the game's forgiving design, it's a challenging task. *Pitfall II* has the most intricate video game world ever seen outside of *Zork* and its text-based ilk, and certainly the most intricate environment ever to in a run-and-jump action game. Crane once again designed about 256 screens for Pitfall Harry to navigate, but here he didn't lay those screens out along an endless horizontal loop. Instead, *Pitfall II* emphasizes verticality. The Lost Caverns span only eight screens across, but that's literally just scratching the surface; the underground now contains a series of caves that descend through a whopping 27 floors.

Pitfall II's caverns interlock and interconnect, becoming a sort of spatial puzzle. You can see multiple levels of cavern on each screen, but you can't always reach the spaces you can see right away. Walls, pits, and ceilings turn the subterranean caves into a maze. The dense caverns underground consist of three large columns of structure separated by a screen-wide gulf of empty air. Pitfall Harry has the remarkable ability to survive a fall from any height, so completing *Pitfall II* becomes a matter of taking bold leaps and plunges in order to cross these chasms and reach otherwise inaccessible areas. An underground river at the bottom of the caverns creates a conduit that allows Harry to cross back to the rightmost column of caves and ladders when the player miscalculates. The game requires patience, but there's a real sense of satisfaction when you finally deduce the path that will help you reach a seemingly out-of-the-way treasure.

Pitfall II is also notable in that it has a goal beyond the point-building treasure hunt. Ultimately, you only need to find a single specific item—a diamond ring—and rescue Harry's niece and pet mountain lion in order to win. The real task at hand here is exploration and navigation of a huge and complex series of caverns.

More than any other early action game, *Pitfall II* truly feels like the proper progenitor to the metroidvania genre. Its world is vastly larger and more complex than that of even *Montezuma's Revenge*; but, unlike *Zork*, its interface and vocabulary are based entirely around action, and not overtly arcade-style action. It's a game that allows you to explore, challenges you to take notes, and gives you the freedom to do so at your own pace. Given the game's late release and the obscurity of the 2600 console in Japan (where it had launched belatedly, around the same time as the Famicom, under the name Atari 2800), *Pitfall II* probably wasn't a direct influence on the core metroidvania games; Sega's arcade and SG-1000 interpretations streamlined the game considerably from its 2600 iteration. But, looking at what Crane accomplished on the humble 2600, it's impossible not to be impressed with his work—and to recognize that adding exploration to action games is a natural, human impulse.

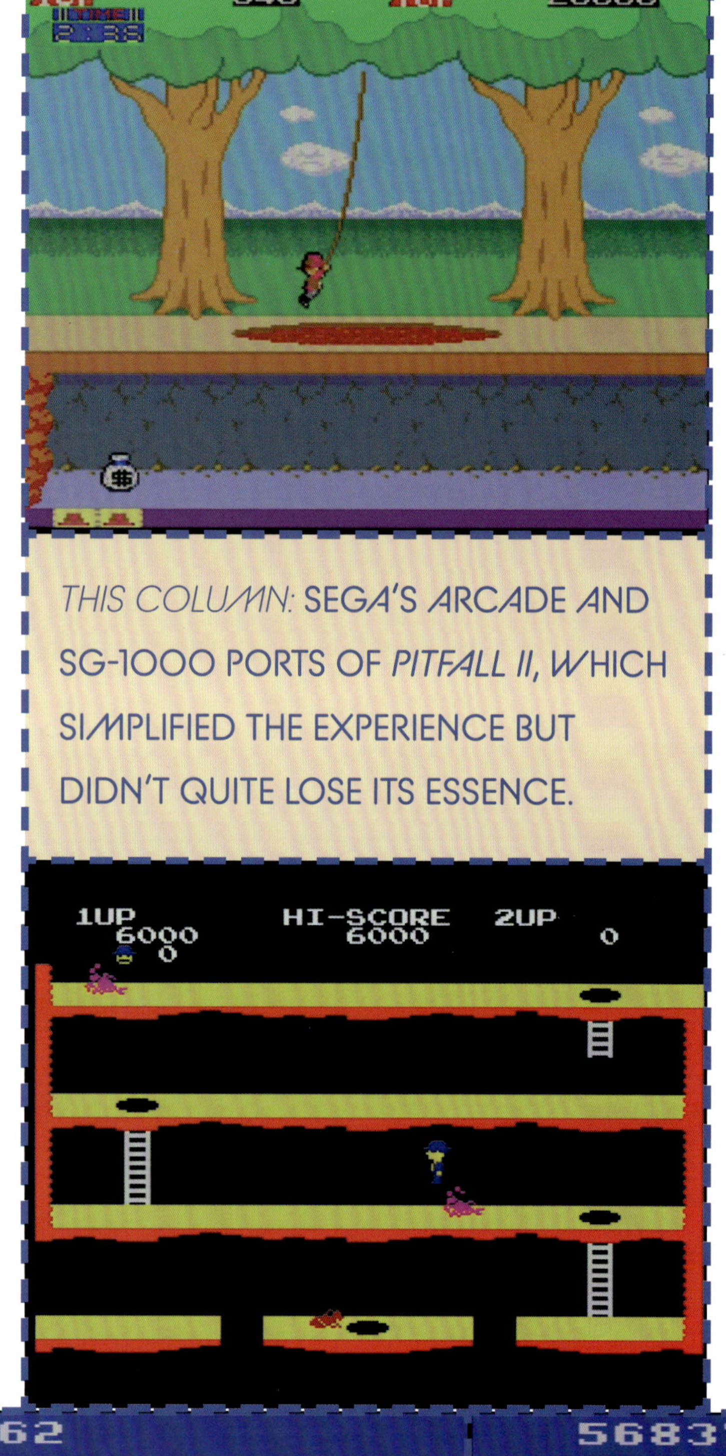

THIS COLUMN: SEGA'S ARCADE AND SG-1000 PORTS OF *PITFALL II*, WHICH SIMPLIFIED THE EXPERIENCE BUT DIDN'T QUITE LOSE ITS ESSENCE.

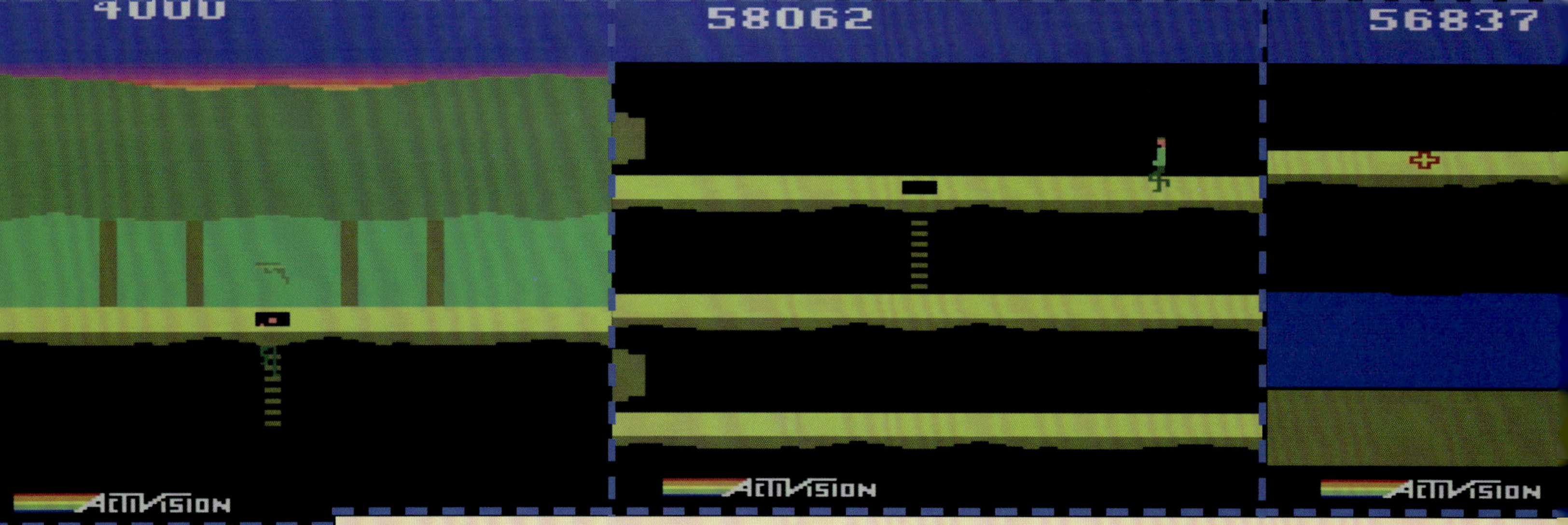

H.E.R.O.

Another groundbreaking Activision release from the waning days of the Atari 2600, *H.E.R.O.* channeled the basic spirit of *Pitfall II*—an adventurer making his way down into the underground—but did so in service of presenting players with a more traditional arcade-style experience. Unlike *Pitfall II*'s arcade incarnation, however, *H.E.R.O.* didn't seek to break the different phases of a journey into standalone levels. Instead, it consists of a single gameplay loop that repeats with every stage, growing more difficult and complicated but never varying from the fundamental format that defines the very first stage. Each level starts with you descending into caverns with a flight pack, armed with a weak laser rifle and a few sticks of dynamite; you must reach the bottommost level without succumbing to predators, running low on flight pack fuel, or becoming hung up on obstructions or trapped behind rock walls.

H.E.R.O. revolves around exploration, but not in the metroidvania sense of the word. You certainly can backtrack, but for only a short distance— after all, each stage only consists of a handful of interconnected screens, and returning to the beginning of a stage doesn't allow you to travel back to the previous level. Rather, you simply need to make your way downward to the bottom of a given stage, where you'll find a trapped miner waiting for rescue. A simple task at first—hover downward with your flight pack, avoid dangerous critters, and follow the seams of the mine—*H.E.R.O.*'s action quickly demands more caution as you advance beyond the first stage. Walls appear, forcing you to squander your limited dynamite supply or else find an alternate route. The creatures inhabiting the mines become more aggressive, evading your defensive laser and homing in on your character. The mines begin to branch, meaning that you can easily commit to a dead end and find yourself forced to burn your precious fuel reserve to jet back upward to the other track. In short, *H.E.R.O.* uses the metroidvania concept of complex, interconnected, contiguous spaces to add exploratory depth to the classic arcade-action game but never loses its momentum. *M*

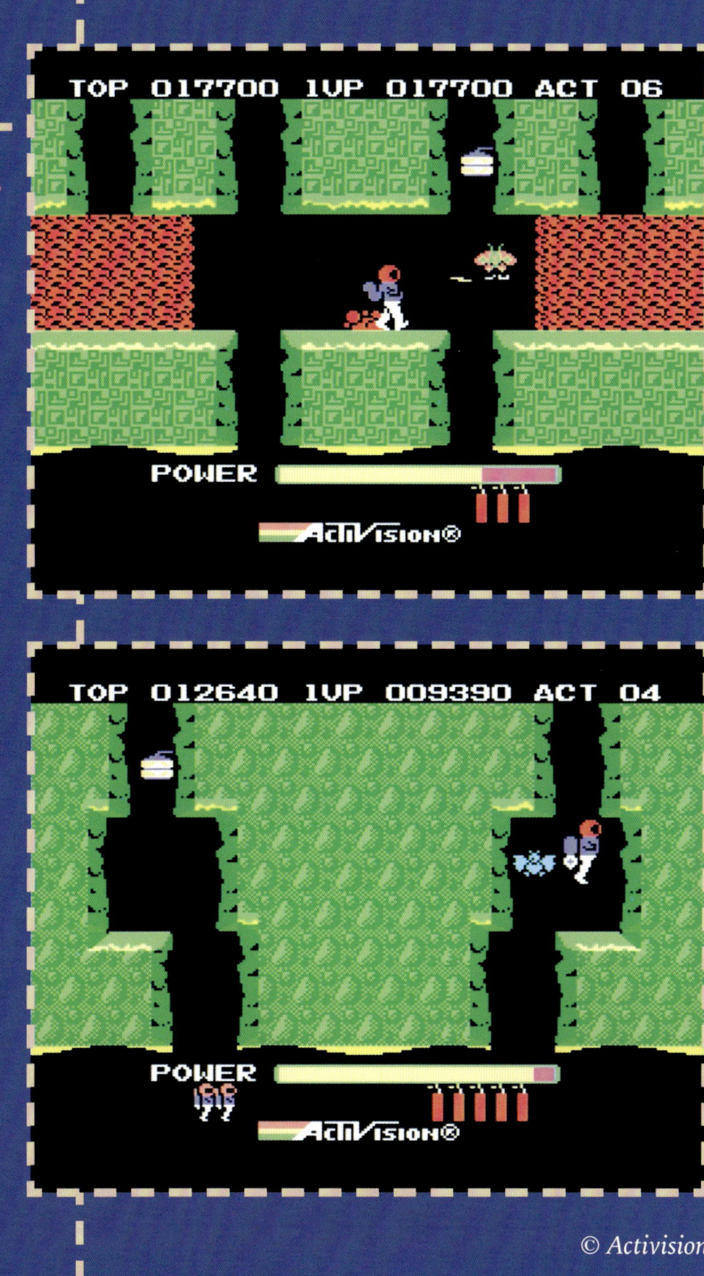

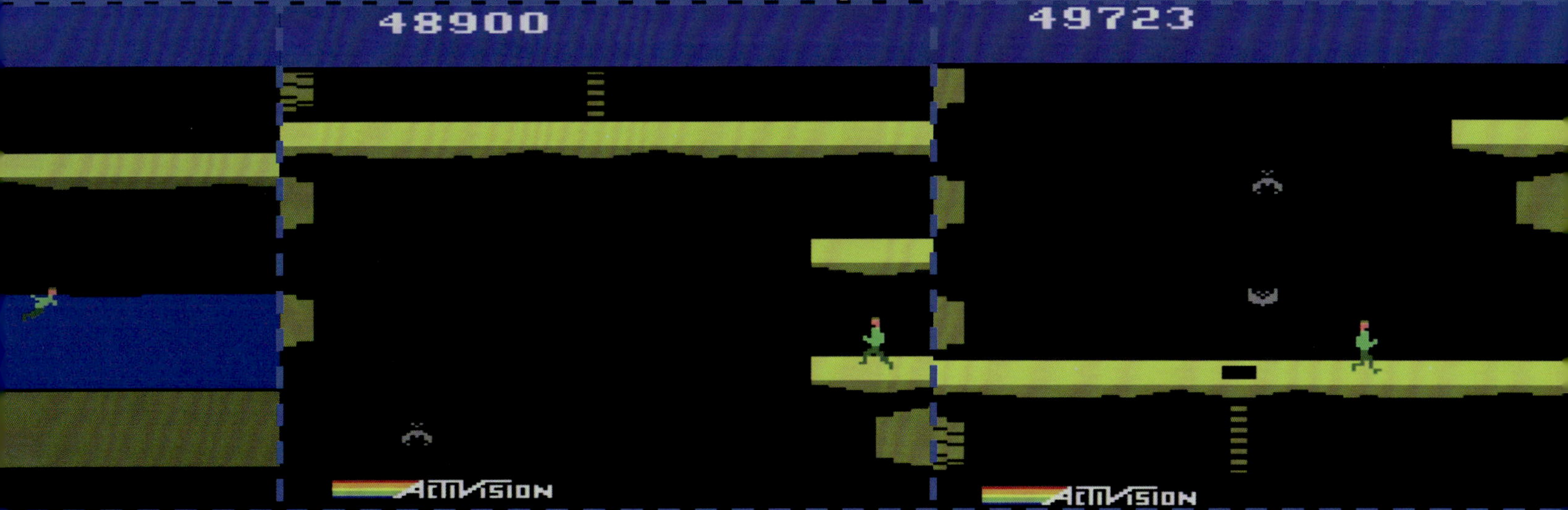

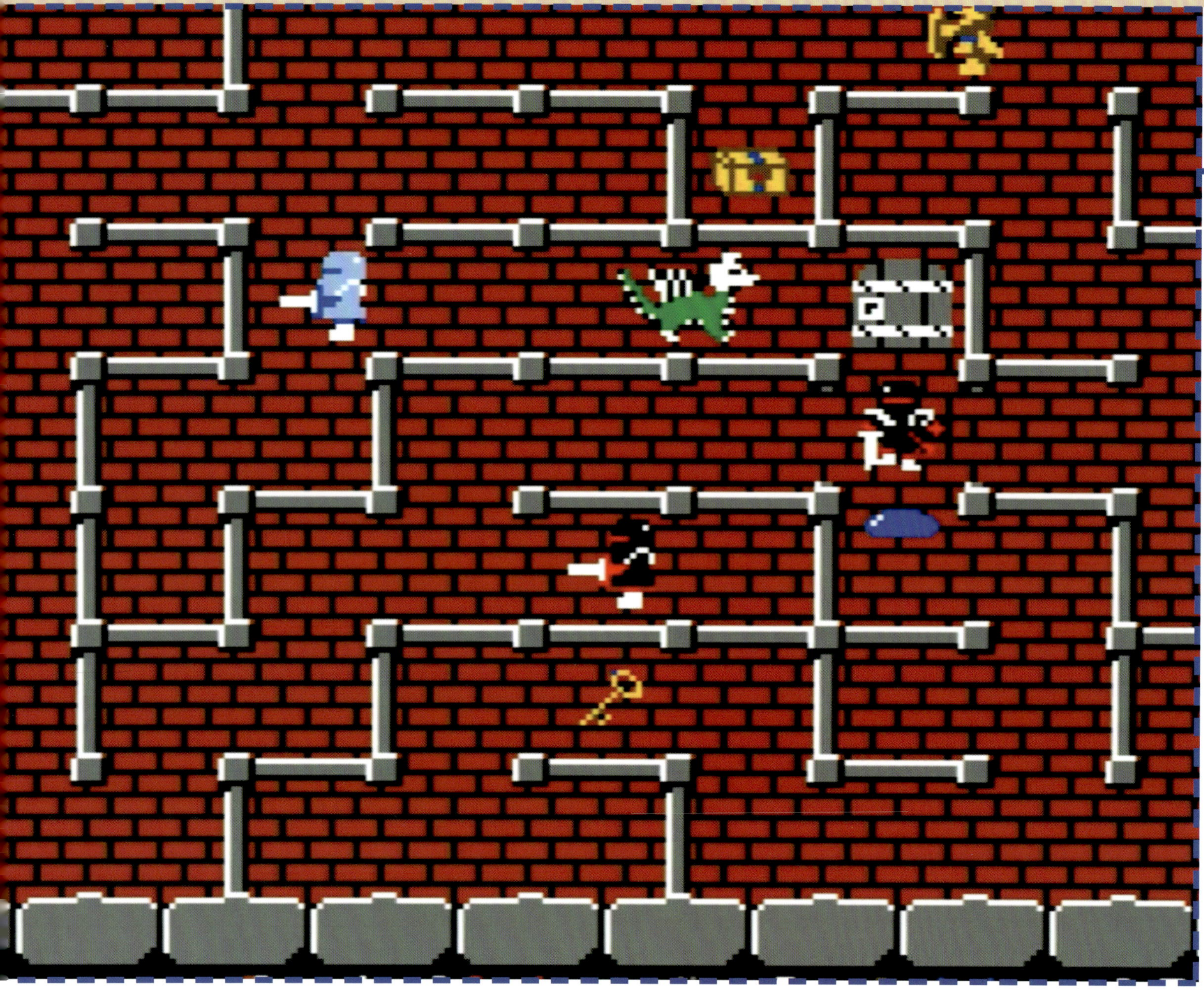

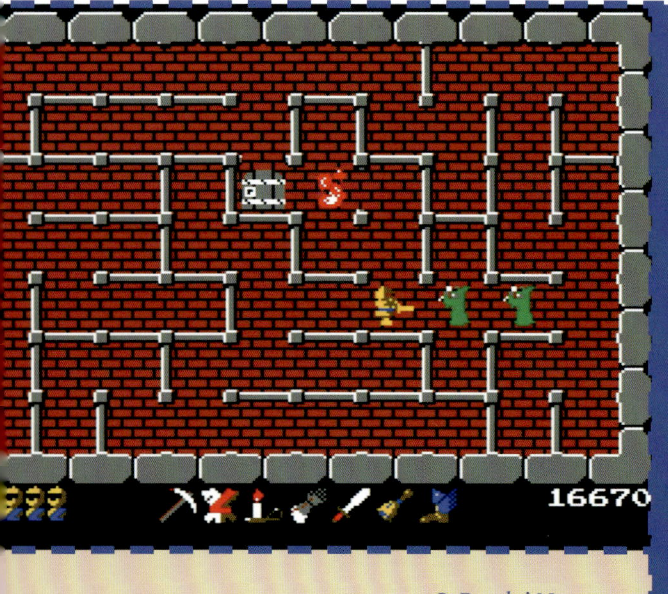

THE TOWER OF DRUAGA

PLATFORM: **ARCADE / VARIOUS**
DEV: **NAMCO** | PUB: **NAMCO**
INITIAL RELEASE: **JUNE 1984**
SHOWN HERE: **NINTENDO FAMICOM VERSION, 1985**

NOTABLE FOR: **TRANSFORMING THE DUNGEON CRAWL INTO A ZIPPY ARCADE GAME**

TOWER OF EMPOWERMENT

Think of *The Tower of Druaga* as Japan's answer to Atari's *Adventure*. It has the same basic concept, presented in a more elaborate fashion, as you'd expect from a game that arrived four years later. *Druaga* once again attempted to distill the role playing genre into a simple, intuitive, single-button action format that worked as an arcade machine. A tall order, but Namco somehow pulled it off, and *Druaga* became an absolute phenomenon in Japanese game centers.

In some ways, *Druaga* is a much simpler game than *Adventure*. Whereas Atari's game only allowed players to carry a single item at a time, forcing them to juggle their inventory and keep track of where in the maze they had left critical tools, *Druaga* does away with the notion of a persistent, interconnected world. Instead, its world spans sixty stages that consist of two screens of mazelike partitions, breaking the action into digestible spaces and doing away with the notion of backtracking.

Everything else about *Druaga* is far more involved than *Adventure*. Protagonist Gilgamesh can and must collect far more equipment than the hero of *Adventure* did. In fact, there's a crucial treasure to be found in each of the sixty rooms of the tower—well, mostly crucial. Some items merely offer minor survival perks; a few actually work against you. But for the most part, the treasures you unearth have enormous value, giving you greater speed or endurance, boosting your attack power, granting you an advantage against certain deadly monsters, or (in a few cases) proving to be critical against the final boss.

You don't stumble across these items by chance, though. Each one has to be uncovered through a series of increasingly complex actions, ranging from killing a fixed number of foes to pressing against a certain wall. These triggers would be more or less impossible for a single player to determine alone, and arcade-goers famously shared tips and solutions with one another back in the day. These conversations were a transposition of the social element that defined the very tabletop games that computer RPGs emulated, all in service of the search-driven design and character growth that would define metroidvania games.

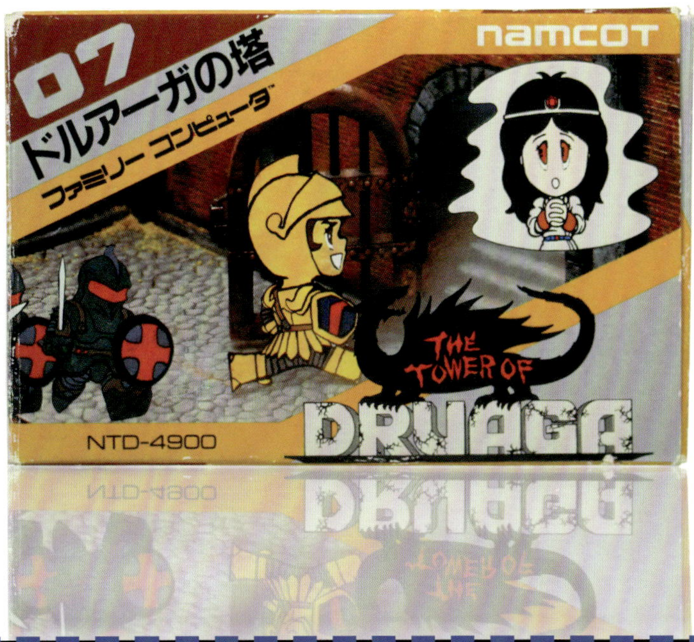

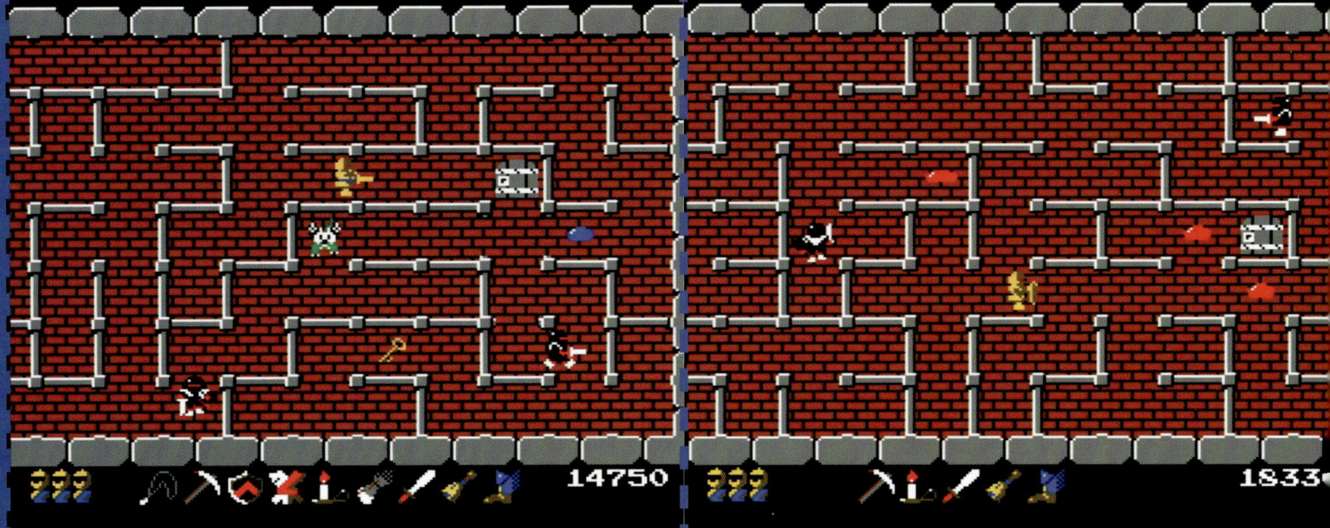

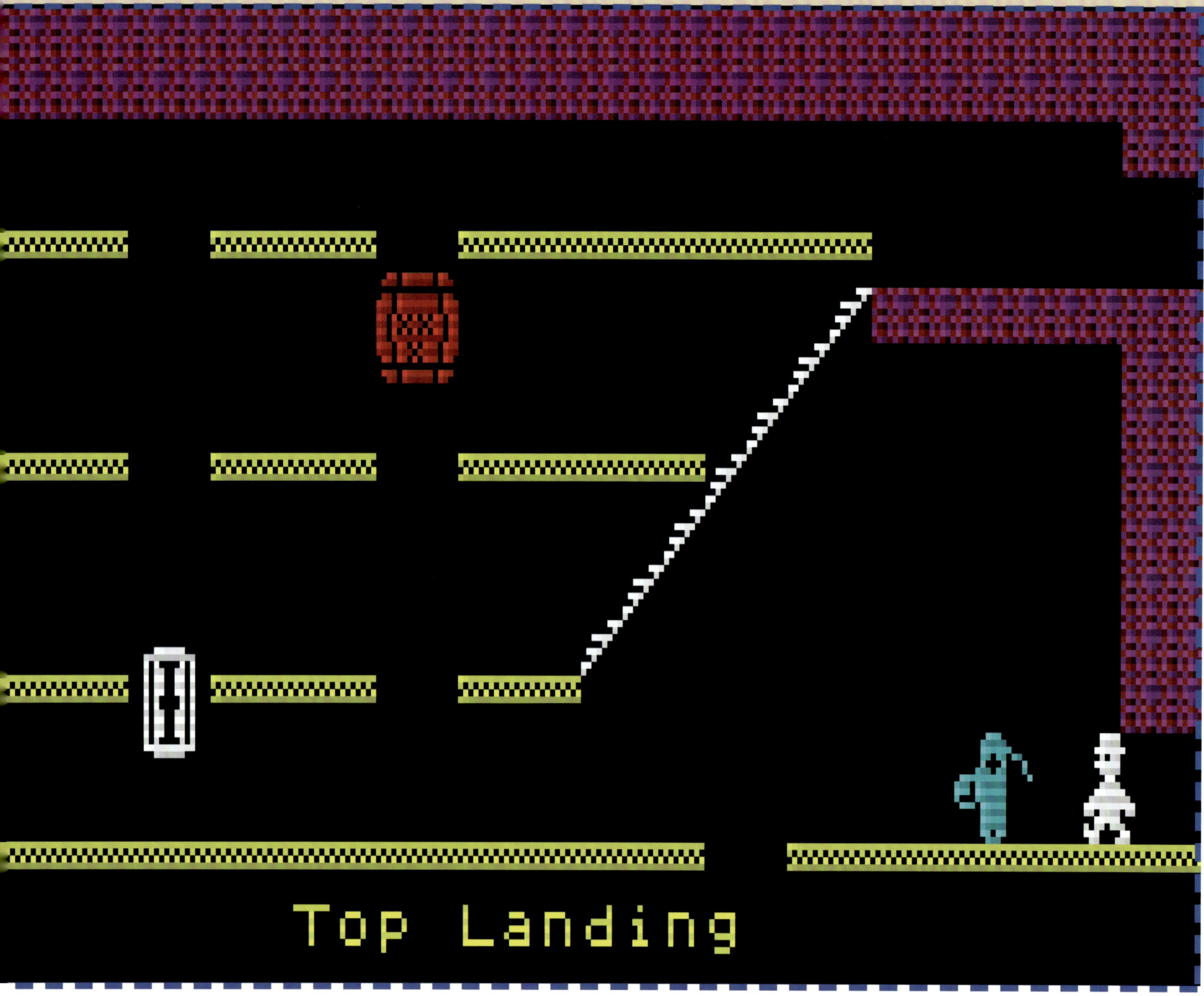

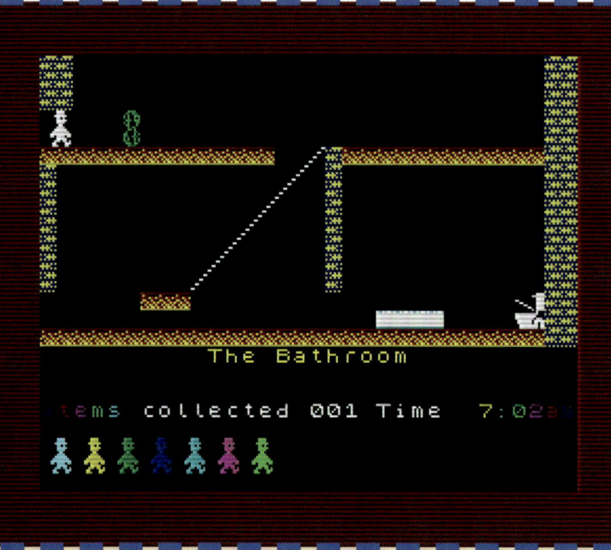

© BBG Entertainment

JET SET WILLY

PLATFORM: **ZX SPECTRUM / VARIOUS**
DEV: **SOFTWARE PROJECTS** | PUB: **SOFTWARE PROJECTS**
INITIAL RELEASE: **JUNE 1984**

NOTABLE FOR: *A WHOLLY OPEN SPACE BUILT AROUND INTENSE PLATFORM CHALLENGES*

WHERE'S THERE'S A WILLY THERE'S A WAY

British microcomputers of the 1980s may well be the Galápagos Islands of video game design. Largely disconnected from the trends and transitions that shaped gaming throughout the rest of the world in those pre-internet times, the UK games industry undertook its own peculiar journey on its own unique hardware. Evolutions and revolutions that emerged in the US and Japan transpired almost entirely independently of the journey that '80s British gaming experienced.

Few British microcomputer creations had quite so profound an impact (felt almost exclusively within the confines of the UK) as *Jet Set Willy*, a sequel to the hit game *Manic Miner*. Where *Manic Miner* had played much like your typical early '80s arcade platformer, presenting players with a series of single-screen tests of skill and reflex, *Jet Set Willy* expanded its protagonist's adventures into a *Pitfall II*-like series of interconnected screens that spanned an entire persistent, contiguous space. In many ways, *Jet Set Willy* improved on *Pitfall II*'s design, with each layout and challenge often differing radically from the previous. That sense of mise en scène permeated the game, all the way down to the fact that each screen had its own name, which established its location within the mansion that contained the adventure.

This mansion-bound setting simply reinforces the profoundly British nature of *Jet Set Willy*: namely, its droll cynicism. Hero Miner Willy, having made his fortune as a lucky miner, has retired to a preposterously oversized mansion. After hosting a housewarming party attended by many friends, he has drunk himself into a miserable state and now has to wander the unfamiliar (and curiously deadly) halls of his new home, tidying up after his guests, while reeling from a hangover. It's a decidedly low-stakes affair (though no less dangerous for Willy if the player fails), with a creative sense of geography about the home's interior that helped make each screen memorable. While lacking any power-ups, *Jet Set Willy* and its interconnected puzzle-box screen setup would influence the exploratory branch of British PC games in the coming years, including another key pillar of '80s UK game design: Ultimate Play the Game's *Knight Lore*. M

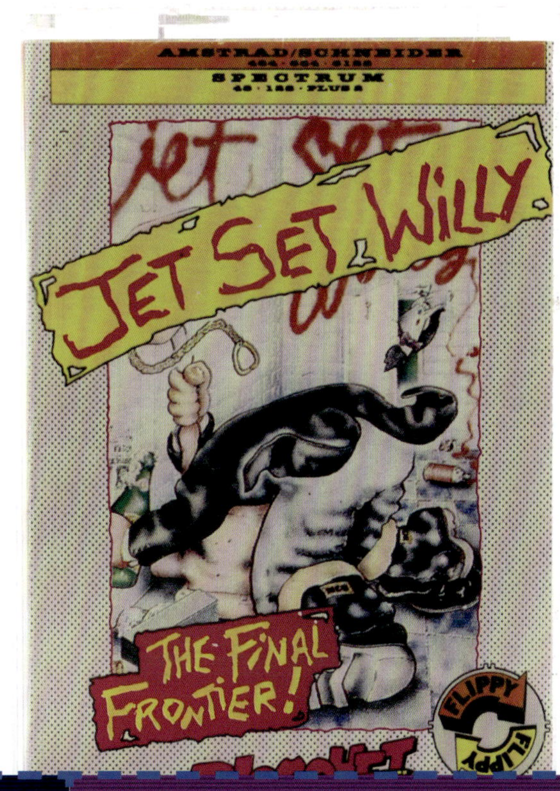

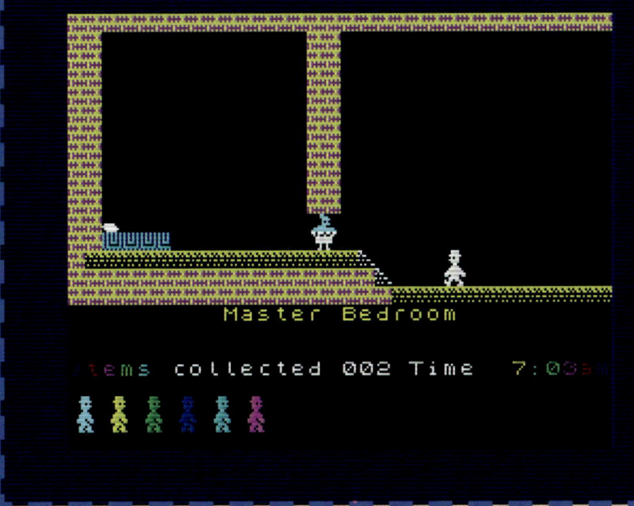

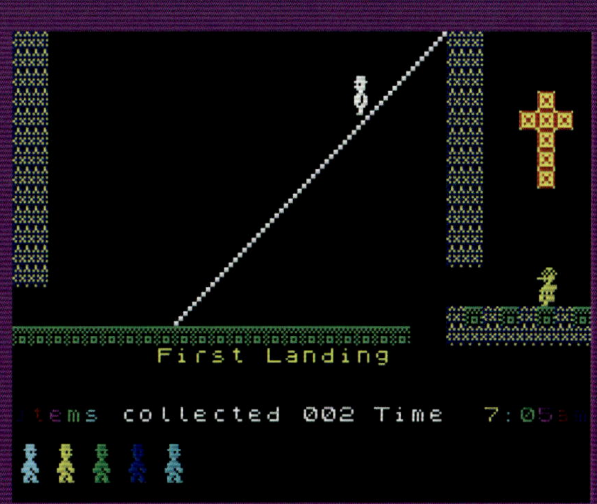

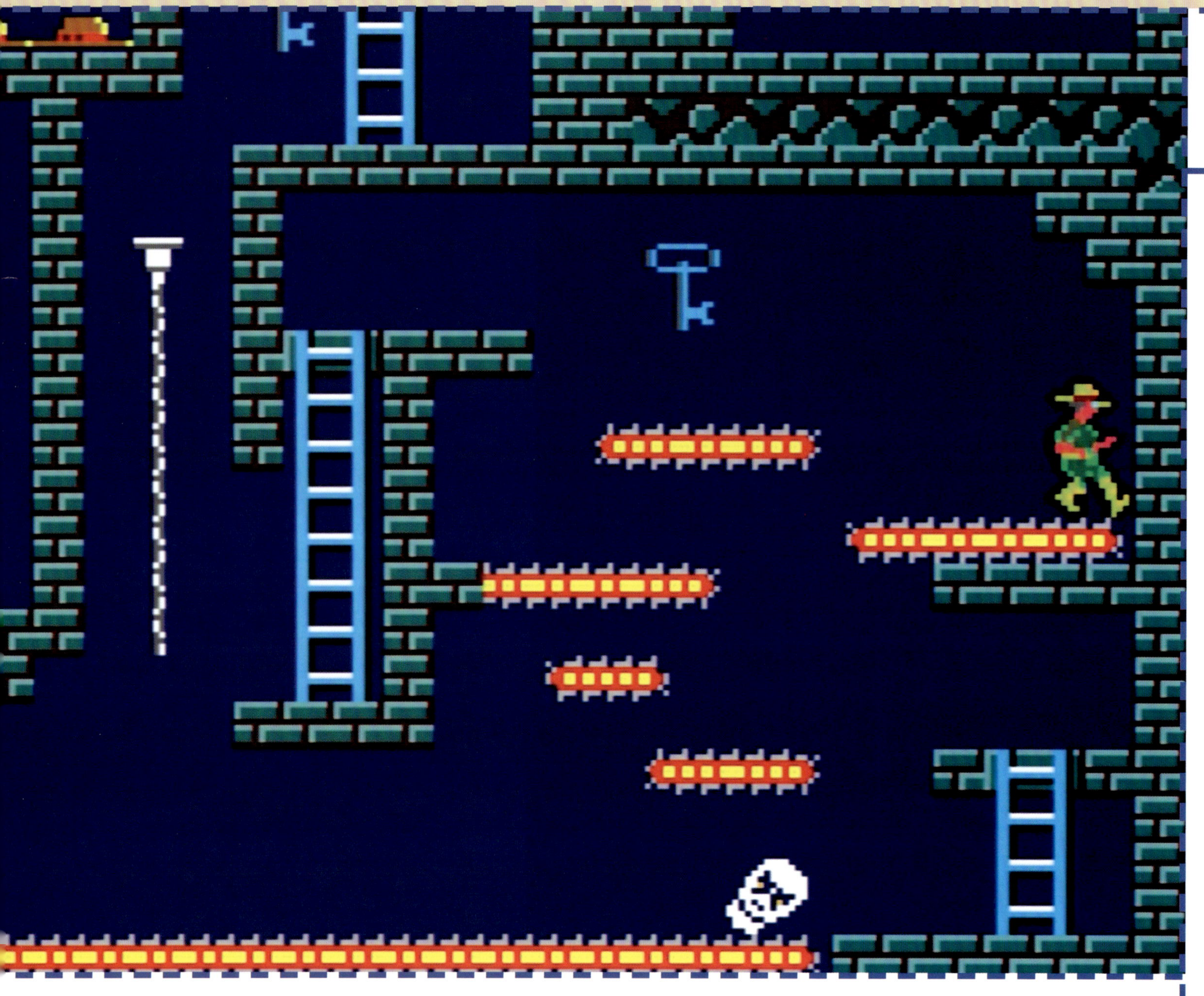

MONTEZUMA'S REVENGE

PLATFORM: ATARI 800 / VARIOUS
DEV: UTOPIA SOFTWARE | PUB: PARKER BROTHERS
INITIAL RELEASE: AUG. 1984
SHOWN HERE: SEGA MASTER SYSTEM VERSION, 1989

NOTABLE FOR: **ADDING A PUZZLE ELEMENT TO THE PLATFORM ACTION GENRE**

THE FUNKY FUNKY GAME FLOW

Pitfall!'s success cemented the concept that platform action games can play out across large virtual spaces rather than being hemmed into single screens and abstract mazes. The sprawling action game seemed like a perfect way to bring arcade-style action games into the player's home, a place where the parsimonious nature of coin-op gaming didn't quite work. The need to pay for the pleasure of playing lent arcade games a special element: real-world consequences for failure. If you messed up, you lost at least 25 cents (or even 100 yen). This created a tension that couldn't exist with a home game, which you acquired for a fixed payment of $20–30. Once you'd shelled out for the privilege of owning the cartridge, there was no way—at least in the halcyon, innocent days before microtransactions—for developers to restrict players' actions with monetary implements.

So then, how do you create an arcade-like sense of tension and motivate people to replay a game when there's no longer any money on the line? The best coin-op games created a sort of compulsive feedback loop. You'd lose, but you'd immediately plunk down your next quarter in the feverish hope of making it just a little farther or earning a few more points next time. Home conversions could get by on the drive to top a personal best score, but that only works for score-motivated players. Even back on the Atari 2600, programmers tended to add a lot of novelty features to keep things fresh. Think *Space Invaders*, which included numerous game variants, such as making the enemies invisible or removing the overhead shields.

Some developers went all-in on frustratingly difficult levels to force players to perfect their skills painfully over the course of weeks, even months, if they wanted to see the end. Others, however, looked to *Pitfall!* and began creating virtual spaces that beckoned players with secrets and a sense of place. One of those, the largely forgotten *Montezuma's Revenge* by Utopia Software, iterated directly on *Pitfall!*: a run-and-jump platform game centered around the goal of collecting treasure while avoiding deadly traps and venomous creatures. However, it forces players to deal with

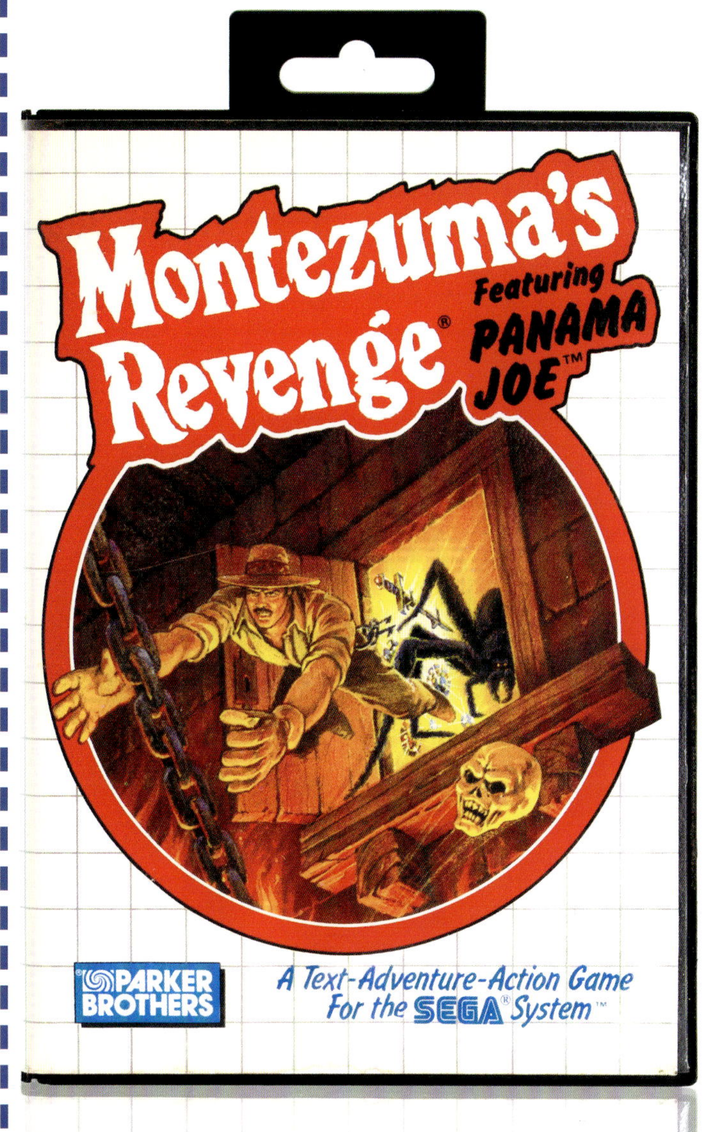

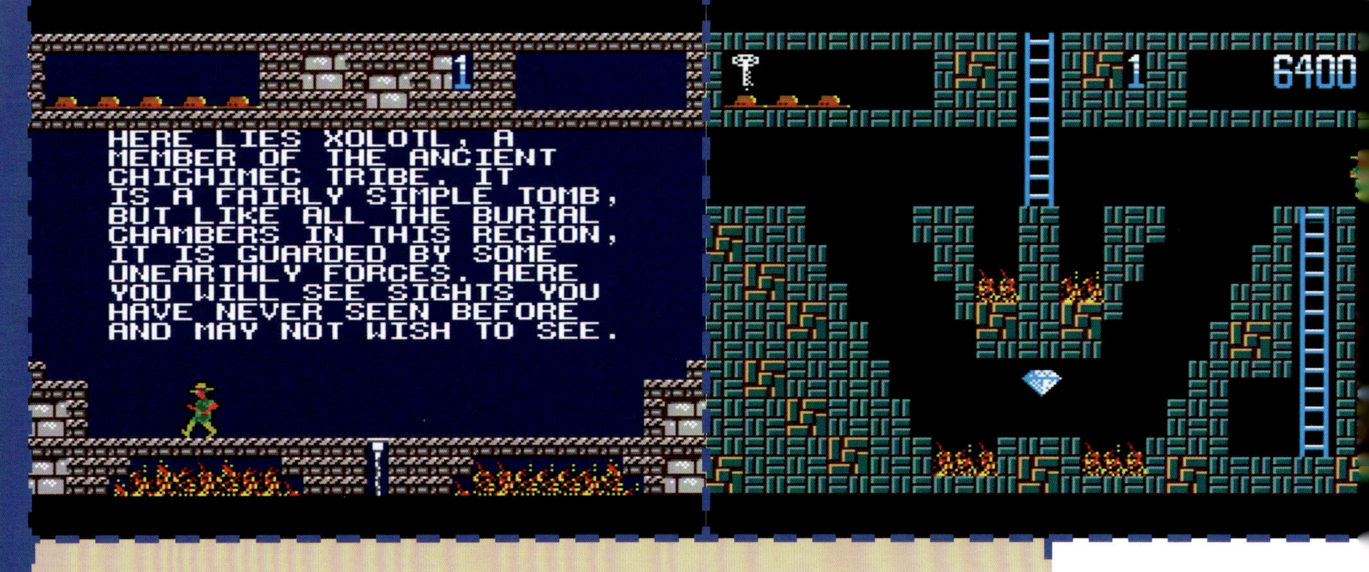

a lot more at any given moment than they had to contend with in *Pitfall!*—and in a far more elaborate and memorable landscape. David Crane had to work within the puny storage limits of the Atari 2600 to create *Pitfall!*'s world, which meant that the entire thing consisted of hundreds of largely identical screens arranged in a straight line. Crane's remarkable hack pushed the boundaries of the 2600, but *Montezuma's Revenge* director Robert Jaeger enjoyed not only the luxury of building on what had come before but also on the capacious memory of a personal computer.

Montezuma's Revenge originally debuted in 1984 on the Atari 800 platform, a far more powerful system than the 2600. While it was subsequently scaled down to fit on consoles as well, even the ROM used for the Atari 2600 port was twice as capacious as *Pitfall!*'s. At the same time, the world contained within *Montezuma's Revenge* is littler than that of *Pitfall!*—a pyramid consisting of between 50 and 160 rooms, depending on the version of the game, versus *Pitfall!*'s staggering 254 screens. Jaeger's decision to build his world at a smaller scale than Crane's, despite the larger storage available, worked to the game's advantage. The resulting screen layouts were far more varied than in *Pitfall!*, while also accommodating greater mechanical complexity and more intricate goals.

Montezuma's Revenge also owes a debt to another game: *The Pharaoh's Curse* by Synapse Software. Released in 1983 for Atari 8-bit computers, *The Pharaoh's Curse* shares much in common with *Montezuma's Revenge*. In both games, you descend into a pyramid consisting of interconnected screens loaded with danger, seeking treasures in an ancient tomb. But *The Pharaoh's Curse* contains a tiny, simplistic world compared to that of *Montezuma's Revenge*. The former encompasses a mere sixteen rooms, with an inventory "system" that amounts to picking up a couple of keys scattered throughout the world to open specific doors. *Montezuma's Revenge* can span up to ten times the size of that game, depending on the version, and there's a lot more going on here. It's also worth noting that Jaegar's game does a better job of exploiting its setting, too—whereas *The Pharaoh's Curse* took place in a "pyramid" built as a 4×4 square grid of rooms, *Montezuma's Revenge* unfolds from the top of a Mesoamerican structure that widens as you descend. The top floor is only one room wide, while the next level spans three screens, and the one below that runs five across, and so forth. The pyramid you descend into grows larger as you ascend through the difficulty levels, with more rooms appearing and new barricades appearing that force you to change your route. This is a game that encourages players to map it out, something previously only encountered in *Pitfall!* and dense PC RPGs and adventures like *Wizardry* and *Zork*. Although the game lacked any RPG-inspired systems beyond a basic inventory system, the size and complexity of Montezuma's tomb gave a clear sense of where action games would be going in the coming years.

You also have to juggle protagonist Panama Joe's limited inventory to advance. There are several items to collect here, ranging from a torch that lights up dark rooms to key that unlock doors. You can also pick up amulets and weapons that allow you to fight back against the creatures that roam the pyramid. Panama Joe can only carry a few items at once, so toting around a sword for protection seems all well and good until it prevents you from grabbing a key you need to advance. To further add to the complexity of the adventure, this is one of the earliest games to include color-coded keys. Keys appear in blue, red, and so forth—and, naturally, each one only works on a door of the appropriate hue. This creates a sort of interlocking puzzle element within the pyramid, as simply possessing a key doesn't necessarily mean you can advance past a door; you need to find the correct key. This forces you to be strategic about which items you collect, since you don't want to load down your inventory with keys that won't work right away. It may not be possible to place yourself into an unwinnable situation, but grabbing the wrong tools can certainly land you in an inconvenient situation, forcing you to retrace your steps until you find the correct key. Gaming hadn't even arrived at its first true and proper metroidvania game yet, but already the medium had begun bumping up against some of the design challenges and perils inherent in the format.

All that being said, *Montezuma's Revenge* is ultimately an action game designed in 1983, and that means it comes with all the attendant frustrations you'd expect. The play physics often feel stiff and uncooperative, even compared to those in *Pitfall!*, and your hero is tragically fragile. There's definitely a sense of MicroGraphic Image's *Spelunker* at work here in the sheer overwhelming difficulty you face, although *Montezuma's Revenge* is a more complex game than that, which can make its interface failings and tendency toward "gotcha" design deeply frustrating. The complexity of the *Montezuma's Revenge* pyramid layouts combines with the overall ferocity of the difficulty level to create a game that requires considerable determination to master. Even on its easiest setting, this is a daunting adventure in which you have only a few lives to

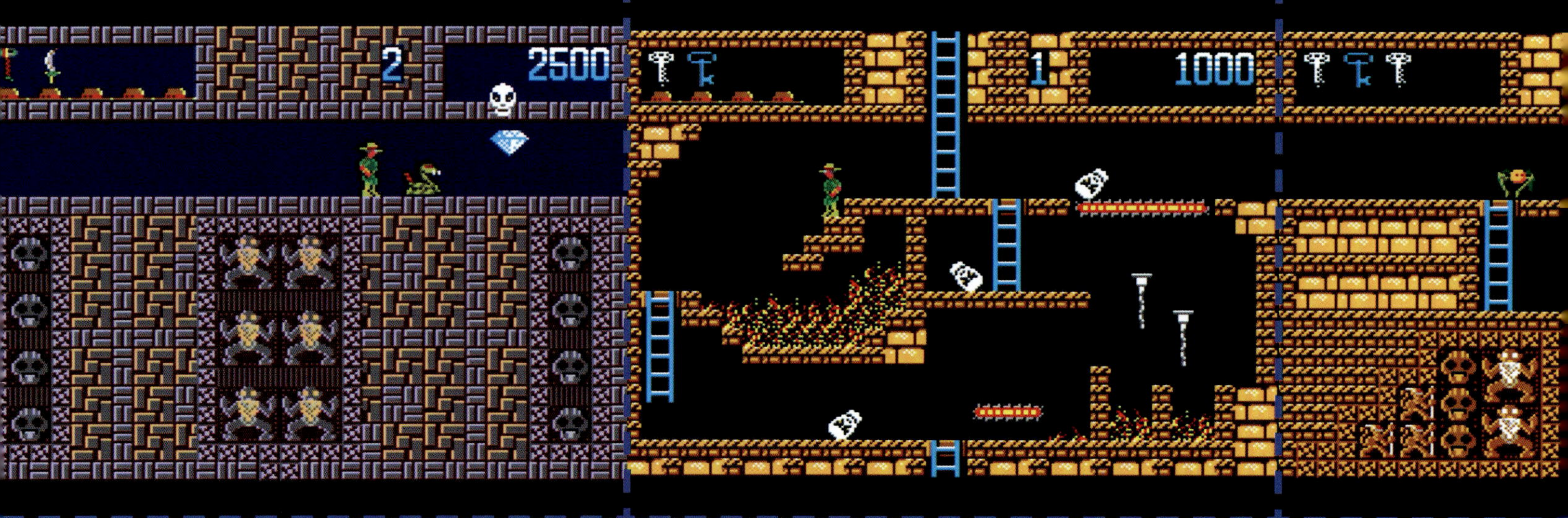

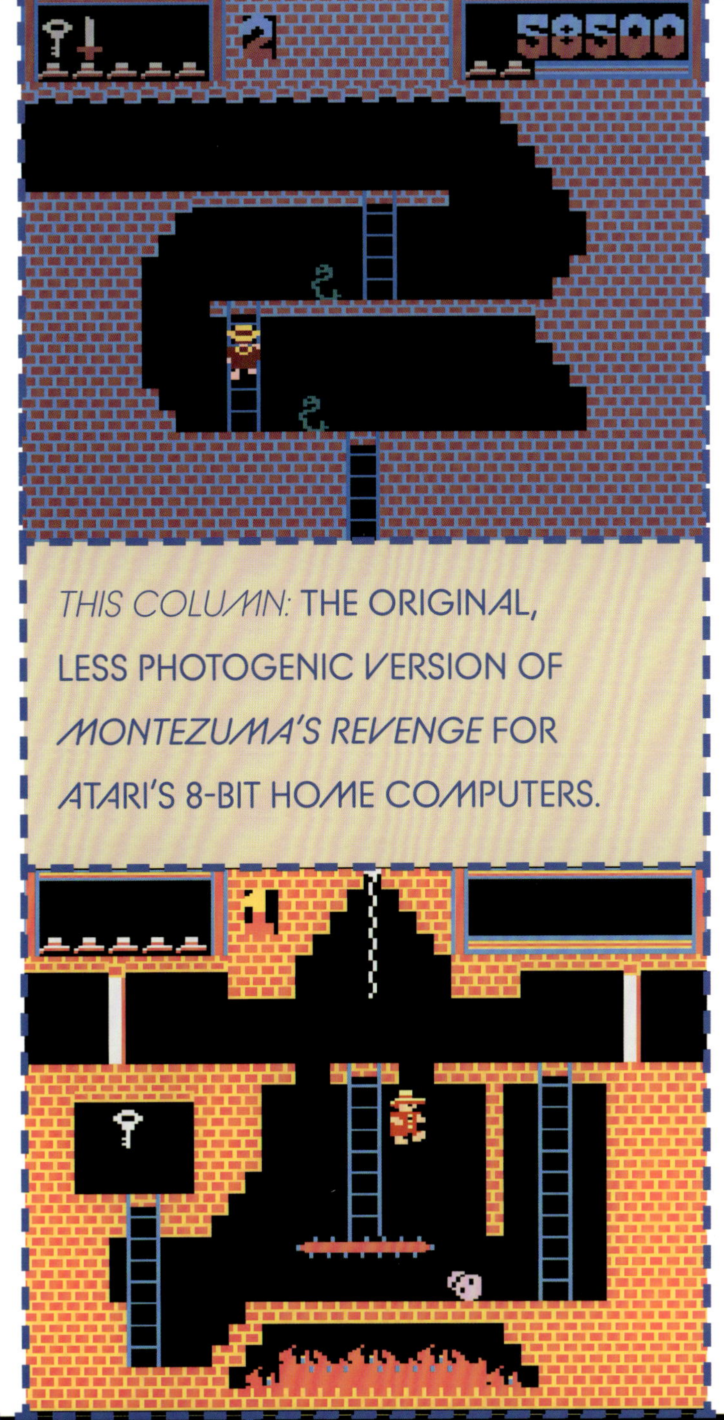

THIS COLUMN: THE ORIGINAL, LESS PHOTOGENIC VERSION OF *MONTEZUMA'S REVENGE* FOR ATARI'S 8-BIT HOME COMPUTERS.

complete a massive puzzle maze.

Successfully completing a run through *Montezuma's Revenge* involves a lot of exploration and collection, and you can only afford to make a few mistakes in the process. Fall from too high of a ledge, fail to leap over a monster with Panama Joe's clunky controls, or screw up the timing of running past a barrier, and boom: that's one life down. It's hard to be too critical, though, because the game presents no shortage of invention when it comes to the challenges you have to survive. Each of the different monsters that roam the pyramid demonstrate unique behaviors. These range from skulls that roll mindlessly back and forth to spiders that can climb ladders in pursuit of Panama Joe, obstructing pathways with their bodies and negating one of the player's key advantages.

Taking another page from *Spelunker*, some versions of the game also introduce a stressful de facto timer to deal with on the higher difficulty levels. If you dawdle too long on a screen, a bat swoops down—an obvious nod to *Spelunker*'s ghost or Berzerk's *Evil Otto* to chase Panama Joe. This feature initially appeared in early prototypes, although it (along with a final encounter with Montezuma himself) was cut for space reasons in the initial Atari 800 release. Montezuma appears in the ZX Spectrum version of the game, while the Master System release omits him but adds in the bats, along with more tools to acquire and use along the way—including parachutes that let Panama Joe glide safely down into pits—along with a greater selection of enemies and hazards.

But whether those updated iterations, the relatively basic original PC release, or even the deeply compromised Atari 2600 version, *Montezuma's Revenge* is characterized by the way its world is packed with impressively complex platforming puzzles. Combine the moving floors (à la *Donkey Kong*'s cement factory) and vanishing blocks together with the wandering enemies and key-based puzzles and you have an intricate, innovative game that represents a huge step forward in platform game design.

Although the game undeniably landed in the thick of the arcade era of game design and reflects those creative and commercial impulses—note its high difficulty level and lack of continues!—*Montezuma's Revenge* embodies gaming's growing awareness of the appeal of treating video game environments as persistent, deliberately designed spaces rather than merely abstract collections of floors and ladders. The shape and structure of the puzzle-box pyramid of *Montezuma's Revenge* offered a glimpse into the future.

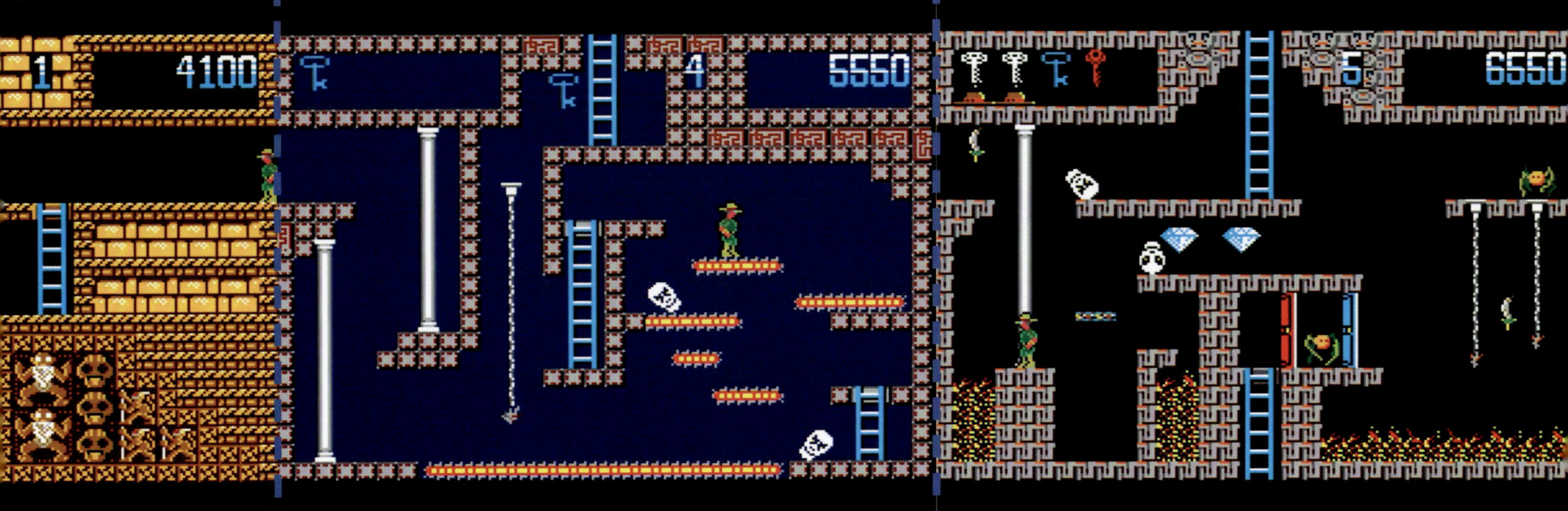

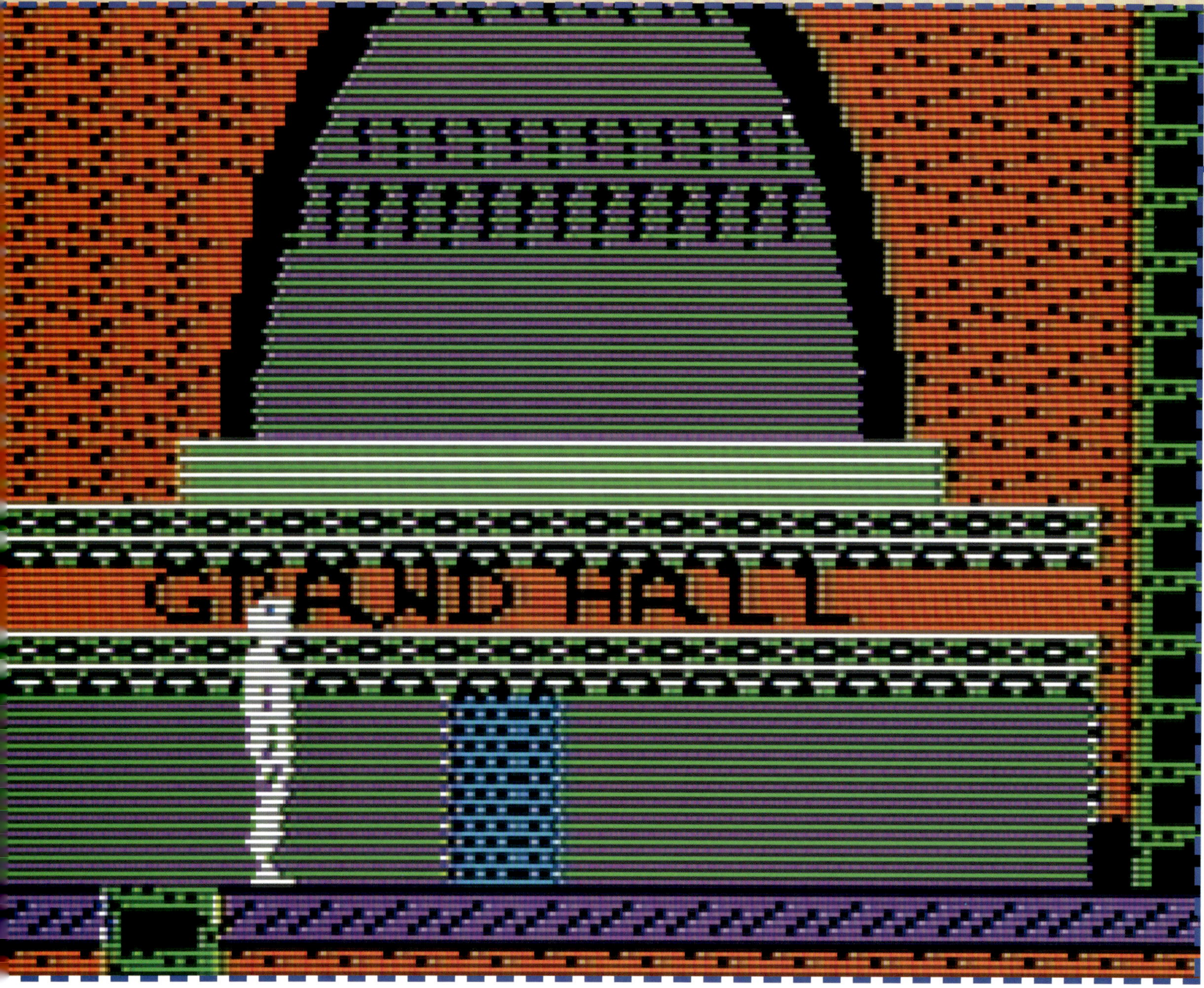

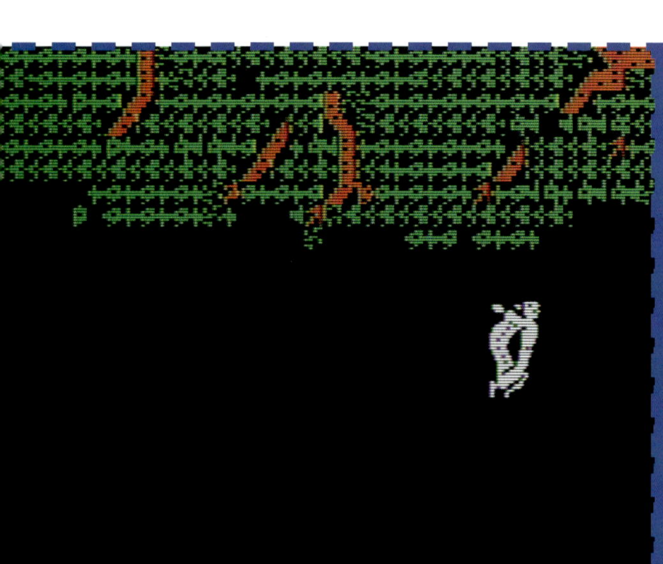

BELOW THE ROOT

PLATFORM: **COMMODORE 64**
DEV: **DALE DISHAROON** | PUB: **WINDHAM CLASSICS**
INITIAL RELEASE: **1984**

NOTABLE FOR: **AN OPEN, IMMERSIVE, NARRATIVE-DRIVEN GAME WORLD**

THE WORLD TREE'S WOE

The irony of *Below the Root* is that it feels years ahead of contemporary video games, yet it takes its inspiration—indeed, its entire concept—from a venerable medium: namely, books. Based on a series of young adult novels by Zilpha Keatley Snyder, *Below the Root* drops players into a fully realized fantasy world set high in the treetops, a sort of elven fantasy kingdom in which the player can empathically communicate with woodland animals and venture into dreams to master fantastic powers.

Structurally, *Below the Root* resembles the likes of *Pitfall II* or *Jet Set Willy*. Players traverse a world of individual, standalone screens that interconnect to create a much larger environment, and many screens present riddles or challenges contained within that space. However, in terms of its actual mechanisms of play, *Below the Root* shares more in common with Sierra On-Line adventure games like *Mystery House* or *King's Quest*. To complete the game, you need to find your way to a specific person in a specific place in order to bring them aid, but the process of reaching their location involves exploring your treetop world, gathering clues from other characters, acquiring essential tools and items for the tasks ahead, and knowing when to perform specific actions and where to use a given item.

In other words, *Below the Root* moves like a platformer, but it works like a graphical adventure, with a hint of role-playing. Your protagonist has to manage their stats—rest, hunger, that sort of thing—over the course of their days-long journey. You make use of items, search, and speak to other characters by selecting commands from a menu. You duck into buildings. You solve navigational puzzles to reach out-of-the-way areas. You refer to the pack-in map to make leaps of faith from the highest branches on the trees. With its minimal emphasis on "action" in the arcade sense of the word— conflict, combat, and twitch skill—*Below the Root* ultimately falls into a different discipline than the classic metroidvania. But it absolutely feels like a predecessor to the genre.

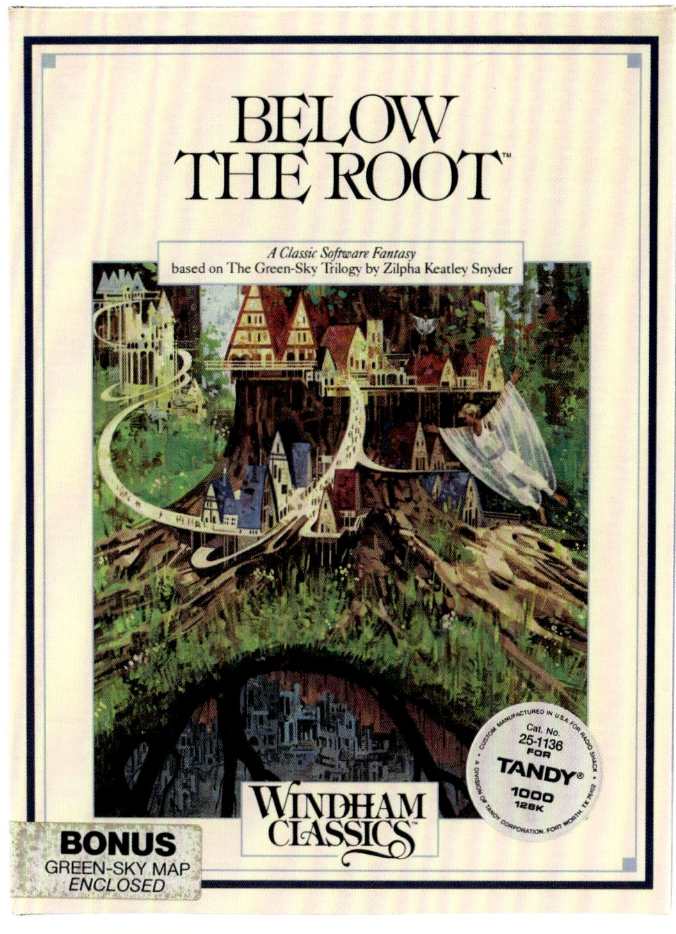

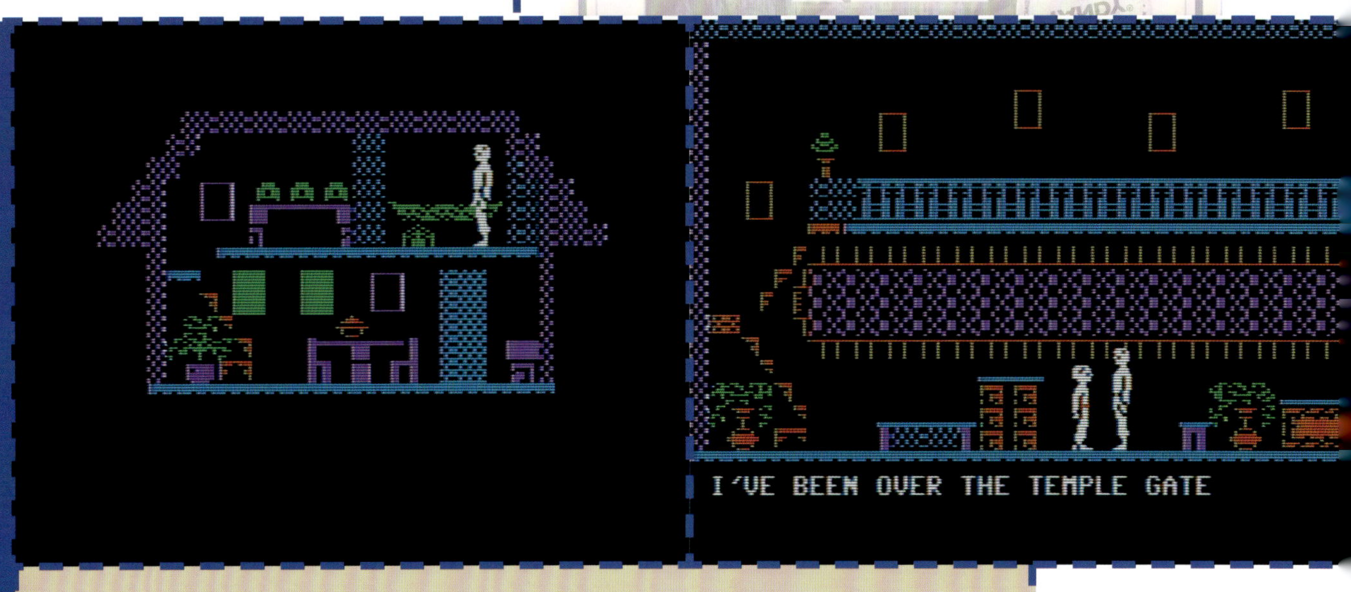

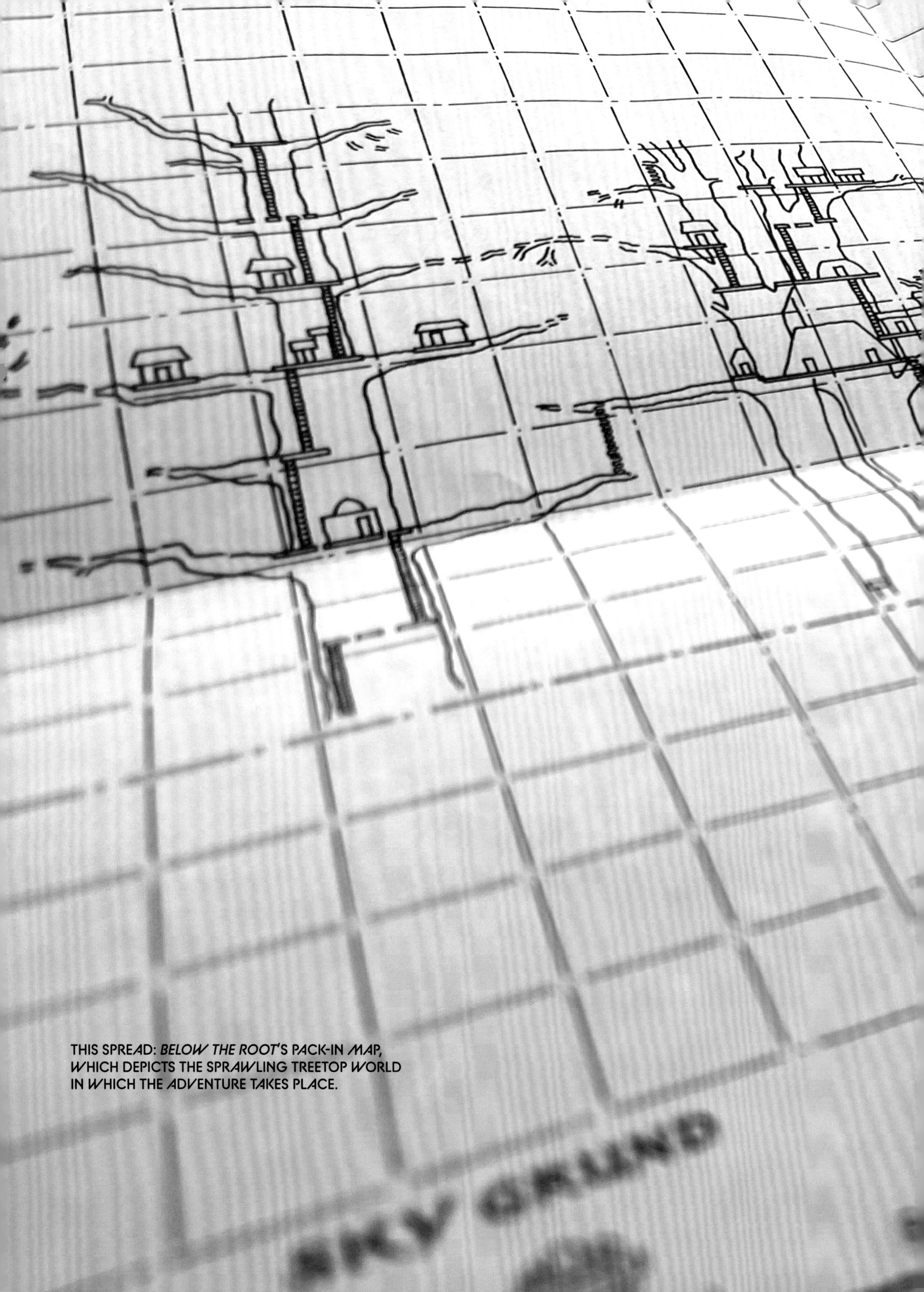

THIS SPREAD: *BELOW THE ROOT*'S PACK-IN *MAP*, WHICH DEPICTS THE SPRAWLING TREETOP WORLD IN WHICH THE ADVENTURE TAKES PLACE.

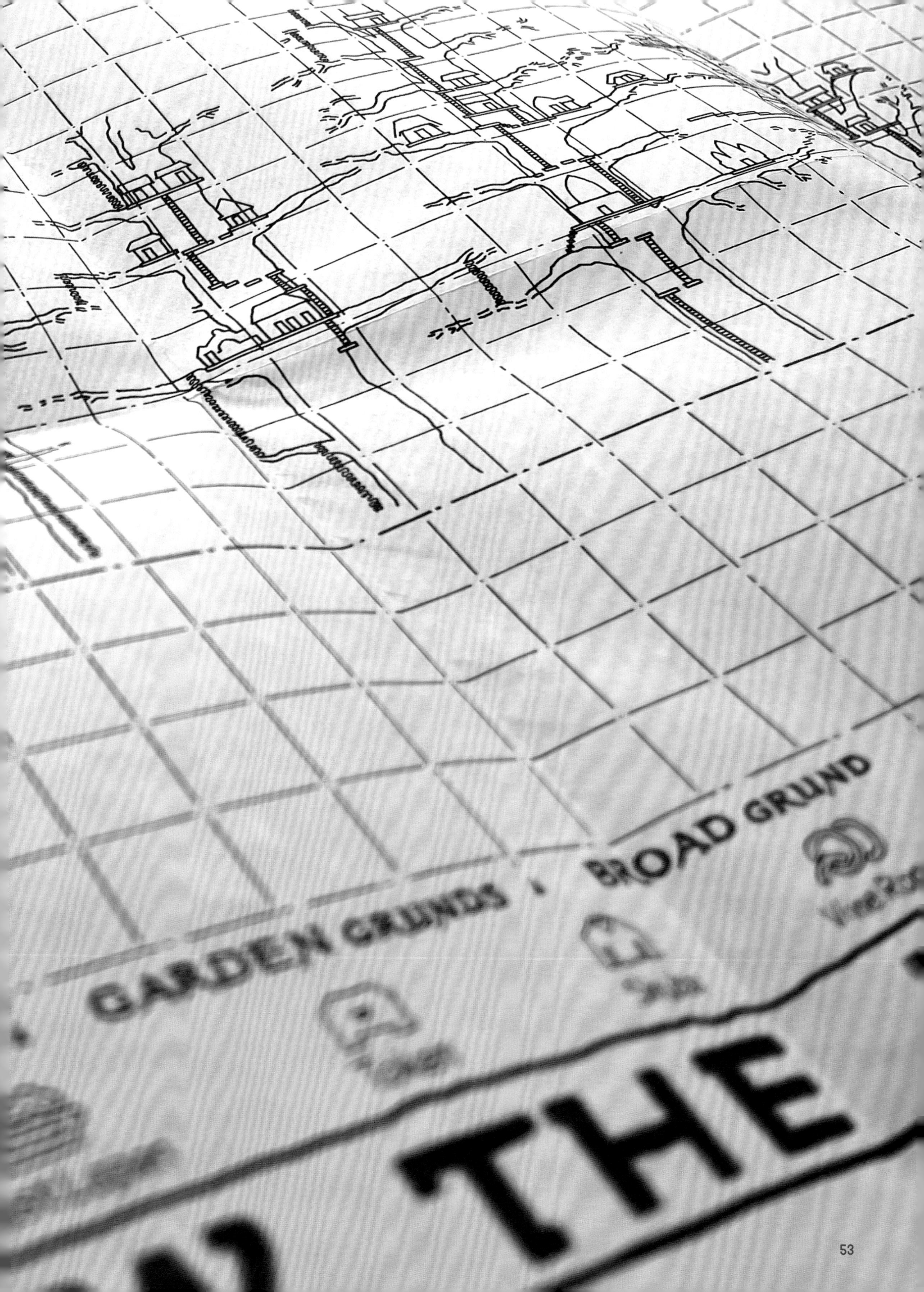
GARDEN GRUNDS
BROAD GRUND
THE

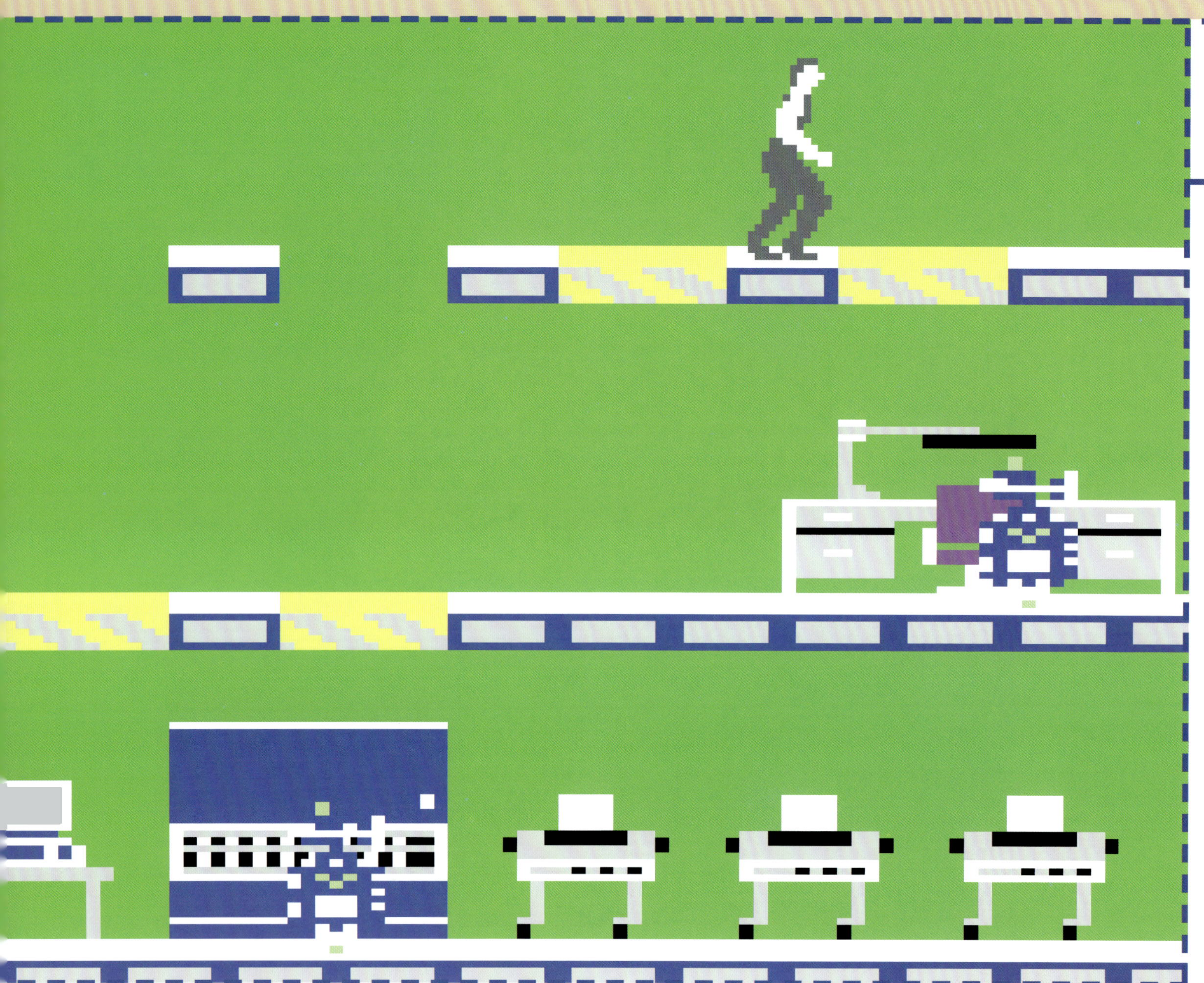

*** SECURITY TERMINAL 09 ***

SELECT FUNCTION

RESET LIFTING PLATFORMS IN THIS ROOM.

==> TEMPORARILY DISABLE ROBOTS IN THIS ROOM.

LOG OFF.

IMPOSSIBLE MISSION

PLATFORM: **APPLE II / VARIOUS**
DEV: **EPYX** | PUB: **EPYX**
INITIAL RELEASE: **SEPT. 1984**
SHOWN HERE: **APPLE II VERSION, 1984**

NOTABLE FOR: **COMPLEX PUZZLE-PLATFORM CONSTRUCTION, PROCEDURAL GENERATION**

ROBOT RAMPAGE

What happens when you combine elements of multiple formative games into a single adventure? If the stars align, you get a game that pushes the state of the art even further ahead. Such was the case with Epyx's *Impossible Mission,* whose creative remit could be summed up as the platform structures of *Donkey Kong* meets the interconnected standalone screen challenges of *Pitfall!* meets the cryptic metaphorical puzzle-and-key systems of *Zork*...maybe with a dash of *Berzerk*'s killer robots. There's more to it than that, of course—Mario never leaped quite so nimbly in pursuit of his simian rival—but you can certainly see the direct connections between those earlier games and the breezy data-collecting quest Epyx assembled here.

Impossible Mission takes place across a series of rooms, each of which exists as its own self-contained, independent space. Every room functions as a puzzle that you need to solve through both action and note-taking. Computer terminals located throughout the enemy base control various functions, such as opening doors or activating elevators, and you need to acquire and input special codes to operate those devices. Doing so often grants you access to new spaces or mission-critical items, unlocking the interconnected network of rooms. But, to actually reach the terminals and move from space to space, you need to evade killer robots that patrol the platforms of the current room. These devices tend to stick to a fixed routine and rarely target you unless you get right up in their way, but a single touch will instantly kill you. This means that you need to plan your actions carefully, timing your movements around the robots' patterns and demonstrating a precise understanding of your own athletic capabilities (such as the ability to take grand, spinning leaps over the machines) and limitations alike. An early take on the puzzle-platformer, the intricate interconnections of *Impossible Mission*'s world made it a huge influence on the metroidvania.

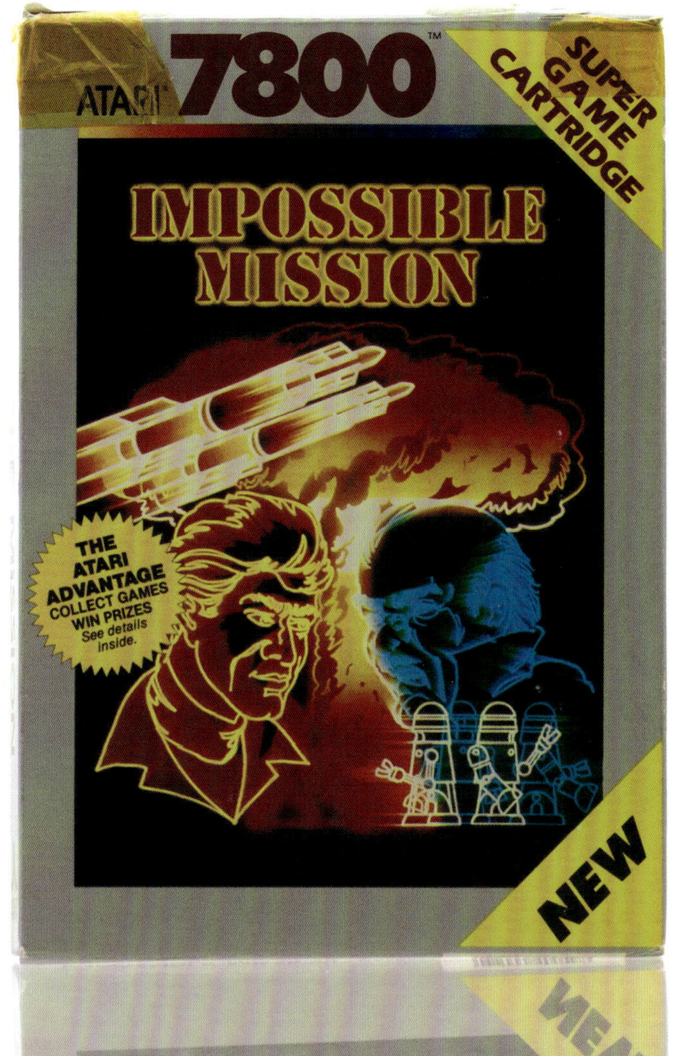

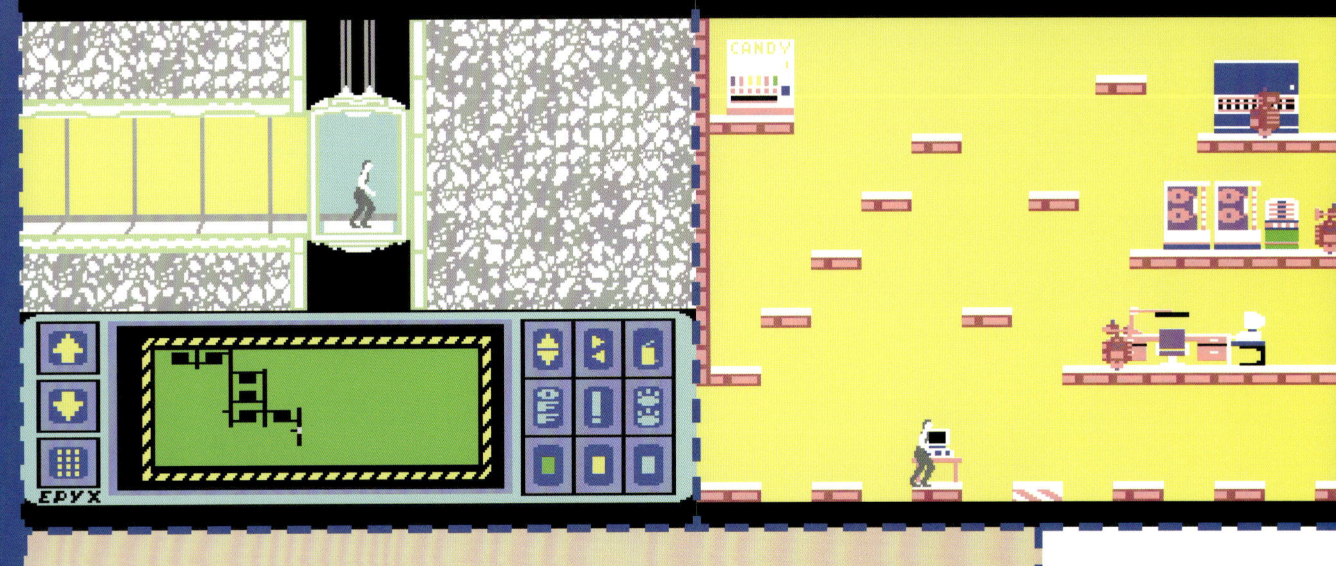

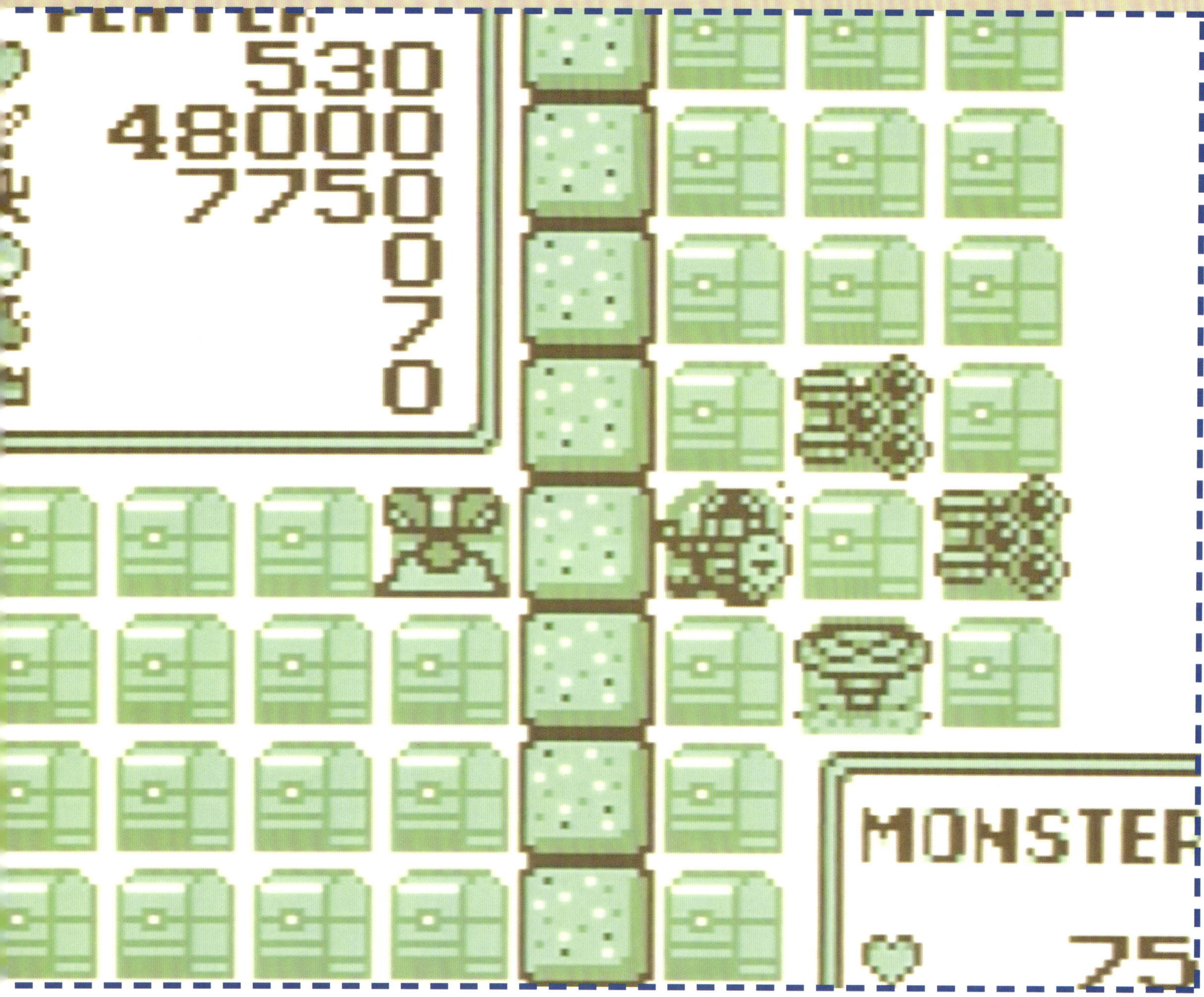

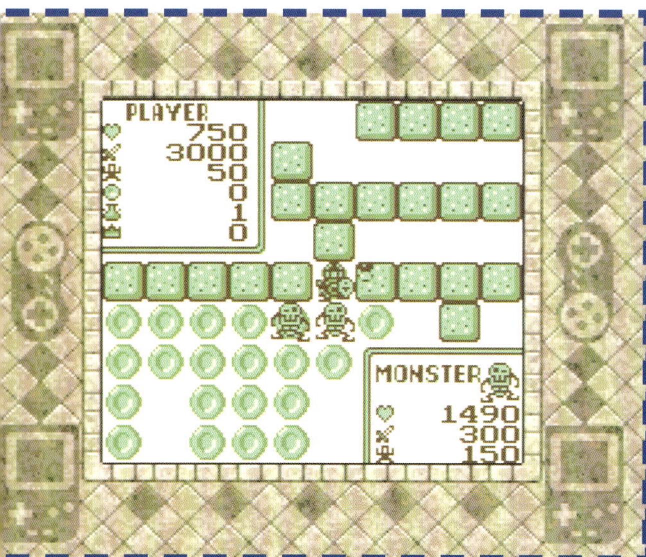

DRAGON SLAYER

PLATFORM: **PC-8801 / VARIOUS**
DEV: **NIHON FALCOM** | PUB: **NIHON FALCOM**
INITIAL RELEASE: **SEPT. 1984**
SHOWN HERE: **NINTENDO GAME BOY VERSION**

NOTABLE FOR: **LAYING THE FOUNDATION OF THE CONSOLE ACTION RPG**

HOME IS WHERE THE EXP. LIES

Debuting around the same time as *Pitfall II*, Falcom's *Dragon Slayer* contributed several crucial ideas to the action role-playing genre, helping establish key elements of the metroidvania. Here, you play as a tiny warrior in a large world, seeking to defeat a handful of deadly dragons.

The core gameplay loop of *Dragon Slayer* revolves around powering up that tiny warrior, who begins the game in a terribly fragile state. The monsters that beset him can tear him to ribbons in seconds until he boosts his experience levels, which you accomplish by retrieving certain items within the maze the warrior inhabits and toting them back to his home to "redeem" for experience. This is an Atari *Adventure*-style simplification of the classic RPG mechanic (e.g., from *Wizardry*) whereby characters couldn't "cash in" their experience and level up until they reached a resting point, like a town or campfire. *Dragon Slayer* takes that a step further by tying the process of earning experience to the resting point. Slaying enemies won't net you experience, and you want to avoid wantonly killing weak enemies because doing so will cause them to respawn as a more powerful creature somewhere in the maze.

Instead, *Dragon Slayer* emphasized navigating the maze space efficiently. Your tiny warrior with his tiny hands can only carry a single item at a time, so completing the adventure involves a lot of swapping and dropping. Your impulse might be to tote the enemy-repelling cross with you everywhere you go for safety, but you can't lug an experience token home while holding the cross. You have to make tradeoffs, which become even trickier as the world opens up and you have to roam farther afield—thus spending more time hauling tokens and being vulnerable to attack—to advance. You do have one advantage, though. The hero curiously has the ability to lift and carry his home around with him, hermit crab–style, which adds another element of complexity to the navigation. It's a strange and often prickly game, but it absolutely feels like a progeny of Atari's *Adventure*, and it demonstrates the continuing evolution of the action-RPG. *M*

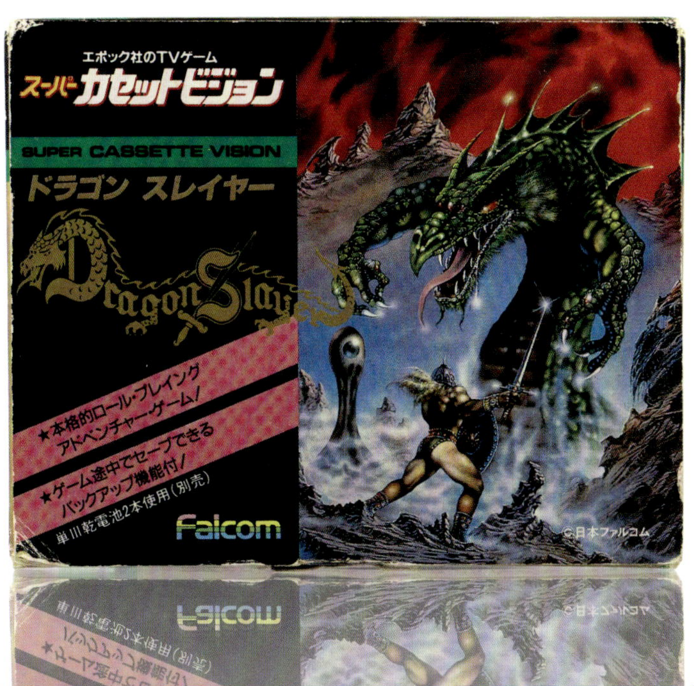

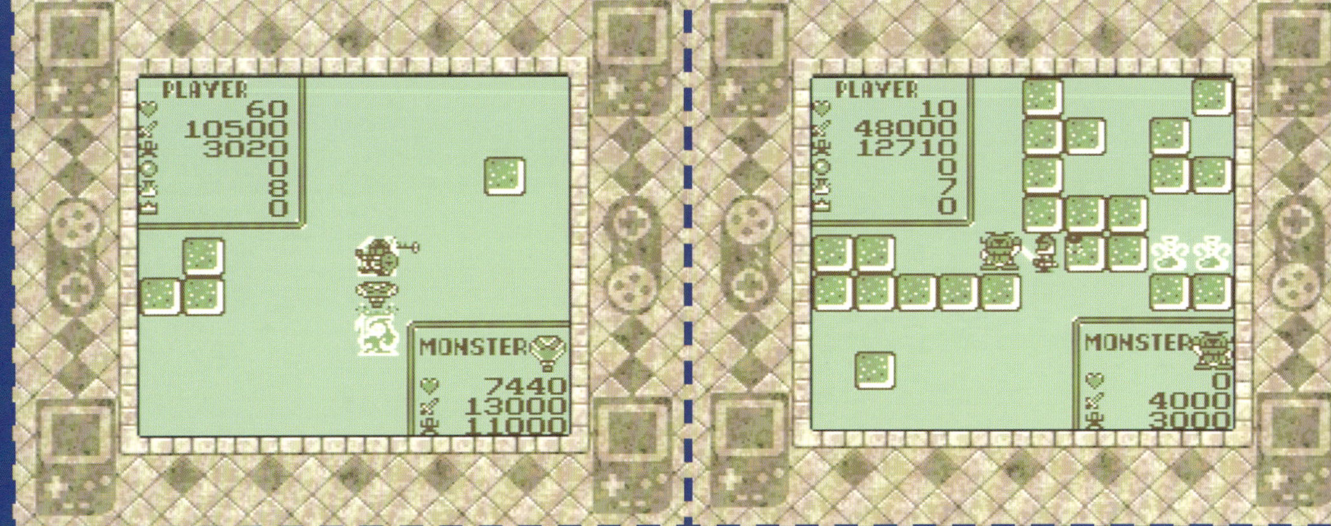

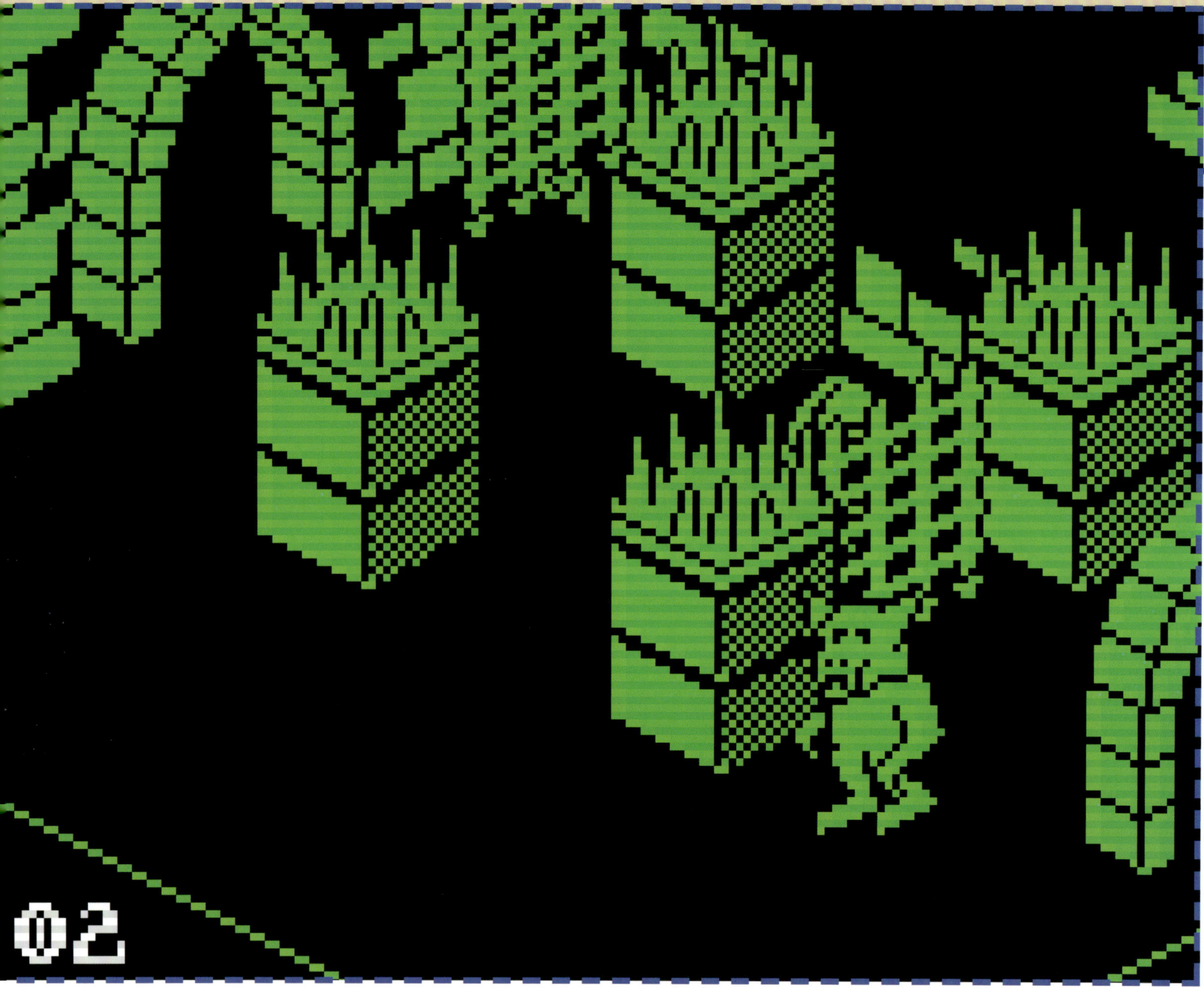

02

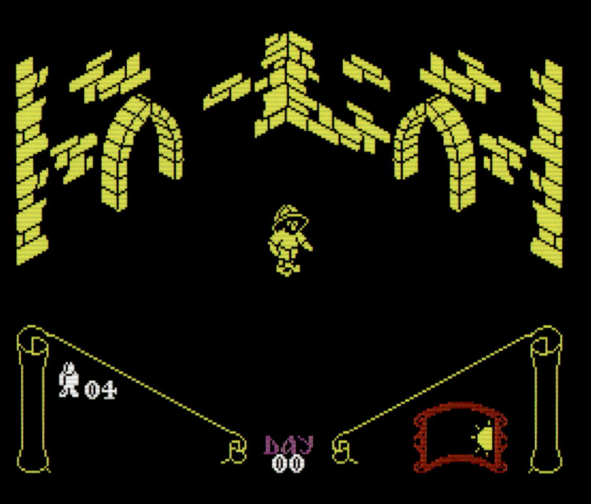

KNIGHT LORE

PLATFORM: **ZX SPECTRUM / VARIOUS**
DEV: **ULTIMATE PLAY THE GAME** | PUB: **ULTIMATE PLAY THE GAME**
INITIAL RELEASE: **NOV. 1984**
SHOWN HERE: **FAMICOM DISK SYSTEM VERSION, 1986**

NOTABLE FOR: **RANDOMIZED EXPLORATION AND ISOMETRIC DESIGN**

LYCAN SEE MY HOUSE FROM HERE

Wizards & Warriors for NES [see *NES Works 1987*, available from Press Run Books] felt like developer Rare Ltd. playing to their strengths while attempting to recalibrate a familiar game concept to better suit the NES platform. Specifically, *Wizards & Warriors* played like a NES-friendly overhaul or spiritual successor to *Knight Lore*, the groundbreaking ZX Spectrum game that put Rare on the map (back when they operated under the name Ultimate Play the Game). In effect, *Wizards & Warriors* took the isometric viewpoint of *Knight Lore* and exchanged it for a side-scrolling viewpoint, but it largely retained the earlier game's aesthetic and overall vibe.

Another similarity: *Wizards & Warriors* moved faster and more smoothly than just about anything seen before it on the NES, whereas *Knight Lore* represented a technical showcase for the Spectrum. Not only did *Knight Lore* feature isometric 3D graphics, it incorporated sprite masking that allowed its characters to appear like they actually belonged to the game environment rather than floating above it like cardboard cutouts. In fact, it was so impressive that Ultimate Play the Game supposedly delayed its release for a year or so to prevent it from cannibalizing sales from a couple of less-impressive releases they had in the works; the world simply wasn't ready for this game. The isometric point of view calls to mind Atari's *Crystal Castles*, infusing depth and height into the action. Where *Crystal Castles* spans a variety of structures with complex slopes and varied surface heights, *Knight Lore* largely takes place on flat planes. However, it retains elements of 2D side-view platformers like *Donkey Kong* and *Pitfall!* While the environments here look predominantly flat, protagonist Sabreman can and must jump over a variety of obstacles to complete his quest. At the same time, he can still move around each room of the game's castle on either the X or Y axis. That is to say, he moves in three dimensions.

This adds a little extra complexity and challenge to the game, forcing players to judge the hero's relationship to the various threats he needs to circumnavigate on multiple axes. Some of this difficulty arises less as a deliberate element of design; Ultimate pushed the limits of Spectrum graphics with *Knight Lore*, but even

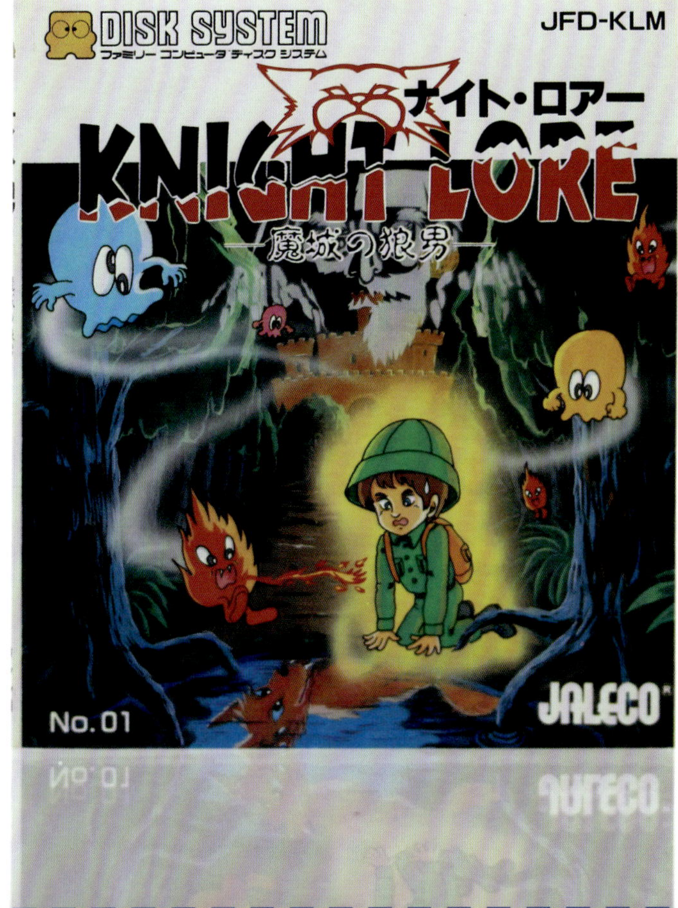

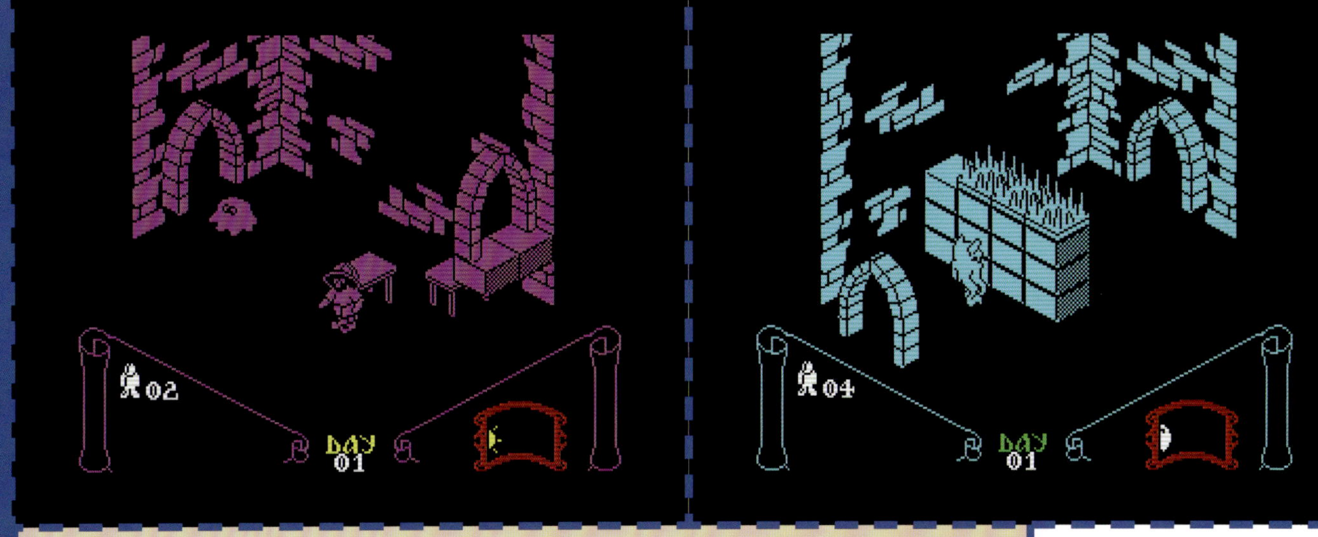

they couldn't integrate shadow-casting. The lack of a shadow on the ground beneath Sabreman makes his relationship to the objects he vaults over slightly ambiguous. Here *Knight Lore* pioneered the eternal bugbear of isometric platformers, even refined ones like Climax's *Landstalker*: Eventually, you have to just kind of guess when to make certain jumps. In Knight Lore, given the high number of fatal spikes you need to avoid, this is a task of critical importance. Still, shadows or no shadows, given the limitations of the ZX Spectrum, these visuals were stunning—they still read well today.

While the graphics drew players in, the gameplay kept them hooked. *Knight Lore* had a lot in common with Atari's *Adventure*, dropping players into a sprawling realm and requiring them to retrieve an assortment of items. In this case, Sabreman has to locate more than a dozen mystical artifacts and return them to a cauldron in order to break the curse he labors under. This involves a lot of roaming around the castle and backtracking.

To keep things interesting, both Sabreman's starting location and the placement of objects—which must be retrieved in a mandatory sequence—are semi-randomized each time you play. To keep things difficult, there's a sort of real-time element to the adventure, and you only have forty in-game days to complete your quest. To make things weird, Sabreman's curse causes him to transforms into a wolfman at night. This doesn't really have any impact on the protagonist's skills or mobility, since you don't gain powers or attack skills, but it does make the world more dangerous. Certain enemies will attack Sabreman when he's in wolf form, including the cauldron where you dump your requested MacGuffins. In other words, you don't simply need to learn the lay of the land and how to navigate it, you must also memorize the various semi-random arrangement of key points while steering clear of aggressive creatures at night and timing your cauldron drop-offs for daylight.

While there's no character growth here to really push this game into the action-RPG realm, *Knight Lore* does represent an essential "root" influence for the metroidvania genre. It's heavy on exploration and requires a fair degree of finger dexterity. Along with *Jet Set Willy* and *Elite*, *Knight Lore* belongs to a holy trinity of sorts for British PC games of the early '80s. Its popularity no doubt has a lot to do with its technical prowess…but it's also beloved for the clever ways in which it builds on the principles of the metroidvania. It's a challenging game, and often a frustrating one, but it has a clear creative direction and a vast world to explore and master. It leaves no question as to its impact on subsequent adventures.. *M*

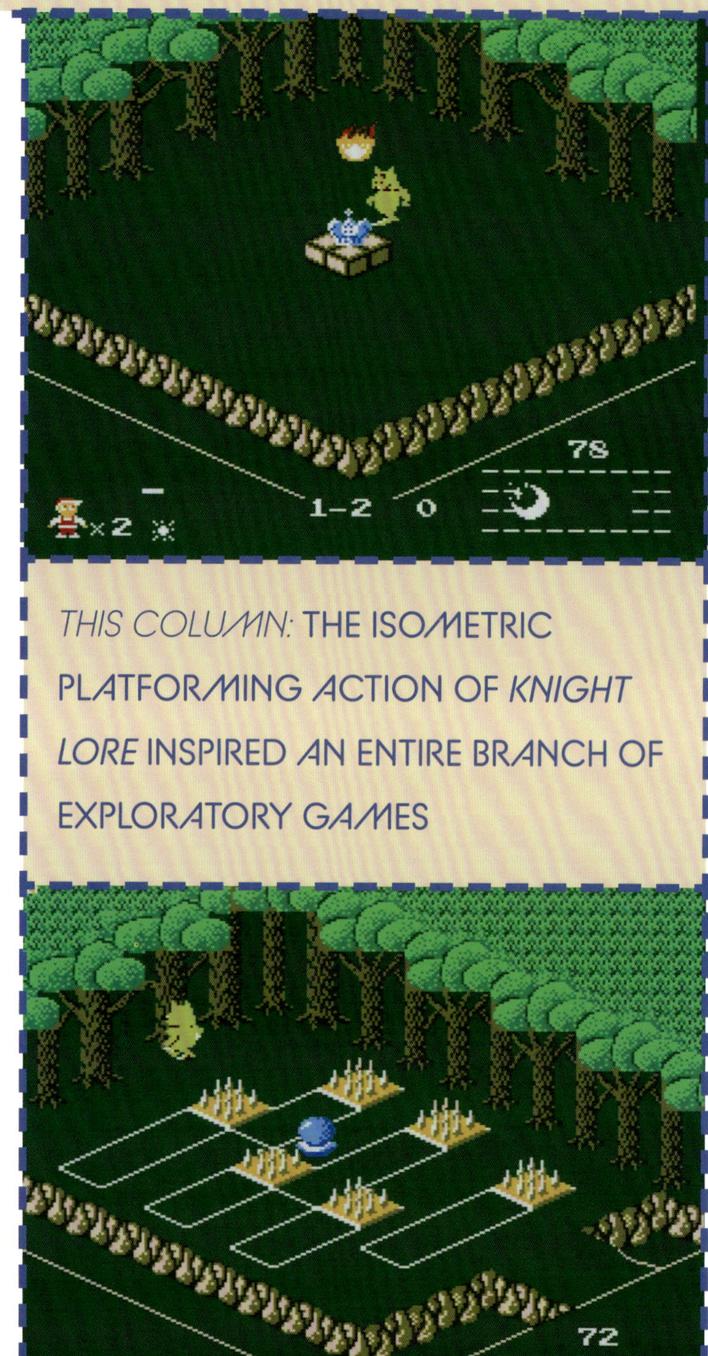

THIS COLUMN: THE ISOMETRIC PLATFORMING ACTION OF *KNIGHT LORE* INSPIRED AN ENTIRE BRANCH OF EXPLORATORY GAMES

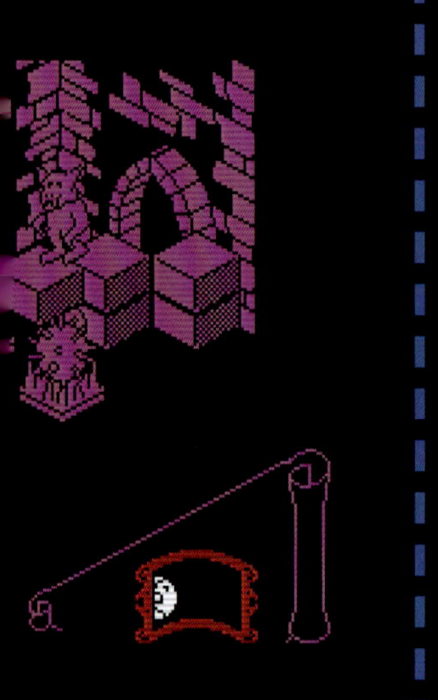

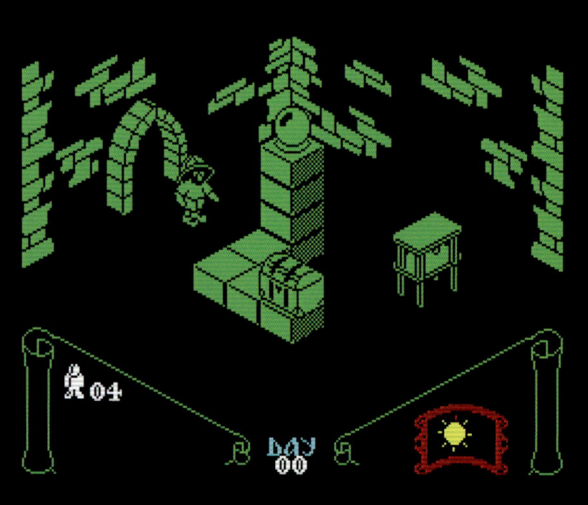

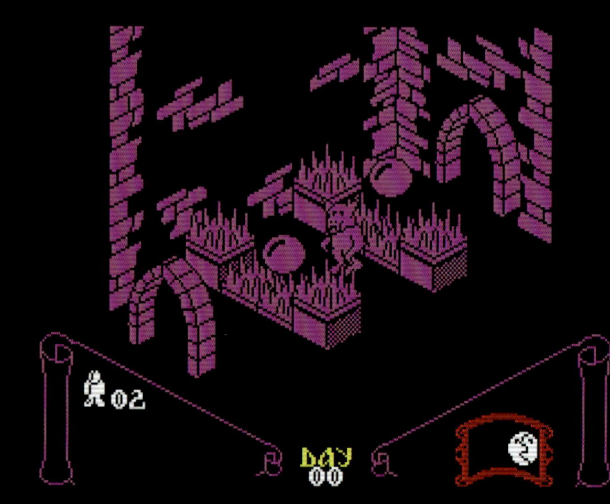

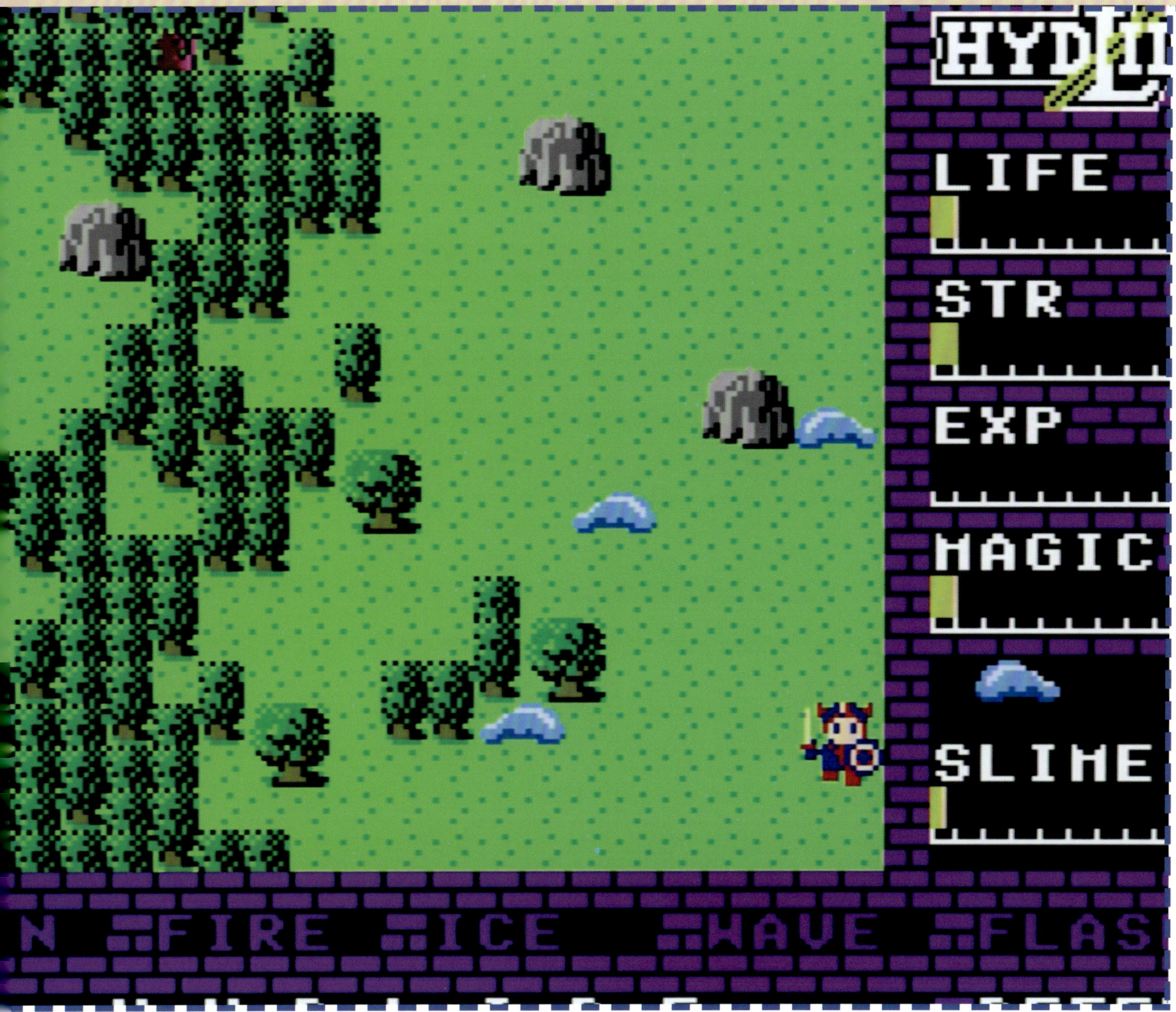

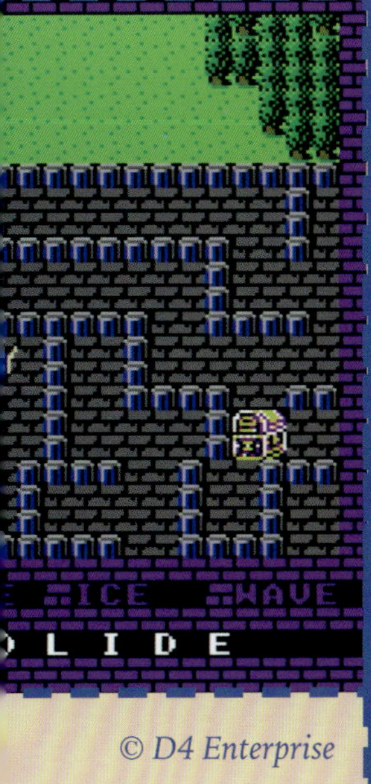

HYDLIDE

PLATFORM: **PC-6601 / VARIOUS**
DEV: **T&E SOFT** | PUB: **T&E SOFT**
INITIAL RELEASE: **DEC. 1984**
SHOWN HERE: **NINTENDO ENTERTAINMENT SYSTEM VERSION, 1989**

NOTABLE FOR: **ALSO LAYING THE FOUNDATION OF THE CONSOLE ACTION RPG**

BUMP AND GRIND

Arriving on the Japanese home computing scene just a few months after *Dragon Slayer*, T&E Soft's *Hydlide* makes for a breezy companion release. Although it was released a little too soon after the launch of Namco's arcade hit *The Tower of Druaga* to qualify as a derivative work, you can't help but feel that *Hydlide*'s designers took some hasty last-second notes from its predecessor.

Structurally, the two games don't have much in common. *Hydlide* takes place in a single open world rather than spanning a few dozen stages. Its overworld consists of a 5×5 grid of screens that loops around in all directions, and it contains entrances to multiple underground passages and dungeons. It's a highly condensed, almost arcade-like, role-playing experience; players stats are depicted by a series of simple meters on the side of the screen. Combat consists of walking into foes with your sword drawn, similar to Namco's *Druaga*, though you can also use magic. Unlike *Druaga*, *Hydlide* employs an experience system. It takes ages to level up your little hero, but you can grind all you want and save your game with a password—at least in the NES version, anyway, which was an enhanced version of the original called *Hydlide Special* in Japan. *Hydlide* reached the US in 1989, well beyond its sell-by date, but the 1984 game was a pretty impressive work for its time. It neatly distilled the essence of games like *Ultima* and *Wizardry* into an easy-to-grasp action format that was richer and more concrete than Adventure.

That said, there's not really much to *Hydlide*. The quest involves a simple chain of progression for key items that need to be used in order to complete the quest. Play time primarily involves grinding for level ups and poking into obscure corners of the world for critical acquisitions. But you can definitely see formative metroidvania concepts at play here, with tools that open new areas and features in a world you can roam freely from the outset. Unlike *Pitfall II*, this game undeniably had an impact on early metroidvanias, having been a sizable hit on Japanese home computers and fueling that nation's collective thirst for exploration. M

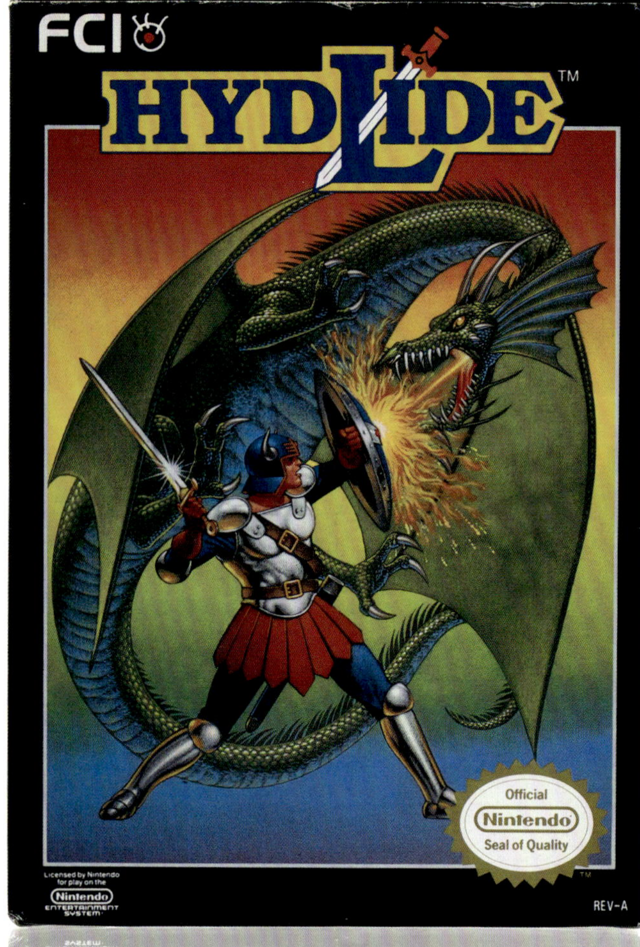

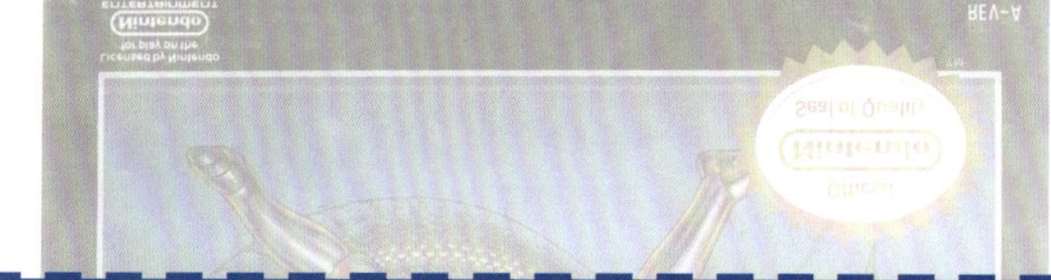

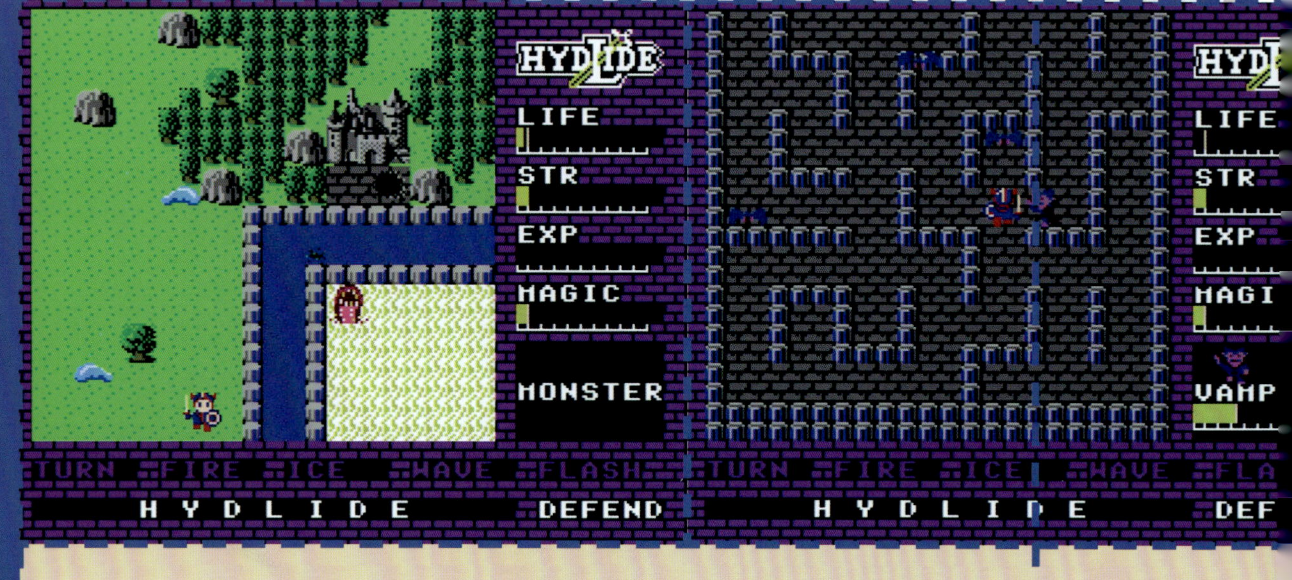

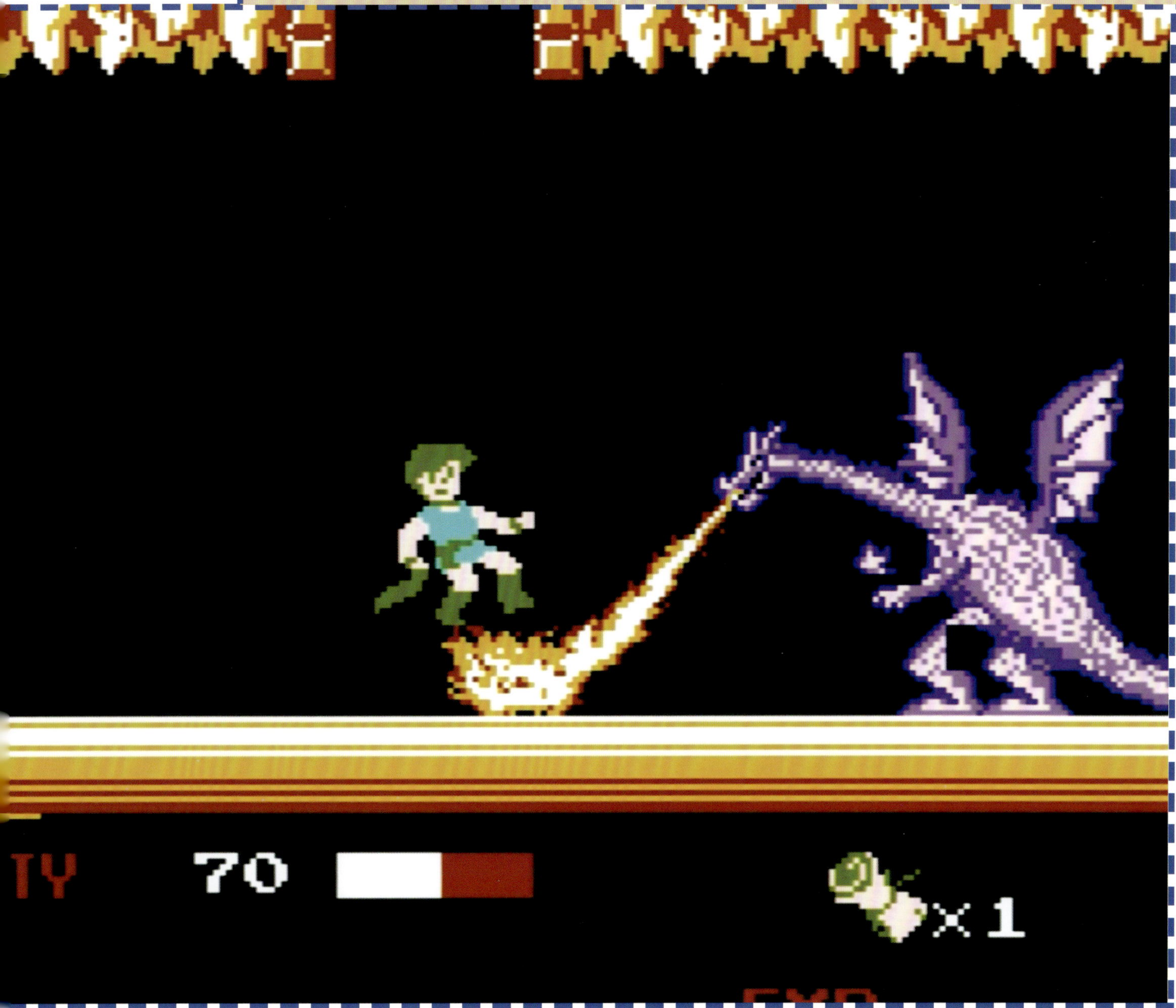

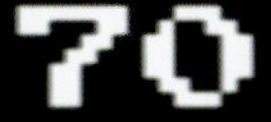

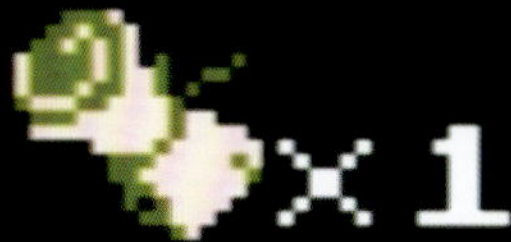

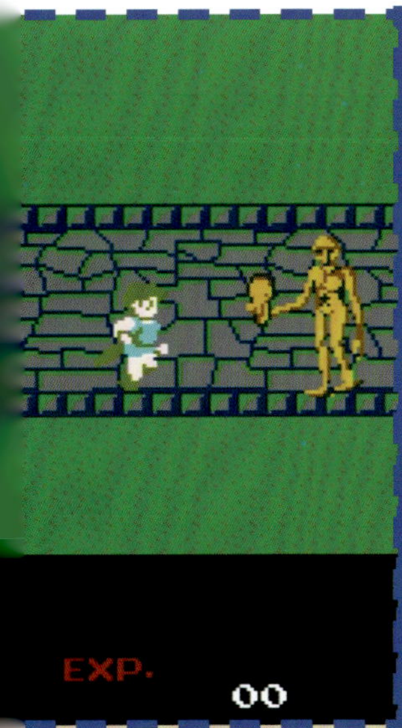

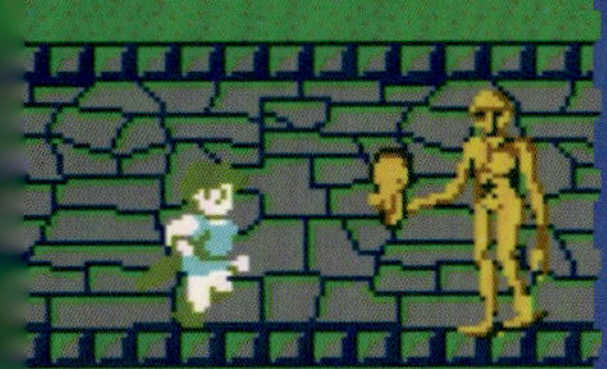

DRAGON BUSTER

PLATFORM: **ARCADE / VARIOUS**
DEV: **NAMCO** | PUB: **NAMCO**
INITIAL RELEASE: **DEC. 1984**
SHOWN HERE: **NINTENDO FAMICOM VERSION, 1987**

NOTABLE FOR: **ALSO LAYING THE FOUNDATION OF THE CONSOLE ACTION RPG**

A LINK TO THE LINK

Although most followers of video game history point to *Super Mario Bros.* as the first great side-scrolling platformer, it was hardly the first of its kind. Aarcade powerhouse Namco delivered not one but two games that featured sidescrolling character action in the waning months of 1984, nearly a year before Mario squashed his first grouchy Goomba. *Pac- Land* arrived first, placing the world's most popular video game character into a *Pitfall!*-like scenario that saw him running and jumping left to right, then doubling back and retracing his steps back to the beginning.

Two months later, Namco followed with *Dragon Buster*, a game that inserted a different hit property into the *Pac-Land* format in place of Pac-Man: namely, *The Tower of Druaga*. While not directly connected to the earlier dungeon crawler, *Dragon Buster* certainly called it to mind with its loose, simple, sword-based combat against spell-slinging wizards and fire-breathing dragons. Like *Pac-Land*, *Dragon Buster* demanded that players run left to right as the screen scrolled along with their movements. But, like *Druaga*, *Dragon Buster* allowed the protagonist to traverse separate paths in search of potions and tools that would enhance their combat capabilities.

The big innovation in *Dragon Buster* arrived in the form of the world map. Upon completing a level, players entered a simple map interface that depicted icons for multiple locations linked by roads, which allowed players to choose their next destination. Although these pathways worked in one direction only, leading the protagonist inexorably toward the dragon's lair at the end of each map, they added variety and replay value to the adventure. Within each icon, players often found themselves needing to explore a far more complex space than anything seen in other platformers to that point. Beyond the first stage, caves and castles sprawled in all directions; these were joined with interconnected and branching paths that contained distinct hazards and treasures. On top of that, the hero could shrug off a certain amount of damage inflicted by his foes thanks to the presence of an RPG-style vitality meter that depicted his current health level. Although not quite a proper exploratory platformer or action-RPG, *Dragon Buster* was a major step in those directions, and was an enormous influence on countless games to come—serving as the bridge between *Pitfall!* and *Zelda II*. M

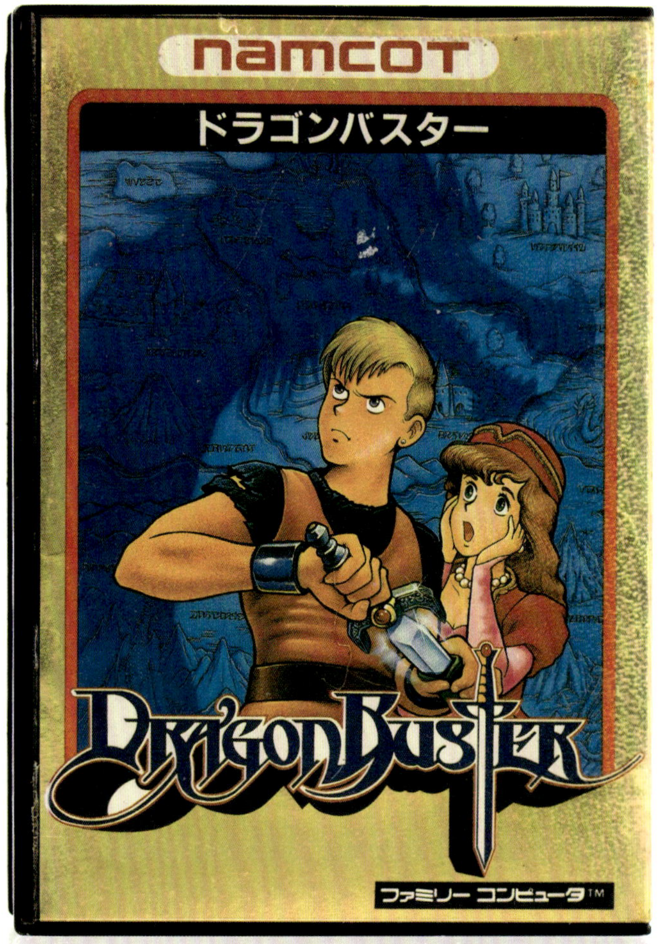

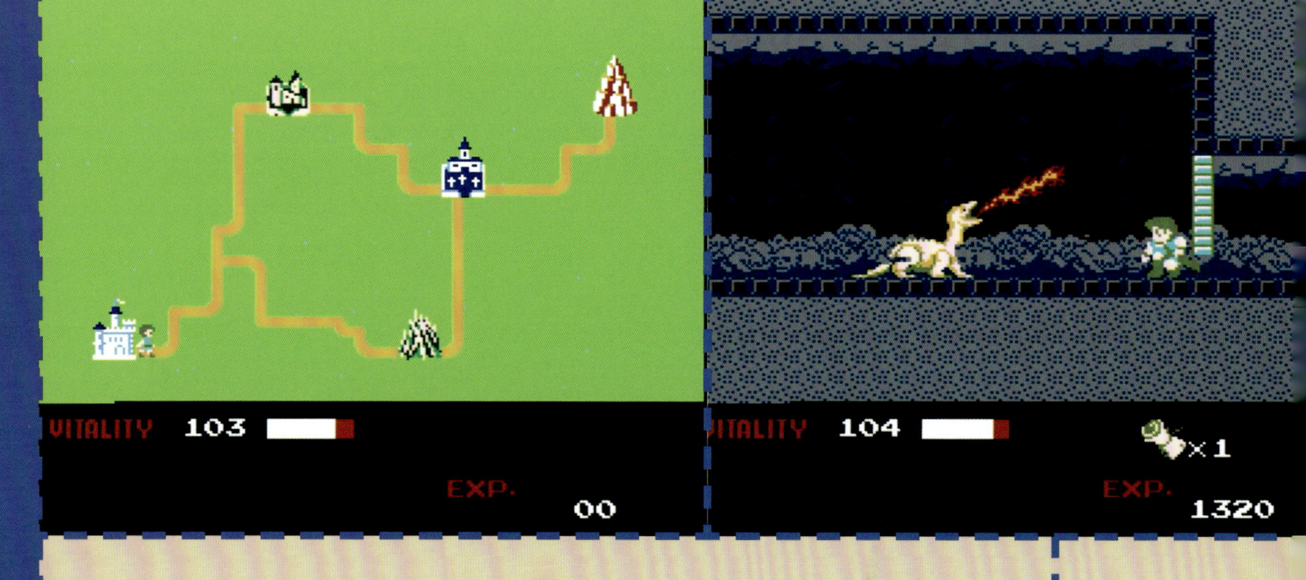

METROIDVANIA TIMELINE 1985-86

After all the turmoil and innovation that gaming experienced in 1984, the following year amounted to something of a re-set. Home computers became more firmly entrenched in all regions, while the Japanese console market expanded radically as third-party publishers made their way to Nintendo's Famicom and began staking out their turf on the platform. Meanwhile, plans to localize the Famicom into Western markets as the NES began to come to fruition with the system's limited American test launch for the holidays.

As a result, very little happened on the metroidvania front in 1985 as publishers and developers recalibrated their businesses to account for the new logistics of the industry. But the following year would be huge, in large part due to a major development for Nintendo's console: the Famicom Disk System, which brought many of the capabilities of home computers to the game system. Console/computer hybrids were hardly a new concept by 1986—even Nintendo had previously explored that option for Famicom with an add-on keyboard, tape drive, and BASIC programming cartridge—but the Disk System took a different philosophical approach to the upgrade process. Rather than turning the console into a low-powered PC, the Disk System simply gave the console access to more storage space and rewritable media without fundamentally changing the player interface. This resulted in pure console game experiences that could support larger worlds, more complex quests, and persistent retention of player progress. Nintendo inaugurated the peripheral with a game that embodied all that the Disk System symbolized: *The Legend of Zelda*, which dropped players into an immense open world and challenged them to unearth nine dungeons in order to defeat the Demon King Ganon and save the eponymous princess.

More games quickly followed, including the two that gave the metroidvania genre its name: Nintendo's *Metroid* and Konami's *Castlevania*. Interestingly, though, it wasn't the Disk System *Castlevania* that represented a milestone in metroidvania evolution. Rather, that honor belongs to *Castlevania*'s companion release, *Vampire Killer*, a more complex, adventure-inflected remix of *Castlevania* for the MSX2 home computer. Both releases shipped under the name *Akumajou Dracula* in Japan, despite their differing localized titles, meaning that Konami viewed them as two sides of a single coin—a duality that would be streamlined into a single unified vision the following year with the games' shared sequel.

Several other landmark titles that shipped in 1986 would go on to steer the design of metroidvania games down the road, most notably *Dragon Quest*. A sort of minimalist take on the role-playing game, *Dragon Quest*'s accessible, streamlined format helped it become a massive hit that other developers would later imitated. But, more importantly, its innovations would manifest in role-playing hybrid works (like metroidvanias), making *Dragon Quest* every bit as influential to the metroidvania as, well, *Metroid* and *'Vania*.

TIMELINE OF EVENTS

July 1985

Commodore Amiga
Commodore's advanced computer offered the most impressive graphical capabilities of any Western PC in the 1980s and became a mainstay for video production...and, of course, gaming.

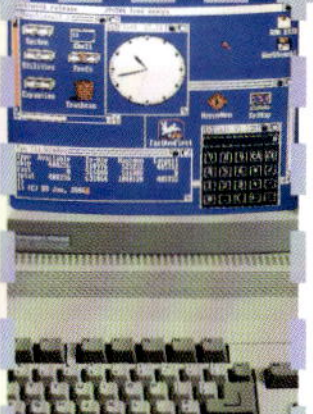

September 1985

Super Mario Bros.
The definitive statement on run-and-jump platforming, *Super Mario Bros.* defined the workings of the tenets of *Donkey Kong* and became the baseline for action games...and action-RPGs.

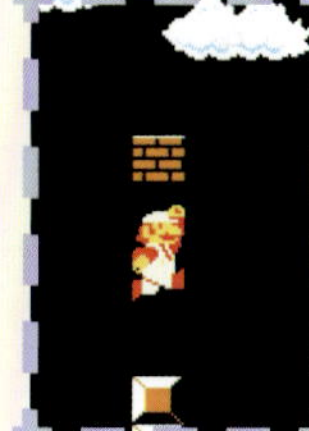

October 1985

Xanadu
Nihon Falcom's take on Namco's *Dragon Buster* led to *Xanadu*, the sequel to *Dragon Slayer*, which, introduced side-scrolling exploratory action while retaining top-down combat.

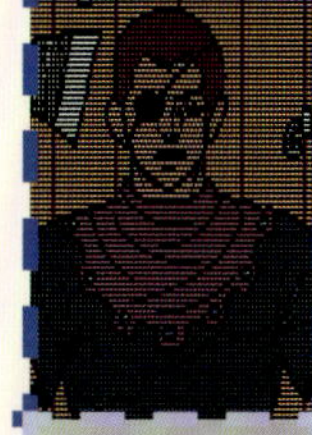

Nintendo Entertainment System
The US release of the Famicom rebuilt the hardware to meet the needs of the evolving industry, resuscitating a moribund American console market.

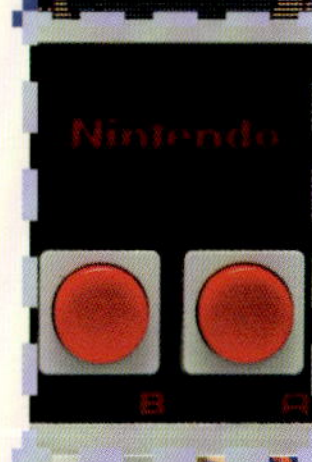

Sega Mark III
Debuting in Japan the same week that Nintendo launched the US NES, Sega's updated SG-1000 added a massively improved graphical chip that made it technically superior to the NES.

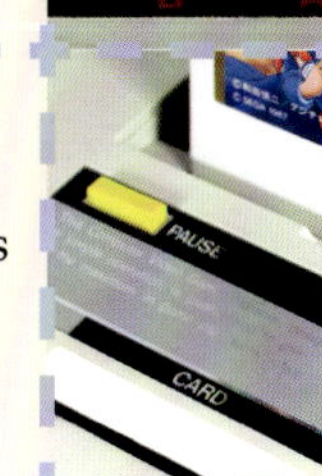

TIMELINE OF EVENTS, CONTINUED

1985 (Unknown Date)

Tetris

While *Tetris* is in no way relevant to metroidvanias outside of a business link to *The Black Onyx*, no video game timeline would be complete without one of the most popular games ever.

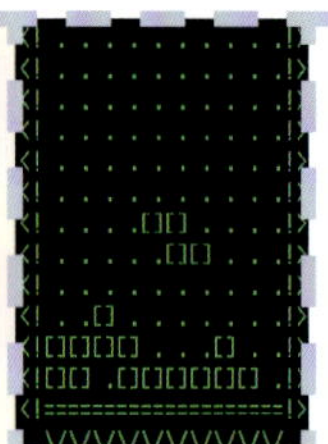

February 1986

The Legend of Zelda

Nintendo presented its own take on the *Hydlide/Druaga* formula with this adventure, designed to take advantage of the powerful, rewriteable Disk System with its persistent world.

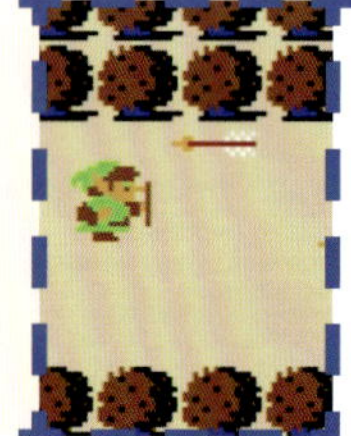

May 1986

Dragon Quest

The world's first true mass-market role-playing hit, Enix's *Dragon Quest* drew on *Portopia*'s interface to lead players through a highly simplified but artfully crafted take on the genre.

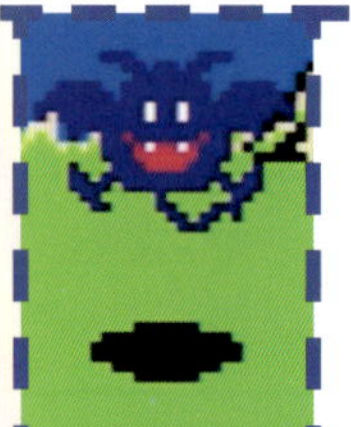

August 1986

Metroid

Nintendo's answer to *Pitfall II*. Like The *Legend of Zelda*, this labyrinthine game exploited the Disk System's media in order to retain quest progression and character growth across play sessions.

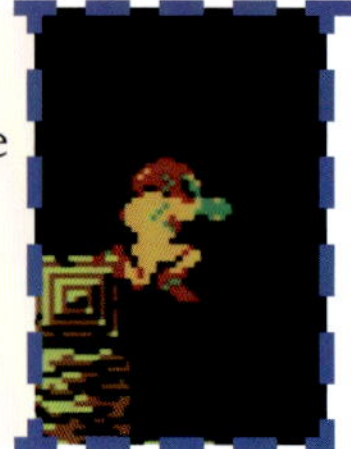

October 1986

Romancia: Dragon Slayer Jr.

Pushing the *Dragon Slayer* series even further from a pure RPG experience, Romancia may have had the look of an action game, but the heart of a PC graphical adventure beat inside.

Vampire Killer

This computer-oriented variant on *Castlevania* retained the action-platforming paradigm of its console sibling but demanded players explore and shop to make their way through each stage.

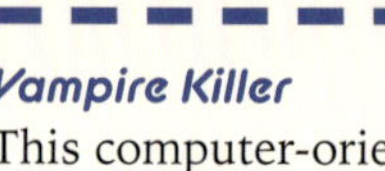

November 1986

Milon's Secret Castle

Arguably learning all the wrong lessons from The *Tower of Druaga*, this puzzle platform adventure emphasized repetitive hunting and aimless blasting in order to complete the journey.

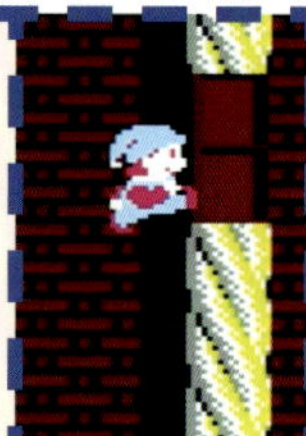

December 1986

Wing of Madoola

Sunsoft's take on the *Dragon Buster* paradigm was rough and often unfair, but it deserves notice for its action-RPG ambitions and for giving the metroidvania genre a rare female protagonist.

Relics

A fascinating if rough-hewn action-adventure game, *Relics* required players to invest time in exploring and exploiting enemies to make progress through its complex world.

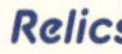

Kid Icarus

While most of *Kid Icarus* unfolds as a purely linear action shooter, players must build up their powers and resources in order to escape the dense labyrinths at the end of each world.

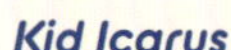

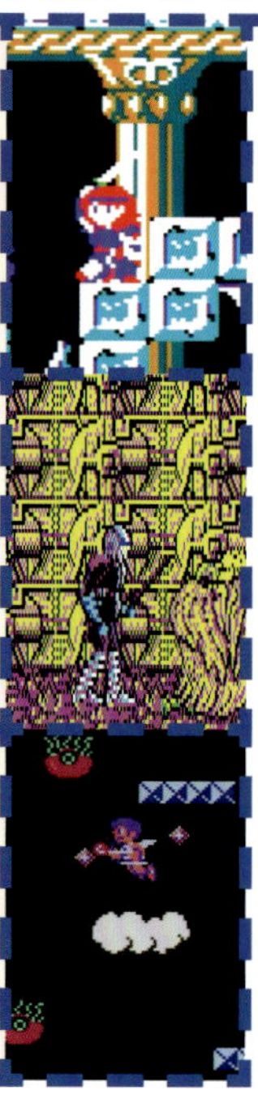

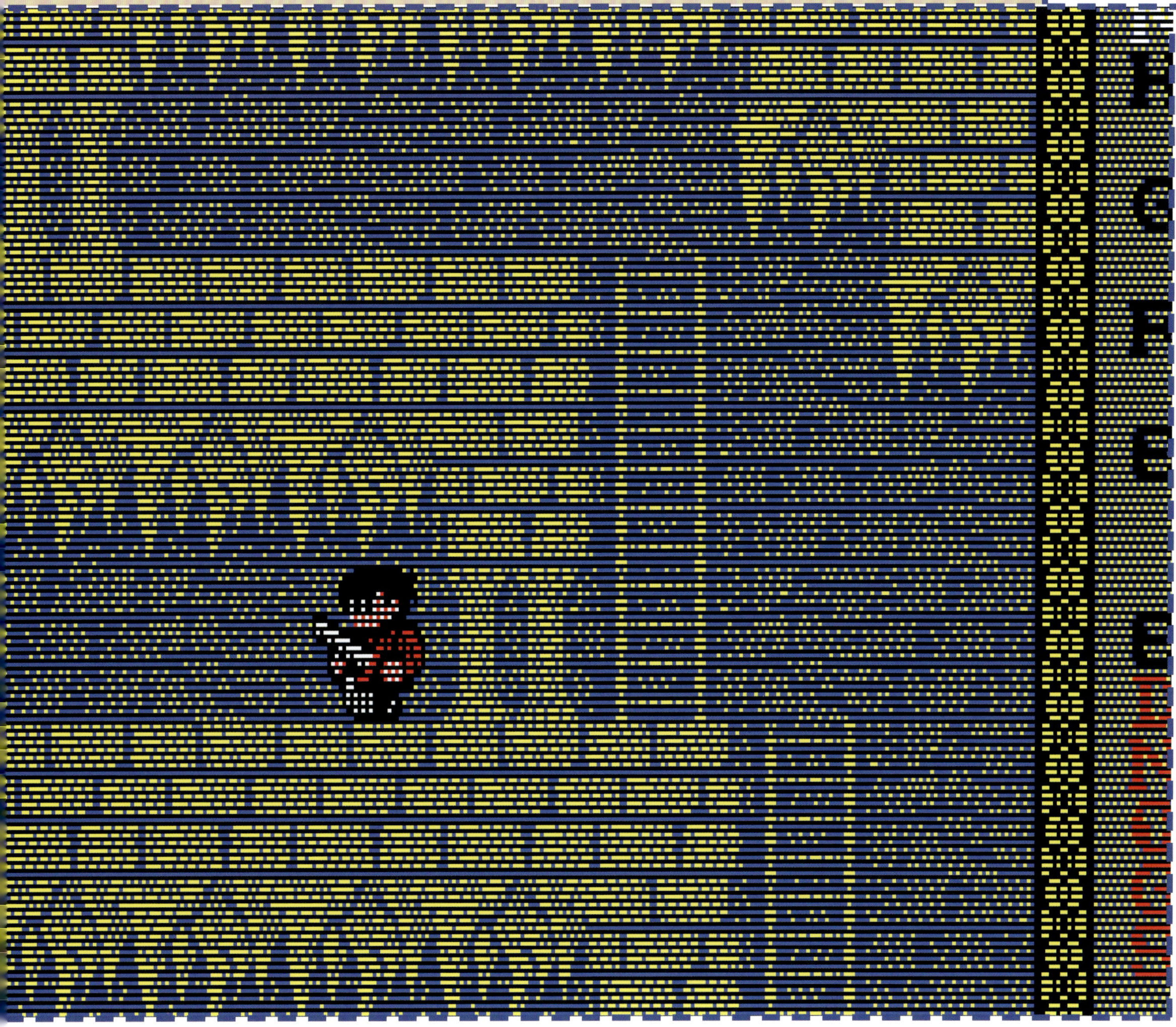

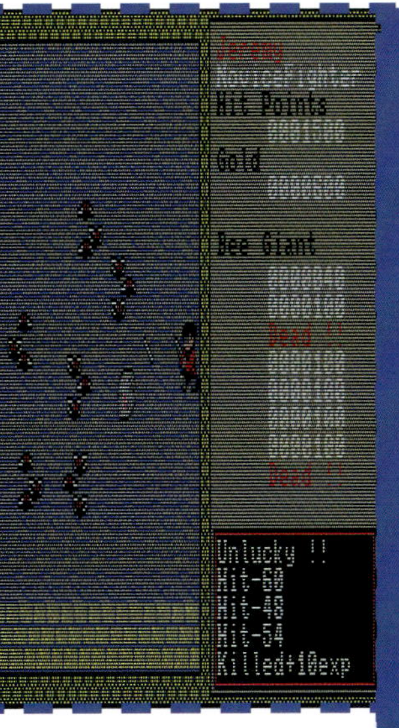

XANADU
DRAGON SLAYER II

PLATFORM: **PC-8801 / VARIOUS**
DEV: **NIHON FALCOM** | PUB: **NIHON FALCOM**
INITIAL RELEASE: **OCT. 1985**

NOTABLE FOR: **COMBINING TOP-DOWN AND SIDE-SCROLLING ELEMENTS**

LEAPING INTO THE FUTURE

By 1985, full-scale role-playing mania had gripped Japan's computer gaming literati. Tech-savvy enthusiasts who frequented the crowded backstreet electronics shops of Tokyo's Akihabara district had braved the hazards of English-language text to poke around primal creations on exotic imported computers like the Apple II and VIC-20. They liked what they saw: turn-based battles against challenging monsters; intricate inventory arrangements, character growth and statistic management systems; and most of all the vast, immersive, imaginary worlds of realms like Britannia and Sosaria. The early '80s saw a variety of rough but earnest attempts by Japanese developers to create their own RPGs, inspired by the likes of *Wizardry* and *Ultima*. The watershed year for the genre proved to be 1984 as Dutch émigré Henk Rogers published *The Black Onyx* through his studio Bullet-Proof Software, and Nihon Falcom finally cracked the RPG nut with *Dragon Slayer*.

Arriving a year after *Dragon Slayer*, Falcom's semi-sequel *Xanadu* feels like the first truly unique take on RPGs to emerge from Japan. Where earlier efforts simply copied existing import titles from top to bottom—*The Black Onyx*, for all the appeal of its Japanese-language text support, did little more than duplicate the structure and beats of *Wizardry*—*Xanadu* combines the elaborate underpinnings of those games with the breezy presentation of arcade-action games. It feels like the midpoint between Falcom's previous work, combining elements of *Dragon Slayer* with the samizdat Western-style RPGs the studio cut its proverbial teeth on.

This is not to say that *Xanadu* in any way feels like an arcade game; this is certainly no *Dragon Buster*, nor even a *Tower of Druaga*. Although *Xanadu* introduces side-scrolling movement into the mix, it works more as a framing device than as the meat of the gameplay. Players navigate the game world by controlling a small hero who walks, jumps, and climbs his way around the underground city and caverns that comprise *Xanadu*'s world. However, these sequences really only serve to move you from place to place.

Xanadu creates a bridge between the standard RPG and the action-RPG style that would become Falcom's trademark and a

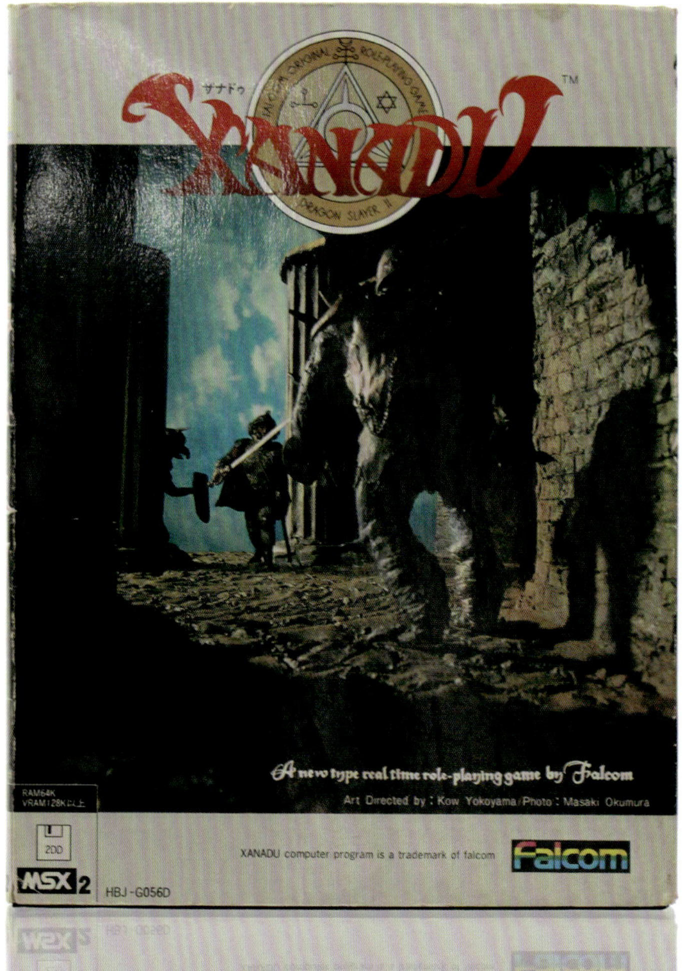

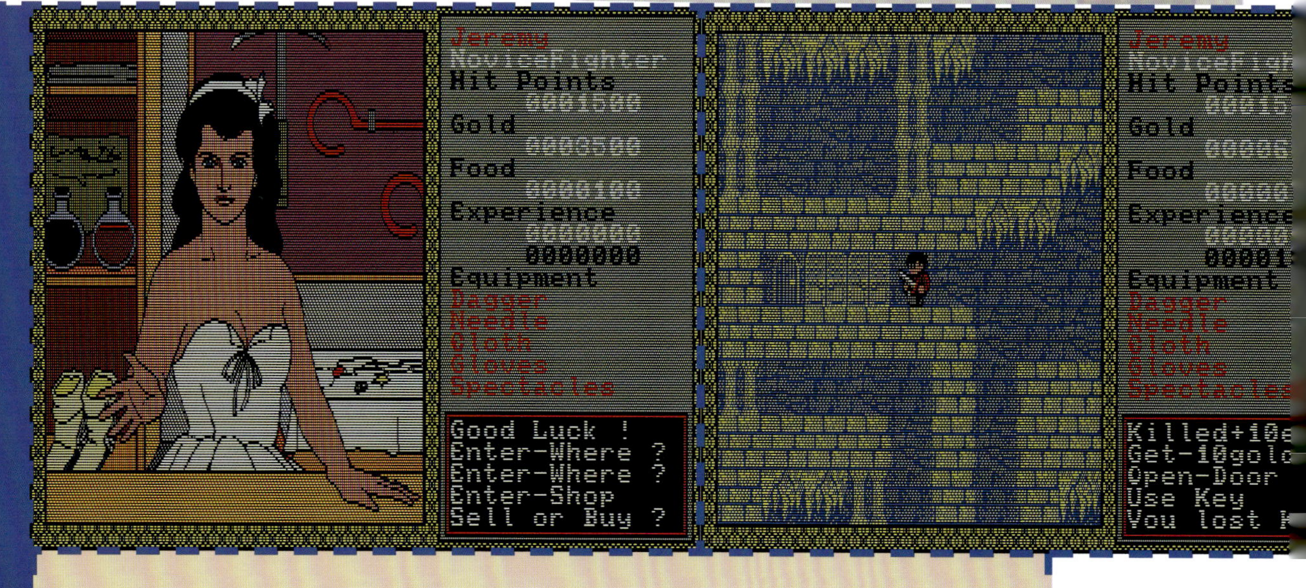

hallmark of the metroidvania format. In a lot of ways, it's the primal font that gave us the likes of *Zelda II*, *Castlevania II*, and *Popful Mail*. It's clumsier and opaquer than any of those games, which is saying something. However, its combination of true role-playing elements—far more substantial than the simple items and health meters of Namco's RPG-flavored arcade-action titles—with two-di- mensional, side-scrolling platform action is a first and would be imitated and refined by numerous developers over the years.

Xanadu begins by dropping players into a town where they can enter buildings to collect money from the king, gather clues, and gear up at shops before venturing into the dungeon. Everything about this game feels like a puzzle, including the simple process of locating the dungeon from the starting town area. Once you find it, you move around the dungeon in the same side-scrolling perspective as you wandered through town, roam- ing around in search of keys and treasures. Unlike in the town area, monsters appear in the dungeon. However, you don't fight them with simple sword strikes à la *Dragon Buster*. Instead, bumping into a foes sends you into a separate viewpoint, the combat mode, which eschews the 2D side perspective in favor of a top-down angle. In this mode, you bump into monsters directly to inflict harm upon them—the point at which *Xanadu* justifies its use of the name *Dragon Slayer*.

XANADU DIDN'T LACK BIG IDEAS AND BIGGER AMBITIONS. FALCOM DIDN'T NECESSARILY REALIZE THEIR ASPIRATIONS HERE, BUT YOU HAVE TO RESPECT THEM FOR PUTTING THEIR ALL INTO WHAT COULD HAVE BEEN A SIMPLE REHASH OF _DRAGON SLAYER_.

Xanadu lacks the grab-and-carry element of its pre- decessor; you don't need to tote tokens back to town in order to earn experience and upgrade your stats. Instead, you'll find a more traditional leveling and gear system, reminiscent of *Wizardry*, where you earn cash and experience after each combat encounter. You then head back to the surface to trade gold for better armor and weapons.

All these efforts funnel into your quest to conquer half a dozen towers located throughout the underground dungeon. Once you enter a tower, the game abandons the side view altogether in favor of an extended top-down combat sequence in which you move screen-by-screen toward that tower's end goal. These portions of the adventure make use of the same bump-attack combat style as the random dungeon battles, but with a certain degree of persistence. The overall structure presages Nintendo's *The Legend of Zelda*, which would ship on Famicom Disk System less than half a year later—almost inevitably a remarkable coincidence rather than a case of creative espionage, given the short gap between their respective releases.

Being a computer RPG, of course, *Xanadu* makes *Zelda*'s most arcane secrets feel almost like giveaways. Falcom invested an enormous degree of player friction into the simple process of discovery and advancement, and *Xanadu* takes no prisoners. It's enigmatic in its design and unforgiving in its difficulty level. Yet it proved incredibly popular, becoming the bestselling Japanese PC release to that point. It even had an expansion disk in the form of *Xanadu Scenario II*, a sequel of sorts that is best known today for giving legendary composer Yuzo Koshiro his start.

Xanadu shipped in many permutations, which often varied substantially from one another. For example, the MSX2 version looked better and moved more smoothly than the original PC 8801 version, though their mechanics largely worked the same. Regardless of its platform, *Xanadu* introduced big ideas and big ambitions. In addition to standard character stats, players also have to manage "Karma," which tracks the types of enemies you kill; slay the wrong foes and your Karma rises, which makes it impossible to level up or acquire the legendary sword needed to defeat the final boss. None of this is explained in the game itself, of course. It's a borderline cruel game, but its grand ideas had enormous appeal in 1985 for players who braved its depths. While admittedly a difficult game to revisit in this day and age due to its daunting design, it was hugely influential on other action-RPGs and did a great deal to establish the tone and design of Japanese games. M

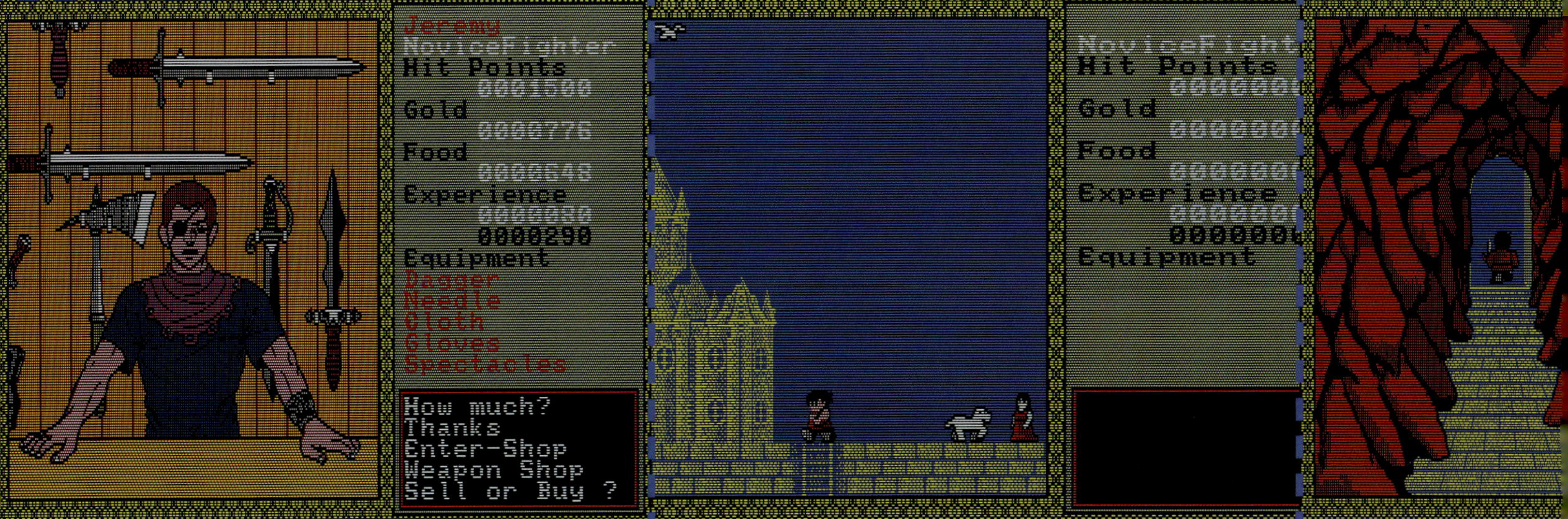

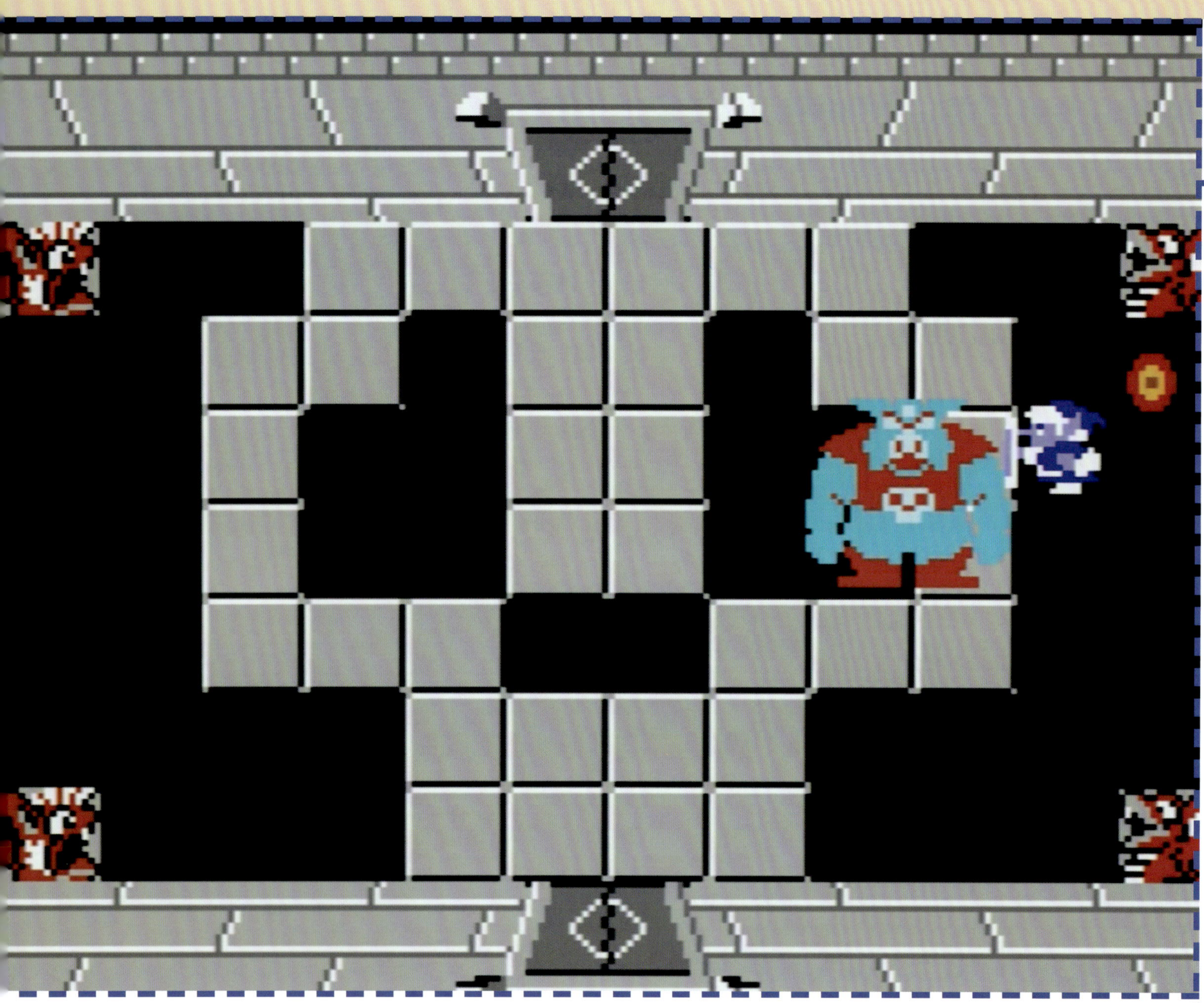

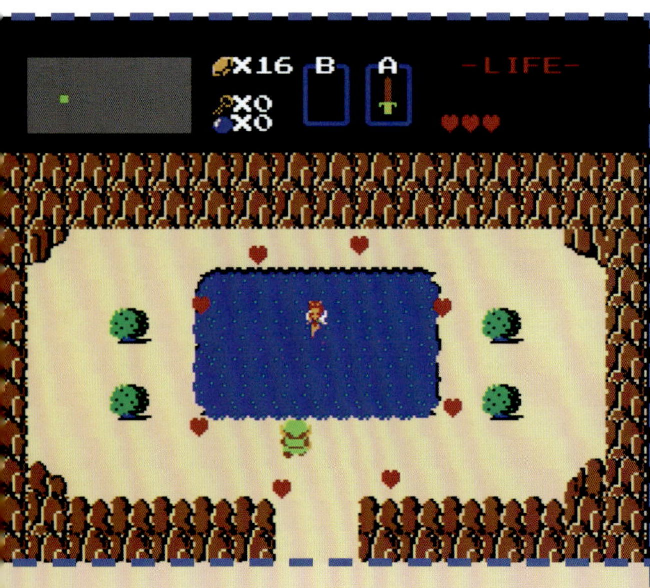

THE LEGEND OF ZELDA

PLATFORM: **FAMICOM DISK SYSTEM / NES**
DEV: **NINTENDO** | PUB: **NINTENDO**
INITIAL RELEASE: **FEB. 1986**

NOTABLE FOR: **TURNING THE ACTION-RPG INTO AN INTERNATIONAL SMASH HIT**

ROLE-PLAYING REDEFINED

Nintendo's designers rarely talk about games that have influenced their own work, which probably stems from a combination of Japanese business etiquette rules and the company's Disney-like drive to create a sense of mystique about its internal processes. Even so, a little light detective work can yield likely threads of inspiration. For example, *The Legend of Zelda* for Famicom Disk System and NES appears to combine a variety of existing role-playing and action concepts into, arguably, the definitive action-RPG. Admittedly, *Zelda* doesn't precisely fit the more pedantic defi- nitions of what constitutes an RPG, because it throws traditional cornerstones (like *Dungeons & Dragons*–derived experience points and character leveling concepts) out the window in favor of a much simpler format that minimizes the need for player calculations and grinding. Despite this departure, you can clearly see those concepts in action beneath the surface of the game's mechanics. It may not look like an RPG in terms of its presentation, but it certainly builds on the genre's ideas.

In broad strokes, *Zelda* plays most like Falcom's *Xanadu*, which undeniably adapted the RPG into a form that was less reliant on abstracted menus. *Zelda* simply takes that approach a step further. Although it doesn't incorporate a side-scrolling action combat view—that would arrive in its sequel the following year—it has much of its structure in common with Falcom's game. It consists of a single massive, interconnected overworld containing multiple self-contained dungeons. The whole game plays out through a top-down viewpoint, just like *Adventure* and *Hydlide*, and the dungeons are extremely similar to those of *Xanadu*'s, though more intricate and complex.

Players can walk anywhere in the world right from the outset in *Zelda*; assuming they can survive long enough to get there. They can even walk immediately to the entrance of the final dungeon. It's very much a sandbox game, with progression gated by a few critical factors. By and large, those factors amount to a handful of tools scattered throughout the dungeons or sold at shops sprinkled around the kingdom. Each dungeon contains at least one treasure that protagonist Link can add to his inventory, many of which double as weapons that help beef up his combat capabilities—bows

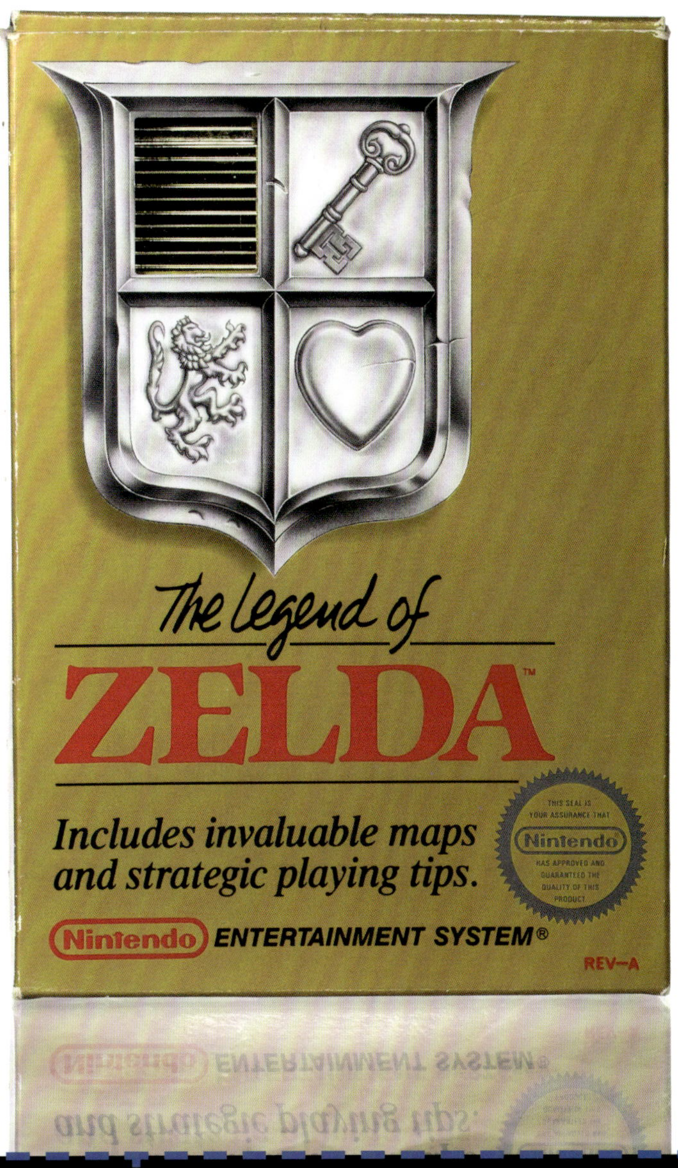

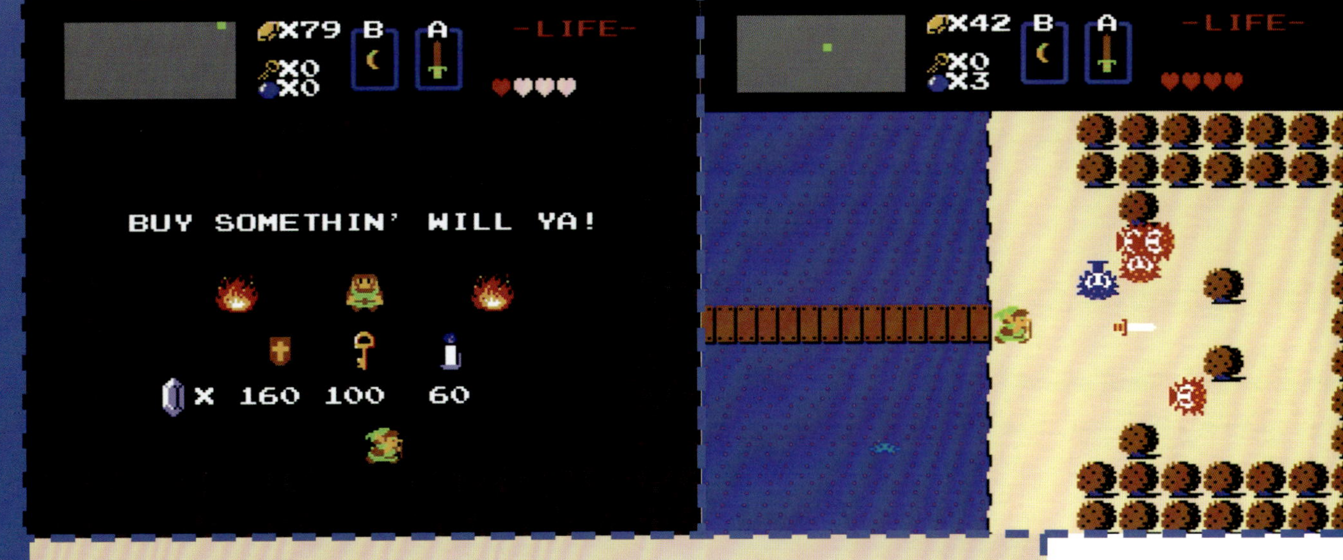

and magic rods and the like. These weapons and consumables help you advance through the quest. Bombs destroy certain foes but allow you to crack open walls, while enemy bait can distract monsters but is also essential for satiating an otherwise implacable foe. At the same time, a handful of treasures have no function besides helping you to overcome obstacles. A ladder allows you to cross gaps, a raft lets you sail across bodies of water, and the eight fragments of the mystical Triforce enable you to access the final dungeon.

Zelda can often be opaque in its design. Some of the game's secrets are only hinted at, such as the means by which you reach the fifth dungeon or reveal the seventh, by way of maddeningly cryptic clues delivered by old men living in unlikely places. At its best, the in-game dialogue offers a riddle. At its worst, it makes no sense at all. Yet the fact that these clues exist at all ultimately make *Zelda* less frustrating than the action-RPGs that preceded it, and its relatively low-friction design is highlighted by the removal of character stats for Link. With no need to worry about your attack strength or defensive power, you never have to level up. You can simply keep your mind focused on your objectives, with no need to grind out experience points to overcome otherwise impossible challenges or to increase your survivability. You can only grow in strength by collecting the three swords hidden throughout Hyrule, and your defensive power only improves when you find life-increasing Heart Containers and buy or find the two mystical shield rings. The only time you need to pause to kill enemies for loot is when you need the money to either buy certain goods or build up your supply of bombs, and both of those elements can be supplemented through alternate means.

These design choices combine to create a slick, low-hassle gameplay loop. The original *Zelda* is by no means a breezy game; your first time through is bound to be a maddening challenge that sends you scrambling for a strategy guide or walkthrough when you find yourself incapable of finding the way forward. Certain dungeons contain particularly challenging enemies, too. There are rooms patrolled by swarms of armored Darknuts that can destroy a careless player in a matter of seconds, and those pale in comparison to rooms where Darknut platoons are interspersed with Bubbles that temporarily rob Link of his ability to wield his sword. In other words, *Zelda* replaces the numerical grind with the need for deft finger work.

Zelda can at times be a cryptic or even punishing game, but it contains no shortage of grand ideas for those who brave its depths. Its lean design and tool-based exploration improved on the games that came before it, and it would prove hugely influential on subsequent entries in the action-RPG format—including *Castlevania*, the series that gave the metroidvania genre its name in the first place. *M*

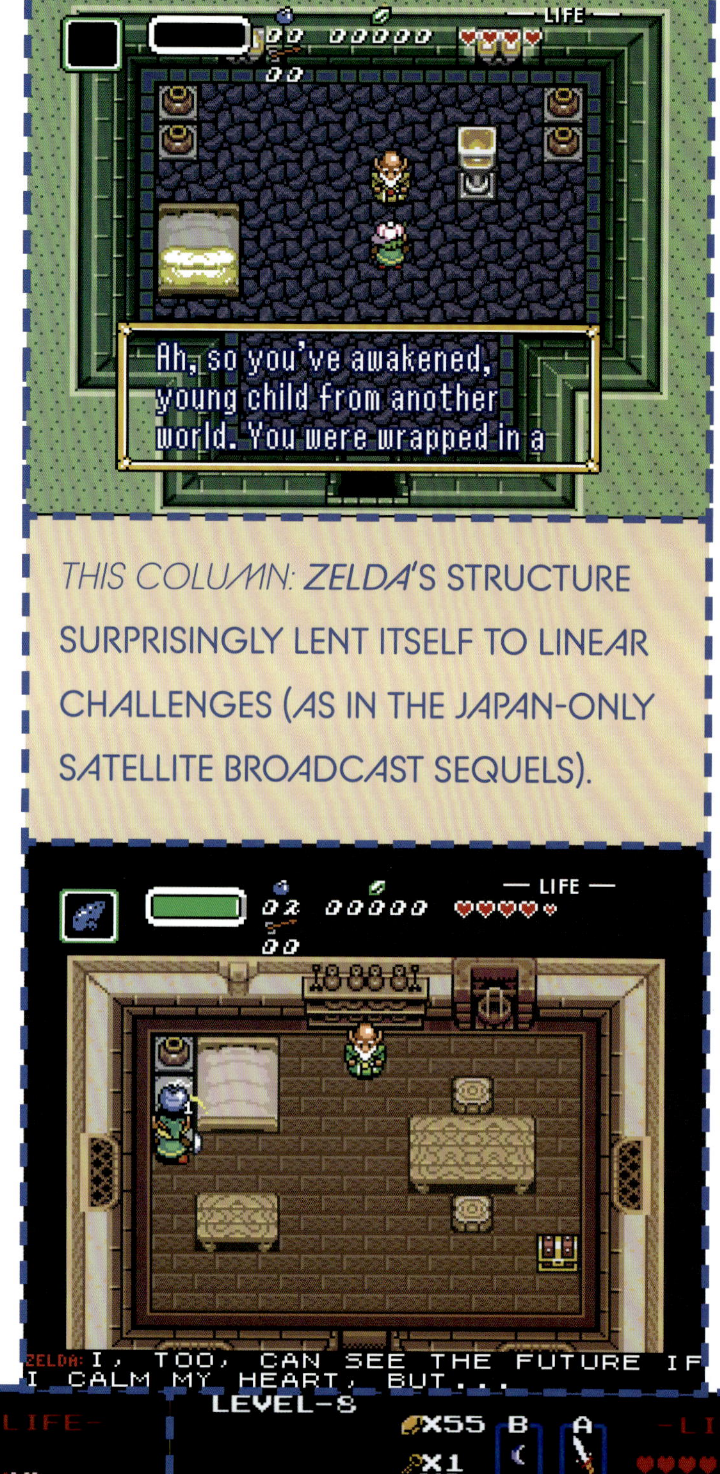

THIS COLUMN: ***ZELDA'S*** STRUCTURE SURPRISINGLY LENT ITSELF TO LINEAR CHALLENGES (AS IN THE JAPAN-ONLY SATELLITE BROADCAST SEQUELS).

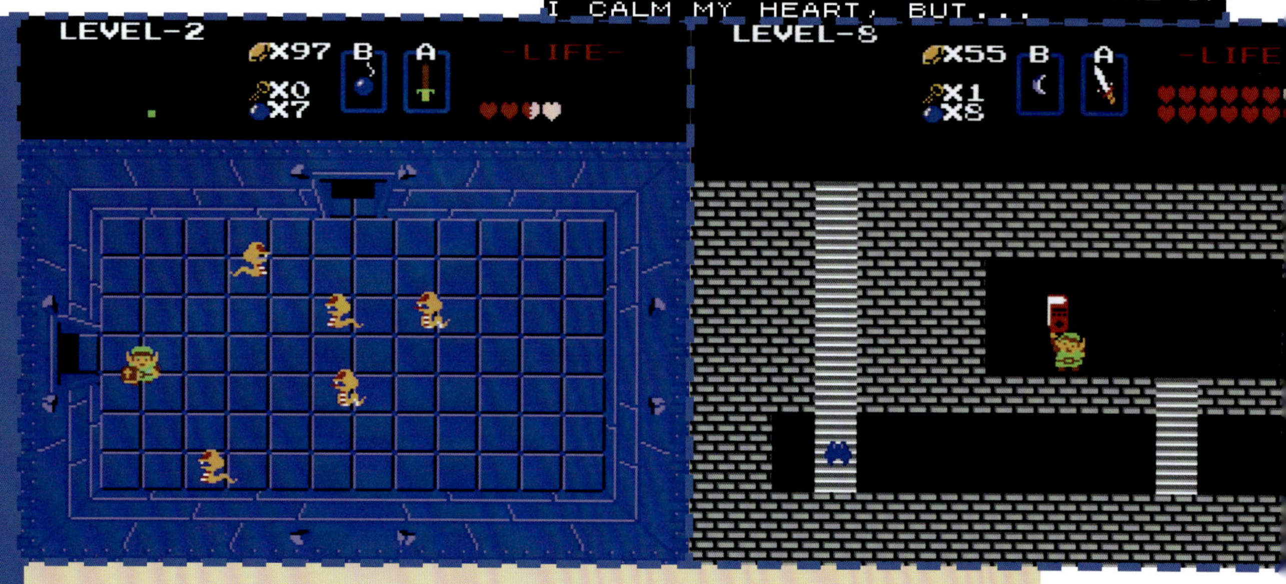

MURASAME AS IT EVER WAS

In some espects, the way for *The Legend of Zelda* was paved by the unlikeliest of genres: military-themed arcade shooters. Although it obviously draws upon the likes of Atari's *Adventure*, *Venture*, *Hydlide*, and the *Tower of Druaga*, *Zelda* also echoes the likes of Taito's *Front Line* and Capcom's *Commando*. The connections go deeper than the simple viewpoint, which streamlined the exploratory top-down style of *Adventure* into a more or less linear march forward—*Xevious* on shank's mare. Like the soldiers in those games, who toted machine guns and tossed grenades, Link wields a primary weapon but can employ secondary attacks with a second button as the situation warrants. *Commando* even included secret underground passages that players could reveal by tossing a grenade at the correct spots!

Not surprisingly, then, a few months after *Zelda*'s debut on the Famicom Disk System, Nintendo harnessed its tech for the sake of a more action-oriented experience: *Nazo no Murasame-jou*, or *The Mysterious Murasame Castle*. Superficially similar to *Zelda* due to its overhead viewpoint and emphasis on sword play, *Murasame* ultimately represents Nintendo's take on the run-and-gun action format, à la *Commando* or *Ikari Warriors*. It's Nintendo's answer to Sega's *The Ninja*, but it gives players control of a noble samurai warrior rather than a devious ninja assassin.

Structurally, *Murasame* falls somewhere between the full open-world roaming of *Zelda* and the more linear style of top-down arcade shooters. With no inventory system and a world broken into multiple stages (each containing a set objective required to advance to the next stage), no one would mistake *Murasame* for a member of the role-playing or action-RPG family. At the same time, it does offer players near-total freedom of movement within the confines of a given level. Each stage contains of a dozen or more scenes consisting of a single screen that flips to the next as you move between them, but you can backtrack freely until you achieve your current objective. This represents far greater freedom than that offered in linear arcade shooters, although many of them did let players scroll backward for a tactical advantage. Nevertheless, while *Nazo no Murasame-jou* tilts too far into the action arena to constitute a proper action-RPG, it represents another step in breaking down the barriers between genres—a central pillar of the metroidvania design philosophy.

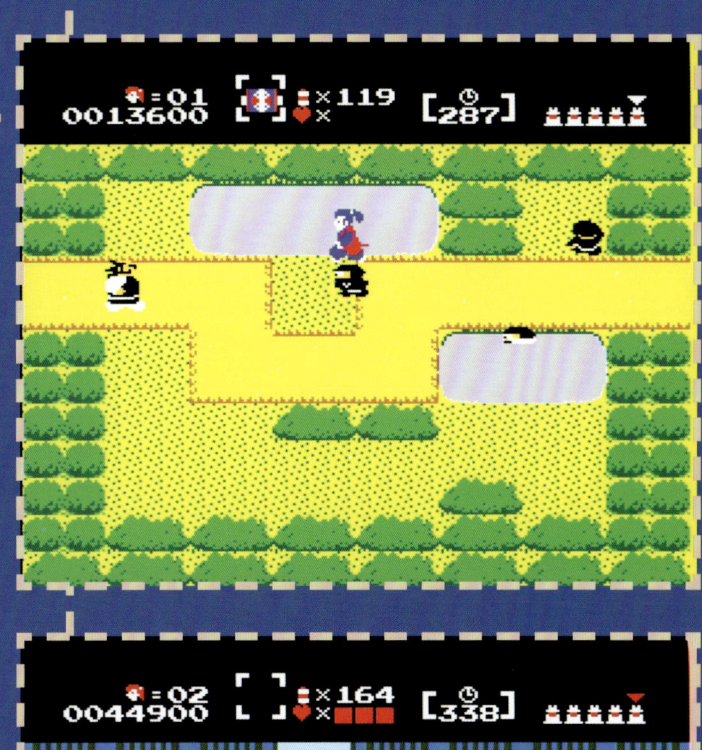

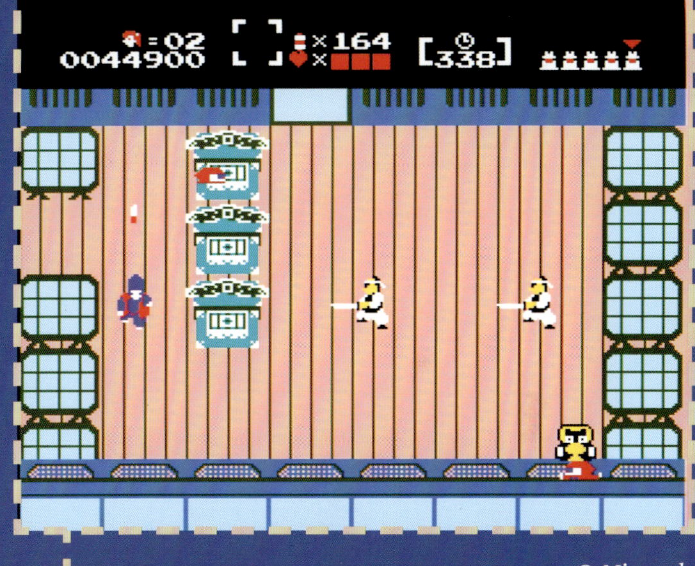

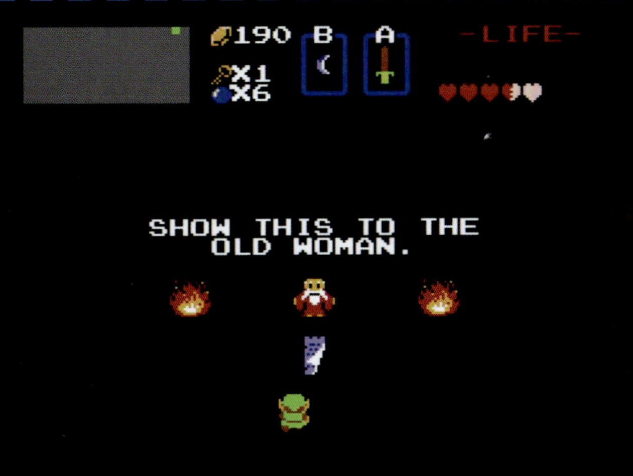

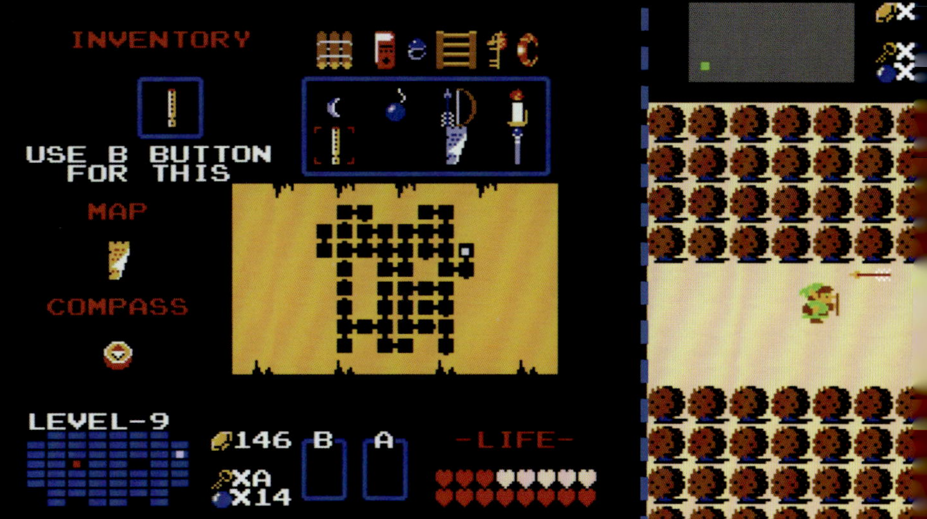

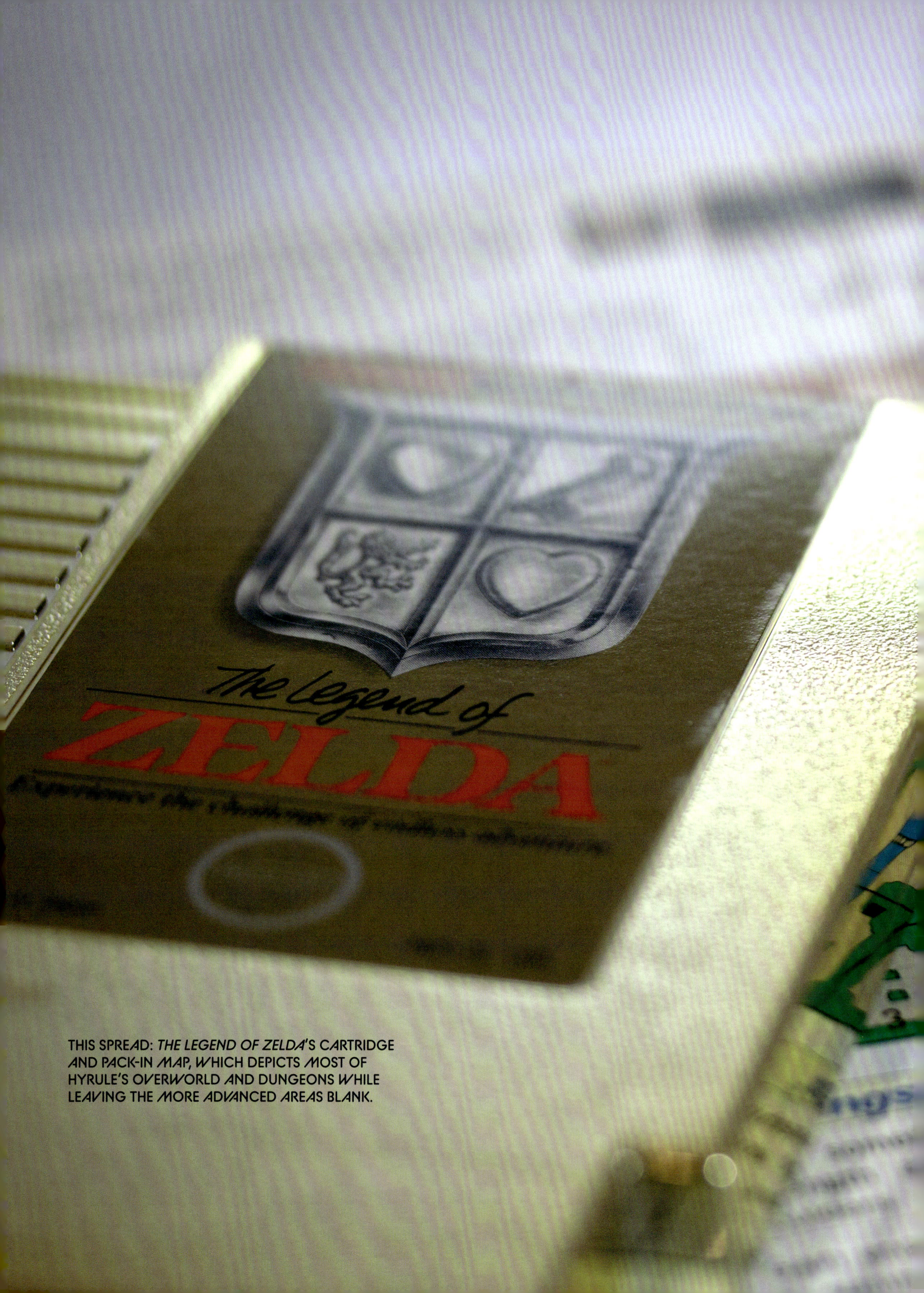

THIS SPREAD: *THE LEGEND OF ZELDA*'S CARTRIDGE AND PACK-IN MAP, WHICH DEPICTS MOST OF HYRULE'S OVERWORLD AND DUNGEONS WHILE LEAVING THE MORE ADVANCED AREAS BLANK.

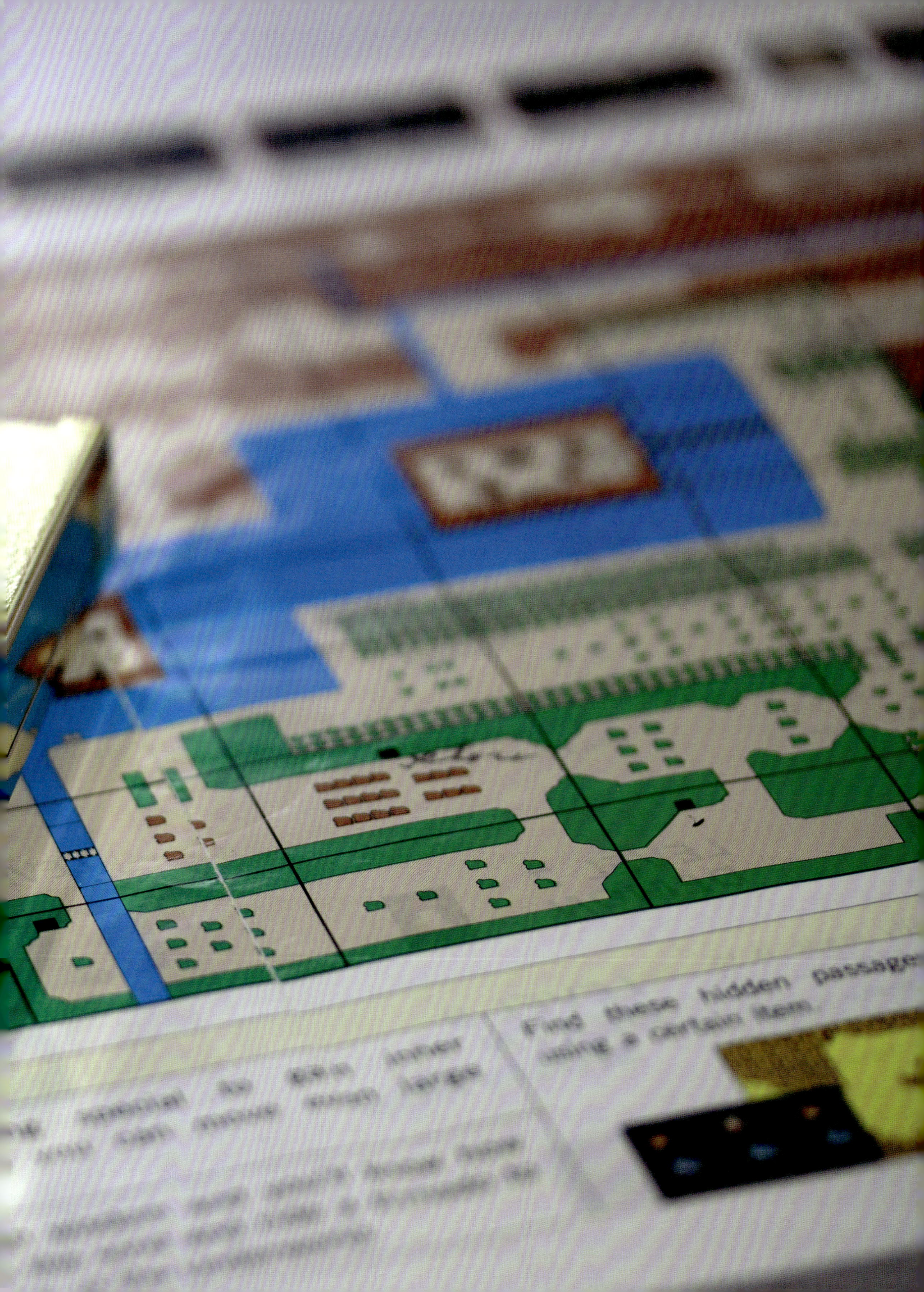
Find these hidden
using a certain item.

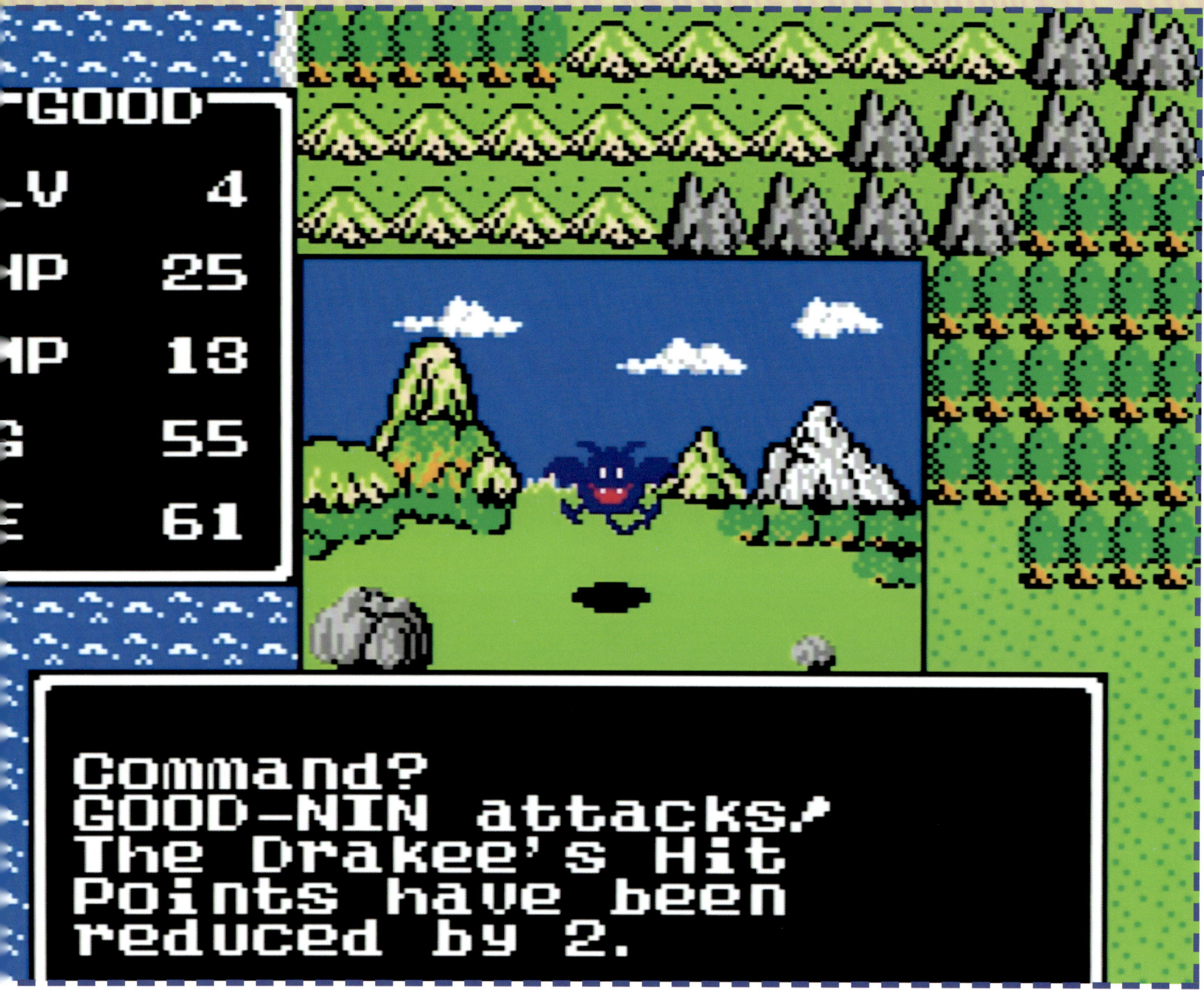

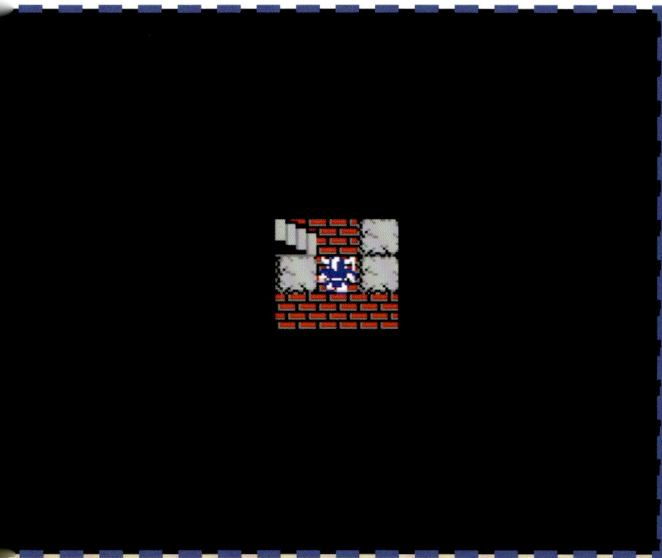

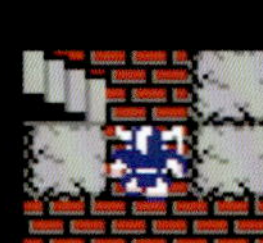

DRAGON QUEST

PLATFORM: **FAMICOM / NES / MSX**
DEV: **ARMOR PROJECT / CHUN SOFT / HAL** | PUB: **ENIX**
INITIAL RELEASE: **MAY 1986**
RELEASED IN THE U.S. AS DRAGON WARRIOR IN AUG. 1989

BUT THOU MUST NOTE THE INFLUENCE

Dragon Quest has very little to do with the platonic ideal of the metroidvania—that is to say, action games enhanced with role-playing elements. Yet being the platonic ideal of console role-playing games, its influence on the metroidvania format can't be overstated. Developer Chunsoft and designer Yuji Horii drew on their experience converting murder-mystery adventure *Portopia Renzoku Satsujin Jiken* from computers to consoles to assemble an RPG that eschewed the genre's usual complexity in favor of a structure that worked with a two-button controller rather than a keyboard. In doing so, they helped tip Japan's burgeoning enthusiasm for RPGs over to critical mass. The genre remains immensely popular there to this day.

In the months and years immediately following *Dragon Quest*'s debut, a seemingly endless succession of imitators hit the shelves, attempting to skim a little of the series' popularity for themselves. More notably, countless games in unrelated genres adopted RPG mechanics as well. Of course, thanks to the likes of *Hydlide* and *The Tower of Druaga*, that trend had begun to take shape even before *Dragon Quest* appeared; Horii's hit simply accelerated the process. By 1988, even Mario's third *Super* adventure offered a passing nod to RPG elements by allowing players to select their path on a zoomed-out world map reminiscent of the one that players explored in *Dragon Quest*. Plus, Mario now had the ability to collect and hold power-ups in a simple queue reminiscent of a role-playing inventory system—one of which could only be deployed on the overworld map with an overt callback to *The Legend of Zelda*.

Although its design felt almost comically simplistic by the time it reached the US in late 1989 (as *Dragon Warrior*), *Dragon Quest* lit the spark that spread as wildfire throughout Japanese console games in the latter 1980s. The fervor for hybrid action/role-playing game design would die down after a few years, but the resulting adventures—the likes of *Wonder Boy III*, *Faxanadu*, *Zelda II*, and *Clash at Demonhead*—would continue to trickle West into the 1990s. These titles would whet appetites overseas for classics like *Castlevania: Symphony of the Night*, and, eventually, the integration of RPG-like systems into every sort of game imaginable.

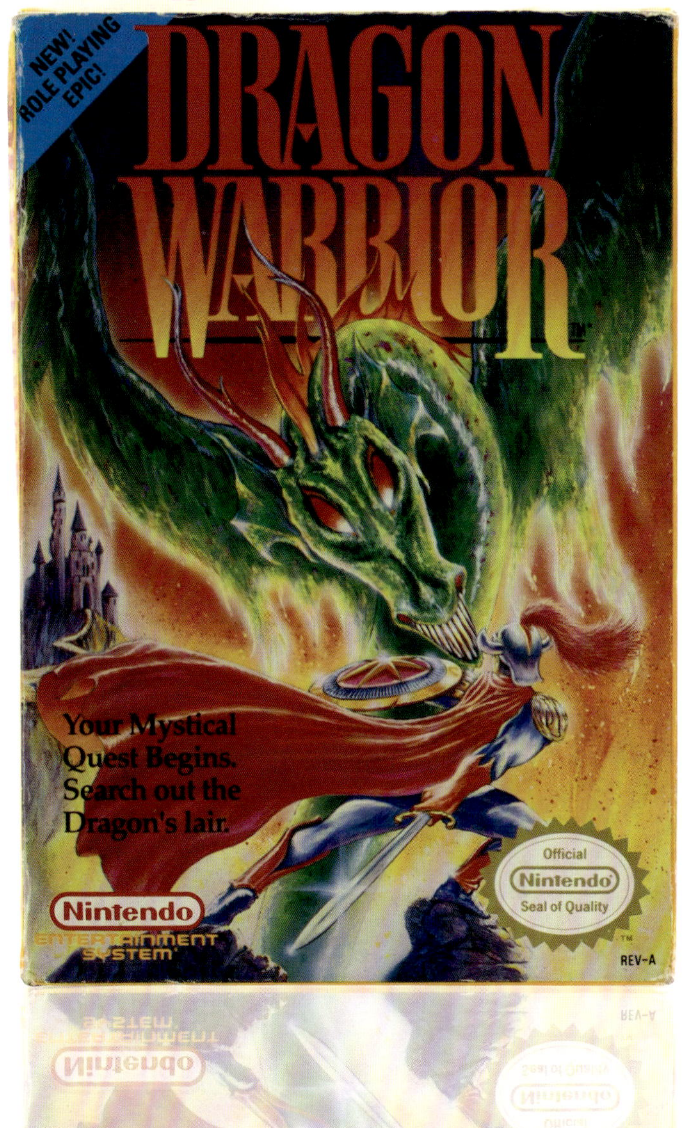

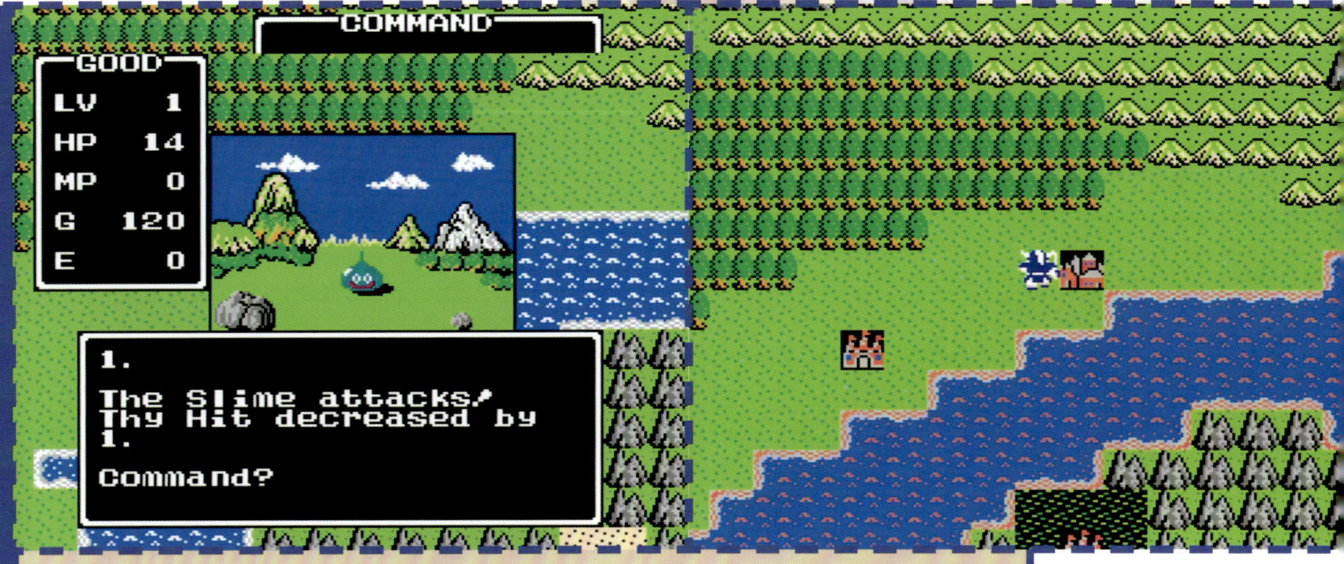

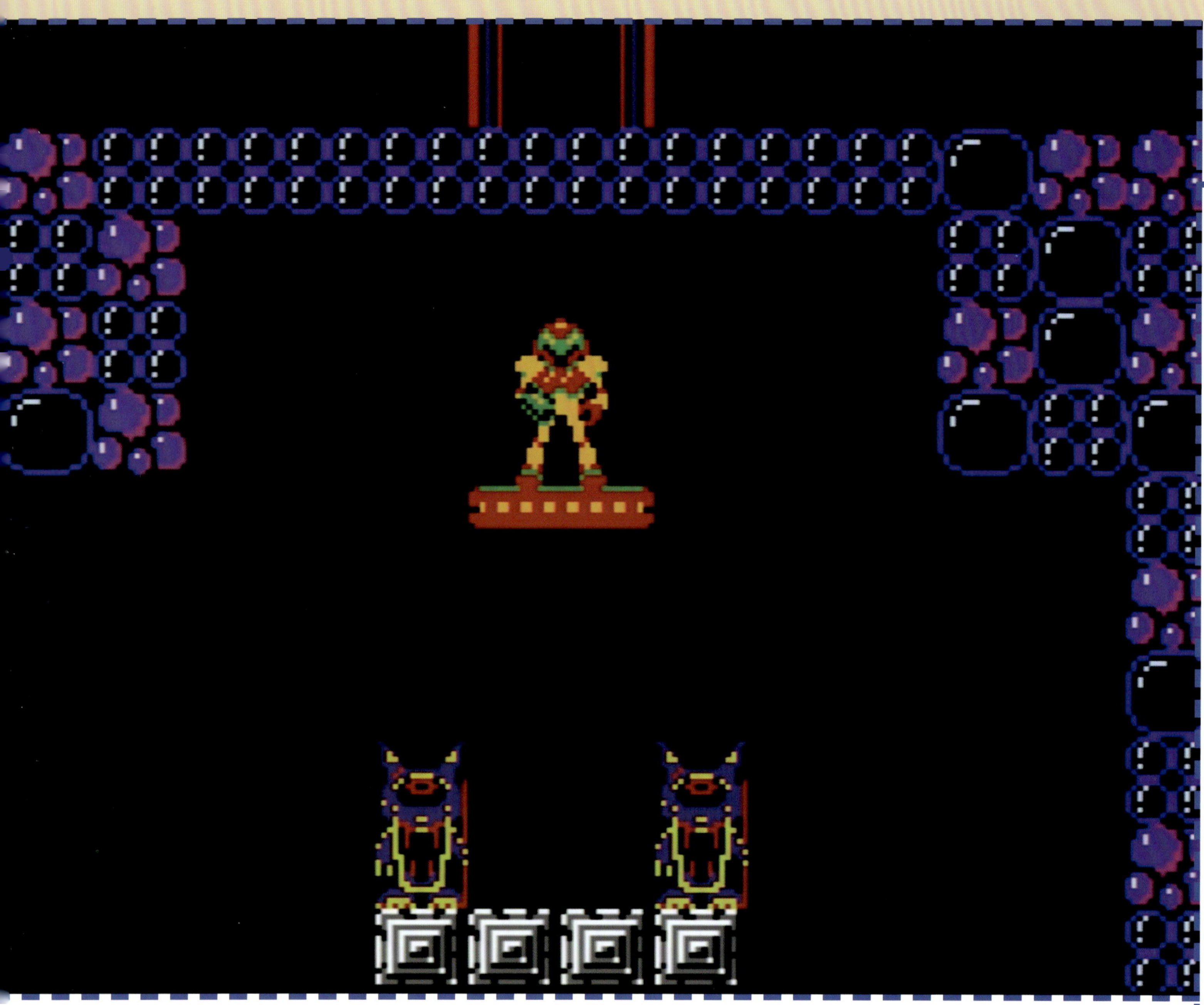

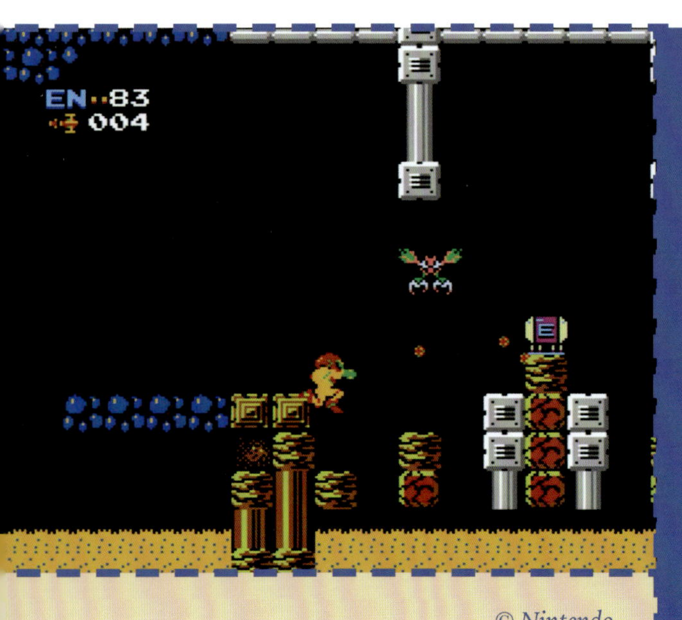

© Nintendo

METROID

PLATFORM: **FAMICOM DISK SYSTEM / NES**
DEV: **INTELLIGENT SYSTEMS / NINTENDO** | PUB: **NINTENDO**
INITIAL RELEASE: **AUG. 1986**

NOTABLE FOR: **STRUCTURED, GATED EXPLORATION IN AN ACTION PLATFORMER**

THE METROID IN METROIDVANIA

Nintendo took a tremendous leap forward for the exploratory action format with *Metroid*, arguably the first action game to incorporate role-playing concepts in a meaningful, elegant way. While certainly not the first attempt to fuse these two disparate genres, the successful action-RPGs before *Metroid* tended to emphasis the role-playing side of the ledger. *Metroid*, however, presents players with a seamless, menu- free action game in which they control a nimble heroine named Samus Aran. A galactic bounty hunter, Samus's advanced spacesuit enhances her capabilities to impressive effect, resulting in a convincing run-and-jump platformer in which the player's capabilities grow progressively over the course of the adventure.

When Samus jumps, her leaps give her enough hang time to allow her to alter her trajectory in midair. But once players find the requisite power-up, she gains the ability to jump even higher and turn her body into a weapon by somersaulting through the air. Samus also acquires tools that allow her to tuck into a ball that can slip through narrow passages and drop explosive bombs along the floor. She can upgrade her primary weapon into a beam that freezes foes or passes through walls, along with the ability to toggle between her basic arm cannon and more powerful missiles at will.

What made *Metroid* unique at the time is that the tools Samus acquired along her journey to defeat the alien menace Mother Brain were permanent upgrades, not the fleeting power-ups found in other action games. Like the inventory system of a sprawling role-playing game, Samus's growing arsenal boosts her strength and survivability, enabling players to explore farther into the labyrinthine depths of planet Zebes by allowing her to face more dangerous monsters as well as reach new areas. Samus's foray into the world is constrained by barriers at the outset, but each new item you acquire allows you to bypass one of those obstacles. The more you explore, the more you acquire, which opens up new avenues for exploration—and acquisition. The entire world exists as a sort of interlocking puzzle, bounded by walls and doors and high gaps, with Samus and her gear being the key to solving that puzzle. All this plays out without the inventory screens found

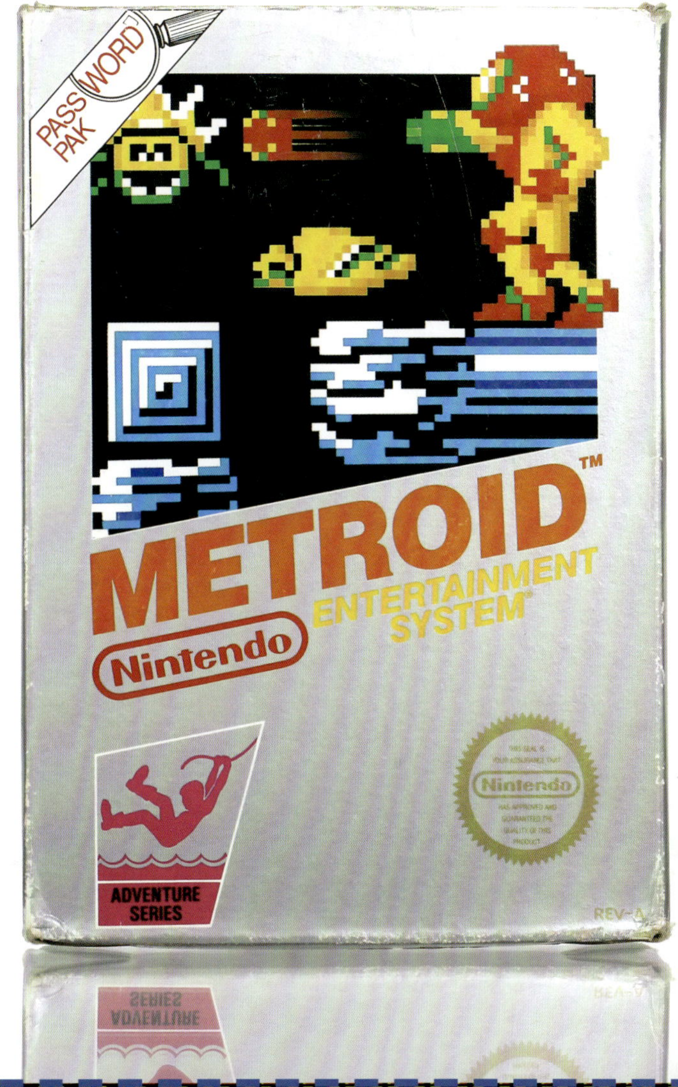

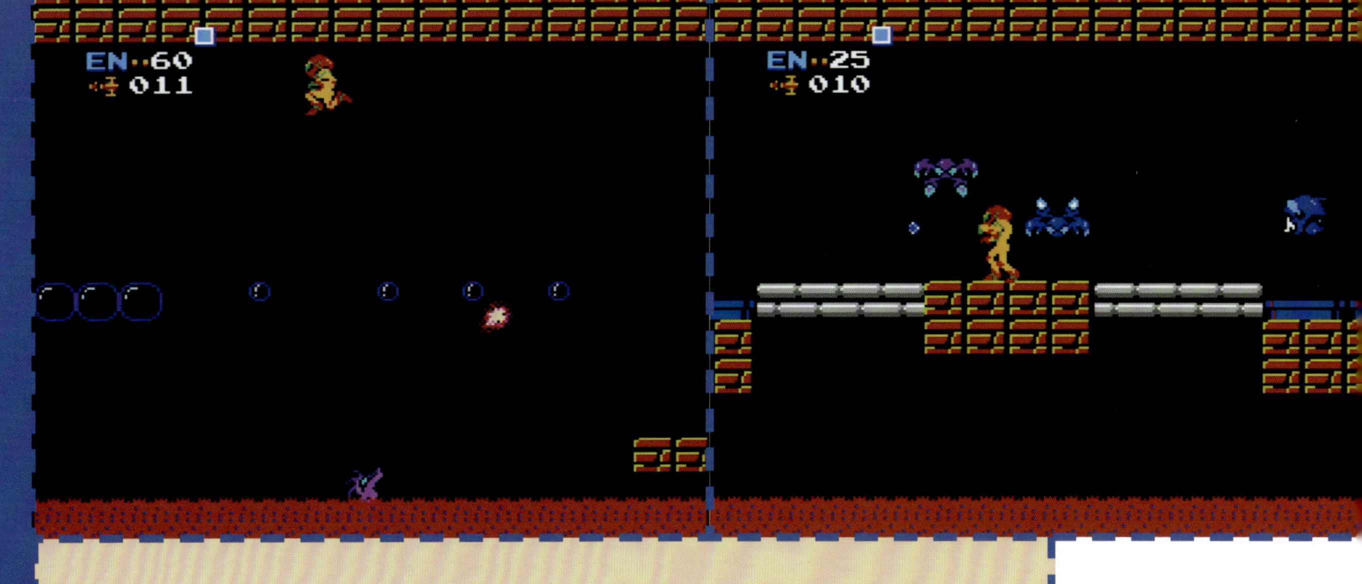

in other action-RPGs like *Zelda* and *Hydlide*. Instead, *Metroid* adopts the streamlined arcade mentality of Namco's *The Tower of Druaga* and *Dragon Buster*, giving players additive abilities. But even though games tracked their heroes' growth with an onscreen inventory bar, *Metroid* does not. When you acquire a tool here, it simply becomes part of Samus's loadout. You don't need to enter a sub-screen when you activate the Maru Mari to duck into a ball, nor do you need to manually swap to the bomb sub-weapon. You simply tap down on the D-pad to cause Samus roll up, and using the attack button while in ball form will automatically activate bombs. The High Jump and Screw Attack skills become integrated into Samus's repertoire once you collect their respective power-ups, and the defense-boosting Energy Tanks and Varia Suit instantly and permanently become a part of Samus herself. The most complex adventure elements in *Metroid* are energy icons at the top of the screen, which denote Samus's current health level and the need to actively toggle between weapon types by tapping Select.

Metroid presents an RPG-inspired structure that's been streamlined to the most minimal form imaginable. Samus's weapons double as tools. Bombs can liquefy barriers to hidden passages as easily as they can monsters. Missiles open doors and destroy powerful foes. The Screw Attack shatters or repulses enemies upon contact, but it can also clear away debris that blocks your way. As Samus gathers new combat capabilities, she also gains the innate ability to navigate the world and reach her journey's end. Her powers unlock new paths as she grows stronger and more durable, allowing her to better deal with the enhanced threats in the planet's deadlier spaces.

Compared to the structure and gating presented four years later in *Super Metroid*, one of the definitive pillars of metroidvania design, *Metroid* is undeniably simplistic. You really will find only a handful of environmental barriers at play here: doors that require missiles to open, walls that must be bombed to open up hidden blocks, and spaces too high or vast to be leaped without the High Jump Boots. Overcome these obstacles and a path to the lair of the final boss awaits, which opens up only after you've defeated her two main subordinates. For a 1986 creation, however, *Metroid* offers remarkable depth in its action and impressive self-confidence for such an ambitious genre mash-up. Despite the limitations of its tech and timing, *Metroid* does an incredible job of merging role-playing elements into a pure action game. It can be clunky and unintuitive at times, yes, but the progressive design of its action and permanence of its heroine's expandable skill repertoire set Metroid apart from the likes of *Pitfall II* and *Jet Set Willy*. It established a new standard for action-RPGs by making the RPG component almost entirely invisible. *M*

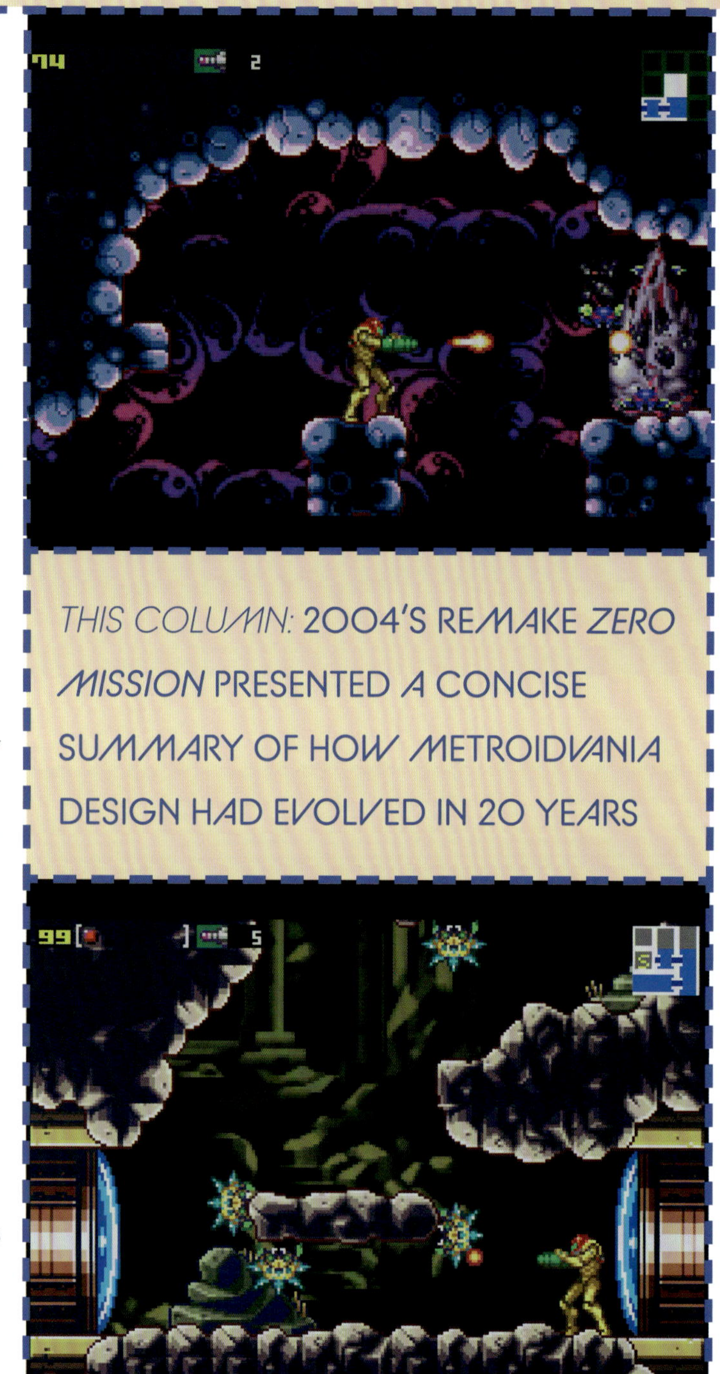

THIS COLUMN: 2004'S REMAKE *ZERO MISSION* PRESENTED A CONCISE SUMMARY OF HOW METROIDVANIA DESIGN HAD EVOLVED IN 20 YEARS

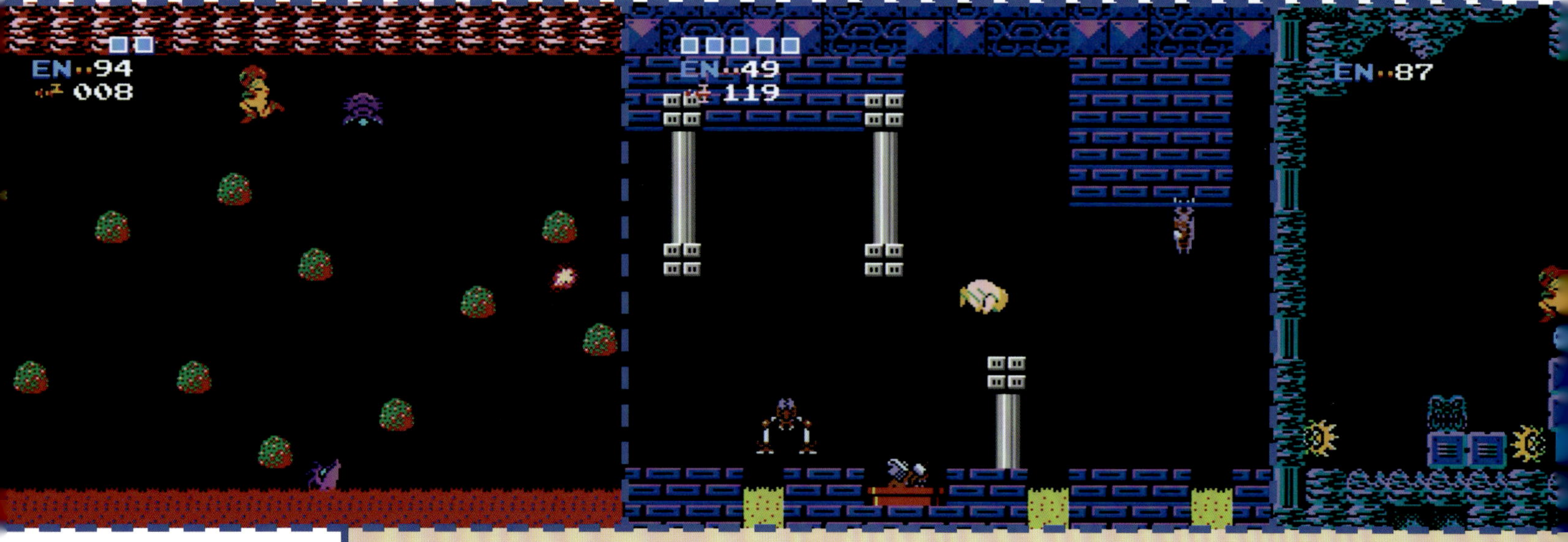

MUGEN SENSHI VALIS

Largely overlooked by chroniclers of video game history, the Famicom release of Nihon Telenet's classic *Mugen Senshi Valis* strayed dramatically from its better-known counterparts for more advanced systems like TurboGrafx-16 and PC-8801. Perhaps to compensate for the relatively meager capabilities of the Famicom, the designers behind this adaptation ditched the original game's straightforward and highly linear design in favor of a rudimentary take on an open-world adventure.

Valis for Famicom resembles its counterparts in the broad strokes. For example, it begins in a modern cityscape in which protagonist Yuuko runs around in her school uniform before transporting her to a mysterious fantasy world in which she dons bikini armor. But where those other versions play out across a series of fast-scrolling stages that can be conquered by dashing left to right and destroying everything in your path, this iteration changes things up from the start. The opening metropolis requires Yuuko to duck into buildings and explore the interconnected backgrounds so as to find the shrine that transports her to another realm. And, once there, she needs to traverse forests and caverns in search of weapons and tools to aid her in her journey to collect the mystical jewels that comprise the backbone of her quest.

As a point of comparison, it plays a great deal like *Rygar* and *The Goonies II*, both of which would make their debut for Famicom about half a year after *Valis*. But where those games tend to be well loved by fans, the Famicom version of *Valis* largely goes overlooked, and not only because it never managed to make its way outside the confines of Japan. Despite its designers' noble intents, this take on *Valis* doesn't quite hold together as an action-RPG. The controls feel a little too slippery, the action a little too punishing, the objectives a little too vague. Unlike the exploratory platformers that would follow soon after, *Valis* suffers from the awkwardness shared by many early Famicom releases that attempt to go beyond single-screen arcade experiences: the tech and collective programming expertise didn't quite match the ambition on display.

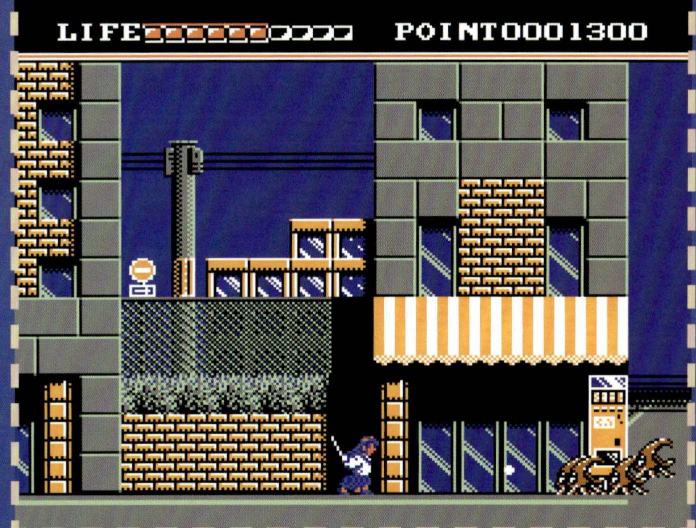

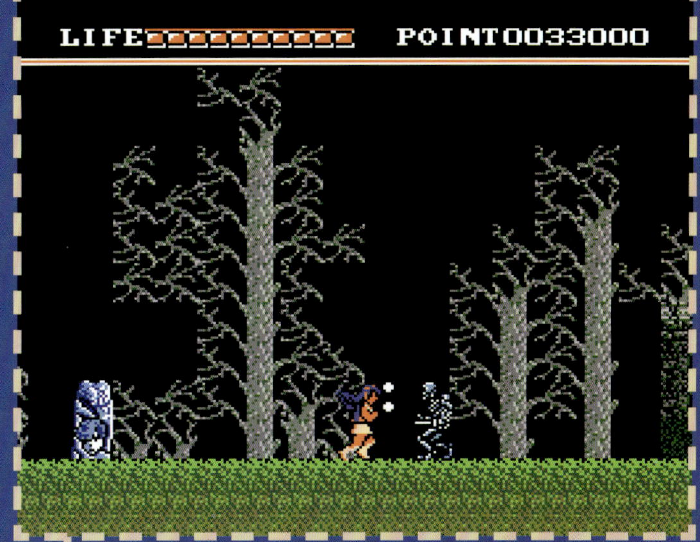

© Edia

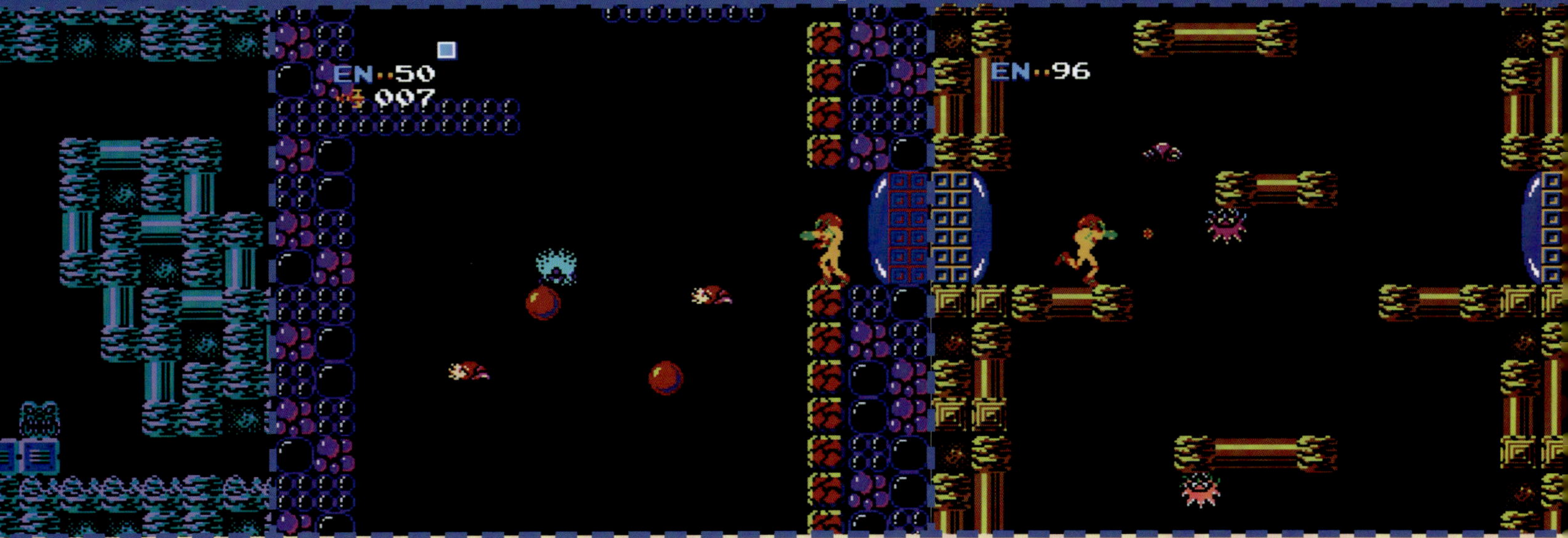

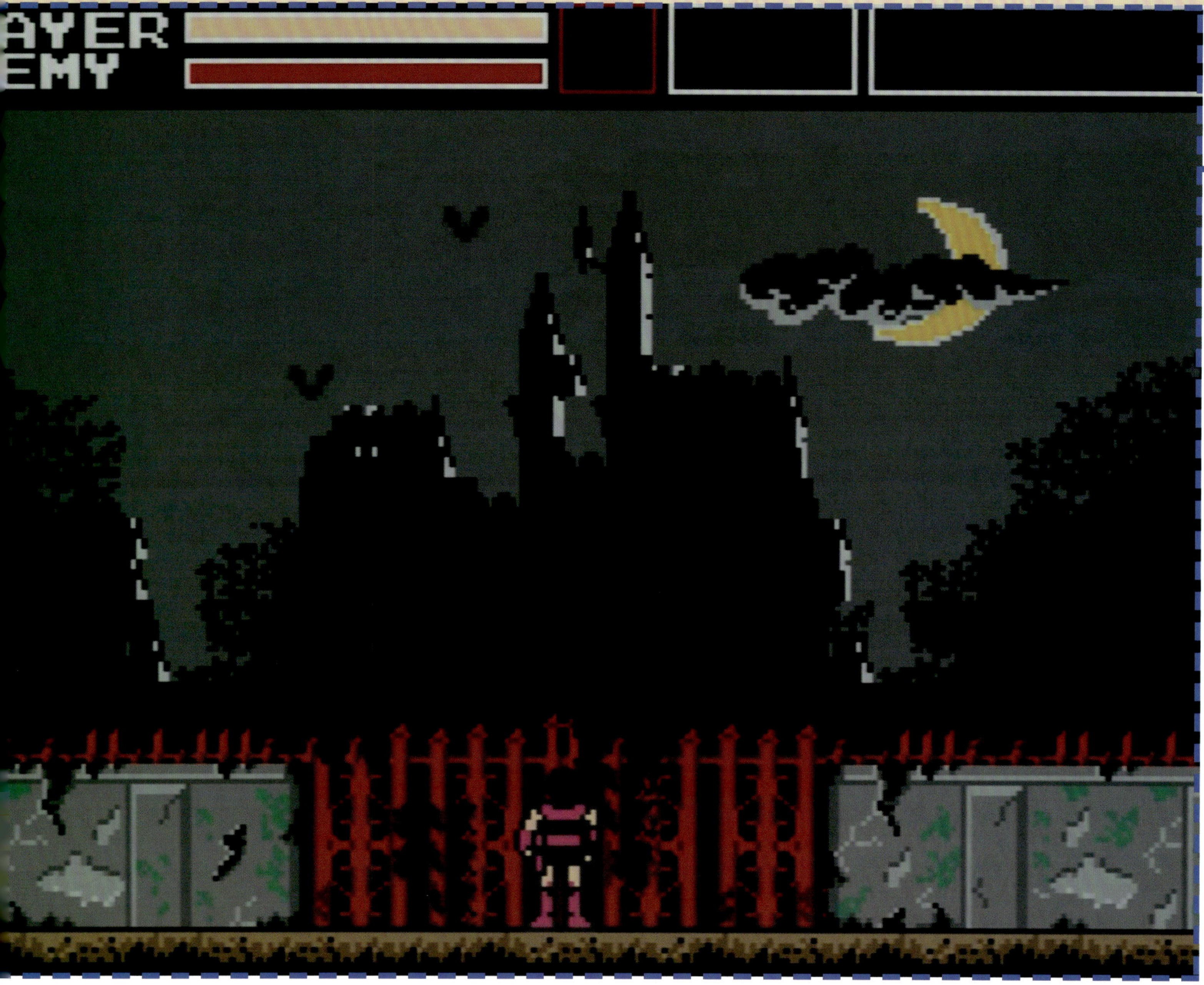

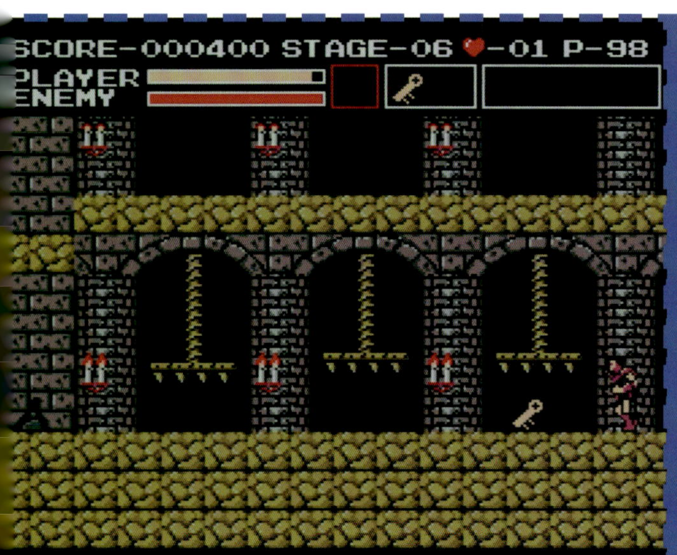

VAMPIRE KILLER

PLATFORM: **MSX2**
DEV: **KONAMI** | PUB: **KONAMI**
INITIAL RELEASE: **OCT. 1986**

NOTABLE FOR: **REWORKING A PURE ACTION GAME INTO AN ACTION-ADVENTURE**

THE VANIA IN METROIDVANIA

Two months after *Metroid*'s Japanese debut, in October 1986, Konami introduced the *Akumajou Dracula* series. In America, the company published this series under the name *Castlevania*, beginning with the original *Castlevania* for the NES in May 1987: a pure, arcade-style action game. However, at the same time the NES title appeared in Japan (making its debut on Nintendo's Famicom Disk System), *Akumajou Dracula* also shipped as a cartridge for the MSX2 home computer (including in Europe, where it appeared as *Vampire Killer*). Although the NES and MSX2 games looked almost identical, in reality they played quite differently.

Whereas *Castlevania/Akumajou Dracula* for NES/Disk System presented players with eighteen stages of precision platforming and tense combat, *Vampire Killer* for MSX2 took a more exploratory tack. It echoes the broad strokes of *Castlevania*, placing you in control of a whip-wielding warrior named Simon Belmont as he infiltrates Count Dracula's castle and battles five guardian bosses across eighteen stages. That's about where the similarities end. *Vampire Killer* takes a less direct approach to action than *Castlevania*. Each of its eighteen stages consists of a self-contained mini-labyrinth. With its use of flip-screen transitions rather than free scrolling, each individual screen of the game exists as a self-contained space that players must unravel. Those screens don't appear in a vacuum, though; you often need to work out the relationship between individual screens to advance. On top of that, most stages exist as an infinite loop on either the vertical or horizontal axis, so that Simon doubles back to the start once he advances too far.

Unlike Simon's extensive NES arsenal, on the MSX2 he can only collect two secondary weapons to complement his main attack: the holy water and the stopwatch. Other sub-weapons, such as the dagger and axe, replace his standard whip attack when gathered; these can be transient, as with the boomerang, which Simon loses forever if he fails to catch it on its return flight. *Vampire Killer* also includes a primitive economy that makes the score-boosting money bags of the NES game literal—though, curiously, it's heart icons rather than cash that function as currency. And Simon must gather keys in each stage to unlock the next. In other

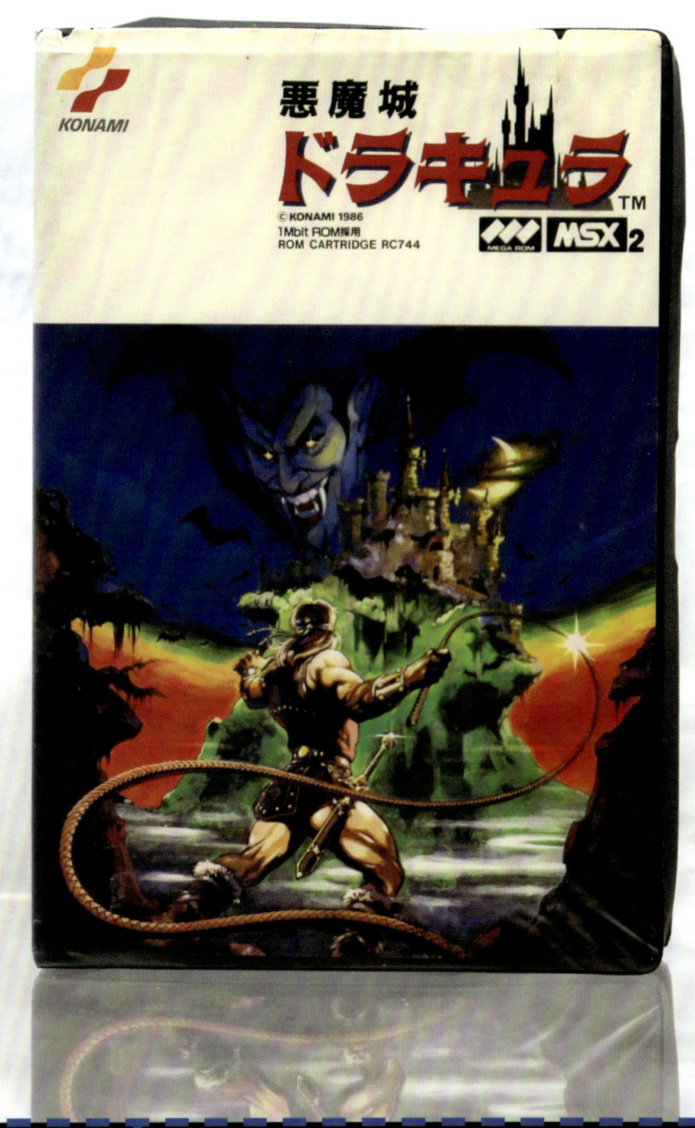

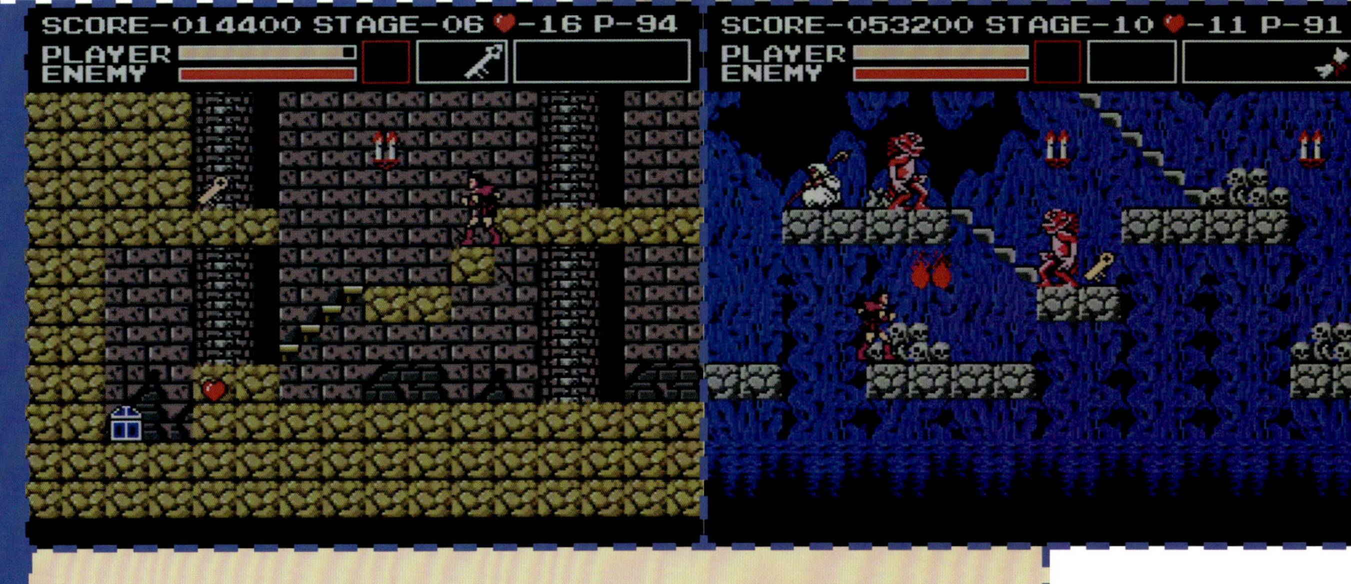

words, *Vampire Killer* tilts more toward "RPG" on the action-RPG scale than toward "action." Although it contains enough action to test any player's reflexes, it balances this with the need for more measured exploration. The added depth of level design comes at a price: the action in *Vampire Killer* is a lot less convincing than in *Castlevania*, and not just because of the flip-screen transitions. Simon doesn't move as elegantly on the MSX2 as on the NES; collision detection works against him; and the level construction lacks the refinement of the NES version, often violating the rules of good game design.

In short, *Vampire Killer* feels exactly like a computer action game of the era: decent enough, but focused on uncovering fussy hidden items and making deliberate progress over a pure twitch experience. As a result, there are many, many more items to acquire in *Vampire Killer* than in *Castlevania*. On the NES, Simon's upgrades were limited to whip power and sub-weapons, with additional hidden collectibles simply adding points to the score tally. Here, you need to unearth several kinds of keys that open treasure chests, semipermanent speed and jump upgrades, merchant discounts, defensive boosts, and more.

As you'd expect for a game in this style from this era, *Vampire Killer* can be pretty obtuse. For example, you sometimes encounter an elderly merchant who will sell you weapons and tools… but, unintuitively, only if you whip her a few times. In fairness, this is balanced out by other factors, such as the way the hallway leading to the encounter with Frankenstein's monster has working doorways that force players to master a complex maze. On the NES, that space consists of nothing more than a straight shot down a short hallway packed with monsters.

Even with its steadier pace and reduced emphasis on pure twitch skill, *Vampire Killer* proves to be a vastly more difficult game than Castlevania. Where the NES game allowed players to continue infinitely upon dying—the FDS version even included the ability to record your progress to disk—*Vampire Killer* gives you only three lives and no continues in which to complete all eighteen stages. Nor do the enemies take it any easier on you here than they did on the NES. This appears to have been a ploy by Konami to sell more copies of their MSX2 cheat device, the Game Master, which included a built-in code to give *Vampire Killer* players ninety-nine lives rather than a measly three.

With a design built around linear progression through standalone, mini-labyrinth stages, *Vampire Killer* is ultimately too limited a game to be considered a proper metroidvania—despite being kin to the game that put the "vania" in "metroidvania." No, that revolution would come a year later, when the Disk System and NES sequel to the action-oriented *Castlevania* took extensive design cues from *Vampire Killer* and expanded on them. *M*

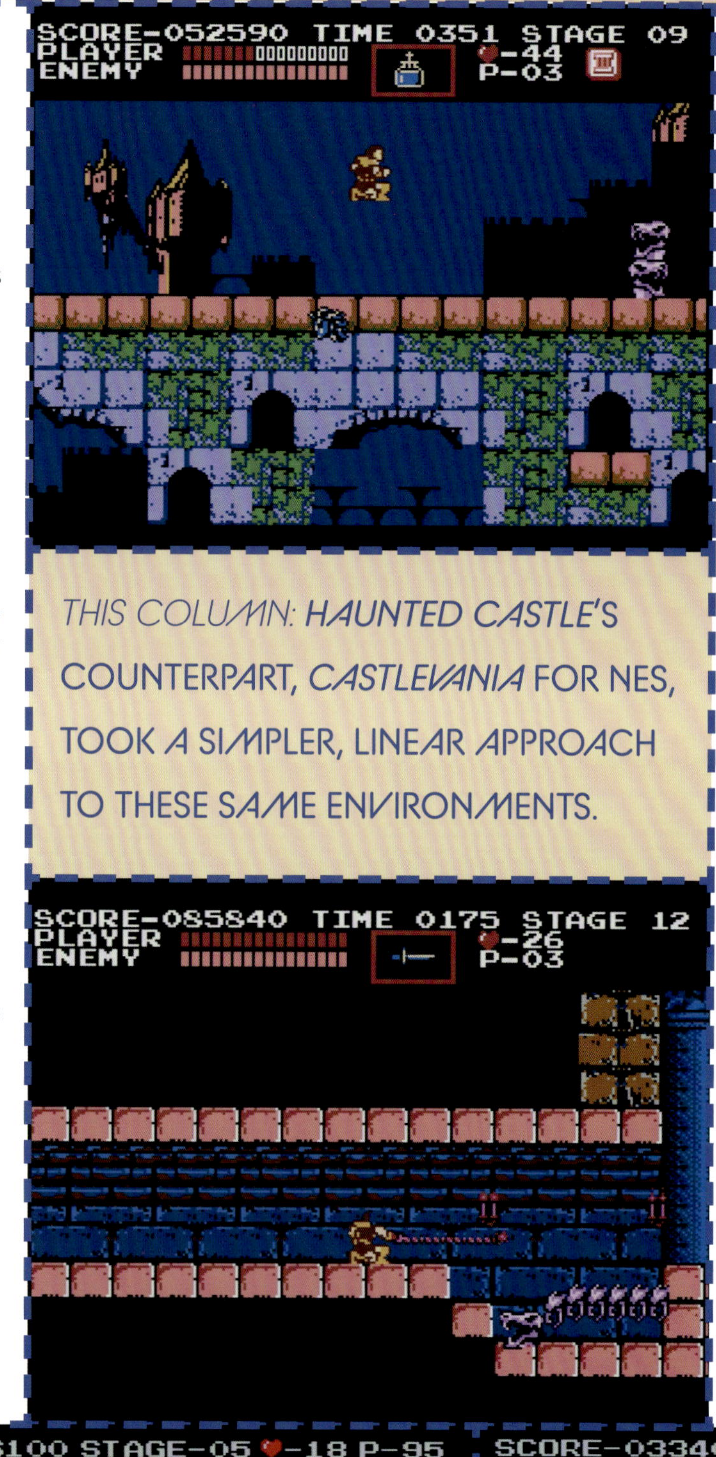

THIS COLUMN: HAUNTED CASTLE'S COUNTERPART, *CASTLEVANIA* FOR NES, TOOK A SIMPLER, LINEAR APPROACH TO THESE SAME ENVIRONMENTS.

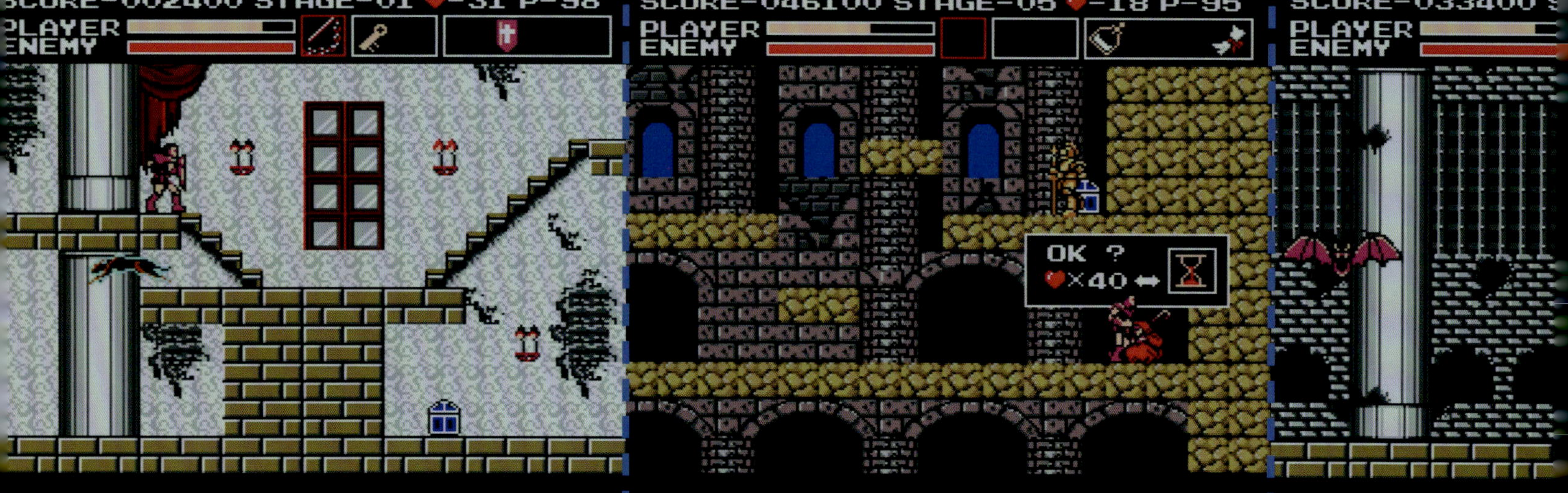

DEADLY TOWERS

Unquestionably the most enormous action game ever created to that point in history, *Deadly Towers* for the NES stands proudly as a nobly intended disaster of a action-RPG. With its prodigious scale across a sprawling, multi-dungeon structure, it truly captures the spirit of *Wizardry* and *The Bard's Tale* in the form of the fast-paced action titles that thrived on Nintendo's console. Unfortunately, it falls well short of being the sort of polished, thoughtfully balanced adventure classic that would stand the test of time.

Deadly Towers suffers from a few unforced design errors. For one thing, it's preposterously difficult, but not in a fun way that makes players feel like they lost because they slipped up and are then encouraged to try again. It's hard because enemies appear out of nowhere, soak up tons of damage, are difficult to strike with the player's sword, and tend to attack by clinging to the hero, whose health saps rapidly rather than allowing the player any sort of temporary invincibility to duck to safety and regroup for a counterattack.

More crucially, it lays out an absolutely massive world to explore—more than a thousand screen of dungeon and palace!—but very little of it offers anything of interest. Players will stumble blindly into hidden warps that fling them into complex labyrinths, which may contain a single item of value across dozens and dozens of screens packed with enemies that drain their health and deplete their resources. Meanwhile, these dungeons feel superfluous to the true thrust of the quest: to visit the seven towers to the north. Players must ascend these towers to defeat a boss and collect a mystical bell to be destroyed as part of a rite to break the vile grip of a cruel sorcerer over the protagonist's kingdom. The towers are more or less a linear upward trek, quite unlike the dungeons, in which players can become lost without ever finding the exit. And while you may indeed find weapons and spells of value in dungeons, your chances of escaping with your health and inventory intact are slim to none. This makes for an ambitious adventure that fails to be fun or compelling—a dead-end for the action-RPG format, was notable only for its sheer scale.

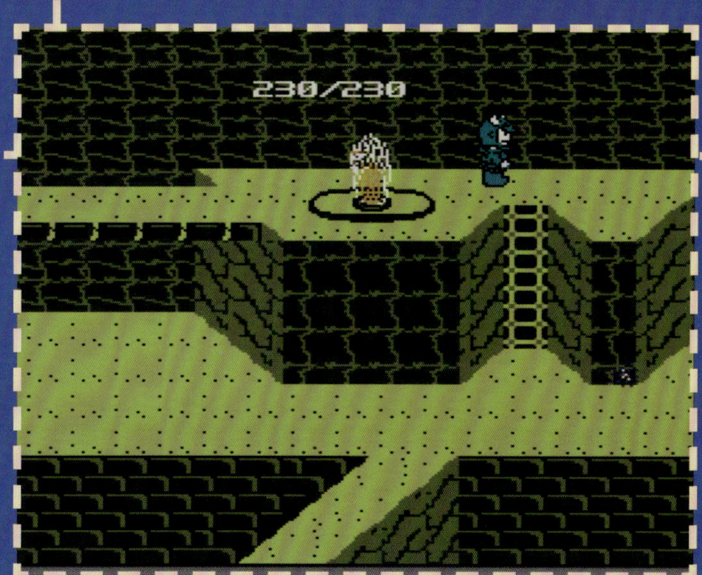

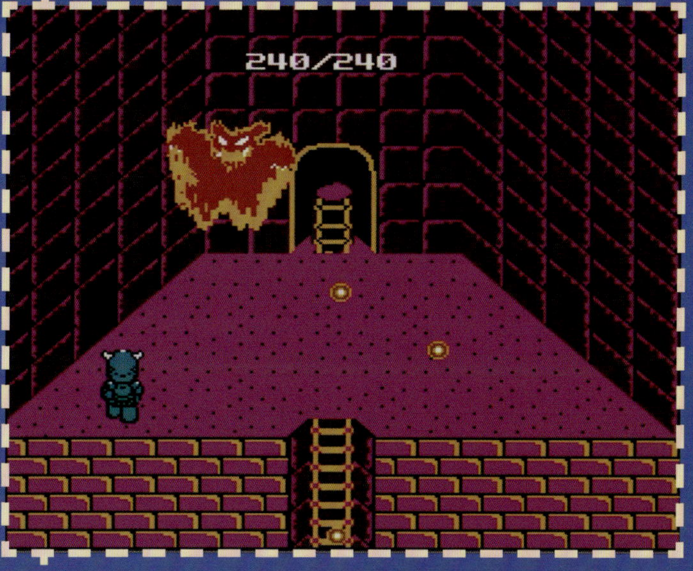

© Irem

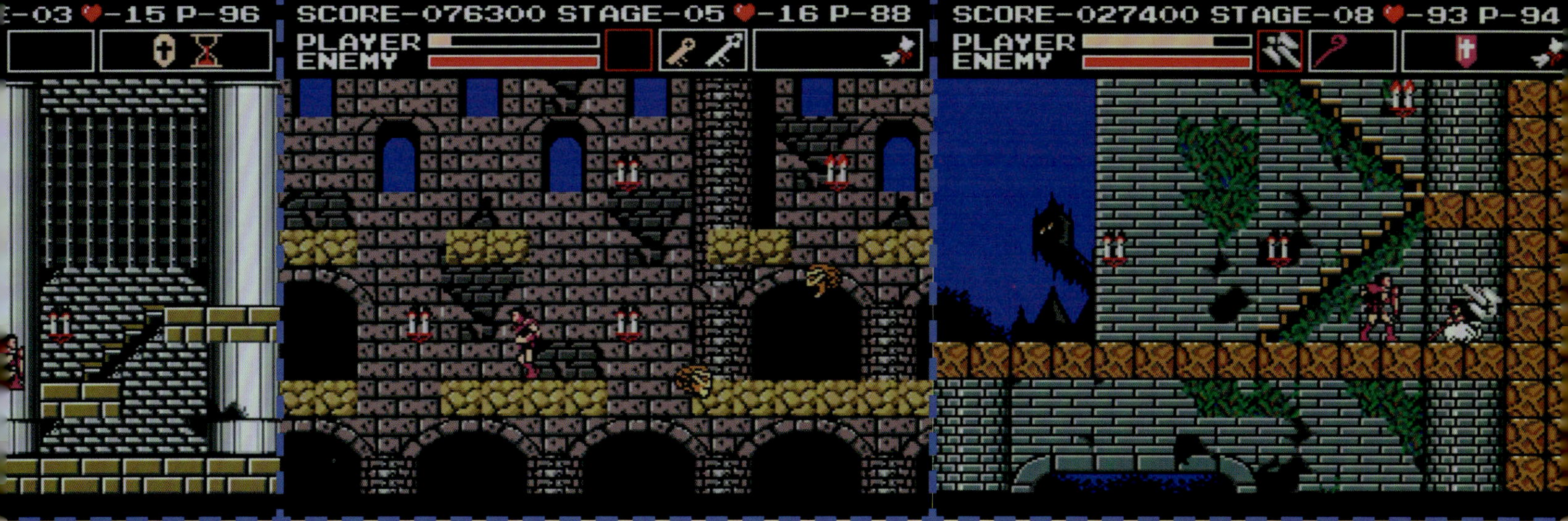

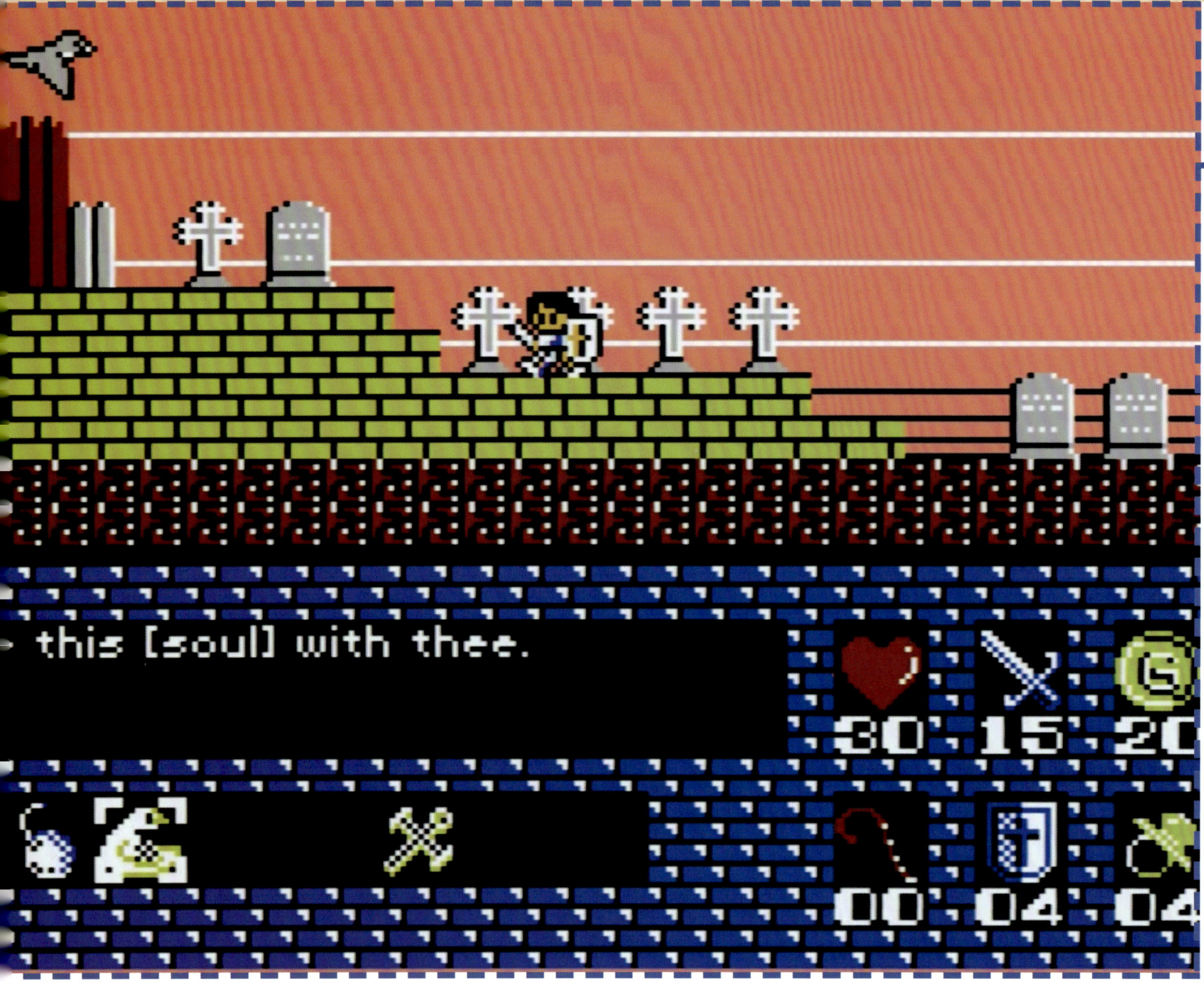

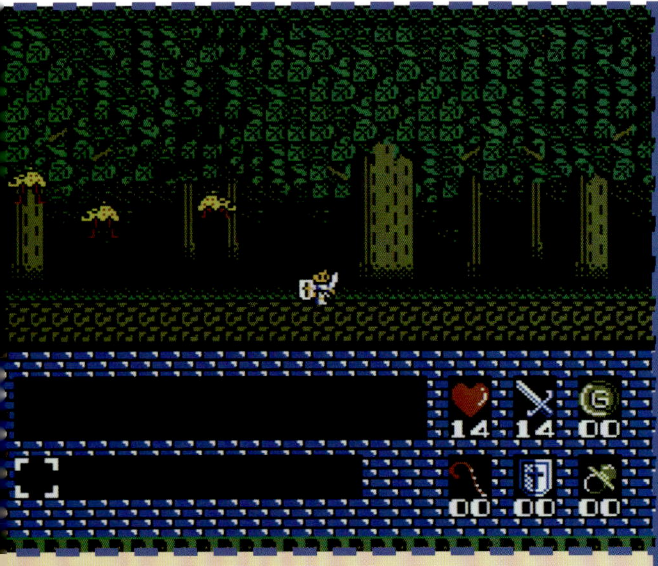

ROMANCIA
DRAGON SLAYER JR.

PLATFORM: **PC-9801 / VARIOUS**
DEV: **NIHON FALCOM** | PUB: **NIHON FALCOM**
INITIAL RELEASE DATE: **OCT. 1986**

NOTABLE FOR: **AN ADVENTURE GAME IN PLATFORMER TRAPPINGS**

SON OF A METROIDVANIA

October 1986 saw the arrival of the third entry in the *Dragon Slayer* franchise on Japanese home computers: *Romancia*, also known as *Dragon Slayer Jr.* In keeping with the throughline of the series to that point, it had little or nothing to do with its predecessors (*Dragon Slayer* and *Xanadu*) besides being an action-oriented take on the role-playing genre. Falling somewhere between an adventure game, an action title, and an RPG, *Romancia* straddled genres much like *The Goonies II* would the following year, albeit viewed through a wildly different lens.

Sadly, the original computer version of *Romancia* is a tough game to play at the time of this writing due to the complexities of emulating vintage Japanese computers. However, Project EGG's EGGCONSOLE service has recently ported the PC-88 versions of several other *Dragon Slayer* games to Nintendo Switch in the West, so *Romancia* might actually have made its way to the English-speaking world in an official capacity by the time this book sees print. (Much of this overview is based on Hardcore Gaming 101's retrospective [hardcoregaming101.net/romancia].)

For the time being, *Romancia*'s most accessible version is the 1987 Famicom release, which can be coaxed to run on NES hardware with the proper cartridge adapter. And for those who don't mind skirting legal means, *Romancia* has an unofficial English localization that greatly lowers the barriers to entry for people who don't read Japanese. Which is not to say that the game suddenly becomes simple or even intuitive with the English patch; Falcom built the game to be opaque, even in its native language.

Still, it's more accessible on the Famicom in more ways than one: the cartridge release dropped many of the PC game's core ele- ments, not least of which was its time limit. Where *Dragon Slayer* and *Xanadu* were designed to be played across multiple lengthy sessions, during which players would gradually build up their hero's statistics and equipment, Falcom intended *Romancia* to be literally impossible to play for extended periods. The original release of the game operated under a strict, thirty-minute time limit. Players had half an hour in which to complete the quest… or less, potentially, if they made poor choices that resulted in their

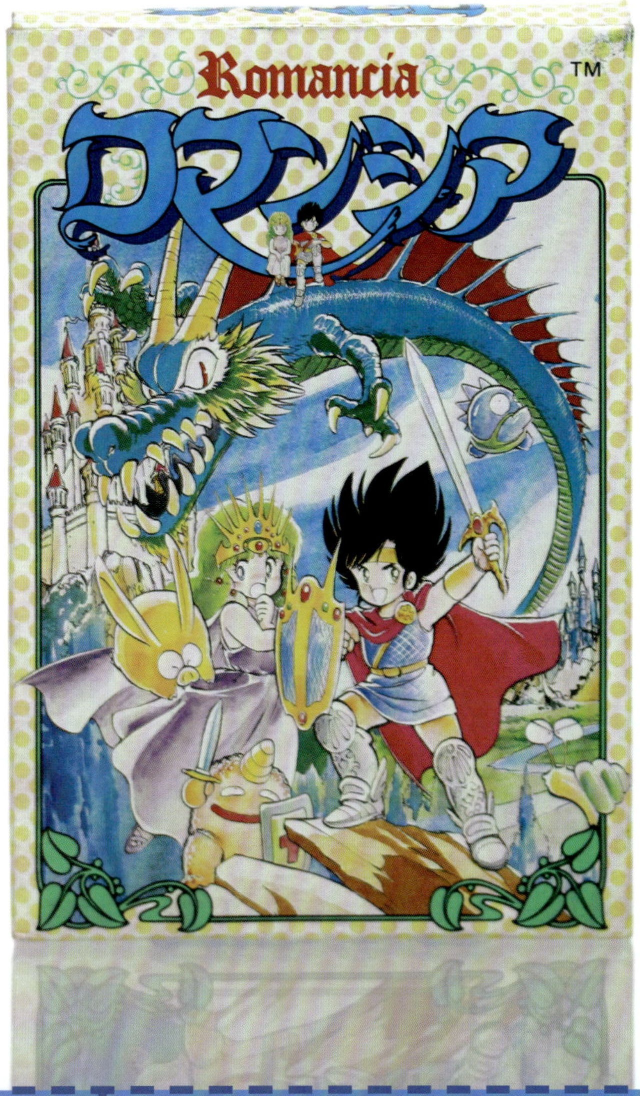

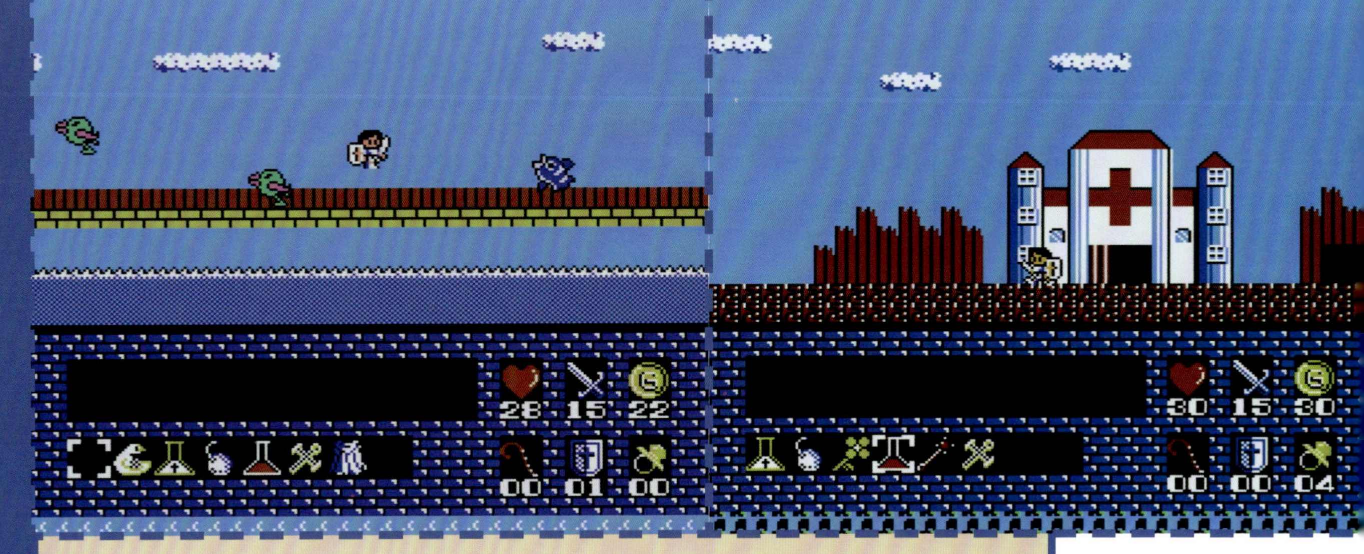

time limit being reduced by 50 percent to a mere fifteen minutes. This is not to say *Romancia* amounted to a single thirty-minute game experience that players could complete during their first attempt. By all accounts, completing *Romancia* could take every bit as long as a full-sized game like *Dragon Slayer*, if not longer.

Rather, Falcom intended for each thirty-minute session of *Romancia* to be an exercise in discovery, allowing players to eke out a little more progress each time. The heart of a roguelike beats inside *Romancia*'s confusing little chest, despite the fact that its highly deliberate design lacks any of the randomization one associates with the particular genre. Yet you can't deny the spiritual connection: As in *Rogue* and its kin, *Romancia* demands a certain degree of curiosity from players, along with a spirit of acceptance for the importance of trial and error. Start a new game, poke around, learn things, hit the time limit; start again and poke around in different ways, guided by the knowledge you acquired in your previous session; repeat. Yoshio Kiya and his team designed the game to be oblique and confusing in the spirit of PC adventure games like those from Sierra On-Line—full of cryptic secrets and poorly telegraphed solutions.

Completing *Romancia* requires a fair bit of finger dexterity, being an action-RPG, but it also expects from players a willingness to experiment, explore, and try counterintuitive actions in every corner of the screen. Every time you figure out the proper steps to progression—where to go, who to talk to, which items to use in different locations—the game throws up a new riddle or barrier to success. It's an experience built around "gotcha!" moments and maddening complications, a game conceived for strategy guides and sharing information with friends. It expects endless patience for overcoming its cumbersome controls and nasty enemy design, and it's confident in its ability to keep players coming back for more based on the dopamine hit delivered by a successful discovery.

In short, *Romancia* saw Falcom dialing down the RPG mechanics of the first two *Dragon Slayer* games in favor of a more *Zelda*-like system where health and strength and sword powers were depicted with simple icons. At the same time, it flirts with adventure game mechanics, replacing the text parser or mouse-and-pointer interactivity with the rugged directness of an action game. All combined, this makes for a stripped-down, bite-sized, action-oriented role-playing and adventure hybrid set in a confusing world that demands to be traversed and slowly unraveled as players attempt to crack its solutions and claim victory. Although largely unknown outside of Japan, *Romancia* feels in many ways like a prelude to latter-day favorites such as *Ico*, *Dark Souls*, and *Metroid Prime*. M

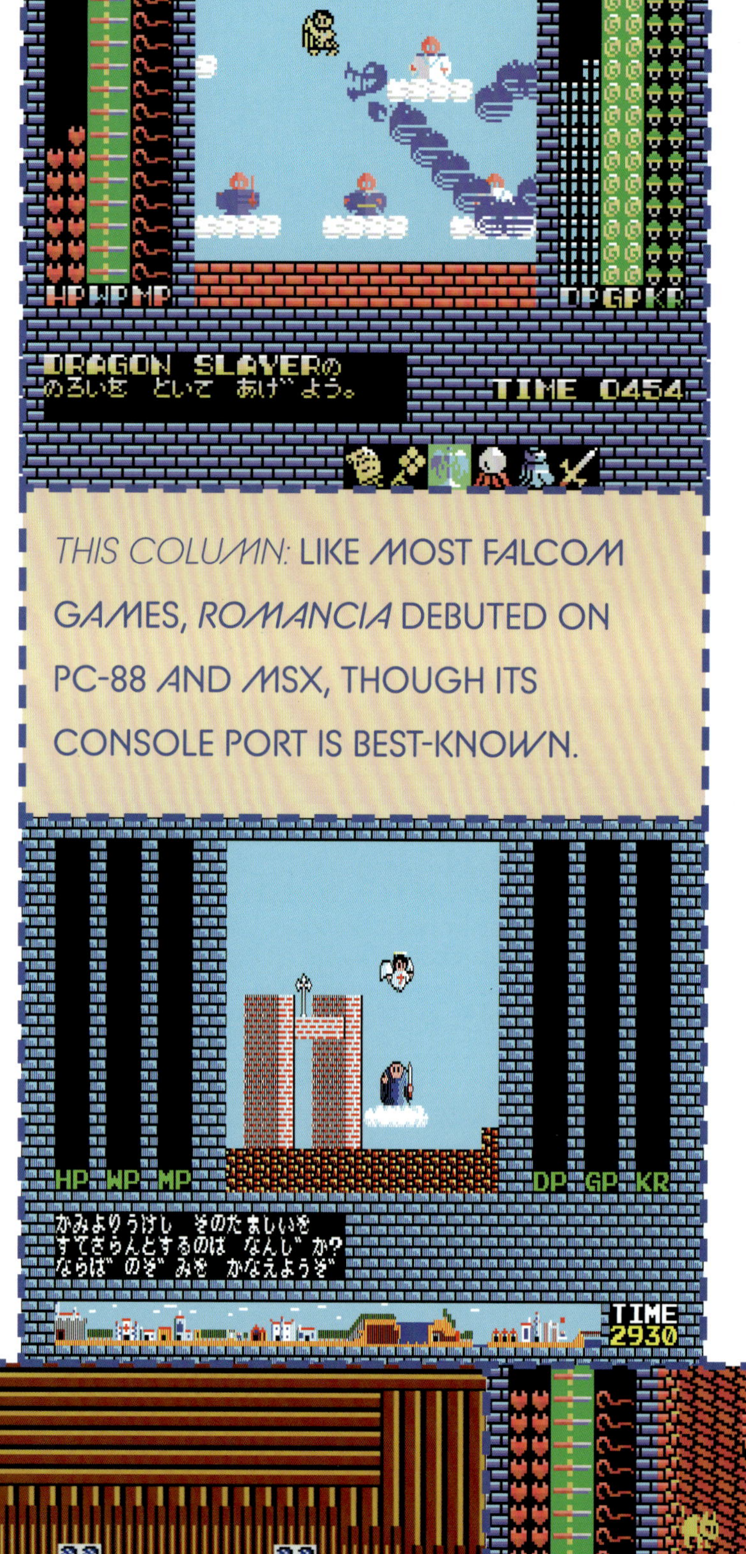

THIS COLUMN: LIKE MOST FALCOM GAMES, *ROMANCIA* DEBUTED ON PC-88 AND MSX, THOUGH ITS CONSOLE PORT IS BEST-KNOWN.

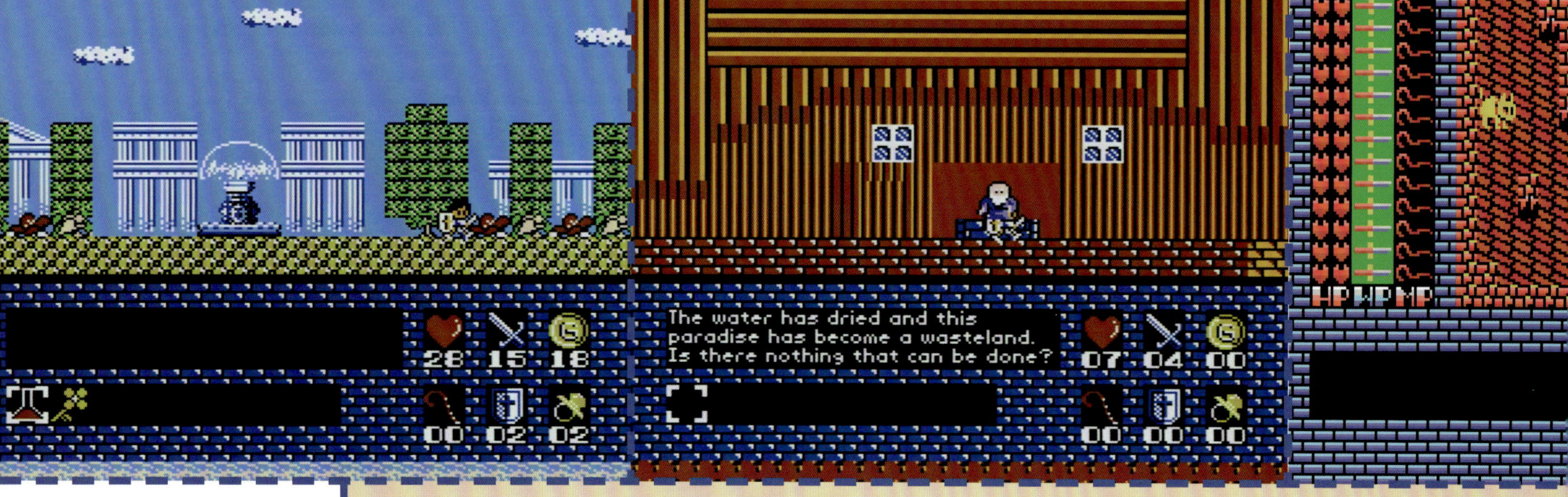

SORCERIAN

When the time came to assemble a fifth entry in the loose coalition of games known as the *Dragon Slayer* series, developer Nihon Falcom effectively took elements of the three most recent entries—*Xanadu*, *Romancia*, and *Legacy of the Wizard*—and combined them into a bizarre take on the role-playing genre. The result, *Sorcerian* doesn't really feature enough action elements or exploration to warrant a place in the historic record of the metroidvania saga, dialing back the emphasis on direct action and free exploration in favor of a more abstract gameplay style built around modular quests, but it still deserves a look.

At first glance, the game bears a close resemblance to *Xanadu* in that players move about the world in a side-scrolling viewpoint. But unlike *Xanadu*, you don't switch to an alternate perspective when enemies attack; you simply fight them head-on. The setting and proportions put one in mind of *Romancia*, an impression underscored by the game's emphasis on complex objectives and narratives, while at the same time the fact that you go out questing with a party of four characters immediately hearkens back to *Legacy of the Wizard*.

However, where *Legacy of the Wizard* involved a single character venturing into the dungeon at a time, *Sorcerian* sends them all in at once. Players control an entire RPG party, but unlike *Final Fantasy* or *Ultima*, this setup doesn't rely on menus or turn-based commands. You control all four heroes simultaneously. When you leap, they all leap. When you attack, they all use their active skills simultaneously. It's a very strange system, but ultimately it comes down to an attempt to streamline a classic role-playing adventure into its simplest form. Sorcerian begins by allowing players to roll their own party of heroes, selecting combat classes and stat perks, and the entire game follows on from that premise. It's a role-playing game stripped down to the bare bones—but only in terms of how the moment-to-moment action works. Unlike, say, *The Legend of Zelda*, it doesn't pare down the underlying systems and mechanics. Like an iceberg, *Sorcerian* looks humble on the surface, but that simply obscures its depths.

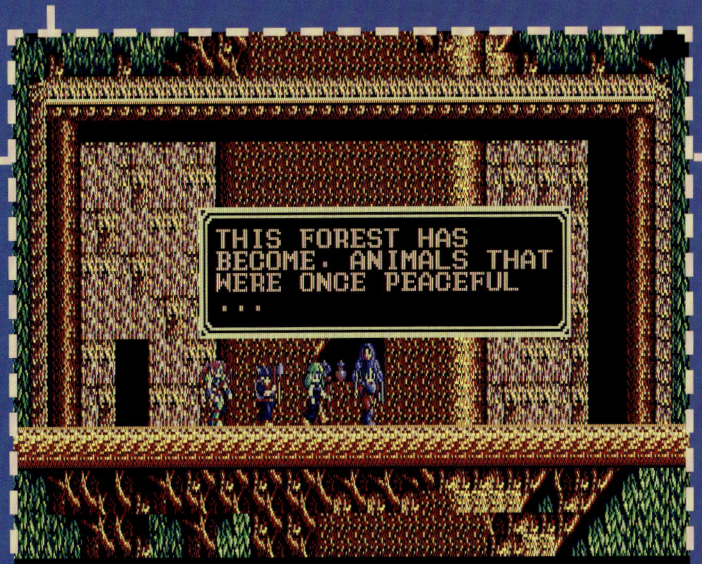

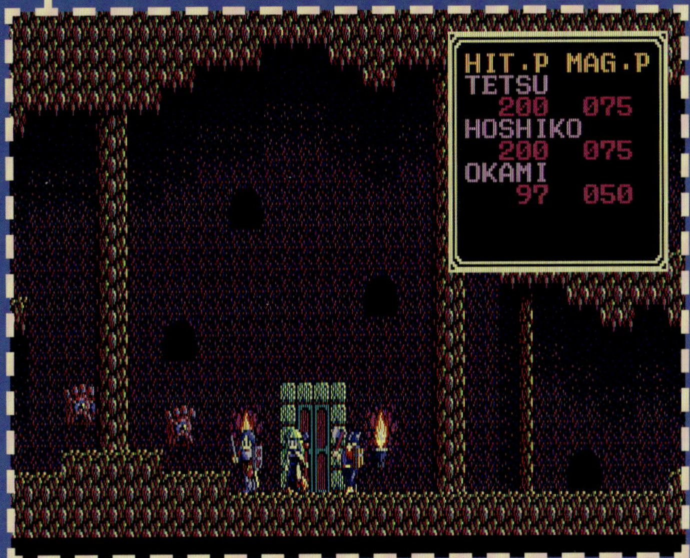

© Nihon Falcom

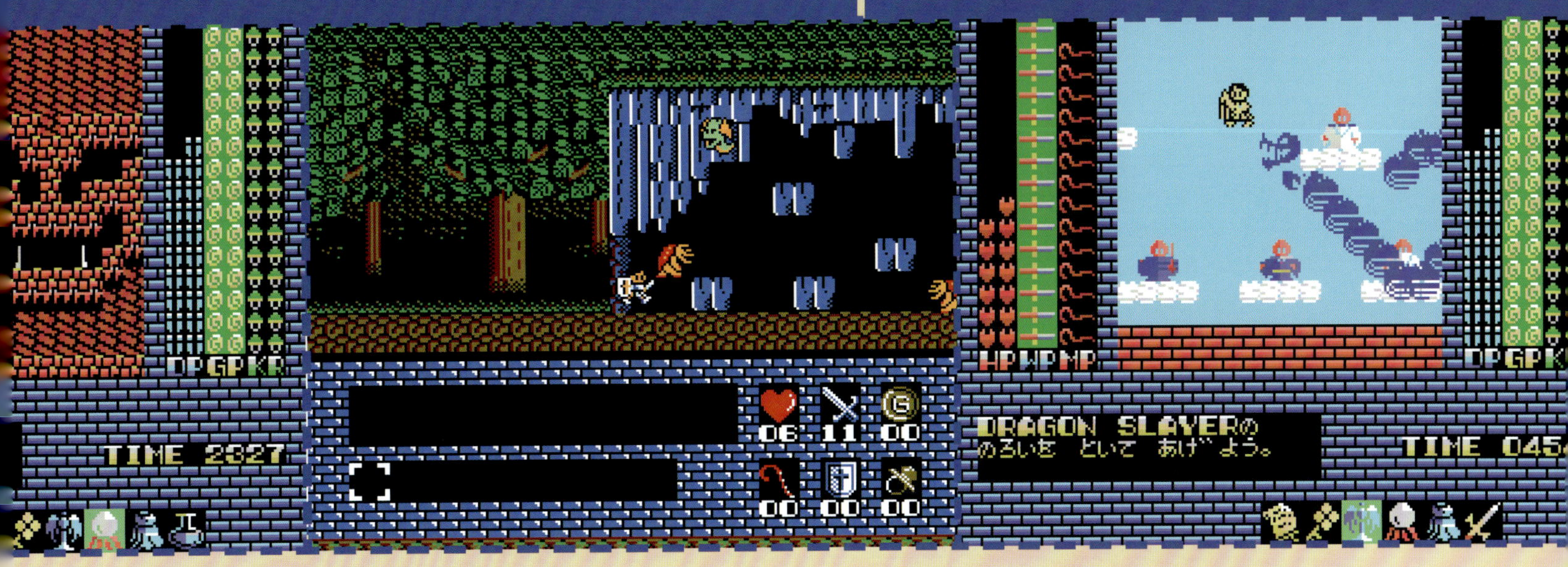

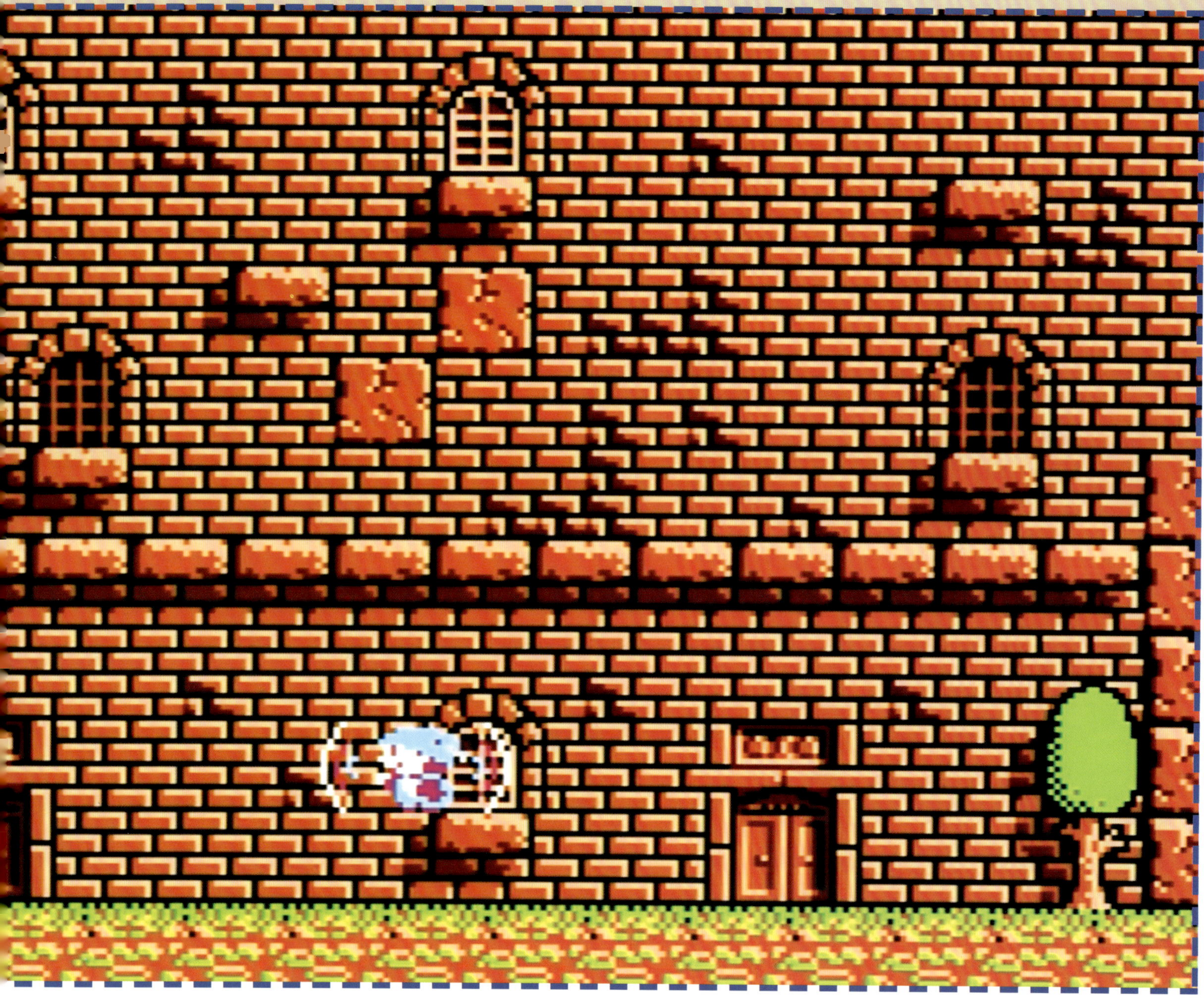

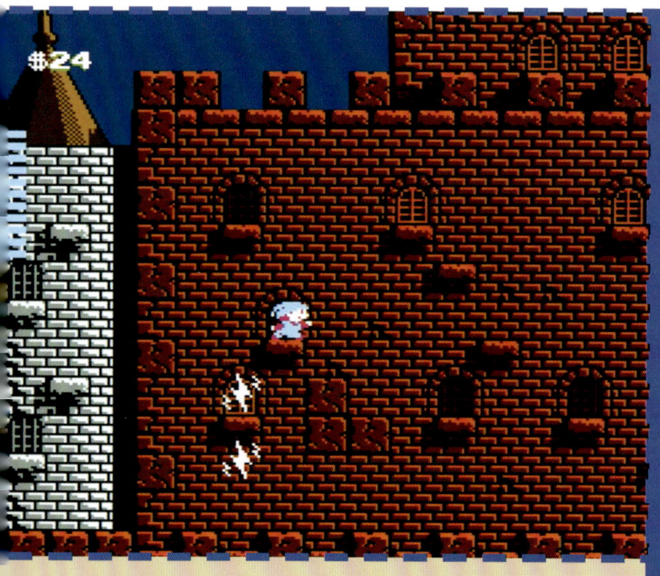

MILON'S SECRET CASTLE

PLATFORM: **FAMICOM / NES**
DEV: **HUDSON SOFT** | PUB: **HUDSON SOFT**
INITIAL RELEASE: **NOV. 1986**

NOTABLE FOR: **A SEARCH-BASED PUZZLE-ACTION GAME**

SOME SECRETS ARE BETTER KEPT

Developers who wanted to create an adventure-tinged action game in the early days of the medium had to work with limited palettes. That proved especially true on consoles, whose consumer-oriented nature demanded compromises compared to expensive personal computers and arcade machines. A $150 device running games that cost $30–50 apiece ruled out high-end tech and high-capacity media in the 1980s. Yet game designers yearned to create more than simple *Pac-Man*, *Galaxian*, and *Donkey Kong* clones, even if they only had four colors, sixty-four sprites, and 16 KB of memory to work with. And so we saw the likes of Hudson's NES adventure *Milon's Secret Castle*: games that expanded on the tenets of simple action and extended the consumer's play time by making everything as opaque as possible.

Released on Famicom shortly after *Vampire Killer* came to the MSX, *Milon's* feels very much of a piece with Konami's game. It's a simple, slightly clunky platformer with a notable element of exploration and acquisition. Players control a kid named Milon, who seeks to make his way from the lower levels of a castle to defeat the monster living at its pinnacle—not unlike Simon Belmont's journey to defeat Count Dracula in his lair above the castle's clock tower. The meaningful similarities with *Vampire Killer* more or less end there, however. *Milon's Secret Castle* lacks a meaningful upgrade path for the hero, and its design lands far from the thoughtful layout that typifies the *Castlevania* series.

Milon's journey takes him through numerous standalone rooms, all locked behind the doors and gratings of a castle facade. You can traverse these rooms freely once you've found the correct key; even after clearing a room of its objectives you can return whenever you like. However, each room works as a sort of trap. The first time you enter a new door, Milon has to find the key to open an exit and return to the main castle. Afterward, you can travel between rooms in the castle exterior, like a less elaborate take on *Xanadu* and *The Legend of Zelda*. You can also find bonus rooms and shops throughout the castle, each offering a different selection of goods, most of which confer permanent upgrades on Milon. Unfortunately, these aren't your typical RPG-style upgrades.

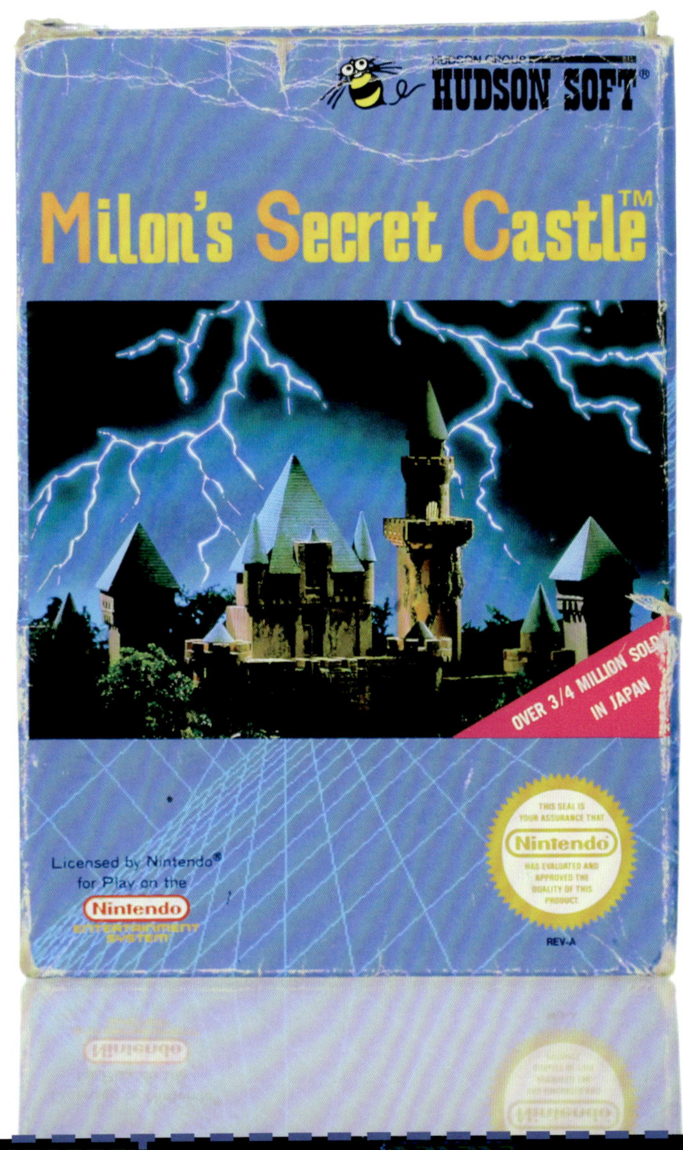

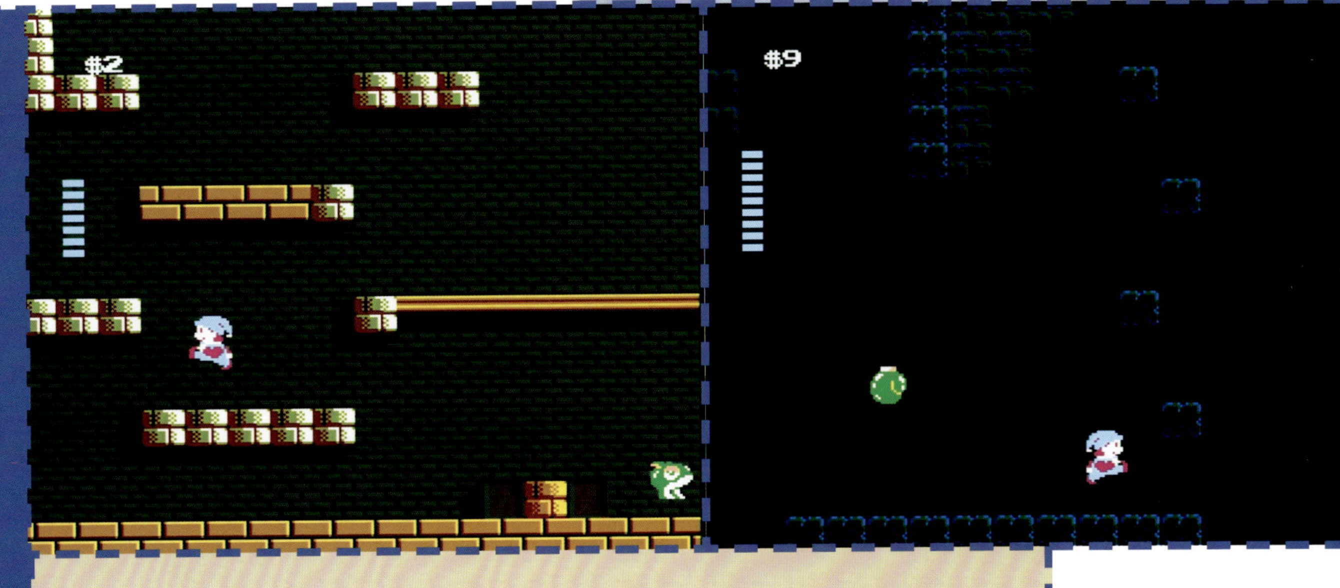

Sure, you can collect a sword (which doubles the power of the bubbles you use to attack) and a lantern (which illuminates dark rooms), but for the most part Milon's upgrades are unique to his quest. For example, a paint can allows him to render invisible blocks opaque. Special shoes enable him to bounce high off hidden, spring-loaded blocks. A hammer and saw let him break through certain windows to open new paths into the castle. And, finally, each boss you defeat drops a crystal granting you a new power.

What makes *Milon's* frustrating, and the thing that prevents it from being regarded as a timeless classic, is the enormous amount of trial and error that it requires. In some ways, *Milon's Secret Castle* feels like the midpoint between *Metroid*—with pure action in a totally open world—and *Vampire Killer*—with RPG-inflected action in a series of self-contained environments. And it looks to both of those games for its central mechanic: hidden and destructible blocks. Every room consists of platforms and structures built of individual crates, stones, and pillars, and any one of these structural items can potentially be shattered by Milon's bubble attacks. These impermanent walls and floors bar forward progress and hide crucial items, so Milon needs to clear them away to complete each stage. But this quickly degenerates into a process of shooting every wall and floor and ceiling in sight in the hopes of revealing something useful. This task is made even more annoying by the unusual angle at which Milon fires his stream of combat bubbles, which makes it difficult to determine whether you landed a square hit on blocks. Certainly, *Metroid* could grow tiresome as Samus rolled around bombing passages in search of secrets, but at least that game's level designs operated under a consistent internal logic that, once decrypted, helped players intuit where they should and shouldn't place bombs. *Milon's Secret Castle* lacks that clarity. It is a game about shooting everything in sight, but not in the hyperbolic *DOOM* sense of blasting hordes of monsters. You literally need to shoot every object on the screen.

For the most part, *Milon's Secret Castle* works reasonably well if you're willing to take it on it its own terms, though even then some of the later bosses are entirely too difficult for their own good. Also, it never puts the ability to backtrack throughout the castle to any particularly interesting purpose; it really just allows you to revisit shops to pick up goodies you inevitably miss during your first pass. Honestly, *Milon's Secret Castle* barely belongs in a chronicle of metroidvania games—it's just interesting to see how the precepts of the genre had begun to trickle into action games like this, even if they didn't always trickle especially well. M

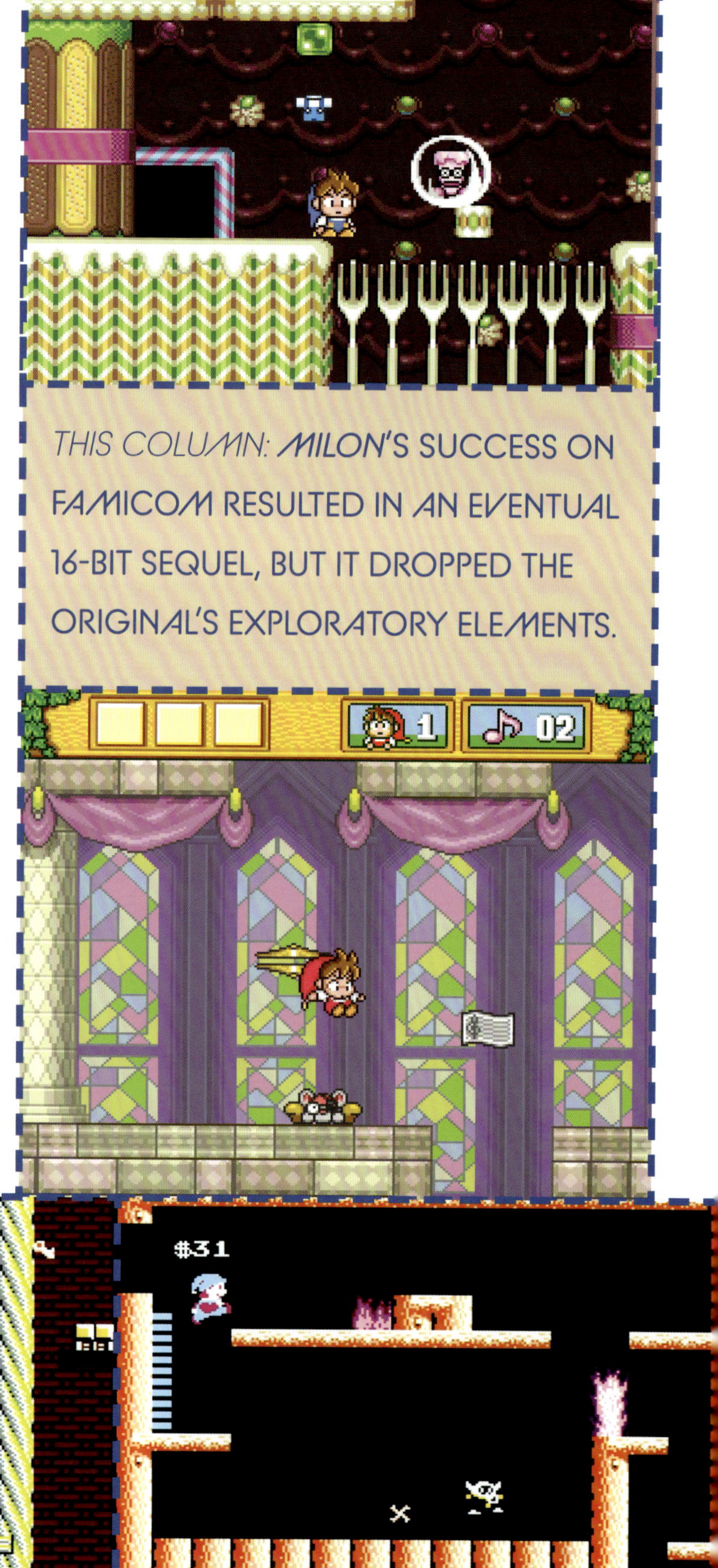

THIS COLUMN: ***MILON'S*** **SUCCESS ON FAMICOM RESULTED IN AN EVENTUAL 16-BIT SEQUEL, BUT IT DROPPED THE ORIGINAL'S EXPLORATORY ELEMENTS.**

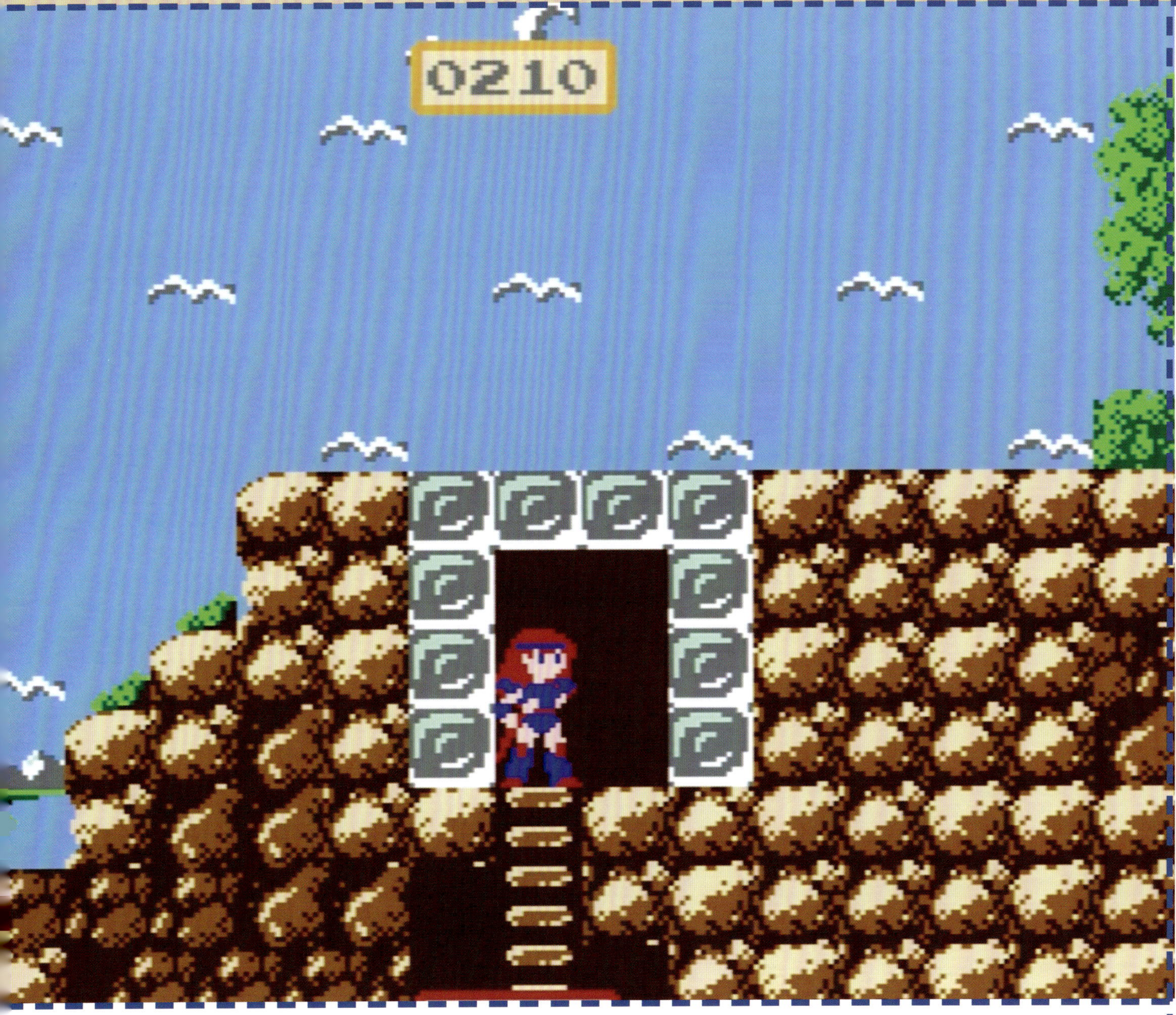

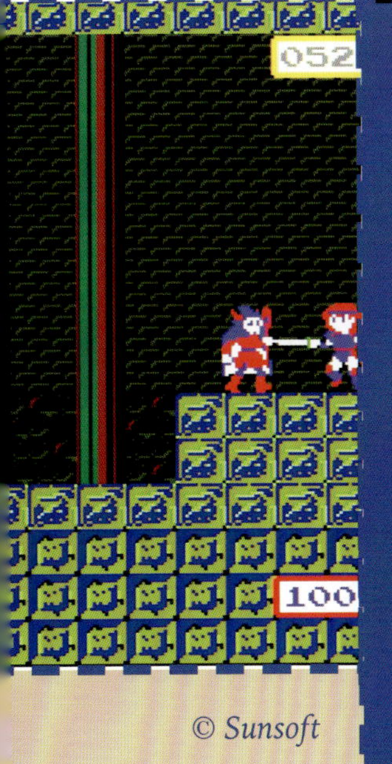

WING OF MADOOLA

PLATFORM: **FAMICOM**
DEV: **SUNSOFT** | PUB: **SUNSOFT**
INITIAL RELEASE: **DEC. 1986**

NOTABLE FOR: ***A MORE OPEN-ENDED TAKE ON DRAGON BUSTER***

FLIGHT RISK

Directly on the heels of *Milon's Secret Castle*, the Famicom received a more notable primal attempt at cracking the action-RPG code: Sunsoft's *Madoora no Tsubasa*, also known (on its title screen!) as *The Wing of Madoola*. Developer and publisher Sunsoft would ultimately go on to produce some of the 8-bit era's most successful works, though *Madoola* doesn't stand among them. Nevertheless, history reveals it to be a critical transition away from the company's simplistic early releases and its meatier later works.

Sunsoft got its start creating arcade games and shifted into the console space by porting those works to the Famicom. The company broke into the US in the early 1980s with its arcade hit *Kangaroo*, which made its way to just about every major console and computer platform at the time. Where the company's early works largely riffed on others' more popular games—Sunsoft produced plenty of *Space Invaders* and *Breakout* clones in its infancy, and even *Kangaroo* came dangerously close to being little more than a samizdat *Donkey Kong*—*Madoola* arrived as part of a push to create more inventive works, such as the feudal shooter *Ikki*, the walking simulator *The 53 Stations of the Toukaidou*, and the infamous *Atlantis no Nazo*. The latter of these deserves mention here for its intoxicating mix of ambitious vision and frustrating design, which drew heavily upon proto-metroidvanias like *Pitfall!* and its sequel. In fact, American publisher Activision very nearly localized it for the US as a sequel to *Super Pitfall*, a game defined by a similar combination of grand ambition and lackluster production values.

While *Atlantis no Nazo*'s granular, level-based structure pushed it a bit too far toward the arcade-action realm to qualify as a metroidvania or action-RPG, it clearly served as the baseline for its follow-up, *Madoola*. Admittedly, *Madoola* also operates under a level-by-level structure, but you can really see the pieces of "action" and "RPG" coming together here, building on *Dragon Buster* in a flawed but interesting way. *Madoola* embodies the shift underway in the mid-'80s, as Famicom and computer game designers in Japan reshaped existing genres to better suit their audience's tastes. Although *Atlantis no Nazo* amounted to a puzzle-heavy take on *Pitfall!* by way of *Super Mario Bros.*, with limited action

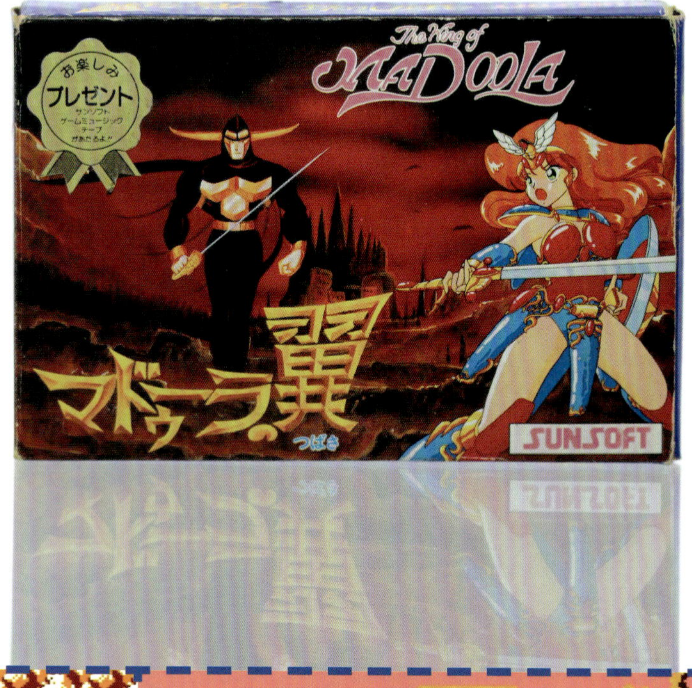

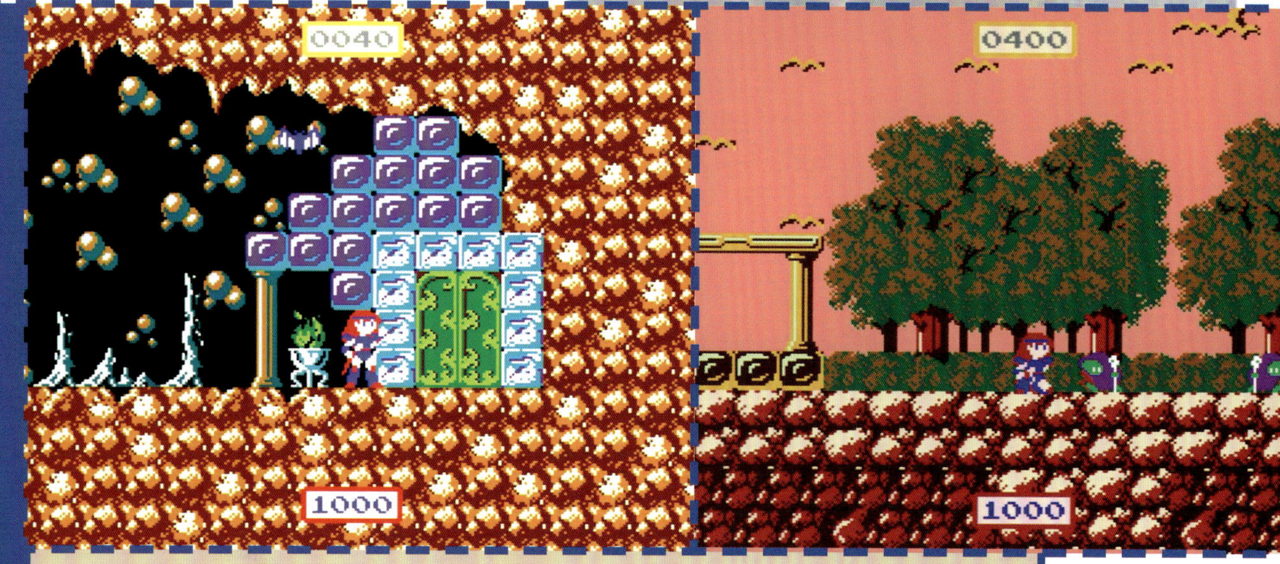

set in 100 small stages loaded with hazards and secrets, *Madoola* takes place across a mere 16 stages, which are far larger and require a considerable amount of exploring due to their confined interior spaces and rambling multistory exterior structures and caverns. Protagonist Lucia, a female protagonist in the scantily clad vein of *Metroid*'s "Zero Suit" Samus and *Valis*'s Yuuko, has a far more varied skill set than her Atlantis-exploring predecessor Wynn. Where he could only run, jump, and drop bombs, she wields a sword, learns magic, and levels up her strength and endurance as she advances.

It's worth noting that *Madoola* shipped about half a year after Enix's *Dragon Quest* made its debut in Japan and reshaped the console industry there with tectonic force. *Madoola* arrived a bit too soon after *Dragon Quest* to have likely been strongly influenced by it, especially since *Dragon Quest* mania didn't really take hold until the sequel appeared in January 1987, a month after *Madoola* shipped. Instead, as we've seen with games like *Zelda*, *Metroid*, and *Vampire Killer*, it likely drew upon earlier games that shaped *Dragon Quest* itself, such as *Hydlide* and *Wizardry*. But this rambling, overly ambitious mess of a game, which feels like it's about to fly apart at any given moment, embodied the way designers had seized upon combining action and RPG concepts as a way to distinguish console games from computer and arcade titles.

Of course, a big part of *Dragon Quest*'s popularity was that it was deliberately designed, carefully balanced to be challenging yet still friendly to players, and programmed with exacting skill. *Madoola*, on the other hand, shares more in common with the other games that tried to bring RPG mechanics to the Famicom in 1987—which is to say, quite rough around the edges. It's honestly not a bad game by any stretch of the imagination, but Sunsoft hadn't quite figured out the meaning of "user-friendly." The game suffers from numerous flaws and quirks that bog it down.

For example, *Madoola* presents players with a huge, sprawling, RPG-inflected action-adventure, but not only does it not allow players to save their progress with a password or battery to approach the game across multiple sessions, it doesn't even allow players to continue when they die without using a hidden cheat code! The game does include a not-so-secret continue feature that allows you to resume progress in the most recent stage you've reach; you need to hold Select while "starting" the game at the title screen. This works like a normal continue, but a frustrated player can easily forget the combo in the heat of the moment after suffering yet another cheap death and simply press Start (without holding Select), accidentally kicking off a fresh game and losing all their progress. This isn't simply a theoretical; *GameCenter CX* host Shinya Arino once did it on camera during his attempt to complete the game.

Why, one might ask, would Sunsoft simply not have just made the continue feature explicit? Why introduce such an unfriendly requirement? But then, this is a game where speedy enemies attack in endless waves from all directions, yet protagonist Lucia lacks any sort of mercy invincibility. While developers at the time could occasionally be too lenient with invincibility, as seen in Nintendo's metroidvania-adjacent *Kid Icarus* (which debuted the same month as *Madoola*), Sunsoft strayed too far in the other direction. Like a proper action-RPG heroine, Lucia begins her adventure with a healthy supply of hit points. However, that reserve of stamina can be whittled to zero in a matter of seconds thanks to the way enemies aggressively sap her health the moment they make it past her guard.

It doesn't help that *Madoola* expects players to be content with spotty controls; Lucia moves about the world with a curiously floppy jump, and she moves stiffly when fighting foes. Although you can deal major damage to enemies (who share Lucia's inability to recover from damage with an instant of invincibility) once you slip into a groove, the game's clumsy design causes the tables to turn on players in an instant. The later stages combine relentless enemies with iffy platform-hopping design, bringing together the worst of both worlds and draining the entertainment value from *Madoola*.

And yet, the game *almost* works! You can see some solid creative instincts at work in *Madoola* beneath all the frustration. Lucia grows in strength as you explore each stage and uncover upgrades. She gains new abilities, which improve her survivability—and some skill boosts are tucked in out-of-the-way locations, so the game gives you a meaningful reason to explore. Each stage unfolds as a self-contained mini-labyrinth of caves and crannies to be uncovered, and the frustration of *Madoola*'s more irritating elements is almost balanced by the satisfaction of actual accomplishment. With more refinement, improved difficulty balancing, and more responsive controls, this could have been a genuine classic.

As it is, you can't help but be frustrated by how tantalizingly close *The Wing of Madoola* comes to being a good game. Instead, it's all potential and promise, a raw heap of ideas and concepts that Sunsoft put to the test imperfectly. This promise would be realized to far more satisfying effect by a number of superior games the following year—beginning just a month later with the January 1987 launch of *Zelda II: The Adventure of Link*, which realized the potential inherent in *Madoola*'s awkward, *Dragon Buster*-inspired combat mechanics to brilliant effect. M

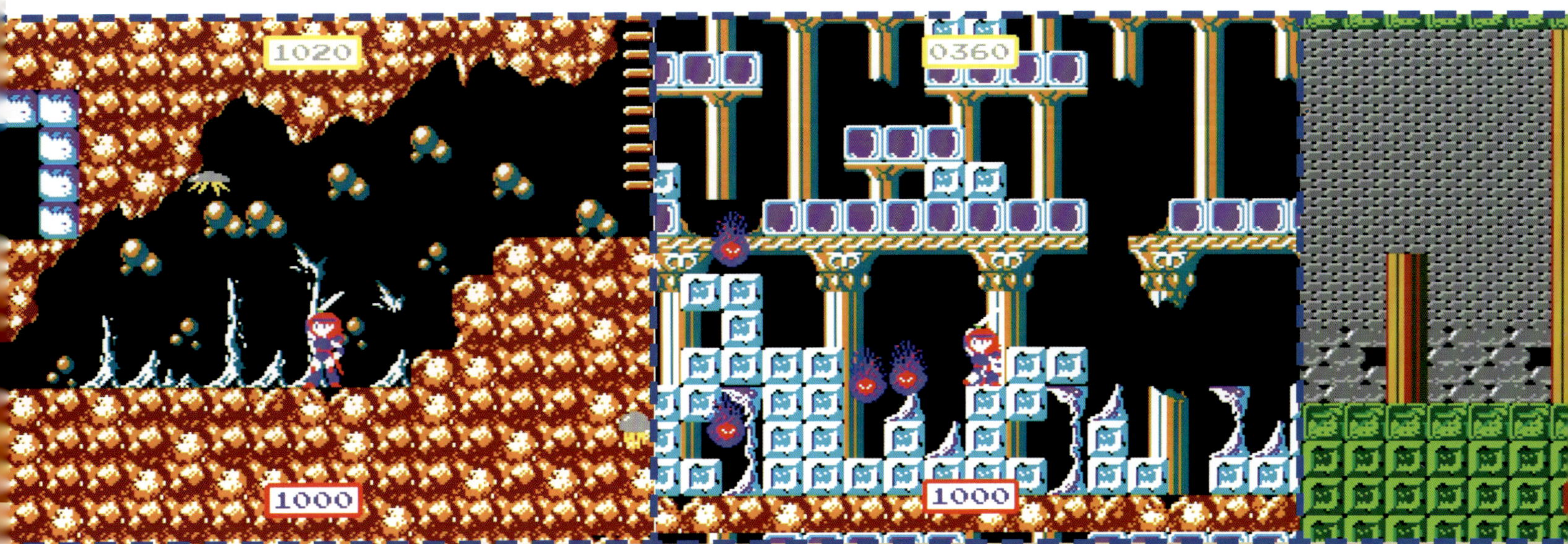

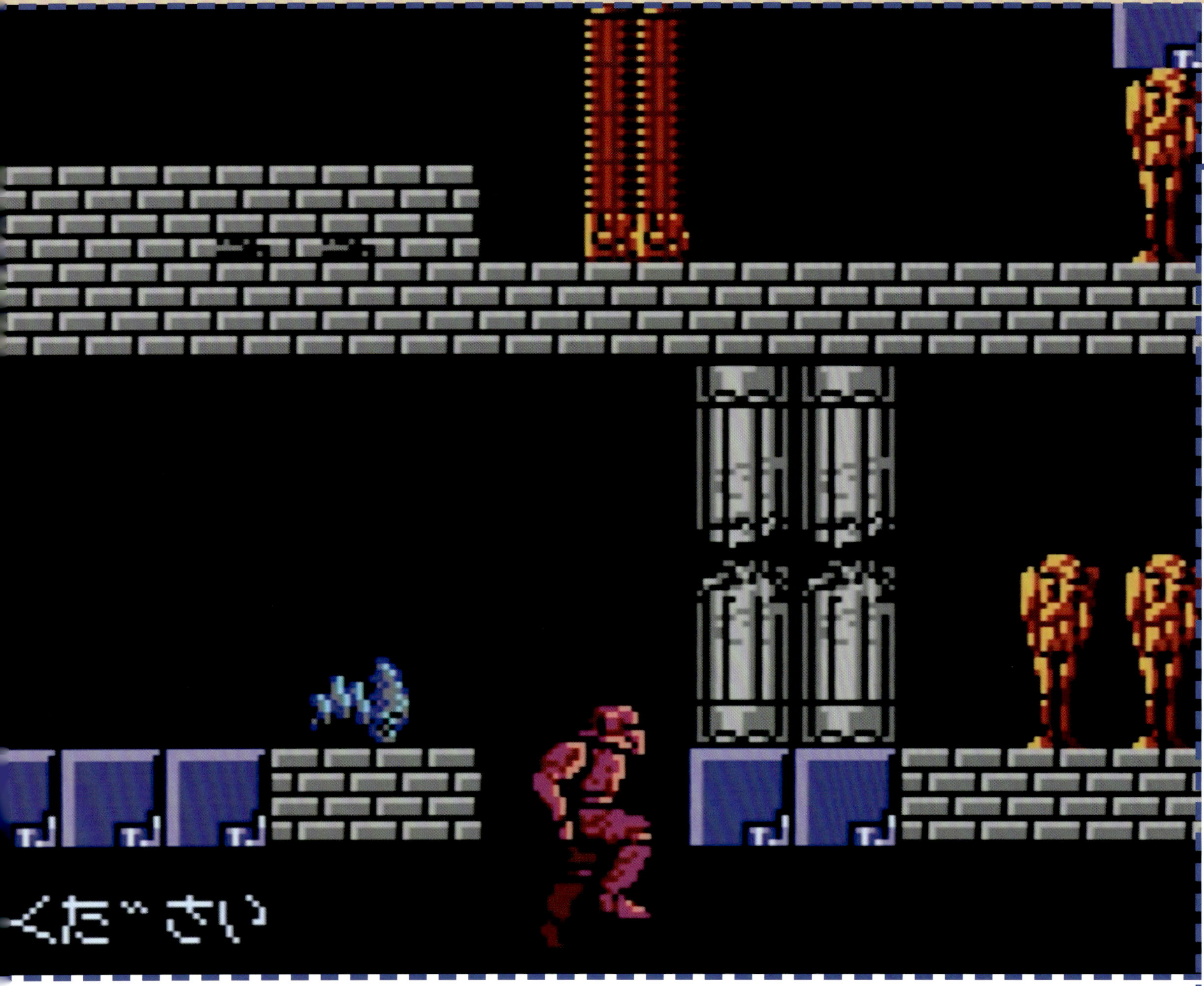

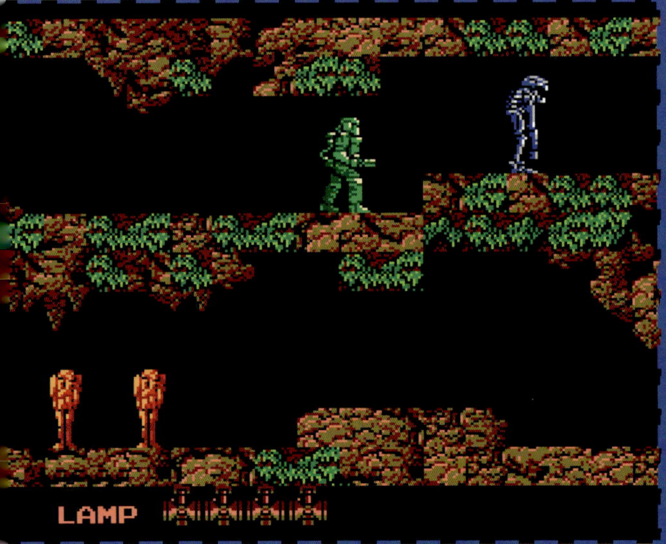

RELICS

PLATFORM: **PC-8801 / VARIOUS**
DEV: **BOTHTEC** | PUB: **BOTHTEC**
INITIAL RELEASE: **DEC. 1986**
SHOWN HERE: **FAMICOM DISK SYSTEM VERSION, 1987**

NOTABLE FOR: **AN INVENTIVE TAKE ON PROGRESSION**

BEST LEFT BURIED

On its surface, Bothtec's *Relics: Ankoku Yousai* looks like a mysterious, *Metroid*-inspired adventure, though it actually debuted on home computers around the same time as Nintendo's game. More likely, both *Metroid* and *Relics* drank from the same font of inspiration: Ridley Scott's *Alien*. Unfortunately, *Relics* falls afoul of the quirks of the Famicom Disk System hardware in the console port that most people know, suffering from some of the most severe disk access issues ever to derail an action game. There's some very ambitious design here, in which players reshape the world around them by destroying walls and floors to reveal secrets and open passages, but that only comes through in the original computer version. Thankfully, the PC-88 original has recently been published to Nintendo Switch via EGGCONSOLE, making *Relics* ripe for rediscovery.

In *Relics*, you control an astronaut exploring the catacombs of an unknown world, with a sci-fi vibe complemented by an element of mysticism. It's one part *Alien*, one part *The Pharaoh's Curse*. The key game mechanic is possession: you need to project your protagonist's consciousness into other bodies to progress here. Games like *Oddworld: Abe's Oddysee*, *Messiah*, and *The 3rd Birthday* would do this better years later, but it's a pretty inventive and clever concept for a 1986 game. Each of the body types you can control wield different weapons and offer distint ways to navigate the world, which combines with the destructible environments to offer an unconventional take on exploratory action.

Unlike in a proper metroidvania, few of your power-ups and skills are permanent. You possess creatures temporary and are limited by the appearance of those creatures in the first place. Your tools—keys, lamps, offensive and defensive power-ups—are similarly impermanent. Even exposed secrets appear to be fleeting, as the walls seem to repair themselves after you blast them. *Relics* is emblematic of some of the more innovative games of this era: full of big ideas and so intriguing you can't help but want to play them, but which are so clumsy you can't bear to play them. Like *Xanadu* and *Hydlide*, this ambitious adventure crawled (at a snail's pace due to loading times) so that later games could run.

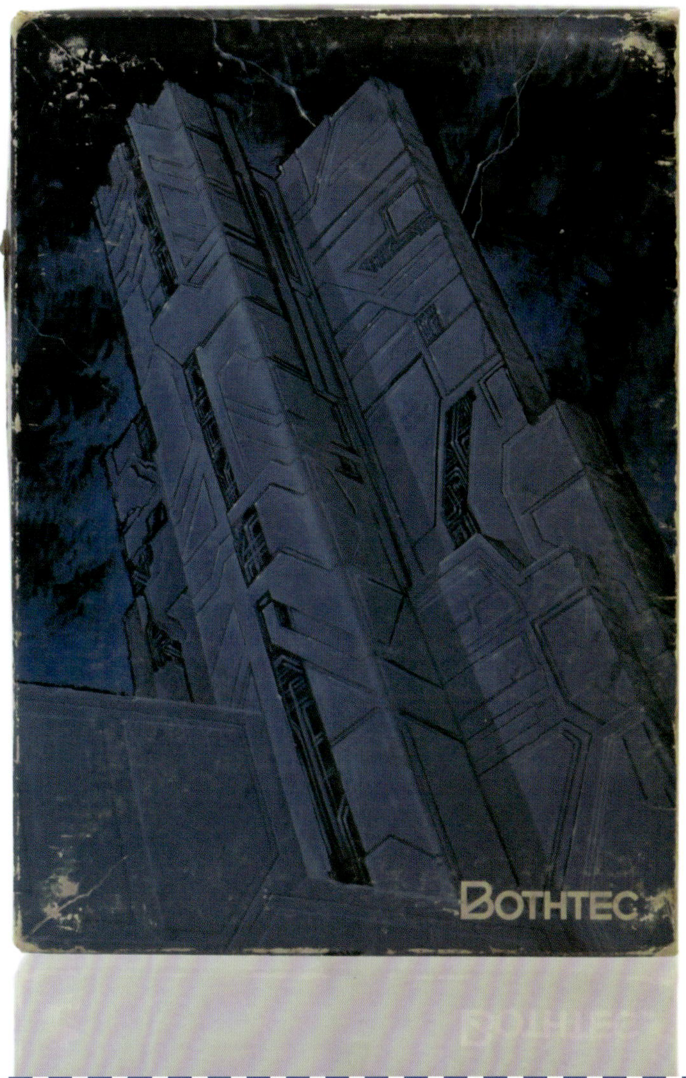

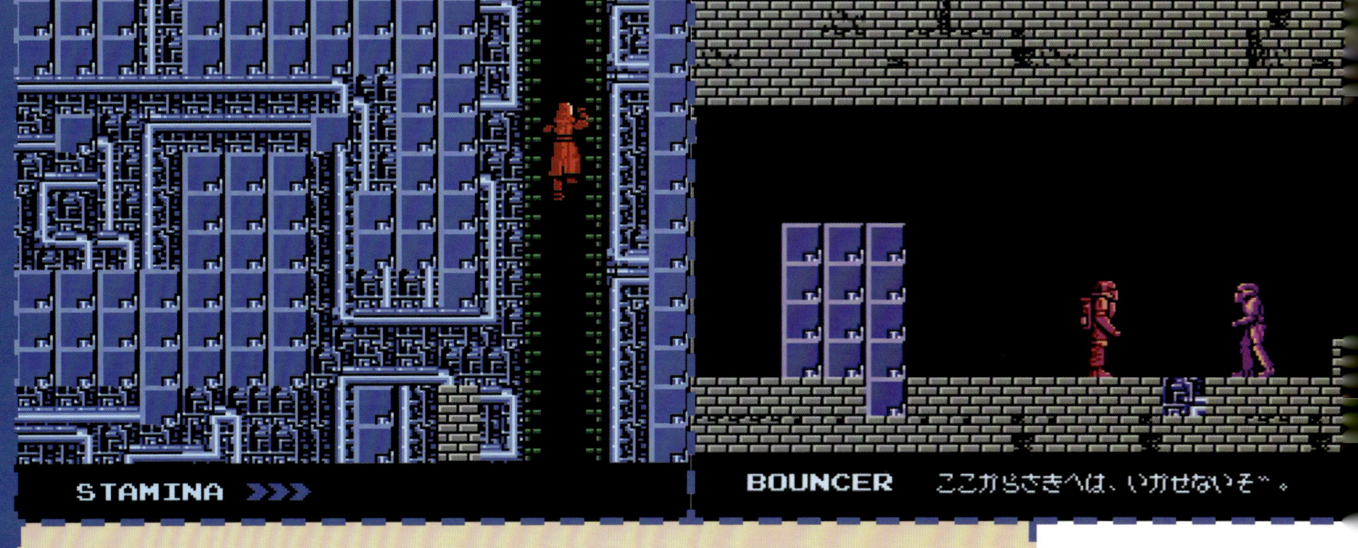

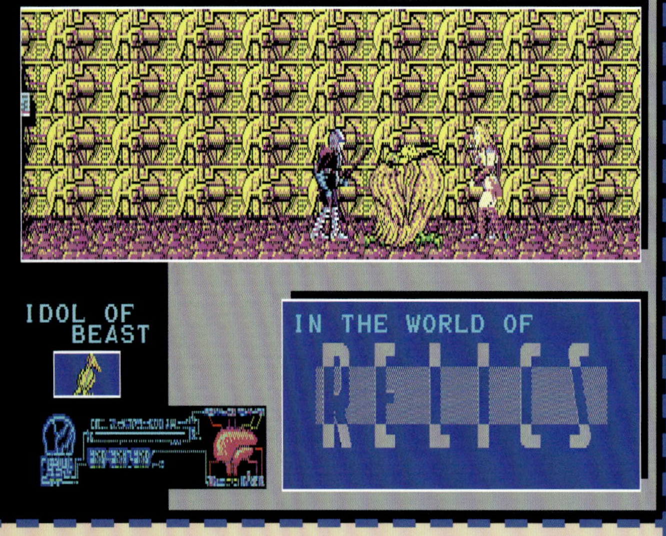

THIS COLUMN: ***RELICS*** BEGAN LIFE ON THE NEC PC-8801, WHERE ITS SLOW PACE AND FOCUS ON OBSCURE SECRETS FELT RIGHT AT HOME.

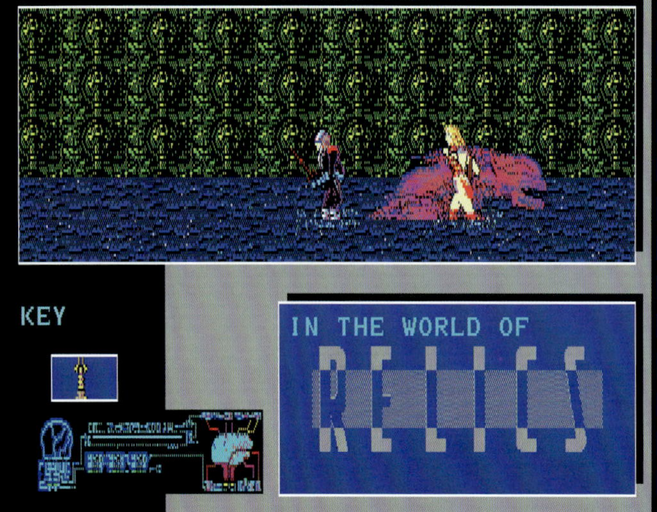

PC CULTURE

Metroidvania games and action-RPGs alike owe a great debt to early Japanese personal computers. Unlike in the US, where consoles crashed out of existence during the formative years of those genres; and unlike in Europe, where consoles had very little traction until the 1990s; the Japanese gaming space saw computers, consoles, and arcade machines uniquely thrive in tandem during the mid-1980s. As a result, the three formats conversed with one another in ways that simply didn't happen in other regions.

Although early arcade games showed up regularly (albeit in compromised form) on consoles and computers in America and Europe, you rarely saw PC software make its way to consoles. Systems like Intellivision and Atari 2600 lacked the power and interface capabilities to run games designed to exploit the potential of Atari 800 and Apple II hardware. Had the US console market survived beyond early 1984, Atari would have launched its 7800 system that year—a platform that eventually received ports of computer hits like *Karateka*, *One on One*, and *Impossible Mission*. But that never panned out, and American console fans largely missed out on mid-'80s computer hits until the end of the decade, once the more powerful Nintendo Entertainment System and Sega Genesis dominated the US market.

But in Japan, the Famicom rose to dominance in 1984, right around the time that action-RPGs truly took off in that market. Leading-edge Japanese home game development largely took place on computers like the Sharp X1 and NEC PC-9801, which offered impressive capabilities even compared to Western systems like the Commodore 64. But the cost and complexity of PCs doomed that market to a relatively modest size, whereas Famicom and other consoles ended up in ten times as many homes due to the low price made possible by their humble tech. As a result, PC developers converted their action-RPG hits to consoles in short order, greatly increasing the reach of those works. Conveniently, many influential computer action-RPGs didn't require much more in the way of interface capabilities than the Famicom controller's four buttons could offer—witness the rudimentary combat of *Ys* and *Hydlide*, for example. This gave the genre far greater visibility than it enjoyed in the West, which goes a long way toward explaining why so many of these games hail from Japan.

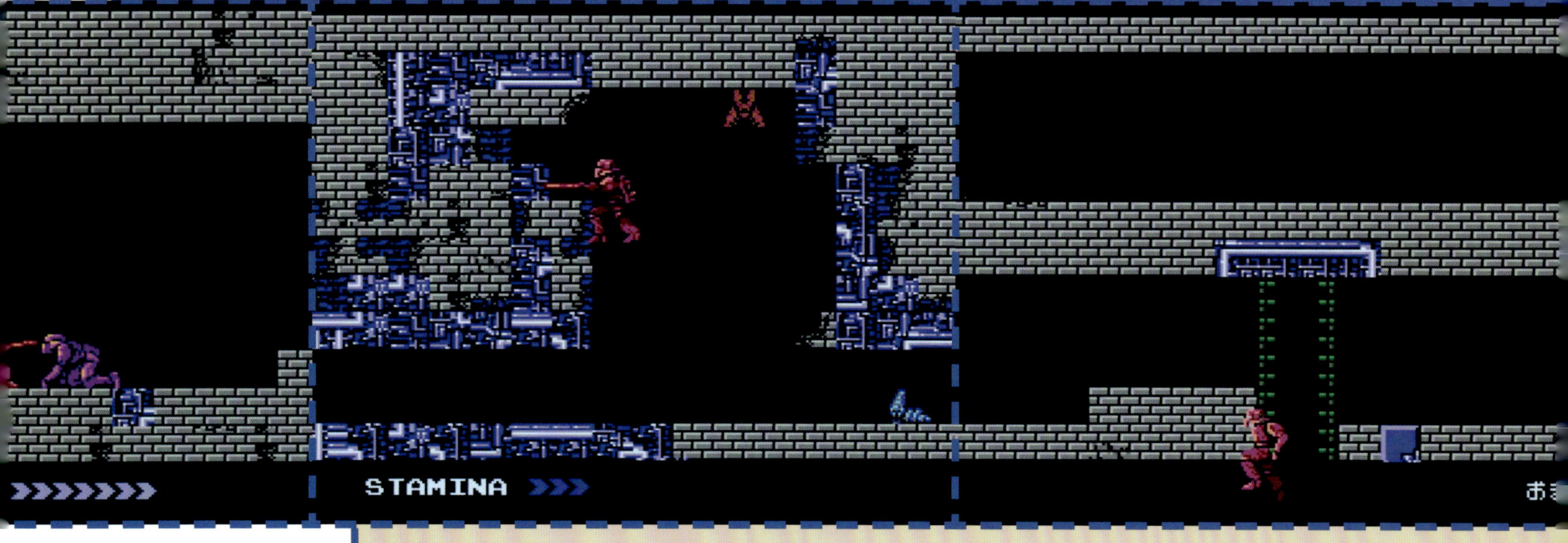

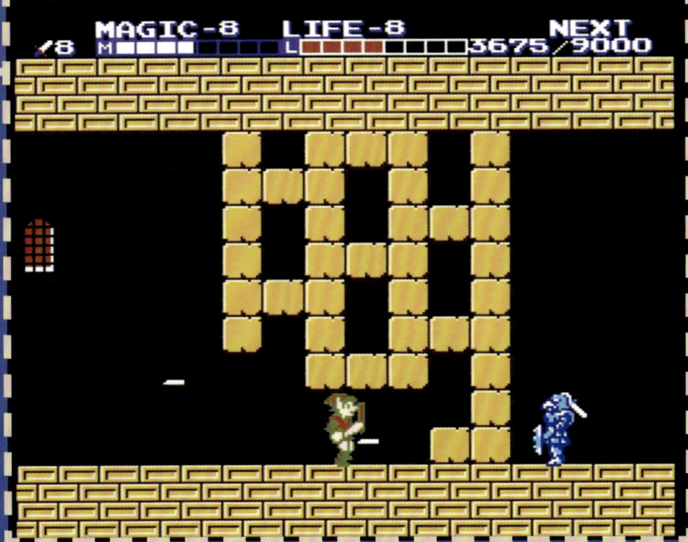

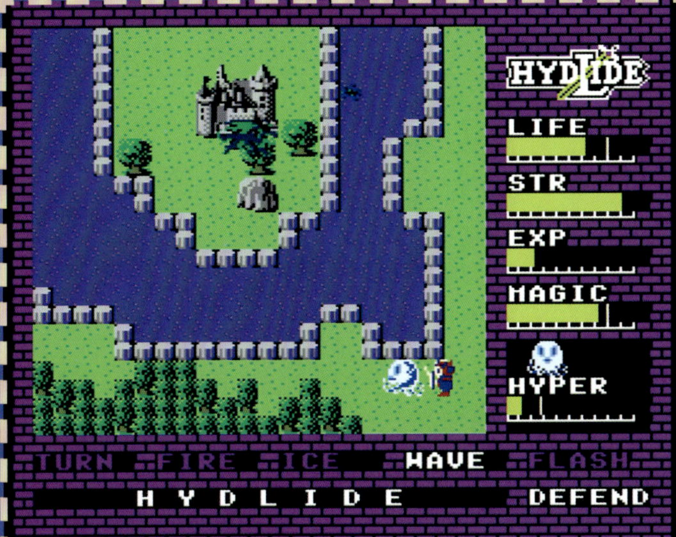

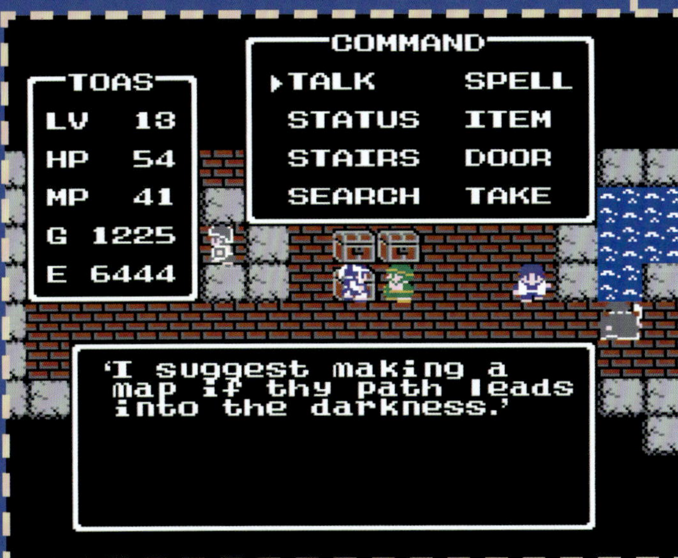

OUT OF SYNC

The chronology that unfolds throughout this book largely describes a logical, progressive chain of evolution for games that shaped the metroidvania format. You can see one build on the next, growing ever more intricate while simultaneously moving closer to what we recognize today as the 1990s golden triumvirate of metroidvania/action-RPG classics: *The Legend of Zelda: A Link to the Past*, *Super Metroid*, and *Castlevania: Symphony of the Night*. And this was the way players would have experienced these works if they followed them at launch…in Japan, that is. In the US and Europe, however, things worked out differently.

Once the Japanese PC and console revolutions got truly underway around 1984 or so, and the American console market crashed, the evolution of these games largely transpired on Japanese systems with games designed by Japanese creators. Which is not to say that nothing was going on in the US or Europe, just that those creations did little to feed into the self-contained conversation that took place in Japan for more than a decade.

That's neither here nor there, but the complexity and increasing focus on narrative elements found in these games meant that their international releases required text and cultural localization to appeal to audiences who didn't read Japanese. Between the slow rollout of the NES in the West relative to its Japanese sales, the complexity of localization within tiny 8-bit memory spaces, and the complications of manufacturing, games tended to ship to US audiences in a wildly different order than they were actually created. Formative works like *Dragon Quest*, *Hydlide*, and *Zelda II* in particular showed up years after countless games that they inspired; *Hydlide* took five years to reach America! This didn't simply rob those games of the revolutionary punch that Japanese fans experienced, it also meant that American and European gamers found themselves flung into the deep end of games like *Rambo* and *Rygar* without experiencing the titles that inspired them as a primer.

METROIDVANIA TIMELINE 1987

Perhaps the single most momentous year in the prehistory of the metroidvania genre, 1987 saw game designers taking radical leaps forward when it came to creating complexity within the action game format. This largely comes down to the maturation of Nintendo's Famicom/NES console. The technical advances made possible by 1986's Disk System peripheral (larger storage capacity, rewritable media) were matched and even exceeded by solid-state cartridges by way of built-in memory management chips that allowed software to greatly exceed the capabilities of the base console hardware. Plus, the introduction of carts with built-in lithium batteries allowed players to save game progress without a disk drive. Now, every Famicom (and NES) owner could enjoy large-scale adventures, allowing the world's bestselling console to date to evolve beyond the simple arcade conversions that had comprised nearly the entirety of its early library.

Nevertheless, the fact that the Famicom and NES had earned so much acclaim on the backs of arcade-style software shaped the direction and nature of the more sophisticated works that began to appear in 1987. Most of the cutting-edge design work that appeared on the system this year resembled the pure action experiences that the console's fan base loved and expected on the surface...but upon closer examination, this new wave of games turned out to borrow liberally from the role-playing and adventure genres that had exploded in popularity on Famicom over the past couple of years. Famicom publishers churned out an almost comical number of games that unimaginatively copied the design and themes of breakout graphical adventure *Portopia Renzoku Satsujin Jiken* and landmark RPG *Dragon Quest*. Yet for every tediously literal clone, you could also find a game that cribbed concepts from those games and applied them to other genres in a truly transformative fashion.

Zelda II took a different approach to incorporating action into the RPG than its predecessor by applying the experience levels and magic spells of *Dragon Quest* into the sword-slinging framework of *Dragon Buster*. *The Goonies II* looked like the original *The Goonies*... until you entered a door, at which point the game shifted to play like an adventure in the style of *Portopia*. *Legacy of the Wizard* adapted the RPG party concept into a single-player action game, allowing players to control a single party member at a time through scenarios that revolved more around solving puzzles than mastering twitch reflexes. And then you had *The Magic of Scheherazade*, which slammed all three genres together into a bizarre, but surprisingly effective, hybrid. Plenty of games predating 1987 shaped the metroidvania's evolution, but it's really here that you begin to see games that closely resemble the form of the medium as we know it today. The genre's mechanical and design innovations came together over the course of this calendar year, resulting in a lineup of games that pushed the boundaries of action gaming in new and exciting ways. *M*

TIMELINE OF EVENTS

January

Zelda II: The Adventure of Link

Improving on *Dragon Buster*'s combat design and adding experience points and character stats, this was the closest *Zelda* ever came to being a true RPG.

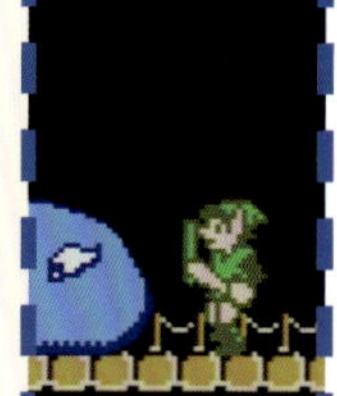

March

The Goonies II

Expanding the previous *Goonies*' free movement within linear stages into a full, open-ended, interconnected world, *The Goonies II* was a pioneering game despite being based on a film license.

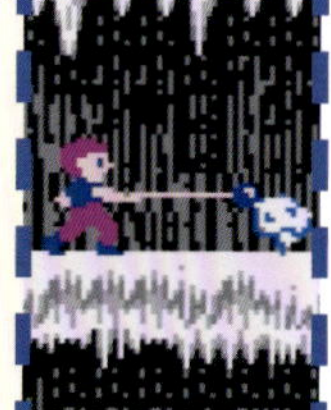

April

Rygar

Barely resembling the arcade game with which it shared a title, *Rygar* for NES introduced the concept of free-roaming action stages connected by a central hub space.

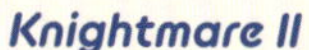

Knightmare II

Playing like a scaled-down version of *Legacy of the Wizard*, *Knightmare II* featured two protagonists who could apply their slightly varied skill sets to an open-ended dungeon.

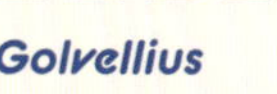

Golvellius

If *The Legend of Zelda* became *Zelda II* inside of dungeons, and thse dungeons played out as an auto-scrolling, twitch-action game, it would resemble nothing so much as *Golvellius*.

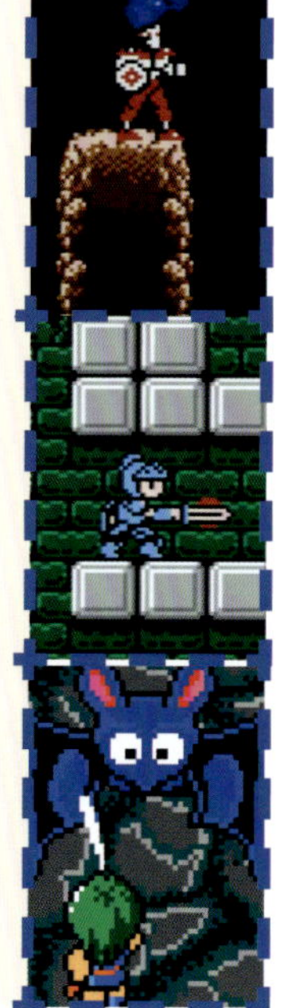

May

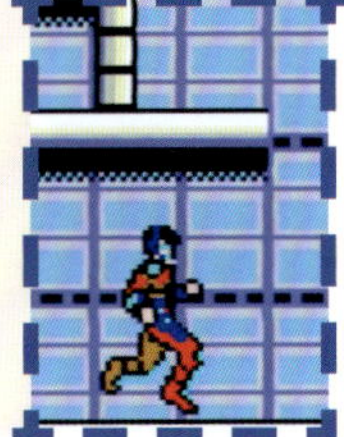

Zillion

Effectively a clone of Epyx's *Impossible Mission*, *Zillion* for the Master System turned a toy and cartoon tie-in into a rescue mission set inside of a vast, intercon- nected alien fortress.

June

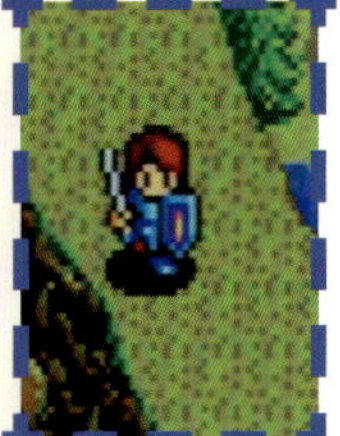

Ys: The Vanished Omen

Nihon Falcom refined *Hydlide*'s format to near-perfection here, with more concrete stat management, a driving storyline, towns and shops, and an improved take on "bump" combat.

July

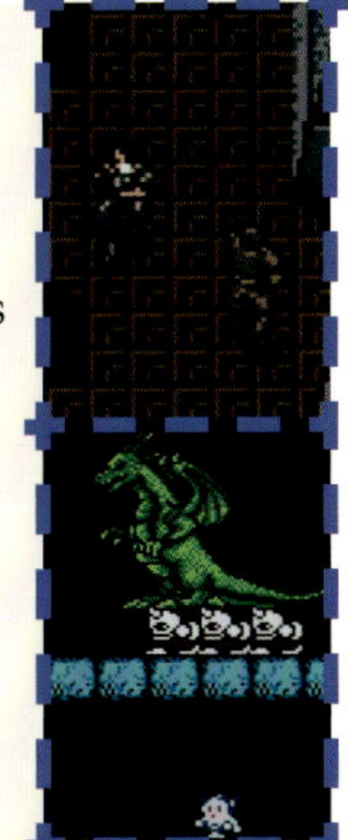

Metal Gear

Zelda with rocket launchers. *Metal Gear* sent players sneaking into an enemy fortress armed only with their wits, making their way with radioed-in hints and whatever tools appeared en route.

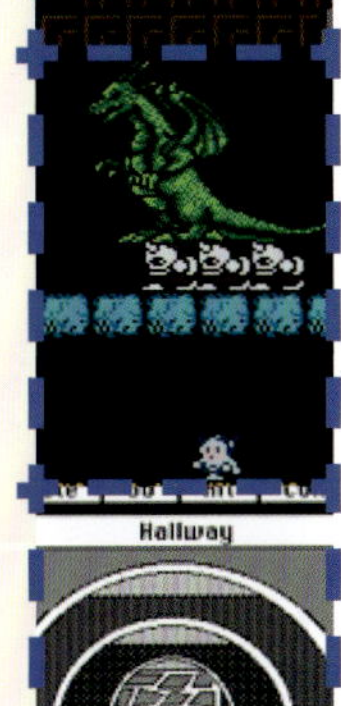

Legacy of the Wizard

The fourth *Dragon Slayer* asked, "What would happen if each member of an RPG party went adventuring alone?" The result: an immense, vexing, nonlinear action-RPG.

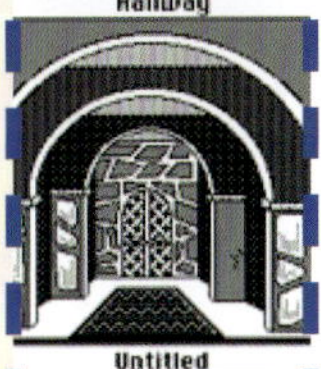

Shadowgate

Taking the *Portopia* menu concept to the next level by integrating a Mac mouse interface, *Shadowgate* turned the graphical adventure into a tricky (and scenery-chewing) test of wits.

August

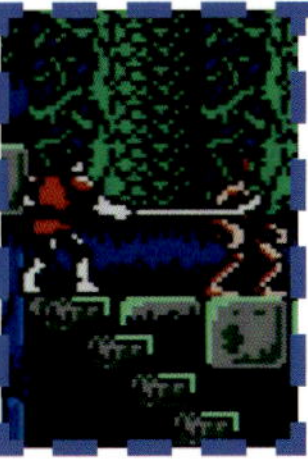

Castlevania II: Simon's Quest

Combining the best of *Castlevania* and *Vampire Killer*, *Simon's Quest* sent its protagonist into five mansions linked by an open, intricate countryside.

September

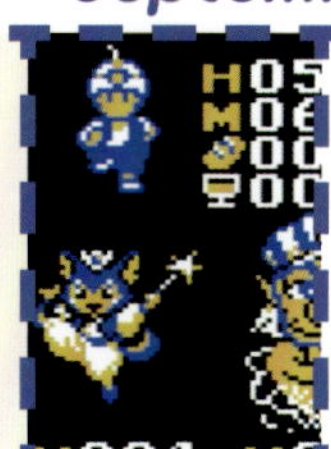

The Magic of Scheherazade

Courageously mixing together elements of role-playing, action-RPGs, and adventure games, this oddball title was far from perfect—but its ambitious innovation is hard to fault.

November

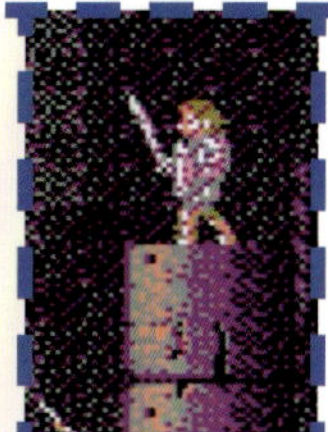

Faxanadu

This console-only offshoot of *Dragon Slayer* plays more like *Zelda II* minus the overhead travel sections; the entire adventure instead plays out through a single, consistent viewpoint.

December

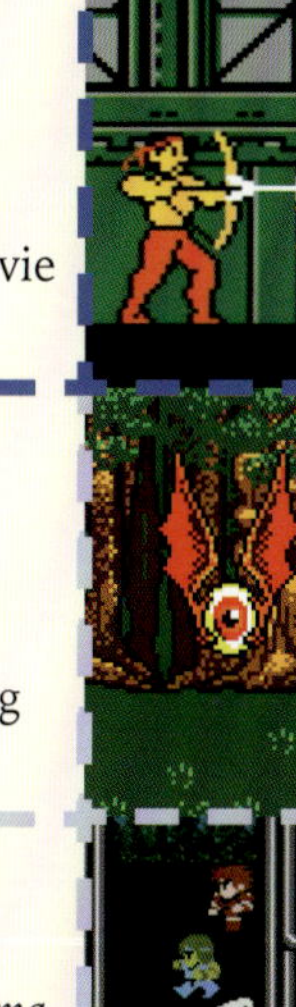

Rambo

An unlikely progenitor of the metroidvania, yes, but there's no denying that in borrowing concepts and mechanics from *Zelda II*, this movie adaptation still fits the description.

Phantasy Star

Sega took a swing at the RPG in cartridge form with *Phantasy Star*, a game that stood apart thanks to its sci-fi themes and technically stunning first-person dungeons.

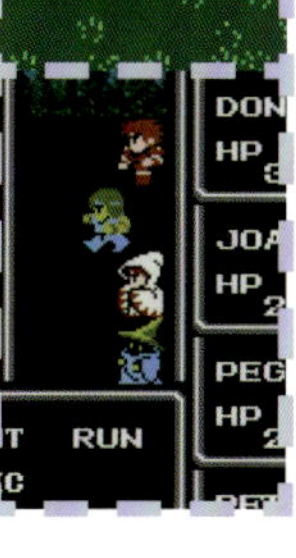

Final Fantasy

Where *Phantasy Star* took its cues directly from Western RPGs like *Ultima* and *Wizardry*, *Final Fantasy* looked to D&D for its combat and bestiary, building on the *Dragon Quest* format.

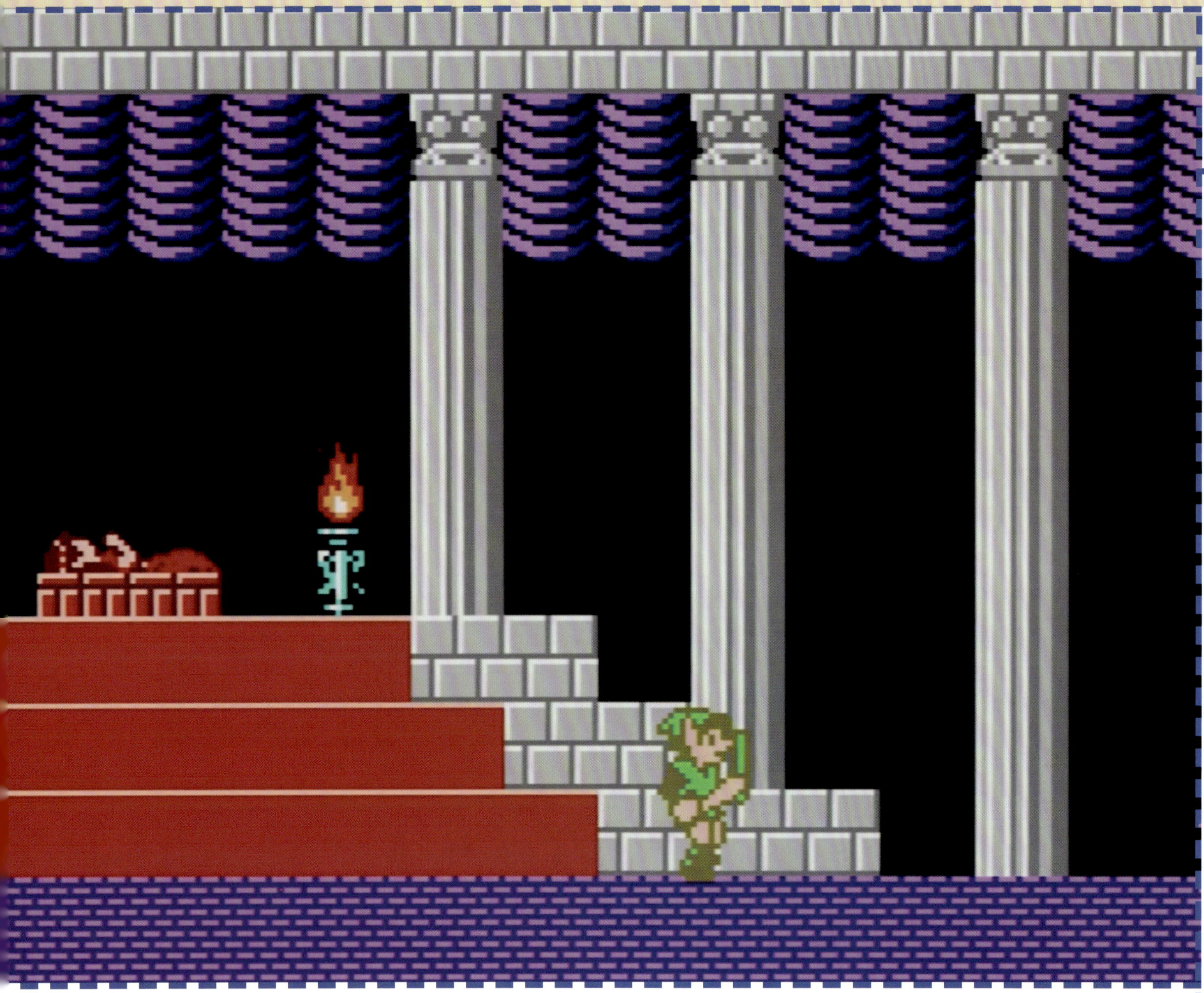

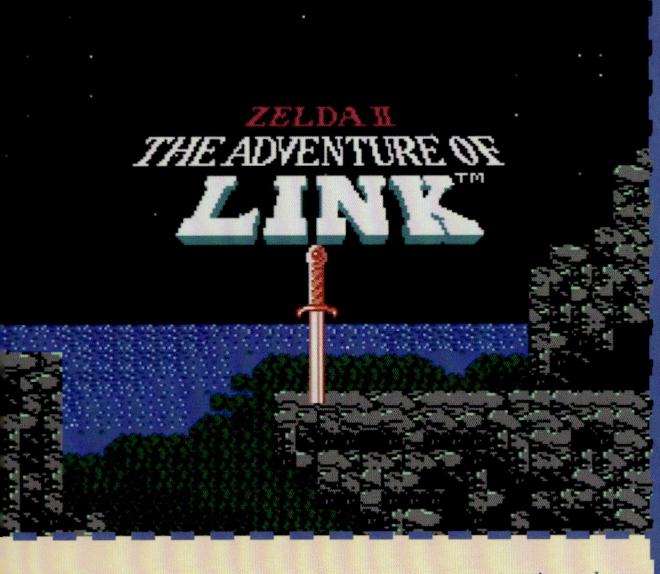

ZELDA II:
THE ADVENTURE OF LINK

PLATFORM: **FAMICOM DISK SYSTEM / NES**
DEV: **NINTENDO** | PUB: **NINTENDO**
INITIAL RELEASE DATE: **JAN. 1987**

NOTABLE FOR: **FULL RPG INTEGRATION INTO AN ACTION GAME**

A LINK BETWEEN GENRES

One year after *The Legend of Zelda*, Nintendo's first sequel to their Disk System masterpiece reinterpreted what an action-RPG video game could look like. The original *Zelda* stood at the intersection of *Hydlide* and *The Tower of Druaga* with just a hint of *Dragon Slayer*, paring down the RPG concept of character stats to the most streamlined form imaginable. Its top-down action visually resembled the combat scenes from *Ultima* or *Xanadu* but played out through real-time, two-button action. *Zelda* reduced the number-management element of those games to just tracking your cash reserve and bomb inventory. Although the stat boosts provided by better swords and enchanted armor rings eased the difficulty of combat, the outcome of each fight was ultimately left to the player's dexterity and grasp of the tools that protagonist Link carried into battle.

Zelda II does not play like that at all. It shifts *Zelda*'s gameplay perspective from a top-down view—at least where combat is concerned—to one that resembles a trendy action-platformer game, à la the exploration (not combat) sequences in *Xanadu*. In a sense, *Zelda* II directly inverts the workings of *Xanadu*; where that game allowed you to run and jump in a side-scrolling perspective as you explored while working your way through battles against monsters through a top-down overview, *Zelda II* switches it up. Here, its exploration that plays out through the top-down view while its combat embraces the side-scrolling action.

The change in perspective is clearly drawn from *Dragon Quest*, but *Zelda II* skips that game's randomized, turn-based encounters. Enemies appear as wandering icons on the overworld, and if you should bump into one of these representations in the top-down view, you shift into the same side-on perspective through which Link navigates dungeons. These side-scrolling scenes require far more dexterity and skill than the original *Zelda* and its kin. In this volume you engage with foes who face off against Link with ferocious attacks in great numbers. They crawl, leap, fly, and

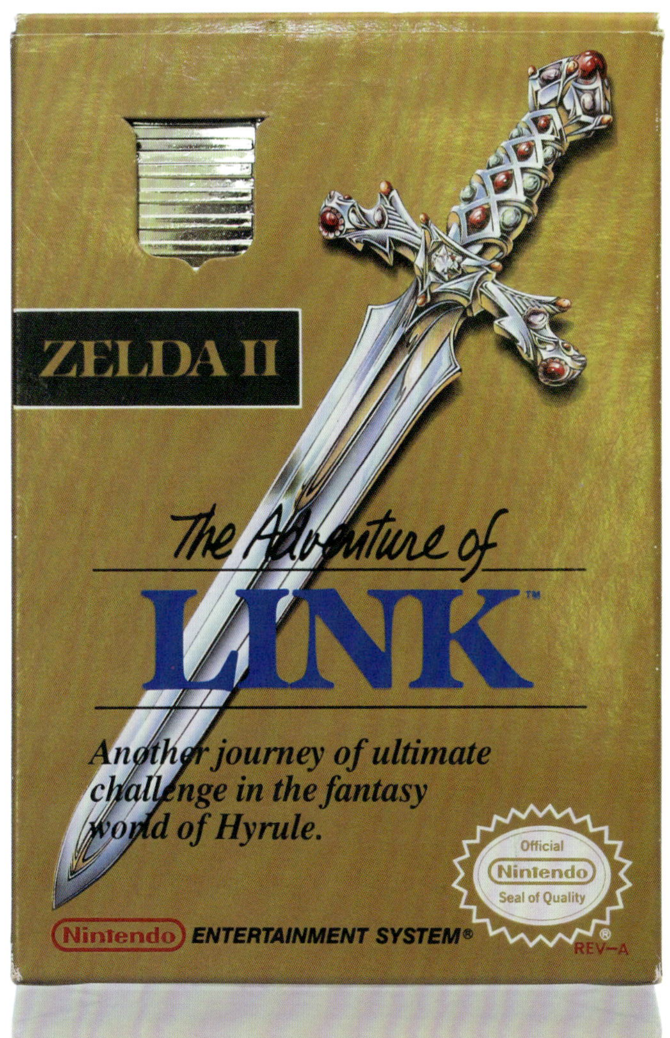

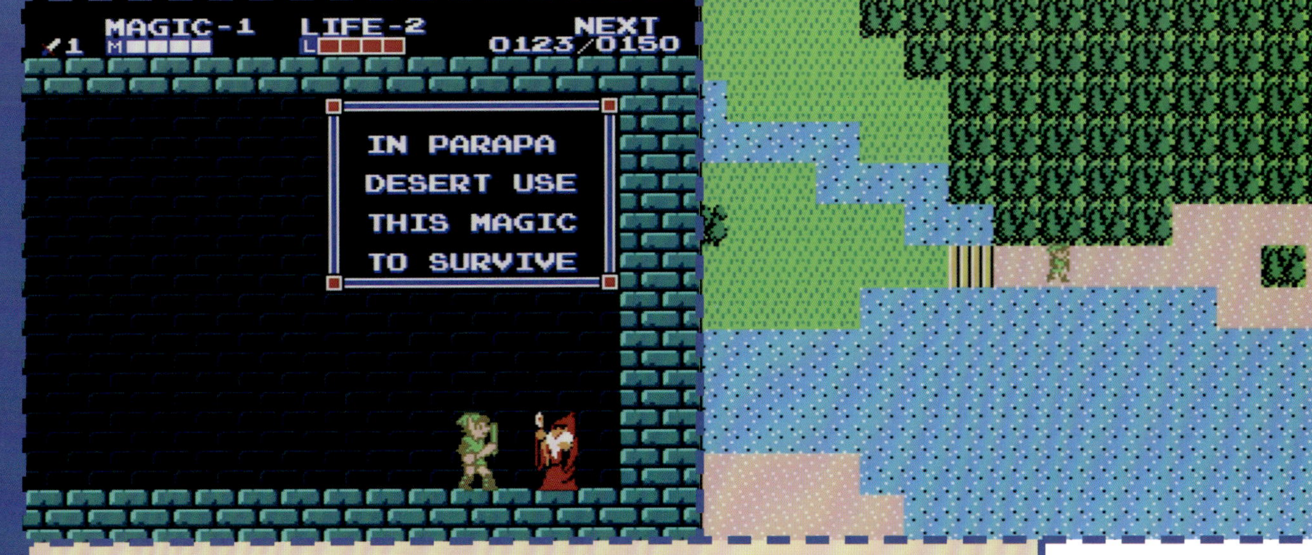

bounce around the room, and many even attack head-on. The game's deadliest hostiles can even go toe-to-toe with Link, challenging him with his own tools and skills: a sword and shield.

While the *Xanadu* connections are obvious, *Zelda II*'s side-scrolling sequences owe everything to Namco's *Dragon Buster*, Namco's 1984 arcade adventure that had ironically made its way to Famicom one week before *Zelda II* launched. Poor timing on *Dragon Buster*'s part, which paled in comparison to the scope and intricacy of Nintendo's game! Yet there's no denying that *Zelda II* would never have turned out the way it did without Namco's work to serve as an example. *Dragon Buster* protagonist Clovis could run and jump, wield a sword, and endure multiple monstrous attacks thanks to his stamina bar. The game essentially set the standard for side-scrolling swordplay action in a platformer perspective, and *Zelda II* builds on those mechanics even more elaborately than *Wing of Madoola* had done just a few weeks earlier.

Like Clovis and Lucia, Link has a life meter here, which allows him to withstand a fair amount of punishment by foes, which he can reciprocate in turn by striking back with his sword skills. Link can wield his sword at two levels, high and low, and when he isn't attacking or running, he holds his shield aloft. This neutral defensive stance allows him to block enemy sword strikes and most projectiles. These more refined swordsmanship capabilities come at a price, as Link abandons the tools of the first game—bombs and boomerangs—in favor of combat-oriented abilities and mystical noncombat enhancements. Link's few tools, such as the Hammer and the Recorder, only come into play outside of combat, in the *Dragon Quest*-style overworld view. In battle, he supplements his sword skills by casting spells, which can double his defense, allow him to leap extra-high, enhance his shield against high-power projectiles, and even transform him into a faerie so tiny it can slip through keyholes.

All this is to say that *Zelda II* engages with the concept of the "metroidvania" far more directly than its predecessor. Link's abilities empower him both as a warrior and an explorer, and if his mechanisms aren't quite as elegant as those of Samus Aran, well, that's because *Zelda II* legitimately is an action-RPG, with all the numbers and menus that entails. For the first (and only!) time in the *Zelda* franchise, Link juggles traditional RPG experience points. Defeating all but the most pitiful enemies yields experience points, and once you hit certain experience thresholds you get to level up one of three skills: Life, Magic, and Strength. Link's stats max out at Level 8 in each category, so you can't over-level him for the final stages of the adventure; on the contrary, the final dungeon is tuned for a fully powered-up protagonist. Ultimately, though, the EXP system isn't meant to be the baseline of Link's capabilities; *Zelda II* still retains the Heart Container mechanic of the first game to increase Link's maximum health, accompanied here by Magic Containers. Rather than raising your skill caps, leveling up in Life and Magic simply improves your endurance and your spell-casting efficiency. The only stat without a collectible equivalent is Strength, as Link already wields the same mystical sword (which would be named the Master Sword in later games) as from the first game. He can also learn a few sword skills from warriors around the land, most notably a downward thrust attack that allows him to stab while descending and makes it possible to shatter certain blocks and reach new areas.

In short, *Zelda II* requires players to manage a lot of different factors in battle, and much of the quest revolves around seeking tools that will open up new pathways. Hyrule has been greatly expanded from the land you explored in the first game (which now occupies a tiny corner of the multi-continent world map), and Link's progress is gated by barriers and obstructions that can only be passed with specific spells and tools. The Hammer smashes boulders and fells trees to reveal new paths; a raft crosses bodies of water; the Jump spell conquers high cliffs; and so on. The game largely avoids *Metroid*-style backtracking, with dungeon-by-dungeon progression carried over from the first game and applied to a classic RPG sense of trekking from town to town and learning new information and skills from the locals. You can wander into areas you aren't yet properly equipped for, such as haunted areas where monsters attack invisibly until you acquire the Holy Cross, but otherwise you rarely need to head back to an area you've previously mastered.

Zelda II was created by a different team than the original game, and it shows. It's a very different experience than both its predeces- sor and its sequels. The next entry in the series, *A Link to the Past*, would revert back to the top-down, EXP-free stylings of the original *Zelda*. You see echoes of *Zelda II*'s sword combat here in the series' 3D titles, but for the most part this was an experiment that Nintendo quickly walked back. Yet it had a profound influence on others, as we'll see down the road in games like *The Battle of Olympus* and *Adventure Time: Hey Ice King! Why'd You Steal Our Garbage?!!*

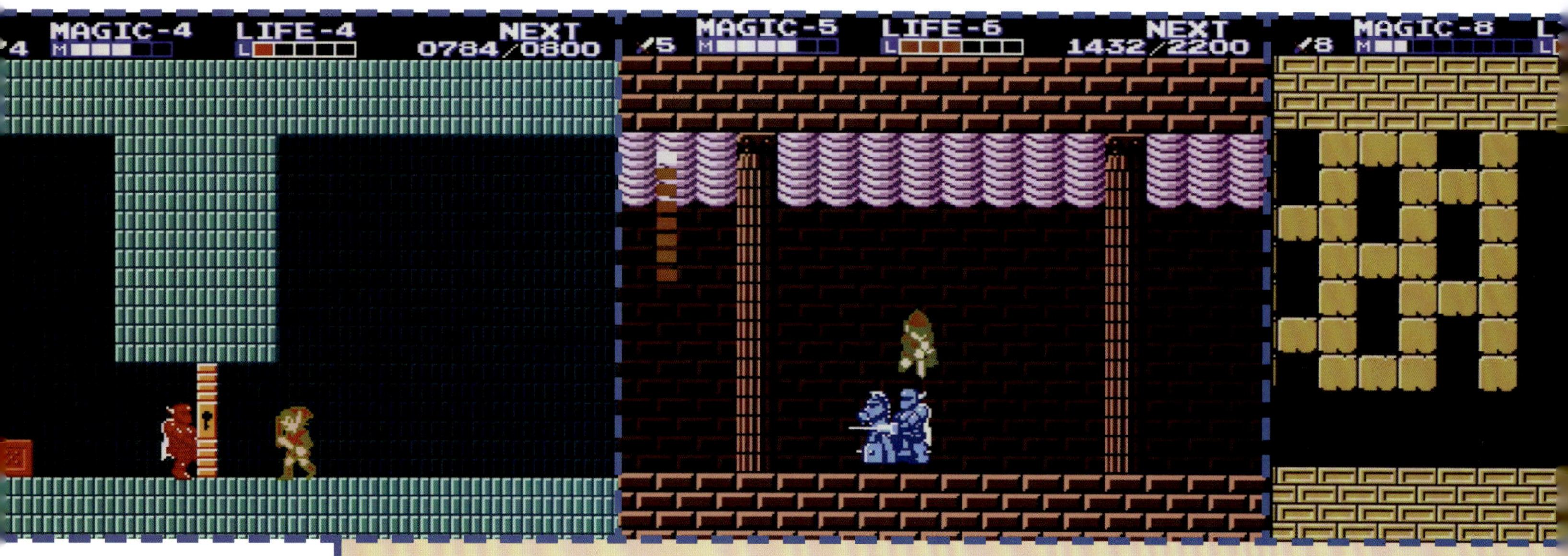

DIZZY: THE ULTIMATE CARTOON ADVENTURE

The next inevitable step beyond *Jet Set Willy*, *Dizzy: The Ultimate Cartoon Adventure* by the Oliver Twins set the hearts of ZX Spectrum owners aflutter with its combination of sprawling, open-world, single-screen action-adventure style, object-based puzzle-solving, and unforgivingly brutal difficulty. It appealed to British Spectrum fans who gravitated toward torturously difficult games: an adventure game that required savant-level arcade twitch skills.

Dizzy differed from *Jet Set Willy* in that it actually functioned as an adventure game in the classic sense of the genre. Where the earlier Spectrum hit simply required players to make their way through a nonlinear mansion packed with death traps in order to collect a full array of items, *Dizzy* gave those items a purpose beyond building toward a game-completing collection of stuff. Nearly every object its eponymous protagonist acquired during his exploration served an alternate function of some sort. For example, a Ghost Hunters Laser allowed Dizzy to make his way past a ghost that blocked a crucial pathway, and you couldn't open a rusty drawbridge without first locating a Can of Oil.

In classic graphical adventure style, very few of these items served an immediately obvious purpose. Indeed, most of the items you acquire in the first half of the game simple go toward concocting a magical potion in a cauldron—and there's no way to intuit what that potion requires in the way of ingredients without reading the instruction manual. But then, that's another adventure game trick: Fighting software piracy by requiring players to reference information contained exclusively in the retail packaging. For modern players who may not be able to get an instruction manual with their copy of the game, this makes an already hard game that much harder…as if its limited number of lives and unforgiving difficulty weren't enough! *Dizzy* hints at the future of metroidvania gaming, but the genre would largely bypass its bloodthirsty, demanding design…at least until recent adventures like *Dead Cells* and *Hollow Knight* made twitch challenges cool again.

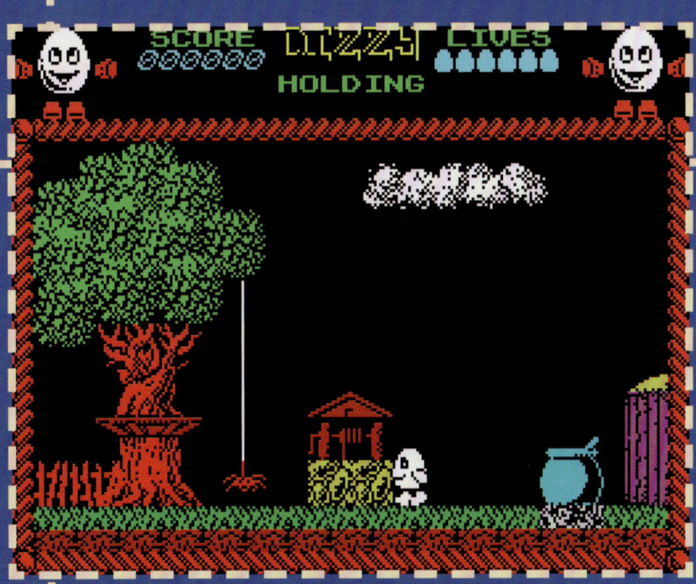

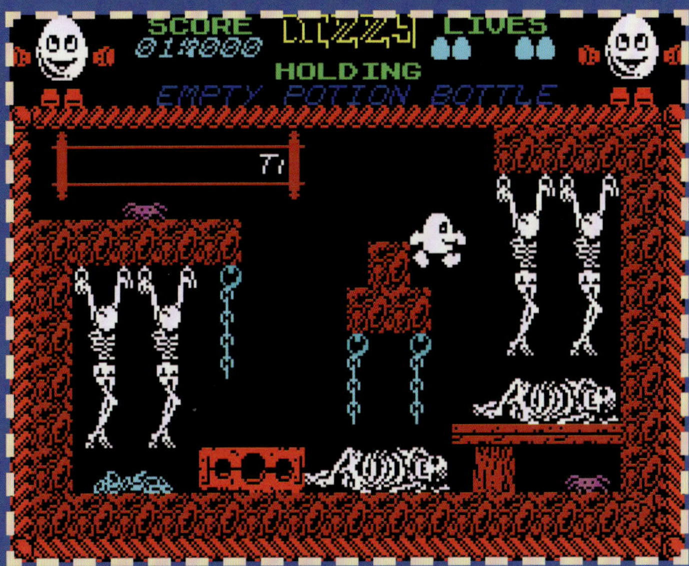

© Codemasters

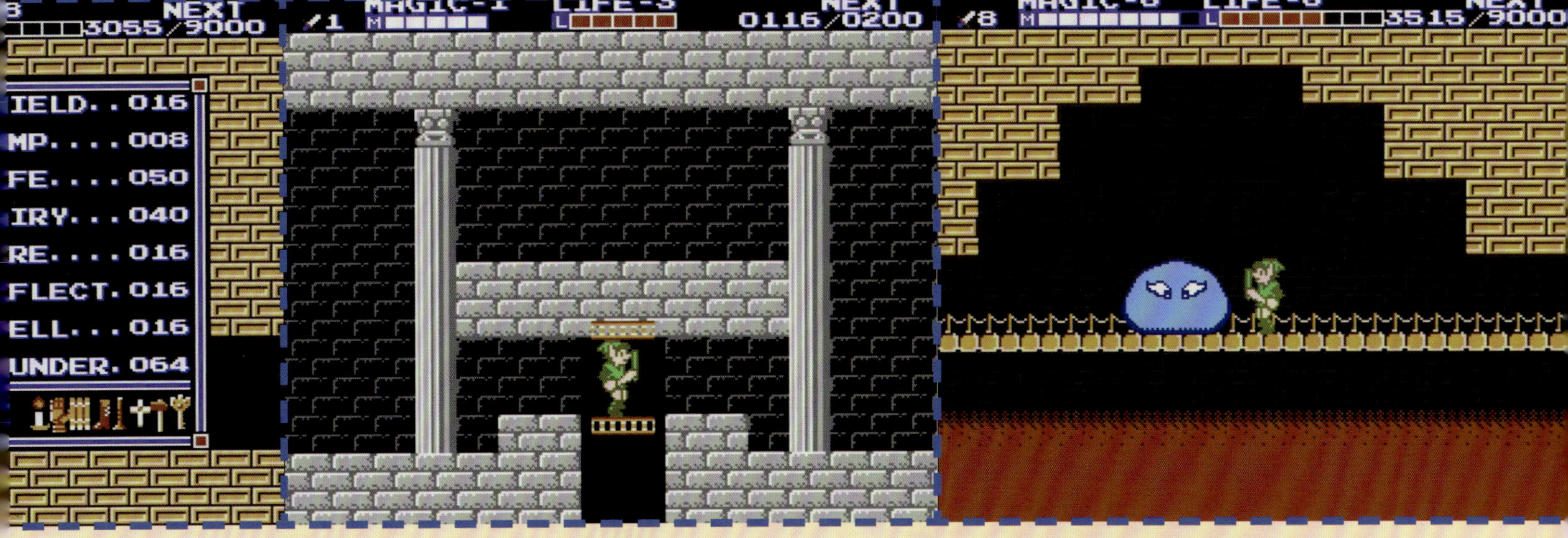

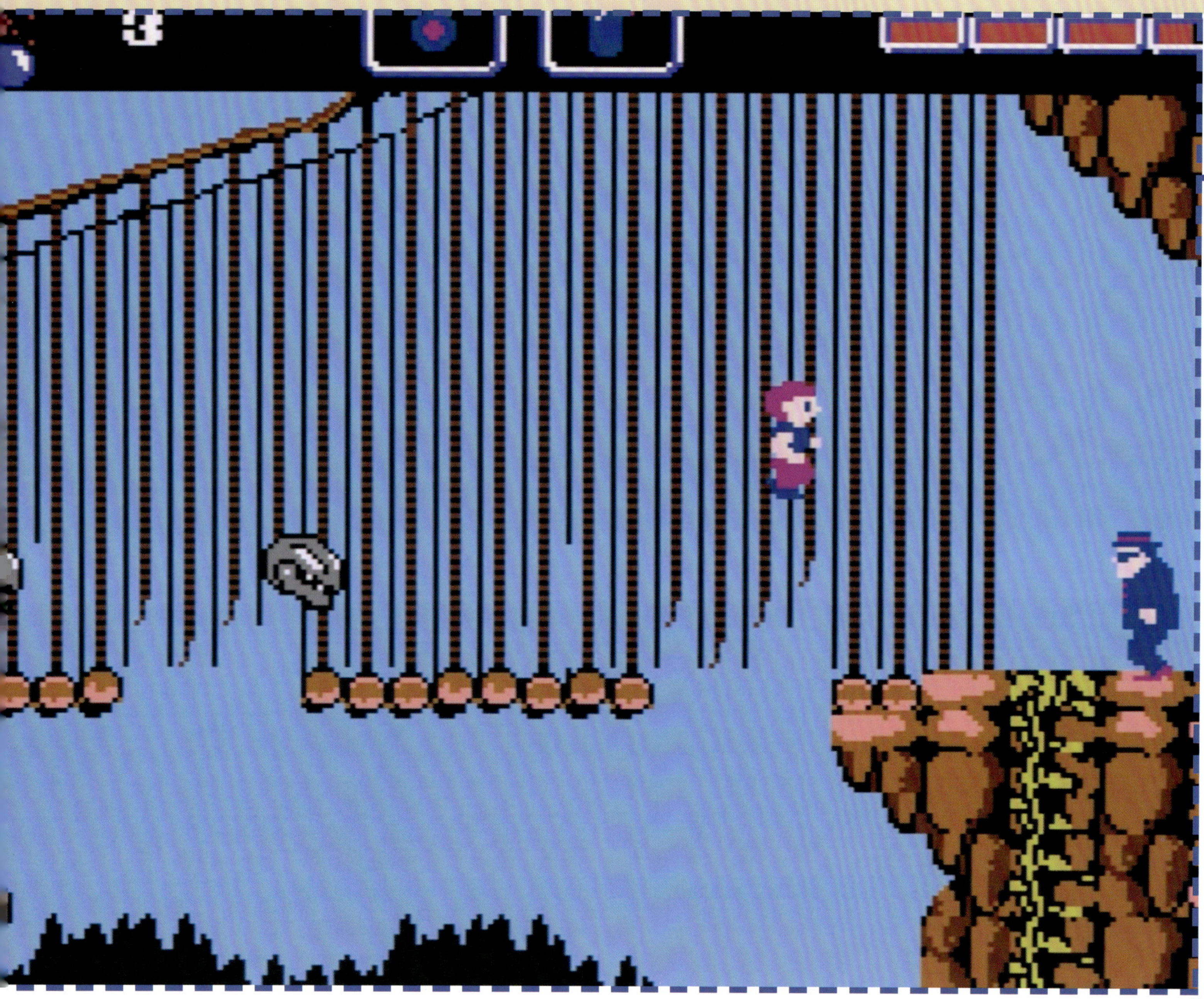

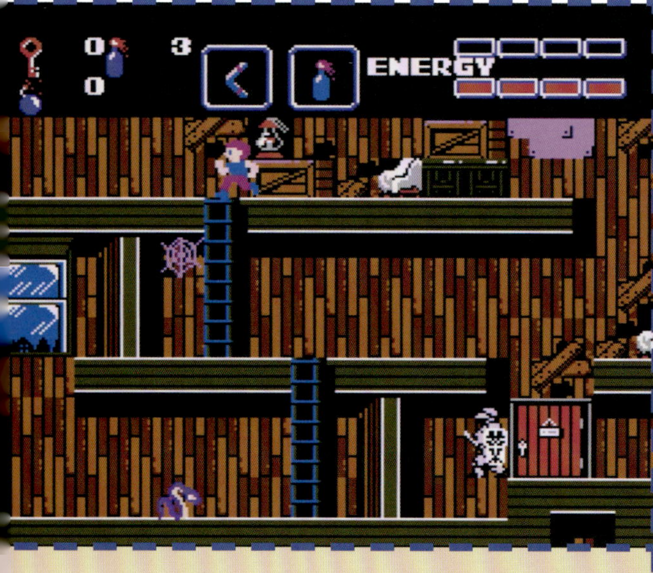

THE GOONIES II

PLATFORM: **FAMICOM / NES**
DEV: **KONAMI** | PUB: **KONAMI**
INITIAL RELEASE DATE: **MARCH 1987**

NOTABLE FOR: **AN OPEN-ENDED ACTION GAME IN A COMPLEX, MULTI-LAYERED SPACE**

GOOD ENUFF TO MATTER

A clever take on metroidvania concepts from Konami, *The Goonies II* offered a more refined and coherent effort than *Vampire Killer* despite being cut from the same cloth. The *II* in the title, incidentally, doesn't indicate a tie-in to some nonexistent sequel to the Richard Donner film but appears because this game is a sequel to Konami's *The Goonies* for Famicom and MSX. That earlier release had involved level-by-level progression, optional power-ups, and the need to explore each self-contained stage by traveling between "layers" of that level through skull-shaped doors. While the tools collected by protagonist Mikey only aided in exploration once, allowing Mikey to leap across a large chasm to unlock a shortcut, ***The Goonies*** contained all the pieces that would come into focus for this bigger, more ambitious sequel.

The Goonies II sees Mikey returning to the hideout of the criminal Fratelli family on a quest to rescue his kidnapped friends. There's also a mermaid involved, for some reason. But while this journey initially appears to take the same shape as the previous game, with the biggest immediate difference being that Mikey now wields a yo-yo as a weapon rather than just kicking giant rats to death, it soon becomes apparent that *The Goonies II* takes a very different approach to exploration. While this journey takes place across a world divided into discrete areas, these zones aren't treated as linear stages; they have no real endpoint, and merely serve as connections to other areas. You can wander through the world and return to any area you've already visited at any time.

In fact, *The Goonies II* makes backtracking mandatory. You often need to return to seeming dead ends once you acquire tools that can unlock a path or secret hidden there. Mikey collects gear as in the first *Goonies*, many of which are drawn from that game. These include a helmet to protect him from falling stalactites; a raincoat to keep him safe from steaming geysers and powerful waterfalls; and a pair of high-jumping spring shoes—now mandatory for progression thanks to a high ledge in a cave across the deadly bridge. However, many of the most crucial tools Mikey acquires this time don't come into play during the action portions of the game. Instead, you deploy them in the so-called Adventure Scenes.

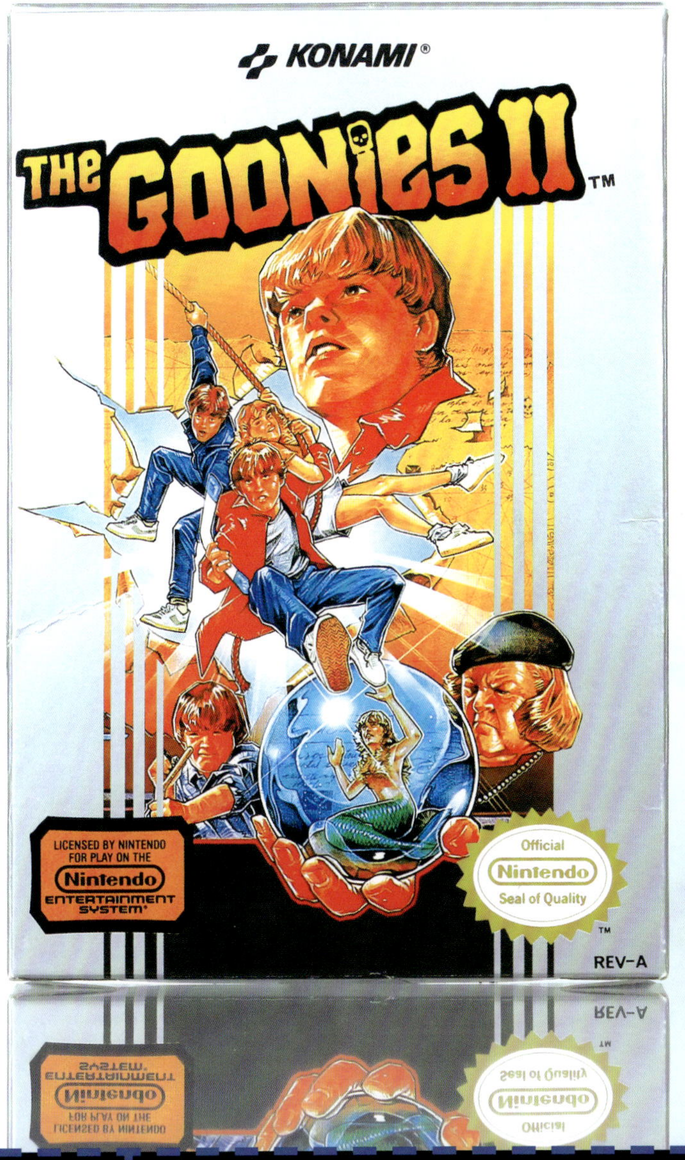

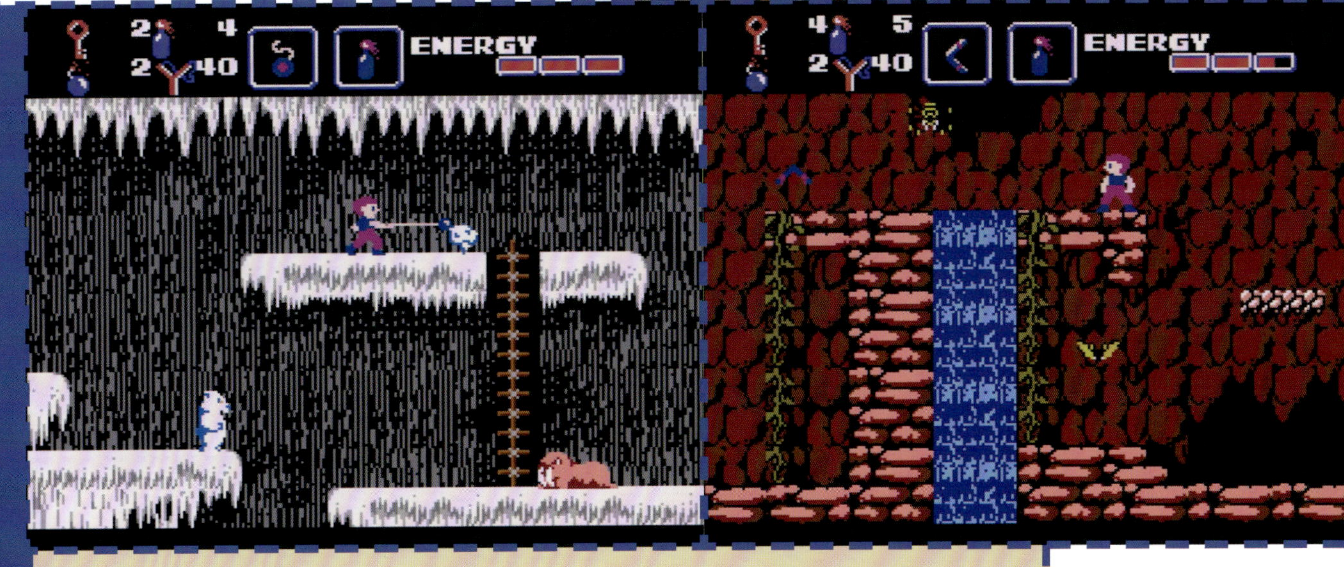

If *Zelda II* draws inspiration from role-playing games, The *Goonies II* takes its notes from a related genre: the adventure game. Since the NES used a two-button controller as its standard user interface rather than a keyboard, it takes less inspiration from *Zork* than it does from Enix's *Portopia Renzoku Satsujin Jiken*. While *Dragon Quest*'s window-and-menu-based interface was adapted directly from Horii and Nakamura's work on the Famicom conversion of *Portopia*, other developers borrowed that concept and applied it in new and interesting ways. Konami certainly came up with a more creative interpretation of *Portopia* here than the flood of banal murder mysteries that popped up in that classic's wake.

Being based in adventure and action rather than RPG, *The Goonies II* doesn't mess around with elements like experience points or character stats. Mikey simply gains an extra point of health every time he rescues a friend. His attack strength never increases; he can simply choose between three different weapons as the situation requires. The game lacks an economy, too. But you do meet plenty of NPCs, who offer you advice and give you important tools for your quest. These encounters all take place in the adventure scenes, which shift the action to a first-person perspective and play out through menu commands and cursors. Here, Mikey can punch walls and don x-ray specs to reveal secrets, smash ceilings and floors with a hammer to open hidden paths, dive into the water with a wet suit, and use keys on vaults and prisons to liberate treasures and his Goonie friends alike. In the finest adventure game tradition, this takes the form of a slow-paced hunt-and-search process in which you spend your time trying every tool in your inventory on every available surface. It's more interesting in concept than execution, as it kills the pace of the surrounding action sequences.

The adventure scenes appear in the game's "in-between" spaces. As in the first *Goonies*, Mikey passes back and forth between the "front" and "back" layers of the world to explore. In the original game, that involved a seamless process where you ducked into a door and appeared elsewhere. Here, once you enter a door, you need to navigate to the other layer by making menu selections and, potentially, revealing a path with tools. It's clumsy but intriguing, essentially turning the progression loop of *Metroid* into a menu-based adventure game—or rather, *back into* a menu-based adventure game. This format didn't make its way into many other games; outside of FCI's *Dr. Chaos*, it was a nonstarter. But it gave Konami another opportunity to kick the tires of the exploratory platformer genre, and it makes *The Goonies II* one of the few action-RPG type games to draw an overt line back to the genre's primal adventure game roots. *M*

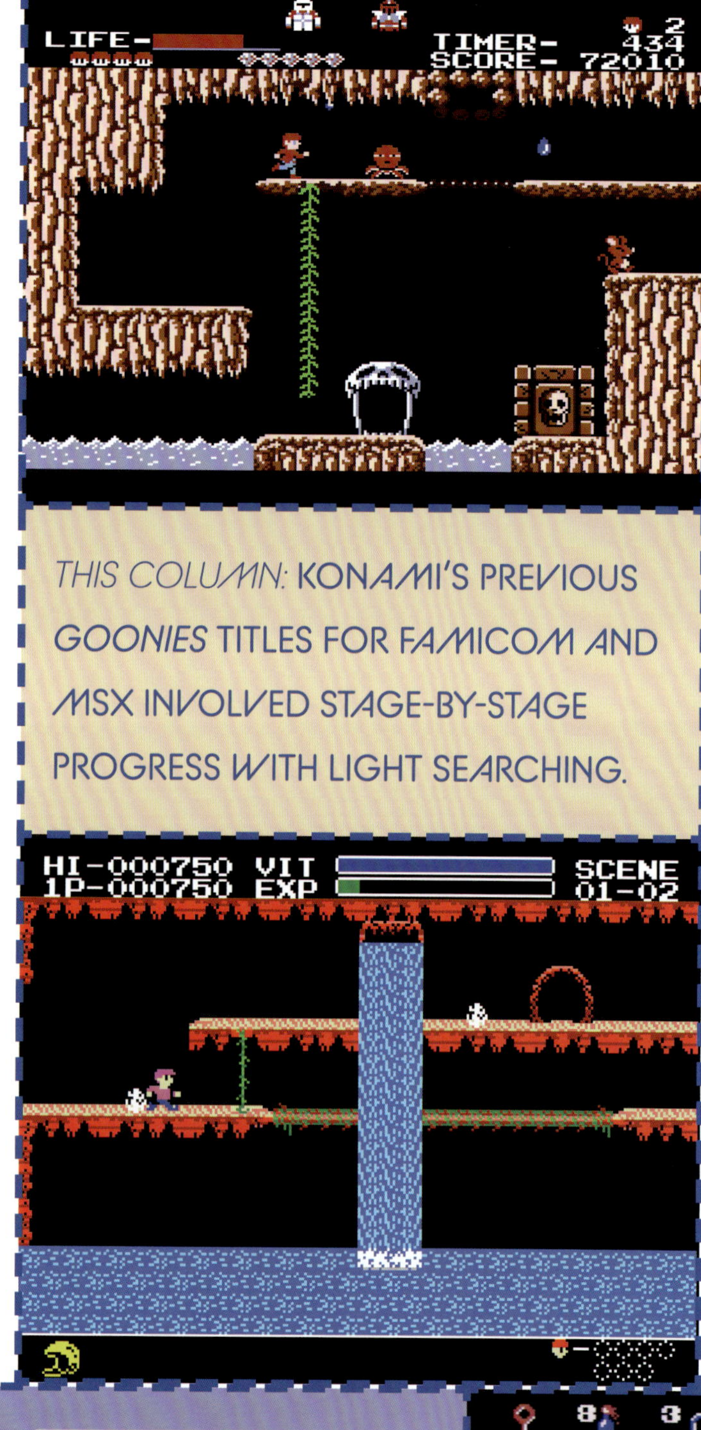

THIS COLUMN: KONAMI'S PREVIOUS *GOONIES* TITLES FOR FAMICOM AND MSX INVOLVED STAGE-BY-STAGE PROGRESS WITH LIGHT SEARCHING.

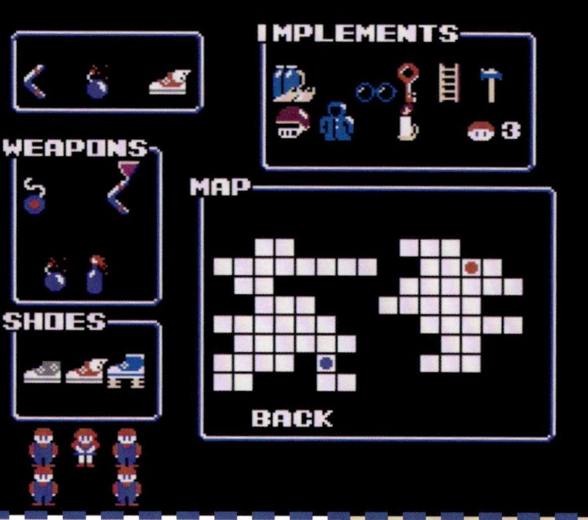

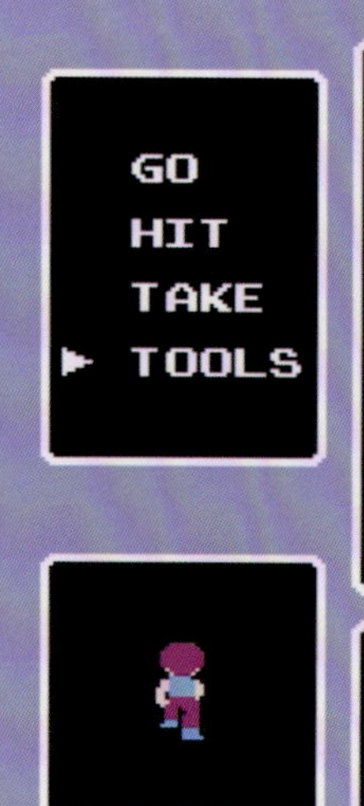

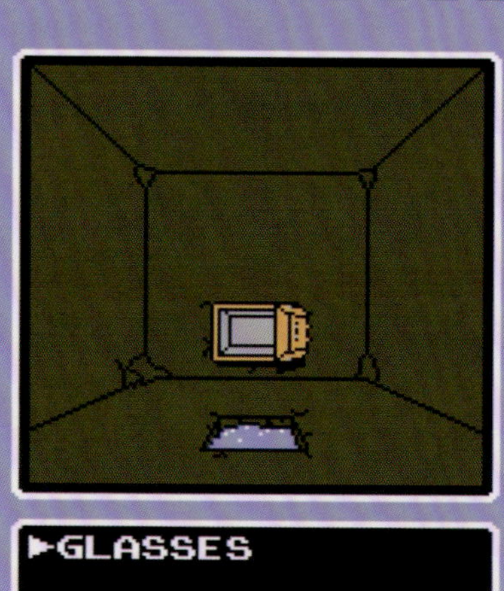

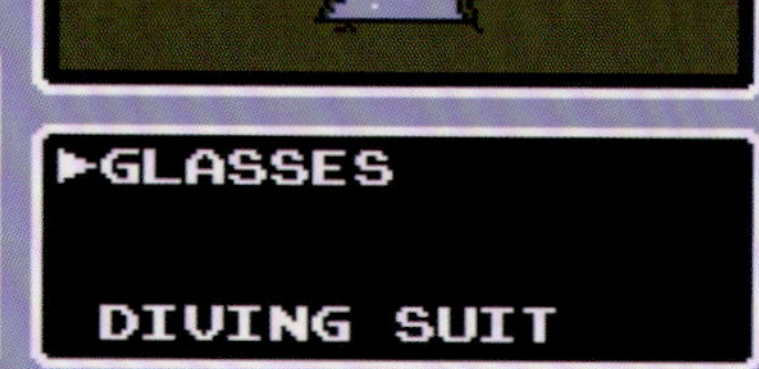

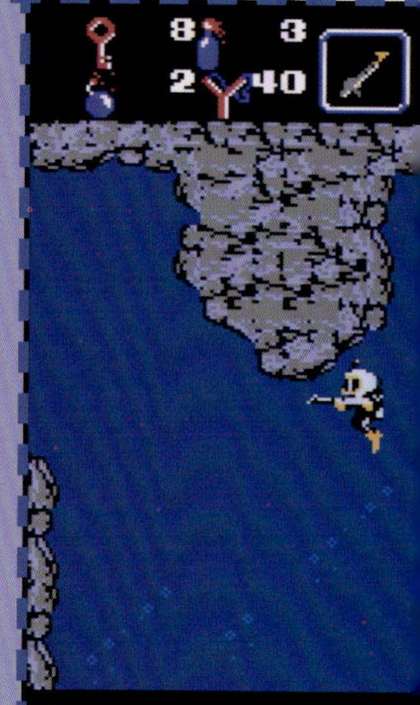

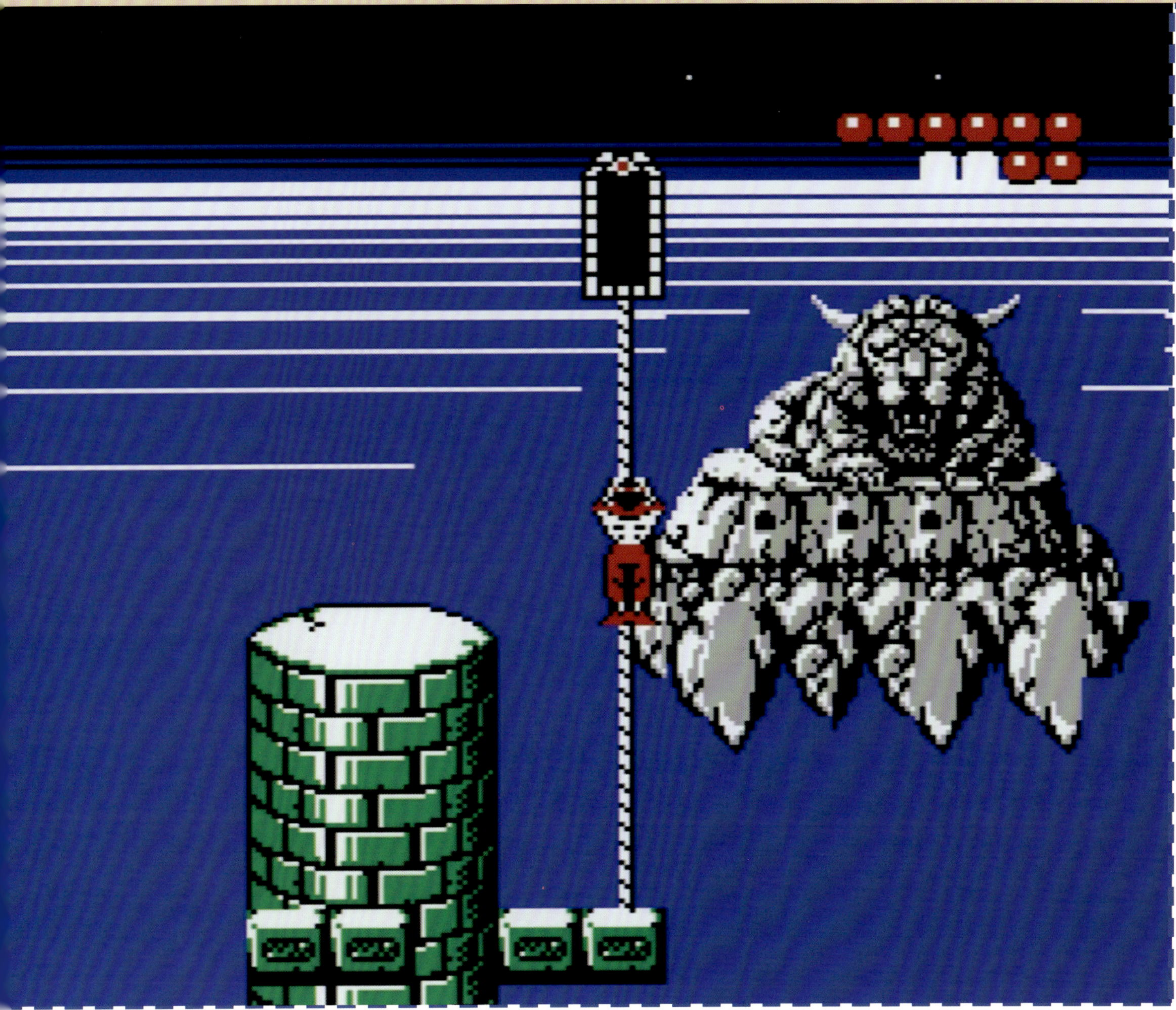

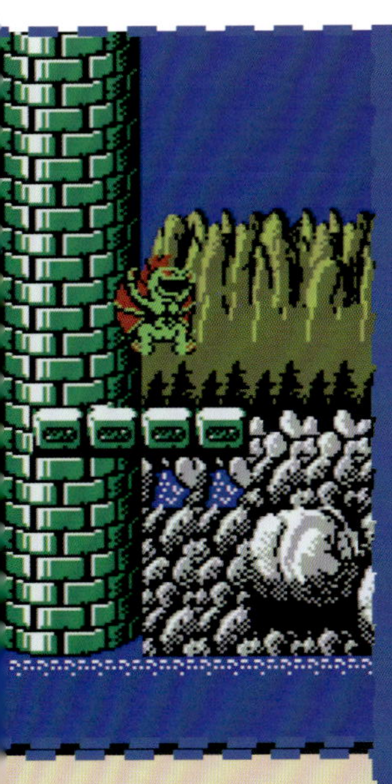

RYGAR

PLATFORM: **FAMICOM / NES**
DEV: **TECMO** | PUB: **TECMO**
INITIAL RELEASE: **APRIL 1987**

NOTABLE FOR: **HUB-BASED WORLD DESIGN**

SUNRISE, SUNSET

A more subtle approach to the action-RPG than *Zelda II*—or maybe just a less confident one—arrived a few months after that title in the form of a game whose exploratory nature amounted to an unexpected swerve. Tecmo's *Rygar* debuted in arcades as a *Conan the Barbarian*–inspired adventure featuring a beefy warrior who ran about the world slashing things up with his bizarre Diskarmor weapon, a chain flail with a large, shield-like disk at the end rather than a spiked ball. It played out across dozens of stages that contained almost no variety from one another save the background wallpaper: a tedious slog of repetition.

Rygar on NES was nothing like that. Besides carrying over the hero, his weirdo weapon, the visual motifs of stage backgrounds, and enemy designs, Tecmo's adaptation for Nintendo amounted to a different game altogether. This Rygar abandoned the arcade's driving premise of running left to right along a monotonous line fighting enemies forever, discarded the notion of a timer, and rejected making enemies indestructible once time was up. Essentially, Rygar for NES became Tecmo's own *Wing of Madoola*.

Of course, having been released a mere three months after *Zelda II* and four months after *Wing of Madoola*, *Rygar*'s facelift almost certainly wasn't inspired directly by those games. Again, it was just something in the air. *Dragon Quest* fever gripped Japan, and developers looked to games like *The Tower of Druaga* and *Xanadu* for inspiration on ways to revitalize arcade games for home release on an aging, underpowered console. Home ports couldn't compete graphically, so instead they promised meatier, more involving gameplay. This would become a recurring theme on the NES in particular, and *Rygar* led the charge of reinvention.

Interestingly, *Rygar* makes use of perspective-switching to distinguish combat from exploration, as seen in *Zelda II*. The line between the two isn't quite as clear as in that game, however. Where Zelda II's overhead view resembled a classic RPG-style abstraction of a map with no direct combat, *Rygar*'s alternate viewpoint retained its fundamental action ethos and required players to battle enemies with the same combat mechanics as the

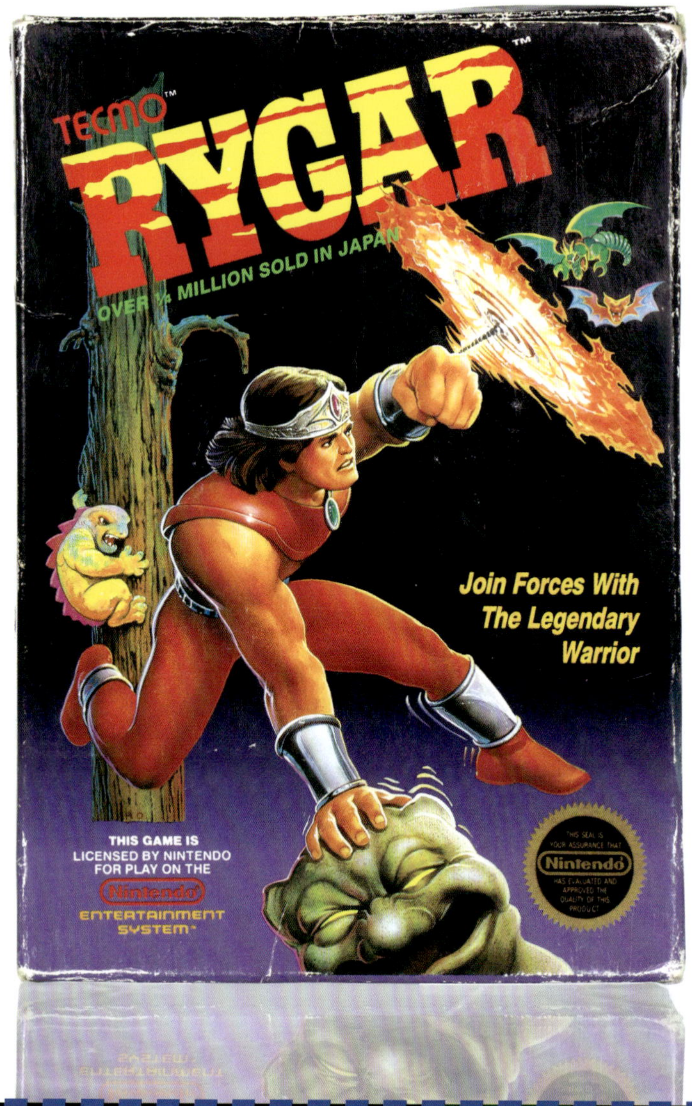

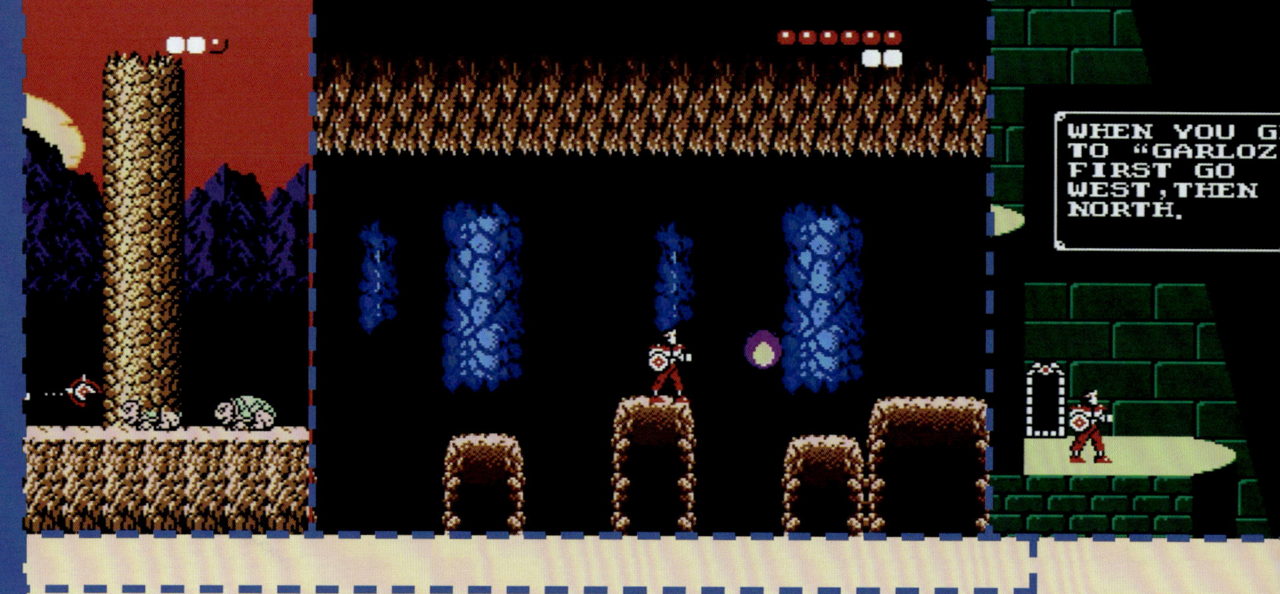

side-scrolling areas. It essentially shifts between *Zelda II* and *Zelda I* in its gameplay, with the many key portions of the adventure playing out through top-down sequences, including its central hub area, Garloz, and the lairs of several boss enemies. Players spend the most time in Garloz, which allows the hero to quickly move between regions of the world. *Rygar* requires backtracking—most notably you need to return to the opening stages once you acquire the necessary tools to explore a robot battlefield in the sky—but rather than forcing you to hoof it through lengthy interconnected platforming sequences, you simply move between areas by navigating Garloz.

The bulk of side-scrolling sequences in *Rygar* work a lot like *Zelda II*'s dungeons, in that you visit them once and need never return after you've completed them. Beating an area boss typically rewards the game's protagonist, the Warrior of Argool, with a device that aids his navigation of the world: a rope, a hook to use the rope as a zip line, that sort of thing. You also need to collect mystic crests, which amount to fancy-looking keys; they exist only to grant you access to other spaces and don't actually have any value or use within the game's toolbox. And, yes, there's an experience system here that allows the Warrior to grow in strength and durability. As you destroy enemies, you gain Tone and Last points—a dual stream of experience. As Tone increases, the Warrior's attacks grow more powerful. Meanwhile, Last grants him additional hit points as it hits certain thresholds. It's a very opaque experience system, but it nevertheless comes straight from the world of role-playing games. The Warrior also gains consumable magic points—Mind—which allow him to cast three spells that he knows from the outset of the quest; at no point does he master additional spells.

Rygar feels clumsy compared to *Zelda II*. The combat can be glitchy, and your navigational tools—which deploy automatically, at least in theory—can be very imprecise, especially in the top-down zones. The murky platform edge boundaries can easily cause you to misjudge an approach to a grappling point and plunge into the water, game over. It can also be tough to judge your relationship to enemies and projectiles in the top-down sequences. Worse, you often need to jump in these scenes—a rarity in action games viewed from this perspective, and understandably so given how shakily it works here.

Even so, you can't help but admire what Tecmo attempted to do with *Rygar*. They took a boring, bog-standard arcade belt scroller and turned it into a rich, multi-format, exploratory platform with RPG mechanics and NPCs to talk to. *Rygar* doesn't seem to have had much direct influence on the design of future games, making it a sort of metroidvania Galápagos, but it's still worth playing.

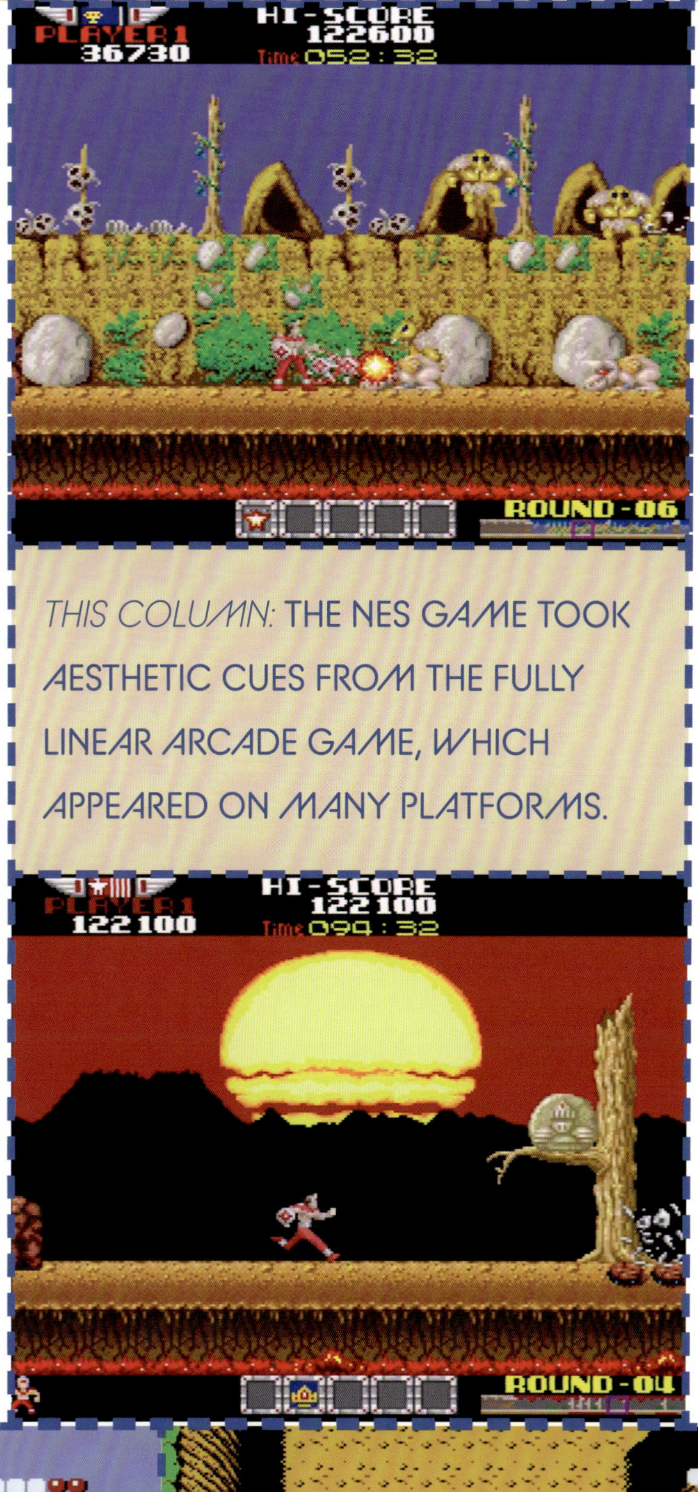

THIS COLUMN: THE NES GAME TOOK AESTHETIC CUES FROM THE FULLY LINEAR ARCADE GAME, WHICH APPEARED ON MANY PLATFORMS.

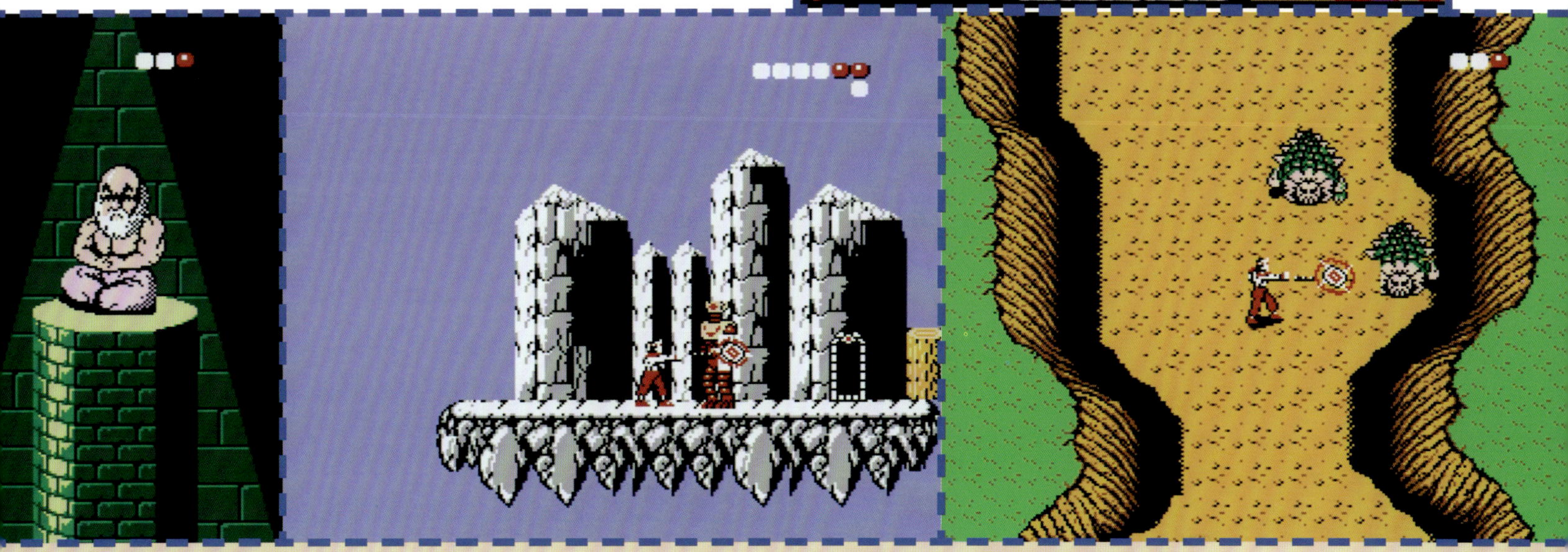

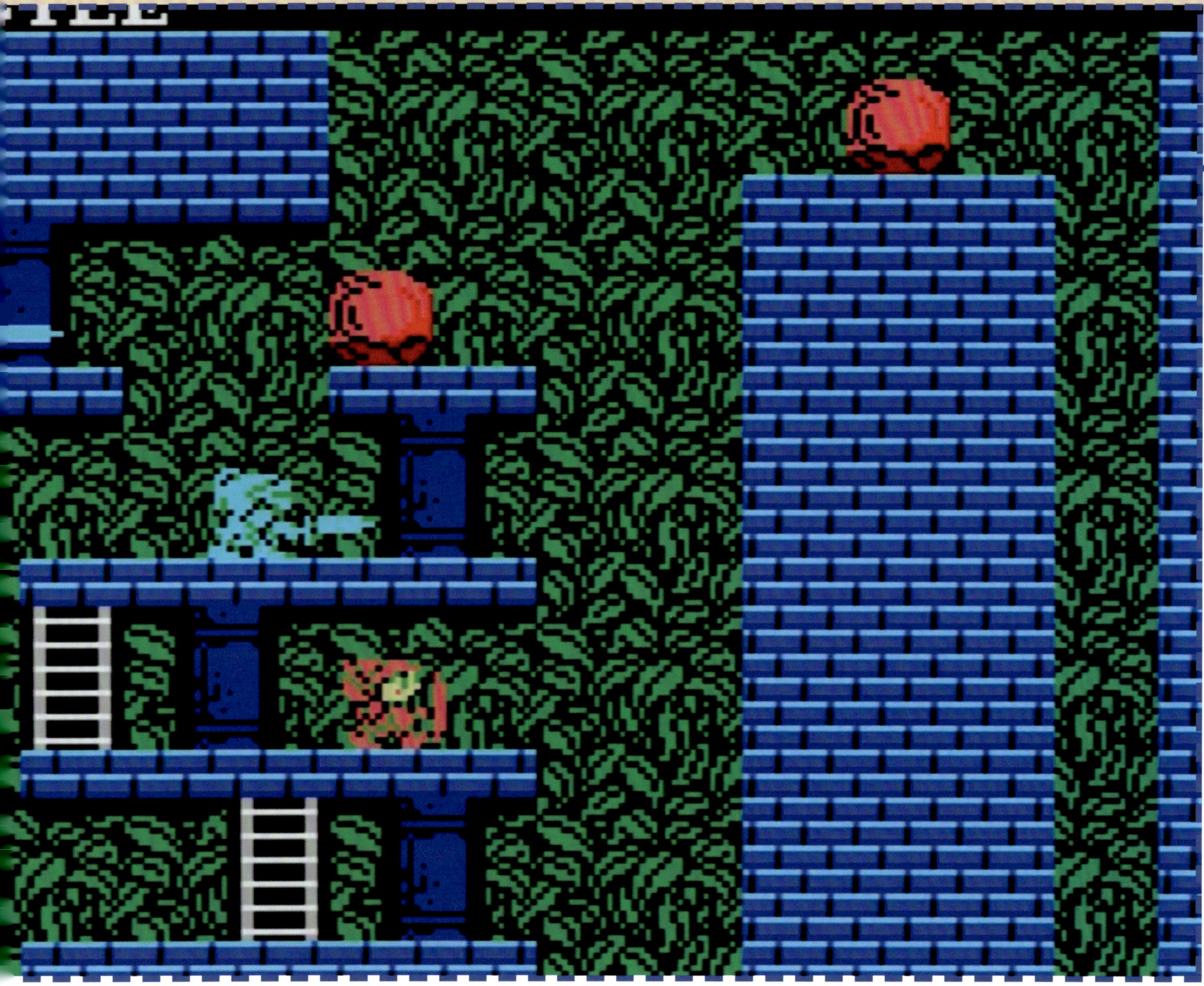

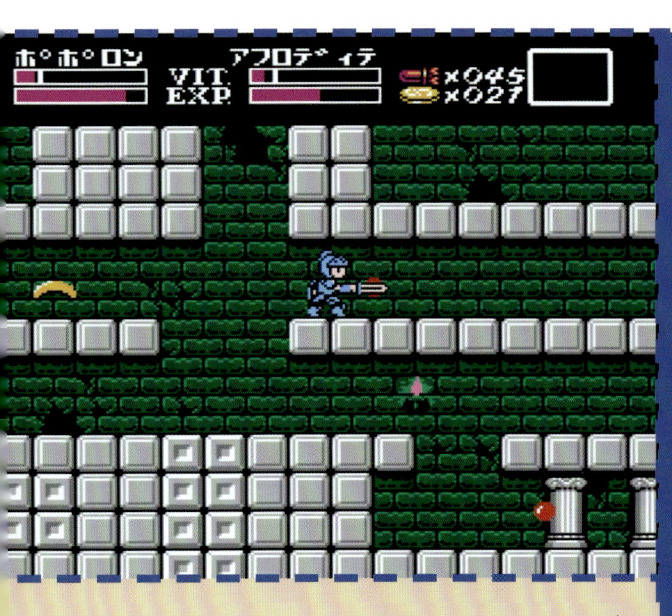

KNIGHTMARE II

PLATFORM: **MSX / FAMICOM**
DEV: **KONAMI** | PUB: **KONAMI**
INITIAL RELEASE DATE: **APRIL. 1987**
SHOWN HERE: **NINTENDO FAMICOM VERSION, 1987**

NOTABLE FOR: **OPEN-ENDED MULTI-CHARACTER EXPLORATION**

LIKE A DREAM

One of the less-heralded moments in the evolution of the metroidvania arrived on MSX courtesy of Konami just a few weeks after they published *The Goonies II*. As with that Goonies sequel, *Majou Densetsu II: Gariusu no Meikyuu* (*Knightmare II: The Maze of Galious*) represents a marked increase in design complexity over its predecessor. The original *Knightmare* had been a simple, auto-scrolling vertical shooter, which stood out for its unusual emphasis on Western fantasy stylings over the science fiction themes more common to the format. Starring a small knight marching ever upward through scrolling fields of monsters, *Knightmare* played pretty much like a standard scrolling shooter, with aesthetics that fell in line with contemporary works like Namco's *Dragon Spirit* and Taito's *KiKi KaiKai* (*Pocky & Rocky*).

Knightmare II plays nothing like that, instead reflecting the hottest trend in Japanese game design for 1987: tacked-on RPG elements. And, rather than playing as an auto-scrolling top-down shooter, *Knightmare II* on MSX unfolds as a side-on platform action game with ample exploration and a bit of inventory management. While largely unknown outside Japan, *Knightmare II* has become something of a cult favorite in its home territory. That's why the game might seem curiously familiar to Western game enthusiasts despite it never having been released in America or Europe: it heavily influenced the design of NIGORO's *La-Mulana* games. The original freeware version of *La-Mulana* in particular feels carefully crafted in the image of *Knightmare II* for MSX: limited graphics, flip-screen scrolling, restricted character movement and controls.

That's how *Knightmare II* started, though the Famicom conversion enjoyed a significant tech upgrade with more detailed and colorful visuals and smoother scrolling. This makes *Knightmare II* an interesting case study. It exists as a transitional point between older, single-screen proto-metroidvania titles like *Montezuma's Revenge* and more contemporary takes on the format, such as *Metroid* and *Castlevania II*.

Knightmare II introduces another interesting first for this style of game: while protagonist Popolon only has one life, which is measured by a single life bar, he's not the only hero of

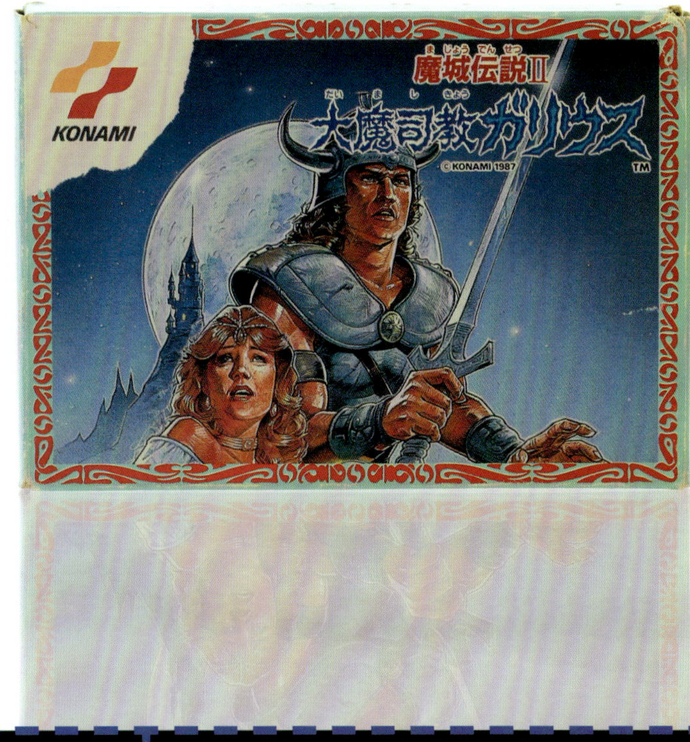

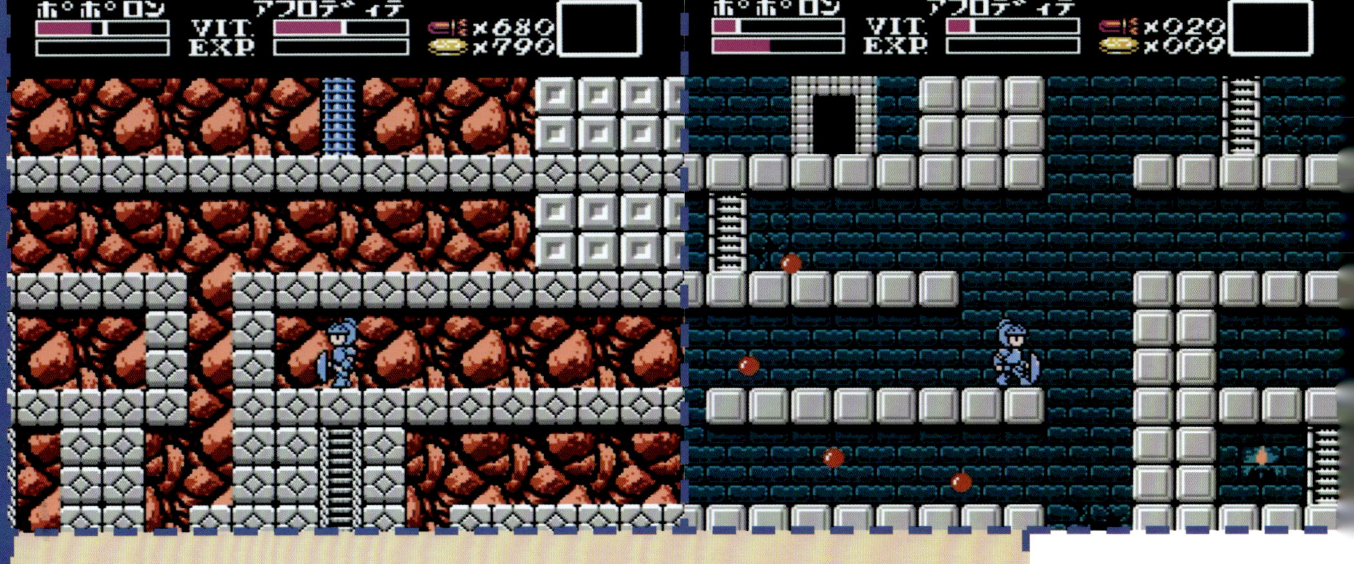

this story. You can freely switch between characters, swapping in heroine Aphrodite (who looks exactly like Popolon, but in pink armor rather than blue) to take up the quest as well. Konami would make frequent use of character-switching mechanics throughout the 8-bit era, as seen in *Konami Wai Wai World* and *Teenage Mutant Ninja Turtles*. As a sort of early conceptual prototype, *Knightmare II* doesn't feel as fully realized as those subsequent works. The differences between Popolon and Aphrodite are less about obvious, unique combat skills (as in Nin- tendo's *Yume Koujou: Doki Doki Panic*, which debuted a few months later) and more about the nuances of their minute advantages. Aphrodite is better at maneuvering through water, gets better prices on goods in certain shops, and handles certain secondary weapons more effectively than her husband. *Knightmare II* encourages you to experiment with the two characters across a variety of situations, exploiting their strengths however you can. It invites players to try and fail repeatedly until they find the best approach for each situation. It's not a punishing game, exactly; more like an obstinate one.

The titular *Maze of Galious* is filled not only with monsters but also locked doors, hidden passages, and seemingly inaccessible areas. Popolon and Aphrodite can make use of a variety of weapons that help them battle enemies while also doubling as tools to forge new paths, in keeping with the tenets of *Metroid*. For example, you can acquire magical devices that basically function as landmines, which are as effective at detonating monsters too low for the heroes to hit as they are at blasting open new passages in the floor. As with *Metroid*, most of the hidden passages and destructible blocks you need to uncover to advance aren't marked or obvious, so you need to work through a process of trial and error—a fact that makes *Knightmare II* a little difficult to revisit in the here and now, the same as many metroidvanias of this primal era.

And really, aside from allowing you to switch between two slightly different characters, *Knightmare II* doesn't break a lot of new ground. Even the seeming RPG elements—namely, the experience meter beneath each character's health bar—feel superficial at best. Maxing out your experience bar doesn't make your heroes more powerful or durable…it just refills your health meter. Still, Konami managed to capture the essential intrigue of dropping players into a massive, hazardous maze and letting them sort things out. This is a slower and less abstruse opposite number to Falcom's *Legacy of the Wizard*, which shipped just a few weeks after *Knightmare II*. You can easily understand how it would have made a big impression on players back in 1987, and why die-hard fans continue to carry a torch for it.

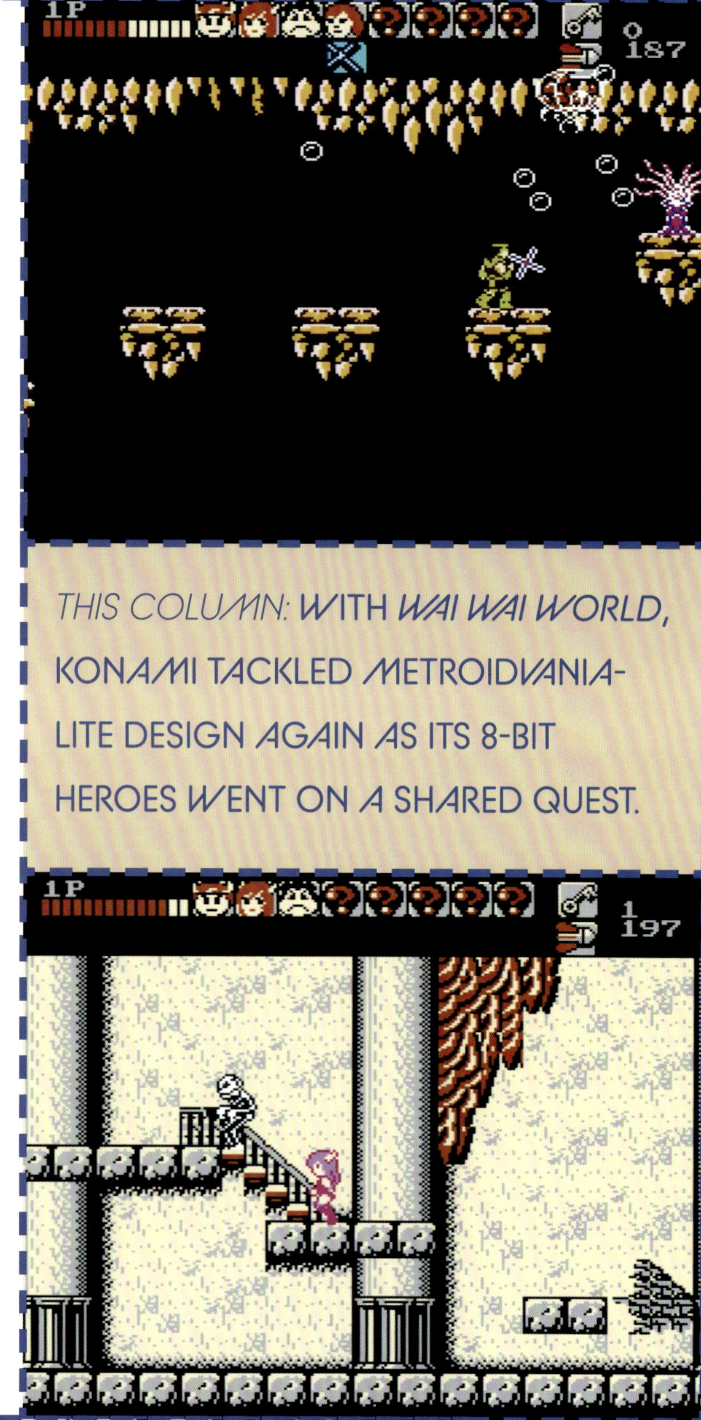

THIS COLUMN: **WITH WAI WAI WORLD, KONAMI TACKLED METROIDVANIA-LITE DESIGN AGAIN AS ITS 8-BIT HEROES WENT ON A SHARED QUEST.**

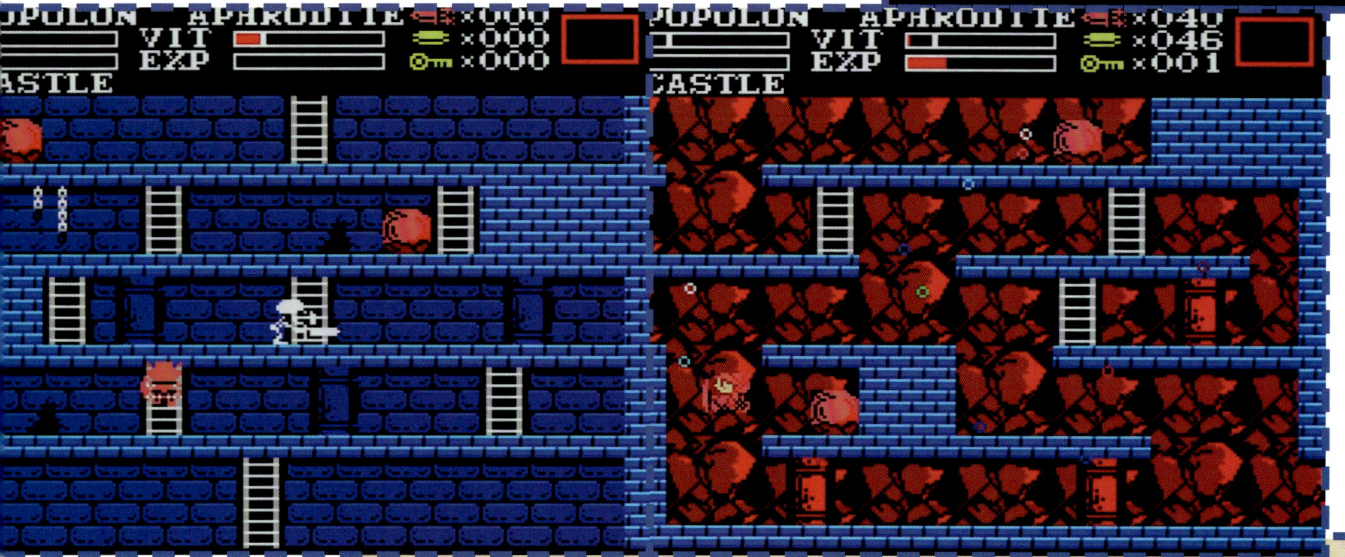

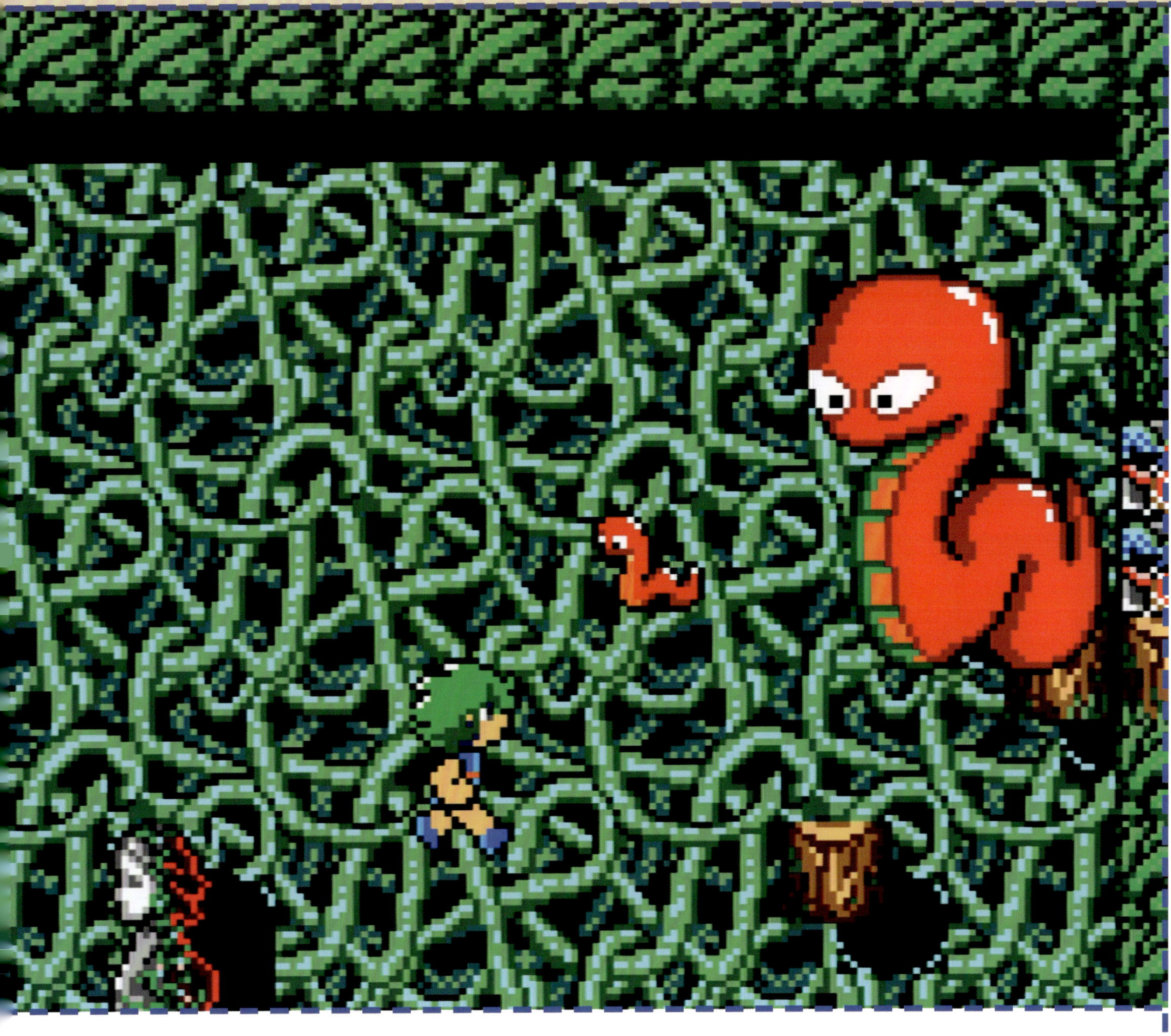

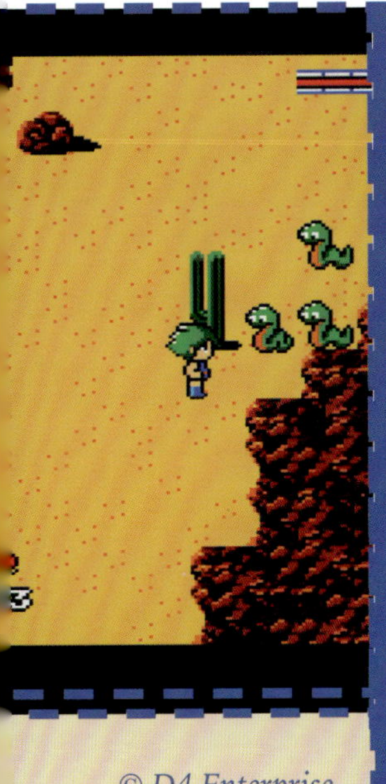

GOLVELLIUS
VALLEY OF DOOM

PLATFORM: **MSX / MASTER SYSTEM**
DEV: **COMPILE** | PUB: **COMPILE**
INITIAL RELEASE: APRIL 1987
SHOWN HERE: **SEGA MASTER SYSTEM VERSION, 1988**

NOTABLE FOR: *A MULTI-FORMAT ACTION-RPG*

A HYBRID OF HYRULE

Golvellius: Valley of Doom is known best in the US and Europe through its port to Sega's 8-bit Master System console. However, this Compile-developed action-RPG originally made its debut on MSX home computers. Many notable Japanese games of the '80s got their start on MSX before making their way to home consoles. Being an action-oriented game, the Master System port of *Golvellius* holds up better than the MSX original available on Nintendo Switch via EGGConsole thanks to the Master System's support for smoother scrolling and animation.

The game's full Japanese title neatly sums up its premise: *Maou Golvellius,* or"Demon King Golvellius" (it's a quest to stop a demon called Golvellius). It plays like a combination of *The Legend of Zelda* and *Zelda II*. The overworld resembles the first *Zelda*'s Hyrule, a grid of single-screen spaces with progression gated by items and quest goal. While you need to purchase most of the keys required to advance, these often only become available once you complete certain objectives—usually defeating a boss that resides in one of the dungeons throughout the land. Rather than taking the form of the top-down mazes seen in *The Legend of Zelda*, however, these dungeons play out more like action games. Think a streamlined *Zelda II*...which is to say, something closer to *Rygar* or *Dragon Buster*.

Some dungeons scroll left to right, while others adopt a top-down perspective. The side-scrolling dungeons make use of a ratchet scrolling effect, meaning that movement only flows in one direction. In fact, if you walk backward and touch the left edge of the screen, you'll actually be kicked out and have to start all over! The same goes for *Golvellius*'s top-down dungeons, which scroll automatically, forcing you to fight as you scramble to stay ahead of the bottom edge.

It's an odd mash-up of arcade-action and a Hydlide-inspired action-RPG, but it largely works... just as you'd expect from Compile, who had a knack for combining genres in interesting ways. While it's not quite a proper metroidvania, despite its emphasis on side-scrolling action, its unusual mixture of elements made for a memorable and decidedly one-of-a-kind adventure. *M*

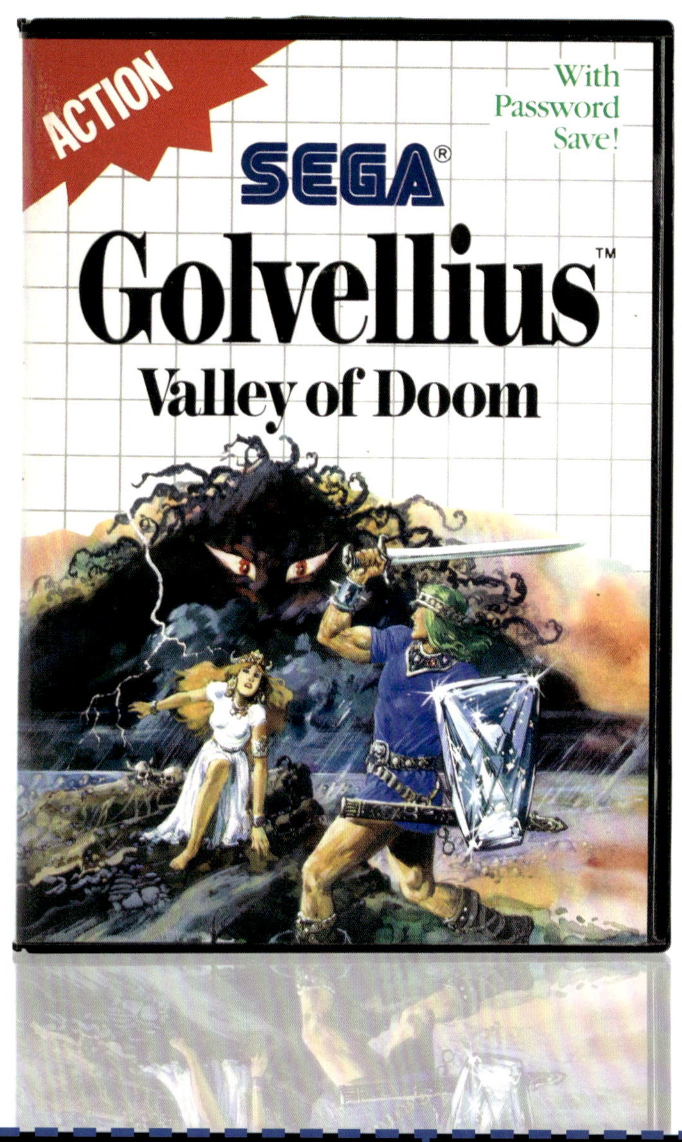

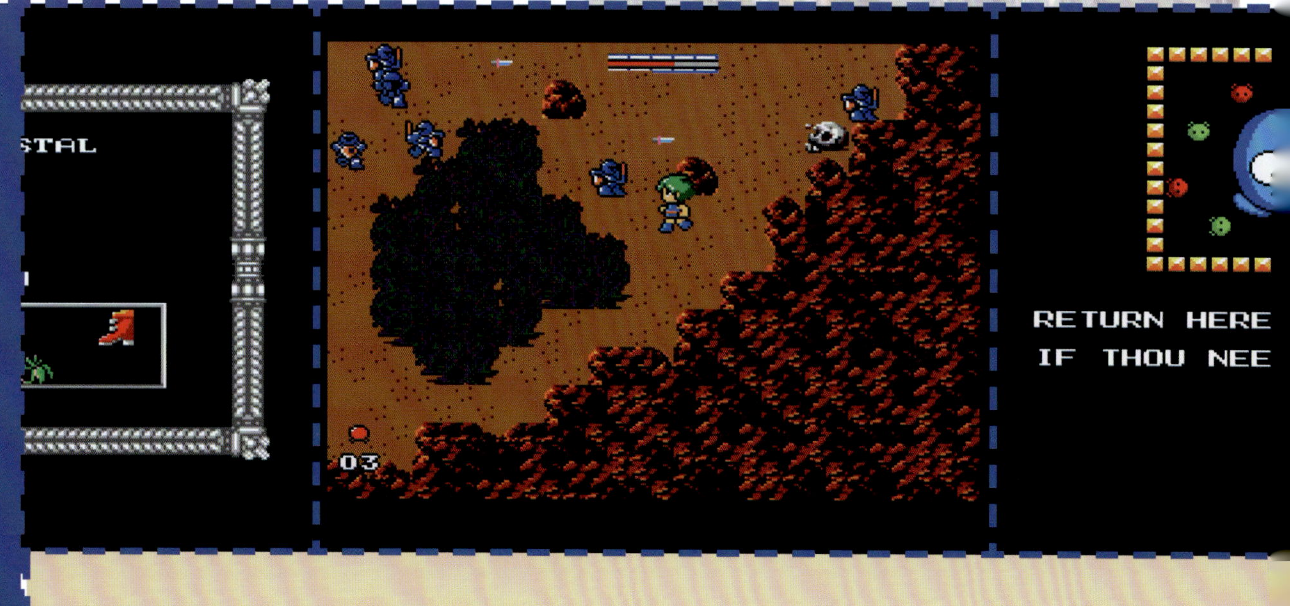

BLACK TIGER

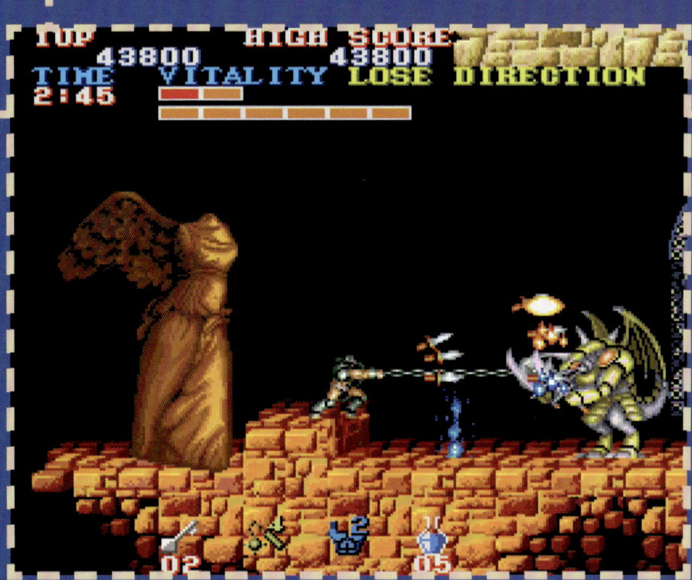

Building on the design of *Bionic Commando*—an arcade game that allowed players to roam large spaces designed as much around vertical movement as the more traditional horizontal—Capcom followed up with a spiritual successor called *Black Tiger*. The connections may not seem obvious as first glance, given the vast thematic gulf between the two works, but look beyond the shift from near-future military action to sword-and-sorcery barbarism and the mechanical and conceptual progression present comes into focus.

Like *Bionic Commando*, *Black Tiger* centers around a single hero who needs to make his way through immense spaces by advancing forward and backward between spells of upward and downward traversal. The protagonist here even flings a chain that resembles the grappling arm in *Bionic Commando*—though the similarity is strictly visual. Here, the hero's chain flail doesn't help him move around the game world; it simply slashes enemies at a remove. To make your way upward, you need to hop across platforms and climb pillars, making this a more grounded form of action than *Bionic Commando*'s.

Black Tiger doesn't break away from the older game's level-by-level structure; like *Bionic Commando*, it consists of a string of sequential stages that require a modest amount of exploration and discovery to complete. Once you finish a stage, you move along to the next. There are more stages here, and they're larger, but what really puts *Black Tiger* on the map of metroidvania history is that it was an early pioneer of bringing role-playing elements to an arcade-platform action game. The hero grows progressively more powerful as he earns experience (read: racks up a high score) and collects cash and spells from fallen foes and treasure chests. You can spend those earnings in shops you find along the way, beefing up the main character even more. Capcom seemingly lifted this concept from Sega games like *Fantasy Zone* and *Wonder Boy in Monster Land*, but it feels more at home here, in a game drenched in RPG aesthetics, than it did in a pastel-colored shoot-'em-up. Capcom would continue to build on the concept with more intricate arcade-action RPGs like *Willow* and *Magic Sword*: grand heroic fantasy.

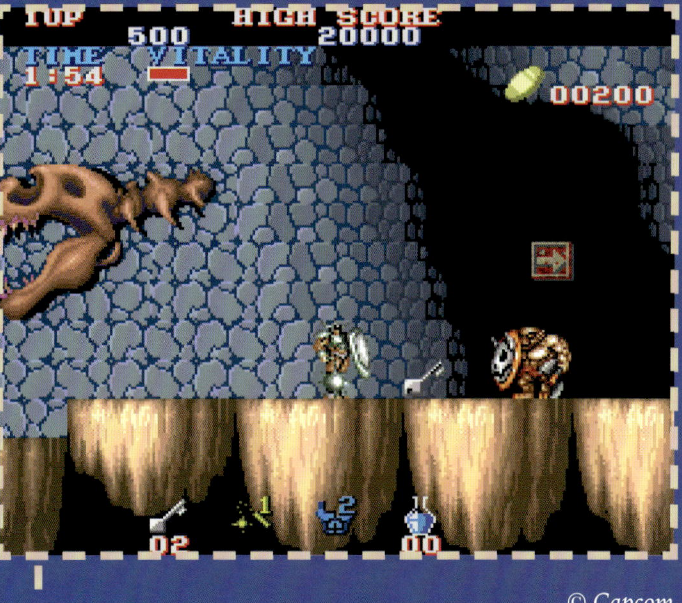

© Capcom

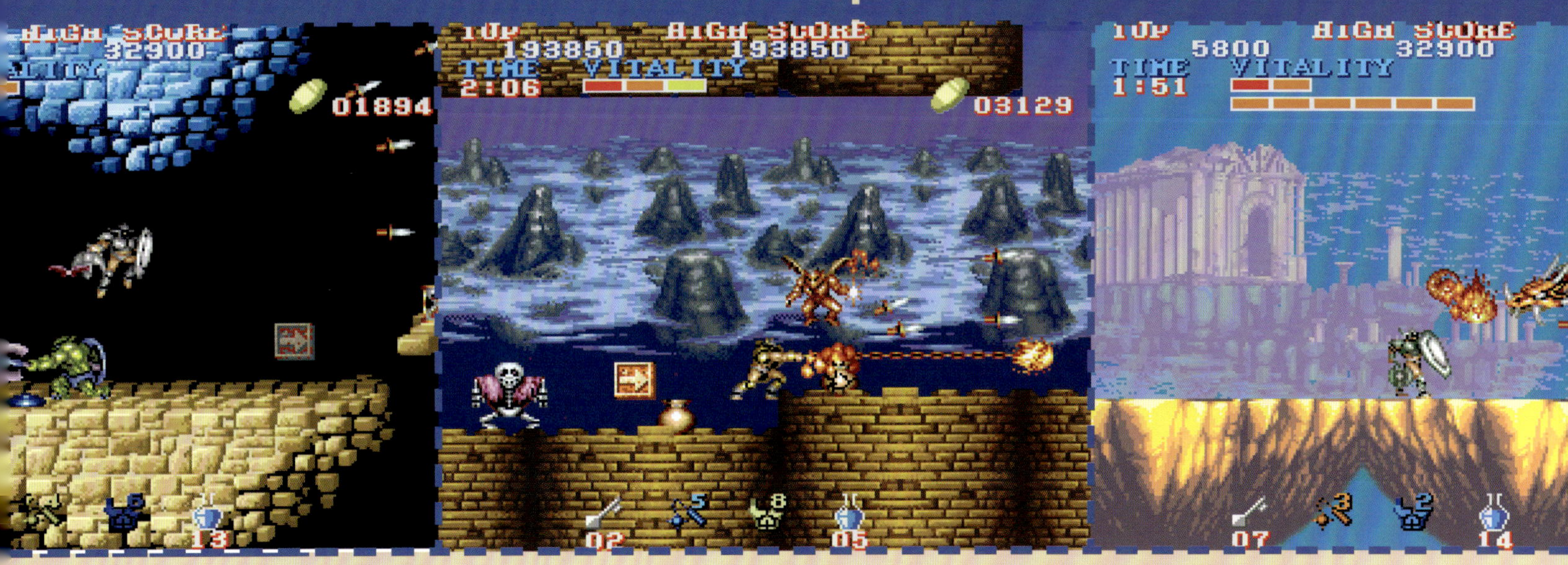

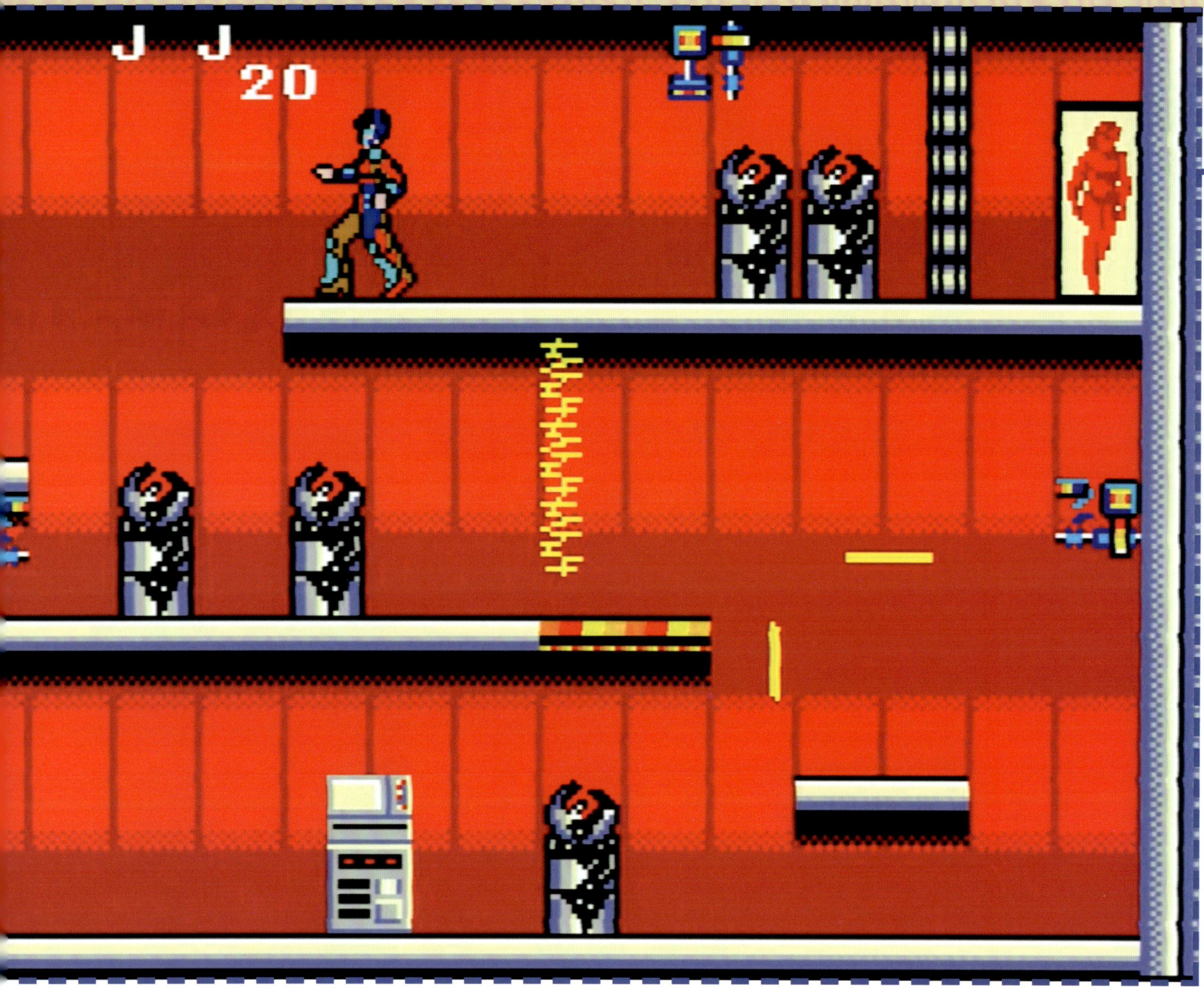

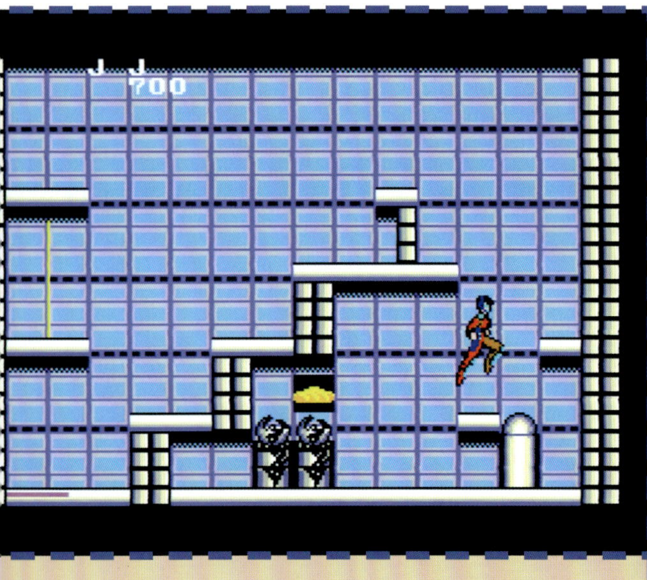

ZILLION

PLATFORM: **MARK III / MASTER SYSTEM**
DEV: **SEGA** | PUB: **SEGA**
INITIAL RELEASE: **MAY 1987**

A ZILLION LITTLE REASONS

Sega's *Zillion* for Master System, with an initial Japanese release in May 1987, tends to be brushed aside as a mere Sega-made *Metroid* imitator. This is wildly incorrect. Aside from its escape sequence (which does appear to be a more convoluted lift of a similar epilogue from *Metroid*), *Zillion* takes almost all its inspiration from Epyx's *Impossible Mission*. Given Sega's propensity for localizing Western computer hits into visually appealing arcade and console releases, as they had done with *Choplifter*, *Pitfall II*, and *H.E.R.O.*, it's entirely possible that the game began life with the intent of directly adapting Epyx's adventure under license. Or, more likely, *Zillion* ended up the way it did because the company held the rights to a different license altogether (a toy light gun complete and its Tatsunoko-produced anime tie-in, *Akai Koudan Zillion*) and the easiest way to create the tie-in game in time for the product launch was simply to crib notes from a proven success.

Whatever the back story, *Zillion* places players in control of the show's primary protagonist, a young soldier named J. J. of the White Knights task force, as he infiltrates enemy bases to put an end to an enemy plot and rescue his missing comrades, Apple and Champ. Although the game initially appears to be a simple run-and-gun scrolling platformer, that turns out not to be the case. After completing the linear introductory sequence, in which J. J. runs right to left from the hatch to his team's landing craft while blasting bad guys, you reach an elevator that leads you to the primary game environment: a massive, sprawling, interconnected maze of a base made up of dozens of individual, single-screen rooms connected by elevators and corridors.

Zillion verges on being a "true" metroidvania. It offers extensive freedom of exploration, and J. J.'s upgrade path allows him to access to new areas as he grows stronger. The core gameplay loop comes directly from *Impossible Mission*: you delve ever further into the maze by activating computer terminals with key codes. The codes here consist of mangled or mirrored arabic numerals. These are randomized each time you play, so you can't simply write down solutions in one playthrough to allow you to skip the code collection process in subsequent attempts. You need

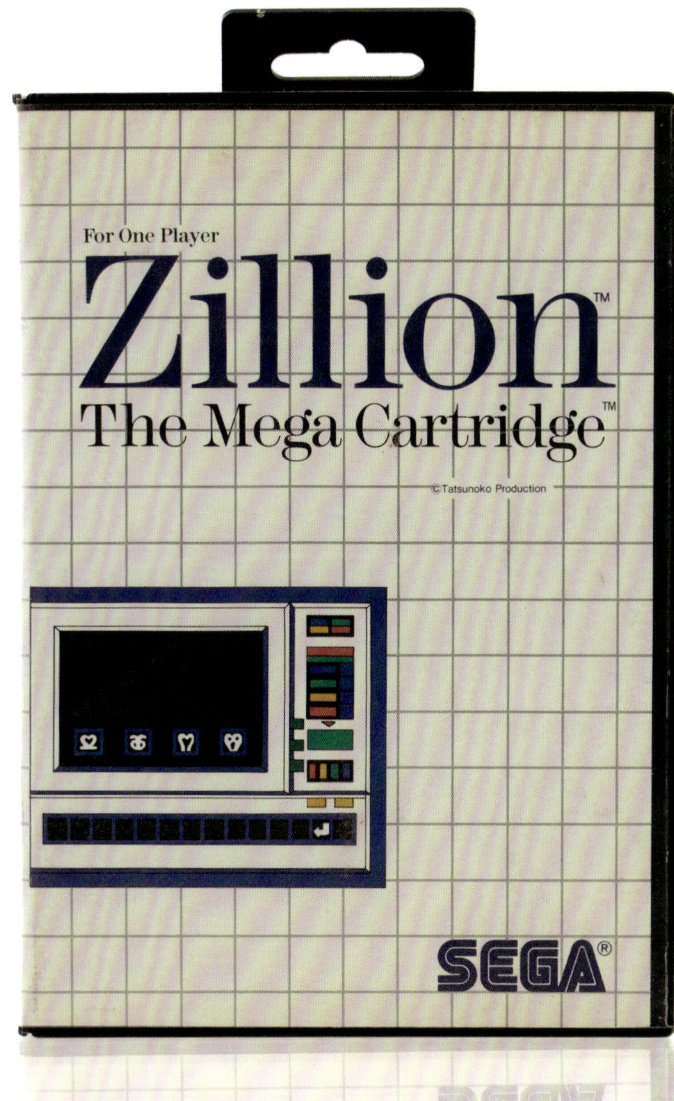

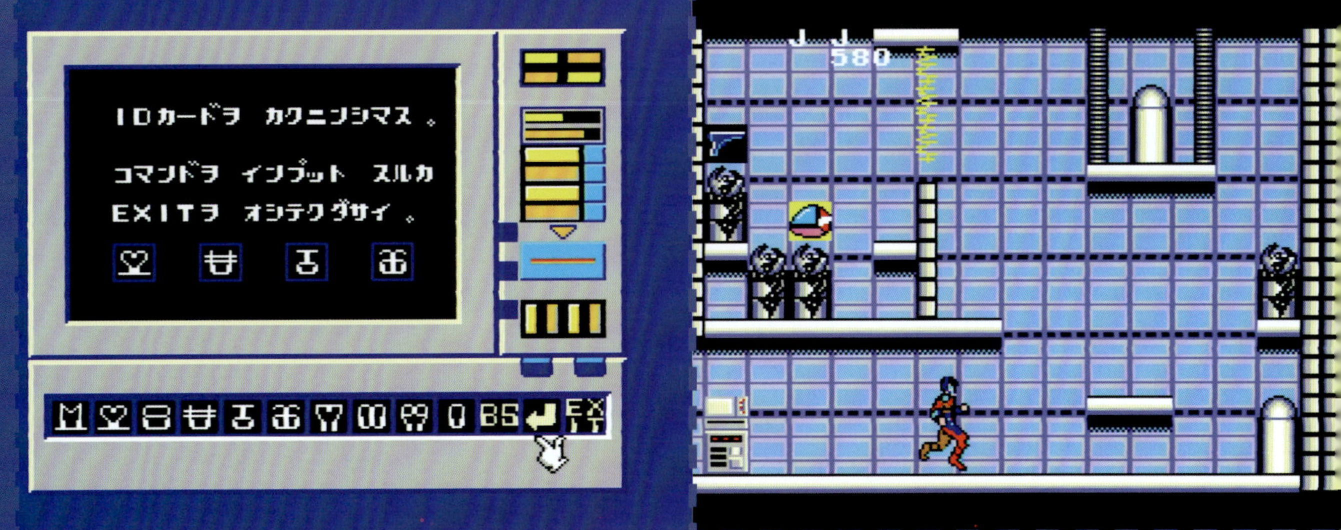

to reveal codes by breaking open containers scattered throughout each computer room. Once you gather code fragments, you punch the correct sequence of symbols into that room's terminal to unlock the doors and elevators leading to adjacent rooms. Containers and terminals serve multiple functions—the former sometimes contain power-ups instead of codes, and the latter allow you to input preset codes that perform alternate actions, such as disabling barriers or sensors. You need to find key cards before can perform terminal actions. Using command codes requires you to insert a card into the computer, and you can only retrieve and reuse a card when you use it to activate the unlock code. Other functions, such as returning to the White Knights' landing craft, permanently expend a card so as to prevent you from relying too heavily on those functions.

More importantly, you'll find J. J.'s two allies, Apple and Champ, imprisoned in the maze. Rescuing them allows you to add them to your playable roster, swapping them into action in J. J.'s place. Not only do the other White Knights work as effective extra lives (since they all have independent health meters and the game ends if J. J. runs out of stamina while exploring solo), they also act as power-ups. Apple, being lighter and more agile than her male companions, can jump higher, while Champ can tank more damage and has greater attack strength than his peers.

Ultimately, your goal in *Zillion* is to destroy the enemy base's main computer, then escape. The enemy's underground complex is a daunting labyrinth divided into three zones. The extremely limited visuals—every room within a given zone uses the same monotonous graphical tiles to define its platforms and walls—makes it easy to become lost among dozens of similar, single-screen rooms. *Zillion* is also hampered by its clumsy controls. J. J. and the White Knights constantly engage in shootouts, but they lack the agility to take out any but the lowest-level grunts without taking return fire. And before too long, even the bottom-tier soldiers learn to counter the most effective strategy of ducking and firing. On top of that, the game is full of annoying, untelegraphed traps that can kill you in an instant without warning.

Still, *Zillion* feels like a step toward something bigger for Sega, building more intricate metroidvania components into the *Impossible Mission* template. That Sega invested so much creative effort into a game ultimately designed to sell toys and cartoons makes its complexity all the more remarkable. It speaks to the collective drive that took hold of Japanese game designers in the mid-'80s, pushing them to turn console action games into something bigger and better than simple arcade-style score-chasing affairs. *M*

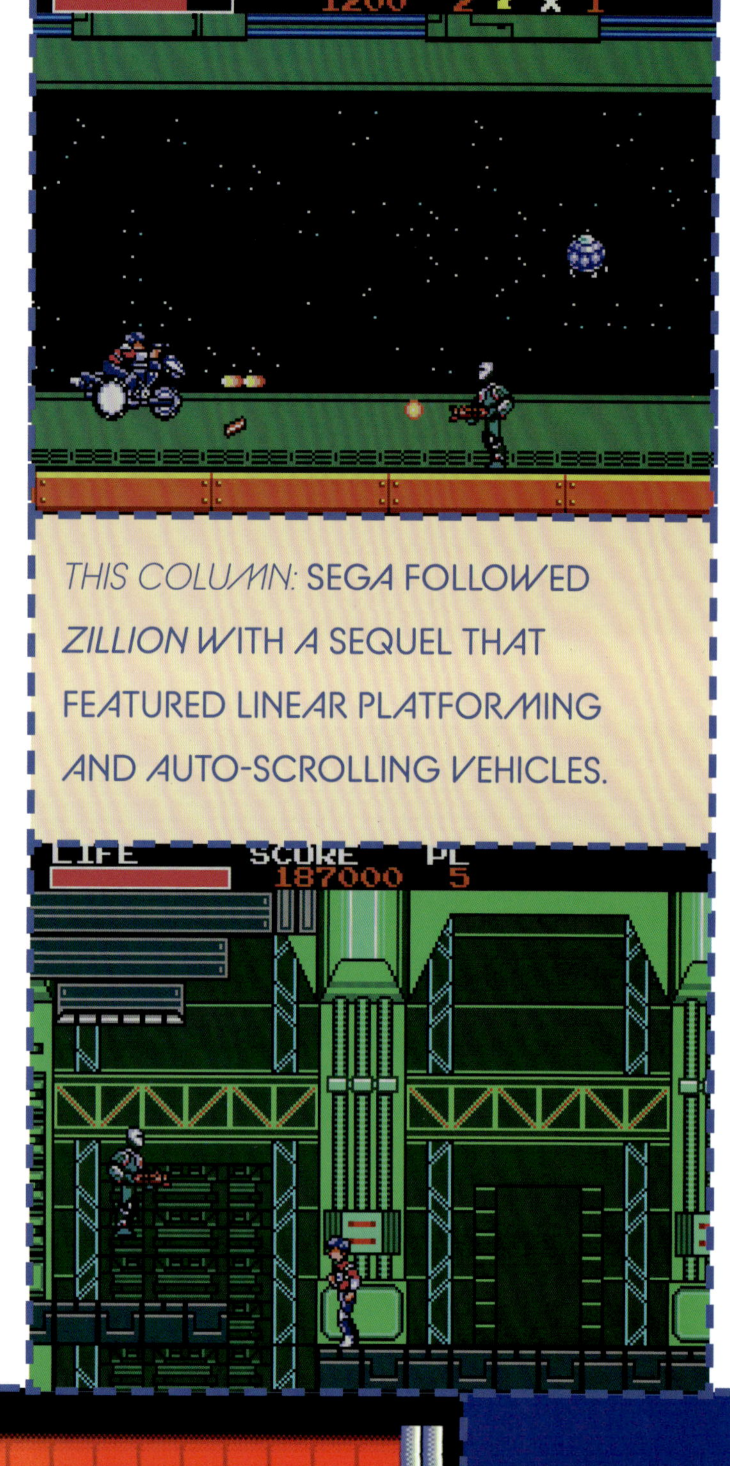

THIS COLUMN: SEGA FOLLOWED *ZILLION* WITH A SEQUEL THAT FEATURED LINEAR PLATFORMING AND AUTO-SCROLLING VEHICLES.

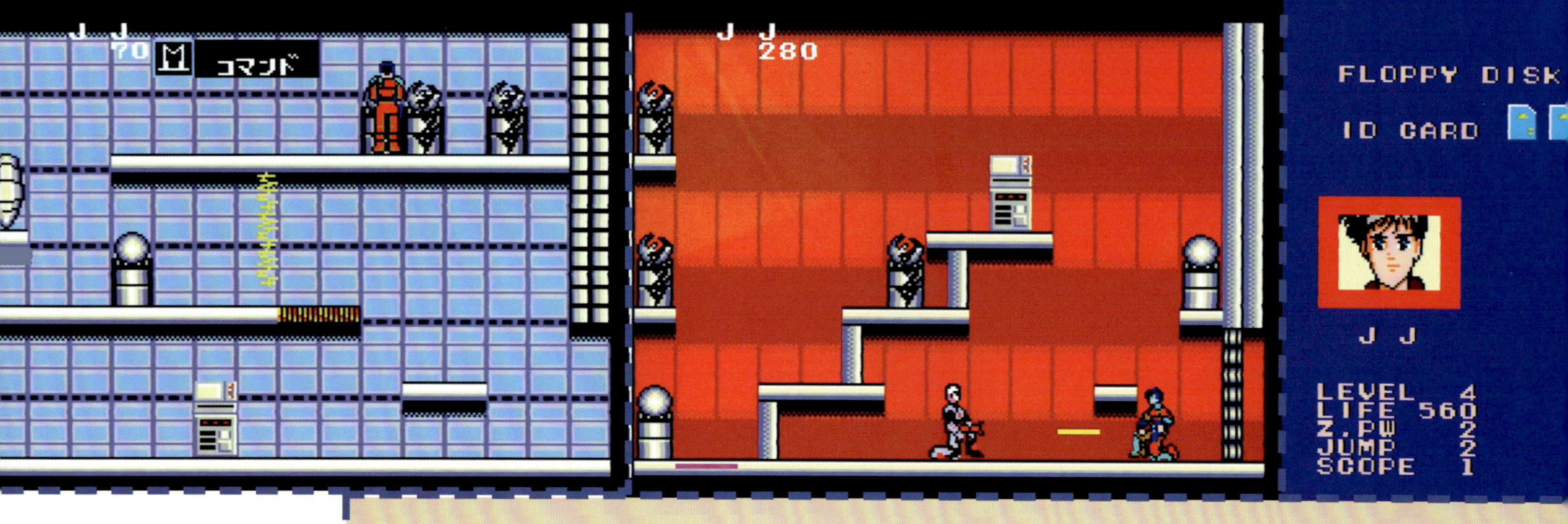

MANIAC MANSION

It's established fact that graphical adventure *Portopia Renzoku Satsujin Jiken* forever reshaped the role-playing genre when its designer and programmer carried forward their streamlined, console-friendly user interface into their follow-up project, *Dragon Quest*. Whether by coincidence or convergent evolution, a small team of designers at Lucasfilm Games functionally reverse-engineered this process the following year when they put together the quirky *Maniac Mansion*, which revolutionized the adventure genre by pulling in RPG elements.

For starters, *Maniac Mansion* introduced Lucasfilm Games's own variant on the menu-based command system seen in *Portopia*'s Famicom adaptation. While navigable via controller and keyboard, *Maniac Mansion*'s menu bar also worked perfectly with newfangled mouse-based inputs as well, making for a wholly adaptable and incredibly accommodative front end for adventure gaming. Players no longer needed to worry about typing commands and guessing at the syntax of a given game's parser; instead, they used menus to construct simple sentences like "USE" "HAMSTER" "ON" "MICROWAVE"—a revolution in friendliness (unless you were a hamster, that is).

Maniac Mansion's friendliness defined its overall philosophy. Although it contained many potential deaths and fail states as players infiltrated a nuclear-powered mansion inhabited by a mad scientist's family living under the influence of an alien force, the game lacked the bloodthirst of other '80s-era adventures. Rather than killing players for their mistakes, most slip-ups merely landed them in the dungeon, where they would languish until another character rescued them.

Yes, here we see that RPG influence at play: *Maniac Mansion* did not concern the exploits of a single hero but rather a trio of kids snooping around the mansion. Players selected their "party" members from a pool of six characters, each with different specialties and skills that allowed them to solve the mansion's puzzles in different ways. Besides introducing the rescue feature (and the ability to carry on even if one or two kids somehow managed to get themselves killed), it also gave *Maniac Mansion* immense replayability by allowing players to take different routes while exploring the mansion.

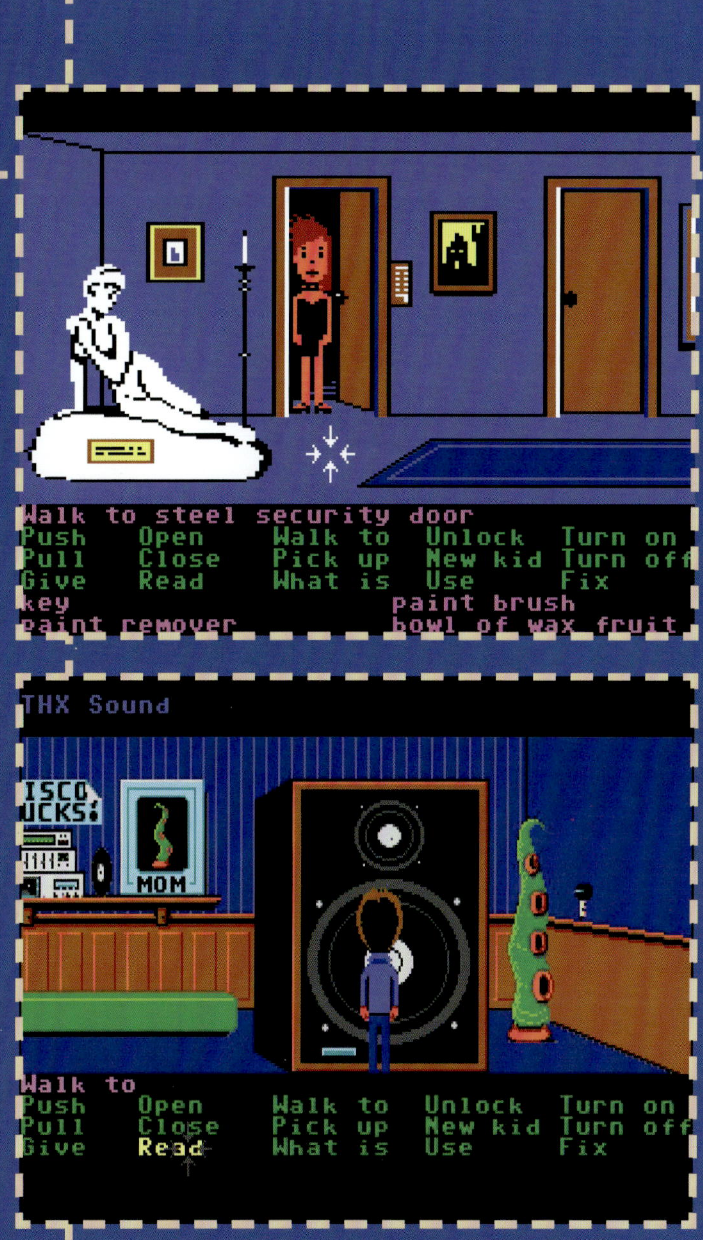

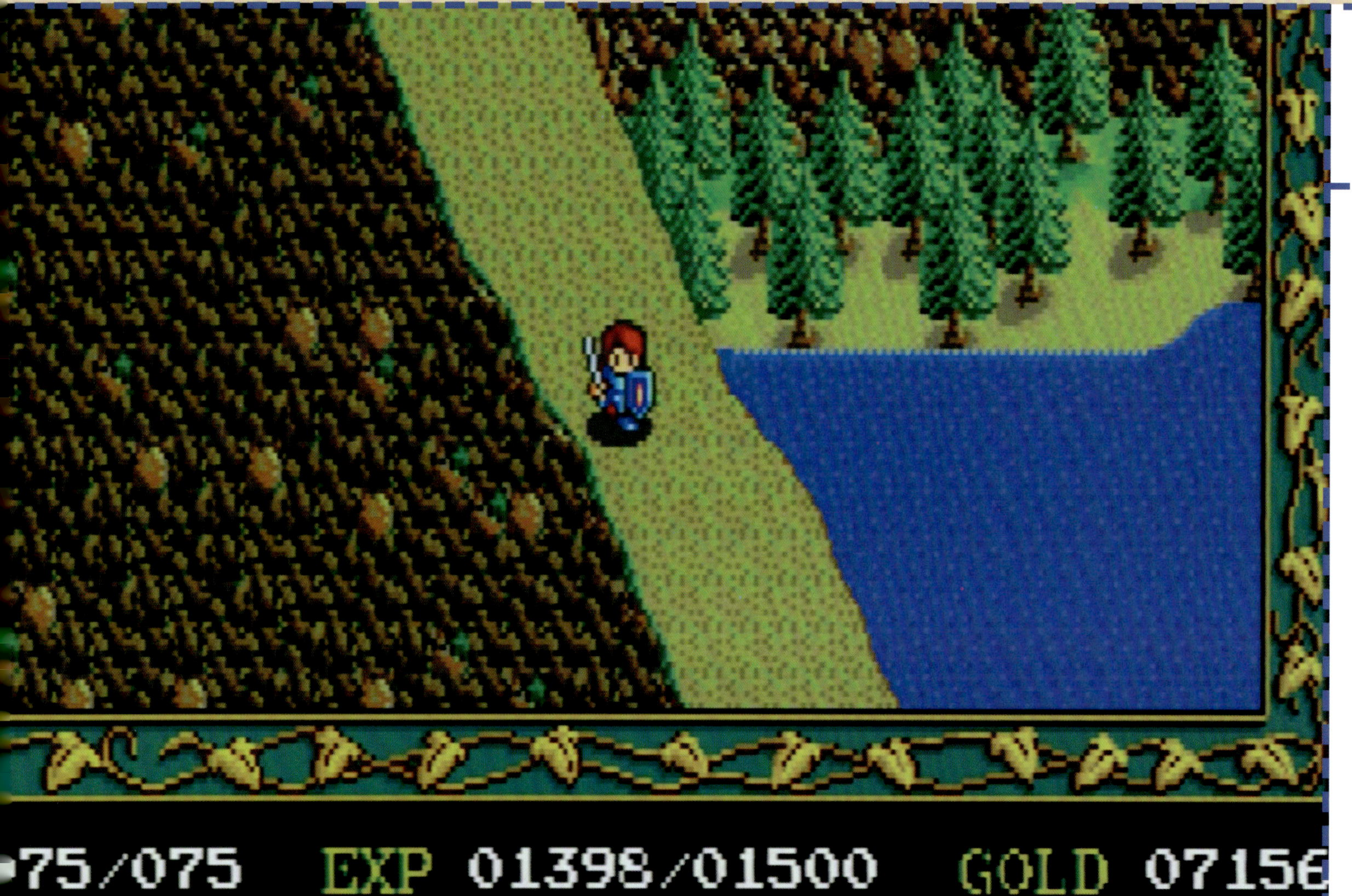

YS: THE VANISHED OMENS

PLATFORM: **PC-8801 / VARIOUS**
DEV: **NIHON FALCOM** | PUB: **NIHON FALCOM**
INITIAL RELEASE DATE: **JUNE 1987**

NOTABLE FOR: **EXPANDING ON THE HYDLIDE FORMAT**

A NEW CHAPTER FOR ACTION-RPGS

An enduring take on the action-RPG, June 1987's *Ys: The Vanished Omens* reached the U.S. a couple of years later on Sega Master System, although it's better known among fans for the Turbo CD release that combined it with *Ys II* into a single super-sized adventure. Falcom found its sweet spot with *Ys*, a fast-paced action game that nevertheless fully embraces its role-playing heritage. Spells and stats and inventory and exploration all factor into *Ys*, even though the game moves at a blazing fast clip. While it builds to some degree on earlier Falcom works like *Romancia*, *Ys* belongs squarely in the same category as *Hydlide* and *The Legend of Zelda*.

As in *Hydlide*, *Ys* uses simplified bump-attack combat mechanics; indeed, you don't even have to press a button to toggle between attack and defense. Damaging enemies is a matter of (1) hitting them at the proper angle and (2) having sufficiently high stats to inflict damage. Victory has more to do with simple numbers than finger skill. The similarities to *Hydlide* end there, though. In terms of overall design and sophistication, *Ys* compares more closely to *Zelda*.

Its overworld lacks the sandbox feel of *Zelda*, but its dungeon-based progression unfolds steadily, with a consistently rising difficulty curve that spikes sharply once you come face-to-face with bosses and encourages you to take time to grind out experience and gain levels. Progression isn't all about stats, though; it's gated by items, bosses, and dialogue with non-player characters you encounter in towns and elsewhere. While *Ys* doesn't offer anything that would have been wholly new in the action-RPG world of 1987, the two chapters combine elements of multiple works that had come before it in a satisfying and intriguing fashion. And, like *Zelda*, the series would attempt embrace a side-scrolling format before the developers realized they'd be better off sticking to their established strengths.

More importantly, *Ys* would influence countless other action-RPGs ranging from Zoom's *Lagoon* to SNK's *Crystalis*—games that didn't necessarily stick to the *Hydlide* bump-combat format yet carried forward *Ys'* brisk action and meaty role-playing systems.

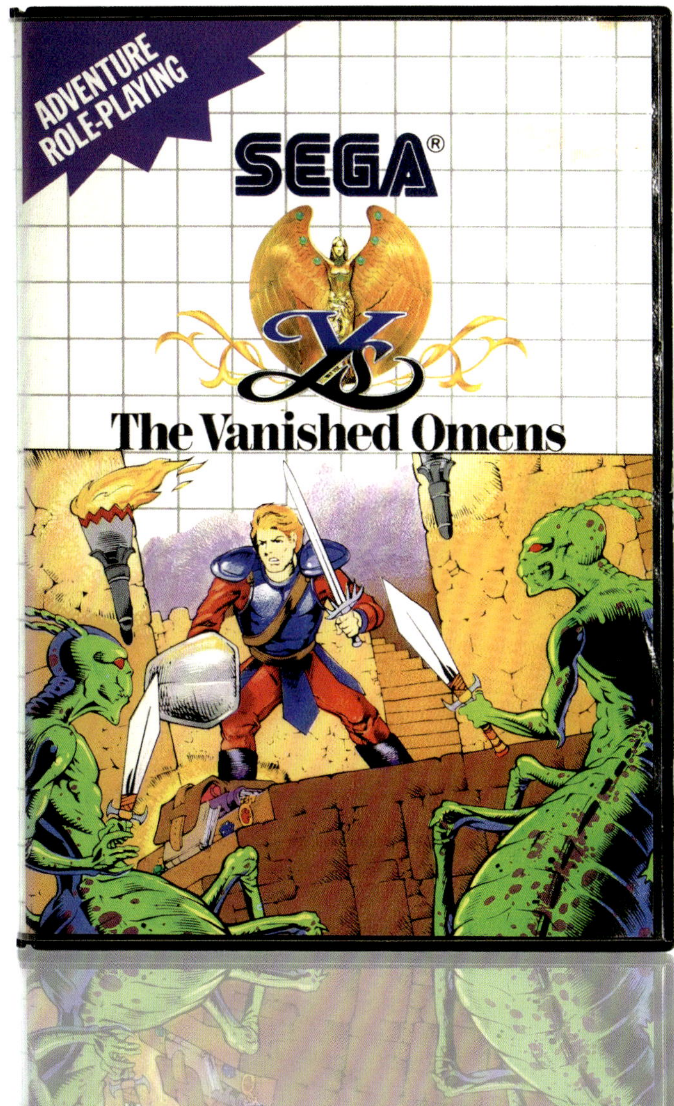

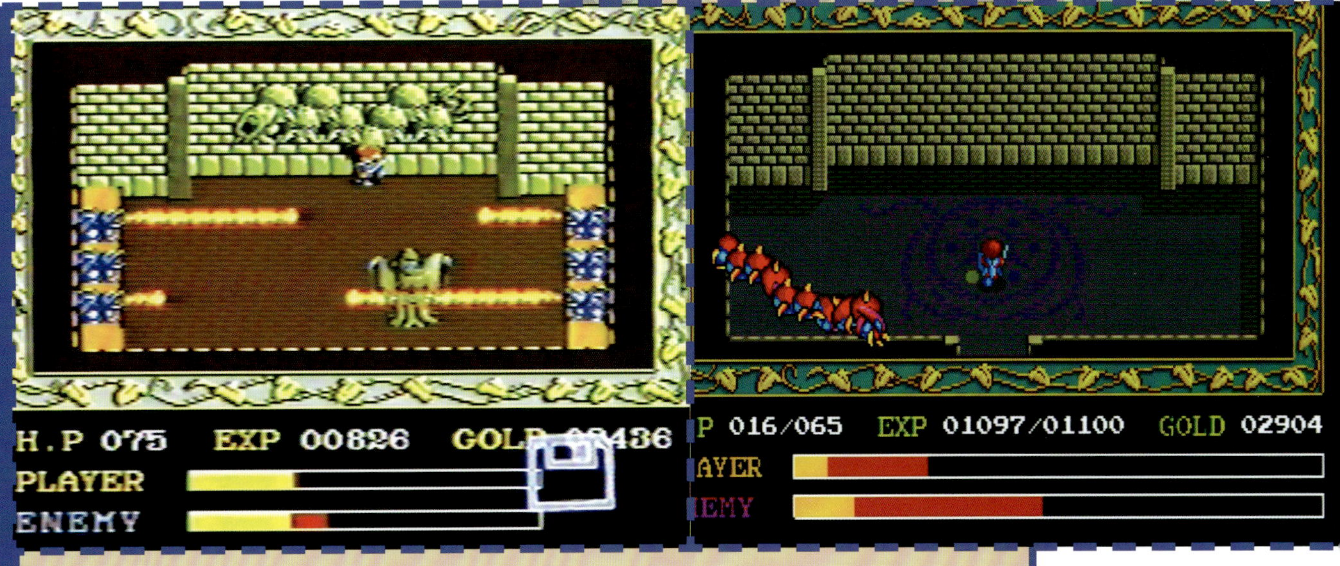

NOTABLE FOR: **THE ZELDA FORMAT AS A STEALTH COMBAT ADVENTURE**

INFILTRATING THE ACTION-RPG

By this point in history—that is, July 1987—*Metal Gear* already felt like a tangent to the evolution of the metroidvania format. Although "metroidvania" wouldn't properly exist for another decade, when *Castlevania: Symphony of the Night* shipped for PlayStation, the action-RPG had already begun to fall into certain patterns and rhythms. You can see the shape of the metroidvania taking form through the likes of *Metroid* and *Zelda II*, and that shape involves side-scrolling action. *Metal Gear* doesn't feature side-scrolling (or any kind of scrolling, in fact). It builds on the format of *Hydlide* and *The Legend of Zelda*, and it's a sort of thematic inverse of the original *Knightmare*: an action-RPG that leaves behind the genre's usual fantasy tropes in favor of sci-fi tinged military elements. Thematically, *Metal Gear*'s premise seems better suited to being an auto-scrolling vertical shooter, while *Knightmare*'s story would have felt more natural as a top-down action-RPG.

Blame the mix-up on the MSX platform. If not for the computer's limitations, *Metal Gear* might well have turned out to be nothing more than a straightforward vertical shooter in the vein of Capcom's *Commando*. But due to the MSX and MSX2 spec's lack of hardware-based background scrolling and limited support for simultaneous onscreen sprites, *Metal Gear* designer Hideo Kojima decided it would be futile to attempt to coax a satisfying pure action game out of the computer. Instead, he opted to turn his shooter project into something slower and more complex.

Metal Gear is unusual for its time in that despite being a military combat game, direct shootouts and conflicts rarely represent the ideal approach to play. The protagonist, a soldier codenamed Solid Snake, can amass quite an arsenal for himself, but even when he's fully decked out, he'll quickly find himself overwhelmed by enemy forces if he takes a head-on approach to combat. Instead, *Metal Gear* emphasizes stealth, encouraging players to stay out of the enemy's view and using lethal weapons sparingly to avoid alerting soldiers with the noise of a gun report or mine detonation.

Now, this wasn't a totally original approach to game design. Muse Software pioneered the concept of military stealth way back in 1981 with *Castle Wolfenstein* for the Apple II, and Firebird Software had enjoyed moderate success in 1986 with a BBC Micro

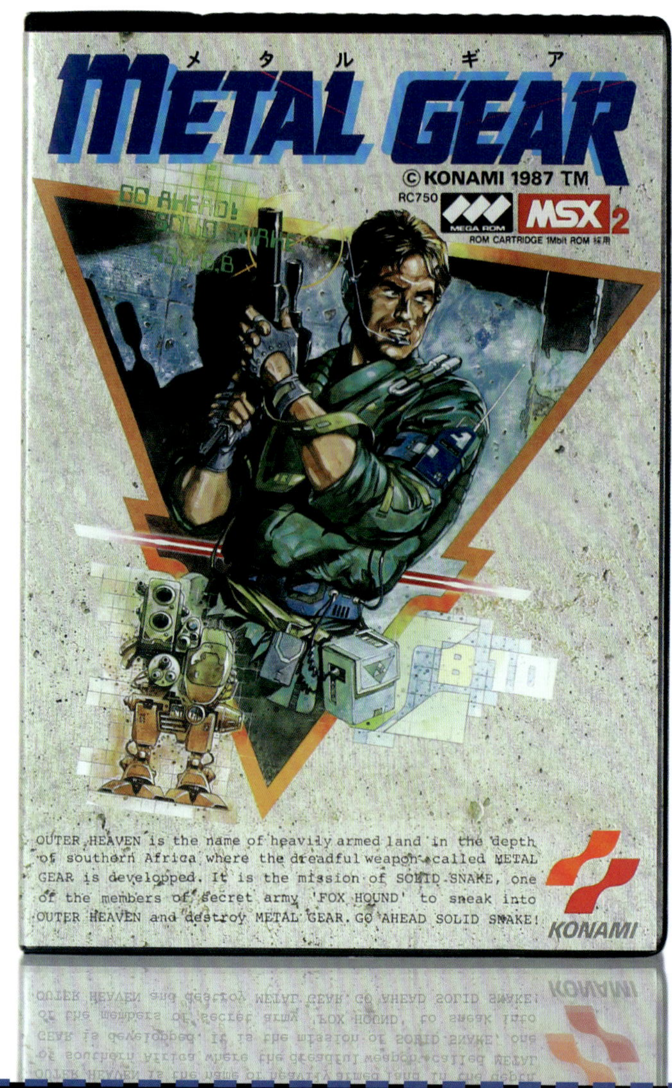

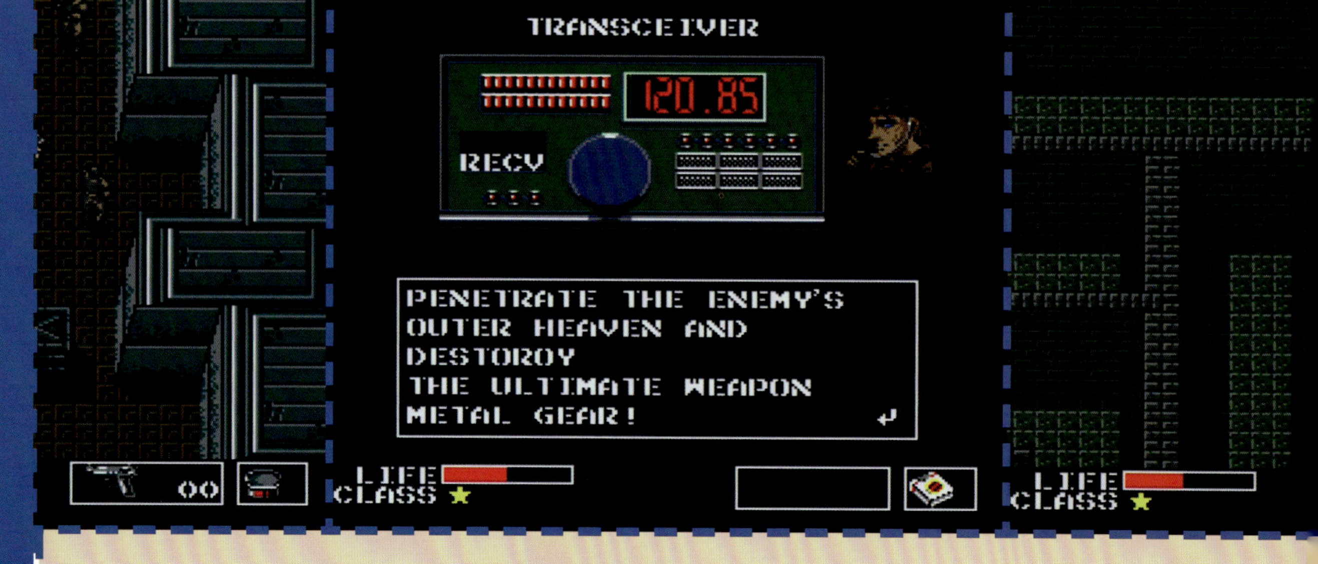

stealth-puzzle game called *The Sentinel*. Around the same time, Pack-In-Video had adapted Sylvester Stallone's film *Rambo: First Blood Part II* into a pair of MSX action games in which the title character had to sneak around the jungle gathering weapons and tools while avoiding detection by staying out of his foes' line-of-sight. Given that Kojima has proven himself a massive nerd for Western pop culture, it's hard to imagine that he would have been completely unaware of a major computer hit like *Castle Wolfenstein*—or that he would have somehow been oblivious to a game adaptation of one of America's biggest box-office hits for 1985 appearing on the same platform that he developed for. But whatever inspiration it may have taken from that prior work, this is no trite, derivative clone—*Metal Gear* is a fully realized work that pushes the action-RPG in new directions.

Arguably the biggest innovation to be found in *Metal Gear* is the addition of its built-in narrative device, Snake's radio transceiver. Set to its own dedicated keyboard button, activating the transceiver takes you to a separate screen where you can send and receive calls to and from a list of radio contacts. As with *The Legend of Zelda* and the MSX version of *Rambo*, *Metal Gear*'s environment—a multibuilding fortress complex called Outer Heaven—is divided up into standalone screens. Just about every screen of the game contains some sort of unique transceiver message, provided you reach out to the correct contact for that screen, and a good many of these messages relay useful information. Mission-critical information comes to you via active calls denoted by a call indicator icon; this icon announces an inbound message from your mission commander, who relays new mission objectives and other essential advice for surviving your journey through enemy territory as needed.

Metal Gear's premise of a one-man infiltration of Outer Heaven lends itself to both stealth and remote guidance. You receive enough dialogue via transceiver (and the occasional in-person encounter) to define the bare minimum of a functional plot, while it also provides a more focused experience than the aimless "poke around everywhere" approach of something like *Knightmare II*. There's admittedly not much to *Metal Gear*'s story, and the cipher-like Solid Snake himself isn't a proper character even by the loosest definition of the word, but the transceiver's steady drip feed of information gives context to the environments and helps justify your scattered mission objectives.

Structurally, *Metal Gear* adopts a classic lock-and-key approach. The passages of Outer Heaven are closed off by eight electronic lock types, each of which can only be opened with the corresponding card key. Acquiring new key cards grants Snake access to deeper portions of the fortress, and you can only acquire the majority of those keys by completing requisite story objectives like boss encounters. At the same time, in the emerging metroidvania style, many of Snake's weapons and other tools also double as keys. Plastic explosives can destroy specific types of equipment (including the eponymous nuclear battle tank), but it can also destroy weak walls. The rocket launcher lets you take out threats from a safe distance, but it can also shatter control panels that power otherwise impassable stretches of electrified floor. An enemy uniform lets you pass unchallenged into the securer areas of the fortress, while a compass is the only tool that will allow you to navigate the sprawling wasteland between buildings. You need a gas mask to bypass rooms filled with toxins, a parachute to safely leap from the highest floors of the fortress to the ground below, and a metal detector to avoid dying in a minefield.

All these tools and devices can be found within the walls of Outer Heaven, and much of your game time is spent hunting for those crucial mechanisms in order to advance. This involves taking a lot of side excursions into out-of-the-way locations like subbasements or backtracking to previously explored areas. In the early going, your mission commander (codenamed Big Boss) guides you directly to the tools you need. The farther you advance, however, the less reliable he becomes. What initially appear to be innocuous slip-ups, like forgetting to alert you to a room flooded with poisonous gas, become more and more frequent, especially once Big Boss changes his radio contact frequency. Of course, it turns out Big Boss (or, as the sequels would have it, Venom Snake) is secretly the enemy leader, playing two sides against each other. Therefore, he's highly invested in ensuring the player's mission ends in failure.

The twists and turns of this running transceiver commentary do a great job of easing players into the rhythms and expectations of *Metal Gear* via Big Boss's instructions before leaving them more or less to their own devices once the mission commander begins to reveal his truly colors at the game's midway point. It makes for an adventure that expects a certain amount of resourcefulness and sharp thinking, yet it doesn't leave you completely adrift—perhaps the most significant move away from the typical mid-'80s gaming mindset of throwing players right into the deep end and expecting them to sink or swim. Certainly, other games from '87—*Zelda II*, *Castlevania II*, and *Faxanadu* in particular—presented players with a fair amount of text, too, but *Metal Gear* gives you the ability to receive (and even solicit) information no matter where you are. And unlike *Castlevania II*'s love for misdirecting players with false information from mean-spirited villagers, *Metal Gear* makes its swerve into deception pretty obvious; even in terse, 8-bit text, Big Boss absolutely hams it up when he does his heel turn, with erroneous instructions and bizarre remarks that amount to enormous red flags.

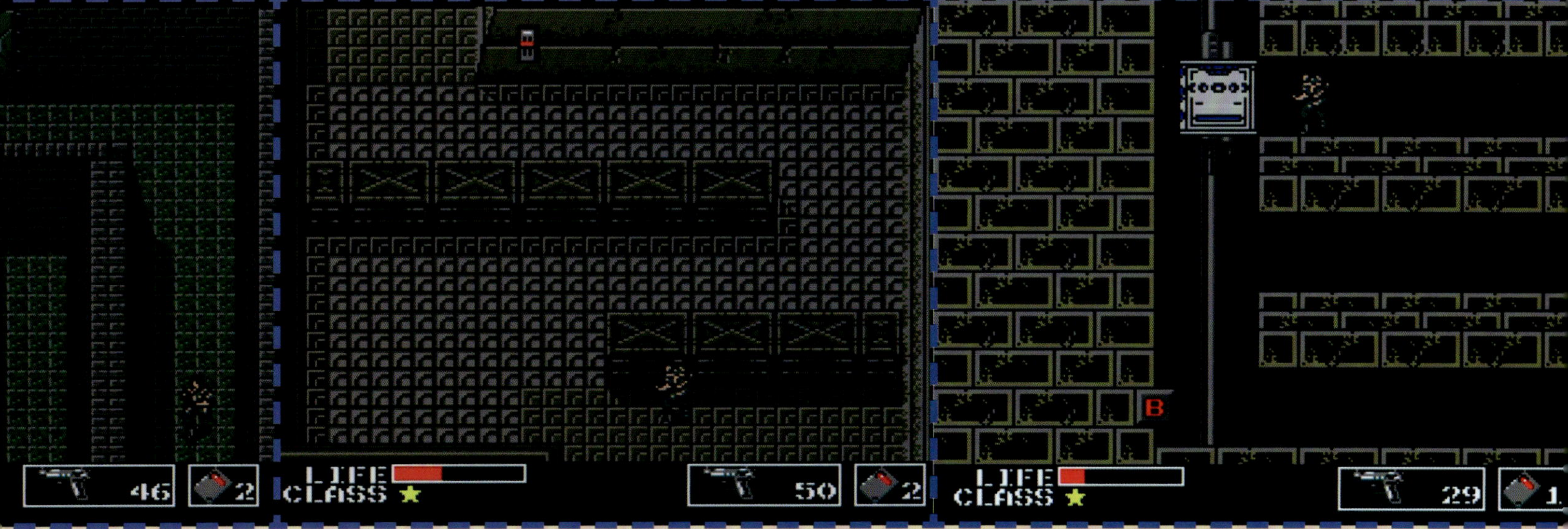

Metal Gear also deserves notice for the way it treats Outer Heaven as a virtual place. While the entire fortress consists of individual, self-contained screen-sized spaces, these areas often blur together thanks to the monotonous design and presence of hidden, connective passages linking several of the buildings. The fortress feels almost puzzle-like thanks to the way the environmental designers arranged the layouts to emphasize stealth action. Solid Snake needs to avoid being spotted as he sneaks about whenever possible, and each individual screen conspicuously gives you an entry point that allows you to enter that space while remaining outside of the enemy's line-of-sight. Patrolling soldiers usually appear in different starting positions depending on where you step onto the screen, meaning you rarely run the risk of being spotted the instant you enter a new area. Although the latter portions of the game do tend to force you into situations that render stealth useless, until that point *Metal Gear* expects you to plan your transitions from one screen to the next by making use of the binoculars, which lets you look ahead one screen to take note of enemy placement. Generally speaking, Outer Heaven patrols reset when you step out of a screen and return, turning the process of advancing and backtracking through the game into a matter of observing patterns and avoiding contact.

METAL GEAR'S

RADIO TRANSCEIVER AND PLOT TWISTS MAKE FOR AN ADVENTURE THAT DEMANDS A CERTAIN AMOUNT OF RESOURCEFULNESS AND THOUGHT FROM THE PLAYER WITHOUT LEAVING THEM COMPLETELY ADRIFT—A MOVE AWAY FROM THE 1980S DESIGN MINDSET OF THROWING PLAYERS INTO THE DEEP END AND EXPECTING THEM TO SINK OR SWIM.

If enemies do spot Snake, endless waves of soldiers come after him. Gun them down and more appear. Shake them off by ducking to the next screen and the alert will carry over with you. Duck into an interior room and the bad guys will flood in after you, guns ablaze. *Metal Gear* places a heavy burden on players to avoid enemy interaction, and while the penalty for mistakes isn't necessarily a game over—it's possible to shoot your way through an alert or to reset the enemy patrols by moving to a different floor or building—it can be tough to recover from combat.

Like the heroes of similar games, such as *The Legend of Zelda*, Solid Snake does have a few opportunities to grow in strength and durability as his quest progresses. Defeating certain bosses causes your military rank to increase a step, which expands both the size of your life bar and the maximum amount of different ammunition types you can carry. You can lose rank by accidentally killing prisoners of war; one particularly nasty boss hides behind hostages to make it difficult to defeat him without suffering a huge and permanent penalty to your character growth. But there is no experience system here, nor is there an economy; in fact, enemies don't drop any sort of loot outside of the occasional health-restoring ration, meaning there's very little incentive to kill the soldiers you encounter—even on screens where there's no way to avoid an instant alert state, you're better off running and avoiding damage rather than stand- ing your ground and wasting health and healing items.

This adds up to an unusual and interesting take on the ex- ploratory action game, one driven by story and defined by the need to avoid conflict as much as possible. Although *Metal Gear* on MSX2 would not have a huge direct impact on gaming, the NES conversion would end up being a sizable hit in the US, which gave the *Metal Gear* name enough cachet to inspire a sequel for NES and return a decade later on the Sony PlayStation, where it completely revolutionized storytelling in video games. Back in 1987, however, *Metal Gear* seemed like little more than an interesting interpretation of the action-RPG model. It embraced a variety of influences to create a military shooter that worked like a sword-and-sorcery adventure while fitting within the technological limitations of its host platform. It's a significant offshoot of the metroidvania genre, but most of all, it showcases the growing divide between the new wave of side-scrolling metroidvanias and the more classic *Hydlide*-inspired action-RPGs.

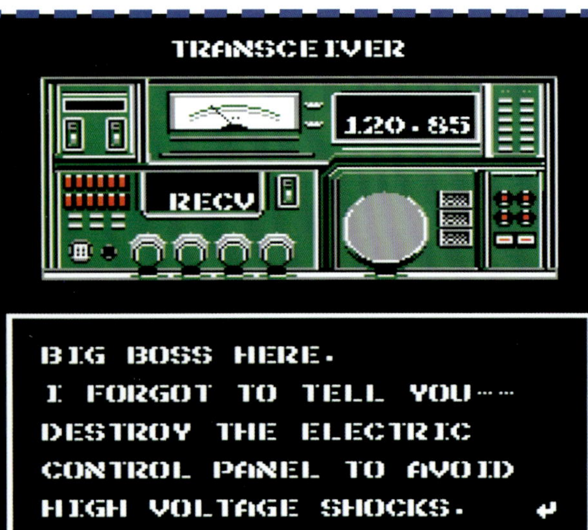

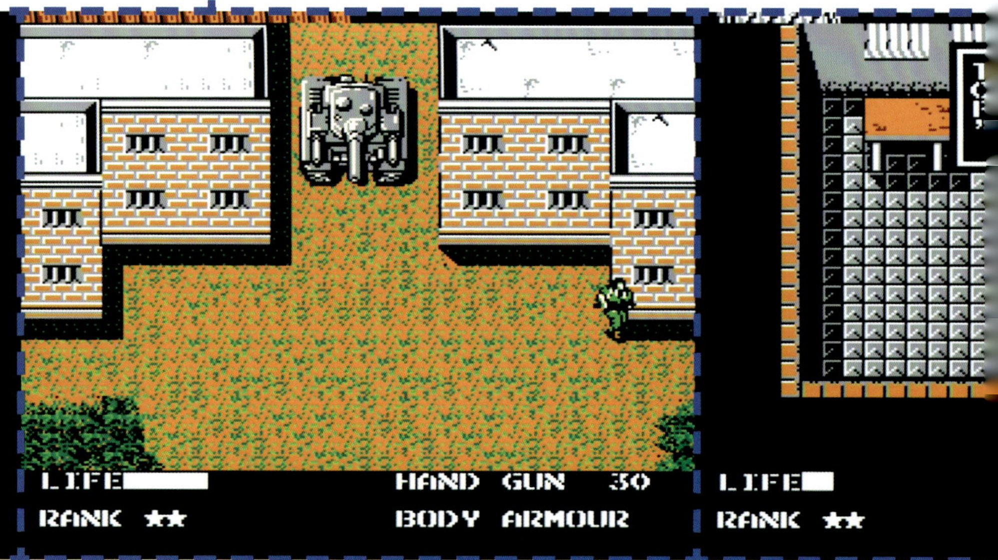

WONDER BOY IN MONSTER LAND

The original *Wonder Boy* saw developer Westone working in pure *Super Mario Bros.* imitation mode: a run-and-jump platformer across thirty-two stages (numbered 1-1 through 8-4) in which you collected power-ups that allowed its protagonist to chuck projectiles or dash forward at high speeds. A fun game, but entirely derivative and reactive, driven by the desire to do *Super Mario* except better—but, ultimately, nothing more than that.

When it came time to pull together a sequel, though, Westone didn't simply settle for more of the same. With its role-playing inspired equipment system and power-ups, *Wonder Boy in Monster Land* bears almost zero resemblance to the original. If not for the title and the presence of a few common enemies, you might never know the two games had any relationship. But then again, the original *Wonder Boy* did include a simple status bar—an almost pointless, vestigial element, but you don't have to squint too hard to get the sense that *Wonder Boy*'s primitive status bar evolved into the more elaborate one found in *Wonder Boy in Monster Land*. That feature makes the sequel's expanded design and ambition clear; the protagonist has a life meter, a pile of cash on hand, gear, and equipment.

The status bar also betrays the fact that, despite taking some aesthetic cues from RPGs (including the addition of shops and an economy), it's still ultimately an arcade-action game. Each stage needs to be completed within a certain amount of time, and each one presents a fairly straightforward path from beginning to ending boss battle. It's a linear arcade-action game dressed up in RPG drag—hardly a metroidvania by any definition of the word. Rather, it's an exercise in evolution. Two years after *Wonder Boy in Monster Land* made its furtive stab at being an action-RPG, Westone delivered one of the finest 8-bit examples of the form in *Wonder Boy III: The Dragon's Trap*.

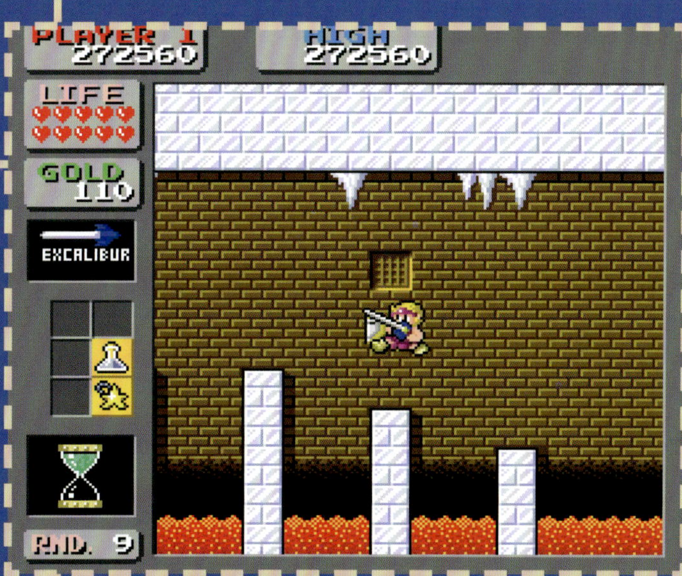

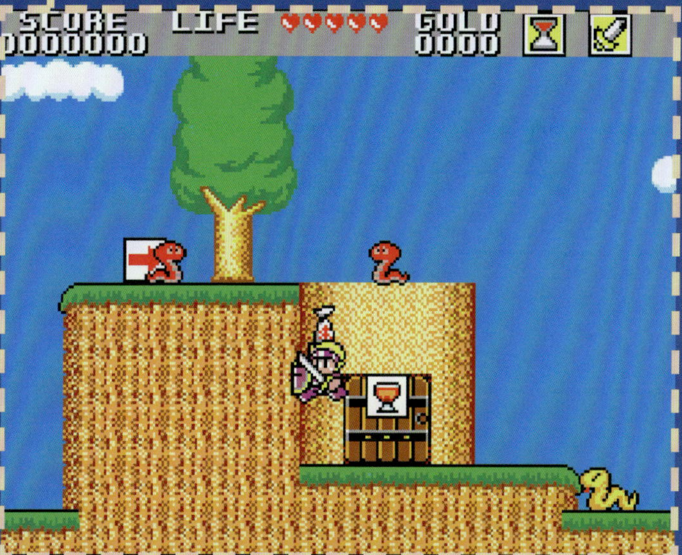

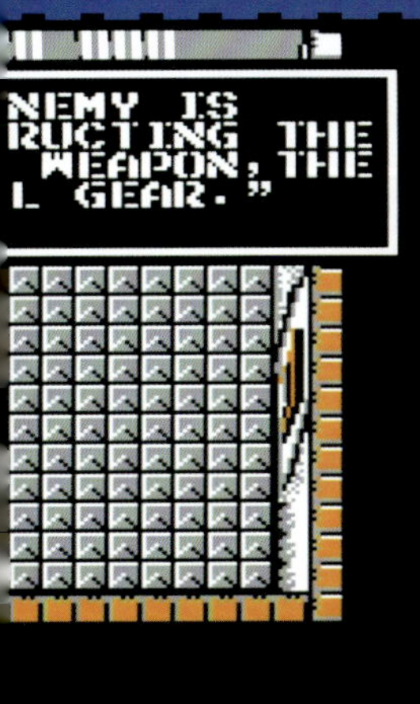

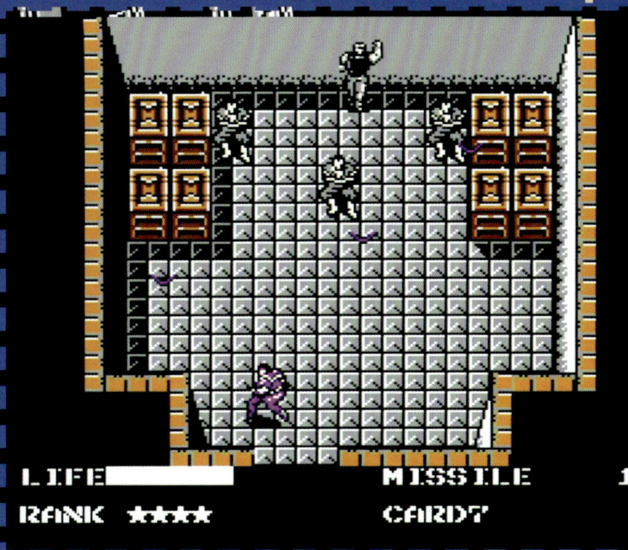

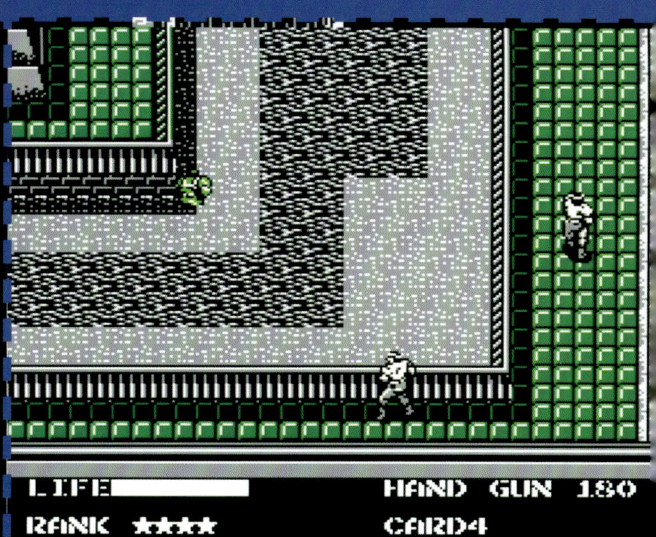

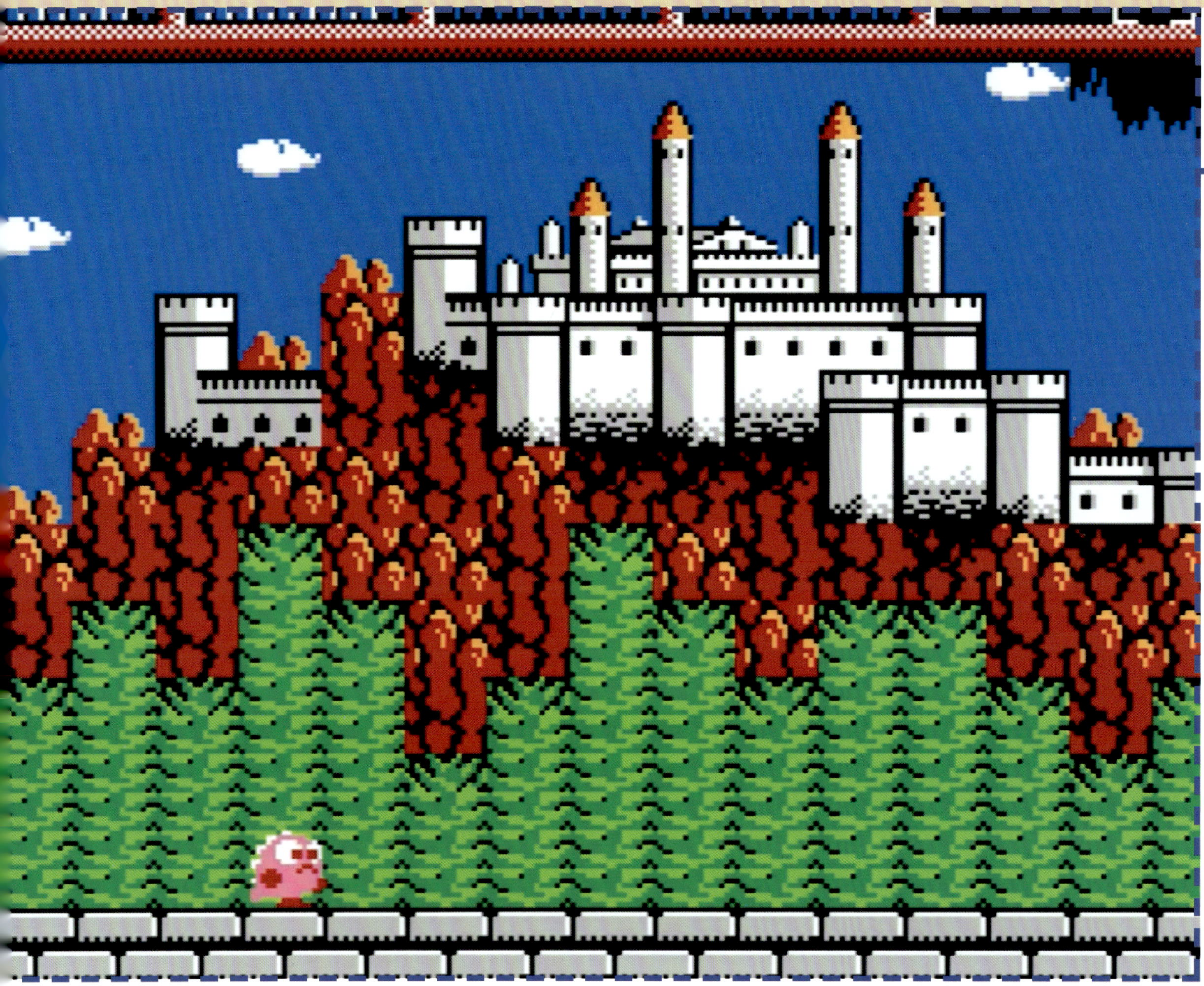

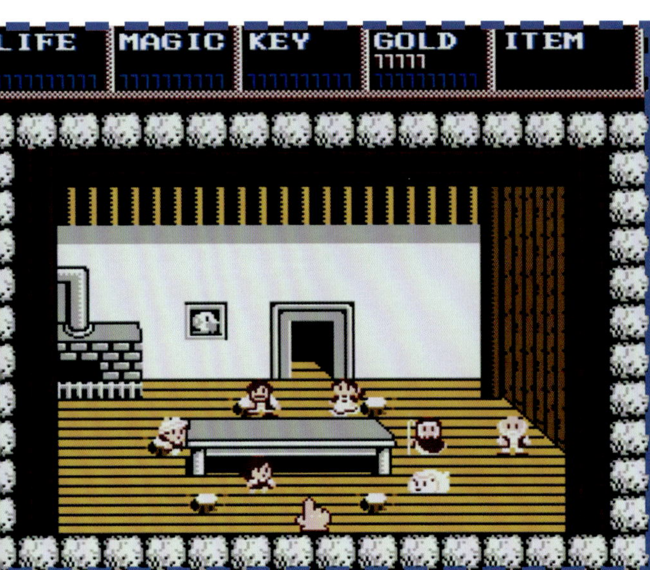

LEGACY OF THE WIZARD

PLATFORM: **MSX / NES**
DEV: **NIHON FALCOM** | PUB: **BRØDERBUND**
INITIAL RELEASE DATE: **JULY 1987**
SHOWN HERE: **NINTENDO ENTERTAINMENT SYSTEM VERSION, 1989**

NOTABLE FOR: MULTI-CHARACTER PUZZLE-ACTION PLATFORMING

FAMILY MATTERS

One month after *Ys* debuted, Falcom debuted the next entry in its long-running *Dragon Slayer* series. *Dragon Slayer IV: The Drasle Family*, localized for America by Brøderbund as *Legacy of the Wizard*, falls more into line with what would become the metroidvania genre than its predecessors *Romancia* and *Ys* did. Not only did *Legacy of the Wizard* take the form of a side-scrolling platformer, it's a side-scrolling platformer that gates progression based on a combination of character skills, tools, and character skills augmented by tools—all core tenets of the metroidvania as we know it today

The entire quest of *Legacy of the Wizard* takes place in a sprawling underground labyrinth comprised of a 16×16-screen grid of screens. That's 256 screens in total, which doesn't seem like a lot until you actually look at the map and realize that *Legacy of the Wizard*'s labyrinth is *dense*, not to mention unfriendly. Completing the game requires exploring the dungeon in its entirety, and the dungeon itself actively conspires to make that difficult. The game world is loaded not only with monsters but also with one-way passages and hidden traps that can send you spilling backward into areas you've already completed, forcing you to retrace your steps.

What really makes *Legacy of the Wizard* tricky is that its dun- geon is divided individually into quadrants that can only be explored by a specific character. However, you don't really know which character is best suited for a given area until you've sorted it out through trial, error, and desperation. This is the big innovation of *Legacy of the Wizard*. The Drasle family referred to in the Japanese title consists of a proper nuclear family, and each member has a part to play. Even the family pet! The father, mother, son, daughter, and pet (a strange pink jellybean of a critter named Pochi) can all take turns to venture forth and uphold their part of the quest.

Each character has their own strengths and weaknesses, and each can only access a specific region of the dungeon. Pochi, for example, is a monster. That's its power. Being a monster, the other beasts of the labyrinth won't attack it, allowing you to travel and explore unmolested until you reach the boss of Pochi's area. Meanwhile, the patriarch of the family, Xemn, has powerful attack

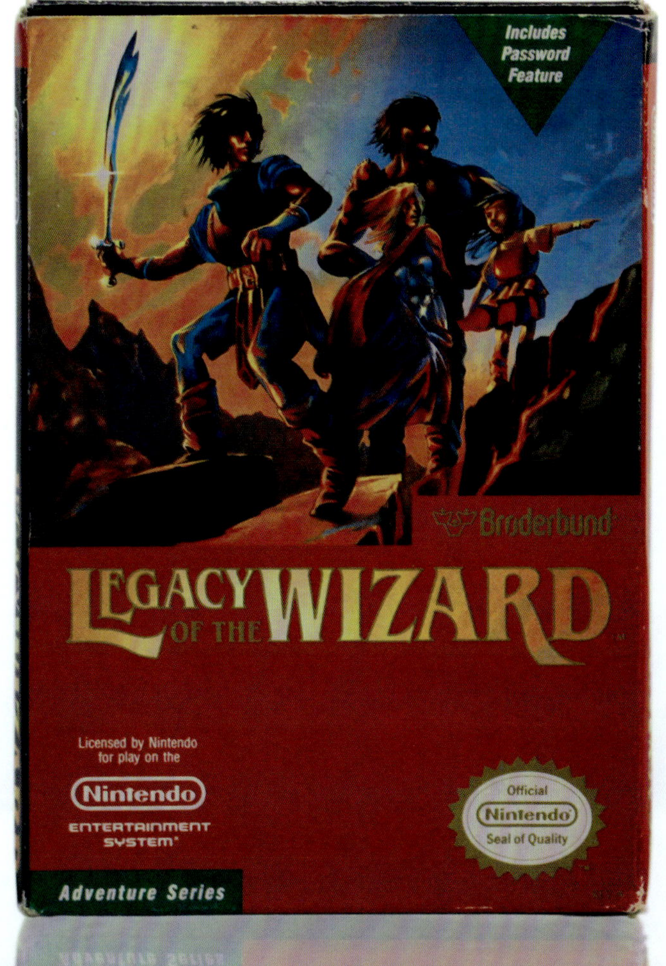

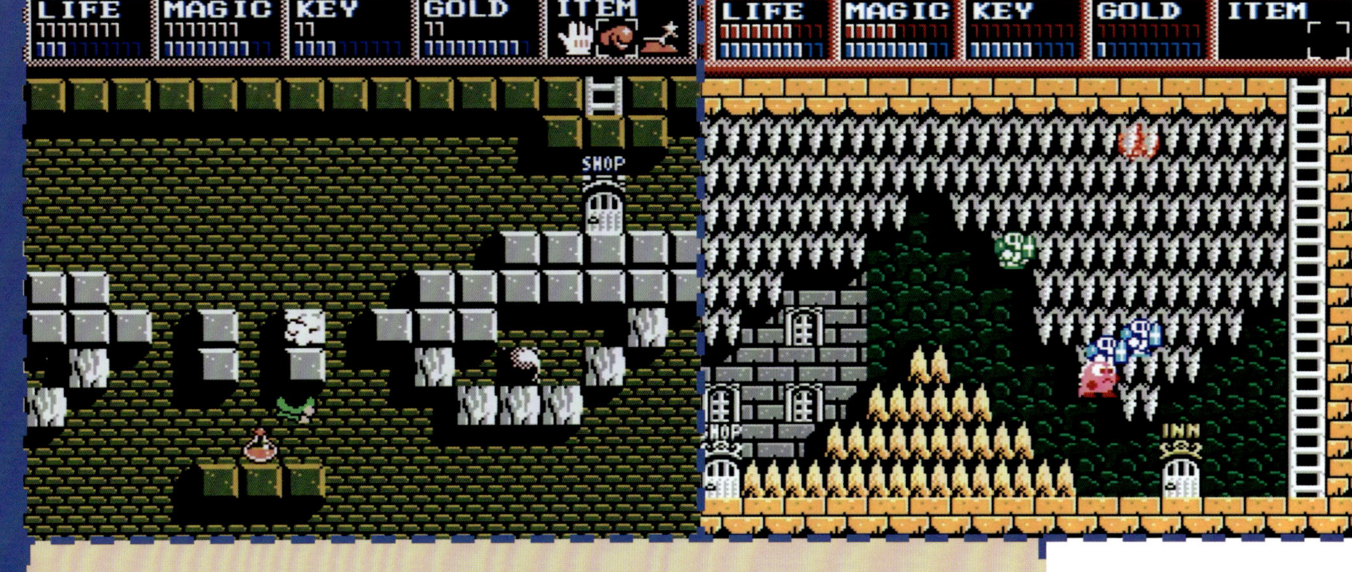

skills and miserable jumping capabilities, which limits the areas he can reach. To balance out this weakness, Xemn has the ability to manipulate certain blocks in the dungeon, turning his areas into something akin to block-puzzler *Soukoban* as an action game. Meanwhile, while the family's matriarch, Meyna, can't wear the power glove, she can wield a wand that allows her to manipulate blocks indirectly. Her daughter, Lyll, can smash blocks with a pickax and augment her excellent jumping skills by equipping a magical winged rod. And finally, the family's son, Roas, basically amounts to dead weight until game's end. Once you acquire the eponymous Dragon Slayer sword, he fulfills the game's title by slaying the dragon as the only character capable of wielding the blade.

Advancement in *Legacy of the Wizard* boils down to a process of exploration and acquisition. Each of the four exploratory characters must conquer their portion of the dungeon (which, again, isn't clearly marked as such) and defeat a boss to acquire one of four mystical crowns that unlocks the *Dragon Slayer* sword for Roas. While each character has their own distinct stats and skills—speed, strength, endurance, range, and jump height—success for every character (except Pochi) comes down to wielding that adventurer's unique items. You can't get far in Lyll's area, for exam- ple, until you acquire the jump shoes. And you won't find the shoes along Lyll's route; instead, you'll need to acquire them while exploring Meyna's portion of the labyrinth. Similarly, only Xemn can acquire the mystic rod for Meyna and the pickax for Lyll.

These requirements hark back to the backtracking and item- based gating established by games like *Metroid*. But instead of building out skills for a single character, *Legacy of the Wizard* distributes your capabilities across an entire RPG party and then forces the party members to explore individually. The idea here is to venture into the dungeon, take note of obstacles while acquiring tools, and regroup to send the character best suited for the situation at hand into action.

> LEGACY OF THE *WIZARD* HEARKENS TO THE ITEM-BASED GATING ESTABLISHED BY *METROID*. INSTEAD OF BUILDING UP THE SKILLS OF A SINGLE PLAYABLE CHARACTER, YOU DISTRIBUTE THOSE ABILITIES ACROSS AN ENTIRE PARTY WHOSE MEMBERS TRAVEL SOLO.

There's more of the puzzle genre here than of role-playing. The integration of a *Xanadu*-style party and a basic economy is as close as *Legacy of the Wizard* comes to being an RPG. Its systems are even more simplistic than those of *Romancia*; each character's various attributes (including their cash reserve) max out at 100 units apiece from the very beginning and never increase. Characters can't earn more maximum hit points or permanently upgrade their strengths; the closest you get to traditional RPG stat improvements is a set of armor that only Xemn can wear to double his defense. Otherwise, the principles of advancement here are shouldered entirely by the act of exploration and key item acquisition.

Legacy of the Wizard feels very much like culmination of the three previous *Dragon Slayer* games. It simplifies the RPG mechanics even further than *Romancia* did; gives you a five-member party reminiscent of the heroes you led around in *Xanadu*; and involves a lot of in-dungeon manipulation and returning to home base as in the original *Dragon Slayer*. Yet the emphasis on four distinct characters (and their tools) pushes *Legacy of the Wizard* well away from pure RPG, through the adventure genre that *Romancia* and *The Goonies II* embraced, and into the realm of puzzle game. It's a puzzle-action-adventure RPG, one that equally emphasizes exploration and intuitive problem-solving.

It's a dense, challenging, often confounding adventure, but it works well. As with everything we've seen from Falcom to date, *Legacy of the Wizard* doesn't go out of its way to accommodate players; on the contrary, it asks much of them and makes little effort to assist their needs. Still, those who take the time to unravel its mysteries can enjoy the satisfaction of completing an impossible task while getting a real sense of the shape that the metroidvania genre would adopt not too far in the future.

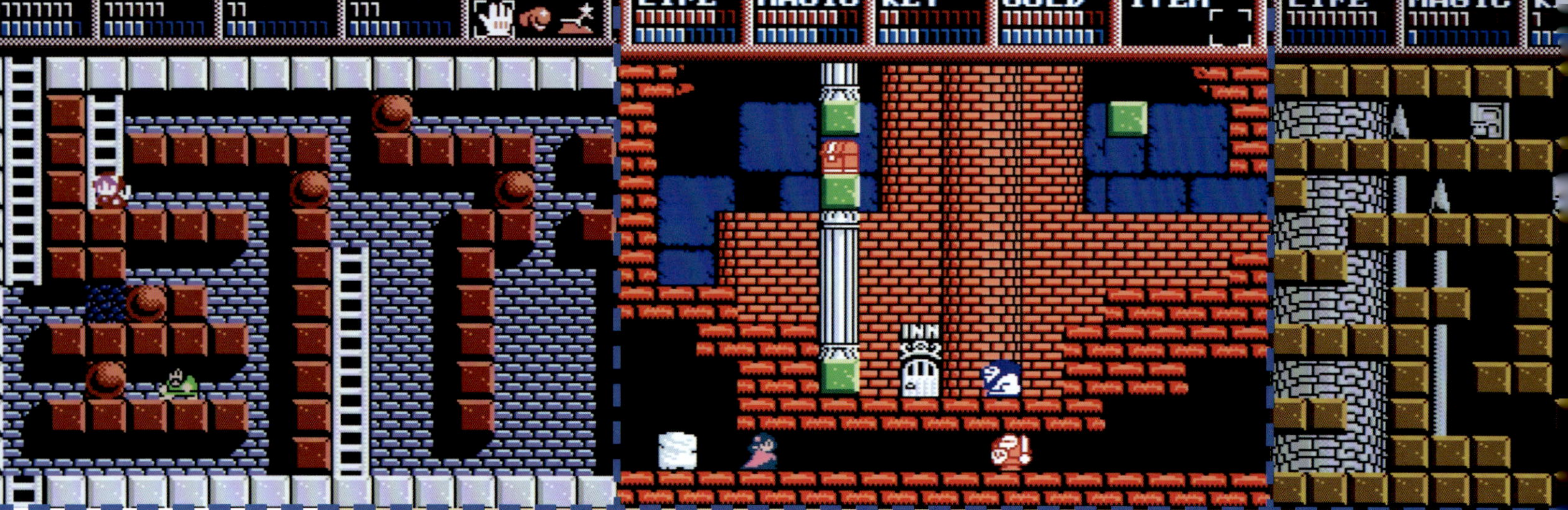

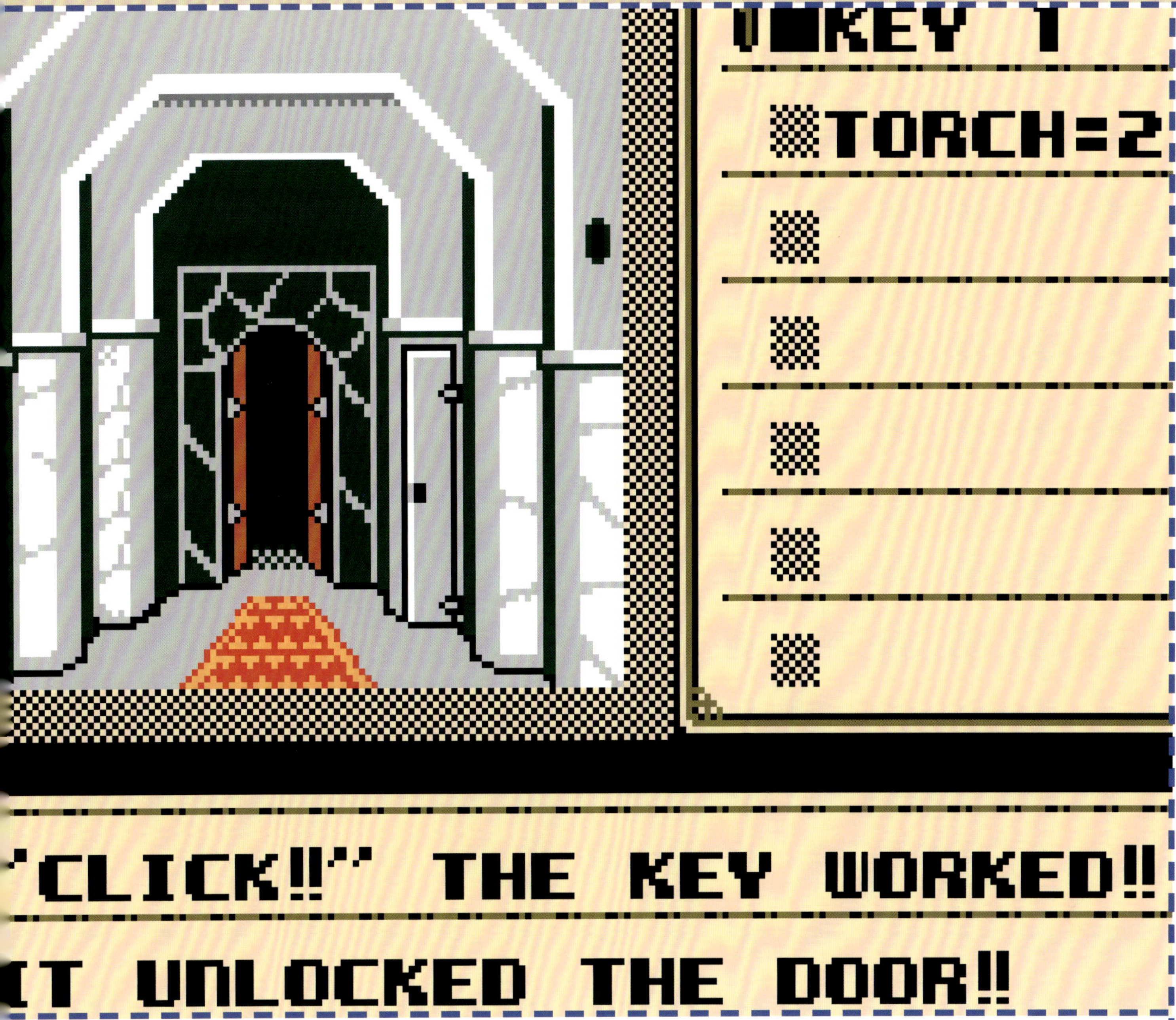

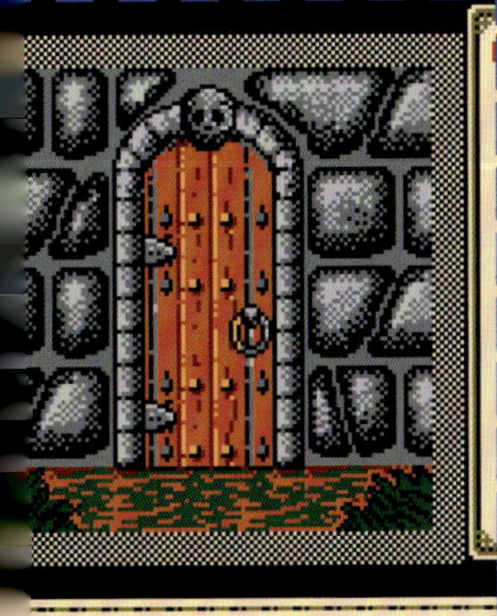

SHADOWGATE

PLATFORM: **MACINTOSH / VARIOUS**
DEV: **ICOM SIMULATIONS** | PUB: **KEMCO-SEIKA**
INITIAL RELEASE: **JULY 1987**
SHOWN HERE: **NINTENDO ENTERTAINMENT SYSTEM VERSION, 1989**

NOTABLE FOR: *A VISUAL INTERFACE FOR THE ADVENTURE GENRE*

SHADOWS TALLER THAN OUR SOULS

The Macintosh home computer should have been the perfect place for video games to evolve. Between its mouse-driven interface and gorgeous high-resolution graphics, the system begged to be put to use for entertainment. And, no question about it, the Mac did give us some wholly inventive creations, ranging from the bizarre *Ballblazer*-like *Shufflepuck Café* to proto-smartphone time-wasters like *Stunt Copter* to Bungie's cerebral pre-*Halo/Destiny* masterpieces *Pathways into Darkness* and *Marathon*.

But, for the most part, the Mac platform struggled to realize its potential as a gaming rig because its own creator hobbled it right from the starting block. Apple cofounder Steve Jobs took a dim view of video games—despite having made his initial fortune as an early Atari employee!—and his peculiar sense of aesthetics forced early Mac models to forego elements that would have been vital for video game support, like internal hard drives. With weak initial sales, the Mac coulda-shoulda-woulda been an incubator for revolutionary games, but those works came few and far between, overlooked by the public at large. Every once in a while, though, a Mac-first masterpiece slipped through and overcame the odds to become a genuine hit. No Mac original fared better than Cyan's *Myst*, a game that made use of the computer's unique tools like the HyperCard visual programming platform and QuickTime video to revolutionize adventure gaming. But even that wasn't the first truly groundbreaking adventure to work its way free of the Mac bubble. Years before *Myst*, a company called ICOM Simulations created a tetralogy of adventure games specifically for Macintosh tech, the *MacVenture* series: *Déjà Vu* and its sequel, *Uninvited*, and *Shadowgate*.

Of the four, *Shadowgate* commands the greatest legacy among classic gaming enthusiasts, thanks largely to its console ports. The Nintendo Entertainment System version, ported by Japanese publisher Kemco-Seika, hit at the peak of the NES's popularity and offered the system's owners a new experience within its generally action-driven library. Kemco sold hundreds of thousands of copies, which meant that (through the tendency of a single NES cartridge to circulate among several friends and classmates over the course of its life) easily more than a million people have played the game.

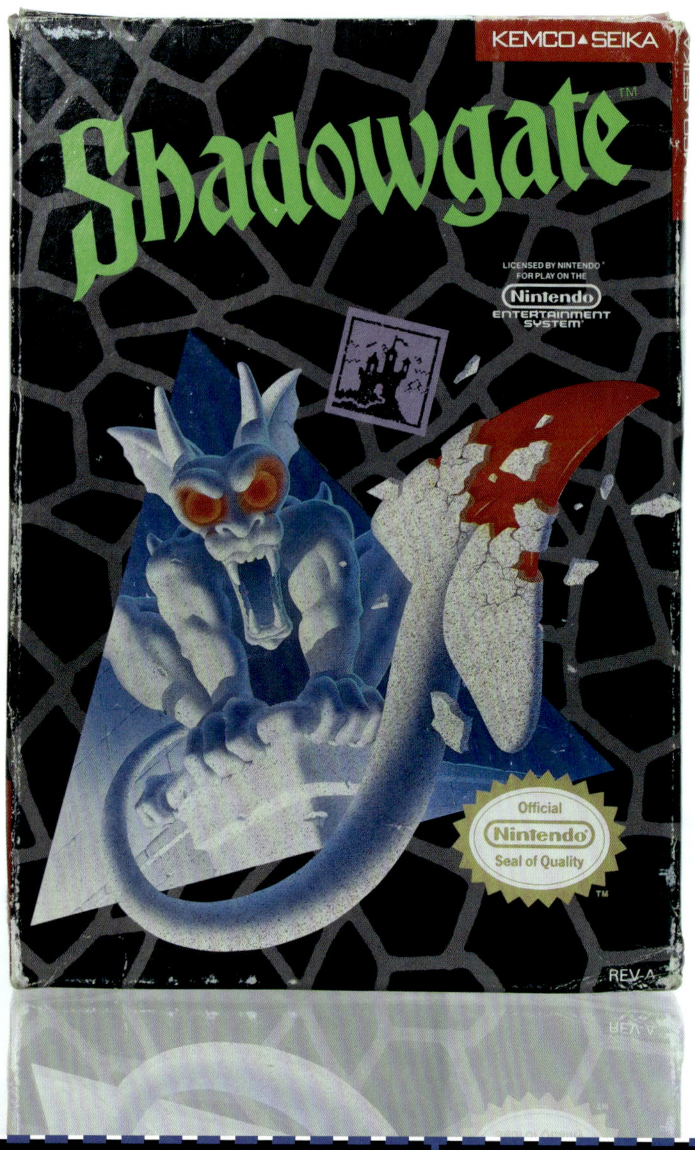

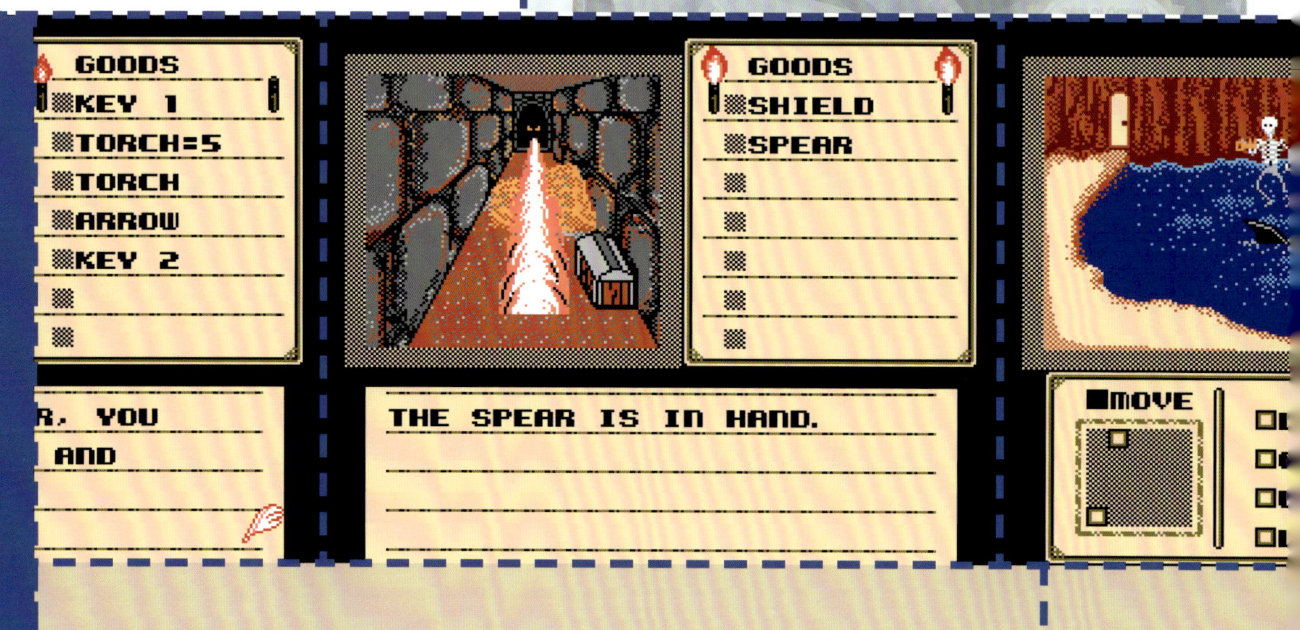

And that's not even taking into account its unknowable reach in the age of emulation, where the NES conversion of *Shadowgate* is the most easily accessible rendition of the game. (Kemco also released this port in Japan, where it gained a different sort of repute thanks to the frenzied, over-the-top tone of its localization.)

Admittedly, *Shadowgate*'s NES adaptation loses much of the Mac game's elegance. ICOM designed *Shadowgate* around the Mac's vocabulary: point-and-click, drag-and-drop, and multi-window viewpoints. Every inch of the screen presented vital information—the current location view and name, a mini-map presenting that node's exits, and a brilliant inventory window—all discretely tucked into their own space. All the elements that would normally require players to take a few turns inquiring after appeared in *Shadowgate*'s play space to be taken in and parsed in mere seconds, realizing the potential of graphical adventures in a way that its predecessors had only hinted at. Players could spend less time fussing with the particulars of their current status and focus on solving puzzles. The inventory window in particular felt like a leap into the future. It dedicated a portion of the screen to the player's ever-growing pile of items as icons that players could apply to in-game objects by dragging them from one window to the other.

The NES version had to tone things down considerably, reverting to a text-based menu system closer in nature to that of *Dragon Quest* due to memory and resolution limitations. Still, the fundamental appeal of *Shadowgate* came through. It's a tricky adventure set in the castle of a diabolical mage, which players needed to traverse by solving puzzles as wicked as the villain. More often than not, puzzles amounted to trial-and-error experimentation, with seemingly intuitive actions leading to cunning traps. This "gotcha!" design would have been vexing if not for two details. First, players could save their progress nearly anywhere, meaning that a cautious approach would result in little lost time, even in the face of a cheap trap. Second, the writing was every bit as punchy as *Zork*'s, full of cheeky sarcasm and ironic wit. Practically every form of death one could encounter in *Shadowgate*—which was a lot!—came with its own droll description, which blunted the sting of failure.

But ultimately, *Shadowgate* worked because it further developed the spirit of metroidvania discovery. Castle Shadowgate contained dozens of interconnected rooms that begged to be explored, with progress gated by puzzles; even the monsters you had to fight amounted to riddles that needed to be bypassed with the proper combination of tools! Most of those puzzles required you to delve deeper into the castle's depths to find the necessary tool before backtracking, mapping the paths and taking notes along the way. The game was another small evolutionary step for the genre. And an awful lot of deaths. *M*

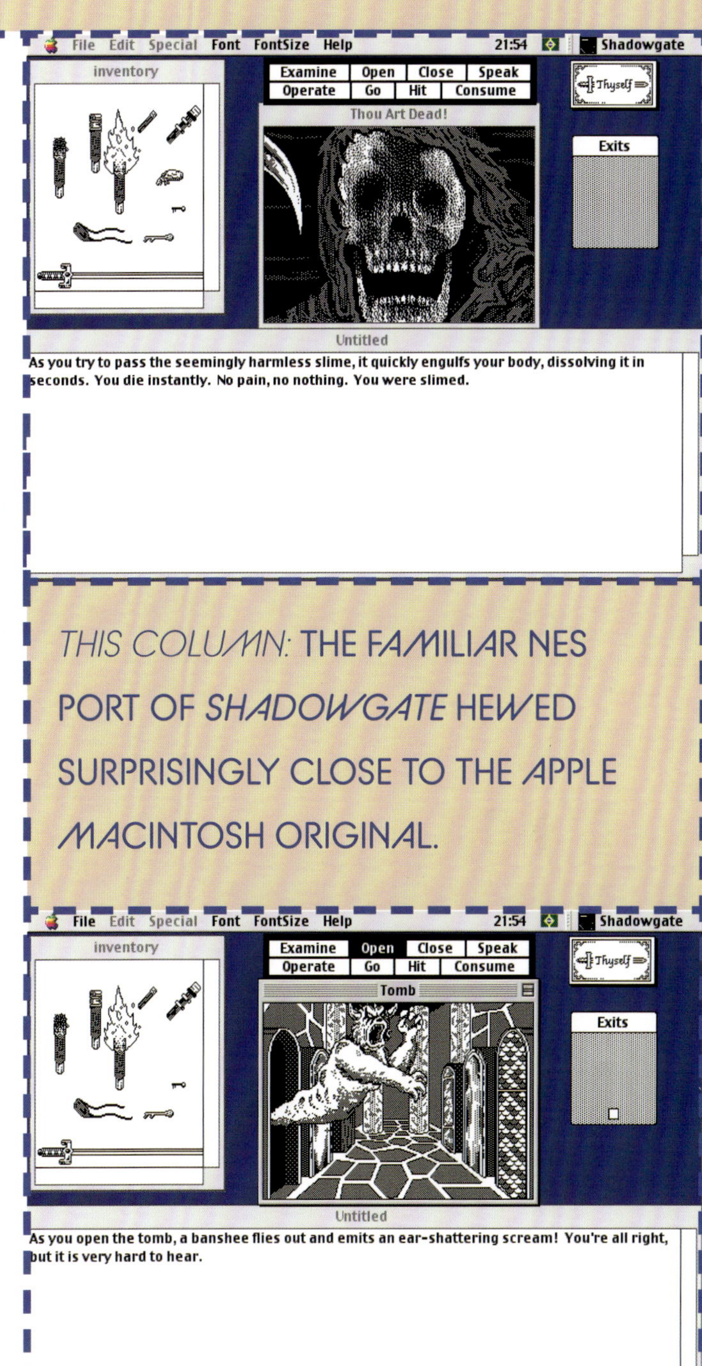

THIS COLUMN: THE FAMILIAR NES PORT OF *SHADOWGATE* HEWED SURPRISINGLY CLOSE TO THE APPLE MACINTOSH ORIGINAL.

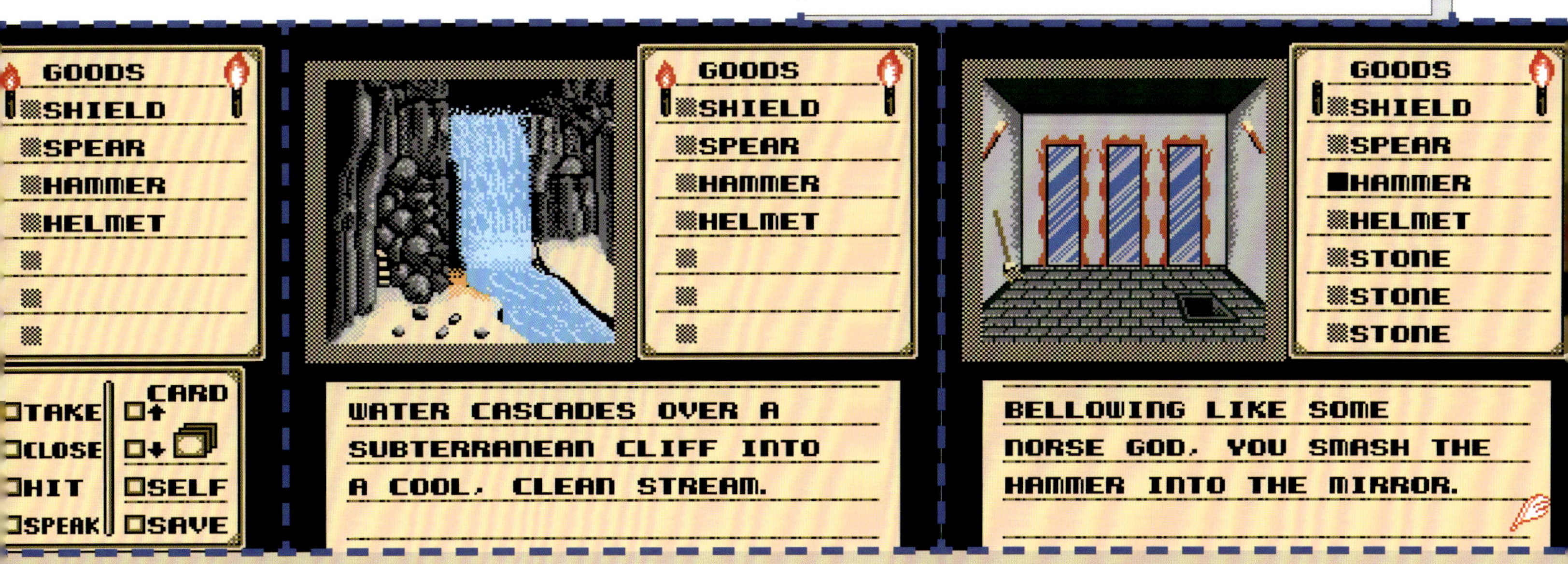

THE DRAGON SLAYER SERIES

Nihon Falcom launched the *Dragon Slayer* games in 1984 as a cutting-edge effort to distill the rudiments of the role-playing genre into a simplified, accessible form. The series abandoned that premise almost immediately. The second *Dragon Slayer* title, Xanadu, may have offered a lean combat system, but everything else about the game took a decidedly unfriendly approach that demanded players give their all. Aside from the platformer-like *Legacy of the Wizard*, the *Dragon Slayer* games grew progressively harder with each entry, steadily discarding action principles and mechanics in favor of meatier, more involved, and more abstract approaches.

Dragon Slayer came incredibly close to presenting a proper metroidvania with the fast-paced exploratory action of *Legacy of the Wizard*. However, Falcom followed that up with *Sorcerian*, a game that opened with a proper RPG character generation system and used its seemingly action-driven interface as a distraction from the intricacy and complexity of its underlying systems. The next game in the series, *Lord Monarch*, moved even further away from the fundamentals that had driven the design of the original *Dragon Slayer*. Rather than distilling classic role-playing elements into the workings of a pick-up-and-play action game, *Lord Monarch* ventured into the realm of the simulation RPG—an abstract, high-level format in which "god's-eye" views of large battlefields are the standard, and players generally order entire units or armies around while worrying about resource gathering and constructing buildings. Of course, being a Falcom game, *Lord Monarch* offered an interesting twist on this format; nevertheless, you'd barely recognize it as a Dragon Slayer title.

Today, the *Dragon Slayer* series lives on, albeit under a different name, in the form of the *Trails* games. *Dragon Slayer VI: The Legend of Heroes* took the form of a fairly standard menu-based RPG, and it fared so well that Falcom has created something like a dozen sequels under the *Legend of Heroes* moniker, which further splintered into the *Trails* series (e.g., *Trails in the Sky* and *Trails from Zero*); the latest of these titles, *Kai no Kiseki*, saw a 2024 release in Japan.

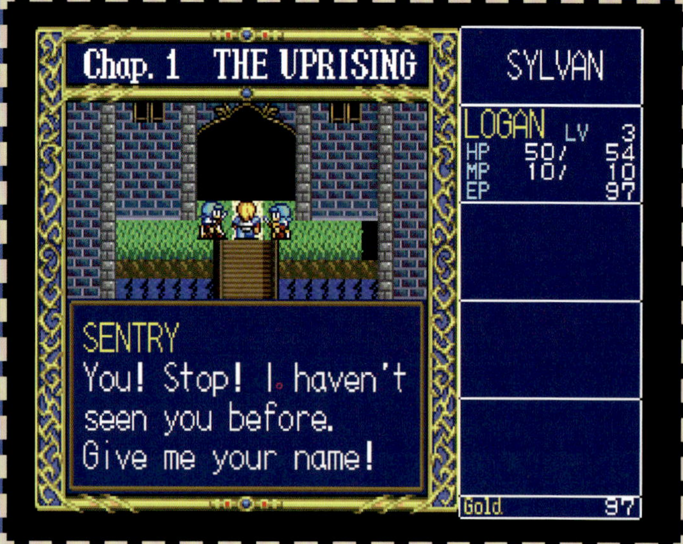

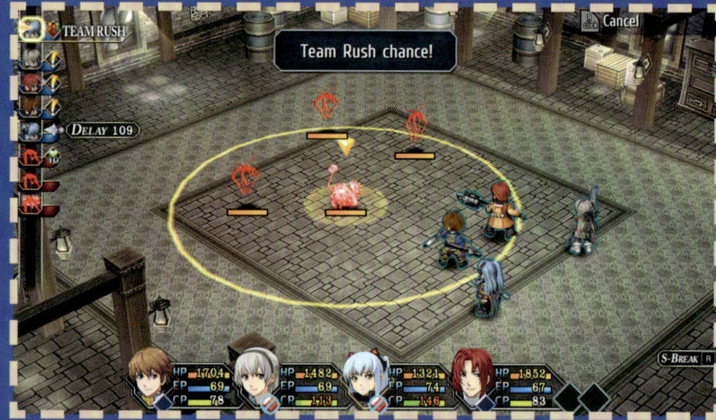

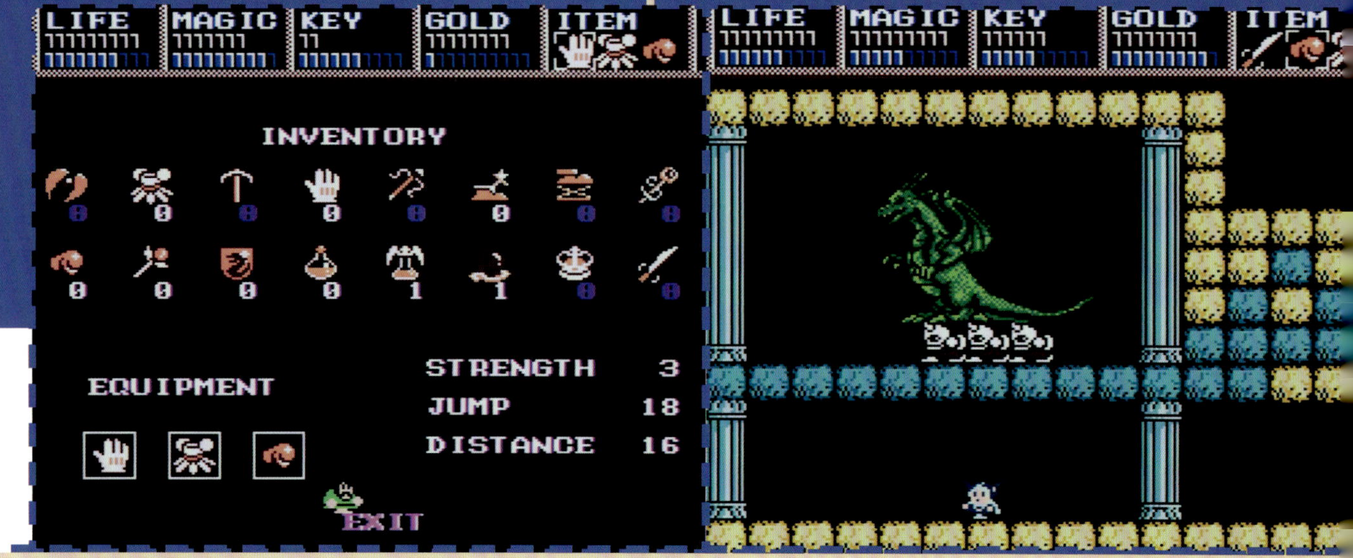

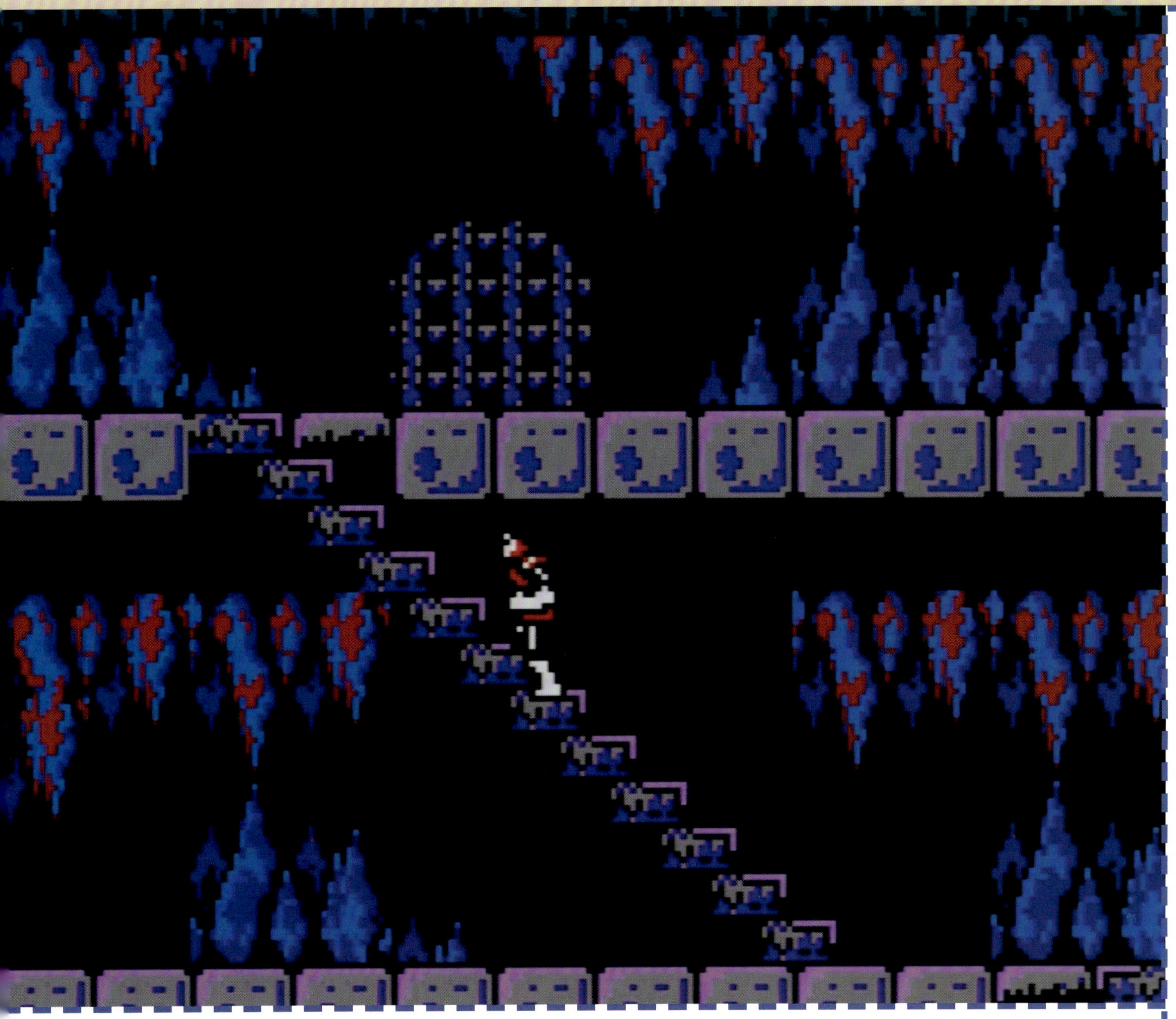

CASTLEVANIA II: SIMON'S QUEST

PLATFORM: **FAMICOM DISK SYSTEM / NES**
DEV: **KONAMI** | PUB: **KONAMI**
INITIAL RELEASE: **AUG. 1987**

NOTABLE FOR: **OPEN-WORLD ACTION WITH FULL EXPERIENCE RPG SYSTEMS**

THE BELMONT STAKES

The word "metroidvania" mashes together two trademarked names into a barely legal portmanteau: *Metroid* and *Castlevania*. Originally coined to specifically describe *Castlevania* games whose structure and interface design appeared to nod toward elements of *Metroid*, "metroidvania" has come to represent free-roaming, exploratory, RPG-inflected action games in general. But it's not as though both of the series that gave us this neologism were destined for their place in this particular slice of history. *Metroid* may have offered open-ended exploration from day one, but *Castlevania* took longer to warm up to its noble task.

The original *Castlevania* was as non-exploratory an action game as you could hope for, a six-stage arcade-style march through a haunted castle along a definite, finite path. It had no character upgrade system besides a boost to the hero's base weapon that vanished each time the player lost a life, and the closest the player ever came to backtracking was if they needed to double back half a screen to grab some hidden goods. But around the same time that *Castlevania* debuted on Disk System and NES, Konami published a somewhat more open-ended interpretation of the same content, *Vampire Killer*. Although that MSX2 adventure didn't truly focus on exploration with its eighteen sequential stages, each individual level required some degree of curiosity and backtracking on the player's behalf. It even demanded a bit of inventory management.

When the time came for a sequel a year later, Konami seemed uncertain whether to work in the NES mode of pure action or to take the MSX2 hybrid approach. In the end, that follow-up—*Castlevania II: Simon's Quest* (a.k.a. *Dracula II: Noroi no Fuuin*, or "The Accursed Seal")—ends up splitting the difference. Since it shipped for Disk System and the NES rather than the MSX2, it incorporates NES-style visuals and control mechanics, but the overall feel of the adventure draws heavily on *Vampire Killer*. In fact, takes the MSX2 game a step further in terms of nonlinearity, presenting players with an adventure that spans the entirety of Transylvania and leaves them to find their own way across the countryside.

Despite shipping under the name *Castlevania*, in truth Dracula's eponymous castle only appears for the finale, having

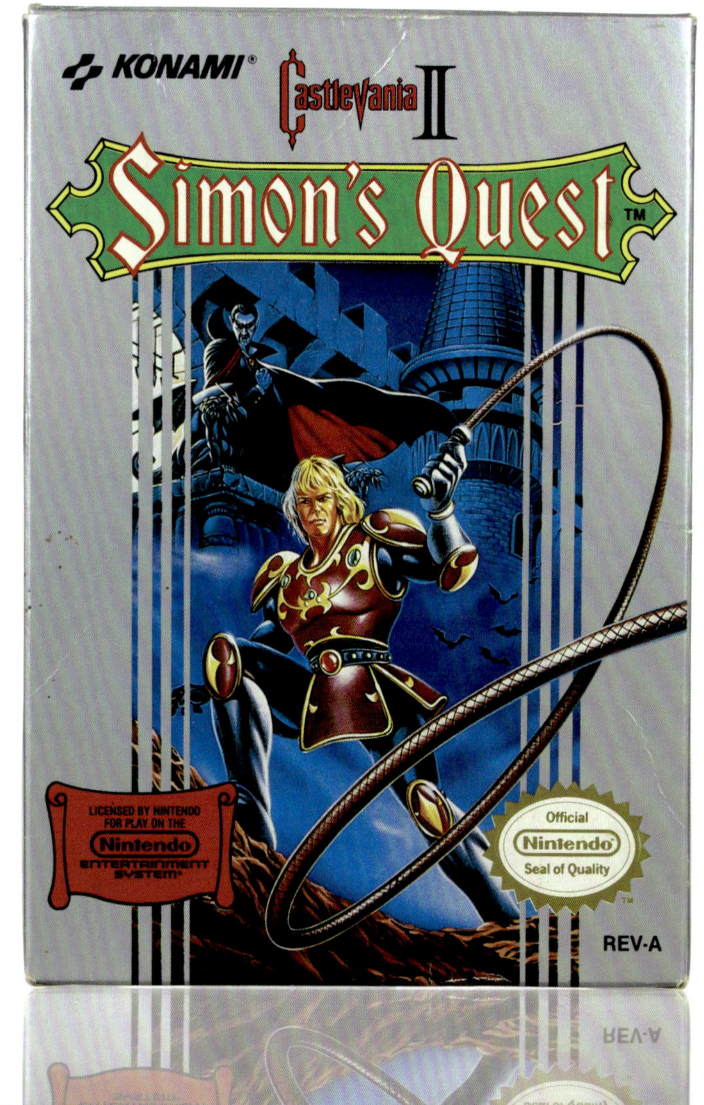

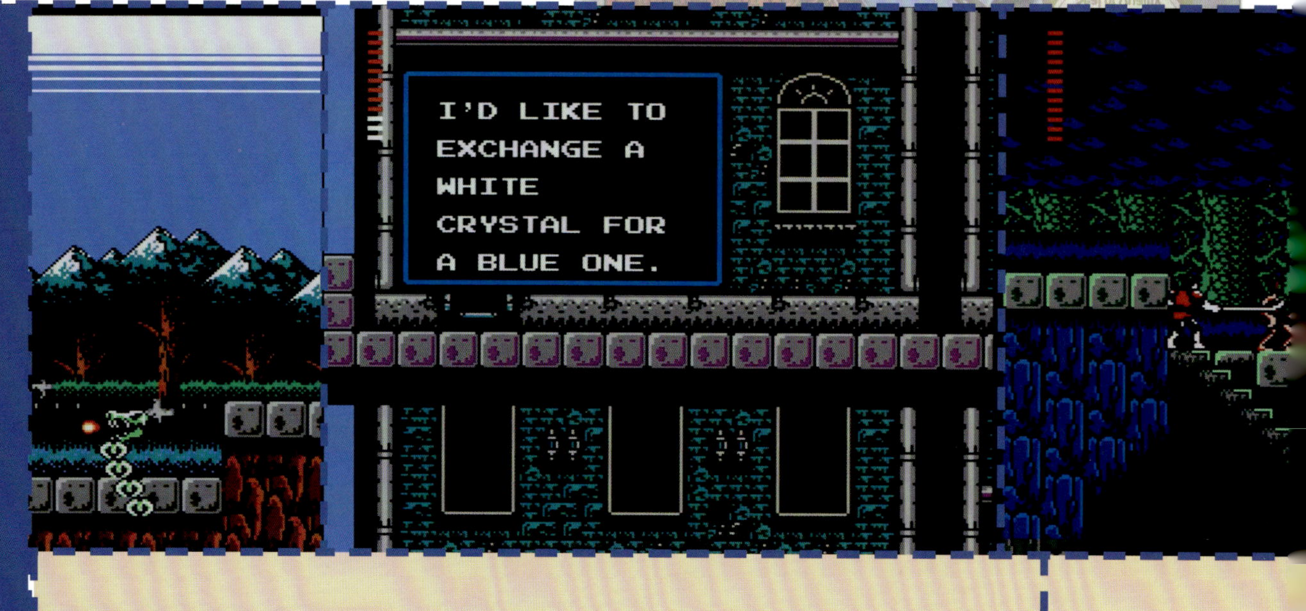

been reduced to a heap of rubble at the end of the first game. There's not much left to do in the ruins besides dig into the basement and burn Dracula's remains on an underground altar. Rather than stalk castle corridors, Simon instead roams the forest and swamps of Transylvania, stopping into villages and seeking essential tools and permanent weapon upgrades to improve his survival odds and allow him to destroy the evil count once and for all. The game most closely resembles *Vampire Killer* when you venture into the five cursed mansions located around the land. Each mansion contains a piece of Dracula's mortal remains (which Simon must collect before burning), and each one plays a great deal like alone stages of the MSX2 game. Every mansion encompasses a self-contained space. These lack the infinite-loop scrolling that defined many stages on the MSX2 but otherwise consist of familiar elements. There's plenty of up-and-down advancement between different floors of the mansion via staircases, moving platforms, and occasional leaps into the unknown. Many of the mansions require Simon to puzzle out hidden or invisible passages, either by using Holy Water to dissolve fake blocks or by wielding Dracula's Eye to reveal illusory walls. The Dracula relic in each mansion has been secured in a mystic orb, which can only be shattered with the use of an Oak Stake, which in turn must be purchased with Hearts from merchants hiding inside each mansion. These shopkeepers appear to have been inspired quite directly by the merchants in *Vampire Killer*.

SIMON'S QUEST STANDS APART FROM ITS PREDECESSOR *VAMPIRE KILLER* NOT ONLY IN THE OPEN-ENDED LANDSCAPE THAT LINKS MANSIONS AND TOWNS, BUT ALSO BECAUSE COMPLETING THE QUEST INVOLVES HUNTING FOR PERMANENT UPGRADES THAT ENABLE SIMON TO EXPLORE TRANSYLVANIA FURTHER.

Still, *Simon's Quest* stands apart from *Vampire Killer* not only due to the open-ended landscape that links the mansions and town, but also because completing the eponymous quest involves hunting for and collecting permanent power-ups and tools that enable Simon to explore Transylvania further. These must be purchased, traded for, or simply uncovered, and Simon can't complete his quest without them. For example, Simon can purchase a White Crystal in the town where he begins his quest, though this item's purpose isn't immediately apparent. (Then again, pretty much nothing in *Castlevania II* is immediately apparent; it's a game designed to be opaque and borderline impossible without using strategy guides—quite a step backward from the intuitive *Faxanadu*.) It turns out that if you happen to equip the White Crystal in the first mansion, you'll suddenly be able to see a crucial moving platform at the very entrance of the building that allows you to enter the mansion proper. The platform is always there, and you can leap onto it even if you can't see it, but without the White Crystal in hand the mansion appears to enter directly into an impassable pool of water.

In gameplay terms, that's all the White Crystal is good for. Yet it still plays a crucial role in your quest even after you've completed that first mansion; somewhere in the world, you can trade it for a Blue Crystal that, when held, allows you to reveal a false lakefront that hides a second mansion. Later, you'll meet someone seeking a Blue Crystal who will happily accept yours in trade for the Red Crystal they own. This third crystal will allow you to summon a whirlwind that carries you to yet another mansion.

The game's other tools prove to be every bit as vital to your trip as the crystals. That includes Holy Water, which breaks through false blocks and obstructions, and the laurels, which render you briefly invincible—handy in combat, essential in traversing vast swaths of poisonous swamp. And, in proper metroidvania style, even the remains of Dracula often do more than simply act as a key to access the final battle. While Dracula's Heart truly is nothing more than a key (show it to the ferryman and he'll take you to—you guessed it—a mansion) and Dracula's Ring only lets you cross the boundary into Castlevania's ruins, Dracula's Rib works as a shield that can reflect enemy projectiles, just like the shield item in *Vampire Killer*. Dracula's Eye

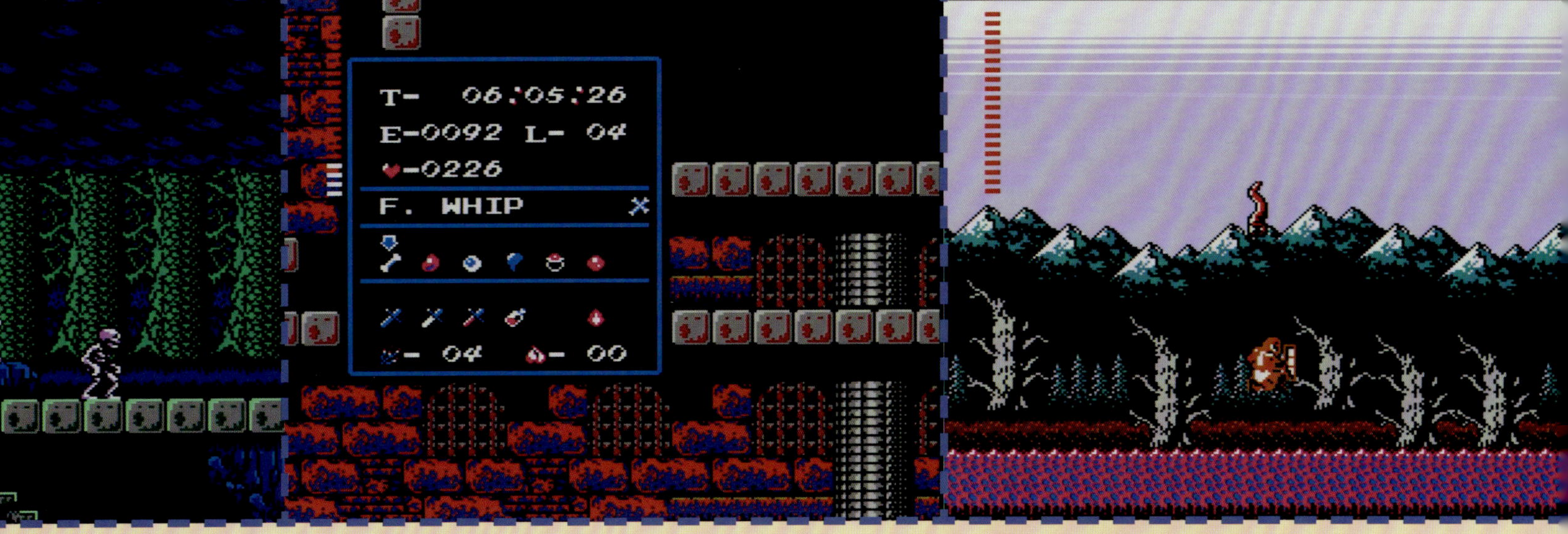

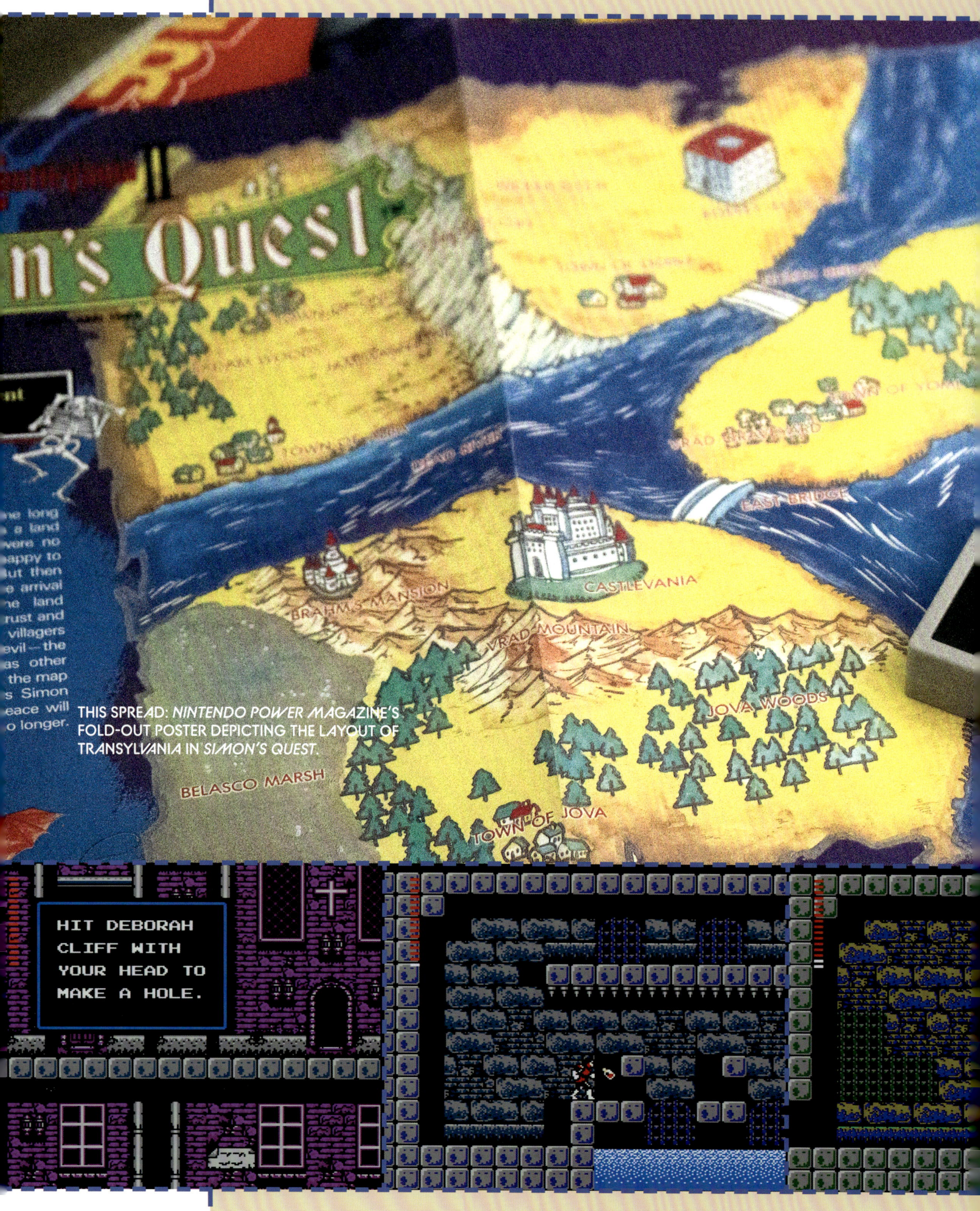

THIS SPREAD: *NINTENDO POWER MAGAZINE'S* FOLD-OUT POSTER DEPICTING THE LAYOUT OF TRANSYLVANIA IN *SIMON'S QUEST.*

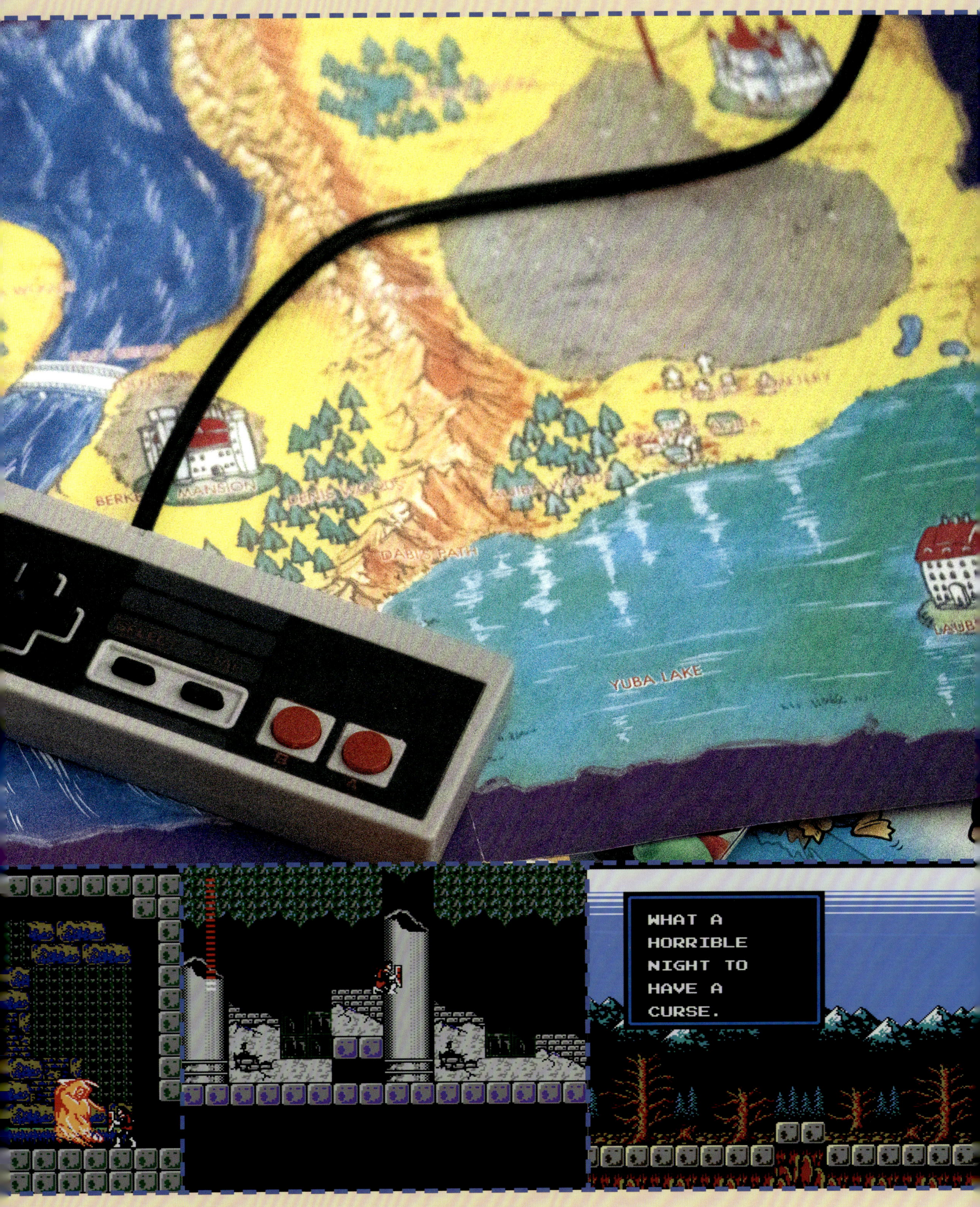
MANSION
DABI'S PATH
YUBA LAKE
WHAT A
HORRIBLE
NIGHT TO
HAVE A
CURSE.

reveals false passages, and his Nail imbues your whip with the power of Holy Water, allowing it to shatter false blocks. A fair portion of *Simon's Quest* involves crisscrossing Transylvania to collect these items and either put them to use or trade them for the next tool in a "Straw Millionaire" chain. You also accumulate Hearts, which no longer simply function as ammunition for sub-weapons, such as the Holy Water, daggers, and the Diamond, did in *Castlevania*. Here Hearts double as currency, just as in *Vampire Killer*. They're essential not only for purchasing Crystals and Oak Stakes, but also for buying permanent upgrades to your whip, consumables like garlic and laurels—and upgrading Simon himself. Enemies drop different values of Heart (one, five, or ten) depending on that foe's power level. Collecting these Hearts also provides Simon with experience points to add a legitimate hint of traditional by-the-stats role-playing here: as Simon gains experience points, he levels up.

Don't mistake *Castlevania II* for a full-scale RPG, though. Boosting Simon's level doesn't do much to increase his combat prowess, giving him a modest hit point boost. There's no power bump or defensive buff beyond extending his life meter slightly. The benefits of leveling up are greatly limited in *Castlevania II*, as are the means: Enemies in a given area only yield EXP until you reach that zone's limit. Once you've hit that point, you receive no further experience from grinding. There's a hard level cap for the game—which is just as well, since it's not particularly difficult. The only real challenge in completing *Simon's Quest* comes in the miserable task of navigating the clues Simon receives from the townspeople he speaks to along the way. Several critical tasks are utterly unintuitive—kneeling at a cliff for ten seconds while holding the Red Crystal, for example—and the NPCs offer murky guidance at best.

This impenetrable dialogue is by design. Even in the Japanese version, conversations amount to a succession of cryptic riddles and outright misdirection. And so, as exploratory adventures go, *Castlevania II* isn't a total win; again, *Faxanadu* offered a more cogent example of how clear quest objectives and smart gameplay structures could make for a compelling adventure. Still, *Castlevania II* has its charms, and a big part of that comes from its intriguing marriage of action and role-playing elements in the style of *Zelda II*. *Simon's Quest* probably shipped too soon after *Zelda II* to be fully inspired by that game—or by *Metroid*, for that matter. Its director, Hitoshi Akamatsu, has cited Konami's own *Maze of Galious* for MSX, which debuted on Famicom a couple of weeks before *Castlevania II*, as the greatest influence on *Simon's Quest* design. The simple fact of the matter is that action-RPG mania swept Japanese computers and consoles in 1987, and *Simon's Quest*—despite its shortcomings—demonstrates the appeal of a meandering action game bursting with great graphics, music, and environmental design. M

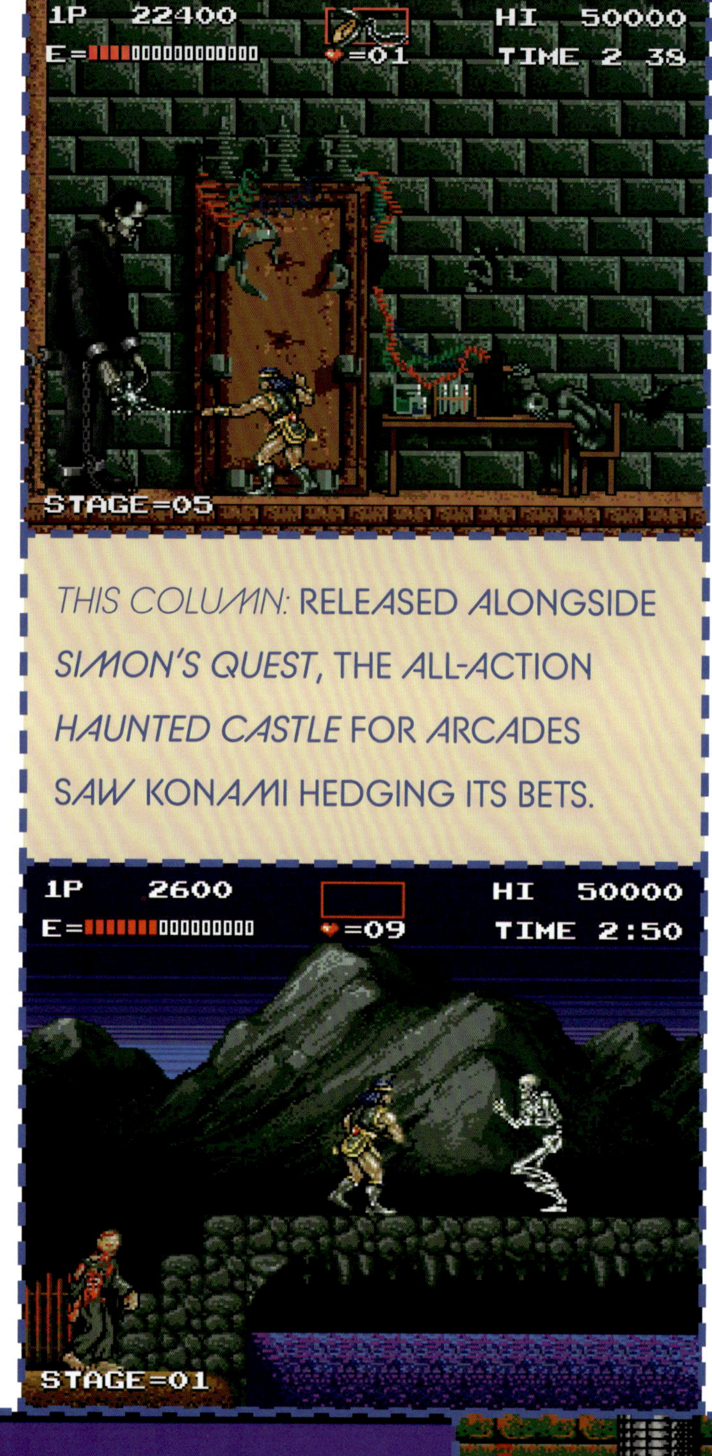

THIS COLUMN: RELEASED ALONGSIDE *SIMON'S QUEST*, THE ALL-ACTION *HAUNTED CASTLE* FOR ARCADES SAW KONAMI HEDGING ITS BETS.

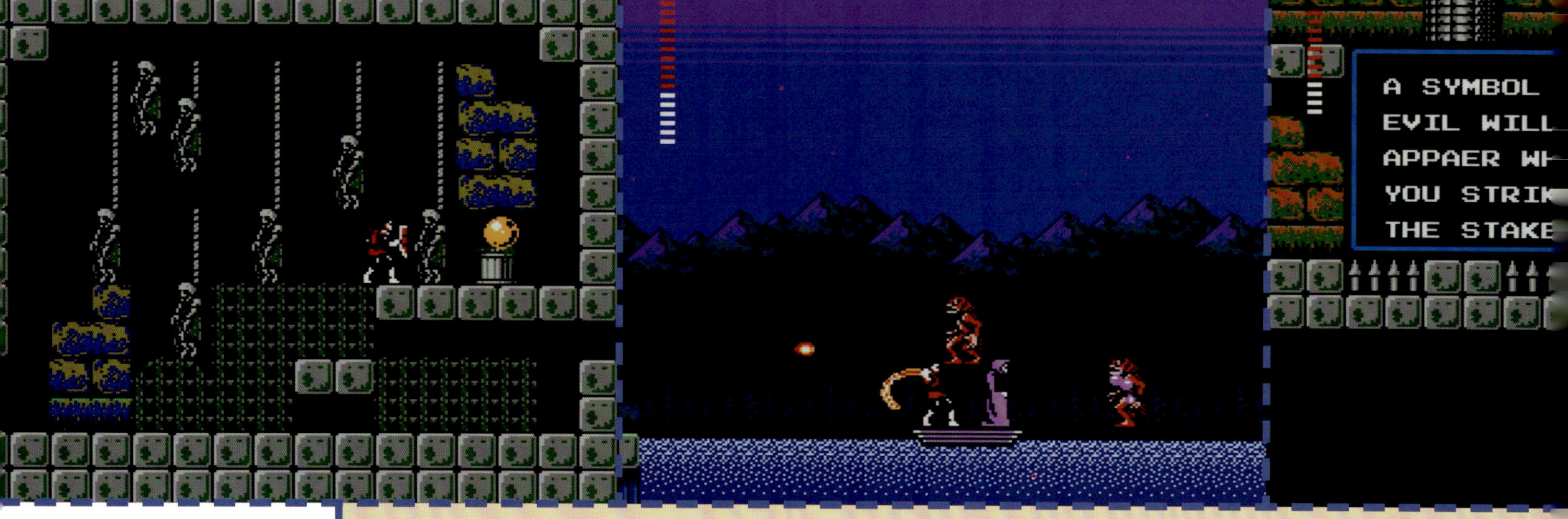

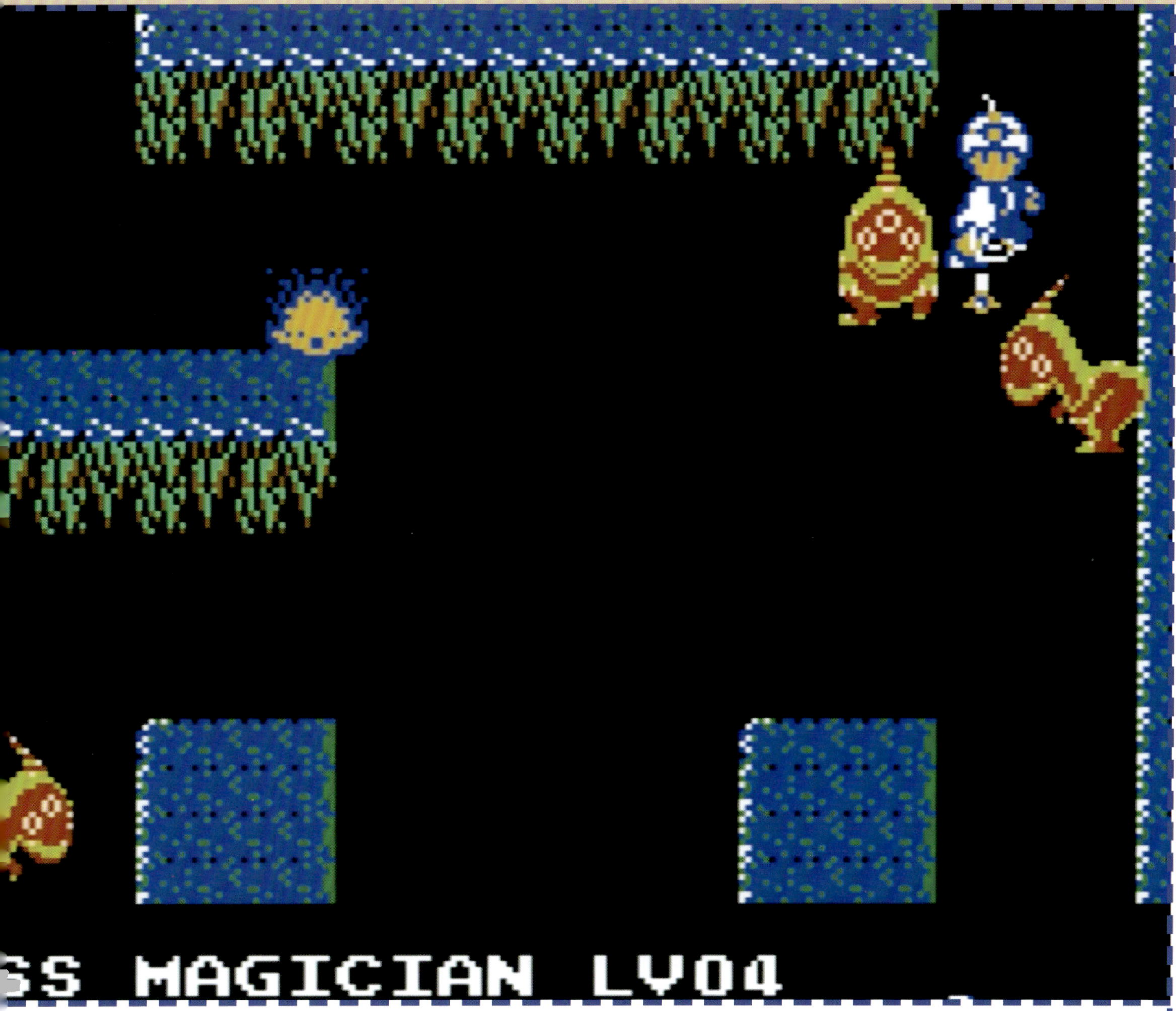

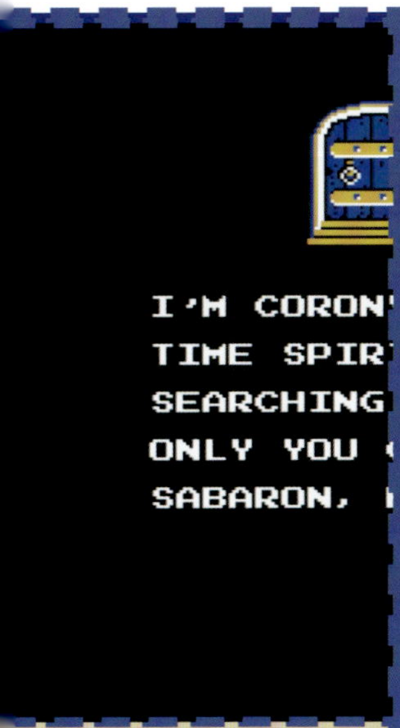

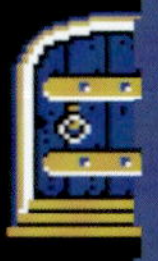

THE MAGIC OF SCHEHERAZADE

PLATFORM: **FAMICOM / NES**
DEV: **CULTURE BRAIN** | PUB: **CULTURE BRAIN**
INITIAL RELEASE DATE: **SEPT. 1987**

NOTABLE FOR: **OPEN-WORLD ACTION WITH FULL EXPERIENCE RPG SYSTEMS**

A LINK BETWEEN GENRES

With *The Magic of Scheherazade*, Culture Brain dared to ask: What if *Zelda II* had played more like the original The *Legend of Zelda* in places? But not in the way that *Golvellius* approached that question? The answer they came up with is an action-RPG in a remarkably pure sense of the word.

Culture Brain was a relative newcomer to the console video game business by the time it made its first proper bid at this ambitious genre. Despite their inexperience, they went about it sensibly; *The Magic of Scheherazade* draws upon the developer's previous work for inspiration and direction rather than simply drafting off someone else's style. This isn't to say that it doesn't owe anything to anyone else, of course. But, fundamentally, The *Magic of Scheherazade* feels like the developer took one of its older games—namely, *Kung Fu Heroes*—and reworked it to incorporate more role-playing elements.

The bulk of this adventure takes place in a three-quarter perspective viewpoint in which you can walk about freely, attack foes with weapons and magic, use tools, and even jump around. Structurally, these areas closely resemble the overworld of *The Legend of Zelda*, though the action has a brisker pace and more elaborate geography that puts one in mind of *Zelda*'s samurai-themed companion release for Famicom Disk System, *Nazo no Murasame-jou*. Despite these similarities, look beneath the surface and you'll find a game whose flow and structure have more in common with *Dragon Quest* than Zelda or *Kung Fu Heroes*. For example, any time you enter a new region, your first order of business should always be to stop at the nearest town, where you'll spend time gathering information, buying equipment and items, and training up new skills.

Once you strike out into the world, your rollicking, action-packed journey takes you across fields and rivers, through deserts, up mountains, and into dungeons and palaces. It also takes you across time, as each chapter involves zipping through the fourth dimension into other periods of history in pursuit of princesses, monsters, pieces of equipment, and—most crucially—additional party members. Your nameless protagonist doesn't have to go

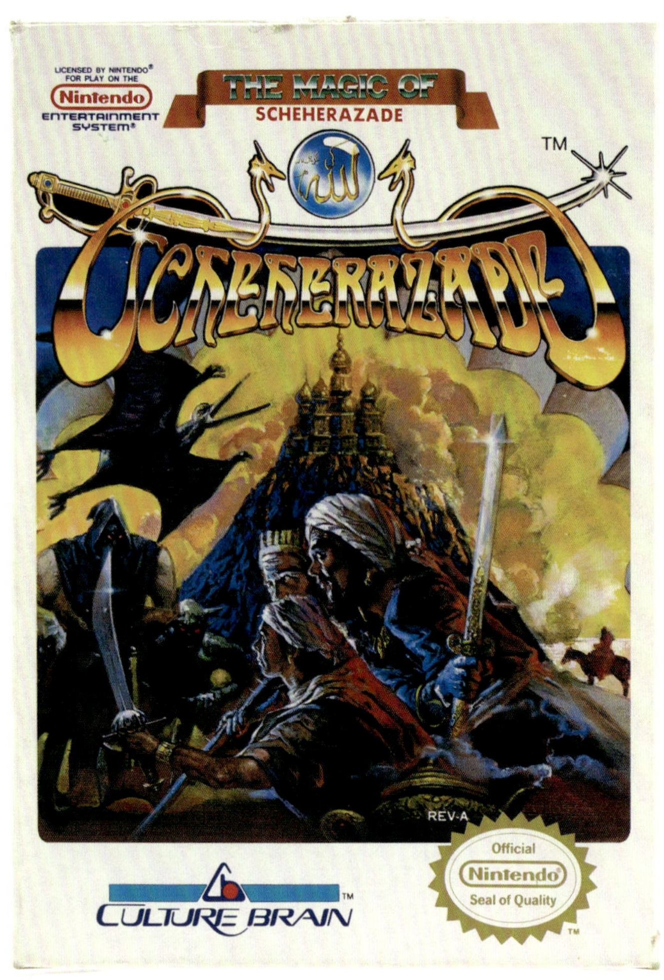

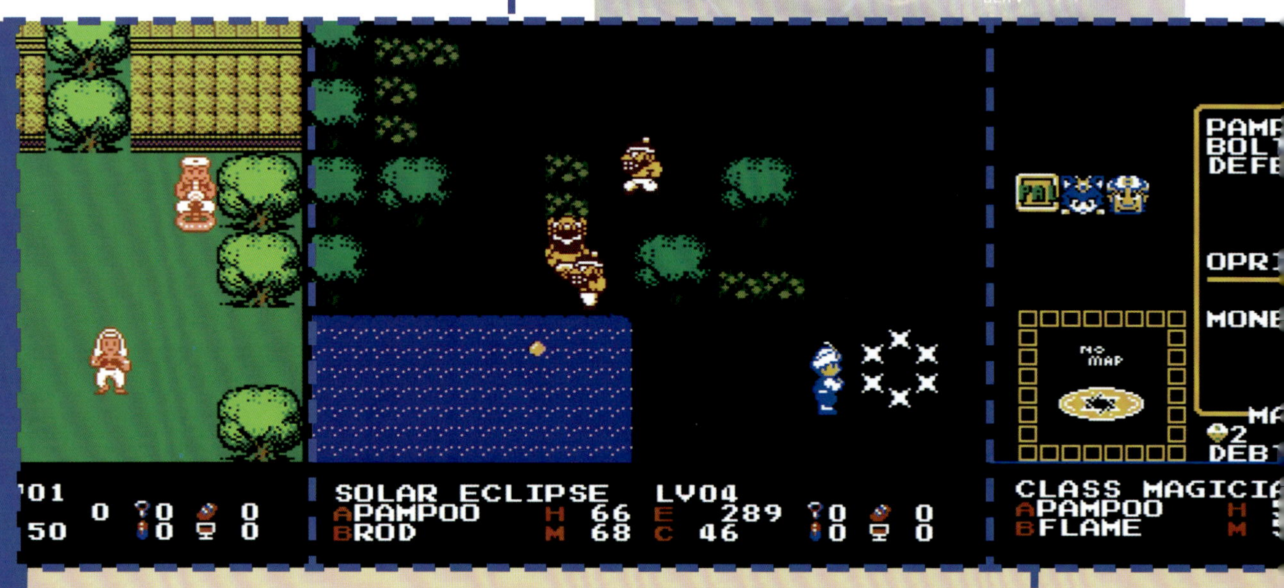

it alone here. Although only the main character appears during exploration and town sequences, the oddball companions he collects along the way play crucial roles in the adventure. They allow Val to cast healing magic, they reveal hidden items and entrances, they attack foes directly, and more. They also play a crucial role during solar eclipses by allowing players to travel the world via flying carpet.

The companions also factor heavily into the portions of the game that derive directly from *Dragon Quest*: the turn-based battle sequences. The party will randomly find itself whisked into turn-based combat against mobs of monsters, something that happens more frequently during eclipses. At these moments, you can assign a team of specific companions to assist you in your fight.

The Magic of Scheherazade doesn't entirely work. It pulls together a lot of different influences and tries to do a remarkable number of different things all at once. This ambition can leave the game feeling overstuffed with ideas that never gel. For example, the game has a sort of real-time element that manifests through solar eclipses, and certain special events and magic spells only become available during those eclipses. You can change the hero's class between fighter, magician, and saint, a class that allows you to use special items. You team up with nearly a dozen different allies, most of whom have little function in combat and only hang around to perform a specific task from time to time. You can swim, fly, and even attend universities where you learn specialized information like how to arrange your party into distinct battle formations that only work against unique sets of enemies. You travel through time! There's a casino years before that would become a mainstay of the *Dragon Quest* franchise!

In summary, there's a lot in here for an 8-bit game. Despite the game's haphazard design, you can't shake the sensation that Culture Brain was a few years ahead of the rest of the industry with *The Magic of Scheherazade*. The hybrid format and structure of this 1987 release wouldn't be matched until the 16-bit era brought forth the likes of Quintet's *SoulBlazer* and SquareSoft's *Secret of Mana*. And even then, those games dropped many elements featured in *Scheherazade*, like turn-based battles, in favor of a more streamlined design and greater focus on direct action. It's hard to believe that a title as ultimately obscure as *The Magic of Scheherazade* had any particular influence on these later works. Still, even if it amounted to a group of designers shouting into an empty room, Culture Brain's creation is noteworthy for allowing you to see all the disparate elements of the action-RPG genre on such clear display at once. It's a game that showcases how the metroidvania sausage would be made, eventually.

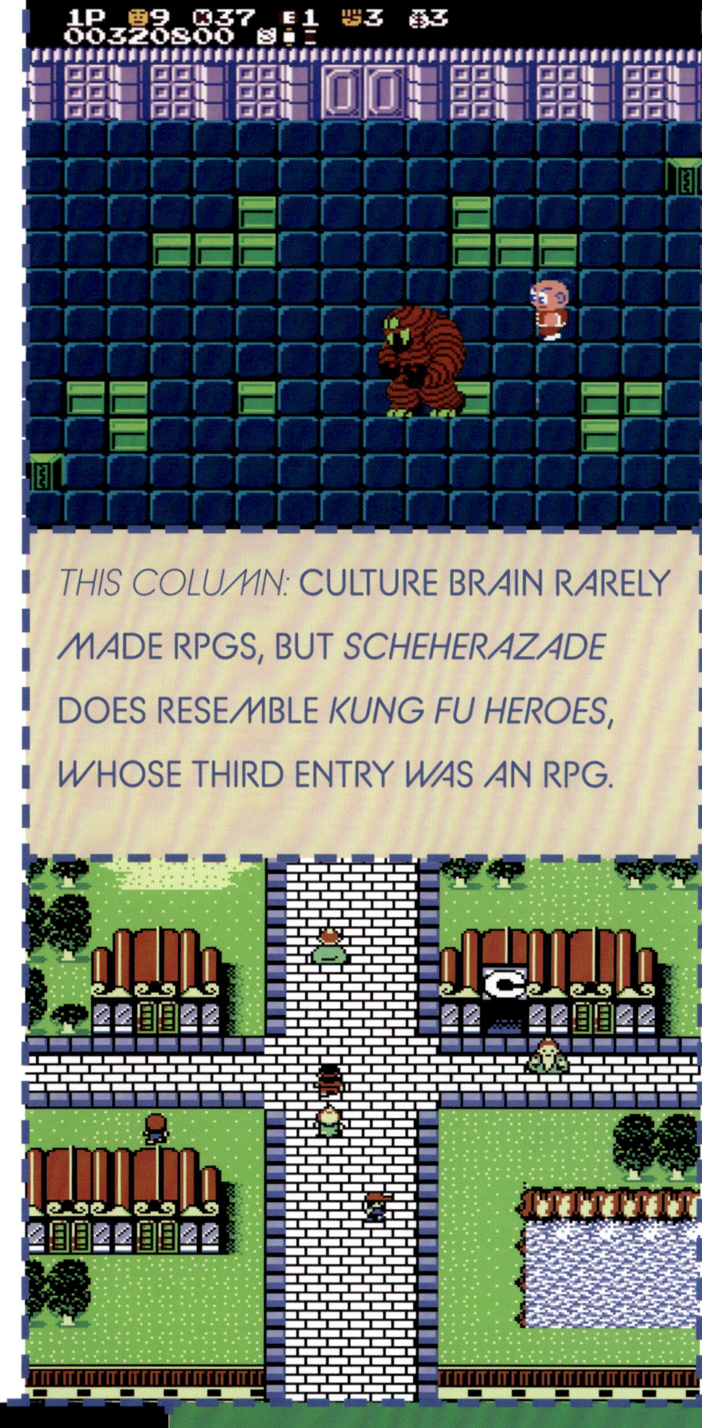

THIS COLUMN: CULTURE BRAIN RARELY MADE RPGS, BUT *SCHEHERAZADE* DOES RESEMBLE *KUNG FU HEROES*, WHOSE THIRD ENTRY WAS AN RPG.

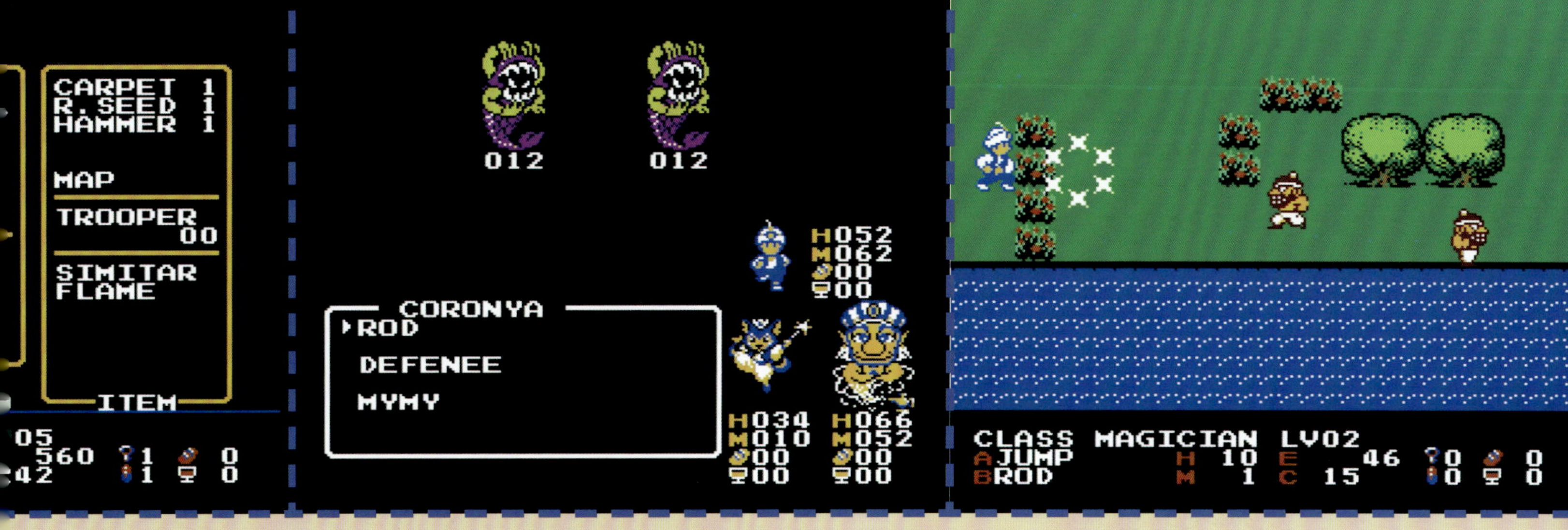

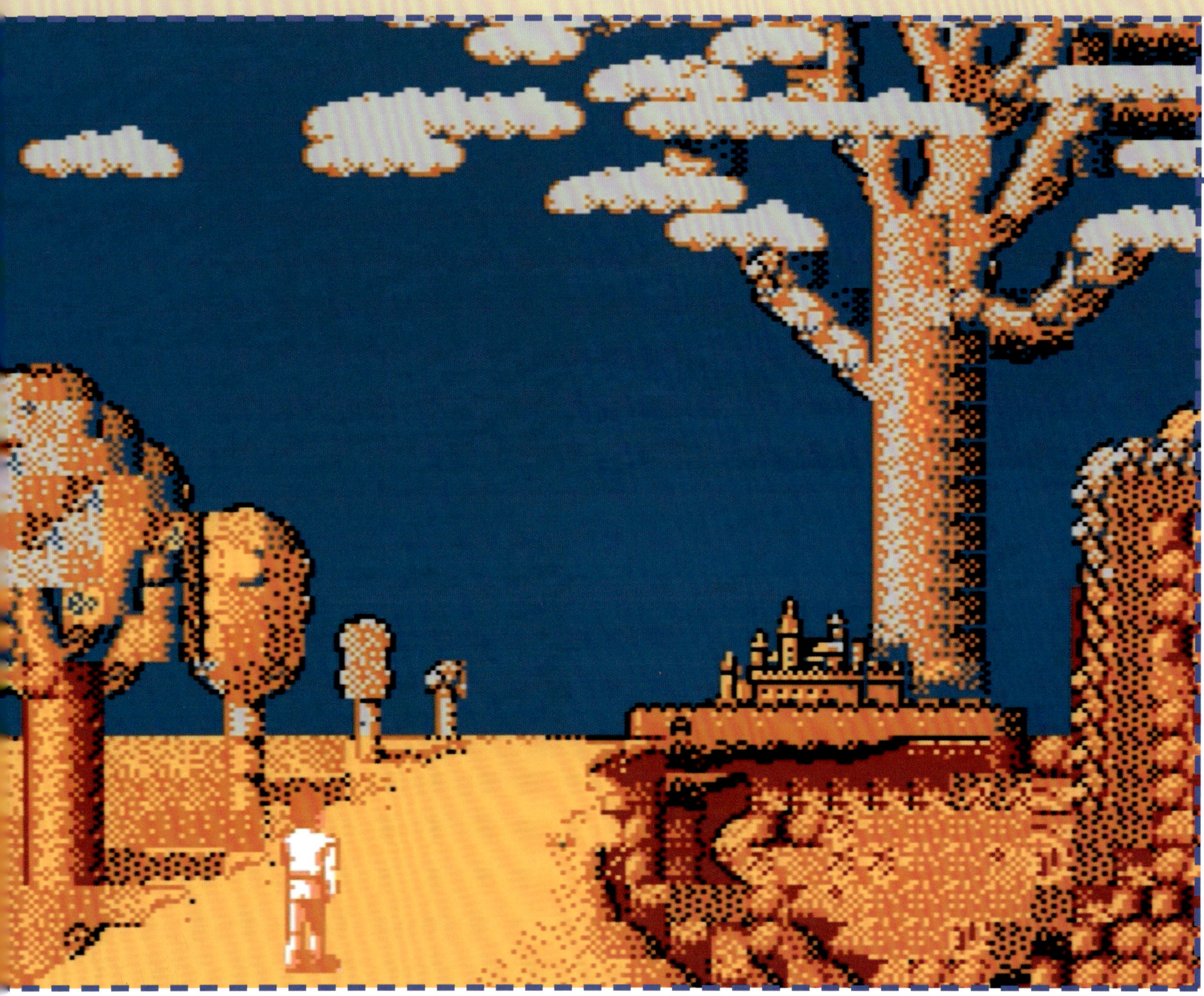

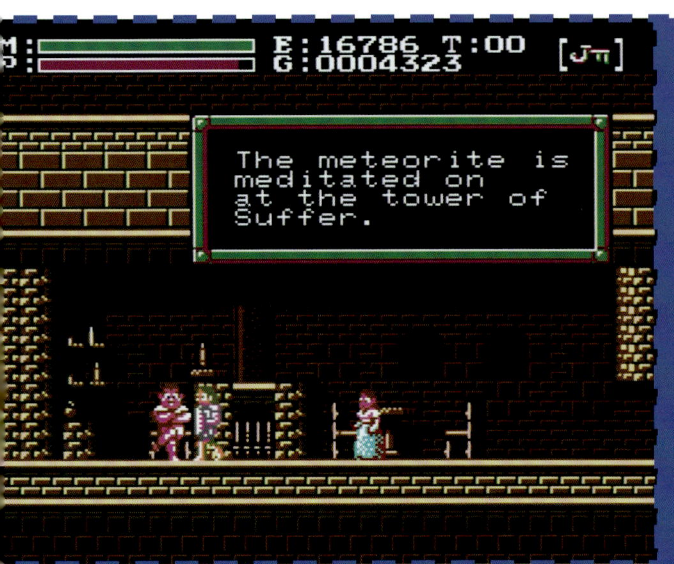

FAXANADU

PLATFORM: **FAMICOM / NES**
DEV: **HUDSON SOFT** | PUB: **NINTENDO**
INITIAL RELEASE DATE: **NOV. 1987**

NOTABLE FOR: *A PLATFORM ACTION-RPG WITH FULL EXPERIENCE AND ECONOMY SYSTEMS*

THE WORLD TREE'S WOE

Falcom seemed almost determined to redefine the action-RPG in 1987. In addition to *Ys* and *Legacy of the Wizard*, the company also gave us Faxanadu for Nintendo Entertainment System… sort of. Although Nihon Falcom signed off on this inventive action-RPG experience, and although title is an abbreviated version of "Famicom Xanadu," *Faxanadu* was designed top-to-bottom by Hudson Soft, fresh off their work on *Milon's Secret Castle*. Fortunately, *Faxanadu* holds up far better today than *Milon's Secret Castle* does. It involves no muddling around in obscure corners, nor the need to blast every block and tile onscreen in the hopes of finding some random hidden object or passage.

In fact, *Faxanadu* may be the most refined, most polished, least oblique game yet to appear in this prehistory of metroidvania games—the most modern work in sensibility and design alike. The game communicates the player's objectives clearly at every turn, dispensing quest objectives and gating irrelevant areas to prevent players from wandering lost for hours in search of a clue or key capable of moving the plot ahead. *Faxanadu* controls work reasonably well and the game gives you a decent challenge without every seeming unbalanced or unreasonable. It even includes an element of forgiveness that was uncommon in this era of software: if you ever run out of cash, you can return to the starting town to ask the king for more.

Now, this clarity of design does come with some limitations. *Faxanadu* doesn't really offer much in the way of opportunities to explore the world; it's fairly linear in its structure. The adventure takes place entirely within the interior of the World Tree, which is slowly dying due to the malign influence of a cosmic force, and you journey through the tree by moving from town to town, taking side excursions into small fortresses and dungeons along the way to complete the various objectives you need to move on to the next region. Dungeons typically contain a boss and some sort of tool you need to advance to the next part of the tree, or else a token you need to trade in exchange for a vital combat tool or key.

Villagers offer critical advice along your way, revealing the secrets of the World Tree; healing the player; providing passwords for saving progress; and, of course, selling essential weapons,

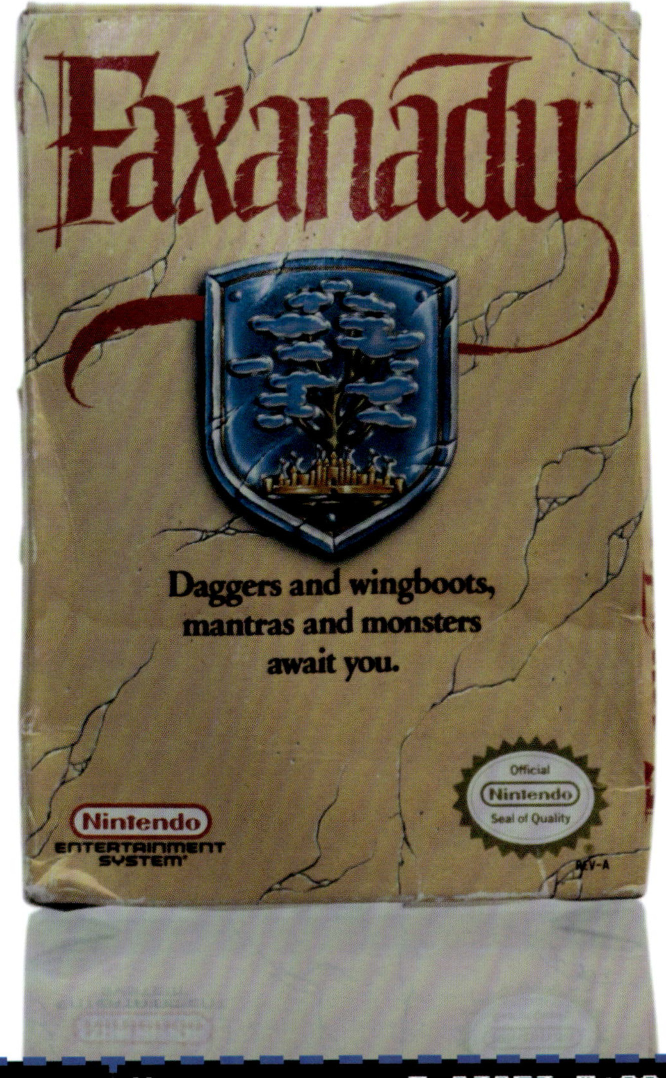

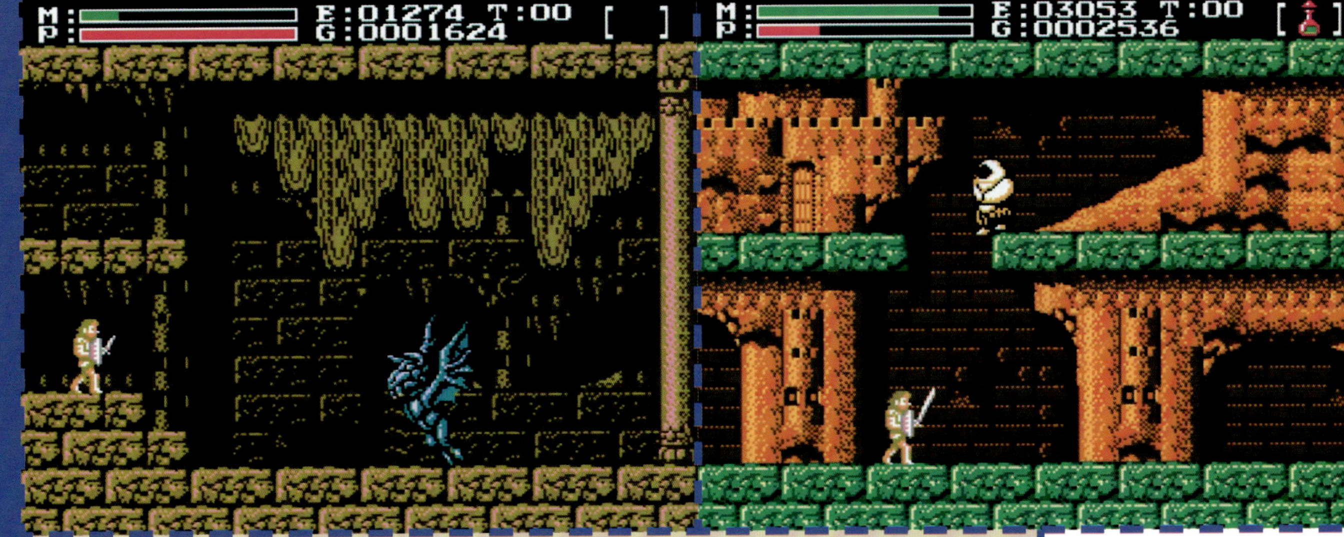

spells, and gear. Faxanadu largely relies on its economy to keep the player moving. Not only do you purchase most of your weapon and armor upgrades, you need to buy magic spells and even the different types of keys that open passages and gates into fortresses. Unsurprisingly, this does result in a moderate amount of repetitious play in order to grind for experience and cash, but *Faxanadu* seems tilted toward generosity in most respects versus most games of its vintage. Income flows at a pleasantly reasonable rate, and pricing on the gear and skills you need to pick up varies enough that it gives you some flexibility on how you build out your hero. You'll rarely have enough cash on hand to buy all the fresh upgrades on offer once you arrive at a new village, so you need to strategize your focus on offense, defense, and magic—not unlike the upgrade options in *Zelda II*, though presented through a decidedly different mechanism.

In the early areas of the adventure, you'll occasionally spot a powerful, expensive magic spell or piece of equipment. This presents another conundrum: How and when should you buy it? Do you stick around and grind for cash by killing weak monsters in the outer areas of the World Tree, which offer pitiful cash rewards? Do you bypass the item for the moment and double back through the tree later on in the game? Or do you just write it off as a lost opportunity and move along without that precious bit of additional combat proficiency? The innate play rhythm of *Faxanadu*, with its barriers to progress and spur-of-the-moment quests, turns each town along the hero's journey into a sort of waypoint, which in turn means that each town's shopping opportunities bookend your stay in a given section of the World Tree.

As in *Metroid*, the nameless hero of *Faxanadu* becomes a walking arsenal by adventure's end. Yet the game embraces the action-RPG genre even more fully than *Zelda II*, forcing you to consider the need not only for experience points but also for cash. Like Link, this hero has a magic meter that limits his spell-casting capabilities. Grinding for power feels like an inevitable outcome here, though as in most previous grind-heavy NES action-RPGs—*Zelda II*, *Rygar*, and *Castlevania II*—there's a firm level cap on your stat-boosting efforts. You can't whittle away hours leveling up to preposterous stats so as to steamroll the final boss. Then again, you don't really need to. *Faxanadu* is not an especially difficult game, especially by NES action game standards, which is another way you can tell it wasn't developed internally at Falcom. As long as you stay on top of your spell and gear upgrades—and in a nice touch, each new bit of gear you equip is a visible part of your hero's appearance—you can hold your own against the bad guys.

AS IN *METROID*, THE NAMELESS PROTAGONIST OF *FAXANADU* BECOMES A WALKING ARSENAL BY ADVENTURE'S END. YET THE GAME EMBRACES THE ACTION-RPG EVEN MORE FULLY THAN *ZELDA II*, FORCING YOU TO PAY ATTENTION TO BOTH EXPERIENCE POINTS AND CASH.

Admittedly, *Faxanadu*'s quirky hit boxes and spell capabilities take some getting used to, but on the whole it's a highly approachable, streamlined take on the action-RPG. In fact, Nintendo picked it up to sell as a first-party title in the US—an honor they ex- tended to only a handful of games during the NES era. This puts *Faxanadu* in the same rarefied space as the original *Dragon Quest* and *Final Fantasy*—impressive company to keep. Although *Faxanadu* certainly doesn't have the cultural cachet of either of those games today, at the time it genuinely did push forward the action-RPG format in terms of structure, depth, and accessibility. And it was no slouch on the aesthetic front, either. It had muted, yet detailed, graphics that created a sense of mystery underscored by its atmospheric soundtrack. Given the capabilities and limitations of 8-bit console hardware, *Faxanadu* overperformed.

While it's probably a little too straightforward to constitute a true entry in the metroidvania pantheon, *Faxanadu* marks a turning point for the action-RPG: it's the first that doesn't seem to actively work to thwart or bewilder the player at every opportunity. There's something to be said for accessible design… and it's no small irony that one of the pioneering works on that front descended from the series that gave us the maddeningly opaque *Xanadu* and *Romancia*.

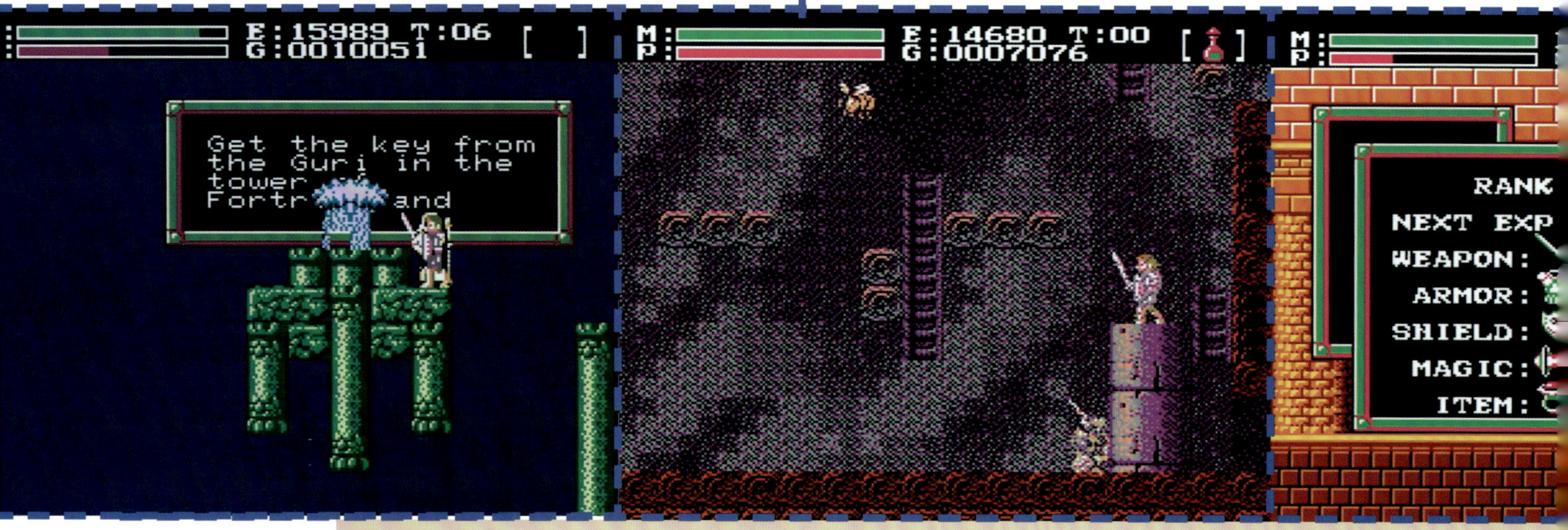

SUPER HYDLIDE

As the Ys series veered off in a wildly different direction for its third entry, the franchise that inspired it—*Hydlide*—chose instead to double down on its existing structure and design. *Super Hydlide*, or *Hydlide 3: The Space Memories* as it was known in Japan, stuck with the top-down action-RPG design seen in the original *Hydlide* and its sequel, though it did replace the older game's limited bump-attack combat system with something a more contemporary. And then! It just kept going, ladening a seemingly simplistic take on the role-playing genre with some of the most complex systems to be found in any game of the era.

Some of *Super Hydlide*'s elements came from the first game, such as its viewpoint and the central role that faeries play in the quest. Others come from *Hydlide 2*, most notably the morality system that punishes you for killing "good" monsters by basing the price of purchasable items on your current Moral Fiber rating. Still others, however, appear for the first time here. *Super Hydlide* introduces a time-of-day system, like that of *Castlevania II* but vastly more limiting. The passage of time ties in with the game's stamina/hunger system, and your protagonist requires regular meals (twice per in-game day). Fail to feed him according to his body clock and he'll experience starvation, which reduces his health.

To further complicate matters, the food system ties in with the game's encumbrance mechanic. Every item you collect or purchase in the game has a weight attribute, including coins you gather from fallen foes! If your protagonist acquires too much stuff, he'll become overloaded and will begin to move slowly, making him vulnerable in combat. Food has weight, so the rations you carry add to your encumbrance. Plus, you may find that wielding a weak, small weapon in combat works better than attempting to carry a more powerful (but heavier) blade. This can be managed, somewhat, by assigning a character class with high strength levels to your hero, such as Thief or Fighter…though these come with drawbacks of their own.

Considering *Hydlide*'s emphasis on breezy simplicity, it's surprising to see so many complex factors at play in its sequel. *Super Hydlide* is a strange game, and not necessarily a great one, but you certainly can't accuse it of playing things safe.

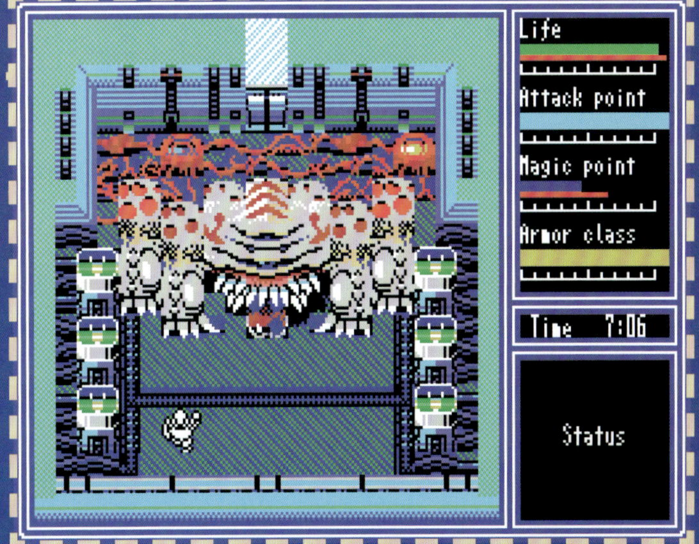

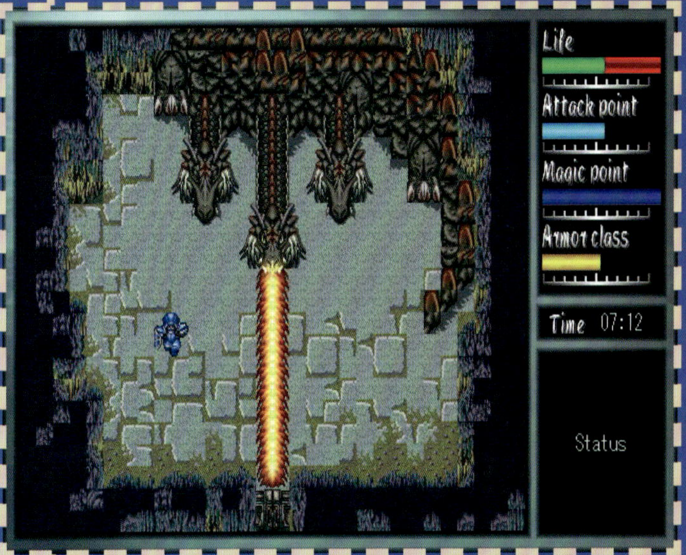

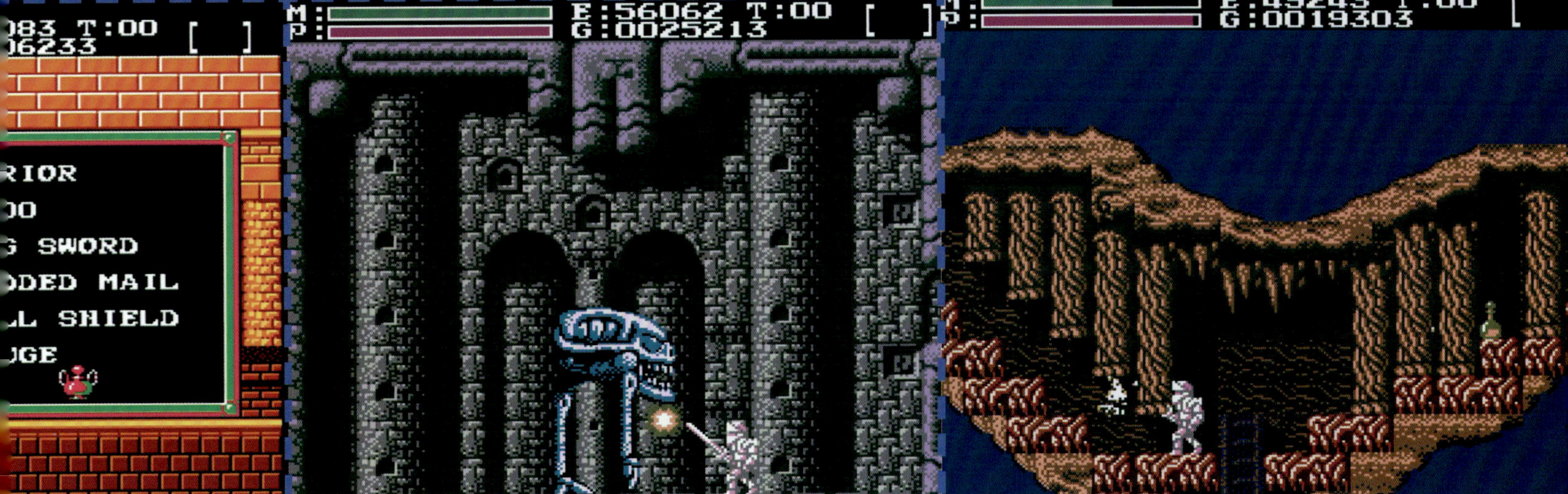

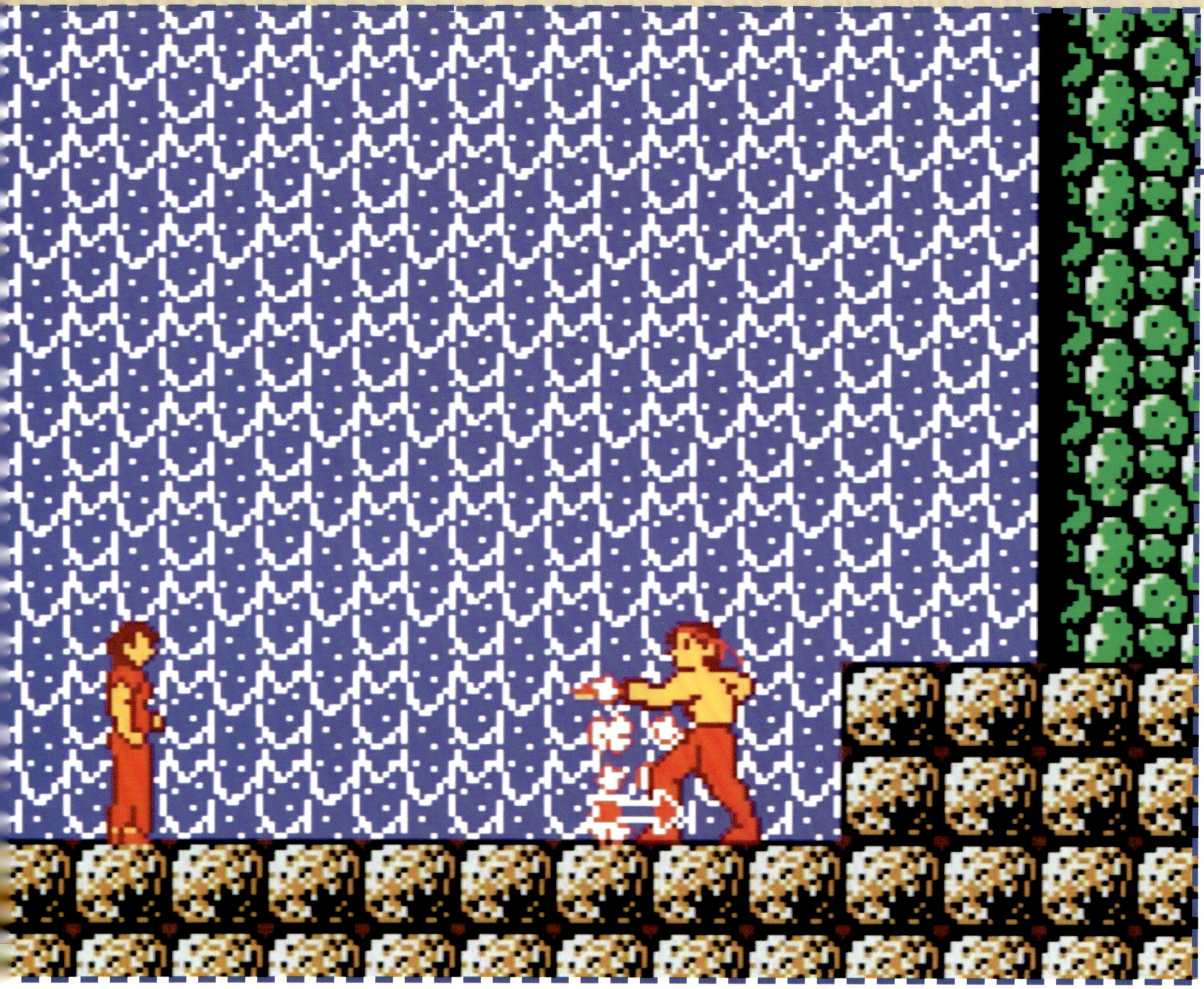

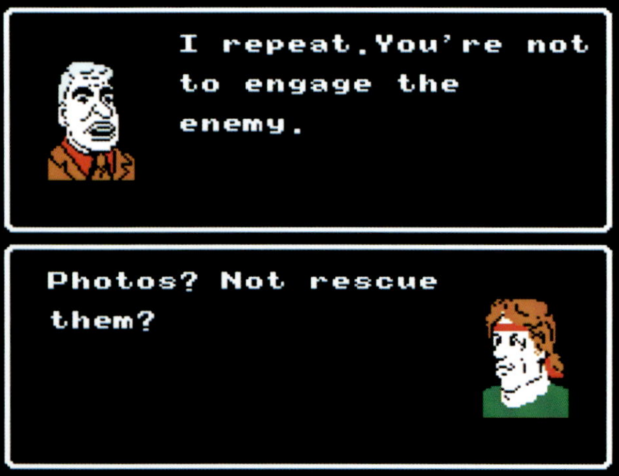

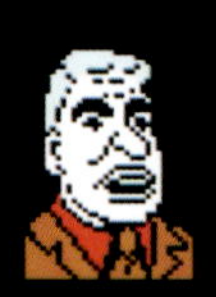

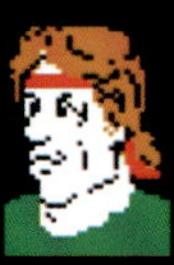

RAMBO

PLATFORM: **FAMICOM / NES**
DEV: **PACK-IN-VIDEO** | PUB: **ACCLAIM**
INITIAL RELEASE DATE: **DEC. 1987**

RAMBEAUX-ARTS

Although *Zelda* fans tend to look back at the second game in that series and write it off as a misfit, an ugly duckling, in reality it had a fairly significant impact on its contemporaries. Many other developers imitated the design of *Zelda II*, some more overtly than others. The first truly overt *Zelda II* knockoff strangely featured one of the least compatible subjects you could possibly imagine: Sylvester Stallone's John Rambo.

Publishers around the world rushed to produce games based on the 1985 hit film *Rambo: First Blood Part II*. In Japan, those rights belonged to a Japanese firm called Pack-In-Video. Like a lot of companies that produced video games for the Japanese market in the mid-1980s, Pack-In-Video leveraged an existing businesses to exploit the "Famicom boom" that gripped the country in the wake of *Super Mario Bros.*'s success. At least Pack-In-Video's move into games represented a lateral shift compared to some of the weirder entrants into the Famicom space (which included educational publishers and textile firms). According to the website *Glitchwave*, Pack-In-Video got its start in 1970 as a video distribution venture. The company's earliest video games featured their import licenses—not only *Rambo* but also Jim Henson's *Labyrinth*, *Predator*, *Space Camp*, *Young Sherlock Holmes*, and *Knight Rider*. Parlaying video distribution deals into video games made for a fairly tidy transition, giving Pack-In's initial releases a level of mainstream visibility that many competitors lacked as they dealt in console conversions of third-string arcade games and esoteric PC creations.

Pack-In-Video launched its game business with an MSX title based on *Rambo*, which would be the first of several different takes on the film by the fledgling studio. The MSX *Rambo* played like a slower, clumsier clone of Capcom's *Commando*. This was followed by *Super Rambo Special*, a game that broke away from pure linear design in favor of an early foray into the top-down military stealth that Konami would perfect a year later with *Metal Gear*. If *Metal Gear* and *Super Rambo Special* were The *Legend of Zelda* with modern army action vibes, it seems only fitting that the company's next attempt at *Rambo*—which made its debut on the Famicom in December 1987—would pursue the second *Zelda*'s format.

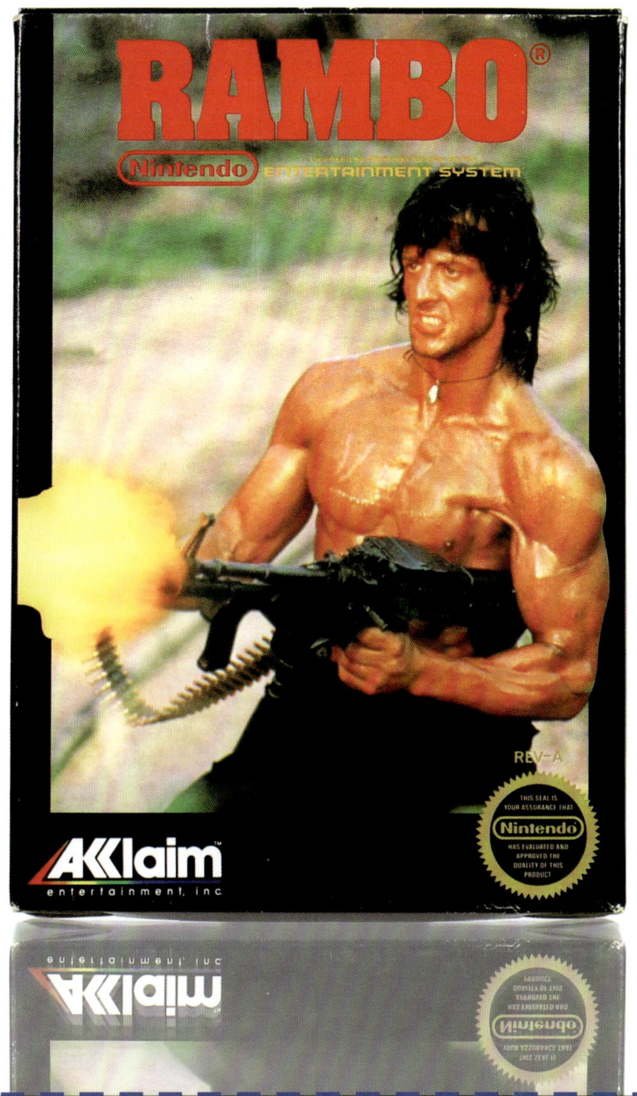

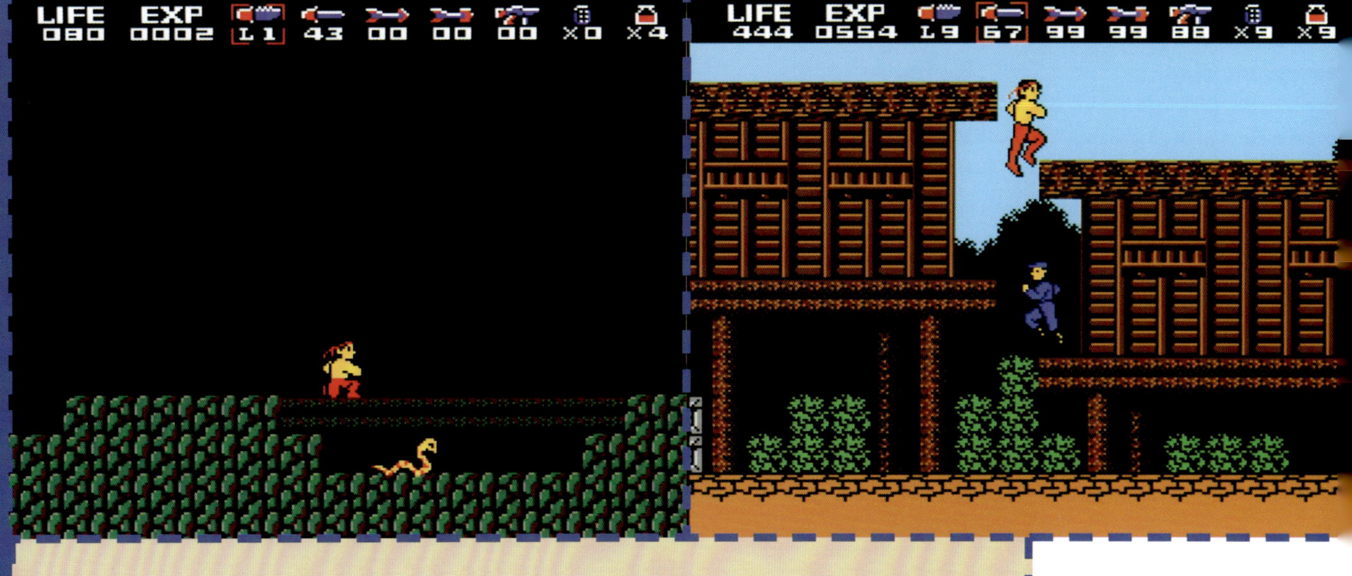

Copying a huge, complex adventure like *Zelda II* was a bold plan for such an untested developer; perhaps not surprisingly, it didn't entirely work out. Yet you can't write off *Rambo* for Famicom and NES as a complete failure, because it swings for the fences. It almost manages to connect. For starters, it directly adapts the film into video game form, playing out as an open-world, side-scrolling platform-shooter driven by a linear plot. You genuinely did not see arcade-style action games propelled by a narrative in 1987. Even *Zelda II* and *Castlevania II* had stories that amounted to little more than vague commentary by random villagers. Those games contained premises, not stories, and their in-game dialogue rarely had anything to do with the overall plot. Instead, the fragments of dialogue players encountered simply served to lead them to the next activity they needed to perform, the next place they needed to go, or the next monster they needed to defeat. Villagers handed out little side quests or dropped hints for finding new weapons, skills, and tools, but that's as involving as their text ever got.

COPYING A HUGE, COMPLEX ADVENTURE LIKE *ZELDA II* WAS A BOLD PLAN FOR AN UNTESTED DEVELOPER, AND PERHAPS NOT SURPRISINGLY, THEIR EFFORTS DIDN'T WORK OUT AS WELL AS ONE MIGHT HAVE HOPED. YET YOU CAN'T CALL *RAMBO* A TOTAL FAILURE, AS IN SOME WAYS IT PLAYS AHEAD OF ITS TIME.

Rambo, on the other hand, retells the film's narrative from the opening scene. Before you even begin your quest, you take control of protagonist John Rambo in a military prison, and you can't leave the compound until you speak to Rambo's commanding officer and accept his mission to infiltrate the Vietnamese jungle in search of prisoners of war. Once you enter the jungle combat zone, you can wander freely through much of the game world straightaway. However, you can't actually accomplish much until you complete story-related tasks. At a glance, this doesn't seem entirely different from the way quests worked in contemporary Famicom action-RPGs. For example, the side jaunt that requires Rambo to rescue a lost child from a dark cave appears to have been copied directly from Link's quest to rescue a lost child from a dark cave in *Zelda II*. But look more closely at Pack-In-Video's game and you start to notice the presence of points of no return, pivotal events that change the nature of the adventure by bringing new enemies into the mix. There's even a sequence in which you play as a different character! Story dictates Rambo's progress even more than the in-game checkpoints of *Faxanadu*. The narrative here doesn't merely exist as wallpaper in the background.

Remarkably enough, Pack-In-Video built this interactive adaptation of the film's events into an open-world exploratory action game. Most of the game takes place in the jungles of Vietnam, linking together jungles, swamps, villages, military encampments into a convoluted, continuous world. *Rambo*'s map doesn't simply flow left to right with paths leading up and down to allow you to branch in different directions; it also incorporates a third axis of travel despite its 2D nature.

Rambo's left-to-right movement represents his east–west traversal through the jungle. But throughout the game, you'll spot small squares on the ground labeled N or S—that is, north or south. Step- ping onto these tiles and pressing up allows Rambo to "shift" to another plane of the jungle, continuing his east–west exploration on a parallel tract. It's a fun idea, although it doesn't work smoothly in practice due to the oblique and sometimes abstract nature of these links.

Unlike the Front and Back maps in *The Goonies II*, the connections between the different tracts of the jungle don't always line up. Pack-In-Video's programmers didn't design the jungle as methodically as they should have, and that sometimes makes for a deeply confusing environment. The convoluted layouts are a real source of frustration in *Rambo*, because the game does have a lot going for it otherwise. The developers clearly put real thought into this oddball take on a popular foreign film. In an era when most games based on media licenses played like someone had jammed a recognizable character image into a generic action game, *Rambo* genuinely feels like Pack-In-

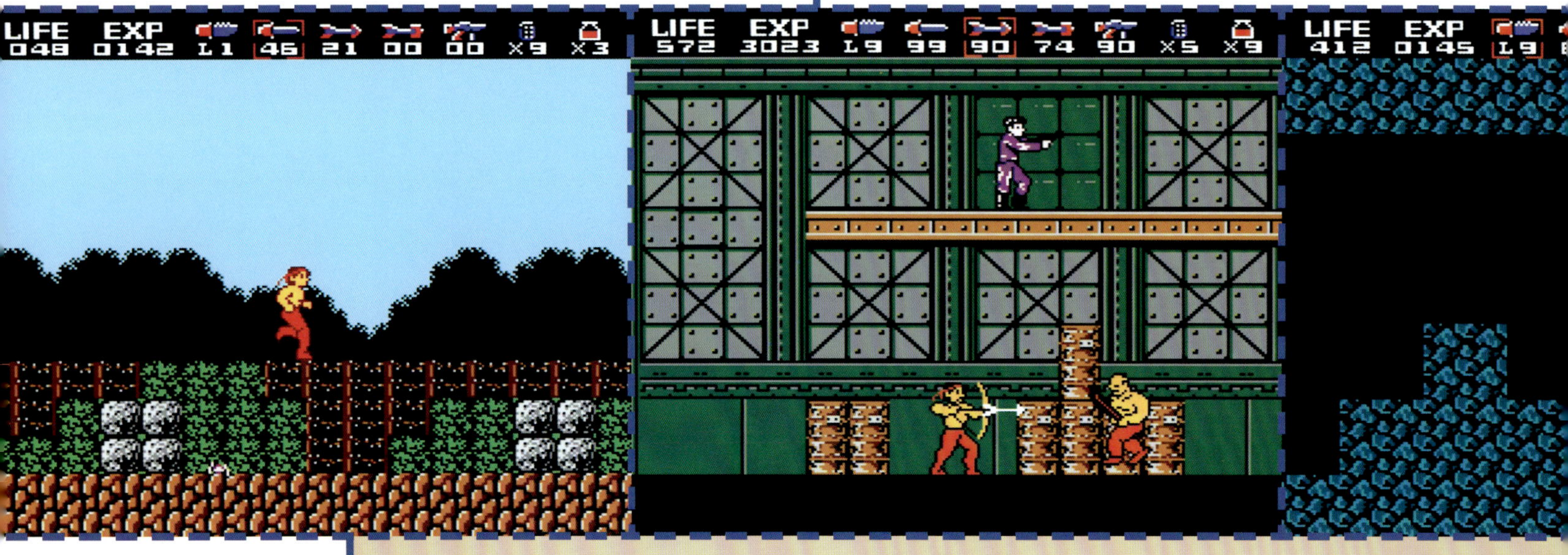

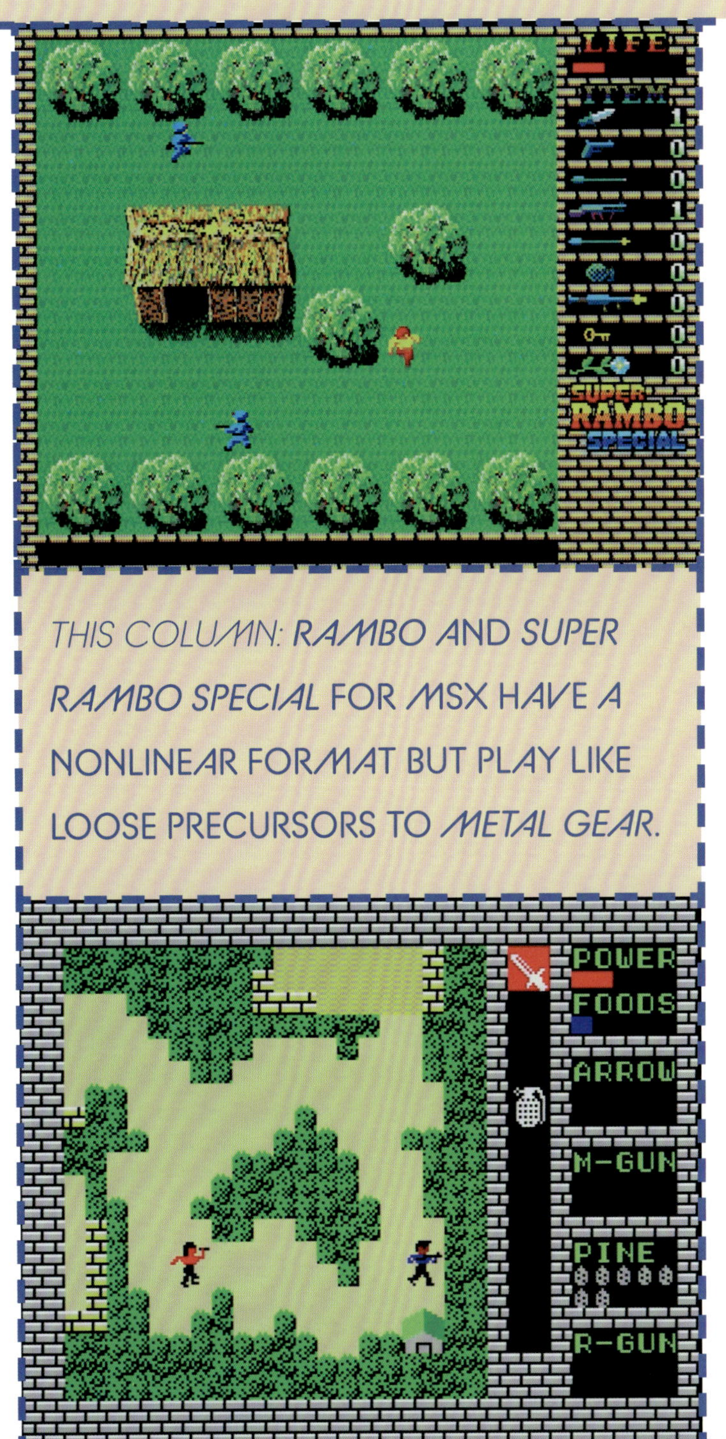

THIS COLUMN: ***RAMBO*** *AND* ***SUPER RAMBO SPECIAL*** FOR MSX HAVE A NONLINEAR FORMAT BUT PLAY LIKE LOOSE PRECURSORS TO *METAL GEAR.*

Video's team tried to create a game that engaged with the material. It's a *Zelda II* clone, sure, but it genuinely radiates a *Rambo* vibe.

Despite the technical limitations of this era of NES software, it stuffs an impressive amount of variety into its meager memory space. Rambo treks through a wide range of environments, including a Soviet base patrolled by futuristic weapons. You travel the countryside by boat and helicopter, return to the jungle to rescue captives in defiance of the US government after the command officers scrub your mission, and even play briefly as Rambo's guide and love interest, Co. The devs also took time to include a handful of strange little visuals gags, seemingly for their own amusement, such as the Russian soldier whose head balloons when you attack him or the way you can scream the Japanese symbol for anger (怒) to transform a sleazy military adviser into a frog. All within a massive interconnected jungle beckoning players to explore it.

Fittingly, given the game's open nature and RPG-like emphasis on narrative, *Rambo* incorporates an experience-based leveling system. As Rambo battles through the jungle, he gains experience points from fallen foes. Indeed, this element seems like the biggest tip-off to the debt *Rambo* owes to *Zelda II*; when you defeat an enemy, you're rewarded with a small numeric icon that denotes your EXP earnings. As EXP accumulates, his durability and combat prowess increase, as does his capacity to stock the var- ious secondary weapons and items dropped by enemies. By default, Rambo battles with a trench knife, which offers decent power but terrible range. Defeated enemies drop expendable tools ranging from exploding arrows to grenades to machine gun ammo. The higher your EXP level, the more of these materials you can carry—this includes medical salve, which restores Rambo's life. As in other games of this era, Rambo has a limited level cap on his experience, which means you can't turn him into a superpowered god. In fact, you don't want to hit the level cap, since the game's simple math causes Rambo's EXP level to roll back over to zero if you exceed its maximum value!

Between the open interconnected world, the central narrative, and the role-playing mechanics, *Rambo* takes gaming another step closer to the realization of what the world would eventually think of as the platonic ideal of the metroidvania. In a lot of ways, the game is a mess, an Icarus of gaming that flies a little too close to the sun and scorches its wings before crashing to its demise. But considering the untested nature of the developer, who could have phoned in a simplistic *Rambo* shooting game but chose instead to forge new ground in the difficult terrain of the action-RPG, you can't help but respect this strange, ambitious little adventure.

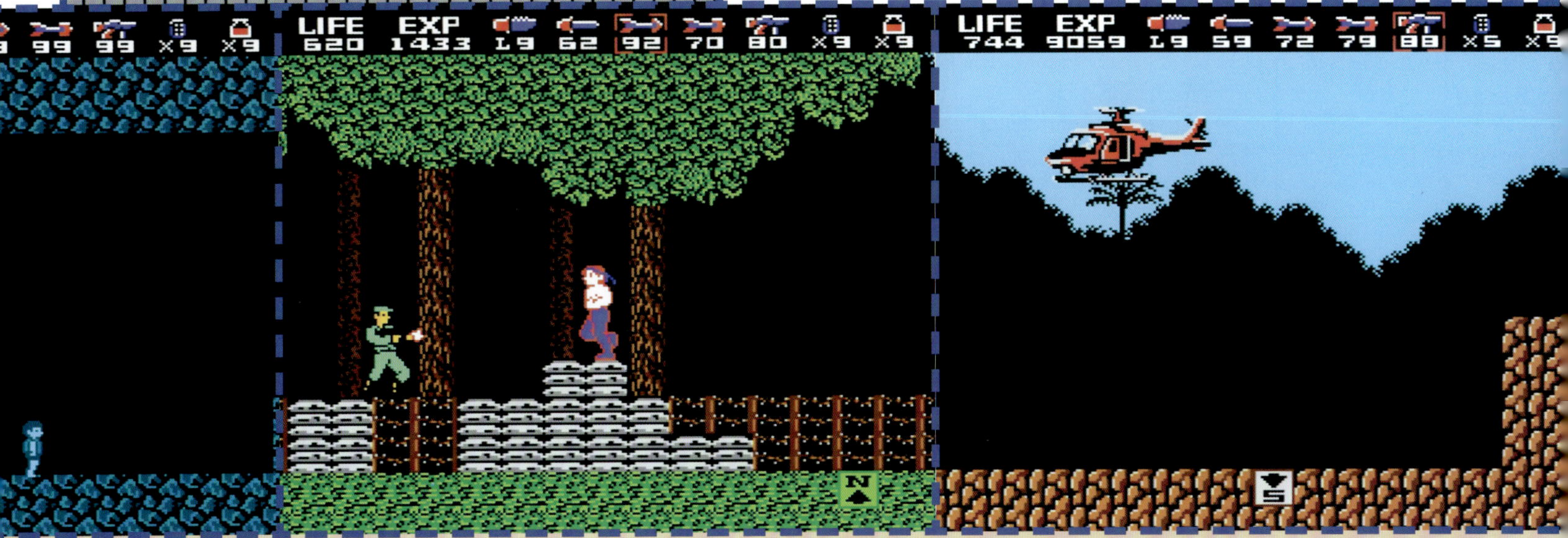

METROIDVANIA TIMELINE 1988

And, just as quickly as it exploded, the 8-bit obsession with exploratory action games began to cool in 1988. Whereas 1987 saw a constant stream of groundbreaking creations (ranging from a greatly expanded interpretation of minor arcade barbarian action game *Rygar* to the debut of the *Ys* series and its ultimate refinement of the *Hydlide* format), 1988 saw console game developers slow their headlong rush into bold explorations in favor of slower, more thoughtful approaches to the proto-metroidvania form. This manifested in a few by-the-number, iterative efforts, such as the *Zelda II*–clone *The Battle of Olympus*, but also more complex genre crossovers. But 1988 also gave us *The Guardian Legend* and *Blaster Master*, two different flips of the same coin: free-roaming action games set in thoughtfully gated worlds where the boss battles played out totally differently from that of the primary quest sequences.

More significantly, the future began to assert itself here. Nintendo's Famicom had been, arguably, the world's single most dominant force in video game evolution for four years by this point—if not in game evolution as a whole, then certainly in the development of the metroidvania format. The console had only just made it big in America (and struggled to gain a foothold in Europe), but in Japan it found itself beset by two undeniable next-generation rivals: Sega's Mega Drive and NEC's PC Engine CD-ROM², better known in the US as the Sega Genesis and Turbo CD. Offering greatly enhanced technical capabilities (more colors, greater speed, expanded storage capacity, etc.), these new challengers would introduce greater technical demands that required larger teams and more resources than the more primitive-looking games of the 8-bit era. Ironically, this would result in simpler games, as the wild freewheeling innovation and multi-format design of Famicom's cutting-edge software proved riskier in these more expensive projects.

That's not to say that the 16-bit generation would put an end to innovation—not at all! But it would see genres solidifying, with platforming and shooting action games pulling back from the RPG explorations that had thrived during the peak of the Famicom/NES era. But, in fairness, this trend began to manifest even on the NES and Famicom here in 1988 when Nintendo launched *Super Mario Bros. 3* in Japan: a game that made modest nods to the ideas of exploration and inventory systems, but which ultimately demonstrated the universal appeal of an action game that was content to simply offer great action. Its massive sales figures had a pied piper–effect on other developers, who eagerly followed in its footsteps. The metroidvania would continue to grow and evolve, but it would become a relatively rare sight throughout the 1990s and into the '00s…at which point kids who had cut their teeth on the exploratory adventures of Famicom's 1987 library grew up and started making their own games in that style, and the indie metroidvania boom began in earnest.

TIMELINE OF EVENTS

January

Konami Wai Wai World

This innovative character crossover gave players the ability to rescue, play as, and upgrade a medley of familiar Konami heroes through a series of free-form stages based on their games.

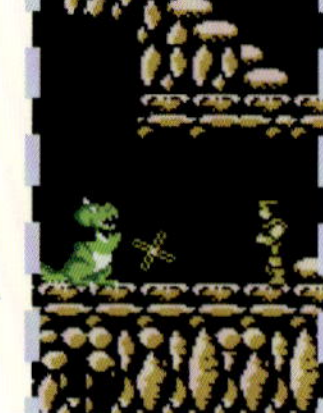

February

The Guardian Legend

Combining top-down scroll-based shooting with top-down action-RPG exploration, *The Guardian Legend* plays like no other game of its era—a metroidvania shoot-'em-up.

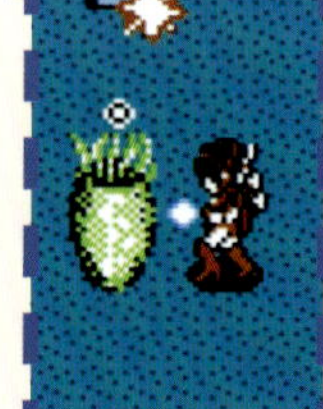

March

The Battle of Olympus

Based heavily on the *Zelda II* template, *Olympus* ditched the numeric stats in favor of item- and cash-oriented upgrades across a fully interconnected rendition of Greek myths.

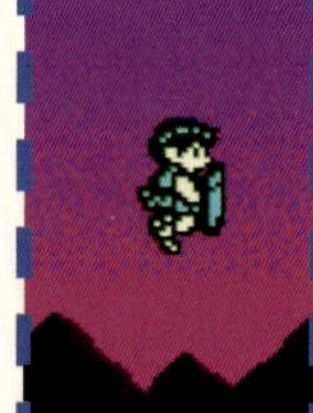

May

Captain Comic

Best known for its unauthorized NES release, *The Adventures of Captain Comic* played best in its original PC form—a rare attempt at an exploratory action game on Western 8-bit computers.

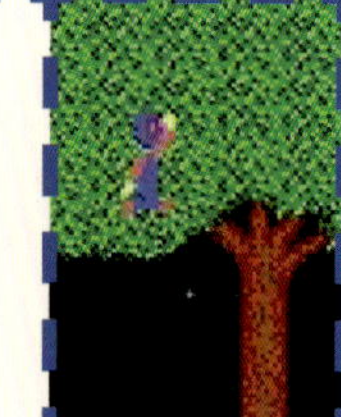

June

Blaster Master
In this inverse to *The Guardian Legend*, players controlled a superpowered vehicle through huge, side-scrolling areas, then ventured out on foot in a top-down view to fight bosses.

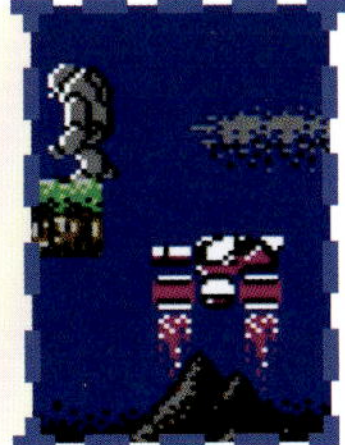

July

Bionic Commando
Best known for its radical overhaul of platform gaming rules (you don't jump, you swing!), *Bionic Commando* also deserves credit for its use of narrative and gear to guide its quest.

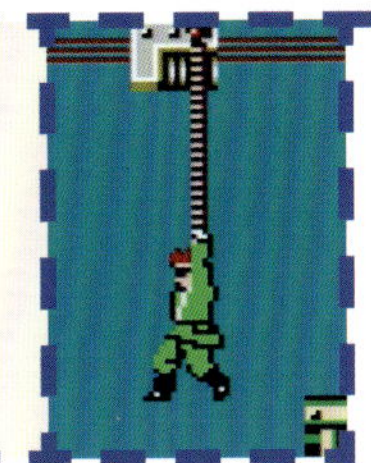

August

XZR
Calling back to *Xanadu*'s dual format, this action-RPG featured zippy action combat but put its core emphasis on the role-playing aspect with a complex story about assassins and time travel.

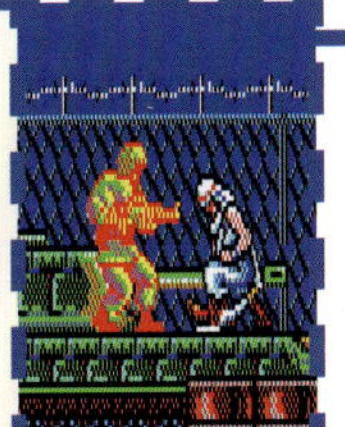

October

Super Mario Bros. 3
This outing of the Mario bros. wasn't a metroidvania by any sense of the word, and that makes it notable. Its success as a pure action game caused platform action-RPGs to fall out of favor.

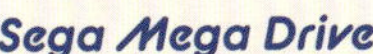

Sega Mega Drive
The first proper next-generation console to arrive in the wake of the Famicom's success, Sega's 16-bit powerhouse opened new horizons, not only visually but in terms of substance, too.

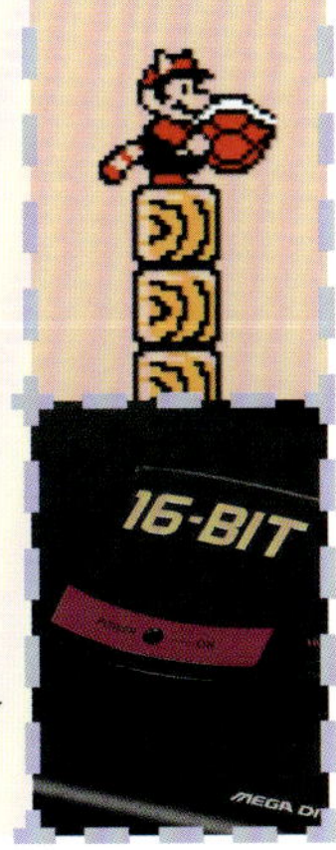

December

PC Engine CD-ROM²
An upgrade to NEC's advanced 8-bit PC Engine console, this groundbreaking device multiplied the capacity for game data by a factor of hundreds—perfect for immense RPGs.

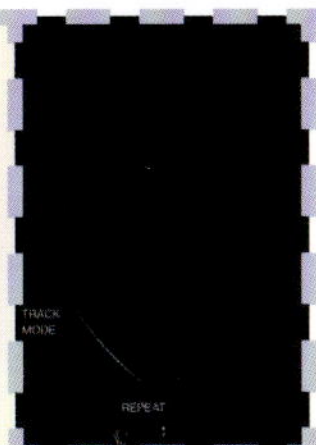

Unknown Date

Exile
Unrelated to *XZR*, this sophisticated adventure left players in a hostile alien environment where they had to contend with dwindling resources and a complex interactive physics model.

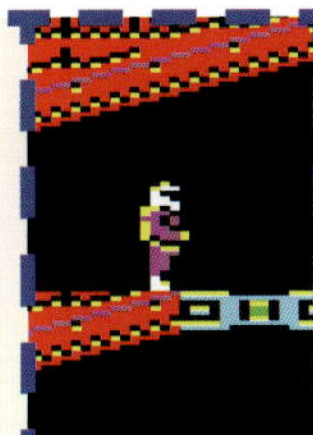

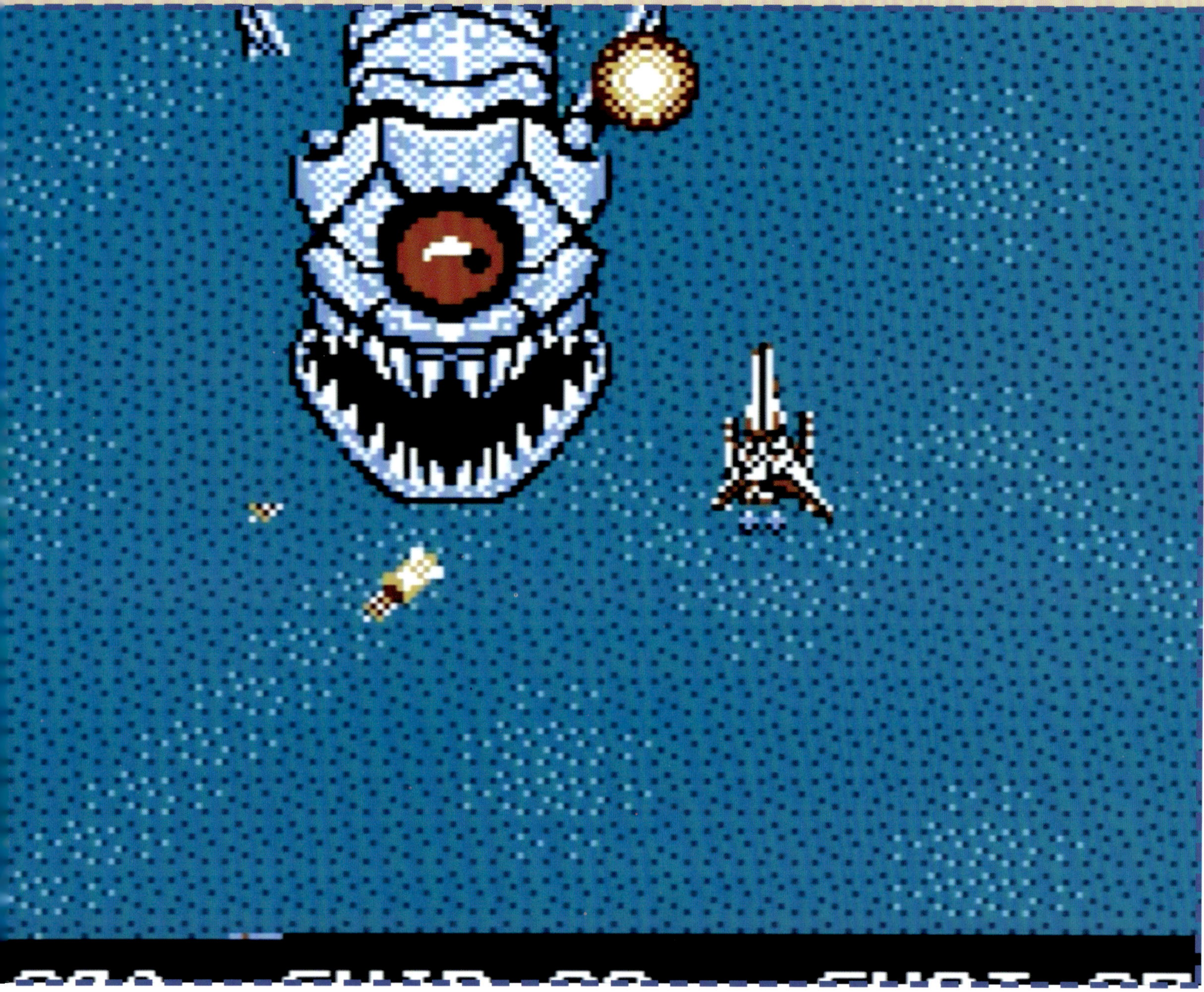

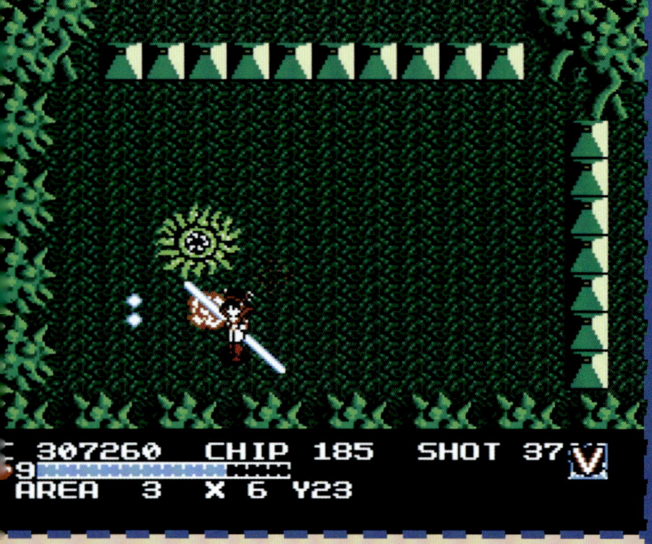

THE GUARDIAN LEGEND

PLATFORM: **FAMICOM / NES**
DEV: **COMPILE** | PUB: **BRØDERBUND**
INITIAL RELEASE DATE: **FEB. 1988**

NOTABLE FOR: **COMBINING THE SHOOTER AND ACTION-RPG FORMATS INTO A UNIFIED WHOLE**

A TRANSFORMATIVE WORK

The Guardian Legend for NES neatly embodies many of the trends that ruled Japan's console gaming market in the latter 1980s. Designed by Compile, a studio that had begun to make a name for itself through technically impressive shooting games like *Zanac* for the NES and *Gulkave* for the SG-1000, the company didn't mind dabbling in big exploratory adventures from time to time—think *Golvellius*. *The Guardian Legend* combines both these genres into a unique hybrid that doesn't even attempt to reconcile its two very different modes of play. You travel and explore in a three-quarters combat viewpoint that moves similarly to *The Legend of Zelda*. But, when it comes time to explore dungeons, those spaces take the form of a top-down, auto-scrolling vertical shooter.

It's a curious combination of workings—*Zelda* by way of *Xevious*—but Compile arrived at this format honestly. Not only does it iterate on *Golvellius*'s structure, *The Guardian Legend* is a follow-up to a shooter called *Guardic*, which shipped exclusively for MSX home computers in Japan. *Guardic* itself broke the rules of the shooter genre, as it involved space ships and aerial combat, yet it didn't include any scrolling backgrounds. The MSX hardware famously had difficulty displaying scrolling visuals, so Compile turned what could have been a vertically scrolling shoot-'em-up into a slower, more methodical game. Players moved screen by screen through *Guardic*, and it demanded a certain degree of exploration as each individual screen is connected to the others through a sort of labyrinthine structure.

You might recognize this approach to adapting arcade experiences for the MSX as being quite similar to that adopted by Konami for *Metal Gear*, which transformed a *Commando*-style shootout into a *Zelda*-esque infiltration mission. *The Guardian Legend* in turn plays as though Compile dropped *Guardic* into a centrifuge to separate out its individual components: a proper on-foot action game and a conventional scrolling shooter. The two styles of gameplay exist separately here, feeding into each other but never actually overlapping. The game begins with a shooter sequence, which is a little tough but not unmanageable. Only after you complete this prologue do you move into the central hub of the game,

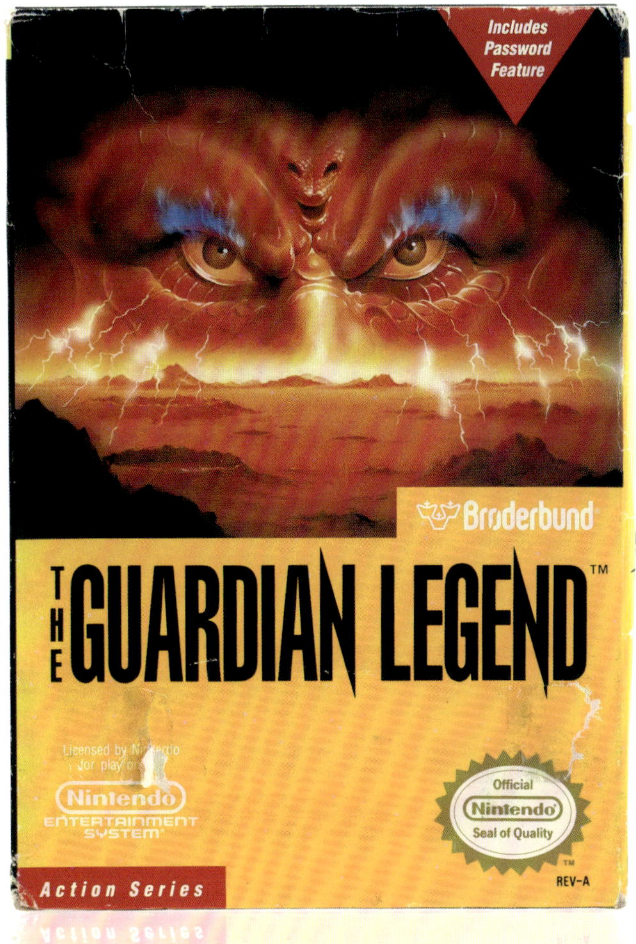

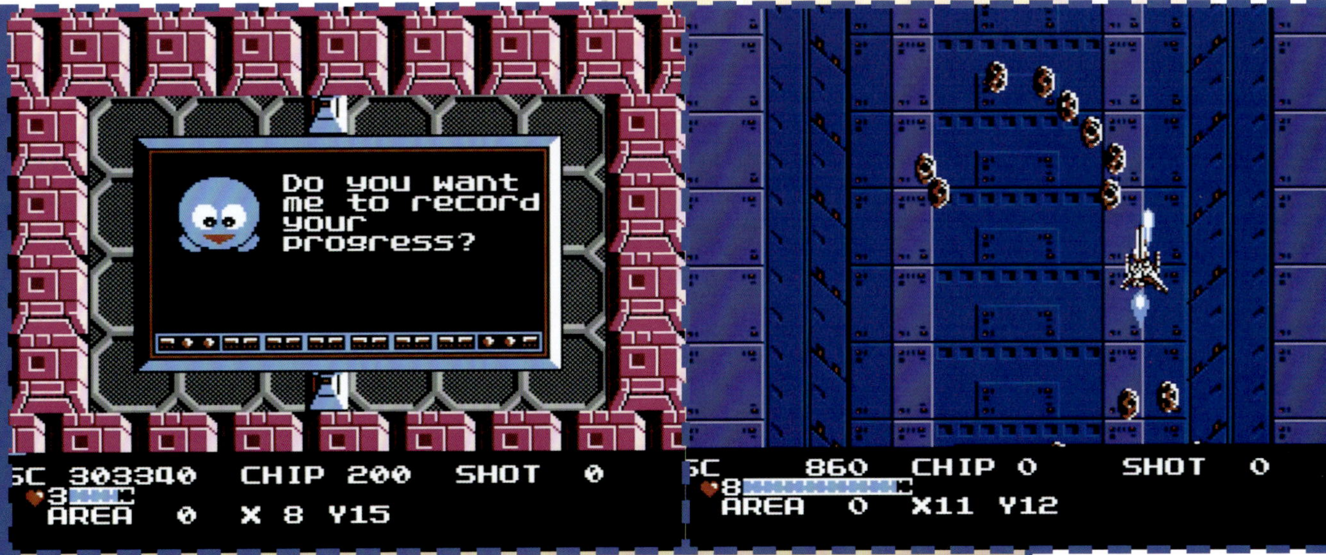

where everything plays out through *Zelda*-style maze exploration. The artificial planet Naju, where the story takes place, consists of a central space with locked-away subsections, which functions like a standard action-RPG overworld. Here, though, the classic underground dungeons take the form of corridors, vertically scrolling spaces in which players control a spacecraft and blast their way to a boss encounter. In order to unlock the gates dividing the core of Naju into separate areas, you need to defeat the primary corridor bosses. Along the way, you can also tackle optional secondary corridors, where you earn permanent power-ups for the protagonist: Miria, a sleek fighter craft that transforms into a cyborg girl wearing an armor bikini. Again, *The Guardian Legend* embodies many trends of Japanese pop media from the late '80s.

Corridors aren't the only place you'll find power-ups for Miria—they appear throughout the Naju hub, often guarded by smaller bosses that you must battle on foot rather than in fighter-craft form. These upgrades include secondary weapons and their progressive upgrades, maximum health boosts, upgrades to Miria's armor and main gun, and modules that increase her capacity to stock a consumable resource called chips. Chips play a crucial role in the adventure, functioning simultaneously as currency, fuel for secondary weapons, and a power enhancer for your main gun. By default, your main weapon consists of a meager single projectile, but you can acquire permanent upgrades to its power and firing rate. As you increase your stockpile of chips, your gun will expand the volume and width of projectiles it can fire at once. But these enhancements can be fleeting if you don't take care to ration your chip consumption. When your current chip count falls below one of your main gun's power-up thresholds, it drops to the next-lowest tier of force until you replenish your chip supply.

THE GUARDIAN LEGEND'S CHIP SYSTEM FORCES YOU TO MAKE TRADEOFFS, ESPECIALLY AGAINST BOSSES. YOU SPEND THE CHIPS THAT BULK UP YOUR ATTACK POWER IN ORDER TO FIRE YOUR SUBWEAPONS. THE MORE YOU RELY ON THEM, THE WEAKER YOUR PRIMARY GUN BECOMES.

This forces you to make tradeoffs during boss fights. As you spend chips to fire sub-weapons, your current chip total drops rapidly when you use your supplemental abilities, meaning that your main weapon loses its oomph the longer you rely on secondary skills. You can't help but lean on Miria's secondary skills because the boss encounters—both the corridor bosses and the hub's mini-bosses—put up quite a fight. They like to crowd Miria to damage her with collision force while also bombarding her with projectiles. Most bosses seem designed to be countered with a specific sub-weapon, even if that means weakening your main weapon.

The Guardian Legend plays slightly rough on the whole, with the game's shooter heritage resulting in wild difficulty spikes that will absolutely create dead ends for players accustomed to the less taxing pace of action-RPGs. On the other hand, the action-RPG component makes for a much easier vertical shooter than fans of the format might prefer; if you find yourself unable to pass a particularly tough boss or corridor, you can poke around the optional corridors to collect critical power-ups to give you more of a fighting chance. You can also swing into shops to buy upgrades from the few friendly creatures that populate Naju. It's not the freeform leveling-up mechanics of a proper action-RPG, where killing enough monsters will eventually crank your stats so high you can steamroll any challenge, but it hints at the shape of things to come.

Most of all, *The Guardian Legend* demonstrates why the bulk of metroidvania innovation happened in Japanese console games. While Western developers of the late '80s largely focused on simulations, tabletop-style role-playing games, or brisk arcade experiences and rarely created games where these concepts overlapped, games like *The Guardian Legend* showcase a collective—maybe even cultural?—enthusiasm for smashing together disparate genres to do unexpected things. Such as turning an action-RPG into oddball hybrid.

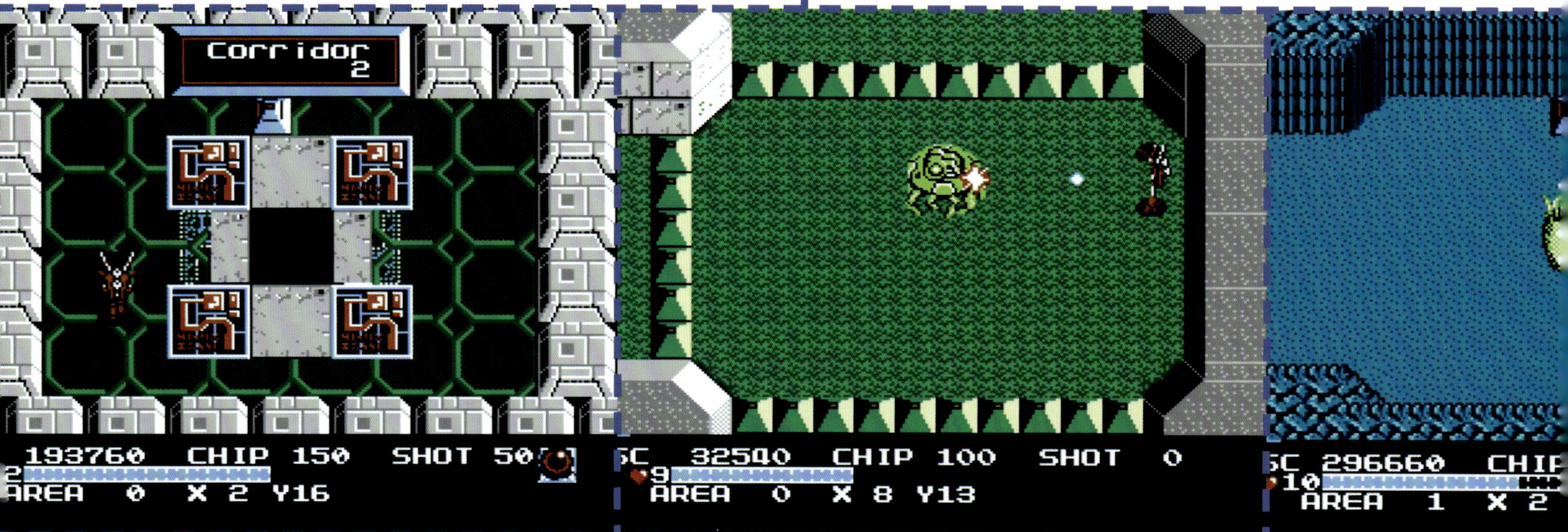

GUARDIC

As a developer, Compile earned a reputation for turning the impossible into reality. The company cut its teeth on underpowered platforms, such as the MSX and SG-1000, and quickly established an aptitude for making limited hardware perform remarkable feats. It didn't hurt that the interests of Compile designers and pro- grammers like Satoshi "Pac" Fujishima lay in technically demanding genres like shooters. The desire to deliver satisfactory takes on those formats inspired them to push the boundaries of humble machines: moving more sprites around, simulating more advanced screen move- ment, refining object collision routines, etc.

Still, even Compile's skilled programmers eventually ran up against the hard limitations of the machines they worked on. So, when their creations began to push up against the upper-end of those platforms, they switched tracks and explored a different form of innovation: creative software design. That's how MSX fans ended up with the quirky *Guardic*, a vertical shooter that sidelined its verticality in favor of a slower, borderline-exploratory design approach.

The MSX struggled to produce vertical scrolling with enough speed to make a satisfactory shooter; *Guardic* defers to this limitation by separating screen movement and combat into distinct phases of play. Shooting takes place in fixed locations, preventing the visual distortion and jumpy sprite movement that result from ratcheted screen motion. Once players clear a screen of enemies, they move along to the next location. But the screen-to-screen movement doesn't automatically propel the player's ship to the next space. Instead, the combat spaces are connected by conduits, and players can move through conduits in any of four directions—even into dead ends, which you'll need to clear of enemies before backtracking to seek the proper path to the end of the current stage. The battle arenas become nodes in a labyrinth, forcing players to chart out the correct route, not unlike the "base" stages of Konami's *Contra* or the NES version of Capcom's *Section Z*. Clearly, Compile wasn't the only developer to envision the shooter as a maze…but with *The Guardian Legend*, they alone took the idea to its ultimate conclusion.

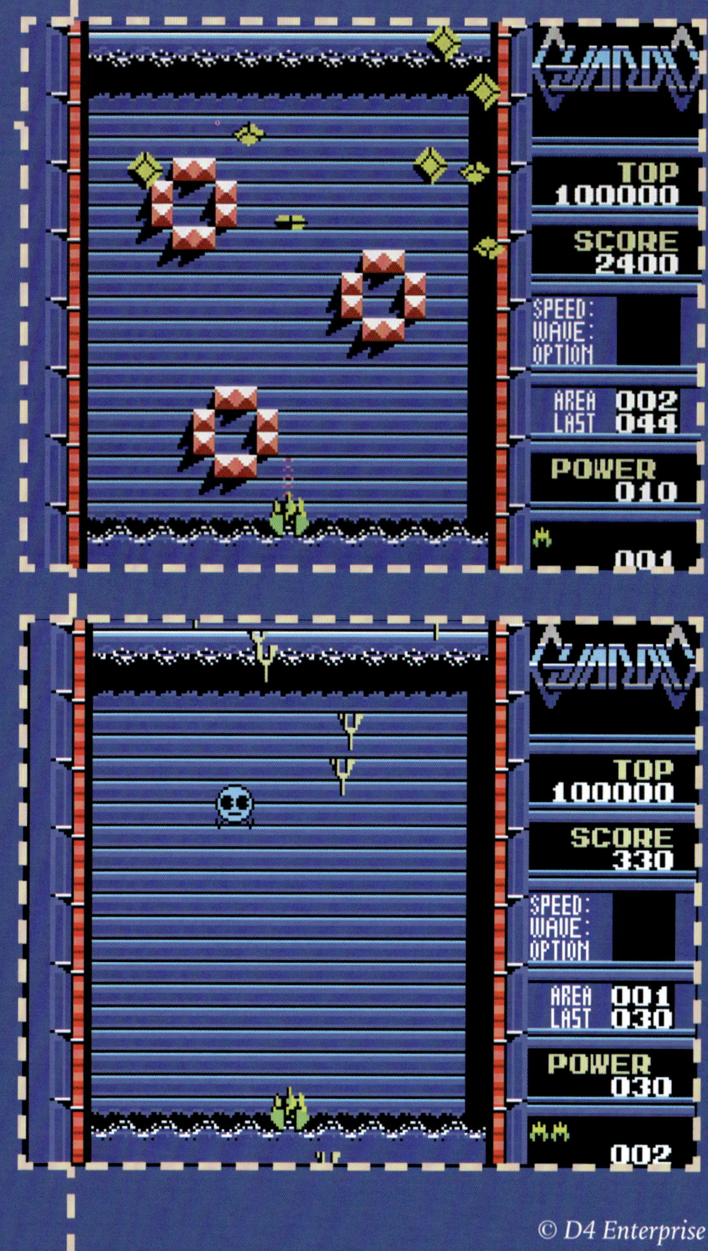

© D4 Enterprise

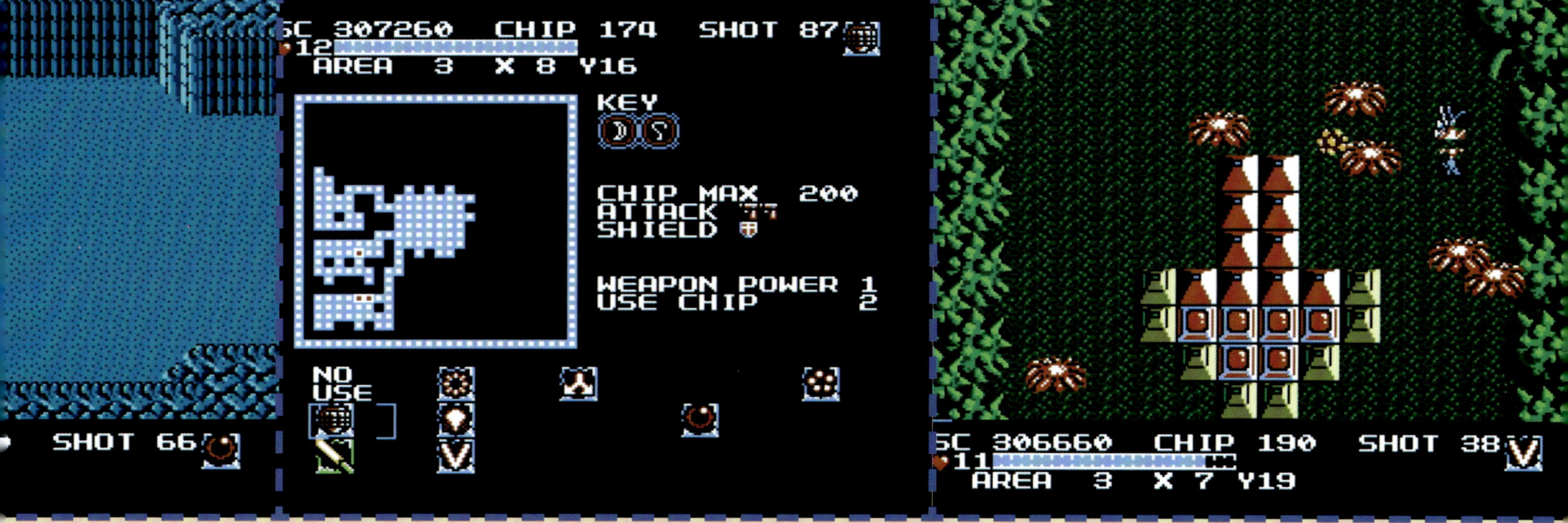

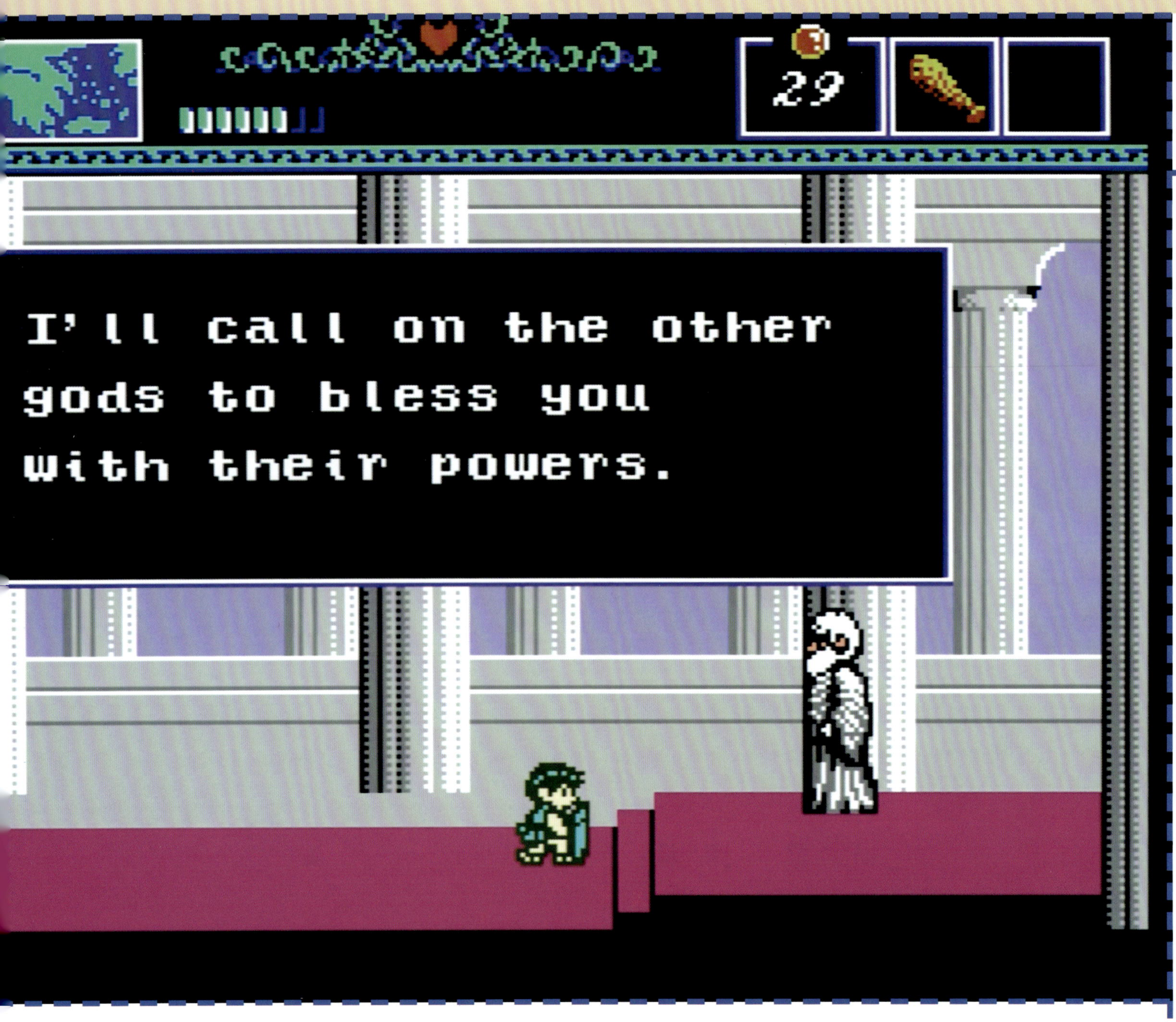

I'll call on the other gods to bless you with their powers.

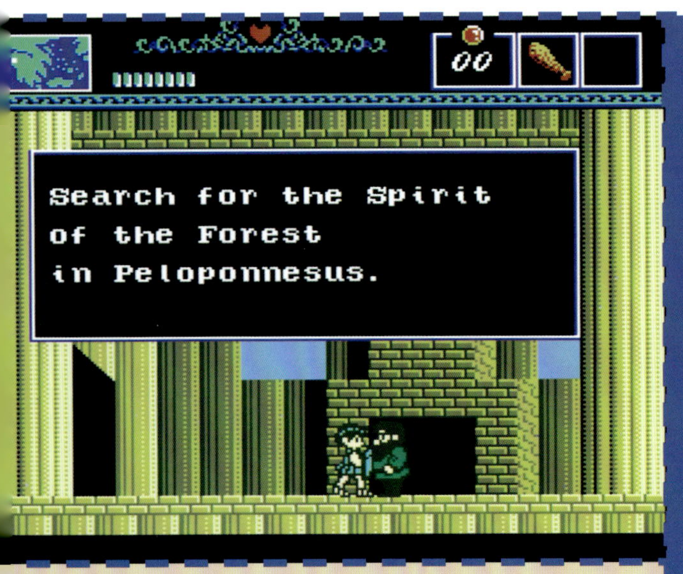

THE BATTLE OF OLYMPUS

PLATFORM: FAMICOM / NES
DEV: INFINITY | PUB: BRØDERBUND
INITIAL RELEASE DATE: MARCH 1988

A LINK BETWEEN GENRES

If Pack-In-Video's *Rambo* was inspired by *Zelda II*, what does that make Infinity's *The Battle of Olympus*, a game that doesn't take inspiration from *Zelda II* so much as conspire to wear its skin. Released a little more than a year after *Zelda II* debuted on Disk System, *Olympus* lifts ideas and aesthetics even more brazenly from Nintendo's hit than *Rambo* had. However, the two games manifest their aspirations in very different ways. *Rambo* cribbed notes from *Zelda II*'s experience system, all the way down to the little EXP point numbers that float upward from defeated foes. *Olympus* took a different tack, eliminating the concept of EXP and leveling altogether, offloading protagonist Orpheus's ability enhancements to items and tools. Its *Zelda II* inspirations manifest more in terms of aesthetics, combat mechanics, and game structure.

In Greek mythology, Orpheus ventured into the realm of the dead to rescue his beloved from Hades's clutches. The game more or less lays out this same quest for players, though some details have changed in the telling from the Greek canon as documented by Edith Hamilton. For one thing, Orpheus has to rescue Helene here, not Eurydice; for another, you don't win her back by moving Hades to tears with the beauty of your lyre but rather by beating in his face with a sword during a battle that mirrors Link's showdown with his enchanted shadow. (In fairness, *Battle of Olympus* preceded the establishment of rhythm games as a genre by a decade, so the idea of musical combat didn't really exist at the time.)

Still, as 8-bit nonlinear action games go, *Olympus* has quite a bit going for it. It does away with *Zelda*'s overworld exploration and random enemy encounters, treating the world map strictly as a visual reference as you switch locations between one region of classical Greece and another. You can think of it as *Zelda II* meets *Kid Icarus*, though you'll find far more of the former here than the latter. Orpheus travels the length of Greece with the starting region of Arcadia acting as a hub of sorts. He travels on foot, mostly, except when he travels by way of Poseidon's dolphins or a Pegasus. From the game's outset, you can duck into different passages to travel to several other areas: Athens, the Peloponnese, and Zeus's temple. However, when he first strikes out on his adventure,

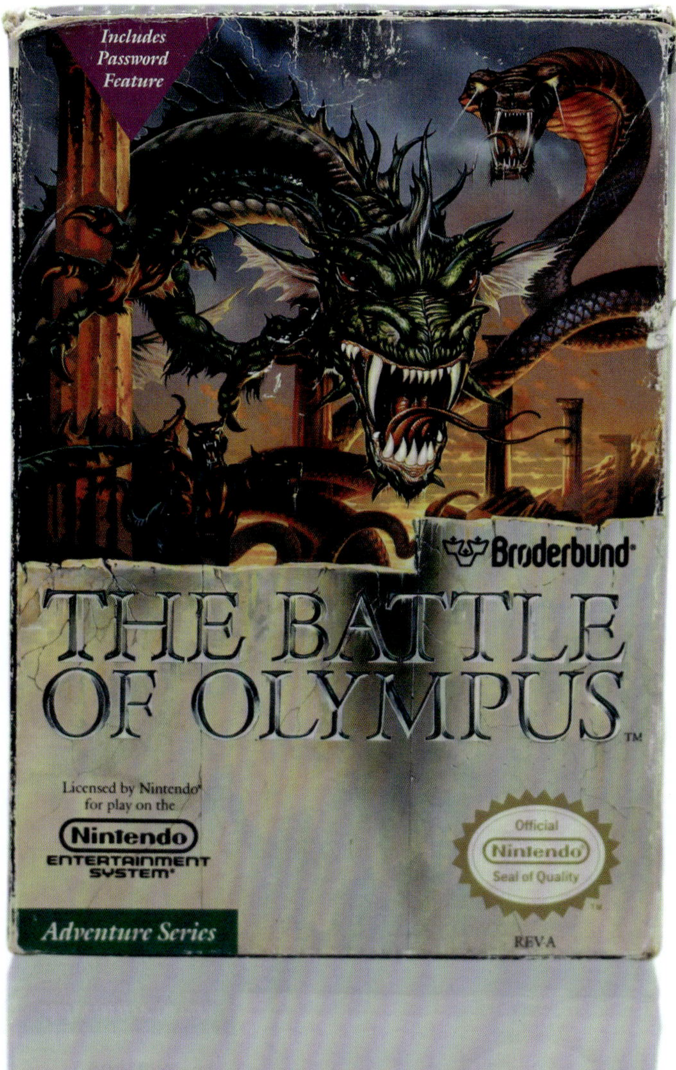

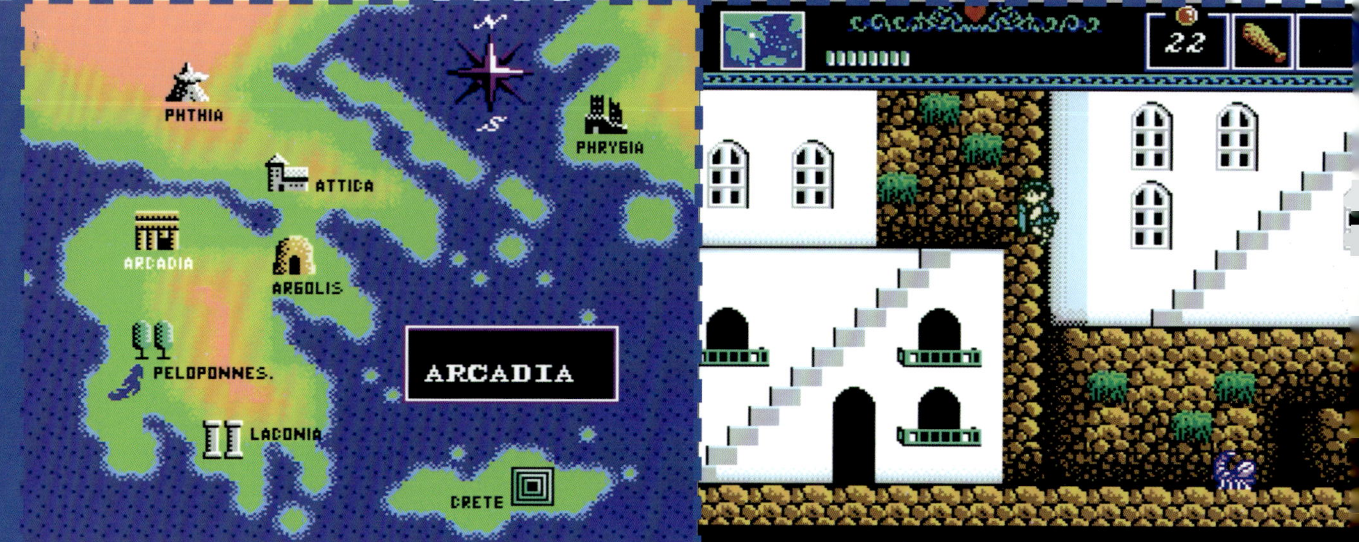

Orpheus is badly overmatched by monsters just about everywhere he goes (an old lady even warns you to stay in your lane), but players are free to try their luck regardless. You won't have much success during combat encounters until you begin to work your way through the central quest, which revolves around finding the equipment Orpheus needs to stand a chance in hell of surviving, well, Hell. The only innate improvements he gains boost his health and durability, which bulk up as you find a handful of ambrosia icons hidden around Greece. Otherwise, Orpheus' durability in combat comes down to his arsenal. Weapons, shields, tools, and musical instruments give him the ability to traverse more of the world, fight stronger monsters, and break through barriers to other regions.

The quest line has a consistent and steady flow. For example, to reach Phthia and unlock the back half of the adventure, you need to open the road that has been sealed by a rock monster named Gaea. This involves finding an ocarina, whose melody will awaken Gaea so that you can destroy it—though you also need to acquire a key that opens the passage to Phthia. You meet the guy with the key early on in the quest, but he won't hand it over until you rescue an abducted nymph, which involves a complex string of other acquisitions. For starters, you need the shield of Athena to survive a fight with the Lamia that has abducted a child—a side quest previously seen in both *Zelda II* and *Rambo*—so that his family will give you the flame-flinging Staff of Fennel. But you can only activate the staff's flames once you learn the secret of fire from Prometheus, who has been locked away in a location that you can only reach once you acquire Hermes's high-jump sandals (which also allow Orpheus to reverse gravity) by visiting the god's shrine. The entire game flows around similar quest chains and prerequisite tasks, with several tools doubling as weapons in the classic *Metroid* style.

UNLIKE METROID OR *ZELDA II, THE BATTLE OF OLYMPUS* INCLUDES A SIMPLE ECONOMY IN THE FORM OF OLIVES: SMALL, RED, GLOWING ORBS THAT CERTAIN ENEMIES DROP AND WHICH YOU MUST USE TO PURCHASE CERTAIN KEY ITEMS IN ORDER TO ACQUIRE THE HEART TOKENS AND REACH HADES.

Unlike *Metroid* or even *Zelda II, The Battle of Olympus* also includes a simple economy in the form of Olives: small, red, glowing orbs that some enemies drop. A few key items can only be acquired by purchasing them with Olives, including a few gifts from the gods under the guise of shrine offerings. Ultimately, you need to seek the best gear to bulk up for Orpheus's battle. Fortunately, most of these appear along the way as you seek out three mystical Heart tokens in order to break through magical barriers to open the path to Hades.

The Battle of Olympus makes no effort to hide the inspiration it takes from *Zelda II*: many enemies move and behave exactly like foes in *Zelda II*; many quest objectives and abilities work exactly like those in *Zelda II*; and the graphics—especially building interiors—could easily have been traced directly from *Zelda II*. This is not an accusation of sneaky plagiarism. Yukio Horimoto, the game's designer, has plainly stated that he simply wanted to make a game like *Zelda II*. He succeeded admirably at this goal while also making some interesting advancements in the action-RPG genre. *Olympus* contains a more concrete and structured world design and quest objectives than similar games that appeared the year before; if it lacks for a certain originality, well, there's no shame in refining existing concepts in pursuit of further advancements.

Although the concept of the *Zelda II*–clone would amount to a fairly short-lived branch of game design that more or less faded into obscurity after *Ys III* and *Wonder Boy III* perfected the format, *The Battle of Olympus* deserves credit for using Nintendo's hit as a springboard into refinement. As a bonus, it takes a playful approach to a setting and theme rarely used in video gaming. Its take on mythical Greek antiquity incorporates thoughtful details, ranging from the way you need to kneel before a god will speak to you to the fact that you fight a Minotaur trapped in a labyrinth on Crete. Perhaps not a major landmark in metroidvania evolution, but worth a play. M

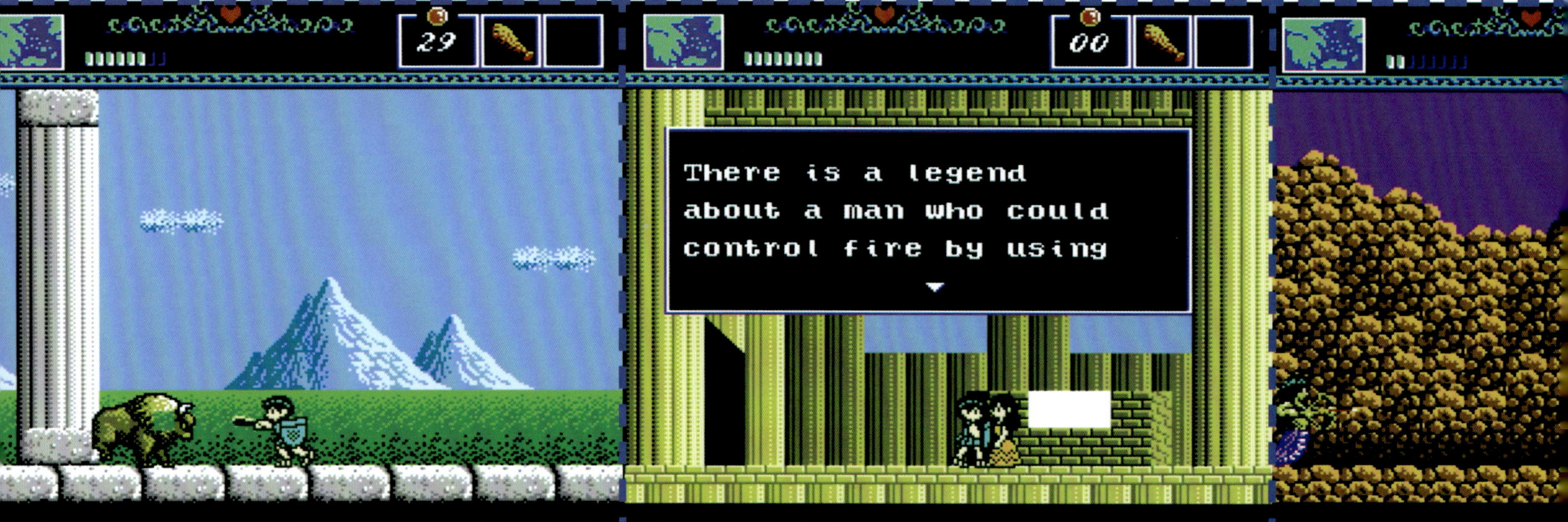

PORTABLE PIPELINE

When Nintendo launched its Game Boy portable system in 1989, it brought all manner of games—including metroidvanias and action-RPGs—to players on the go. But, given the limitations of the system (a tiny resolution and four-tone monochromatic graphics) and the natural play patterns that emerged around the Game Boy (quick bursts of play), only a handful of developers made the effort to produce substantial works that were specifically designed for it. Even after *Pokémon* extended the Game Boy's life in what should have been its twilight days, that second wind didn't result in new portable metroidvanias. *Pokémon* may have been a role-playing adventure in the purest, most *Dragon Quest* sense of the term, but it only led to more turn-based collection RPGs.

For the most part, metroidvania enthusiasts who longed to enjoy nonlinear adventures on the go had few options even through the Game Boy Advance era. *Metroid* and *Castlevania* were well-represented on the GBA, but the handheld metroidvania wouldn't properly take off until the arrival of Nintendo's DS and 3DS. Thankfully, for those who wanted to partake of more than the meager original efforts the Game Boy family had to offer, publishers were more than happy to convert NES games into portable form. By the time Nintendo retired the GBA, quite a few notable 8-bit console releases had made their way to the handheld space via ports and sanctioned emulator carts, ranging from the original *Metroid* (along with the first three *Zelda* games) to *River City Ransom* to the very final Famicom release, the metroidvania-flavored fourth entry in the *Adventure Island* series.

This, it turns out, is *The Battle of Olympus*'s secret legacy: the first NES metroidvania to receive a direct conversion to the Game Boy. Released exclusively in Europe by Imagineer in 1993, *The Battle of Olympus* for Game Boy faithfully recreated the beats of the NES game. It played poorly due to the low power and limited resolution of the handheld, but for anyone jonesing for an action-RPG on the go, it scratched an itch. Its European-exclusive nature has caused it to be largely forgotten by history; even *Olympus* designer Yukio Horimoto didn't know of its existence when I interviewed him in 2015!

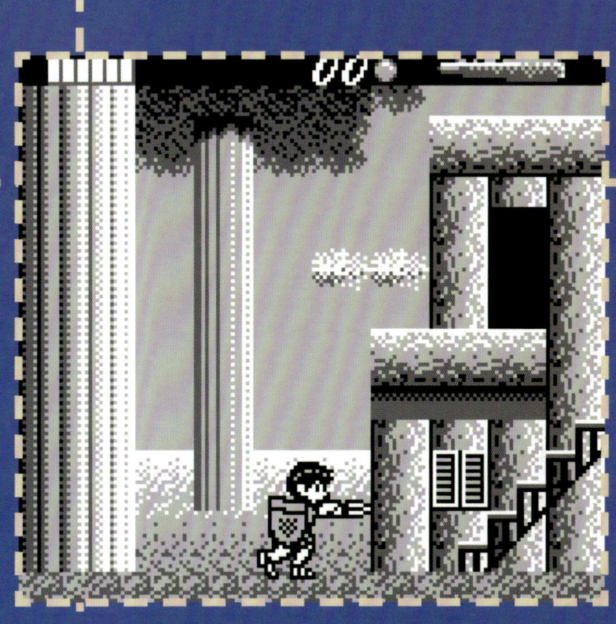

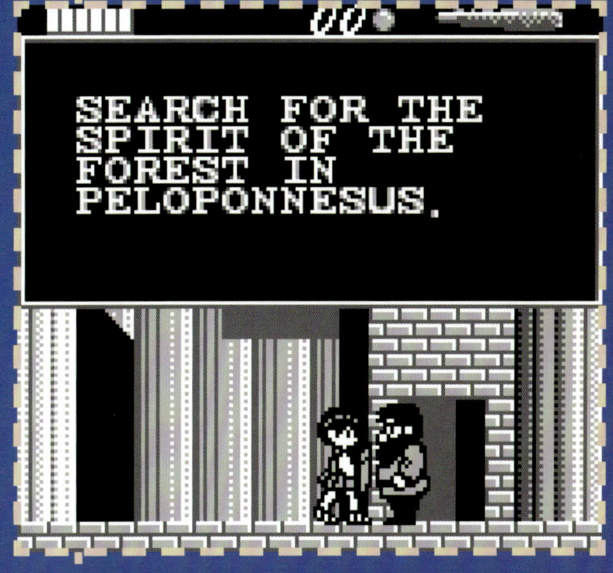

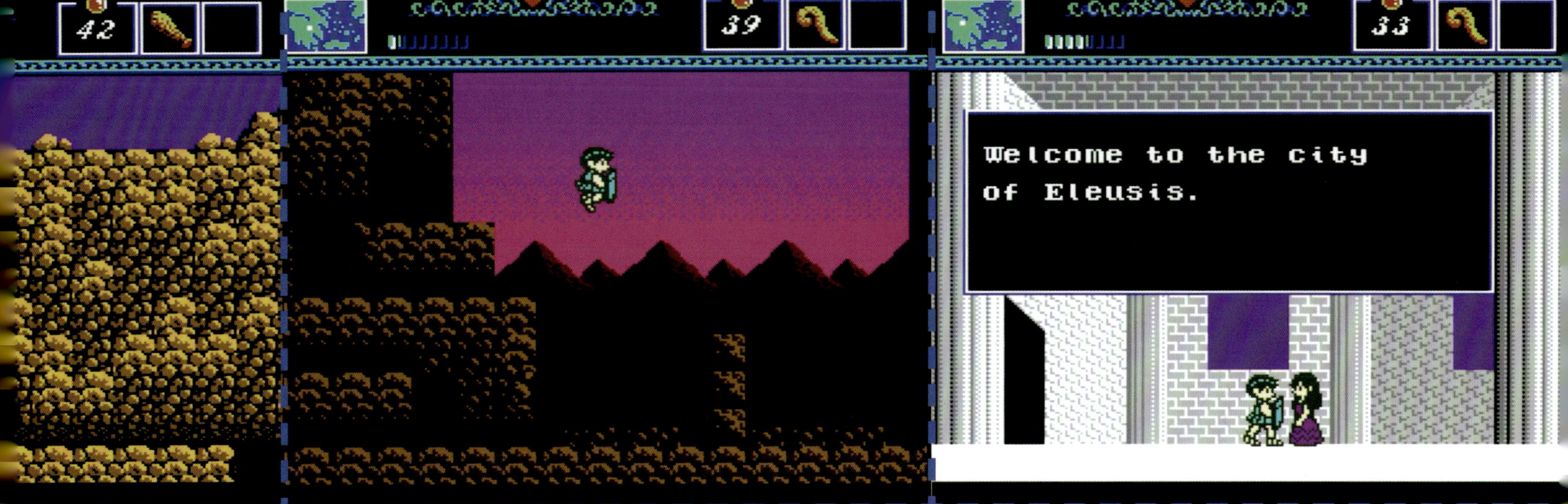

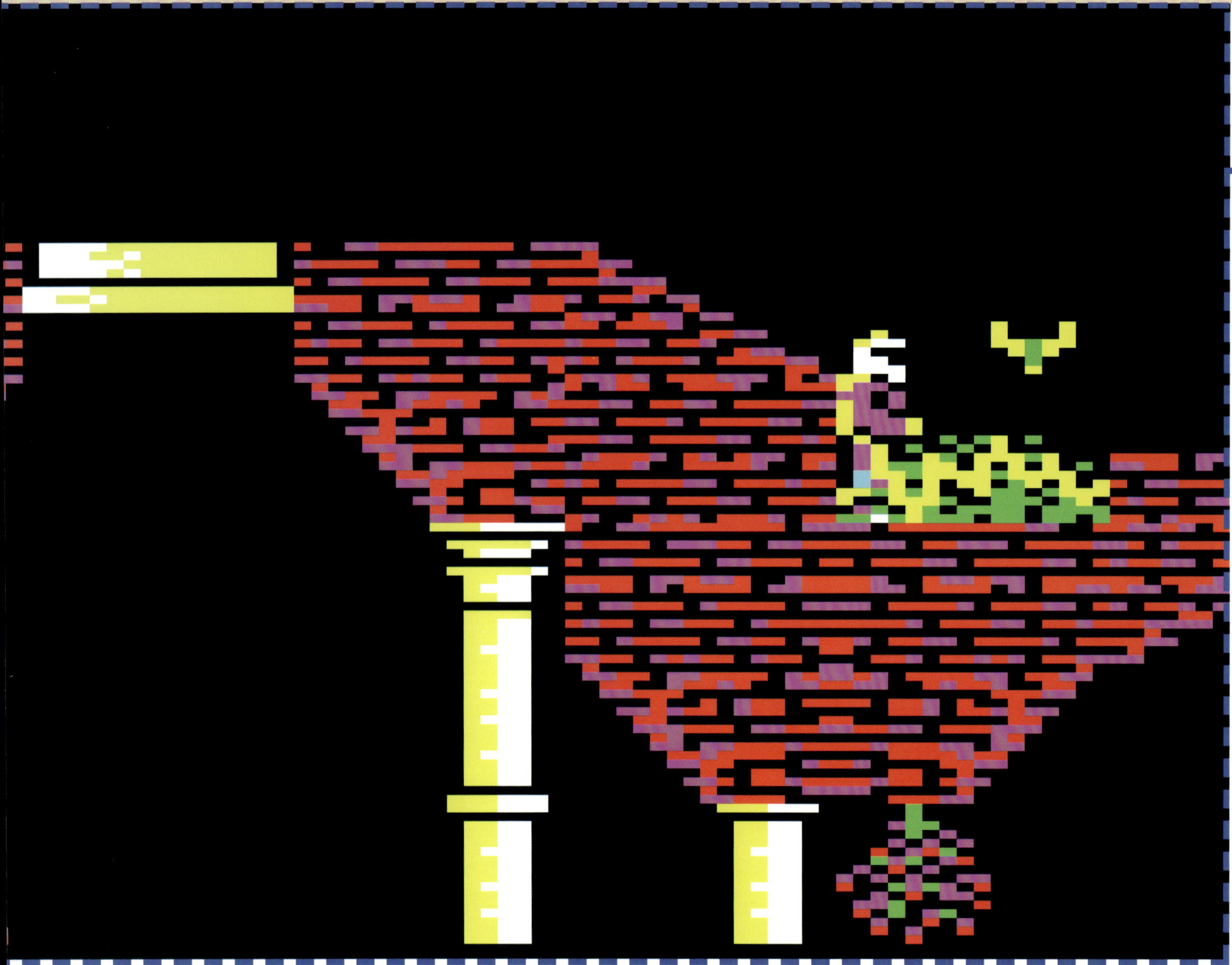

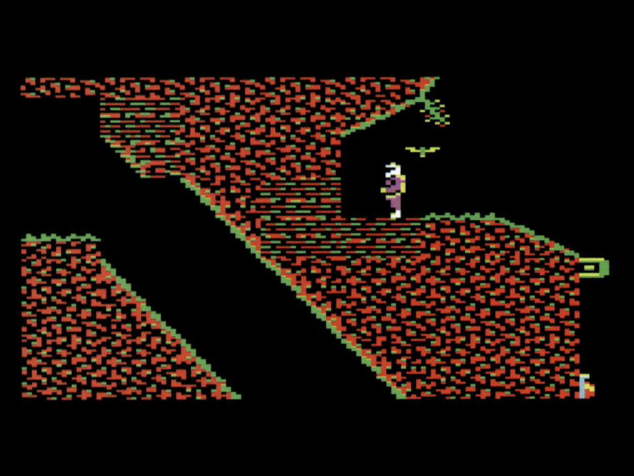

EXILE

PLATFORM: **BBC MICRO / VARIOUS**
DEV: **SUPERIOR SOFTWARE** | PUB: **SUPERIOR SOFTWARE**
INITIAL RELEASE DATE: **1988**

THE EXODUS GENESIS

After getting a meaningful start on American consoles, computers, and arcade cabinets, action-RPG and metroidvania evolution largely shifted over to Japan in the latter 1980s. This isn't to say that no Western developers had any interest in exploratory action games, but certainly they were few and far between. Outside of Japan, consumer tastes simply went in a different direction, leaving creators who loved exploratory action stranded in forgotten tidal pools of the medium that failed to make international headway. Such is the case for *Exile*, a wildly ambitious physics-based open-world action game for Acorn Electron and BBC Micro home computers. Published by UK-based label Superior Software and developed by a team of two men—Jeremy Smith and Peter Irvin—*Exile* is precisely the sort of impossible technical feat that British programmers specialized in for their underpowered computers, cut from the same cloth as *Elite*.

Exile places players in control of an explorer named Mike Finn, who has been tasked with delving into a massive alien world, equipped with a jetpack, a limited supply of energy, and whatever weapons and tools he can forage along the way. The world in question consists of a massive network of interconnected caverns that grow increasingly deadly the deeper into the world you descend. But it seems that the deadliest thing about *Exile* might just be the systems that regulate the world you explore. *Exile* features gravity, autonomous monsters, weapons, physics, and mathematical wind modeling, all in a procedurally generated world. Somehow, all this runs on computers sporting even less horsepower than the NES.

Exile received a number of conversions to more powerful systems, including the mighty Amiga and a Commodore 64 port that fans generally regard as the definitive take on the game. But none of these ports ever reached the Americas or Japan, which means *Exile* has had distressingly little influence on the creators who largely propelled metroidvania design forward through the years; it's more of a novel outlier. Still, a handful of modern metroidvanias have captured a bit of *Exile*'s spirit, such as *Hollow Knight* and *Axiom Verge 2*. Whether by design or coincidence, the pioneering spirit of this mostly forgotten game still lives on in some capacity.

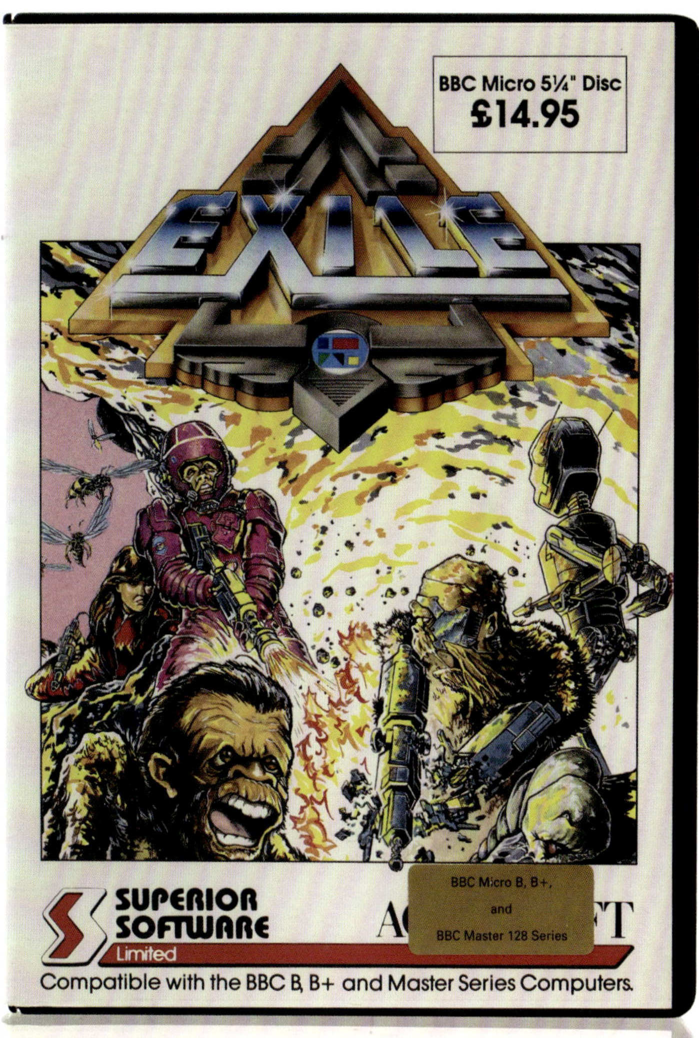

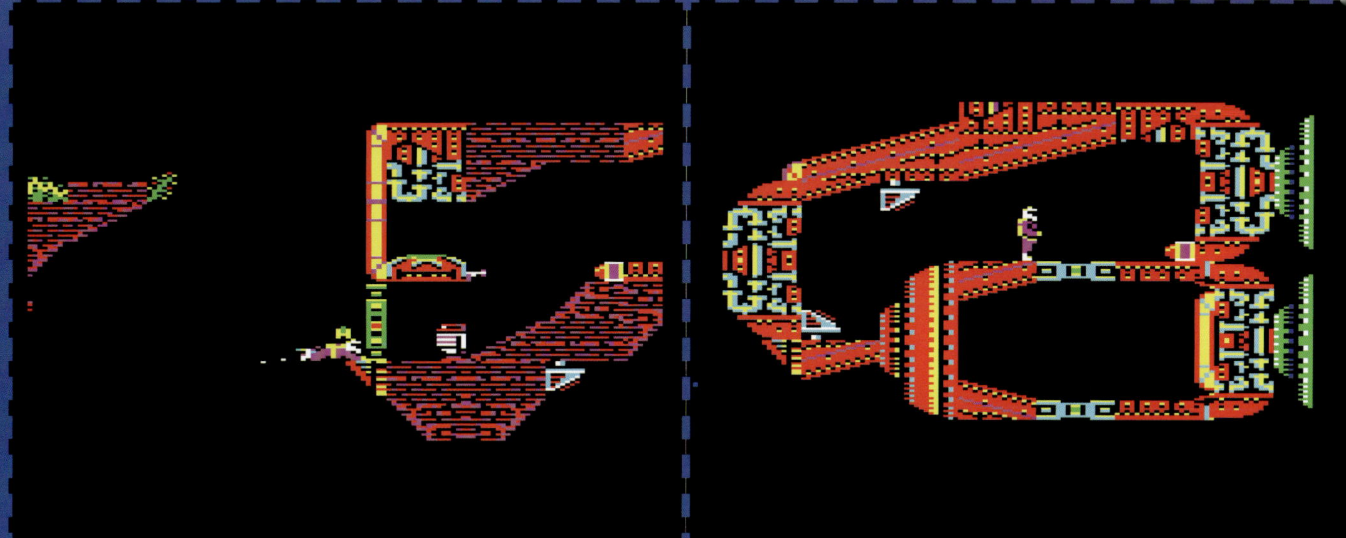

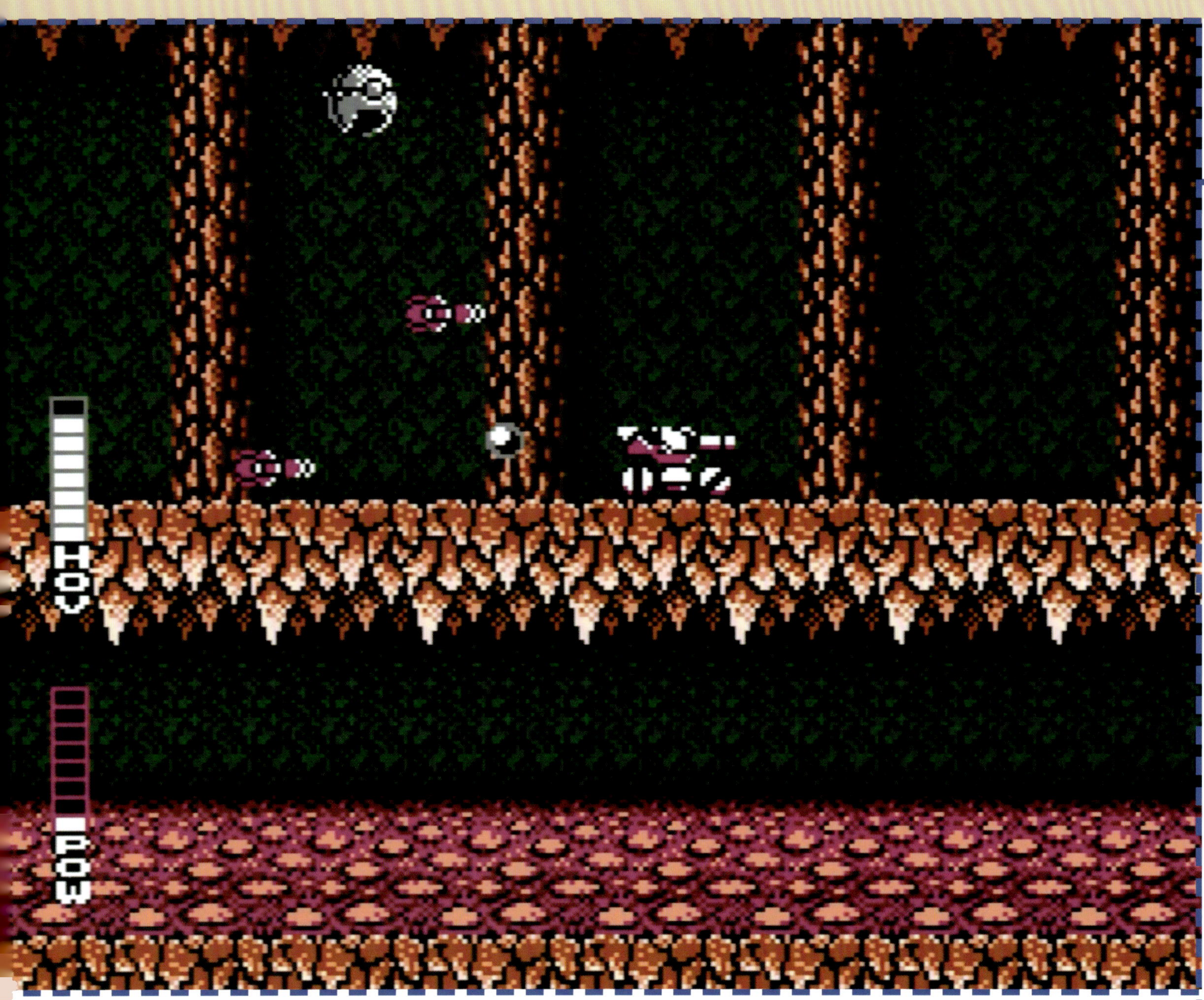

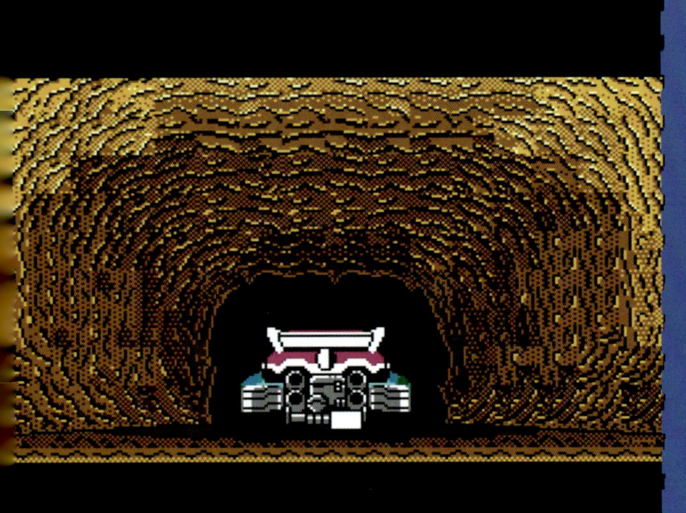

© Sunsoft

BLASTER MASTER

PLATFORM: **FAMICOM / NES**
DEV: **SUNSOFT** | PUB: **SUNSOFT**
INITIAL RELEASE DATE: **JUNE 1988**

NOTABLE FOR: **COMBINING VEHICULAR COMBAT, TOP-DOWN SHOOTING, AND EXPLORATION**

FROG BLASTING THE VENT CORE

Where *The Guardian Legend* combined top-down nonlinear exploration with vehicle-based action-style dungeons, Sunsoft's *Blaster Master* flipped the script, combining non-linear vehicular exploration with top-down action-style dungeons. *The Guardian Legend* treated vehicular sequences as a side excursion from the primary on-foot exploration in the central hub. Transforming into a spaceship to break away from the classic *Zelda/Hydlide* action-RPG perspective allowed the player to build the heroine's power to further her range in the on-foot hub space. Conversely, *Blaster Master* treats the vehicular sequences as the game's core, allowing you to travel through the central hub and relegating on-foot combat sequences to secondary status.

It's a subtle distinction but a noteworthy one. It means that the lively, active shooter portions of *Blaster Master* comprise the meat of the game—a great creative choice that helps the title stand out from its peers. Unfortunately, the on-foot sequences feel more like a chore than the ones in *The Guardian Legend* did. This comes down to the fact that, unlike Miria's powers in *The Guardian Legend*, the abilities you gain for *Blaster Master*'s SOPHIA 3rd combat tank don't carry across modes. When you step out of your tank as the tiny Jason, your pedestrian arsenal consists entirely of a gun and a grenade. That's a marked difference from Miria's ability to use the sub-weapons, power-ups, and skill enhancements she acquired throughout her adventure in both exploratory and combat modes.

It doesn't help that *Blaster Master* attempts to incorporate a dynamic power system for Jason's gun reminiscent of Miria's. But, again, these work differently and to the player's disadvantage. The power of Miria's main weapon was determined by her supply of energy chips—which had a progressively increasing cap—and players could regulate her base firepower through their tactical choices. Jason's firepower falls largely outside of the realm of conscious player choice. He can only upgrade his handgun by finding scarce power-up icons—but any time he takes damage while in the overhead perspective, each hit causes his gun to downgrade in power one step. The more damage you take from

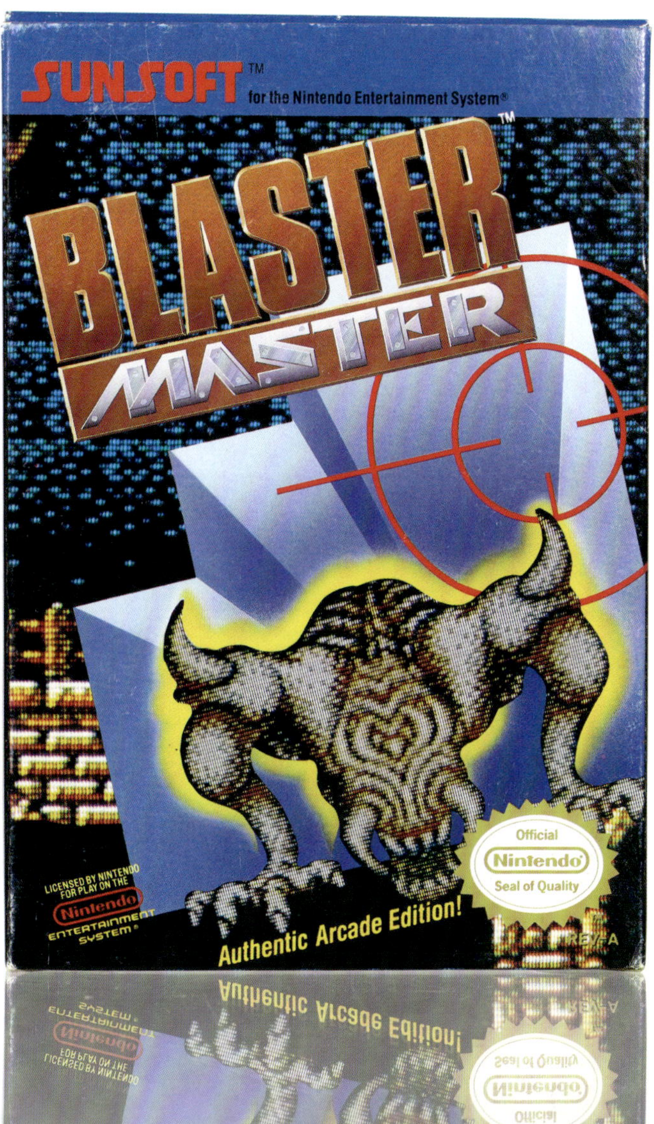

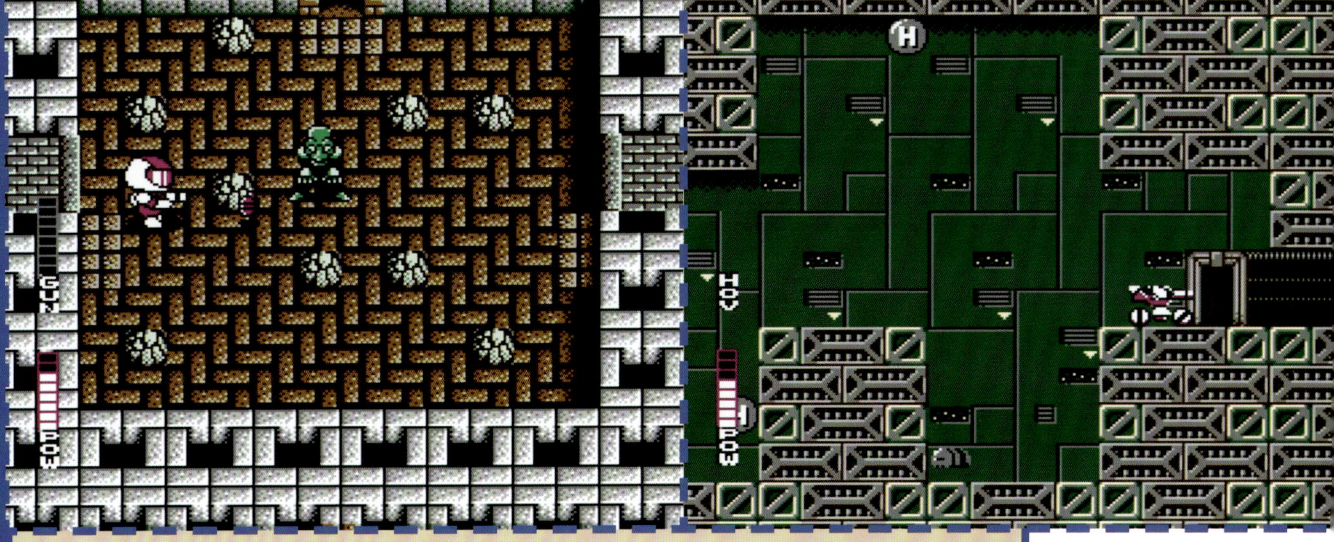

enemies, the more enfeebled you become, and the road to recovering that power is long and difficult. This gives the player a lot less control over their weapon status than Miria had over her weapon output, which lay entirely in players' hands. There is no risk-reward choice here; you simply have to avoid injury. Given that Jason's life bar also decreases when he takes damage, the weapon degradation system feels like salt in the (somewhat literal) wound.

All this also means that *Blaster Master*'s alternate, on-foot gameplay sequences aren't as interesting or effectively integrated into the tank scenes' core metroidvania loop as *The Guardian Legend*'s. That's a shame, because the tank-based portions of *Blaster Master* rank among the absolute best nonlinear exploratory action to be found on any 8-bit platform. In fact, *Blaster Master* introduces quite a few mechanics and concepts that would become fundamental pillars of the metroidvania format. All the permanent skills you earn by killing bosses manifest as tank upgrades, turning a vehicle that begins the game as an impressive, energy-spewing mech with the ability to spring into the air into something even more incredible.

Granted, not all of *Blaster Master*'s power-ups are especially inventive. One of them is a literal key that's only used in a single door, and another gives your tank cannon a power boost that *also* functions as a key by allowing you to break open the door to the second stage. These trifles are balanced by powers like the ability to climb walls, dive into water, and even fly. These more advanced SOPHIA 3rd improvements increase the range and potential of the tank, allowing you to reach new areas and explore the world.

Blaster Master initially appears to be structured as a linear game, with each of its eight zones existing as a standalone space. Once you unlock more of SOPHIA 3rd's potential, however, you begin to realize that the Plutonium Boss's underground lair (where the adventure takes place) is crisscrossed with pathways and connections that allow you not only to backtrack but to take shortcuts once you've fitted the tank with the proper power-up.

The first stage acts as a hub of sorts: a space that you return to throughout the course of the game. You access the second half of the world by returning to the actual beginning of the game and using your hover power to fly up into the open sky above your starting point. Later, you'll return again to Area 1 to use your ceiling-crawling skills to slip through a seemingly impassable barrier that leads to the final zones. *Blaster Master* is perhaps the first game that really and truly dropped tantalizing hints of future traversal—enticingly narrow passages and doors just out of reach—throughout the adventure, giving you glimpses of spaces that draw the eye while making it clear that you couldn't visit those places just yet. Each time you acquire new navigational or combat powers, you can't help but think back: *Oh, I saw something that I couldn't get to before—now, where was that?*

You can almost forgive *Blaster Master*'s failure to include any sort of password or save feature to allow players to bookmark their progress and work their way toward the showdown with the Plutonium Boss across multiple sessions. (Sunsoft tweaked the US version to be even less kind, limiting players to only five continues after a game over before forcing them to restart the entire long, difficult adventure afresh—the mentality of a quarter-gobbling arcade game, not an action-RPG.) The developers clearly didn't expect anyone to complete this game on their first go. Instead, they seem to have assumd that newcomers might get as far as, say, earning the cannon upgrade from Area 2 before running out of continues. But the next time they play, they'd be likely to spot clusters of blocks that the maxed-out tank gun can shatter in some of the earlier spaces of the game, marking those spots with a mental note to return to once they beat the second boss again. They might also notice some barriers throughout Areas 2 and 3 that SOPHIA 3rd can break through at max power, creating shortcuts back to the opening zone. But some of those paths sit too high up for SOPHIA 3rd to reach, despite the tank's impressive ability to leap into the air—meaning you could only reach those areas if the tank could somehow fly. And what's the deal with that spike-lined wall in the Area 1 that's too narrow for the tank to traverse and too high for Jason to clear on foot? It seems to lead somewhere, so you're left wondering how you can possibly pass through it—at least until you gain the ability for SOPHIA 3rd to climb walls and zip right past those spikes...

Blaster Master was certainly a flawed, uneven, and frequently unfair game. But it looked and sounded great, and the tank sequences offered buoyant excitement thanks to the limber-yet-responsive control scheme. From the outset, SOPHIA 3rd moves more nimbly than just about any metroidvania or action-RPG protagonist that had come before, possessing the snappy agility of a pure action hero while also offering the potential to grow in power and abilities by way of upgrades. These compelling design strengths were more than enough to keep *Blaster Master* players hooked despite the lopsided difficulty and overreliance on boring on-foot combat as load-bearing game spaces. Those who took the time to pay attention to the world's interlocking layers and workings, who puzzled out how the different portions of the labyrinth fit together while leaving openings for future improvements, were given a firsthand glimpse of the metroidvania genre's blueprints being drawn. M

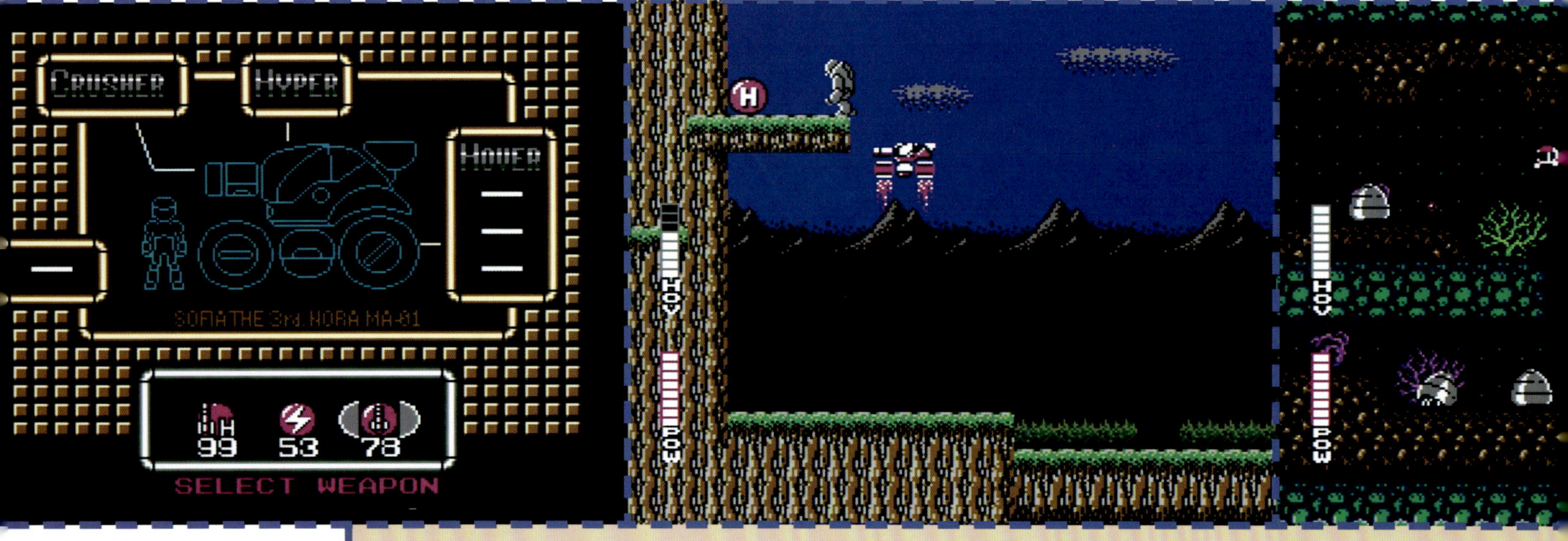

THE ADVENTURES OF CAPTAIN COMIC

Captain Comic has earned a certain notoriety thanks to its trouble Nintendo Entertainment System release, a cartridge published without Nintendo's approval as a licensor. Outside of the Tengen library, NES games that lacked the Nintendo Seal of Quality were more or less guaranteed to fall short of the standards that NES fans expected. *Captain Comic* didn't exactly shatter that paradigm, at least not on the NES. In its original MS-DOS incarnation, however, the game held up considerably better.

Part of that has to do with simple circumstances: at the time of its debut, DOS fans had very few other scrolling platform action games to choose from, and none that contained rudimentary metroidvania elements. *The Adventures of Captain Comic* stood alone, and the fact that a single person—one Michael Denio—created it all on his own made it all more impressive. It's raw, and it controls clumsily, but it demonstrates a remarkable level of ambition given the limitations and precedents of the platform.

Captain Comic does possess a certain metroidvania spirit, albeit in a simplistic fashion. The game's central quest involves hunting for a trio of treasures across a variety of zones, which are somewhat interconnected and allow (indeed, require) the player to backtrack through them to complete the adventure. The eponymous captain acquires multiple permanent upgrades to his skills over the course of his mission, beginning with weapon upgrades; he begins his journey with no offensive capabilities but can ultimately acquire the power to fire up to five rippling blasts of energy at once.

His upgrades come in several navigational flavors, as well. In addition to bog-standard keys that unlock doors, he also needs to locate a lantern to illuminate dark areas; special boots that let him reach high ledges; and even a teleporter that can zap him forward a short distance to clear gaps and pass walls—a rarely seen play mechanic that would appear decades later in *Axiom Verge*! The arcade-like mentality of *Captain Comic*'s difficulty level (five lives, no continues) makes for a short quest, but as a first effort at a metroidvania for American PCs, it does the trick.

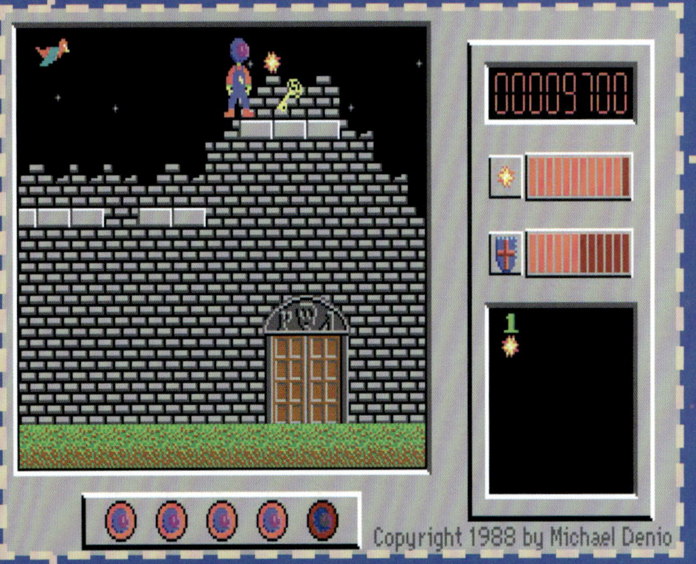

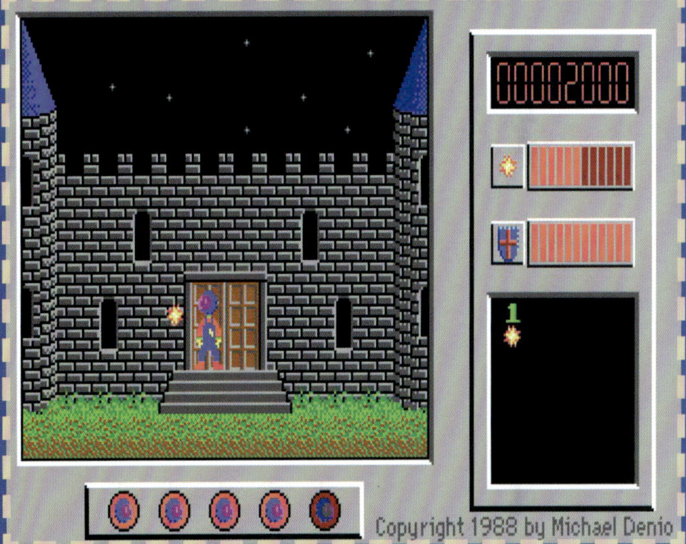

© Michael Denio

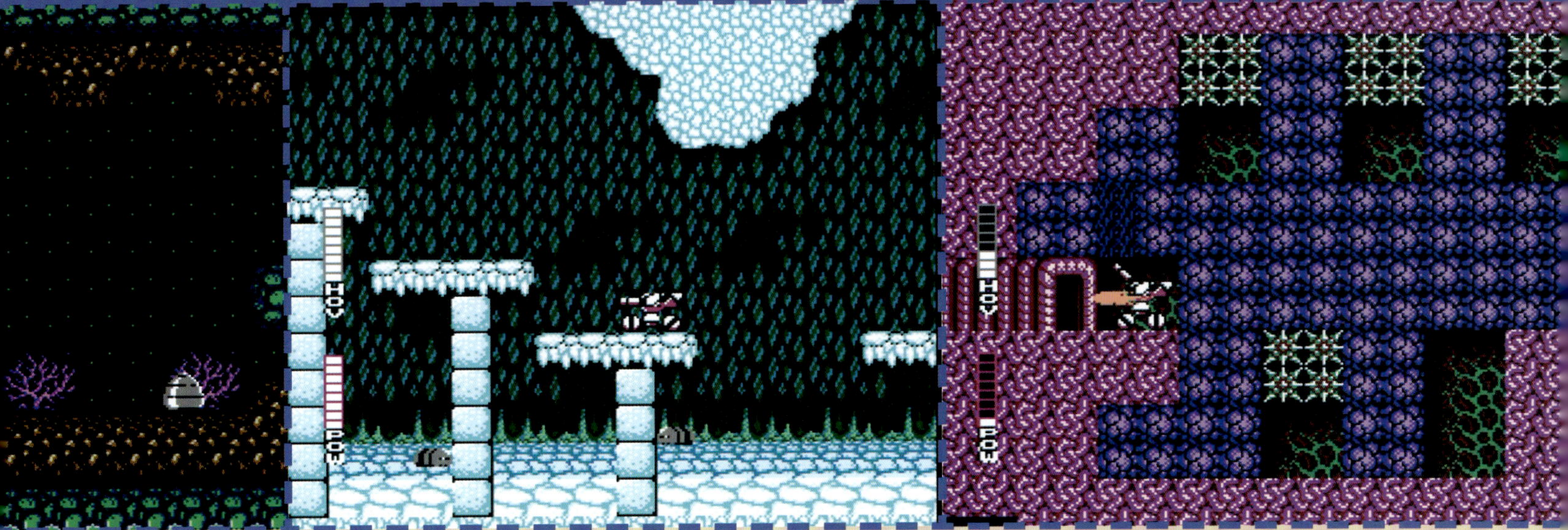

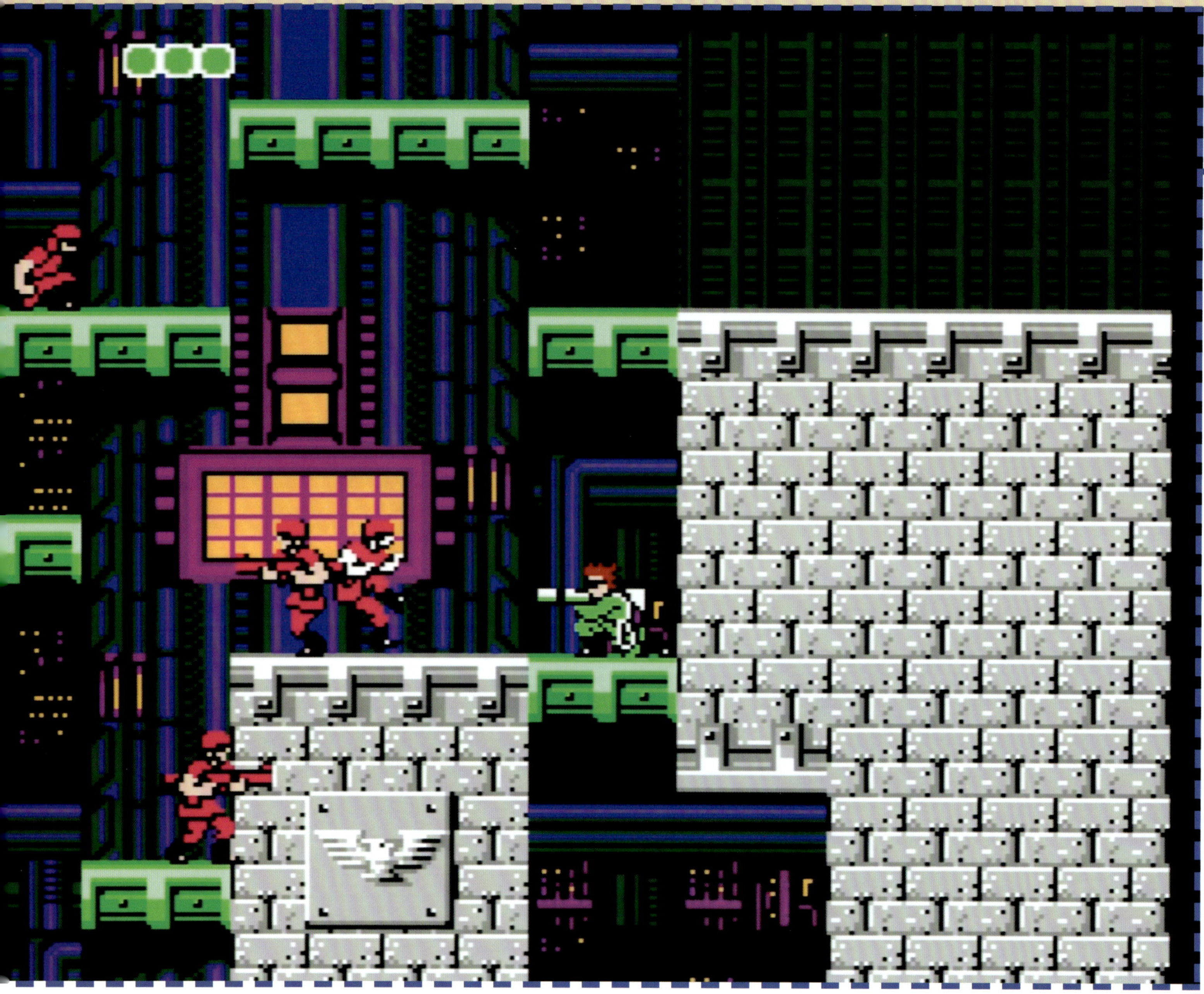

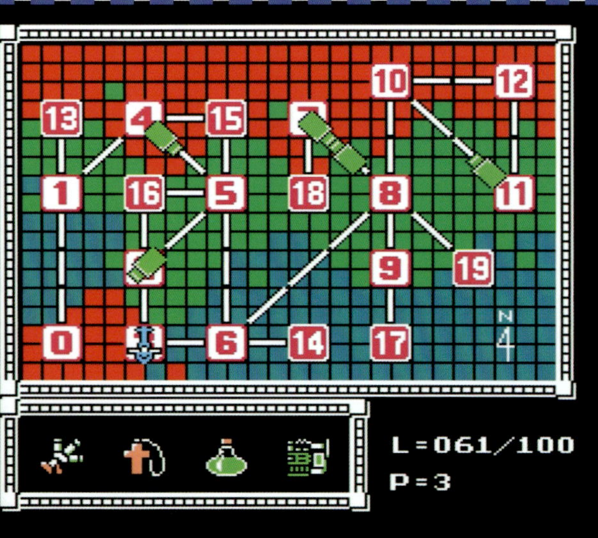

BIONIC COMMANDO

PLATFORM: **FAMICOM / NES**
DEV: **CAPCOM** | PUB: **CAPCOM**
INITIAL RELEASE DATE: **JULY 1988**

NOTABLE FOR: MAP-BASED NARRATIVE-DRIVEN PROGRESSION

GRAPPLING WITH GAME DESIGN

Bionic Commando doesn't fit as neatly into the metroidvania box as something *Blaster Master* does due to its self-contained level structure, a vestige of its coin-op origins. But the spirit of the genre—and of fighting fascism!—absolutely radiates from Capcom's NES version of the game. *Bionic Commando* began life as an arcade game with a fairly simple structure. Players had to fight their way through a handful of levels using their wits, weapons, and a bionic grappling arm that allowed them to zip quickly upward and swing across gaps. The bionic arm introduced an element of vertical space management to the platform game that made the action feel looser and more open than anything that had come before. Bear in mind that it debuted just a couple of years after *Pac-Land*, *Super Mario Bros.*, and *Ghosts 'n Goblins*: the three most influential platform action games of all time, which laid down the rules for how run-and-jump scrolling platformers should work.

Arriving in March 1987, hot on the heels of those landmark releases, *Bionic Commando* burst into arcades with the temerity to get rid of jumping mechanics, making up for its loss by giving players a skill that allowed them even greater freedom of movement. Its stages didn't consist of simple point-to-point reels that moved in a horizontal line from one end to the other. Instead, its levels span upwardly as well as laterally, and its hero can move in all directions through these spaces. The challenge becomes not simply reaching the goal of each level but to find it in the first place. Capcom's arcade team would build further on this concept with *Black Tiger*, which introduced more complex interlocking spaces along with an economy and RPG leveling systems.

In the meantime, Capcom licensed out ports of *Bionic Commando* to other developers, who produced a variety of home computer ports that converted the coin-op material faithfully (albeit with varying degrees of success, given the limitations of PCs at the time). For the NES version, however, the company adapted *Bionic Commando* internally. In the process, their team almost entirely rebuilt the game, using the core mechanics and a few familiar physical spaces to produce an expansive action-RPG that evolved on *Black Tiger*'s design in turn.

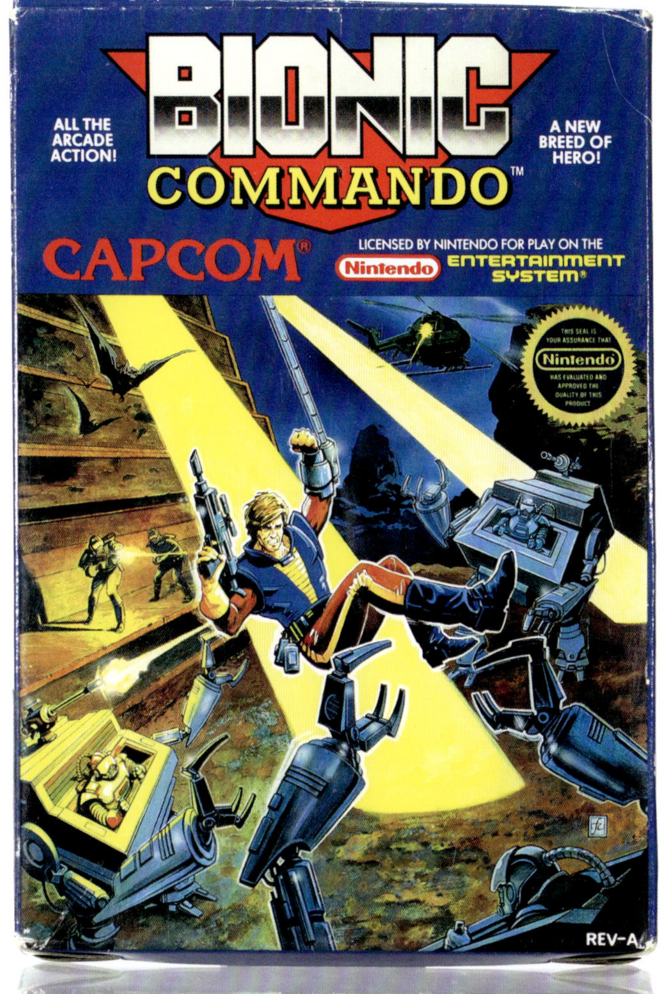

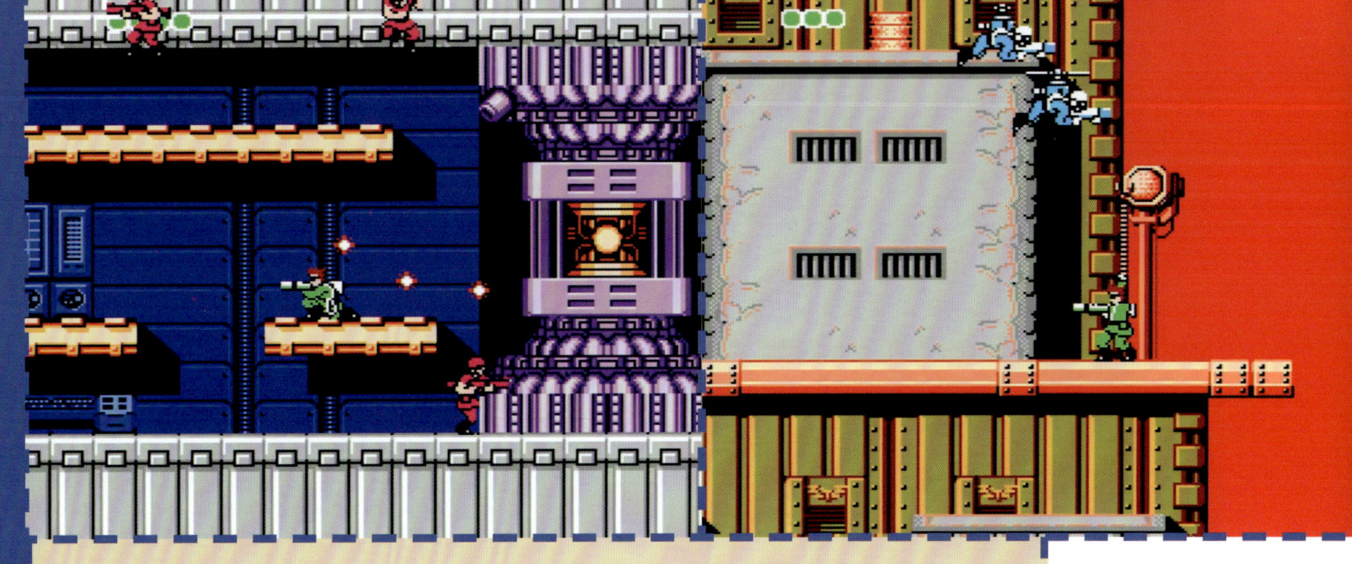

Bionic Commando on the NES works more as a sequel to the arcade game than a direct port. Its action spans a dozen primary stages rather than the coin-op's four. And while these levels still scroll in multiple directions, they have a greater sense of focus and purpose. However, while the game assigns sequential numbers to its levels—1 through 12—you don't play through them in that order; you often need to complete a "later" stage before being able to access one with a lower number. On top of that, players also have to venture into half a dozen additional stages that exist entirely for the sake of storytelling, getting hints, and gearing up. You access these stages through a geographic map that allows you to travel between them more or less at will.

Again, these hard divisions between stages disqualify *Bionic Commando* as a "proper" metroidvania experience since you duck back out to the world map to move between one level and the next. But the heart of an action-RPG beats powerfully here. For starters, *Bionic Commando* features a simple leveling system akin to *Castlevania II*'s: you collect bullet icons from defeated enemies, which act as stand-ins for experience points. At certain milestones, protagonist Captain Ladd gains additional health in the form of an extra pip on his life meter at the top of the screen. You begin with no health pips at all, making NES's *Bionic Commando* initially appear to be a straight- forward, one-hit kill action game like the coin-op. But by the time you reach the first communications room, where you need to interact with NPCs to achieve in-game objectives and open critical paths, players will have collected just enough icons to have added a single health point to Ladd's endurance, allowing him to withstand two hits before he dies.

More crucially, you collect equipment by defeating bosses and interacting with certain NPCs. These fall into three categories: weapons, tools, and communicators. To progress in the game, you need to acquire items in all three categories. Guns expand your combat options, but they also work as keys, with each extra weapon allowing you to break a barrier somewhere in enemy territory. Likewise, you need your full suite of communicators to interface with the encrypted comm systems throughout enemy bases; you can't access a level's boss chamber until you've spoken with one of your allies via that stage's comms room. It's all fairly rudimentary by modern standards, but for 1988 it was a pretty groundbreaking approach to adapting an arcade game, standing right alongside Tecmo's take on *Rygar*.

With rudimentary RPG mechanics, a sprawling storyline that involves rescuing the original game's hero while bloodily exploding Hitler's skull, and some great interlocking quest progression structures, *Bionic Commando* exists next to the platonic lineage of the metroidvania format...but it's an influential work all the same. *M*

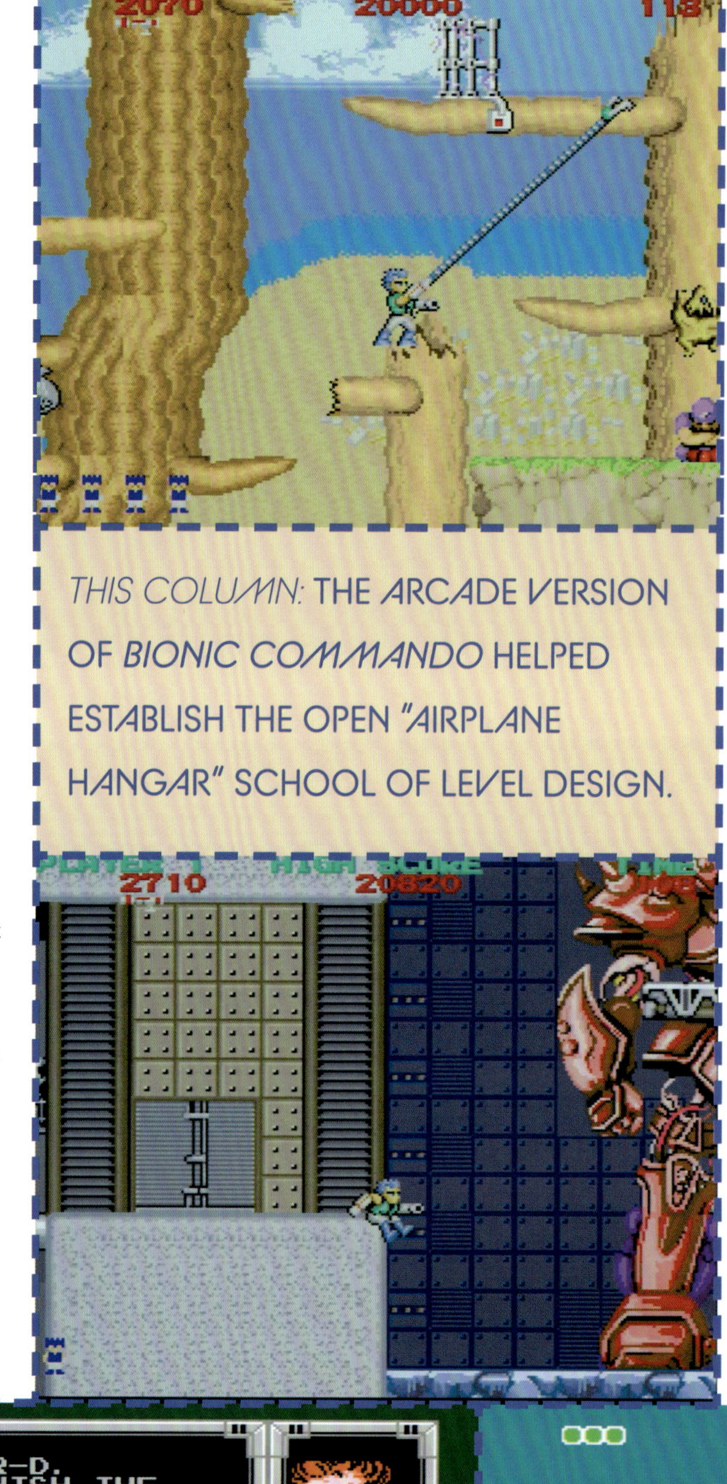

THIS COLUMN: THE ARCADE VERSION OF *BIONIC COMMANDO* HELPED ESTABLISH THE OPEN "AIRPLANE HANGAR" SCHOOL OF LEVEL DESIGN.

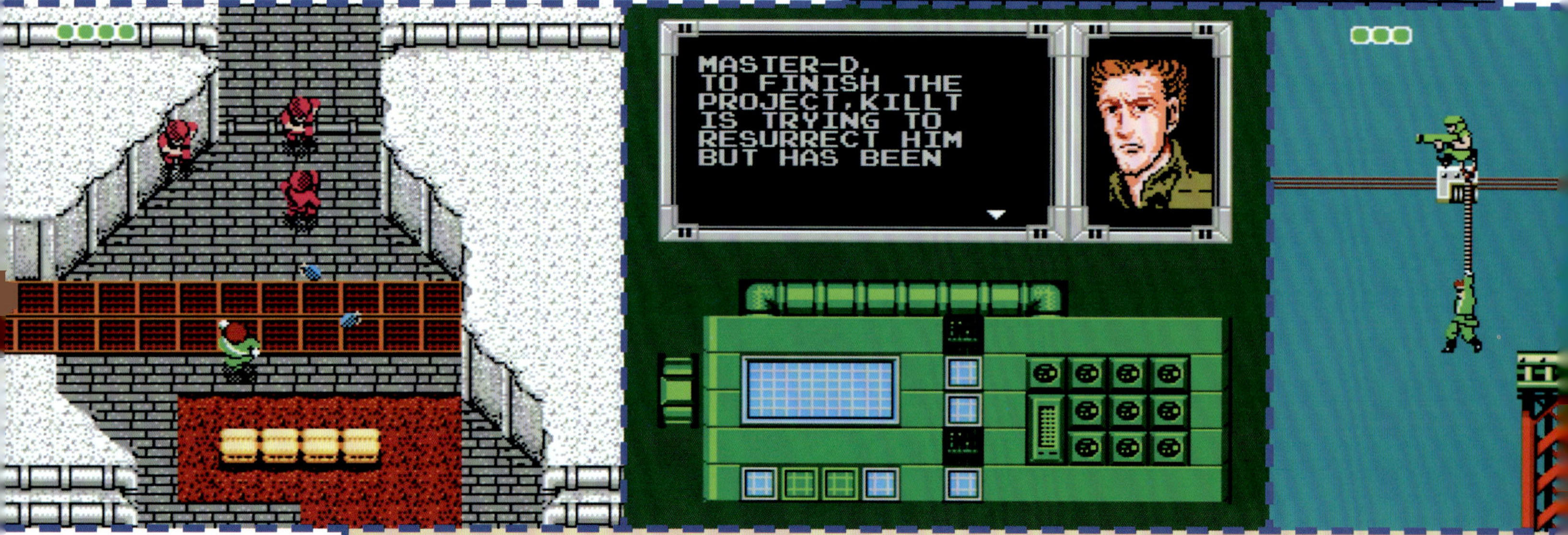

TIMES OF LORE

What if *The Legend of Zelda* had been created for an 8-bit microcomputer like the Commodore 64? Designer Chris Roberts set out to answer this rhetorical question in 1988 when he headed up the wildly ambitious *Times of Lore*. The result that Roberts came up with shouldn't really surprise anyone. *Times of Lore* certainly shares some DNA with *Zelda*, but it undeniably demonstrates a PC-oriented mindset. It's bigger, slower, and vastly more complex than any game ever to appear on an 8-bit console. Well, unless you count the eventual NES port of *Times of Lore*.

With its truncated isometric viewpoint and compact play action window, *Times of Lore* immediately stands apart from Japanese action-RPGs in the *Hydlide* and *Zelda* mold. Even the ones that incorporated windowed interfaces (a trick to minimize processor load and conserve graphical memory) made use of forced, three-quarters perspective that lent an abstract quality to the world. In keeping with American PC sensibilities, *Times of Lore* pursues a more naturalistic feel that suits its open-ended objectives and rambling interactions with non-player characters. Even the windowed interface reflects this, with a skeuomorphic quality to its display elements. The player's current health is denoted by the status of a candle along the right border (a rather literal interpretation of *Macbeth*'s "Out, out, brief candle!"). This manifests in gameplay as well; many of the quest objectives you attain are learned by speaking to NPCs and memorizing keywords, which you can direct back at other characters, opening up new topics of conversation.

And, most of all, *Times of Lore* reflects its nature in the sheer immensity of its quest. The game world covers an enormous amount of space, and key tasks pop up all throughout the world to be discovered and uncovered by the player through exploration and inquiry. The game's real-time combat primarily serves as a distraction or barrier to progress. The scale, openness, and overall vibe of *Times of Lore* would have tremendous influence on Western RPGs as they moved away from windowed interfaces to a more action-driven form, from massively multiplayer online games like *Ultima Online* to *The Elder Scrolls* and *Fallout*.

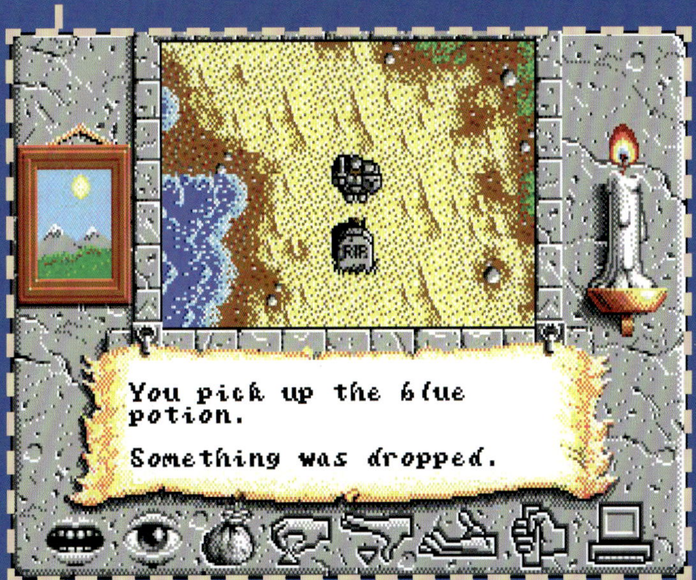

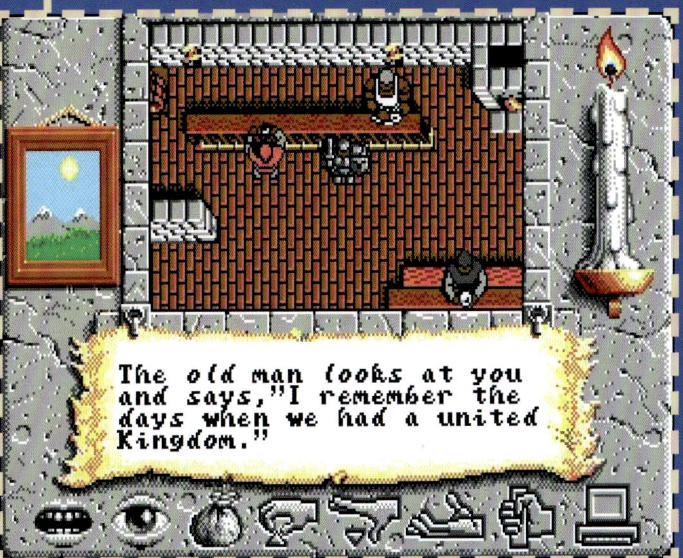

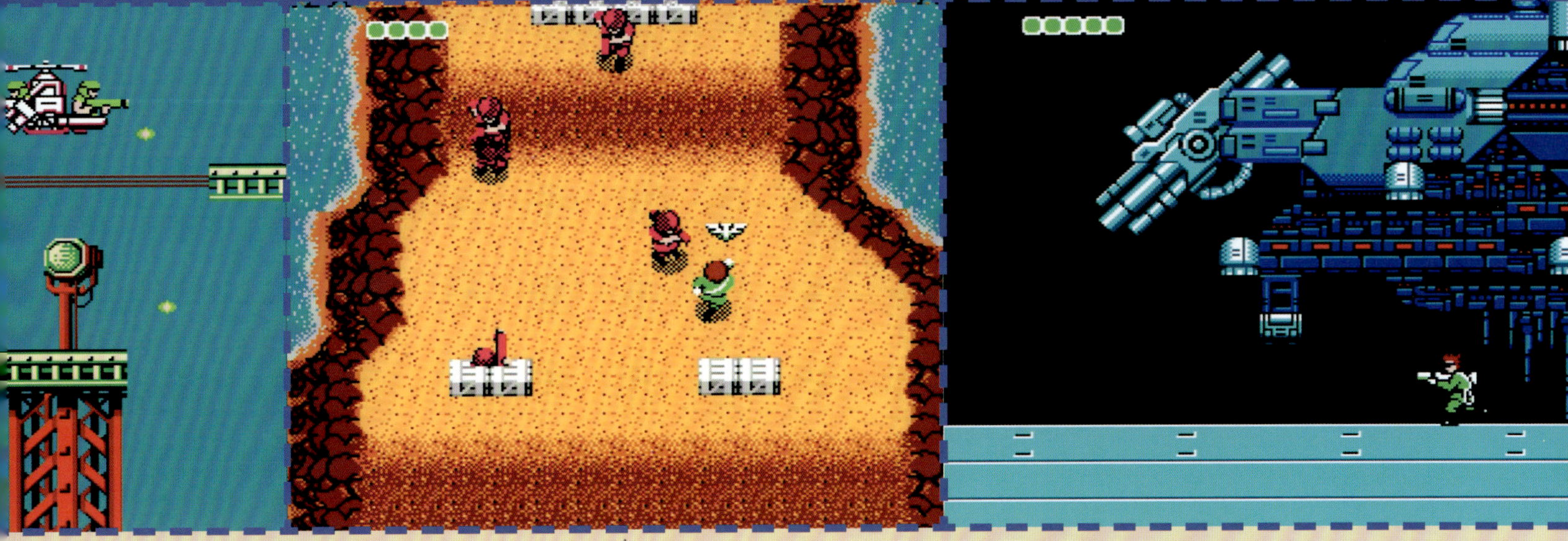

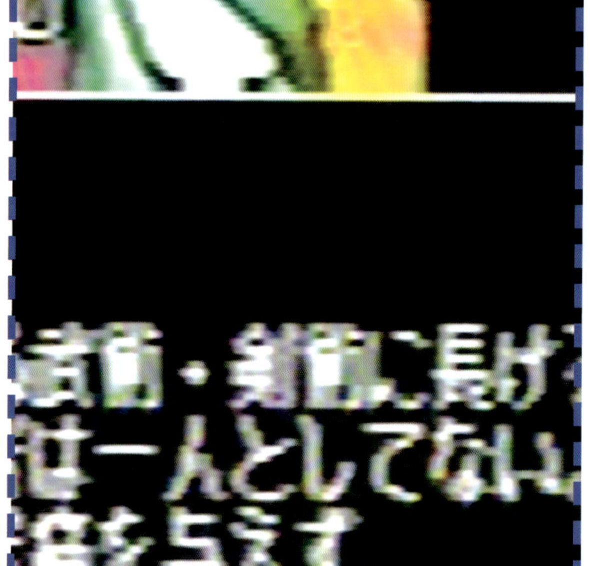

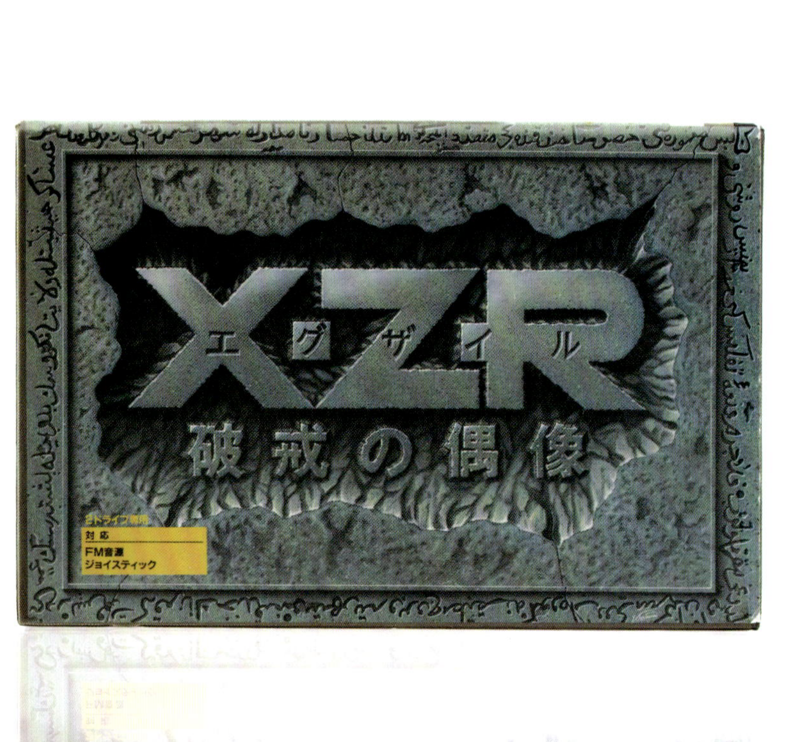

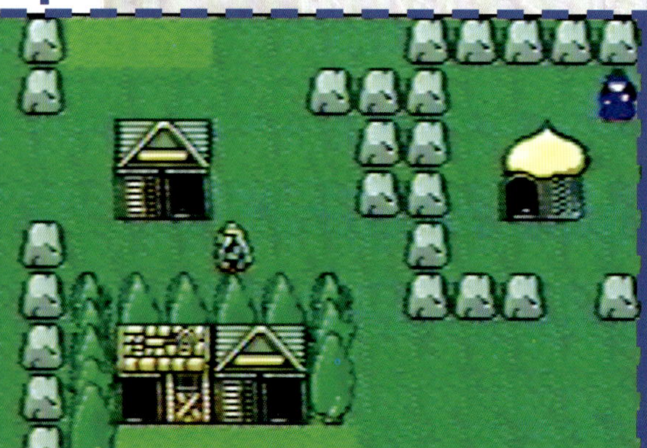

XZR: EXILE

PLATFORM: **PC-8801 / VARIOUS**
DEV: **TELENET JAPAN** | PUB: **TELENET JAPAN**
INITIAL RELEASE DATE: **JULY 1988**
SHOWN HERE: **MSX2 VERSION, 1988**

NOTABLE FOR: ***A FASCINATING TAKE ON THE ACTION-RPG***

SECOND EXODUS

Lovers of the action-RPG format got to enjoy the experience of being Exiled for a second time in 1988 thanks to developer Telenet Japan. The second *Exile*, aka *XZR*, had nothing to do with the Acorn Electron's *Exile*; it's just one of those weird coincidences that both games happened to share a title while furthering the state of the action-RPG art. Yes, the video games industry was smaller in the 1980s, but in those pre-internet days each region worked largely in isolation, resulting in unconnected blips of history like this.

XZR saw Telenet Japan approaching the genre perhaps more literally than anyone before them—certainly more so than their previous effort in this area, the in- triguing-yet-rough Famicom adaptation of *Valis*. In a way, this game feels like an attempt to push the action of *Zelda II* into the deeper, more stat-crunching realm of Falcom's *Dragon Slayer* titles—most notably *Xanadu*.

The core of the action here plays out as…well, it's not quite a side-scroller, since Telenet designed *XZR* for NEC PC-8801 home computers, which lacked hardware-level support for screen scrolling. This game's dungeons consist of static screens that flick from one to the next when players reach the edge of the screen (though the game's MSX2 port does at least feature smooth scrolling transitions). Nevertheless, it captures the overall vibe of *Zelda II* and *Faxanadu*, with sword-and-shield-based combat. However, outside of the dungeons and castles where the primary action transpires, you move from location to location by way of a simple world map in which you choose a destination and go there immediately—just like *Bionic Commando* and *Dragon Buster*. At each destination, you spend much of your time wandering around in a *Dragon Quest*–style town view packed with dialogue boxes. You speak to NPCs for clues; shop for gear; and advance the storyline by walking around a simple, top-down, tile-based perspective. It's only once you connect with critical information and complete specific plot objectives that you can move into the more action-oriented scenarios to explore, grapple with foes, dodge attacks, and cast various spells.

Structurally, *XZR* is nearly as open-ended as *Legacy of the Wizard*, but it places an even greater emphasis on your companion characters. Where Falcom's game sent you out to collect a sword with which to kill a dragon—dealing entirely in established, classic fantasy tropes—*XZR* protagonist Sadler has to locate and team up with his fellow assassins so they can join in his quest to save the Islamic world from crisis. At some point, this involves going after the American president—not exactly a comfortable stroll through Middle Earth clichés.

XZR takes place in a setting entirely removed from any action-RPG to have come before it, with a Middle Eastern theme. It's also considerably less family-friendly than the majority of metroidvania precursors. While most of those games involved combat and destruction, they took an antiseptic approach to killing. Drawing on themes of *1001 Arabian Nights*, Telenet directed their creation at the older audience that gamed on PCs at the time. The developers rooted their adventure in the real-world Order of Assassins, up to and including the warriors' use of narcotics in their works.

If the look and setting of this adventure strike a familiar chord, that's because Telenet would adapt the sequel, *XZR II: Kanketsuhen*, for the Sega Genesis and Turbo CD, where it saw release for the US market under the name *Exile*. *XZR* had a much darker tone—and a looser structure—than those conversions and their sequel, *Wicked Phenomenon*. Released only in Japan, *XZR* is yet another of the many inventive action-RPGs of the late '80s that hinted at metroidvania design concepts but were ultimately too mired in obscurity to exert any real influence on the genre. *M*

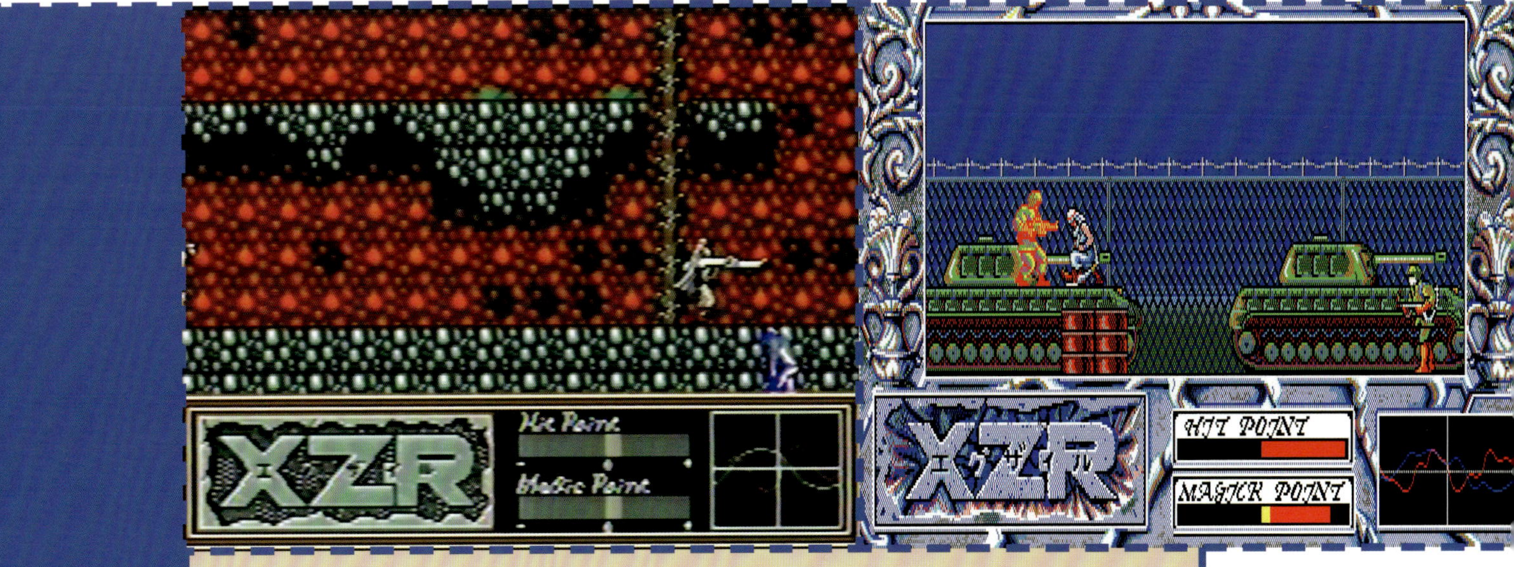

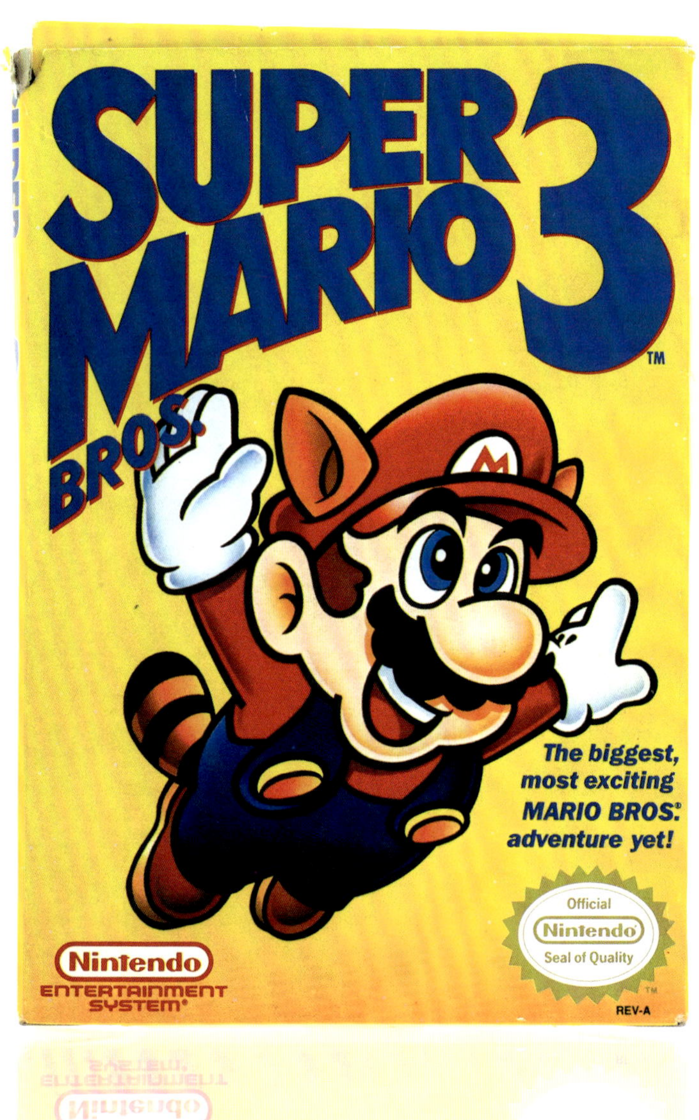

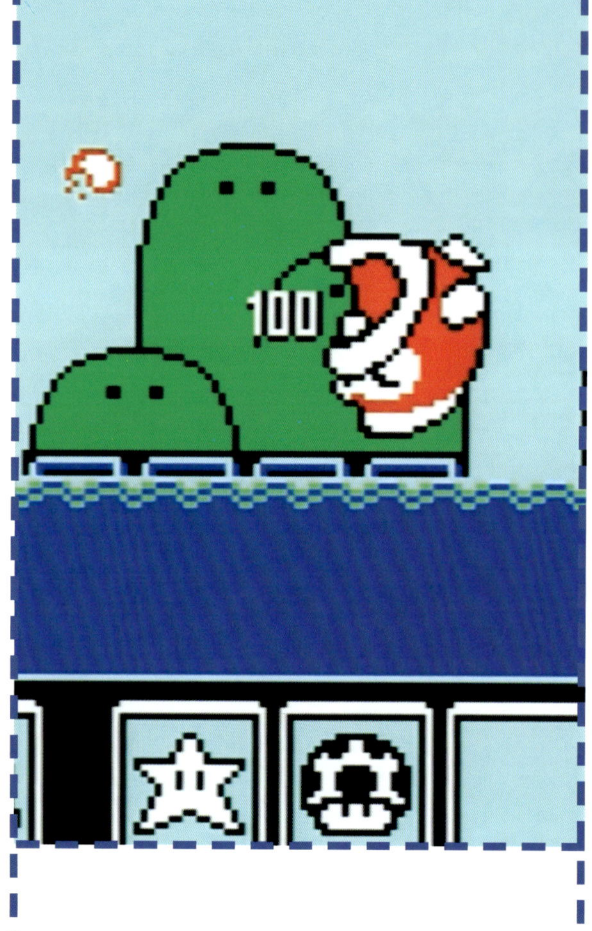

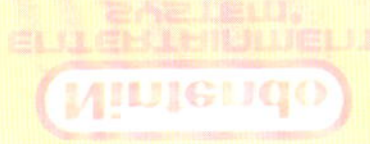

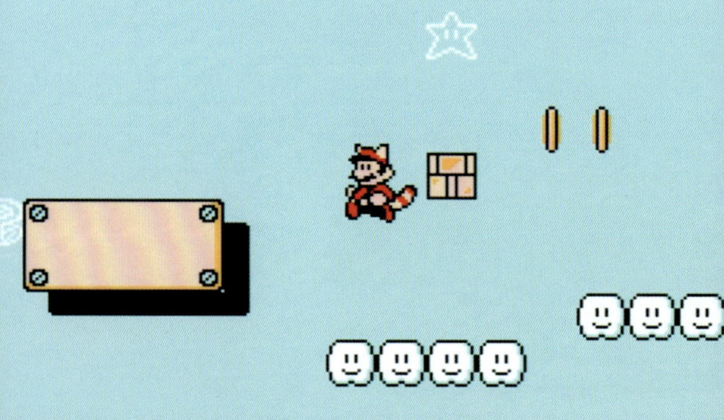

SUPER MARIO BROS. 3

PLATFORM: **FAMICOM / NES**
DEV: **NINTENDO** | PUB: **NINTENDO**
INITIAL RELEASE DATE: **OCT. 1988**

NOTABLE FOR: **HERALDING THE END OF 8-BIT METROIDVANIA MANIA**

END OF LINE?

Super Mario Bros. 3 did not define the metroidvania format in any sense of the word—quite the opposite. So, what is it doing here? Simply put, the game's October 1988 launch in Japan represented a sea change for action-platform gaming. Between 1986 and '88, the idea of big, sprawling, complex platform games featuring role-playing elements and freedom of choice took hold of the Japanese market in a huge way. Then, as 1988 wound down, *Super Mario Bros. 3* arrived and rolled back the platformer genre to focus more clearly on pure action. The result was nothing short of brilliant, and it became a top seller. The entire industry had spent the past three or four years chasing *Dragon Quest*, *Hydlide*, and *The Tower of Druaga*, trying to figure out how to integrate those titles' design principles into action games. *Super Mario Bros. 3* demonstrated that it's enough for an action game to just be a damn good action game, with no calls for exploration, experience systems, intricate narratives, or complex inventory systems. The world took notice.

SUPER MARIO BROS. 3

SET THE JAPANESE SALES CHARTS ON FIRE IN 1988. BY THE END OF 1989, THE DRIVE BY GAME DEVELOPERS TO PERFECT THE METROIDVANIA HAD LARGELY TAPERED OFF IN FAVOR OF CREATING PURE ACTION PLATFORMER GAMES—NOT ONLY FOR FAMICOM, BUT ON SEGA AND NEC'S SYSTEMS.

1989 would see the release of a hefty number of metroidvania-adjacent games, most of which had almost certainly been conceived or greenlit before *Mario 3* set the charts on fire. By the end of that year, the drive by Japanese console titles toward perfecting the metroidvania largely tapered off, and pure action platformers surged once again to the fore on Famicom and its fresh-faced competitors, PC Engine and Mega Drive.

Still, this isn't to say that *Mario 3* drew no elements from the nonlinear exploration games that dominated Famicom prior to its launch. Not only did it drop players into a world map that allowed discretionary movement around board game–like spaces packed with events and unlockable obstacles—very similar to *Bionic Commando*!—it also gave players a rudimentary inventory system and rewarded them for exploring the obscure corners of its action-packed stages even more so than previous Mario games had. But, at heart, *Super Mario Bros. 3* felt like the sort of platformer that had fallen out of favor for a while. Its action centered on pure skill, and its world emphasized creative variety over intricate interconnections.

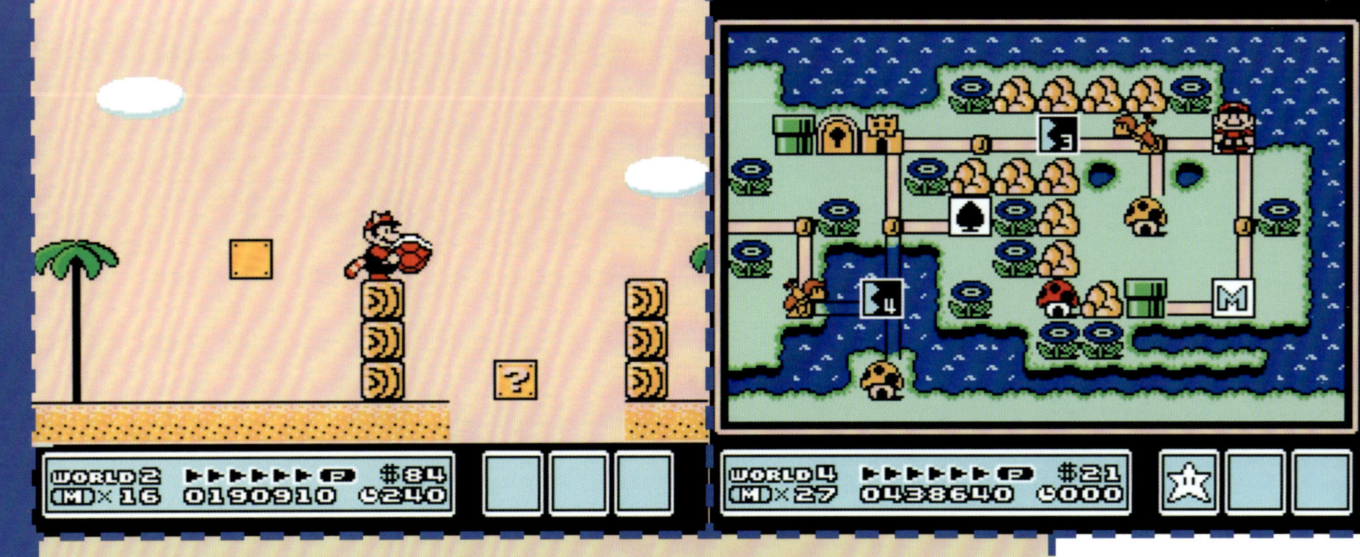

METROIDVANIA TIMELINE 1989

After two years of booming innovation on the action-RPG front, Japanese console developers began to show serious signs of slowing their march to the metroidvania in 1989. It's tempting to point to a single factor as the reason for this shift in game design philosophy (e.g., *Super Mario Bros. 3*), but as with so many things, the truth is more layered. Certainly, the popularity of Mario's third Famicom outing affected how game designers began to approach platform-action game design, but *Mario 3* didn't arrive until October of 1988—meaning its influence couldn't possibly have been seen in titles released in the early months of '89. Even in the 8-bit era, games still took between six and nine months to plan, program, manufacture, and distribute. Generally, you'd see imitators and derivatives of a hit game spring up a year or so after its debut.

No, other factors played in here as well. Perhaps most of all, a lot of the motivation behind early metroidvania innovations in 1987–88 releases came down to the rapid expansion of technology. Thanks to the advent of the Famicom Disk System, cartridge-based memory management systems, and integrated battery-backed save features, games for Famicom and its contemporary competitors managed to break free of the limitations that had previously defined console software. Games could contain larger spaces, incorporate more text for storytelling, and even retain player progress and persistent changes within the world. Presented with these liberating inventions, developers entered a phase of frenzied experimentation, pushing at the boundaries of conventional game design wisdom, failing as often as they succeeded, but always trying new things.

By 1989, most of these enthusiastic game designers had two or three such freewheeling creations under their belts, which meant that they had developed a fairly clear sense of what worked and what didn't. They naturally began to gravitate away from an exploratory mode to one of refinement, building on established strengths and culling less effective creative choices in favor of making their best ideas truly sing. Outlandish genre mash-ups like *The Guardian Legend* and *Blaster Master* took a back seat to games that amounted to better iterations of solid, predictable ideas.

As games grew more complex and incorporated more of this advanced technology, they also became more expensive. Bigger NES cartridges allowed more detailed graphics and intricate elements, which in turn demanded larger creative teams and longer development times. In the early days of the Famicom and NES, a game made by three people in the space of a few weeks could sell half a million copies: an incredible return on investment. As the NES library grew, competition increased, and consumer expectations became more demanding; landing a bestselling hit became a rarity rather than a given. As it became more expensive to create video games, publishers found it harder to recoup their costs, which meant that they pushed developers to produce safer, less experimental games in the shape of proven successes.

All this didn't spell the death of metroidvania evolution, obviously. But it did diminish the industry's collective effort to combine action, adventure, and role-playing games into a single unified form. It's not all bad, though. The action-RPGs that did emerge from this point on would generally feel a lot more thoughtful (and a lot less haphazard) than the see-what-sticks creations of the preceding years. Not always, mind you. But usually.

TIMELINE OF EVENTS

January

Clash at Demonhead
Working around a map hub format akin to *Bionic Commando*'s, this raucous action game let players make their own way through a sprawling enemy land powered by capitalism.

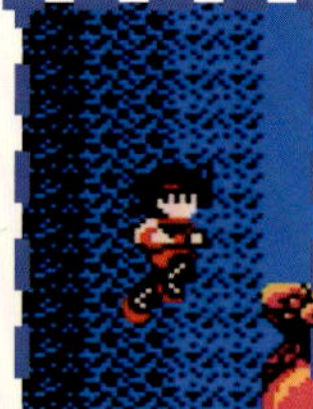

April

River City Ransom
As the cooperative brawler went mainstream with *Final Fight* and *Ninja Turtles*, the format's inventors added role-playing elements, narrative gating, and an open world to the genre.

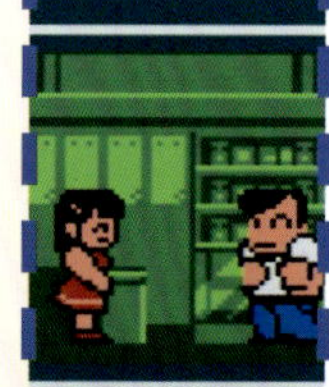

Game Boy
Although portable video gaming had existed since the 1970s, the Game Boy brought proper console tech to the medium, allowing game lovers to enjoy full-scale adventures on the go.

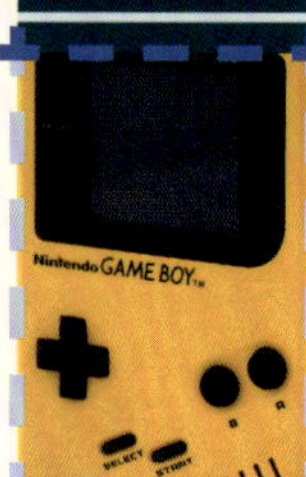

June

Hydlide (U.S. Release)
The game that defined the action-RPG in Japan took fully half a decade to reach the US. its dated visuals and design saddled *Hydlide* with a negative, ahistorical reputation in the West.

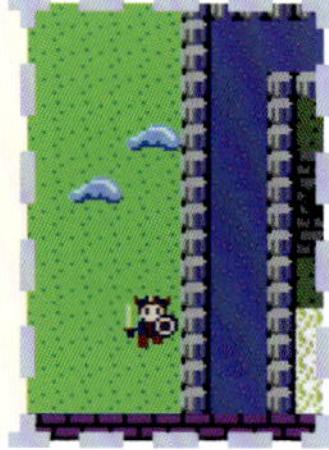

July

Ys III: Wanderers from Ys

The *Ys* series jumped into the side-scrolling format for a single entry, a last gasp for this style of game before the more traditional top-down action-RPG surged back into favor.

Strider

A counterpart to the arcade hit (not an adaptation), Capcom's story-driven action game flirted with metroidvania mechanics but suffered from troubled programming and iffy design.

Willow

Capcom's other licensed arcade counterpart for NES this month, Willow abandoned the coin-op's design entirely in favor of a thoughtfully crafted top-down *Zelda*-alike.

August

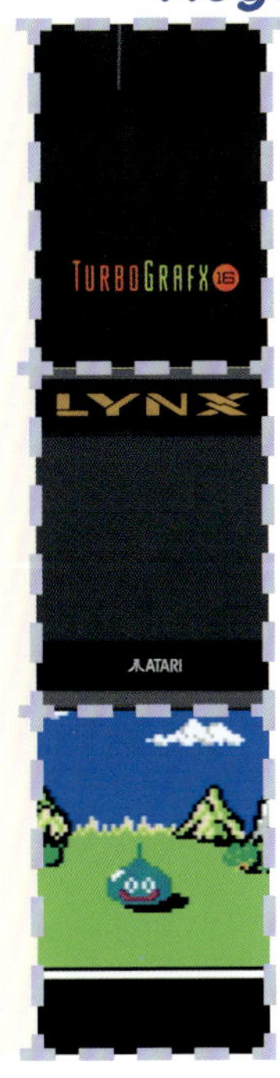

Genesis & TurboGrafx-16

Sega and NEC released their NES rivals into the US simultaneously. This put the older, less advanced TurboGrafx-16 at a disadvantage, but fans still found plenty to love.

Game Boy [U.S.] & Lynx

Nintendo shipped its portable console in the US at the same time that Atari launched its powerful Lynx. Cost and library advantages easily gave Game Boy the upper hand, however.

Dragon Warrior

More than three years after *Dragon Quest*'s debut, the game that hooked Japan on RPGs reached America with a new name. It felt almost as dated upon arrival as *Hydlide* had.

September

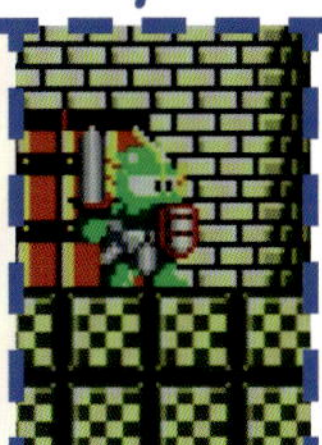

Wonder Boy III: The Dragon's Trap

Sega's Master System was headed for retirement in the wake of the Genesis's arrival, but this masterpiece proved the old system still had impressive chops.

November

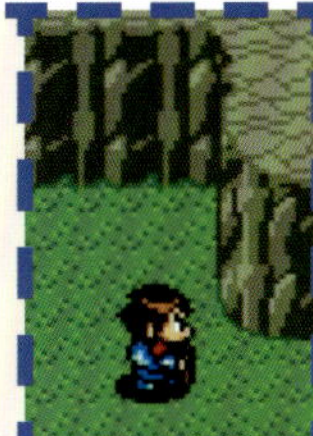

Neutopia

Hudson's answer to *Zelda*—a decidedly literal take on Nintendo's game that did little to push the genre forward outside of its spiffed-up visuals and bite-sized world structure.

December

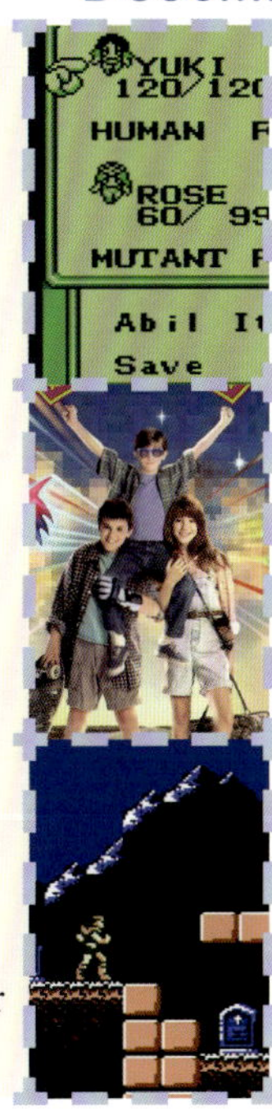

The Final Fantasy Legend

This *Dragon Quest*-style role-playing game included no action in its menu-driven interface, but it deserves mention simply for being the world's first true handheld RPG.

The Wizard

An epochal event for young Nintendo fans, this movie centered around NES competitions and teased the upcoming *Super Mario Bros. 3*—the world's grandest video game commercial.

Castlevania III

Walking back the action-RPG style of *Castlevania II*, this sequel reverted to pure action. Still, with branching paths and companion characters, player choice remained in the foreground.

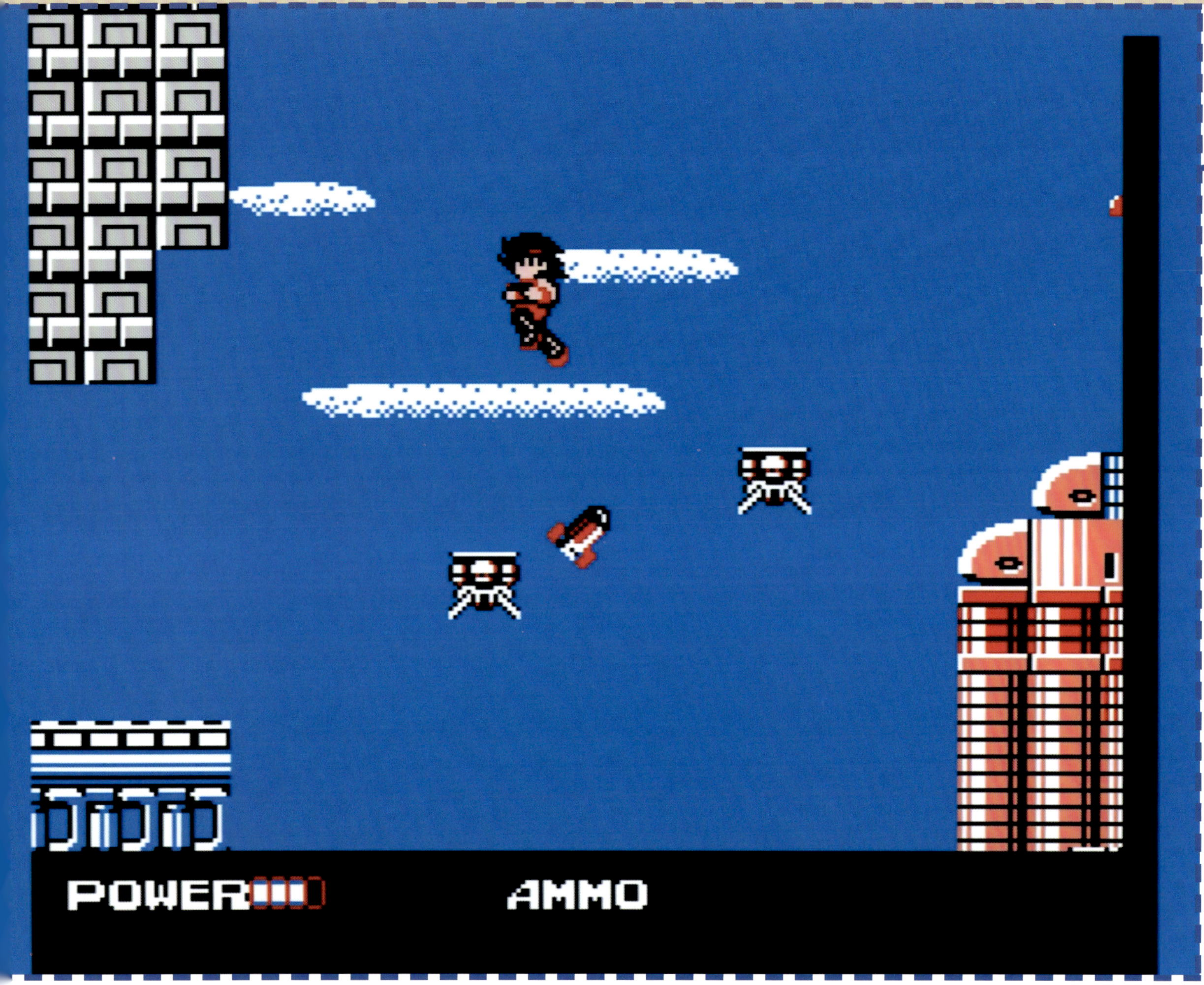

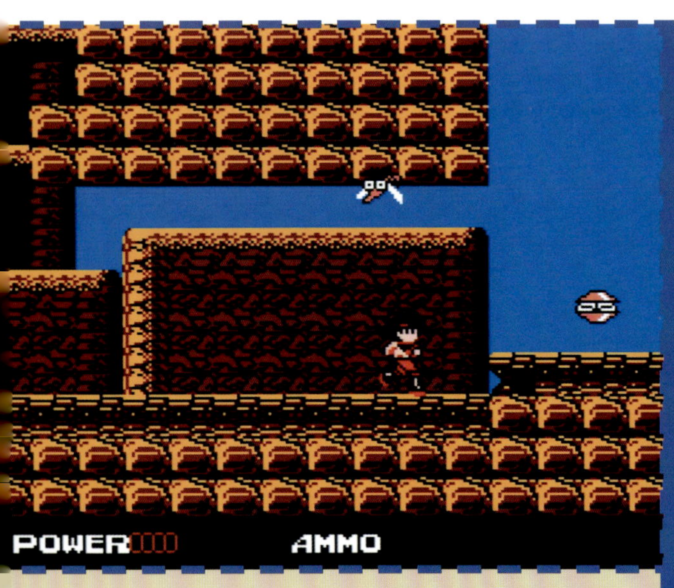

CLASH AT DEMONHEAD

PLATFORM: **FAMICOM / NES**
DEV: **VIC TOKAI** | PUB: **VIC TOKAI**
INITIAL RELEASE DATE: **JAN. 1989**

BANG ON

Arriving about half a year after Capcom revamped *Bionic Commando* for the NES, Vic Tokai delivered an impressive case of convergent evolution. Grappling hooks notwithstanding, *Clash at Demonhead* incorporated many of the same structural and narrative concepts as *Bionic Commando* but did a better job of creating a contiguous, interlocking world with them. *Demonhead* presents its adventure through a world map that works much like the one found in *Bionic Commando* and canonized by *Super Mario Bros. 3*. Although its core action takes place on foot as a side-scrolling run-and-gun game, you freely move between different combat zones by selecting destinations on an abstract map.

However, *Clash at Demonhead* put its own distinct spin on things. The numbers you see on this map don't indicate the area number of your destinations but rather the identity of the routes that run between them. Unlike in *Bionic Commando*, in which you traveled to destination points on the map itself before entering the area labeled with a number, each point here indicates a junction where you return to the overview map and select a new direction to journey in. While it's a subtle difference from the *Mario 3*/*Bionic Commando* approach of setting action stages in the map points themselves, it makes a difference to the game's structure, as everything in *Demonhead* truly is interconnected.

You never see your character moving around the world map here. If the game were to take away its map view and simply give you multiple in-stage exits once you reach the end of a route, it would work the same and become a seamless open world. The map simply makes navigation more manageable by giving players a quick break from the action and providing a visual representation of their current location in the world. And this truly is an open world, even more so than *Castlevania II*'s—a rare case of legitimate freeform traversal on the level of the original *The Legend of Zelda*, in the shape of a platformer.

It even restates the journey northward and upward seen in *Zelda*: you begin the adventure at the southern edge of the map and make your way up the map through increasingly difficult hazards to a grand mountain where the greatest dangers lie in wait. In

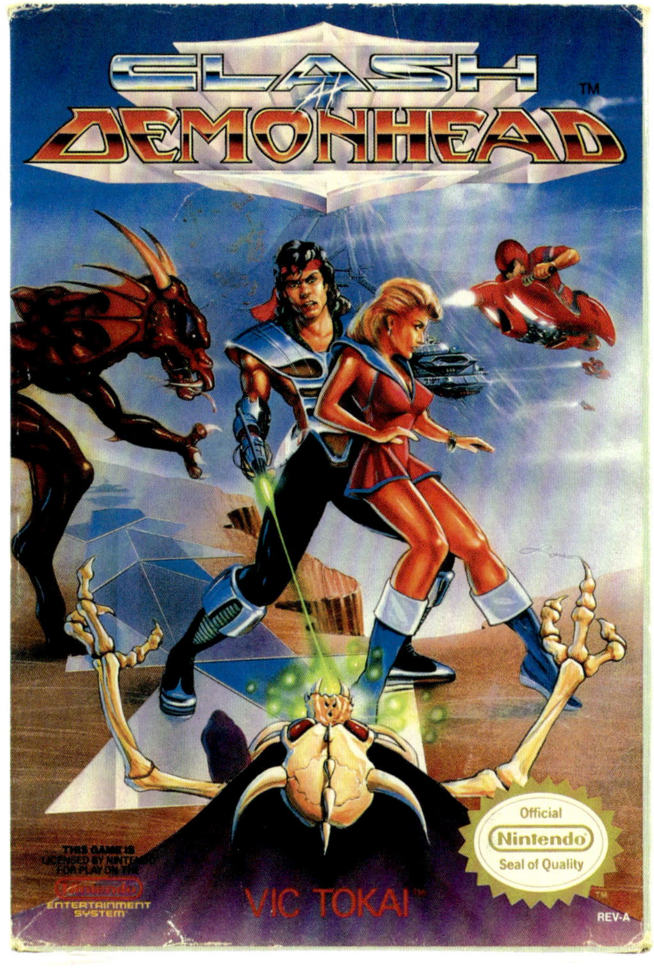

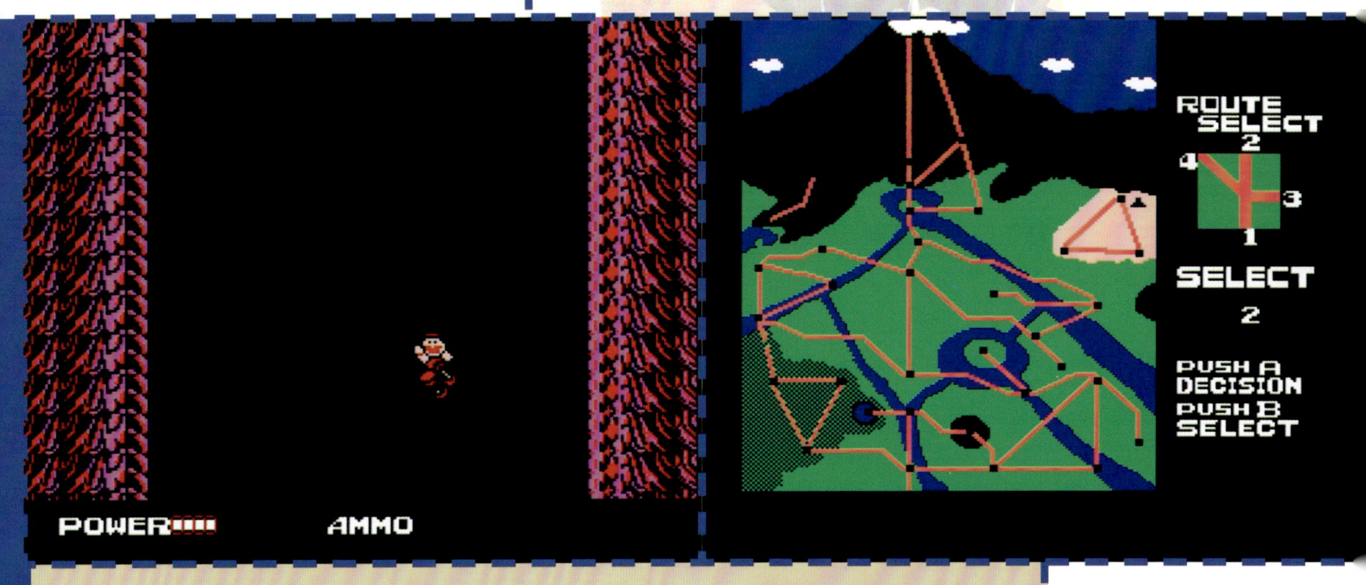

order to complete *Clash at Demonhead,* you need to achieve a variety of objectives like defeating bosses, earning MacGuffins, rescuing captives, and acquiring better stuff. But you can more or less do all those things at any time, that is, provided you can find the proper NPCs to talk to first. You may stumble upon the hidden entrance that leads to the endgame once it's unlocked, if you poke around in the correct route. You can even face off against most of the main game bosses straightaway, since they all operate from fixed locations at the end of specific routes. The question is, can you actually defeat them before you've bulked up protagonist Billy "Big Bang" Blitz?

Bang only gains a few permanent improvements throughout the game. In addition to buffing up his max health, he also learns five magic skills called Force powers from a kind hermit. Otherwise, though, everything in *Demonhead* revolves around its cash-based economy. You can acquire all manner of cool gear and tools, ranging from secondary weapons to health refills to navigational equipment. On offer are a lot of impressive tools that open up the world even more. Bang can use super boots that extend the range of his jumps, a Jet Pack that lets him fly freely, and scuba gear and a Super Suit that enable him to swim through water and magma, respectively. However, none of these abilities remain with Bang permanently. You acquire them as expendable tools that you work for a limited time.

These items all come from the same place: a single shop located on Route 5. You can purchase many of Bang's navigational tools right from the start (although some only become available after a certain amount of time has passed) provided you have enough cash on hand. However, once you use one, it's gone forever, and you have to pick up a new one from the Super Shop. You even need to buy an expendable tool to receive a password and save your progress! It's cutthroat capitalism here in the world of *Demonhead*. But, on the plus side, cash flows freely here from defeated foes. And you can come by money even more readily once you locate the Gold Exchange where you can trade gold nuggets for cash. The game makes extensive use of its "open concept" design, as there's no such thing as a bottomless pit or death by falling. While many pools of water and lava are only as deep as the current screen, others allow you to dive right in and swim to new areas. You may drown in these spaces, but only if you're not properly protected; *Clash at Demonhead* doesn't contain a single location where you can fall into a "bottomless" space and instantly die. You can take advantage of this design element as early as Route 5 from the moment you leave the Super Shop. The shop always drops onto the screen above a flooded conduit, and you need to climb the exterior of the reservoir to reach the shop. You can see hints of enticing underwater passages as you make your way to the top, which will tempt curi- ous players to make the Aqua Lung (a dive suit that lets them breathe underwater) their first major purchase. Equip your new gear, dive into the water beside the shop, and you'll come to a space where you can collect gold nuggets. This find more than covers the cost of the Aqua Lung...once you find the Gold Exchange, of course.

If you spend too long in the water without an Aqua Lung, or take a magma dive without the proper protective equipment, it's game over for Bang. But if he merely falls into a pit, he won't die; he simply plunges into an underground passageway that leads him back to the world map and allows him to try completing that route again. If you keep falling into same pit, well, that's your sign that you need to buy some Jump Boots or a Jet Pack from the shop and brute force the situation. The penalty for a game over is remarkably forgiving, too: the game simply kicks Bang back to the most recent world map junction with no loss of equipment or cash. Thus, allowing you to throw yourself at challenges over and over again...or to farm a load of cash for better temporary gear.

By and large, the central gameplay loop in *Clash at Demonhead* amounts to traveling the world, hunting for the bosses. Defeating the bosses earns you the medallions you need to take on the final boss. Meanwhile, NPCs relay critical information about the land and the location of critical items and bosses. And, of course, you need to seek out and gather gold and cash in order to acquire tools and weapons. The interconnected routes can take a while to traverse the normal way (at least until you acquire the hermit's teleportation Force skill), but many routes contain secret shortcuts for canny shoppers. For example, you can use Route 27 to take a quick trip into the northern mountain rather than slogging through multiple routes by taking the long way around... but only if you have a Super Suit on hand to protect you in the magma that's flooded the path.

Nothing else on NES played quite like *Clash at Demonhead,* and its amateurish graphics and raucous sense of humor belie a remarkably ambitious approach to freeform design in an 8-bit action title. This was hardly the most influential game on the platform—in fact, I'd go so far as to say that no one except *Scott Pilgrim* author Bryan Lee O'Malley has ever been influenced by it at all—but Vic Tokai created a pretty incredible combination of a true open world in *Clash at Demonhead*: an action-platformer that incorporates numerous key RPG concepts. It makes for a bold early entry in the metroidvania canon, a forward-thinking game for the '90s, inexplicably wrapped in goofy 1970s shounen–manga aesthetics. **M**

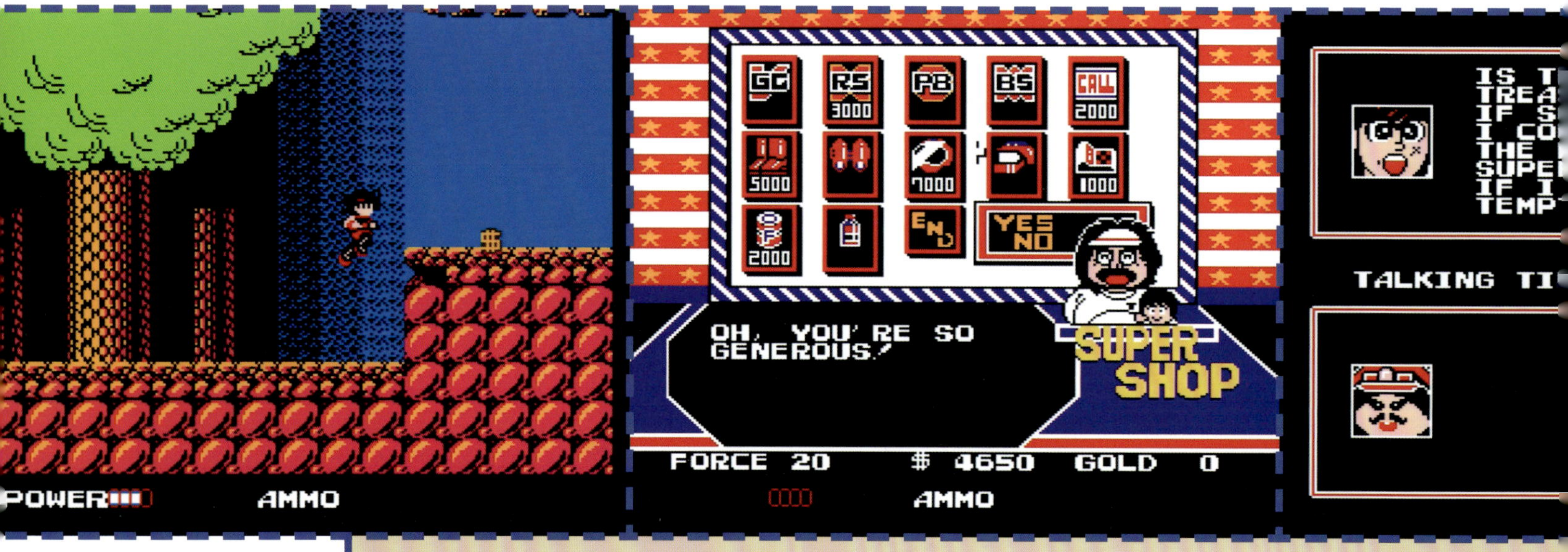

CASTLEVANIA III: DRACULA'S CURSE

Perhaps no single work better represents the way Japanese developers began moving away from nonlinear platform adventures following the bestselling success of *Super Mario Bros. 3* than the third entry in the Castlevania series. After *Castlevania II* had done so much to advance the side-scrolling action-RPG as an art form, *Castlevania III*'s shift back toward a linear focus on pure action that was reminiscent of the original *Castlevania* felt almost like, well, a stake to the metroidvania's beating heart.

And yet, as with *Super Mario Bros. 3*, what appeared to be a complete about-face of game design theory turns out not to be a total repudiation of the NES era's creative advances. *Castlevania III* consists of about three times as many stages as the original *Castlevania*, all of which stand alone and plot a straightforward march from start to finish. At the same time, the overall structure of the game has more nuance. *Castlevania III* still incorporates the Transylvanian countryside that Simon Belmont had to conquer in *Simon's Quest*, and it allows players to plot their own route to Dracula's castle. Do you take the frontal route and make your way across the aqueducts and up the battlements of the structures surrounding the castle? Or do you take the back route and slip in through the catacombs? *Castlevania III* allows you to do one or the other, but not both; you must choose a path to Dracula's lair, and there's no turning back. The game even fakes you out early on. If you attempt to enter through the clock tower at the castle's periphery, defeating the boss there causes the tower to collapse, burying the passage and forcing you to double back.

These alternate routes have another benefit, too: they allow you to meet prospective allies who will tag along and lend you unique powers like flight, wall-climbing, and environment-changing spells. It may not quite be a metroidvania, but *Castlevania III* doesn't abandon the dream entirely. Its structure would directly shape that of *Castlevania: Rondo of Blood*, which would in turn provide the foundation for the platonic ideal of metroidvanias: *Symphony of the Night*.

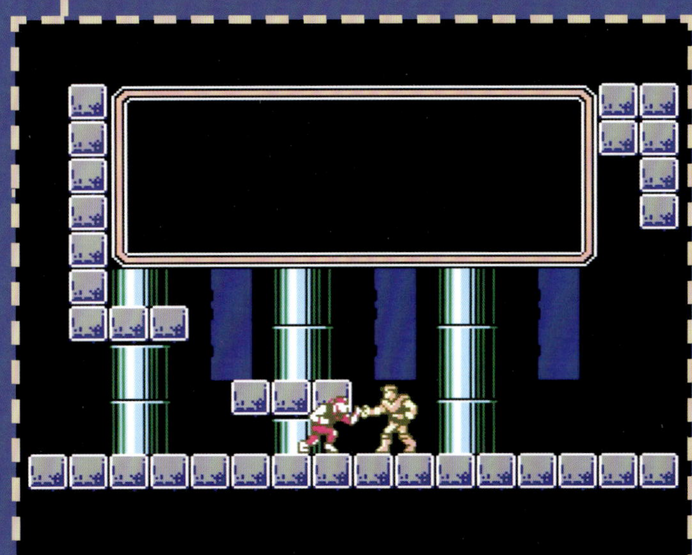

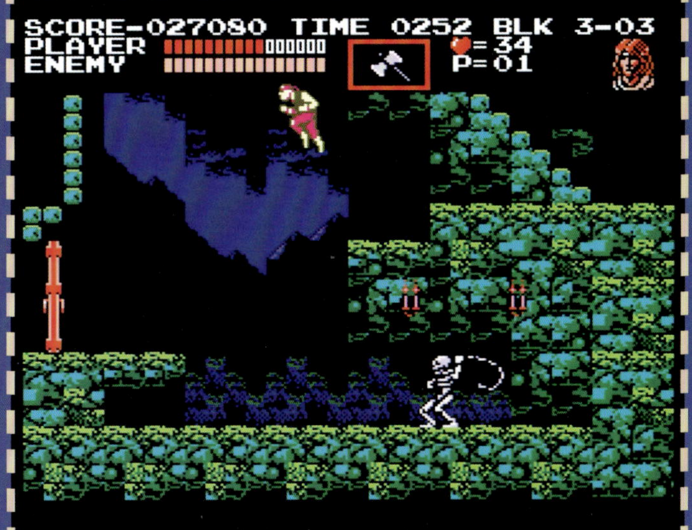

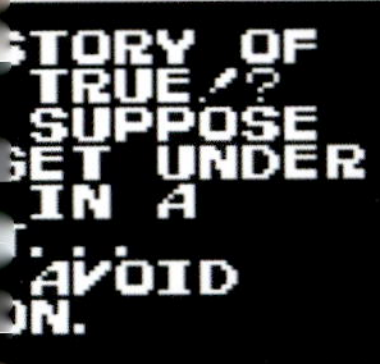

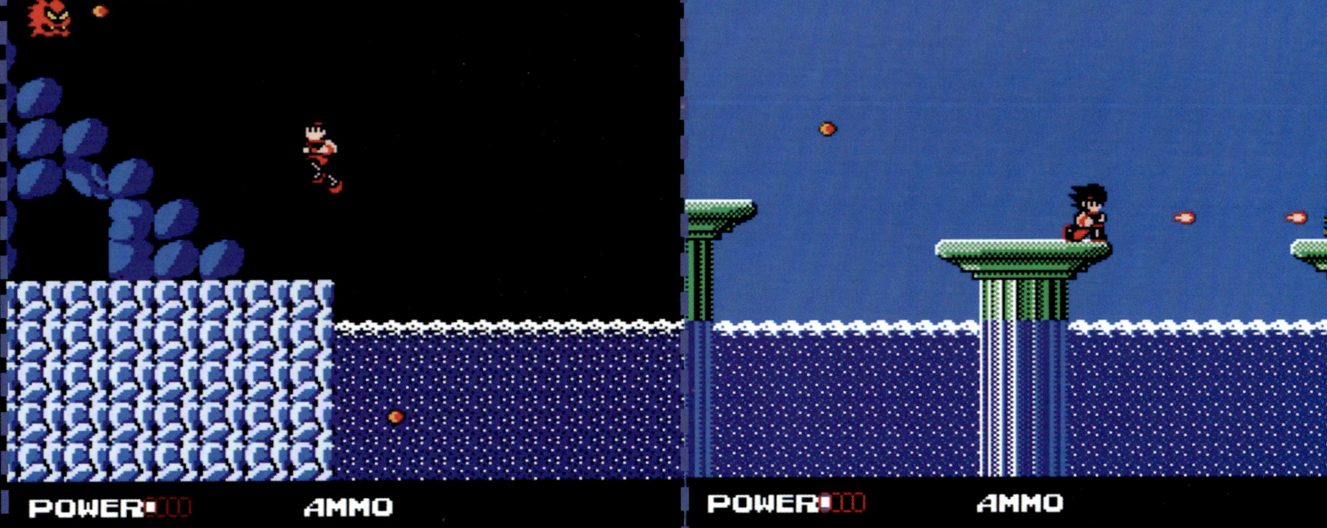

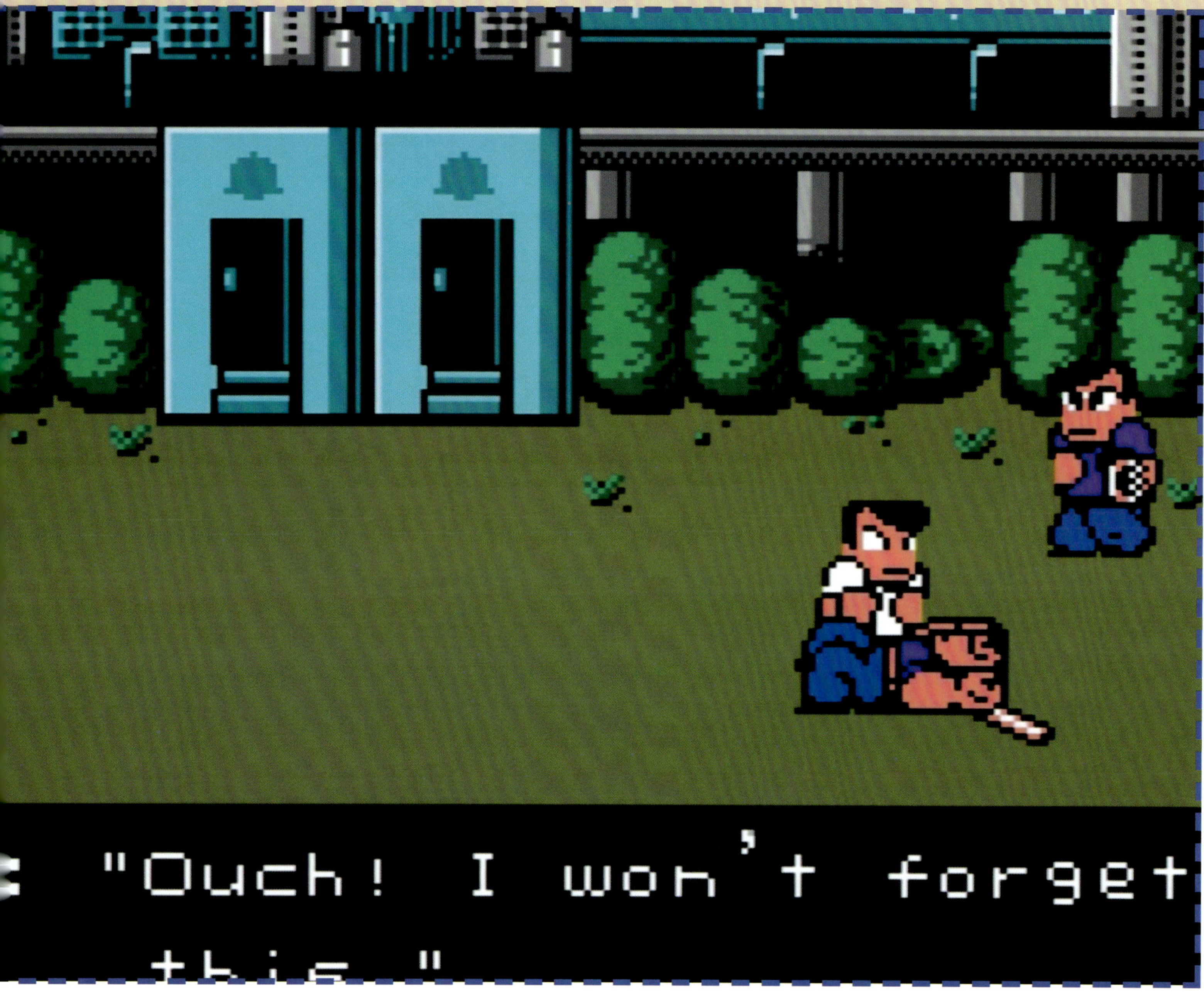

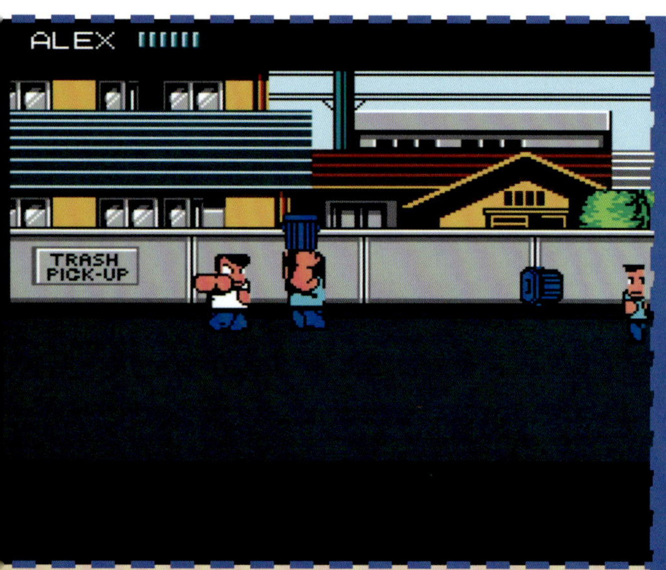

RIVER CITY RANSOM

PLATFORM: **FAMICOM / VARIOUS**
DEV: **TECHNOS JAPAN** | PUB: **TRADEWEST**
INITIAL RELEASE DATE: **APRIL 1989**

NOTABLE FOR: **INCORPORATING OPEN-WORLD RPG ELEMENTS INTO THE BRAWLER**

TOKYO DRIFTERS

A cooperative brawler, a sequel to *Renegade*, and a counterpart to *Double Dragon*: What is a game like *River City Ransom* doing on a timeline of metroidvania action-RPG evolution? Somehow, despite the odds, it belongs.

Technōs Japan's *River City Ransom* shipped on Famicom as the direct sequel to 1986's coin-op beat-'em-up *Renegade*. The sequel introduced cooperative two-player support to the series while completely breaking away from the linear, stage-by-stage design of its predecessor—and in fact of the entire burgeoning brawler genre that had emerged in *Renegade*'s wake. *Double Dragon* factors in there as well, being the "other" sequel to Renegade, and the original pioneer of two-player cooperative design for the genre. It played more or less like *Renegade* with the addition of a second player and the removal of the bike chase scenes, at least in arcades and in most of its home ports. However, the development team behind the Famicom and NES version of *Double Dragon* either lacked the ability to incorporate simultaneous cooperative play into that release or else chose not to. To make up for the removal of that key game component, they added a handful of forward-thinking bonus elements in its place. For one, the NES port included a one-on-one fighting mode where two oversized characters (or rather, two oversized versions of the same character) could beat each other up in a small arena. It was primitive, but it was one of the first takes on what we would consider a modern-day console fighting game in the wake of Capcom's 1987 arcade game *Street Fighter*.

At the same time, *Double Dragon*'s main four-stage story mode also underwent a significant change to compensate for the loss of a second player. A solo session of *Double Dragon* lacks much of the core appeal of the game, which involves raucously strategizing with your partner to corral foes and rescue each other from tight spots; without the social component, the game feels unbalanced and anemic. Recognizing this, Technōs looked to the role-playing mania that had seized console game makers across Japan and added an experience-based leveling system to the NES version of *Double Dragon*, locking all but the most basic of the players' skills behind

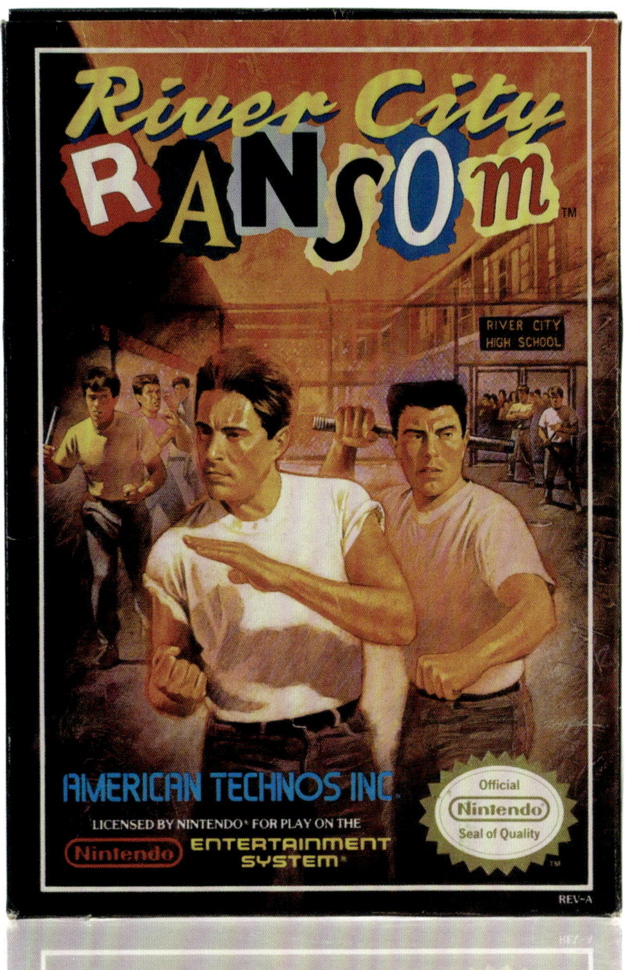

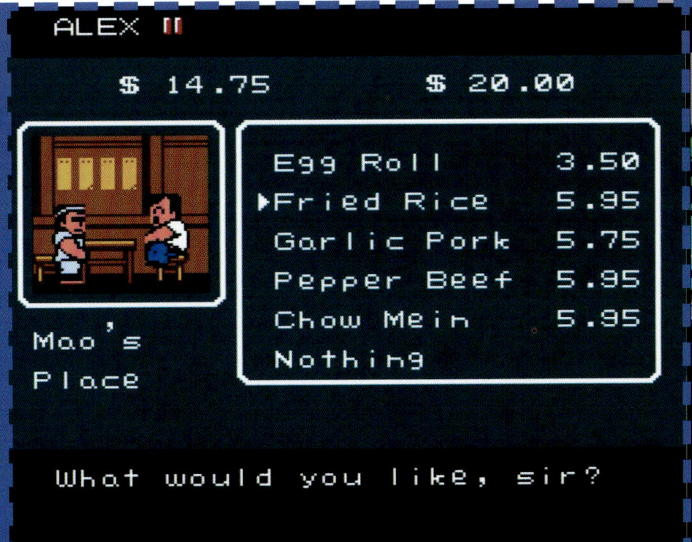

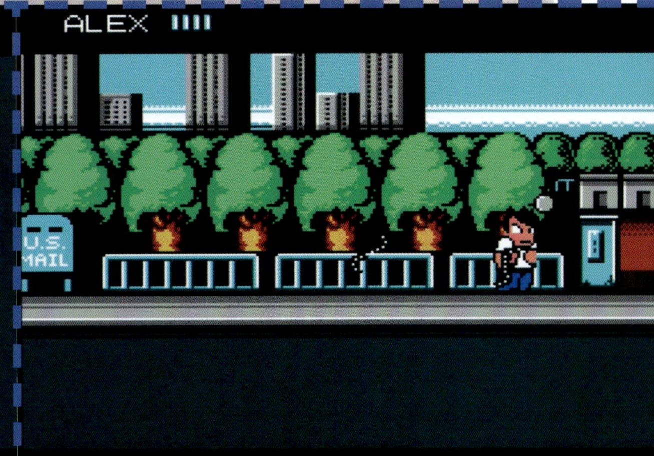

performance-based objectives. Players earned a certain amount of experience for each action they performed, earning bonus points for pulling off more difficult moves. Once their experience tally reached a certain point, they'd level up and learn a new ability to add to their repertoire. Whereas arcade players could access all those skills from the outset, the NES game sent poor Billy Lee into the fray armed only with basic kicks and punches, forcing players to work their way up to flying elbows and spinning kicks.

It was an interesting idea, though in practice it didn't really lend itself to freedom of play; after all, *Double Dragon* consisted of four stages that players could reasonably complete in fifteen to twenty minutes. All the leveling system really accomplished was to pad out play time by encouraging players to stand around and grind for skill points through repetition.

When it came time for Technōs to return to *Renegade* and produce a proper sequel featuring the original characters and setting, the team looked to *Double Dragon* for the NES and decided to do those raw ideas proper justice. *River City Ransom* made those RPG-inspired growth mechanics a central underpinning of the game rather than a way to ration out core design elements. The result is by far the most sophisticated brawler of the 8-bit era. Frankly, it's a title that's unrivaled by most other efforts in the genre throughout the 1980s and '90s, outside of Technōs's own projects and a few standouts like Capcom's *Dungeons & Dragons* arcade games and Treasure's *Guardian Heroes*.

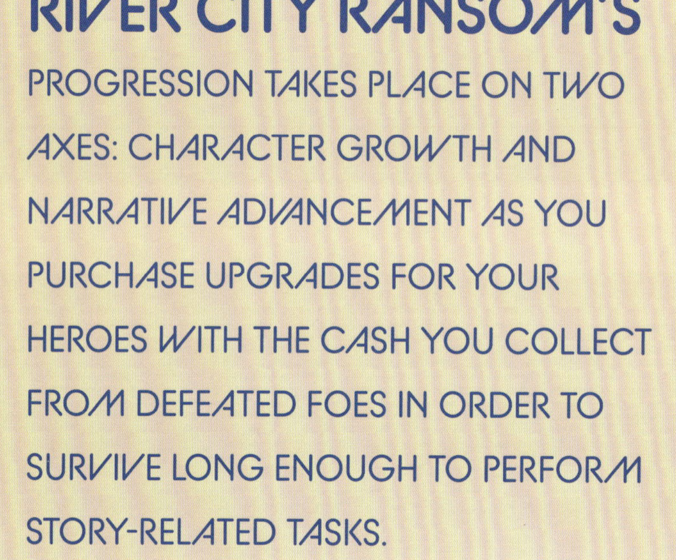

River City Ransom incorporates an actual economy, permanent skill and stat boosts, an open game world consisting of safe areas where you can refill your health and buy upgrades or consumable items. It even manages to add back in the cooperative play that *Double Dragon* lost. It is an RPG in every meaningful sense of the world, but one in which actively punching, kicking, and throwing random debris replaces menu-based combat—an RPG where your party members are controlled by you and your human friend.

River City itself (a generic American city in the US localization, but a suburban portion of the Tokyo metro area in the original Japanese release) more or less consists of a long straight line from the journey's beginning to its end. Laid out on paper, it looks a lot like the world of *Simon's Quest*, minus the eventual loop back and baffling dead ends. This means that, on a very fundamental level, *River City Ransom* works a lot like a normal brawler. You move left to right across various environments, beating up guys and crushing bosses so as to gain access to the next level. The difference between *River City Ransom* and, say, Konami's *Teenage Mutant Ninja Turtles* (which debuted in arcades soon after this game arrived in shops as a Famicom cartridge) is that you have full run of River City from the outset. You can theoretically travel the breadth of the town from the moment the action begins—assuming you can survive against increasingly powerful mobs of enemies who lurk beyond the opening zone. Realistically, you'll find that random low-level thugs halfway through the game can wipe out protagonists Alex and Ryan in a single punch. Those toughs' speed and defense traits are so highly attuned that it's impossible to even land a counter-blow. The only solution is to level up.

Progression in *River City Ransom* takes place on two axes: character growth and narrative advancement. You upgrade your characters with the power of capitalism. You need to collect cash from fallen enemies, which you can then spend at shops to acquire items that confer statistical gains or teach you new techniques. In the early going, Alex and Ryan have only basic combat abilities—not unlike Billy at the outset of NES *Double Dragon*!—and they can't take much of a beating. But, as you invest in enhancements, they don't simply learn new moves; they grow in speed, power, and technique as well.

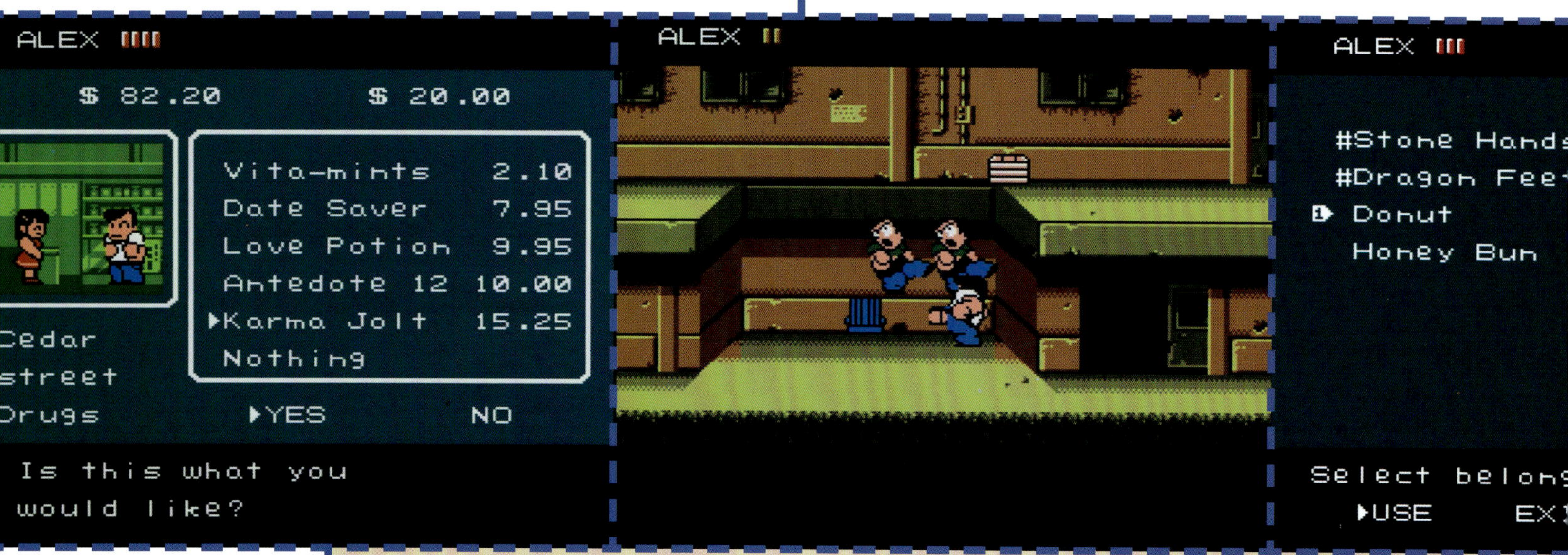

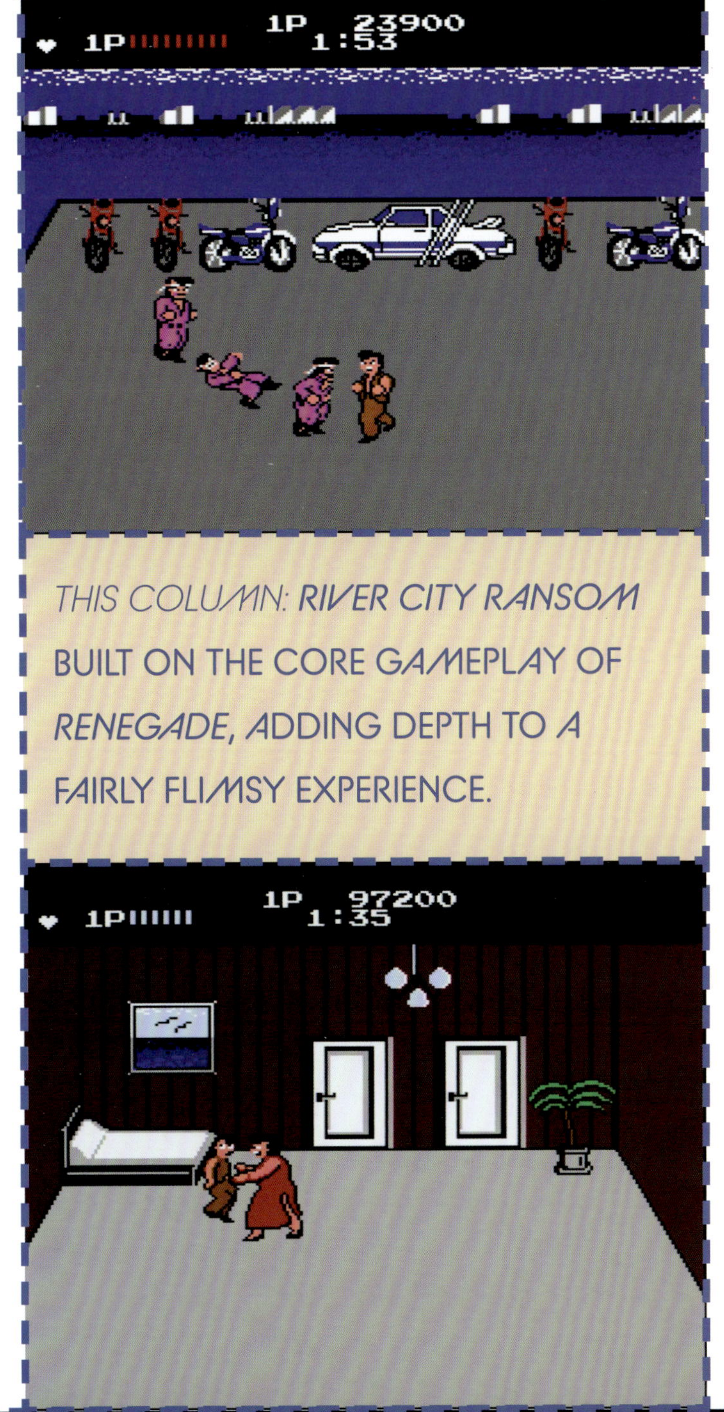

THIS COLUMN: RIVER CITY RANSOM BUILT ON THE CORE GAMEPLAY OF *RENEGADE*, ADDING DEPTH TO A FAIRLY FLIMSY EXPERIENCE.

Narratively, it doesn't matter if you manage to somehow fight your way to the end of the game from the moment you first enter the fray. Like reaching Death Mountain before you've conquered a single boss in *The Legend of Zelda*, all you get for your hard work of fighting past devastating enemies is a locked-down final dungeon—that is, school building—that you can't enter until you go back and complete certain prerequisites. Before you can face the final boss, you need to meet with allies and defeat enemies around town. In a standard brawler, you could achieve this feat in something like fifteen–twenty minutes. Here, the RPG-style systems woven throughout the game's fabric make this easier said than done. Even the first boss can KO you if you approach them with default stats and skills, and you can forget about besting the more powerful later bosses.

So, you need to spend time earning the cash to buy skill boosts that will enable you to stand toe-to-toe with the enemy. That means you need to do a lot of brawling against standard mobs, since they drop money when defeated. The grinding never feels as rote as in many pure RPGs, though, because it offers more involvement, forcing you to manage mobs and fight with skill. (Well, at least until you learn all the advanced techniques that allow you to automatically rapid-fire your way through mobs and bosses alike.)

River City Ransom doesn't necessarily fall into the metroidvania genre, but it's worth mentioning as an action-RPG sidebar simply because it offers the best demonstration we've seen to date of the potential inherent in hybrid role-playing mechanics. Bringing stats, freedom, and persistence into the brawler format not only breaks the game from the rote rigidity that had already begun to define the genre, it brings more purpose and enjoyment to the underlying premise of the brawler. It also opens up the game to more casual players. You might not be able to beat the hardest parts of many challenging 8-bit action games, but *River City Ransom* allowed players to build up their stats and skills to the point that their hero's sheer innate power overwhelmed all foes without any need for dexterity. Lowering barriers to accessibility was a huge part of *Dragon Quest*'s appeal, and a significant element in making its many derivatives so popular. Accessibility would be an integral component of the "true" metroidvania games many years later, which allowed players to buff up their heroes via determined repetition to minimize the need for actual skill. Capital-G Gamers can argue about the validity of this design philosophy all they like, but either way, it's certainly given *River City Ransom* a longer life than any other brawler of the 8-bit era, making it the reference point for countless modern-era brawlers. Clearly, Technōs did something right here.

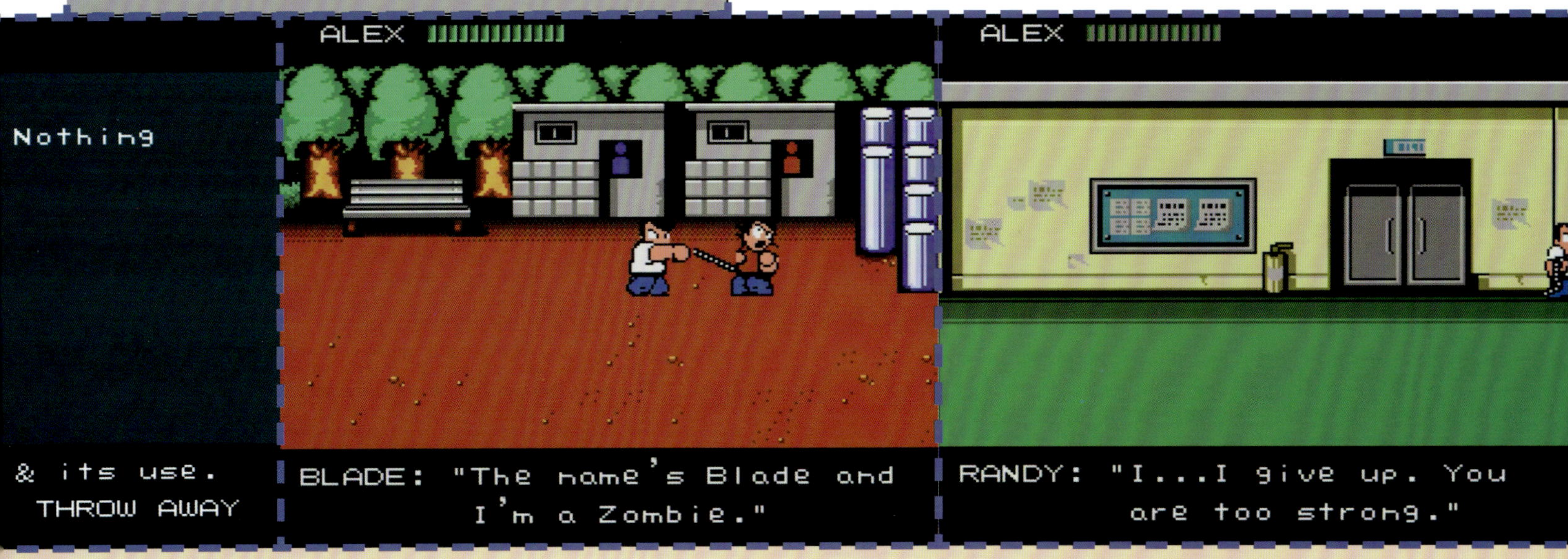

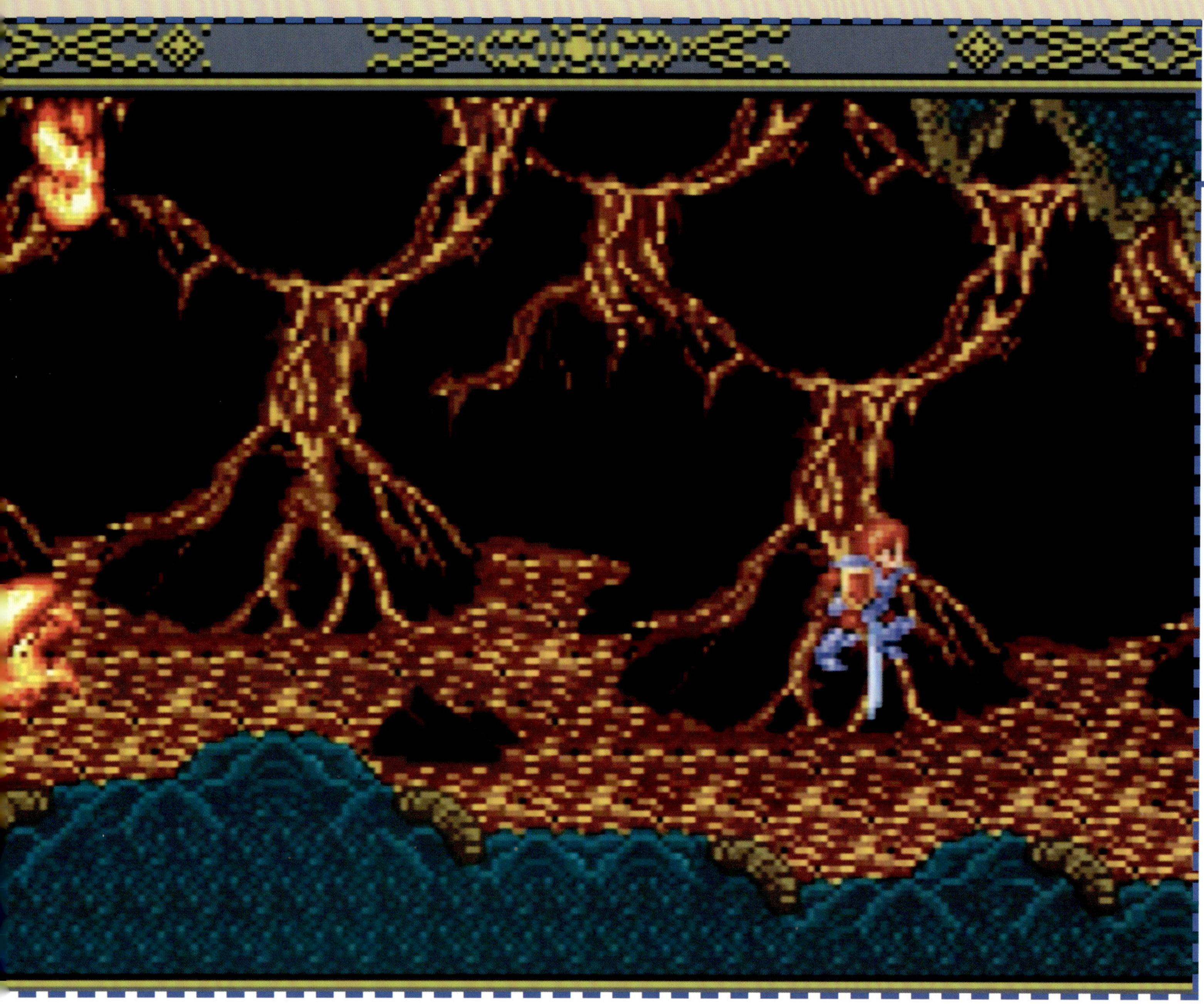

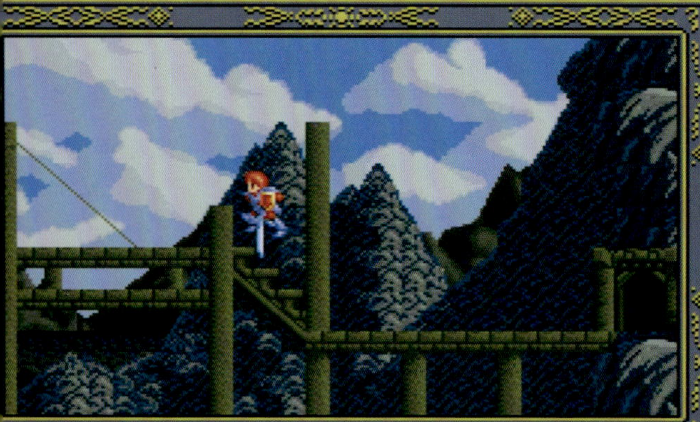

YS III
WANDERERS FROM YS

PLATFORM: **PC-8801 / VARIOUS**
DEV: **NIHON FALCOM** | PUB: **NIHON FALCOM**
INITIAL RELEASE DATE: **JULY 1989**
SHOWN HERE: **NINTENDO SUPER NES VERSION, 1992**

NOTABLE FOR: **THE YS STYLE, BUT IN PLATFORM ACTION**

A SENSE OF UN-YS

As RPG fever gripped the Japanese console market, the result was a succession of interesting genre mash-ups. Few of these efforts came off as rote or by-the-numbers, as each one seemed built around a different source of inspiration. By 1989, the concept of the "role-playing game" had been distilled by some of these proto-metroidvania creations to such a degree that they barely resembled actual RPGs anymore. For example, *The Battle of Olympus* took most of its design notes from *Zelda II*, which in turn combined *Dragon Slayer* with the original *Zelda*, which in turn owed much of its personality to *Hydlide* and *The Tower of Druaga*, which themselves seemed like a mélange of Atari's *Adventure*, *Wizardry*, and a few other primal works from the 1970s.

So, when *Ys III: Wanderers from Ys* shifted gears to take the series from high-speed *Hydlide* to side-scrolling sword-slinger, you could be forgiven for assuming that developer Nihon Falcom had simply decided to churn out another *Zelda II*–knockoff. And perhaps that was the original impetus behind the series' format shift—*Zelda II* ended up being widely imitated in the latter half of the '80s. But calling *Ys III* a mere *Zelda II*–clone would be too reductive, too inaccurate. No, *Ys III* undeniably belongs to the franchise whose name it bears. It gamely adapts the essence of *Ys* and *Ys II* into side-scrolling form, with all that such a description entails.

Structurally, it truly does resemble the earlier games. It's a fairly compact adventure containing only a few dungeons and bosses. Protagonist Adol Christin manages his gear by way of an inventory grid whose limited setup hints at the brevity of the quest, and he ventures into sprawling dungeons of such ferocious difficulty that no normal human could possibly hope to complete them on a first attempt. *Ys III* incorporates the full totality of the vintage *Ys* experience into this new format, and that even includes—improbably enough—interpreting the original game's "bump combat" into side-scrolling form. The original *Ys* games featured blazing fast battles that consisted of Adol ramming into enemies at full steam, either inflicting damage on his target or smacking into that monster at the wrong angle, causing his sword to miss its mark and resulting in Adol dying almost immediately.

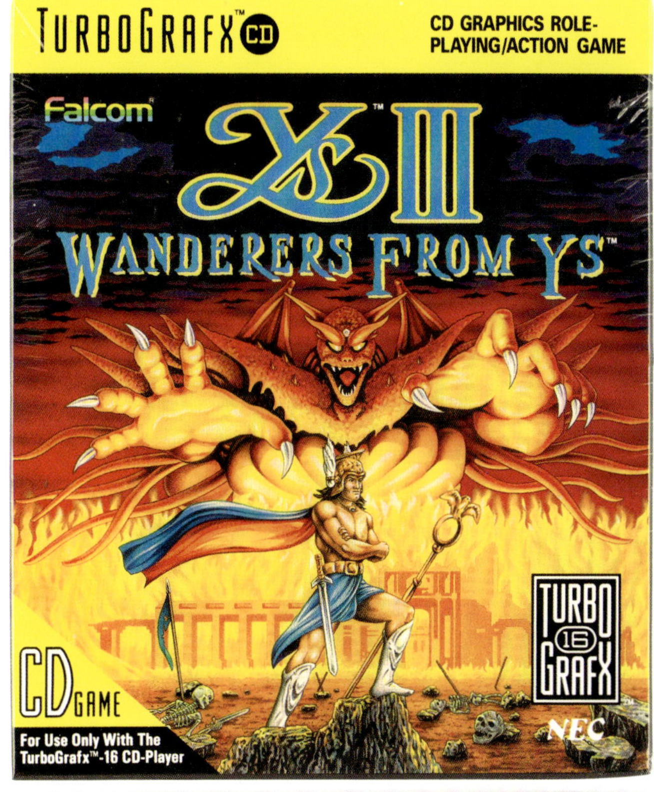

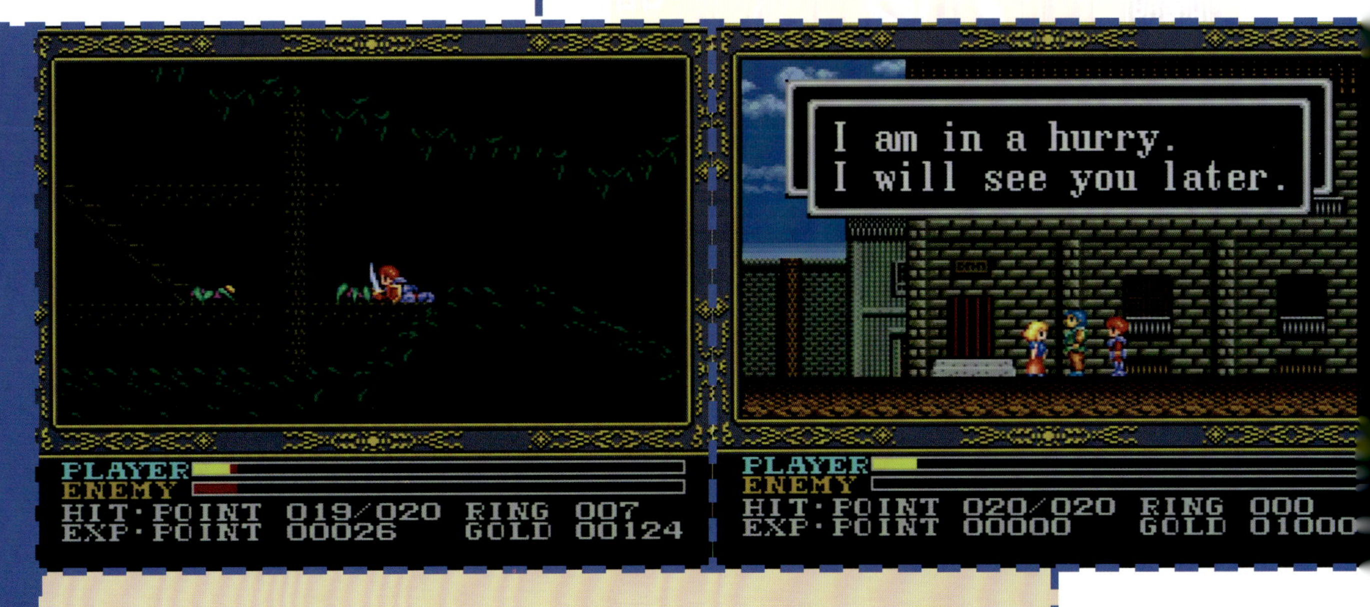

That approach wouldn't make much sense in a game where Adol runs and jumps while enemies largely attack along perpendicular planes to his position. So, instead, *Ys III* turns Adol's sword skills into something akin to an auto-battle ability. Unlike in *Ys* and *Ys II*, you need to press the attack button to brandish your sword; Adol doesn't automatically wield it here. But unlike in slower-paced games, you can turn strikes into a rapid-fire attack by simply holding down the action button. Adol still has Link-like sword tech- niques, including a downward aerial thrust, but the bulk of combat in *Ys III* comes down to walking around with the fire button depressed so that Adol trails behind a perpetual swipe of bladed death. This allows you to set up auto-leveling farms pretty easily: place Adol in a location where he can safely reach enemies, secure the attack button, and let nature take its course for an hour. Far from being an exploit, it appears to be a deliberate, even crucial, design choice.

Moving ahead by even a single experience level makes a massive difference to Adol's physical attack power and his defensive strength. When the game first opens, he's practically guaranteed to be killed on the first screen by mindless insects that zip past; they take multiple hits to destroy while absolutely demolishing Adol in a few hits. As *Ys III* carries forward the older games' lack of any real mercy invincibility when you take damage, you can literally wade through the ten-minute opening cut scenes and town exploration only to die a few seconds into the first dungeon. So, *Ys III* demands that you grind for experience. The grinding here feels different from that of *Willow* for NES (which arrived in store just three days after *Ys III*) because the two games have a radically different perspective on the nature and outcome of leveling. In *Willow*, level ups boosted the hero's maximum hit and mana points but otherwise had no impact on strength or endurance. Protagonist *Willow* had to rely on his gear to improve his numerical combat prowess. Instead, his experience levels manifested in a tangible, almost tactile way by giving him greater skill with the powerful swords he acquired along the way. By tying *Willow*'s actual in-game dexterity to his weapons in a meaningful way, the game forced players to make hard choices about their sword selections, and rewarded them for leveling up without making them feel like they needed to stand around and grind.

Ys III adopted a very old-school perspective when it came to its experience systems. Raising your levels also boosts your max HP, but it doesn't change anything else besides the mathematical formulas applied to your collisions with enemies. But this is by design, just as the ideal way to play is to always hold down the attack button. Even in 1989, Falcom approached the action-RPG with an emphasis on RPG. In particular, the designers took inspi- ration from the vintage strain of the genre that the company's designers had cut their teeth on—*things* like Wizardry, which sent players into the dungeon as weak as a newborn and forced them to linger and fight at the very outset of the adventure to beef themselves up enough to make a proper foray into the world. *Ys III*, like *Ys* and *Ys II* before it, reinterprets this mindset through an action lens, imposing that archaic requirement on players but cranking up the speed to maximum so that it takes hardly any time at all to work your way through the process. It was a dated game design philosophy by 1989, but Falcom adopted it deliberately. The developer put plenty of thought into the balancing of *Ys III*. Once you raise Adol's levels to the point that he can steamroll the generic mobs in a dungeon, he'll have reached the precise point at which bosses can still annihilate him in a matter of seconds if you don't know how to approach them while still giving you a fighting chance against them.

But did *Ys III* have any real impact on the evolution of the metroidvania? Probably not; it's more of an isolated tidal pool of game design beyond perhaps influencing the shape of largely forgotten action-platform adventures on Japanese computers that were already nearing obsolescence. Like a lot of games around this time, *Ys III* abandons the idea of a fully interconnected world in favor of allowing players to select destinations on a world map. Unlike in *Bionic Commando* or *Clash at Demonhead*, you have only a few destinations to choose from, and they only become available once you complete specific story objectives, leading to a linear adventure. In a nice nod to series conventions, though, each standalone locale does include an outdoor space where Adol can step away from the dungeon and swiftly regenerate his hit points. Between these little grace notes of design continuity and the emphasis on grinding for levels and auto-attacking foes, *Ys III* doesn't really feel like an attempt to advance game design so much as an effort to reframe the rules of the Ys series to keep it up to date with contemporary trends.

Similar to the *Zelda* series, *Ys* would revert to its earlier style in the sequel, though by *Ys VI* much of the innate character of the franchise had vanished. Thankfully, *Ys VII* struck the perfect balance for the series, introducing on-the-fly character shifts and instant evasion to the speedy action—a style that eventually carried into an excellent remake of *Ys III* called *The Oath at Felghana*. But even if *Ys III* didn't do much to drive the evolution of core metroidvania design philosophies, it remains an interesting experiment in combining foundational RPG thinking with high-speed side-scrolling combat. The metroidvania reworked into a dungeon crawler.

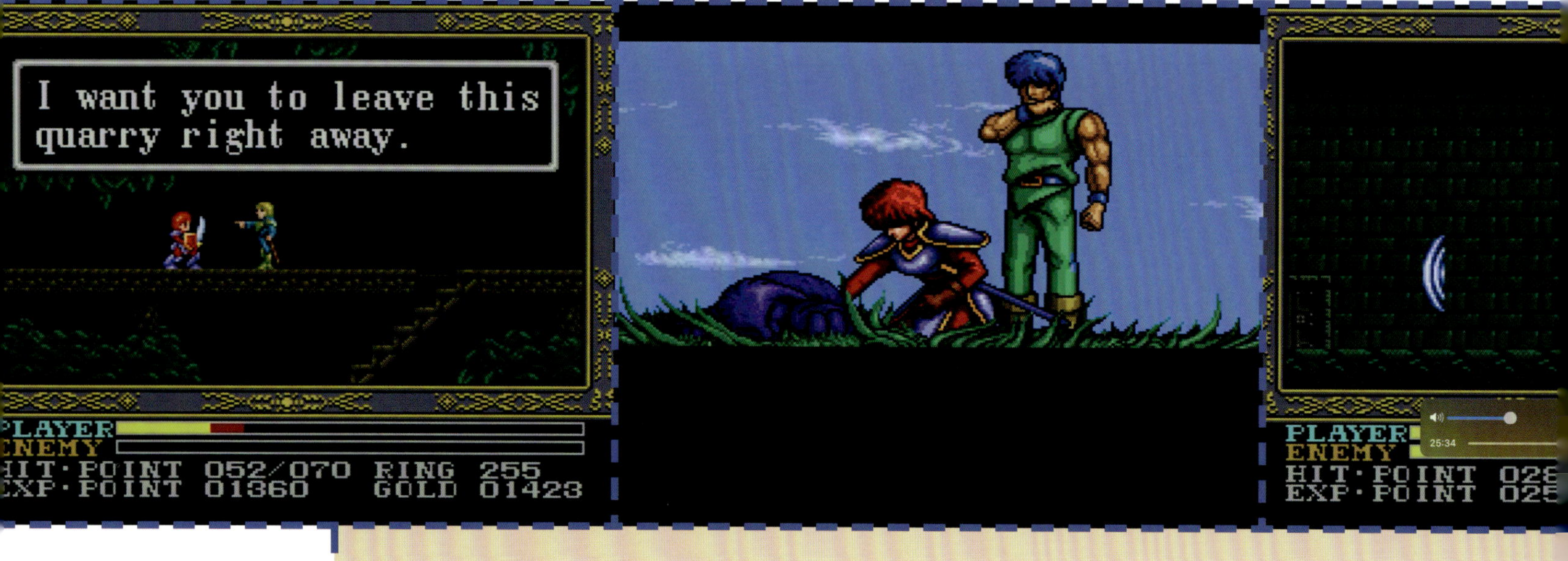

TEENAGE MUTANT NINJA TURTLES

While not a metroidvania by any stretch of the imagination, Konami's first *Teenage Mutant Ninja Turtles* game nevertheless flirts with the principles of the genre and has some deep metroidvania-adjacent roots. Created by the same talent behind *Konami Wai Wai World*, *Getsu Fuuma Den*, and *Castlevania III*—all games that leavened generally straightforward action with opportunities for players to explore alternate paths—*TMNT* consists of six sequential stages that demand a not-insubstantial amount of exploration. All but the final stage involve multiple side-scrolling action environments linked by a top-down overworld, reminiscent of *Zelda II* or Hudson's rambling 1985 Famicom adventure *Challenger*. The Turtles need to wander each overworld, avoiding hazards and ducking into doors and manholes in search of the path forward and, to a limited degree, the items necessary to make further progress.

The tool-based progression here admittedly doesn't begin to compare to the likes of *Metroid* or *Wonder Boy III*. Again, this doesn't even qualify as metroidvania-lite. The four Turtles (Mike! Raph! Leo! Don!) each wields a unique weapon and has individual strengths and weaknesses, but they never gain skill or power upgrades beyond consumable subweapons like shuriken and boomerangs. The navigational tools you need in order to make your way around the city (and beyond) don't have any real role in normal combat: the rope allows you to cross long rooftop gaps, and missiles allow your van to blow open barriers (or wreck enemy robots), but there's no real permanence of character growth here.

Which is fine. *TMNT* isn't meant to be a truly exploratory action-RPG sort of game. The depth and variety of the action here comes from the innate skills of the four Turtles, and balancing their traits and combat capabilities with the need to keep them alive (and understanding how to rescue them when you fail) keeps players on their toes. But you can see hints of metroidvania aspirations at play in this game, and while most *Turtles* games would fall into the brawler or fighter categories, Konami would indulge the quartet's exploratory leanings in 1993's *Radical Rescue* for Game Boy.

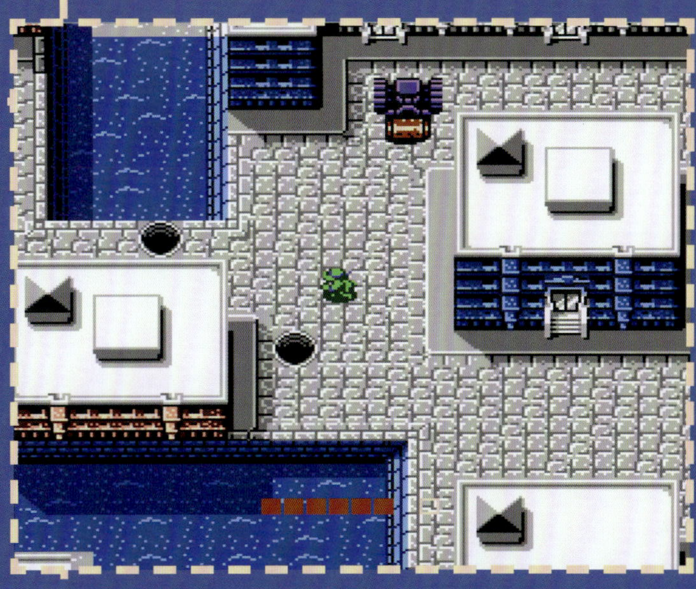

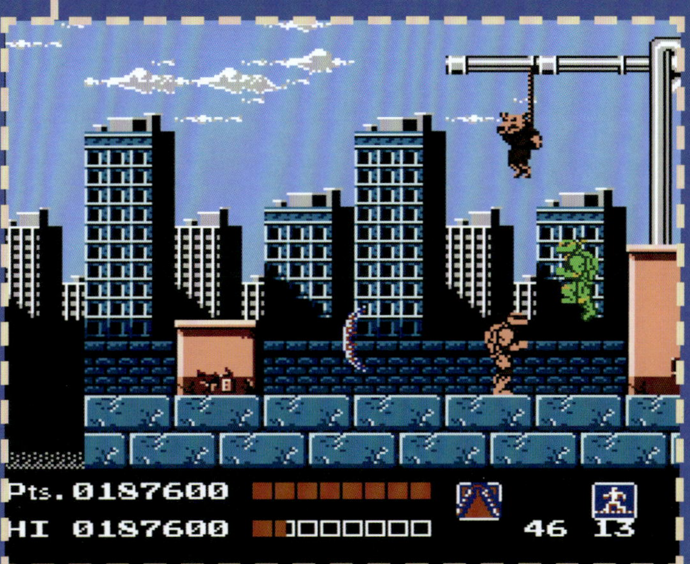

© Nickelodeon / Konami

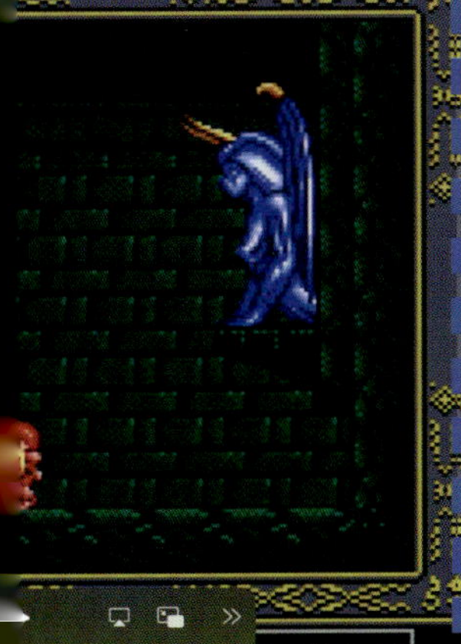

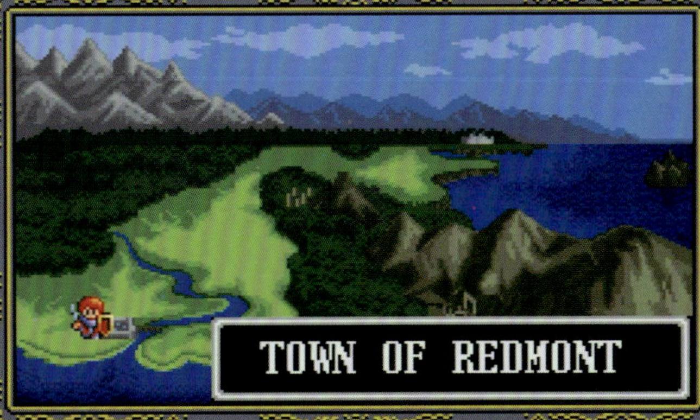

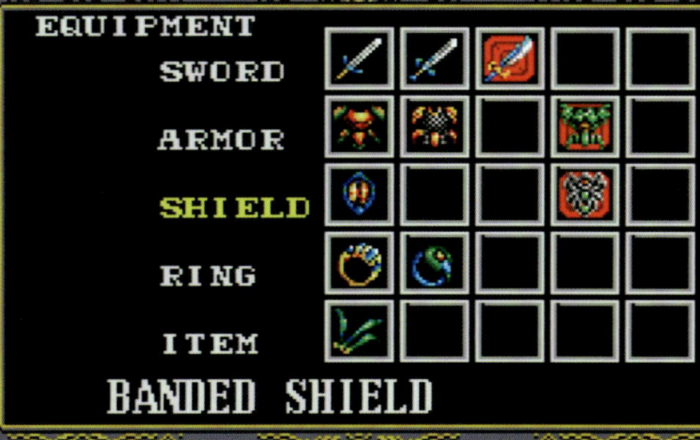

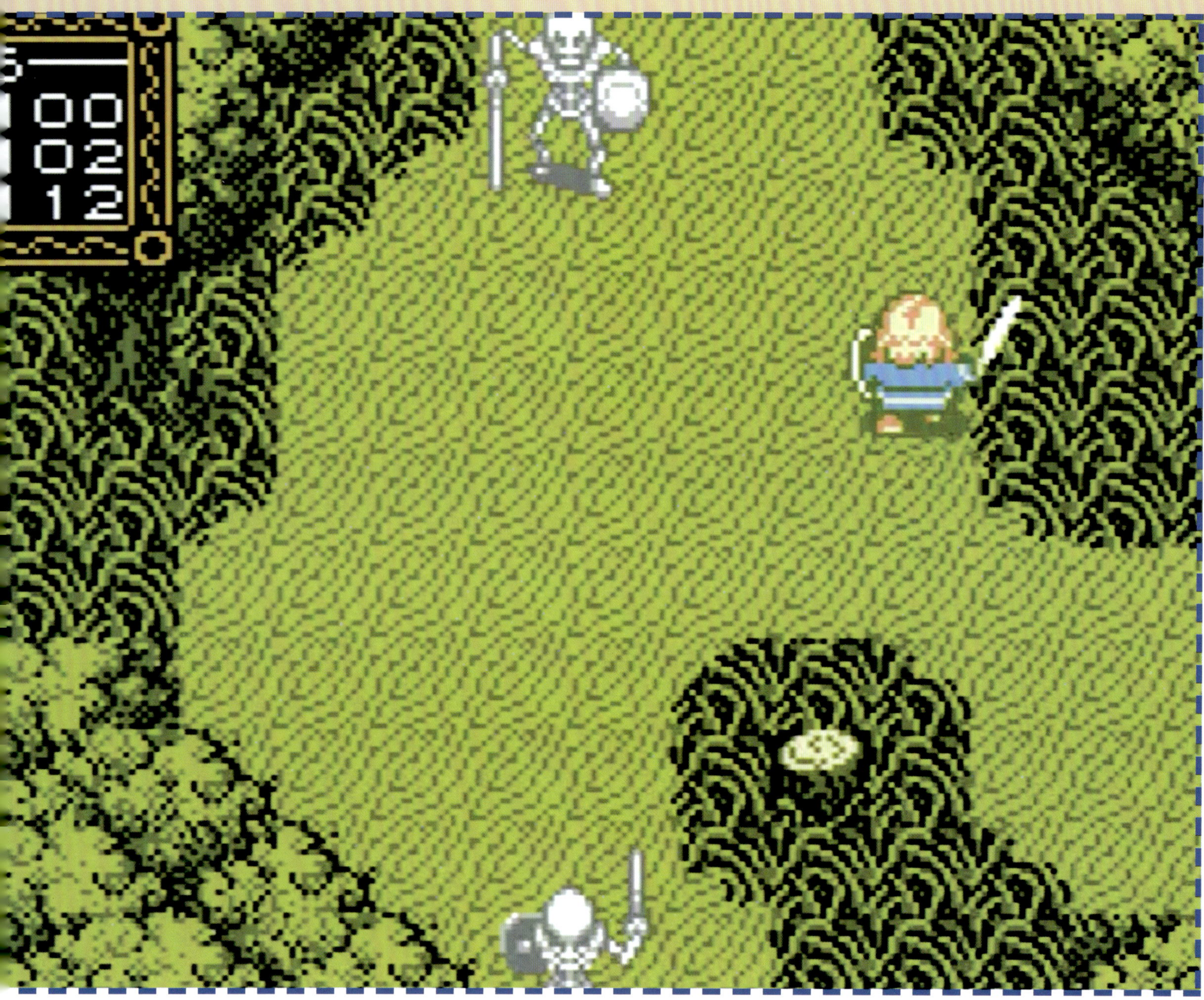

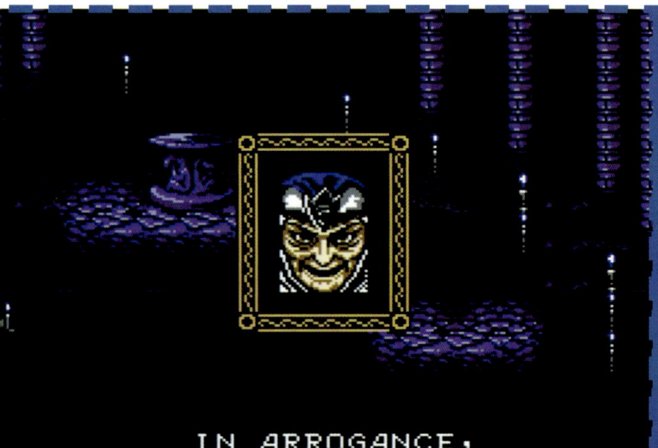

WILLOW

PLATFORM: **FAMICOM / NES**
DEV: **CAPCOM** | PUB: **CAPCOM**
INITIAL RELEASE DATE: **JULY 1989**

A DECLARATION OF WARRICK

In July 1989, Capcom converted two arcade games to NES, re- working them into experiences that had little to do with their coin-op versions: *Willow* and *Strider*. Of the two, *Willow* makes the more convincing standalone work. It has almost nothing whatsoever to do with the arcade cabinet by the same title outside of the presence of the Lucasfilm Ltd. movie license, but that disconnect works in its favor. The arcade adaptation of *Willow* played like a sort of half step between early Capcom action platformers like *Ghosts 'n Goblins* and the company's more recent RPG-inflected adventures like *Black Tiger* and *Magic Sword*. More a platform-shooter than a melee brawler, *Willow* allowed players to take control of Madmartigan (a sword-slinging Daikini warrior) and Willow Ufgood (a diminutive Nelwyn mage).

By contrast, the NES game puts you entirely in control of Willow and shifts the action from smooth side-scrolling to top-down flick-screen progression; this version lands at a pretty solid approximation of *The Legend of Zelda*. The original *Zelda*, that is, not *Zelda II*, making *Willow* the first new game in a few years to adopt the pure top-down action-RPG approach without attempting to make a genre hybrid in the process. *Willow* borrows from *Zelda* in its viewpoint, screen-by-screen progression, and its division into overworld and underworld. Even the combat works the same: like Link, Willow wields a sword and shield with one button and uses the other button to cast spells or brandish tools. Yet *Willow* has no interest in being a tepid, uninspired retread of the Nintendo classic. It simply uses the original *Zelda* as the launching point for a more cohesive interpretation of the term "action-RPG." Along the way, it manages to advance the genre. It even explores concepts that would appear in Nintendo's next entry in the *Zelda* series, 1992's *A Link to the Past*.

Consider the way Willow wields his sword. Rather than simply stabbing forward as Link did in the first *Zelda*, he attacks one of two ways. First, pressing the D-pad as you attack results in a stabbing thrust in that direction. Second, attacking from a neutral stance causes Willow to swing his blade in a wide arc that looks almost identical to the sword strikes in *A Link to the Past*. Likewise, Willow uses tools to cast magic—including acorns that stun foes

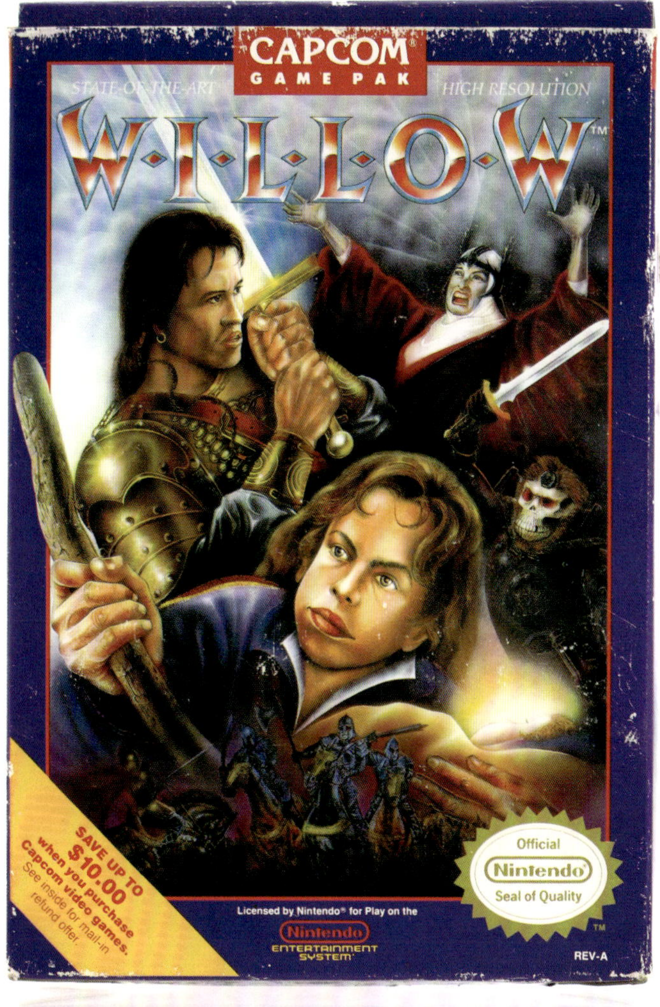

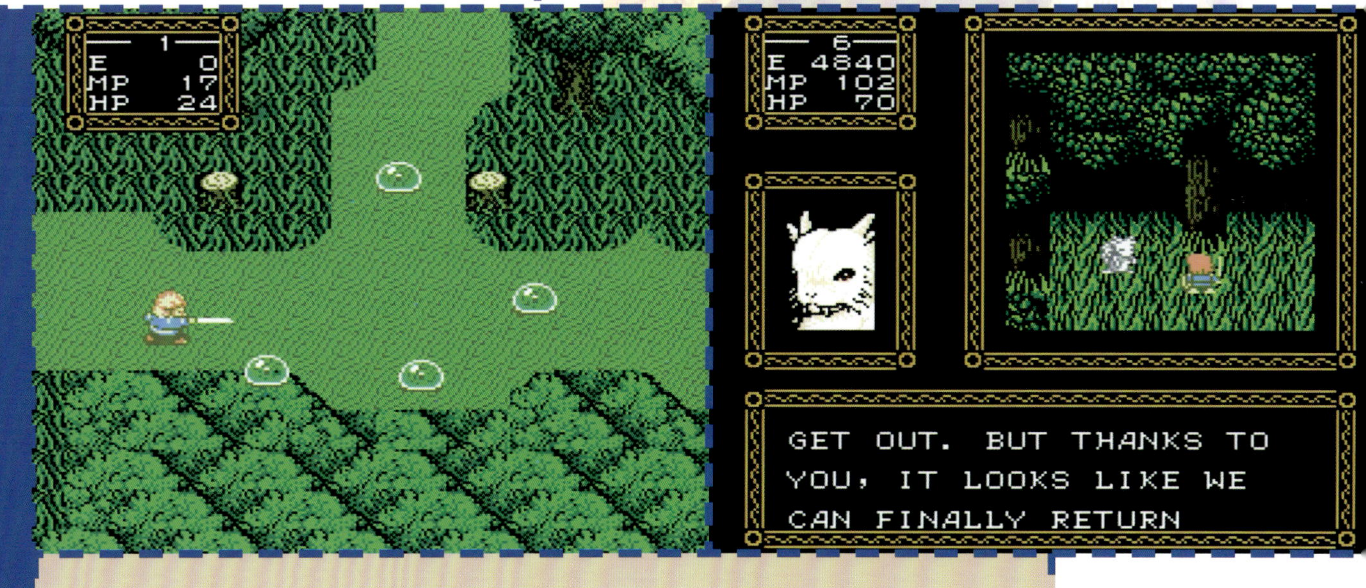

and a staff that casts a healing spell—but rather than using these implements infinitely or expending coins to activate them, Willow draws upon his reserves of mana, depicted by a meter.

In any case, Willow couldn't use money to power his spells, because the game lacks an economy. Willow doesn't need to buy things; the citizens of the realm will simply give him the items he needs for his quest. Otherwise, they make him undergo a fetch quest in order to trade. And there's always the possibility that he'll simply find the things he needs in chests throughout dungeons and forests. The lack of an in-game economy has its benefits, as you never need to stand around grinding for money, which is nice, and you can often acquire a weapon that offers massively more power than you might need at a given moment.

However, this is not to say that grinding doesn't exist at all in *Willow*, because the game simply replaces its cash economy with an experience system. Willow's strength can grow through sixteen levels, and you earn experience by defeating monsters. Obviously, as Willow's level increases, so do his max hit points and mana reserve. However, the experience system also affects the moment-to-moment action in a clever way: each weapon Willow acquires has its own de facto level requirement. The more powerful the blade, the higher Willow's experience level needs to be to wield it effectively. But that's not to say you can't wield it at all. Rather, you can use it clumsily until Willow reaches the required skill level for a given sword.

WILLOW BRILLIANTLY DISTILLS THE ENTIRE CONCEPT OF CHARACTER EXPERIENCE AND SKILL LEVELS INTO A PRACTICAL REAL-TIME FRAMEWORK: UNTIL HE REACHES CERTAIN EXPERIENCE MILESTONES, THE HERO CAN ONLY SWING THE SWORDS HE ACQUIRES CLUMSILY, ADDING AN ELEMENT OF RISK TO WIELDING THEM.

In practice, "clumsy" sword skills amount to sluggish attacks that leave the hero vulnerable to enemies. Once Willow masters a sword, he develops the ability to swing and thrust it quickly. But with a sword whose mastery exceeds Willow's current experience, you can only thrust and stab at a fraction of master speed, with more downtime between attacks. This introduces some important tactical considerations into the mix: Do you venture into battle with the lower-level swords you've already mastered and settle for weak but effective strikes against foes? Or do you stick to a harder-hitting blade that you've yet to master, inflicting greater damage on enemies but running the risk of taking hits in return?

It's a brilliant distillation of the EXP concept into a practical real-time framework, a clever take on what it means to be an action-RPG that would carry over, albeit less elegantly, into SNK's *Crystalis*, which would also apply an EXP-gain level system and spells into a *Zelda*-style format. *Willow*'s interpretation of the RPG facet of the action-RPG draws entirely on the interpretation of the genre that had evolved throughout the 1980s on Japanese consoles. Unlike the original *Zelda*, *Willow* doesn't dump you into a vast world and let you sort your way through it. It guides you with boundaries, gating, and barriers. You can't venture west beyond the starting area until you defeat the first dungeon, since the bridge leading from Nelwyn to Dew has been cursed by the boss who lurks there. You need to bring tokens and items and complete other tasks to open up pathways and gain access to later dungeons as well, making for a linear journey where the kind souls who refill your health and magic energy act as base camps for each region.

Still, *Willow* does incorporate some degree of backtracking, en- couraging you to return to previous areas once you acquire certain items. But for the most part, it sends you on your way, always seeking out new areas and new interactions, a progressive march toward Nockmaar Castle rather than a sally to unearth new challenges within an open area. Overall, it's one of the better action-RPGs of the era, integrating multiple trends and concepts into a cohesive whole that makes no effort to copy the beats of the film but simply attempts to capture its spirit. And, in the process, it introduces a few elements that would show up in later, more famous action-RPGs.

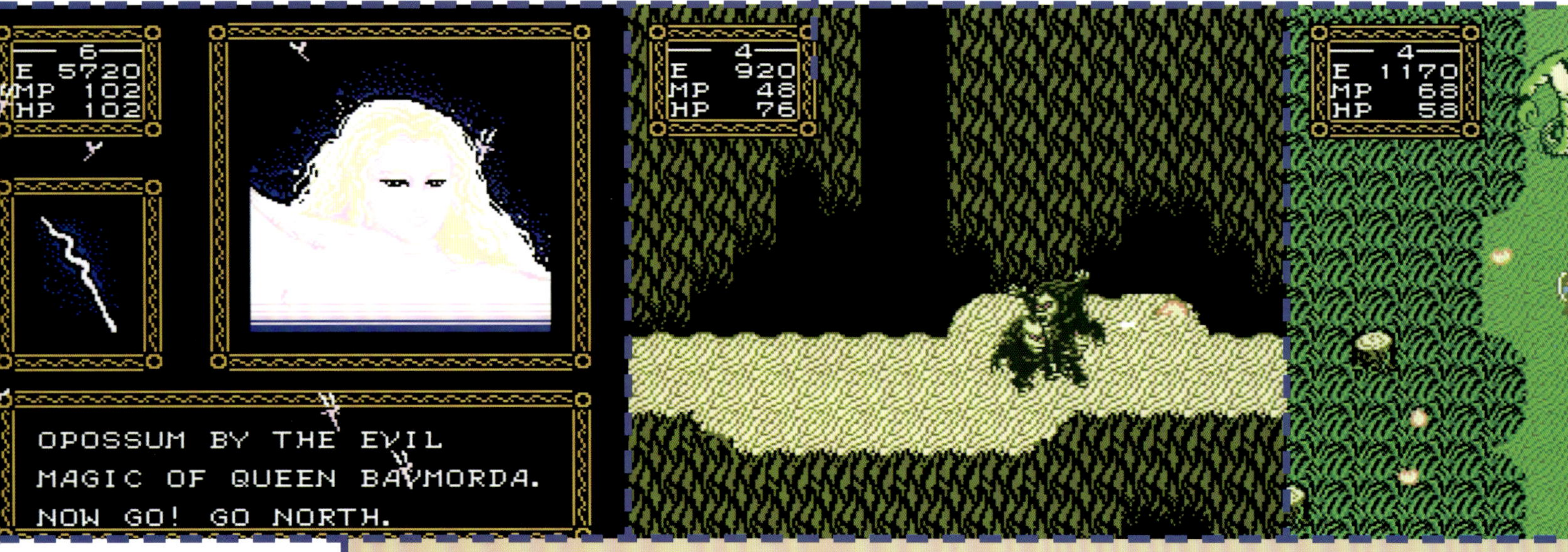

THE SWORD OF HOPE

One of the more unusual business practices of the games industry in the 1980s saw publishers localizing or adapting another company's work and then filing off the serial numbers to produce their own very similar, derivative version…often to great success. Midway did it with *Pac-Man*, creating unauthorized sequels like Ms. Pac-Man without creator Namco's consent. Hudson did it with Tecmo's *Star Force*, which it published on consoles and reworked into the suspiciously similar (and considerably more successful) *Star Soldier* series. And then you had Kemco, who converted ICOM's *MacVenture* trilogy to the NES to great success and who decided to run with that play style for a trilogy of their own.

Beginning with 1989's *The Sword of Hope*, Kemco's derivative works immediately established themselves as something distinct from *Shadowgate* and *Uninvited*. These games all shipped for Nintendo's brand-new Game Boy system, a platform even more limited in comparison to the NES than the NES had been compared to the Macintosh line. This necessitated some fundamental changes to the games' design, such as the removal of the inventory window. That loss unavoidably compromised the central *MacVenture* conceit of presenting players with a constant visual representation of all active game factors; so, rather than attempting to foist a diminished echo of their inspiration upon players, Kemco instead reworked the concept to incorporate elements of the adventure genre's closest cousin: the role-playing game. (It didn't hurt that RPGs had reached peak popularity in Japan the previous year with the launch of *Dragon Quest III*.)

The Sword of Hope largely eschews the puzzle-centric design of the *MacVenture* games in favor of a simplified experience system, basic combat, and a streamlined economy: brute numeric force in place of clever solutions. Still, there's no mistaking the fundamental structure at work here. The node-based presentation, complete with a mini-map of available exits, comes directly from *Shadowgate*. Kemco even reworked it to better fit the dynamics of the RPG: in addition to showing available moves, the mini-map also indicates probable combat encounters, allowing players to avoid or engage dangerous monsters. Given the two genres' common roots, *The Sword of Hope* represents an interesting reconvergence.

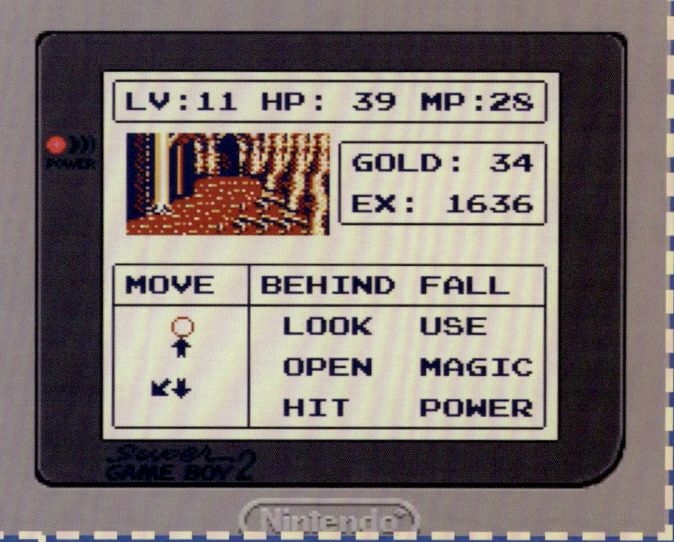

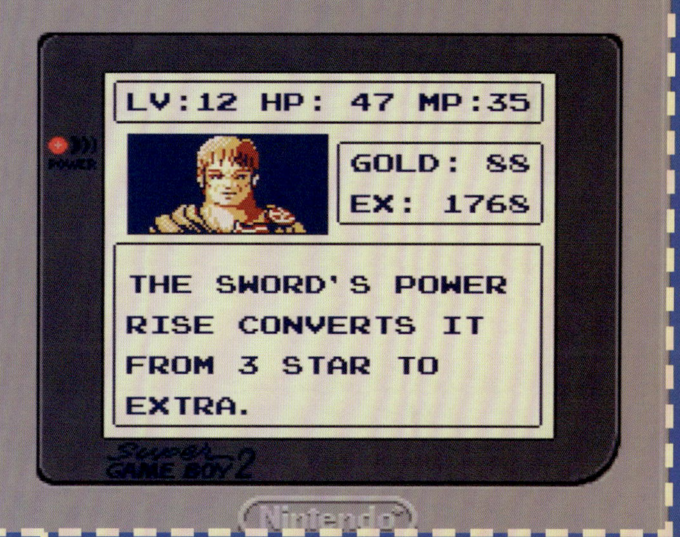

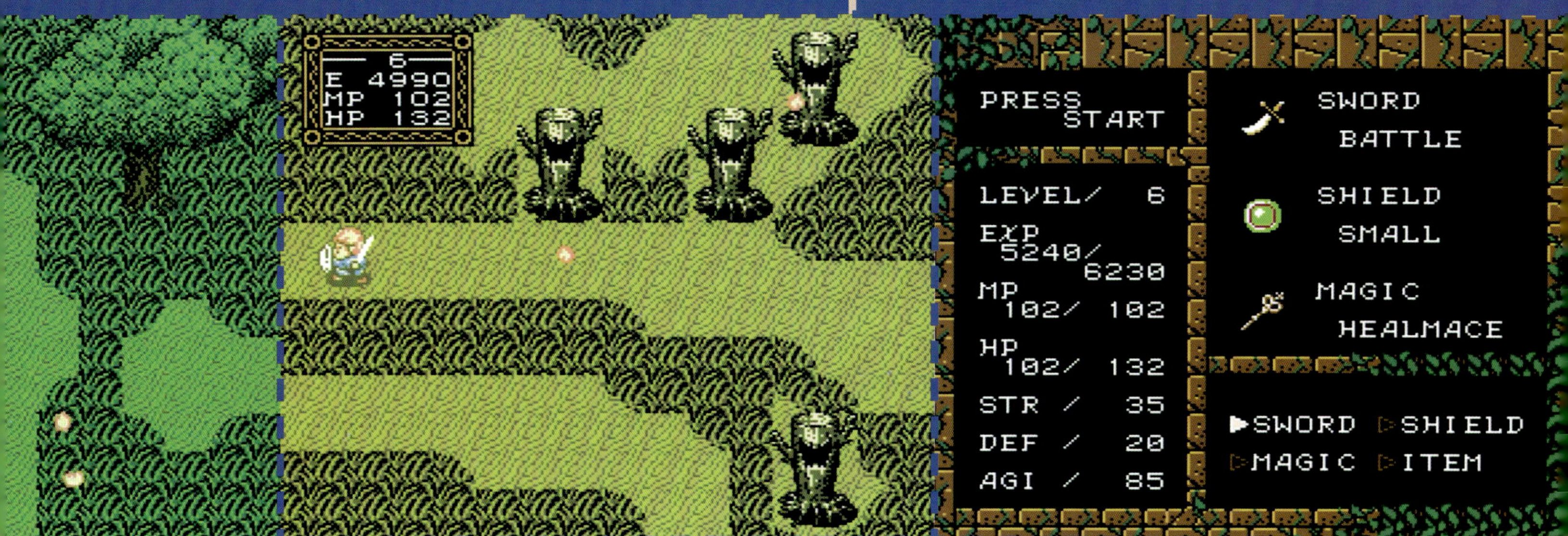

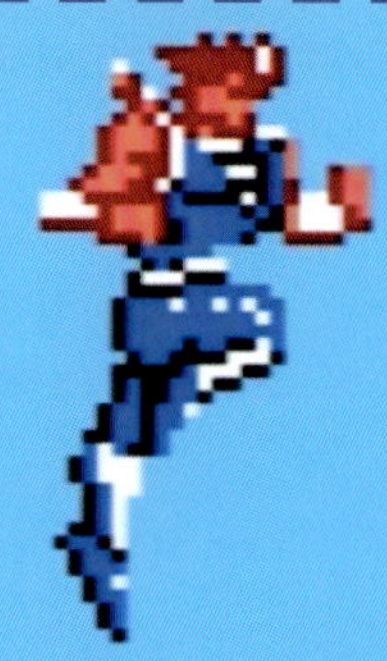

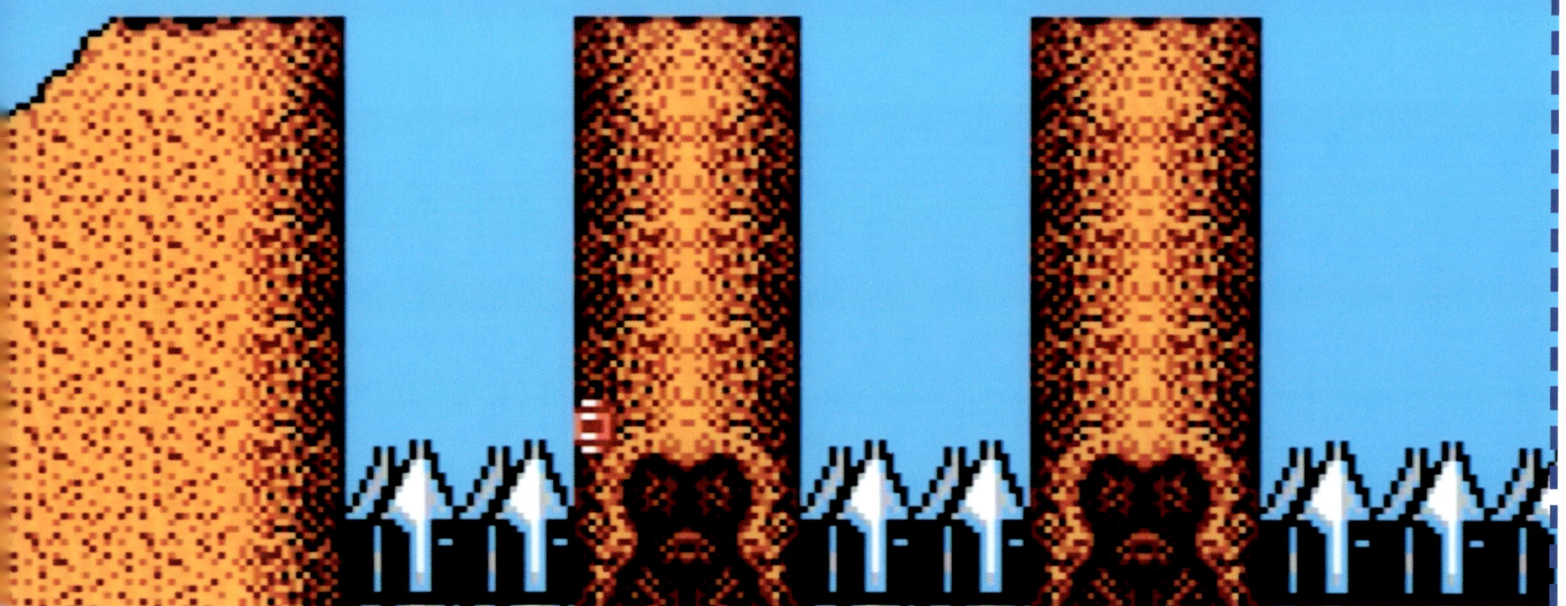

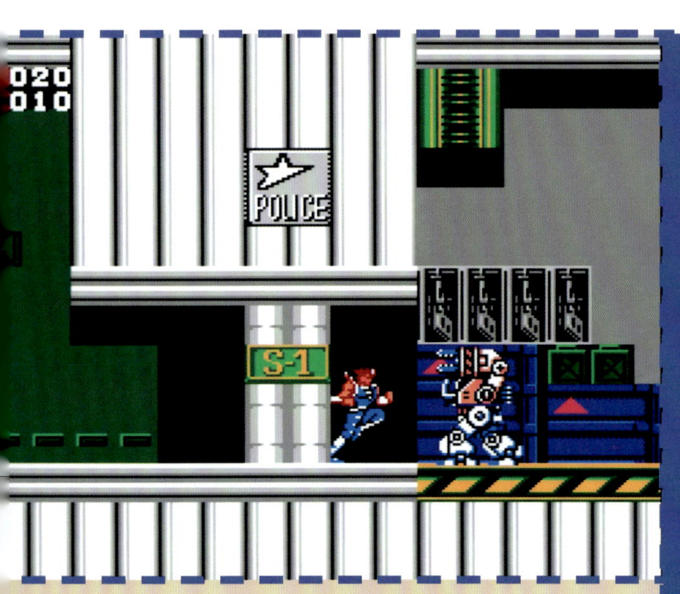

STRIDER

PLATFORM: **NES**
DEV: **CAPCOM** | PUB: **CAPCOM**
INITIAL RELEASE DATE: **JULY 1989**

NOTABLE FOR: **NARRATIVE PROGRESSION IN AN ACTION GAME**

LOSING STRIDE

Like *Willow*, *Strider* comes to the NES via Capcom, ostensibly based on an arcade machine by the same title. But, also like *Willow*, *Strider* contains very little material taken directly from the coin-op release. Capcom opted not to convert these arcade games directly for NES but rather to build entirely new games from scratch. This top-to-bottom reinvention is quite evident in *Willow*, which went from being a *Black Tiger*-style action-platformer with light RPG elements to a top-down, *Zelda*-style action-RPG on NES.

By contrast, *Strider*'s move away from the coin-op doesn't stand out obviously at first glance. The NES release initially seems like nothing so much as a profoundly sloppy take on the incredible arcade title. In truth, Capcom developed it in parallel to the coin-op version rather than basing it on that work. The two versions resulted from completely different teams adapting an external media property into video game form, which explains why they appear to share so many elements while still playing so differently.

The *Strider* coin-op presented itself almost as an action film, thrusting players into a nonstop succession of high-tempo set pieces. On the NES, *Strider* takes a more leisurely approach, sending Hiryu around the world to some of the same settings as those seen in arcades, but in a less linear fashion. Like the arcade game, this *Strider* begins on a platform in Kazakh, which is somehow still a Soviet Socialist Republic despite the adventure's far-future setting. (In fairness, the fall of the Berlin Wall caused an awful lot of late '80s sci-fi to become wildly dated overnight.) The protagonist, a futuristic ninja named Strider Hiryu, runs forward and slashes robots and Cossack guards with his plasma sword Cipher, just as his arcade counterpart. From here, however, the two games quickly diverge in style. The overall structure of the NES game falls somewhere between that of a proper metroidvania and a console adventure game. In this sense, it shares a lot in common with Capcom's 1988 NES action-RPG *Bionic Commando*: each area of the world is self-contained, and you unlock access to different regions by gathering items and story clues.

Where *Strider* differs from *Bionic Commando*—and in fact nearly every other exploratory NES adventure outside of *Metroid* and

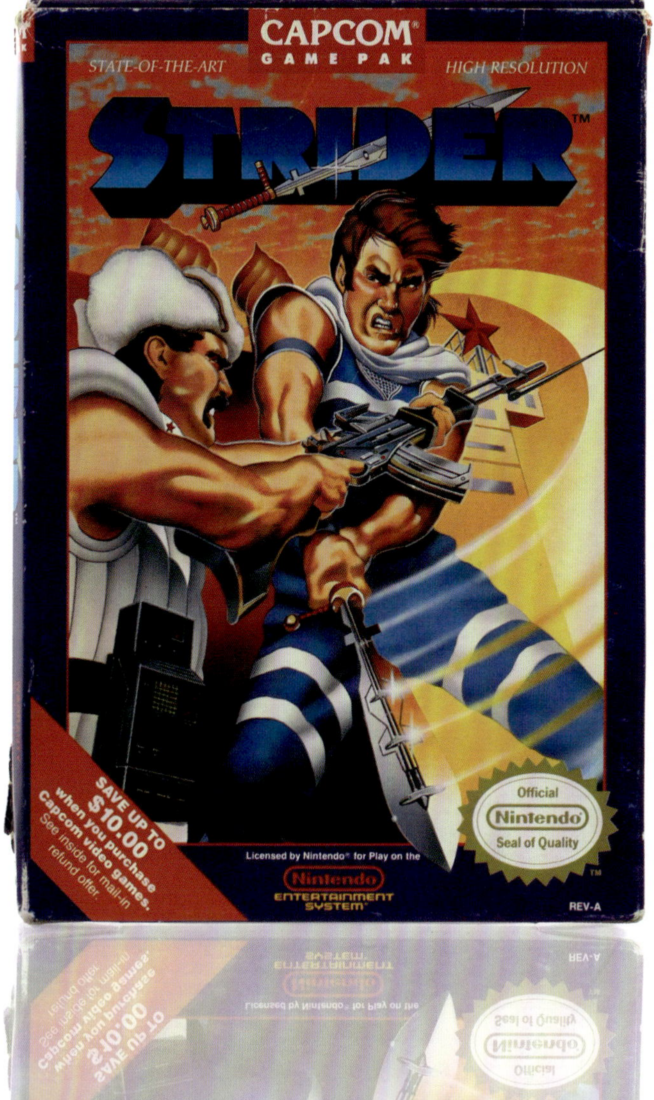

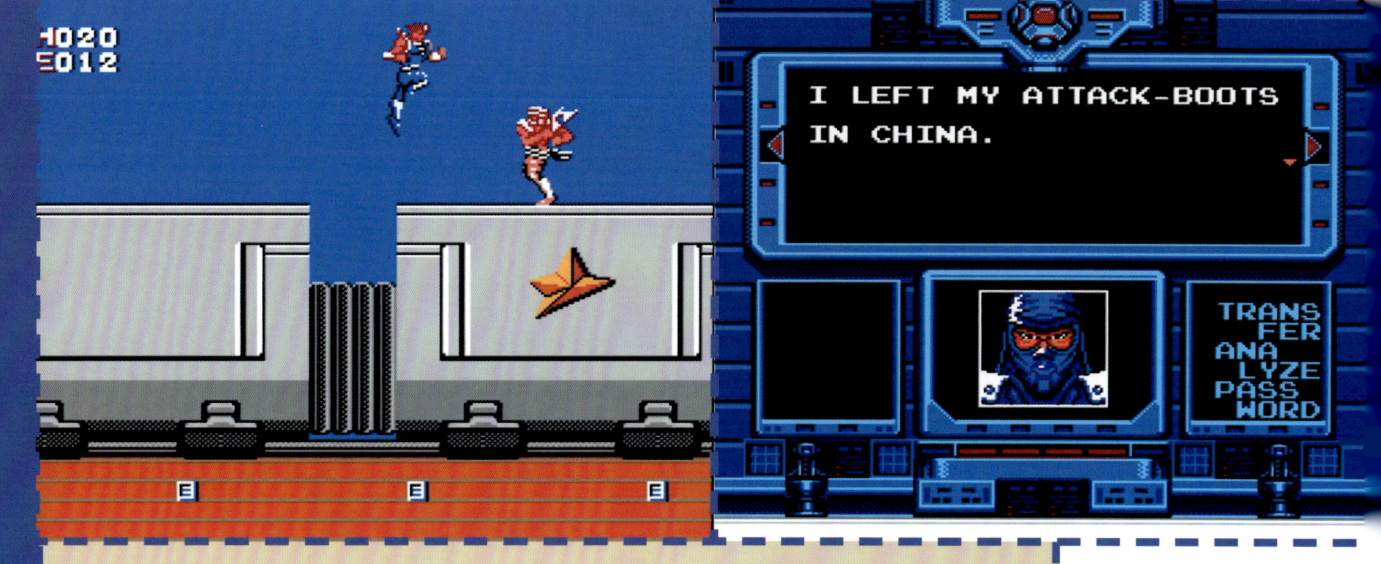

Blaster Master—is that you need to revisit many areas of the game to explore new corners of those locations. Like *Metroid*'s Brinstar and *Blaster Master*'s Area 1, Kazakh functions as a hub, divided up by barriers and partitions that you can only clear once you've ven- tured into different locations to collect clues and acquire gear capable of opening those locks. Some of these barriers work more elegantly than others. The most straightforward and uninteresting of the gates are literally that—gates—which bear a numeric code and can only be opened once Hiryu finds the corresponding key; these aptly appear in your inventory as a comically literal key-shaped item…again, despite the far-future setting.

All told, Hiryu needs to gather about half a dozen of these keys to gain entry into several locations that you can see straightaway upon beginning the adventure. Most vexingly, a Level 3 gate shows up right inside the Kazakh base but it can't be accessed for an hour or two into the adventure. Hiryu tends to discover the existence of multiple destinations at a given time as he explores the early portions of the game, which raises the question of which zone to explore next and gives his quest a nonlinear feel.

In reality, this boils down to a matter of appearances; the game has a less open-ended design in practice. For example, as you make your first foray into the Kazakh base, you'll find a pair of data disks that contain files leading you to two new destinations: Australia and Egypt. Once you analyze the disks in your orbital dragon-shaped satellite home base, Hiryu gains the ability to teleport down into both locales… but going to Australia does you no good, because you immediately reach the dead end of a Level 5 door that doesn't serve any purpose until the very end of the game. On top of that, several locations turn out to be almost entirely immaterial. Japan, for example, consists of three rooms that you can clear in about five minutes.

STRIDER'S SEEMINGLY OPEN-ENDED WORLD DESIGN AMOUNTS TO MERELY A MATTER OF APPEARANCES IN PRACTICE. FOR EXAMPLE, KAZAKH YIELDS DISKS THAT LEAD YOU TO AUSTRALIA AND EGYPT… BUT GOING TO AUSTRALIA LEADS YOU TO A DEAD END UNTIL YOU FIND THE LEVEL 5 KEY, HOURS LATER.

The reality is that *Strider* as a whole just doesn't have much substance. Its half-dozen or so locations are either incredibly tiny or else designed in such a way that you really only have a single pathway through the setting each time you visit. The level design attempts to obfuscate the game's modest size and straightforward level layouts by dropping you into large, sometimes confusing spaces that appear to contain multiple corridors. Yet in almost every instance like this, you'll find that venturing outside of the critical path either leads to an immediate dead end or else simply doubles back around and drops you back to where you were a moment before, accomplishing nothing besides wasting your time.

It also doesn't help that *Strider* suffers from technical flaws. The program code appears to be glitchy, making the game difficult to play—a surprise considering that it comes from the same Capcom who gave us rock-solid NES masterpieces like *Bionic Commando* and *Mega Man 2* around the same time. You won't find the buttery animation and silken controls of those games here.

Unlike his arcade counterpart, a stylish ninja who set a new standard for character animation and control capabilities, this Hiryu moves clumsily. His Cipher has no reach to speak of and can't be extended or powered-up the way it can in the arcade, despite permanent inventory and level-up systems that would seem an obvious hook for such enhancements. Hiryu also lacks the ability to pinwheel acrobatically through the air; climb walls; or stick to ceilings. He can't do much besides run and jump, with a few alternate abilities like a sliding kick and running on water coming into play once you acquire the requisite boots for those powers.

Hiryu does possess one unique innate skill on the NES: the triangle jump. Meant as a replacement for his arcade counterpart's ability to use his short blade as a climbing piton, the triangle jump ostensibly allows players to reach different areas by leaping at a wall

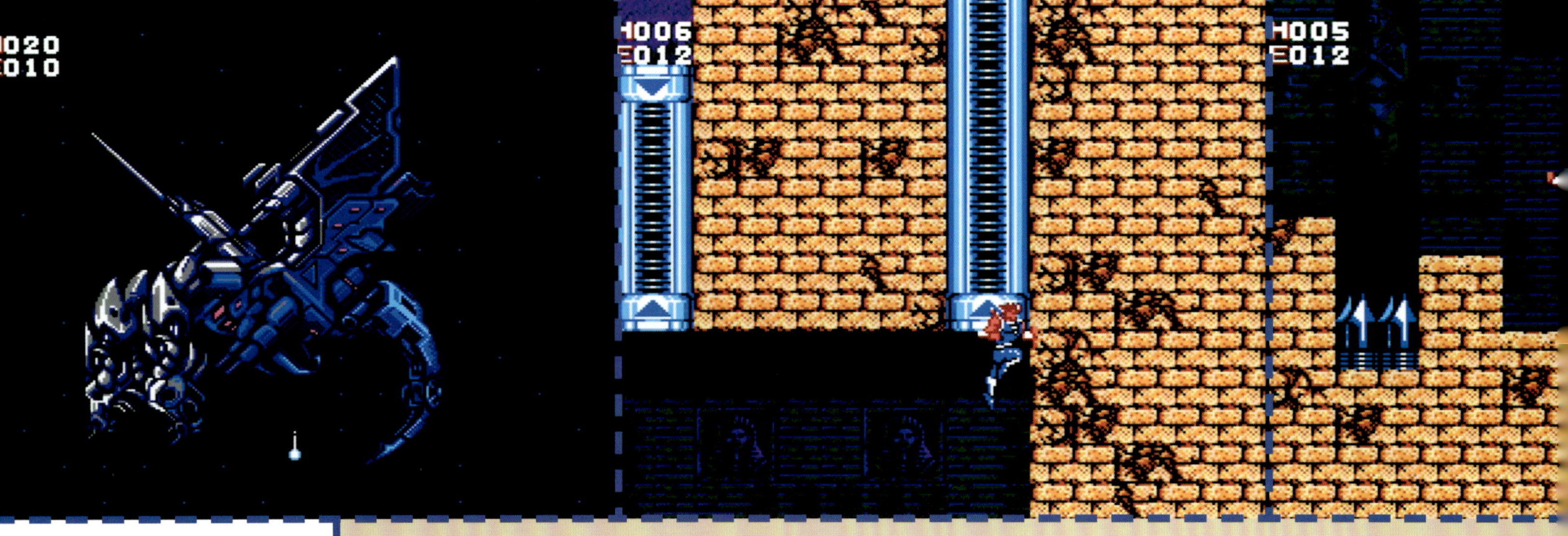

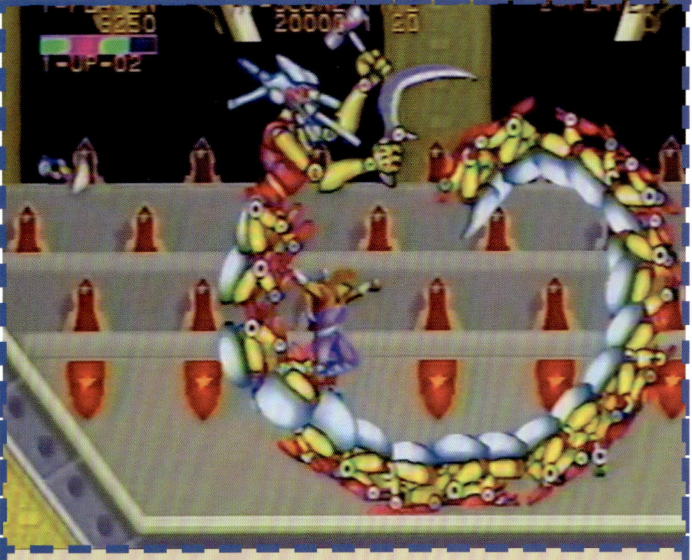

THIS COLUMN: THE ARCADE VERSION OF *STRIDER* FOCUSED ON SPECTACLE OVER EXPLORATION—AND DID A TRULY BRILLIANT JOB OF IT.

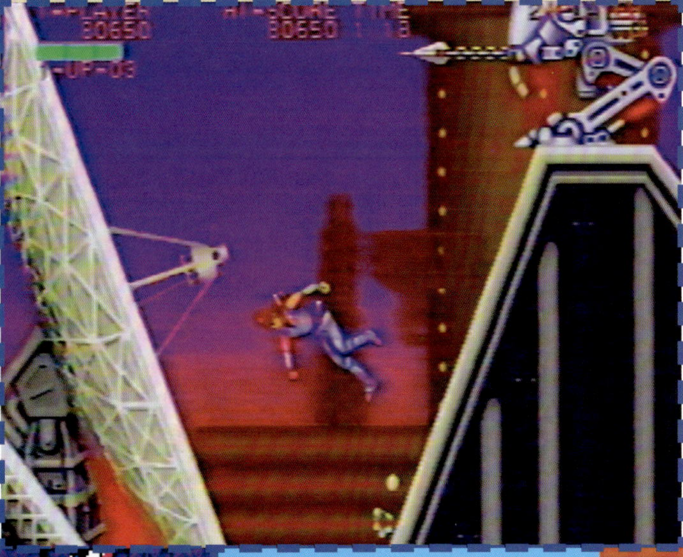

and using it as a springboard. In theory, you can chain this ability infinitely, allowing you to climb shafts by bouncing from one wall to the other, rising a little higher with each leap. In practice, the sloppy programming gets in the way. The triangle jump requires almost frame-perfect timing, demanding you tap the jump button and press the opposite direction from the wall at the precise moment that you make contact. Although you can use this skill repeatedly (and in fact you need to do so in order to complete the game), it always feels like a matter of pure luck when you manage to pull it off.

The triangle jump hardly represents *Strider*'s only control failing. Hiryu has a difficult time with jumps in general, frequently hitting invisible barriers right above the ground when attempting to leap. Slopes prove particularly challenging, as jumping from an angled surface almost invariably causes Hiryu to hit one of those nonexistent barriers or else go sailing into the air twice as high as normal. There is no in-between! It's a mess of a game, in a technical sense, and this jankiness likely accounts for the fact that Capcom didn't bother to release the NES game outside of the US despite *Strider*'s popularity worldwide. That's a shame, because the rambling mess of a story that drives your progress through Hiryu's quest only makes sense if you read the original manga that inspired the games…a work that Capcom only published in Japan. Add to that the weird loading pauses; the abysmal boss battles; and the clunky, tin-eared translation and you have a game that, despite some interesting ideas, feels like a step backward for the metroidvania genre. Capcom's own *Bionic Commando* did this story-driven action format a year earlier with far greater success!

No, *Strider* is likely the first game we've seen in the metroidvania's evolutionary timeline that feels like a genuine step backward. Rather than advancing the state of the art, it plays more like a throwback to *Wing of Madoola*: rough, glitchy, unbalanced, and obtuse. Such clunky design and barely-held-together tech may have flown in 1986, because no one knew how these things were supposed to work. But in mid-1989, *Strider* becomes a lot harder to justify given all the, well, strides that so many developers made in the action-RPG format throughout the latter '80s.

I guess that's not the worst thing in the world. It's good to see that even as things progressed forward, the metroidvania genre still had its setbacks and challenges…sometimes from top-tier studios. Despite its flaws, *Strider* for the NES wasn't a total loss. Developer Double Helix Games used it as their starting point for a greatly improved 2014 release by the same name, finding the good in a troubled work. It only took a quarter of a century!

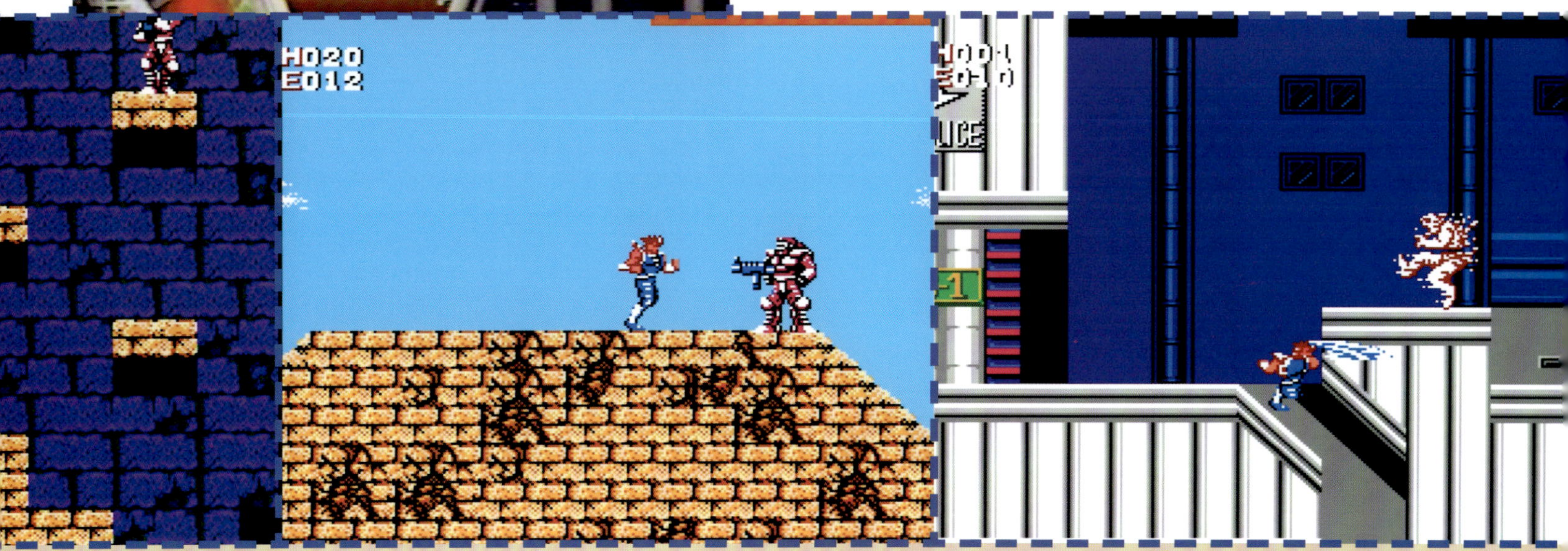

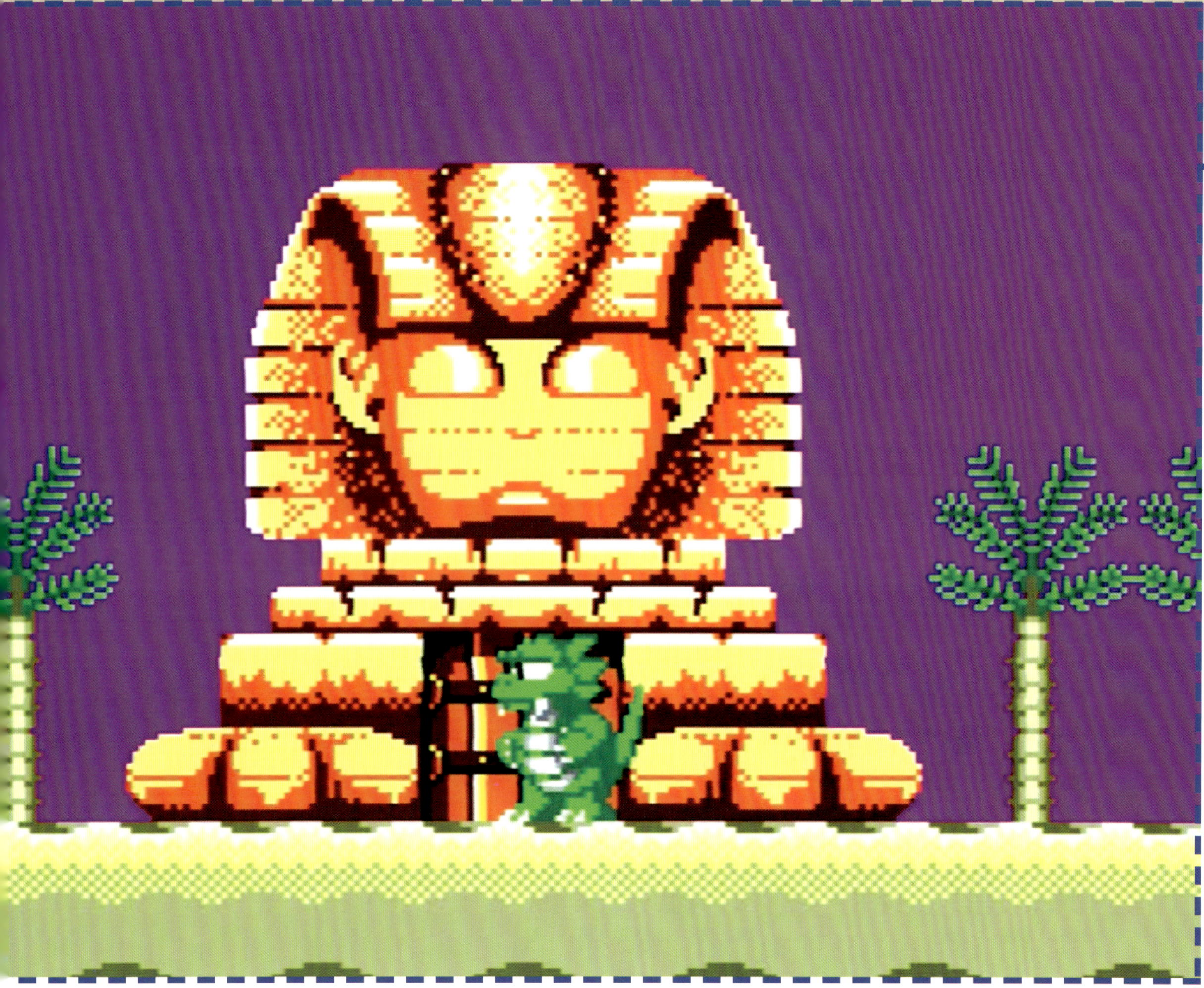

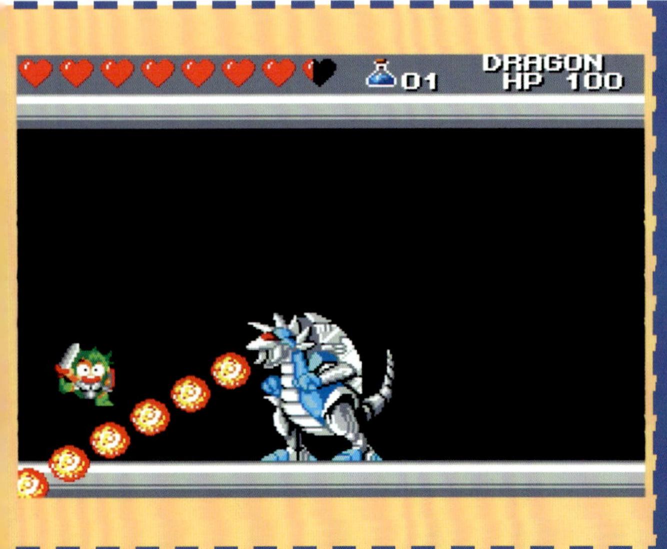

© Sega / Westone

WONDER BOY III
THE DRAGON'S TRAP

PLATFORM: **MARK III / VARIOUS**
DEV: **WESTONE** | PUB: **SEGA**
INITIAL RELEASE DATE: **SEPT. 1989**

NOTABLE FOR: **REFINING THE PLATFORM ACTION-RPG**

THE BLESSING OF A CURSE

Someone must have forgotten to give Sega and Westone the memo that exploratory platformers had fallen out of favor in Japan by late 1989, but that's OK. *Wonder Boy III: The Dragon's Trap* exemplified a genre growing passé, but it's a masterpiece all the same: a strange, wonderful little burst of isolated genius.

Also, Sega didn't actually release this game in Japan, despite giving it a Japanese title screen and adding a special alternate soundtrack for the Master System's Japan-only FM Sound Unit audio enhancement peripheral. The console version of *Wonder Boy III* only shipped in the Americas and Europe, where games like this were still on the upswing due to the localization gap of the 8-bit era. Because complex games tended to be slow to make their way into other languages, metroidvanias had only just begun to catch on in the West even as they languished in Japan.

A great game is always a great game. *Wonder Boy III* gives us the purest, most robust distillation of the metroidvania concept yet seen to this point—and probably the most polished as well. Although it barely resembles the original *Wonder Boy* (a wholly linear attempt to recreate the *Super Mario Bros.* experience all the way down to its format of thirty-two stages across eight worlds), *The Dragon's Trap* came by its design naturally. In arcades, *Wonder Boy* featured an onscreen status bar that depicted the hero's current weapon selection. This element evolved into a proper inventory system, complete with an economy, for the sequel, *Wonder Boy in Monster Land*. That game felt very much in keeping with the likes of Sega's *Fantasy Zone* and Capcom's *Black Tiger* in that it gave players some light RPG trappings, in the form of shops in which to purchase upgrades, while still maintaining a linear flow.

Wonder Boy III builds on that game, quite literally! It's a direct sequel; the title screen for the unreleased Japanese version calls it *Monster Land II*, not *Wonder Boy III*. It begins by dropping players into the final battle of *Monster Land*, fully kitted out with weapons and gear and massive health upgrades, and lets them duke it out with that game's final boss in a fight tilted to be more or less impossible to lose—a gimmick that Konami would borrow nearly a decade later for the definitive metroidvania, *Castlevania:*

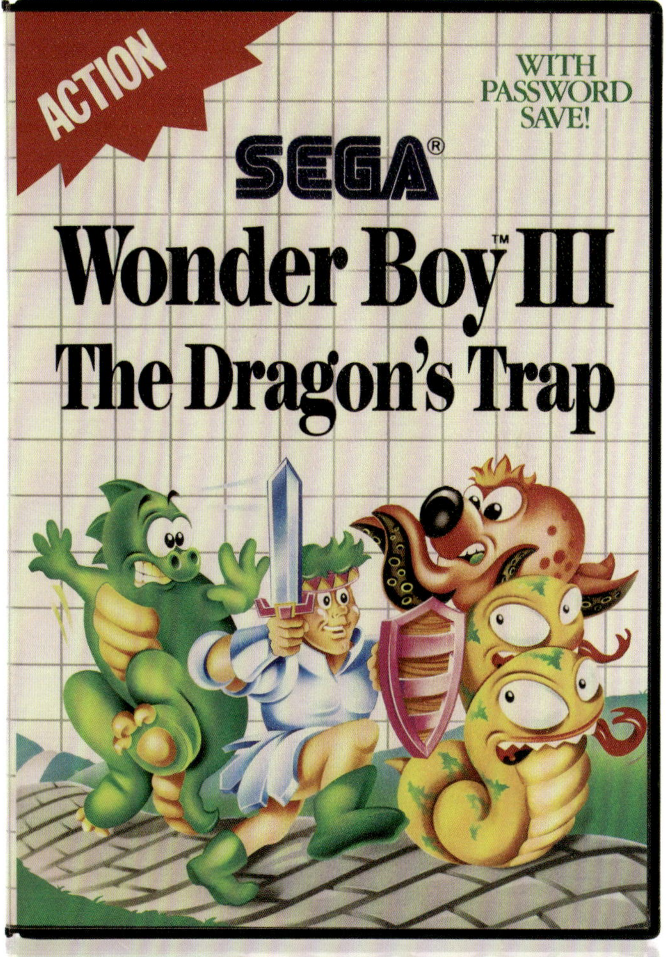

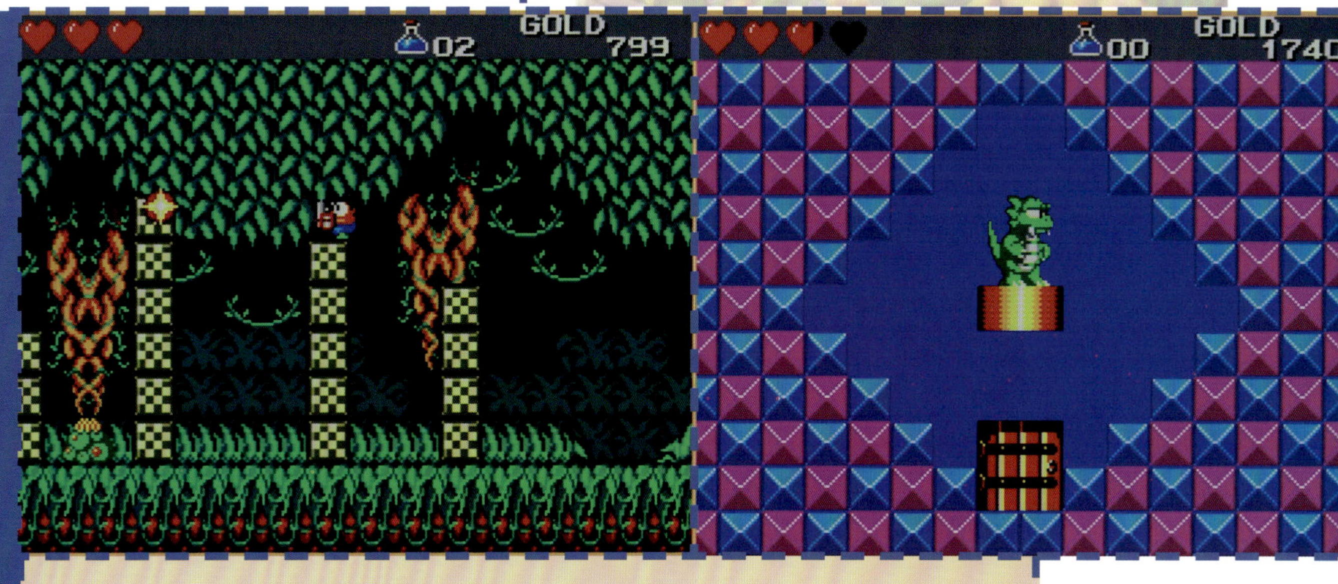

Symphony of the Night. However, it retcons *Monster Land*'s ending by afflicting the protagonist with a curse upon defeating the "final" boss, MEKA dragon. Canny readers will observe that this conceit had previously appeared in *Castlevania II: Simon's Quest*, in which Simon Belmont set out to purge himself of a curse Dracula placed on him (also via retcon) at the end of the original *Castlevania*. Clearly, the two series existed in conversation with each other. But however much *Wonder Boy* and *Castlevania* may or may not owe each other, this game has a tone and feel all its own. The prologue ends with a curse transforming protagonist Tom-Tom into a Lizard-Man with terribly reduced stats, rushing to escape the collapse of the dragon's castle in classic *Metroid* style, before striking out on an all-new adventure that spans a huge and largely open world. *Wonder Boy III* leaves the player to their own devices to complete the quest that the curse has thrust upon them. A few NPCs appear throughout the game world, but they tend to be utilitarian in nature, selling you equipment and health restoration.

From the outset of the adventure, you can venture forth along multiple paths from the central town that serves as the hub of the quest. To the east, you have a series of islands reminiscent of the original *Wonder Boy*; to the west, a desert that ultimately leads to a pyramid. Along the way, you can spot inaccessible caves, underwater grottos, and building interiors, all designed to draw your eye and entice you with the prospect of exploration…eventually…once you figure out how to access them. This process involves lots of traveling and poking into out-of-the-way corners while battling hosts of monsters, gathering cash, and buying cool new gear.

At the most basic level, the keys you need to open new areas are simply that: keys. Find a key, unlock a door that grants you access to a new building or activates a portal to a new space. But your primary means for opening new areas to explore come in the form of something hinted at in the game's title. The dragon's trap may have cursed Tom-Tom, but that curse also grants him unique abilities. As you venture through the world and defeat the various dragons who rule the land, Tom-Tom will find himself stricken by additional curses that turn him into different beastman forms.

These alternate bodies don't simply change your appearance, though—each one grants the hero new physical attributes that open up more of the world to exploration. For example, each monster form can only equip certain types of gear. You begin the main ad- venture as a Lizard-Man who breathes fire as his main form of offense and who can't fully benefit from the power boost conferred by swords. Yet, as a tradeoff, the Lizard-Man form can unleash ranged attacks, giving him the safety of distance from foes. By contrast, the diminutive Mouse-Man form has terrible range with his tiny little sword, which means he can only attack by getting in close to foes. But only the Mouse-Man can slip through tiny gaps in the level design and cling to walls and ceilings, granting him the ability to venture into areas that the other forms can't. The Piranha-Man form can move with agility underwater, meaning you can venture into new areas by swimming through lakes and underwater pools. And so on, and so forth.

WHILE YOU NEVER STOP RELYING ON LITERAL KEYS IN ORDER TO UNLOCK CRITICAL SPACES LIKE BOSS CHAMBERS, *WONDER BOY III*'S EMPHASIS ON THE PROTAGONIST'S PHYSICAL FORM AND INNATE ABILITIES TO OPEN UP FURTHER EXPLORATION IS A GREAT EXPRESSION OF ONE OF THE METROIDVANIA'S BASIC TENETS.

While you never stop relying on literal keys to unlock critical spaces—especially boss chambers—*Wonder Boy III*'s emphasis on the protagonist's physical form and innate abilities to open up further exploration is a great expression of a fundamental rule of the format that goes back to Samus Aran and her morph ball. It's quintessential metroidvania, especially once you gain access to the ability to transform between bodies at will.

Ultimately, of course, you want to get your protagonist back to the human form he started out in, but the dragon's curse doesn't seem quite so bad when you stop to consider how it drives the core gameplay loop. And while *Wonder Boy III*'s world may appear at a

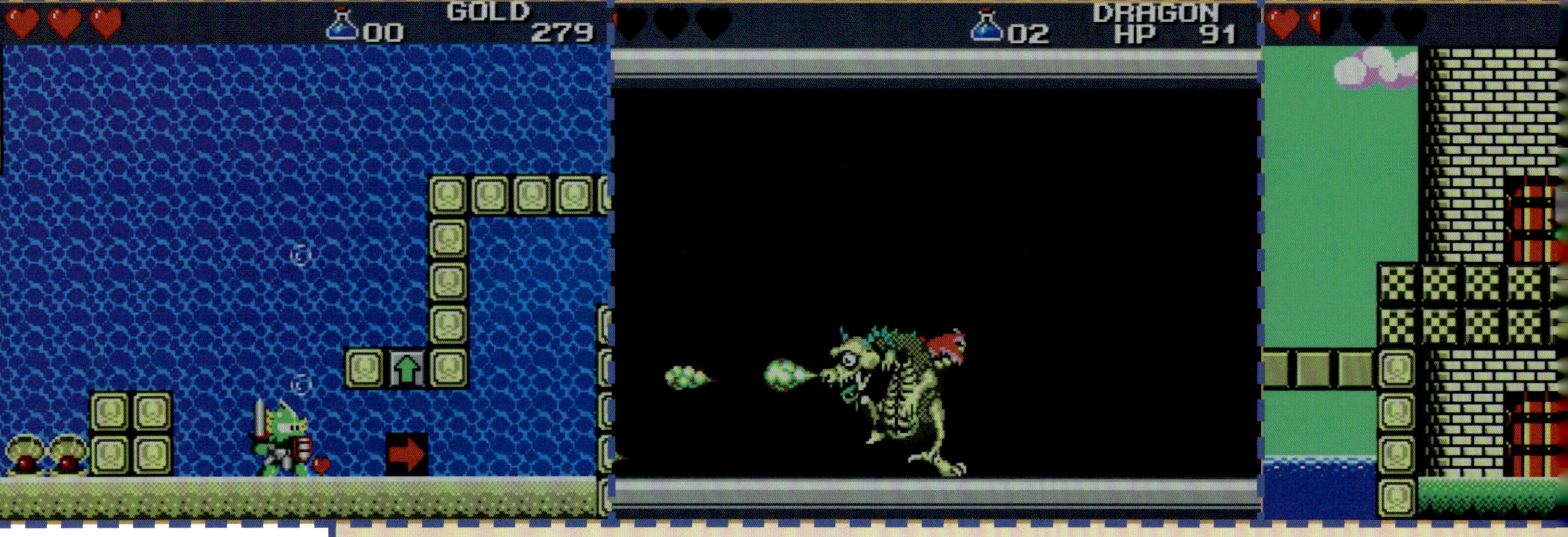

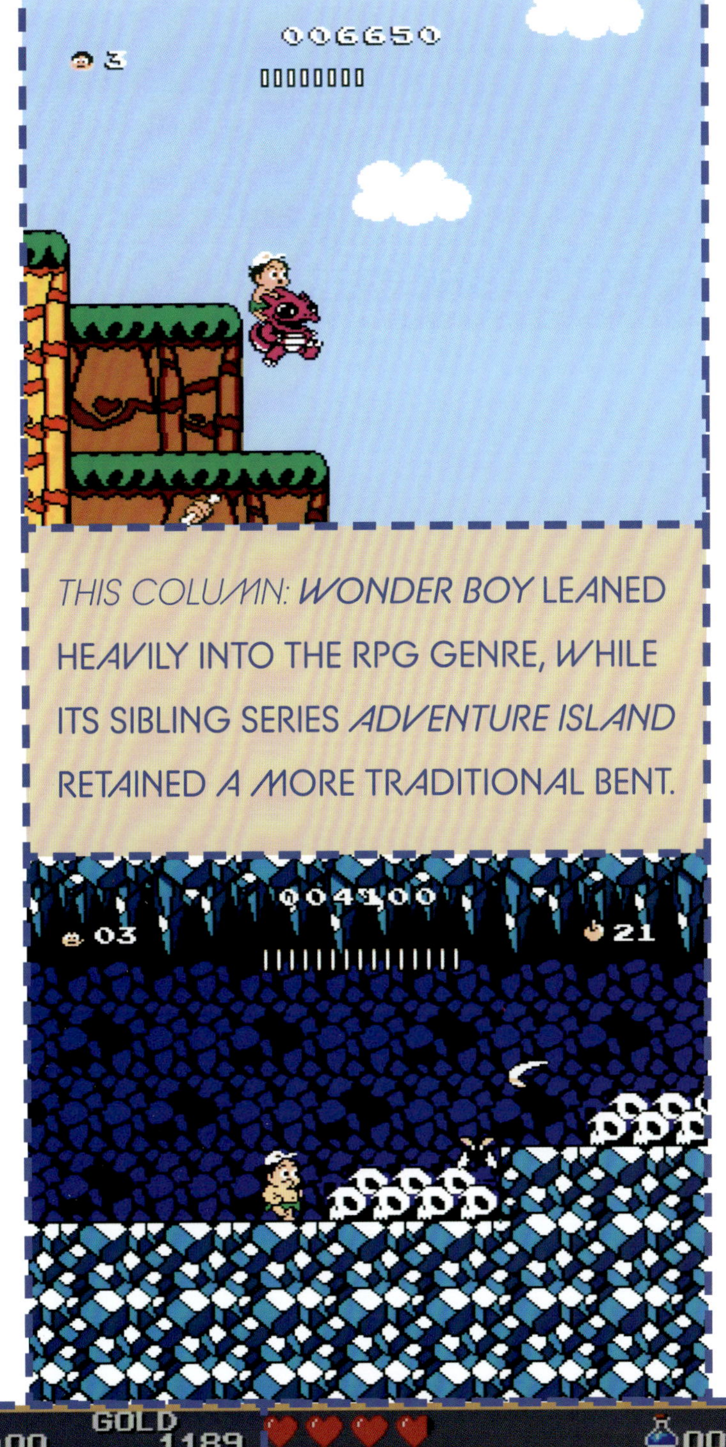

THIS COLUMN: *WONDER BOY* LEANED HEAVILY INTO THE RPG GENRE, WHILE ITS SIBLING SERIES *ADVENTURE ISLAND* RETAINED A MORE TRADITIONAL BENT.

glance to consist of nothing but long horizontal passages, once you begin to pick your way through its spaces, you realize that they contain plenty of intricately interlocked passages. Here there are tantalizingly visible-yet-inaccessible spaces that beg the player to revisit them once they've acquired the necessary skill or body.

Wonder Boy III rewards the attentive player in a way that no game before it had. Consider the tower in the hub town, which contains a single wall of checkerboard blocks rising out of sight. The first time you spot this wall, you may not even notice it; you have no reason to think that particular wall has any significance, since the town's structures contain many different blocks and tiles. But once you become Mouse-Man, you realize that your new form can use checkerboard blocks to scramble up walls and along ceilings. So that structure at the outset of the adventure turns out to contain a secret that only becomes relevant once you defeat the first boss. Likewise, the Piranha-Man form can acquire a special sword whose mere presence in the player's inventory allows you to break a certain type of nondescript block. Once you comprehend that blade's power, your mind immediately begins to race as you review the world and consider where you may have seen that style of block before.

Wonder Boy III empowers players who go out of their way to explore. Drop into a pit or plunge into the water, jump off the top of the screen, nudge a seeming dead end: more often than not, you'll earn something for your efforts, whether it's extra health and consumable sub-weapons or as vital as a permanent health upgrade.

Westone created a true classic in *Wonder Boy III*: one of the best-designed 8-bit games ever made. It was so good, in fact, that its visually enhanced remake for modern platforms in 2017 did very little to change the underlying content and mechanics besides adding crisp new art and animation, yet it still felt like one of the best metroidvanias of the era. That's true timelessness.

Even at the time, Sega and Westone knew they had something special. *Wonder Boy III* shipped for a variety of 8- and 16-bit platforms under an assortment of names and properties, but the core action, systems, and world design remained fundamentally consistent. The game proved especially influential in Europe, but it had its share of fans in the US and Japan as well, including among the game development community. Consider Takeru's NES cult favorite *Little Samson*, which featured the ability to swap the human protagonist for a team of different beast allies, including a mouse with more or less the same skill set as Mouse-Man. Although the game industry's 8-bit explorations into the metroidvania form had begun to wind down by the time *Wonder Boy III* appeared, at least it didn't fade away. Thanks to Westone and Sega, it rather went boldly into that good night.

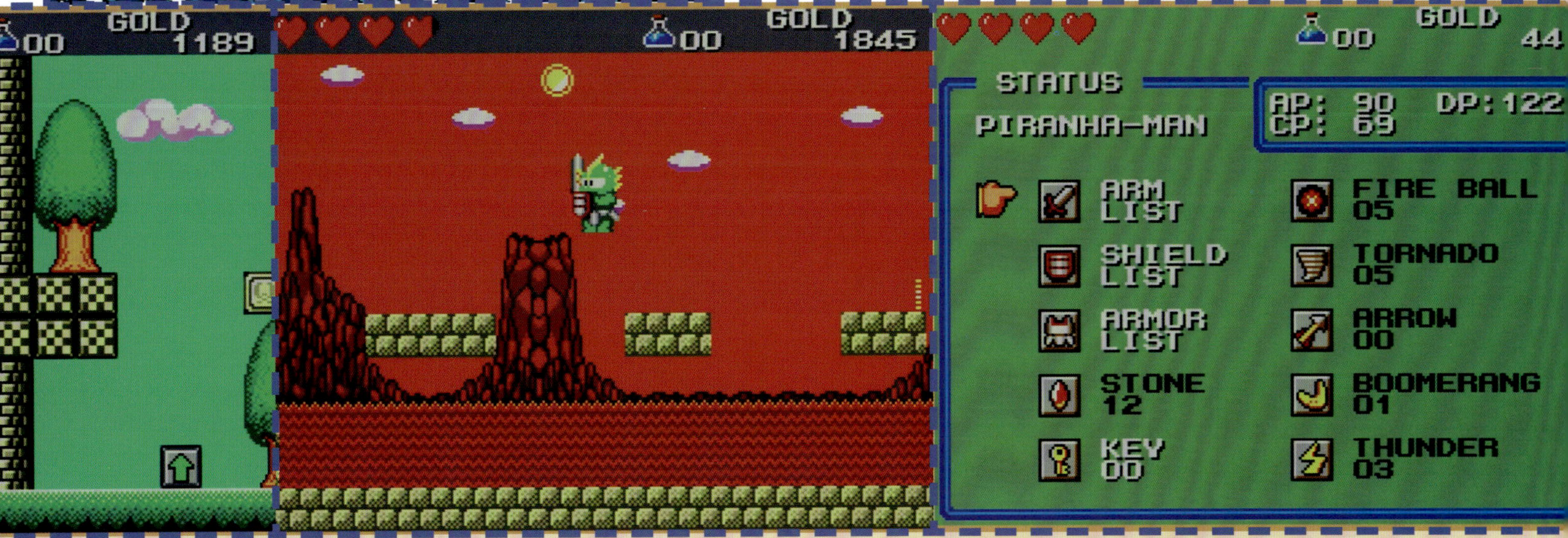

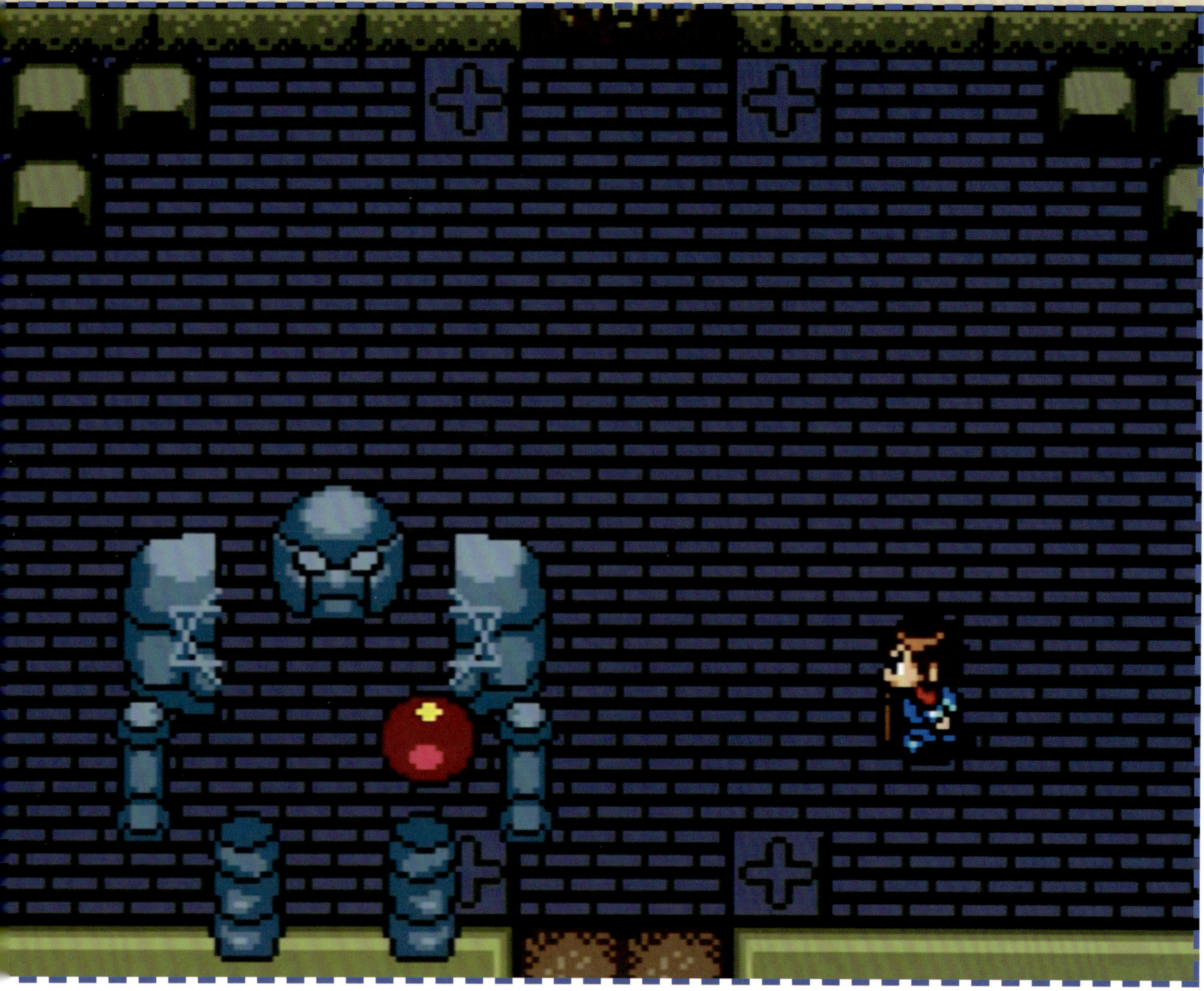

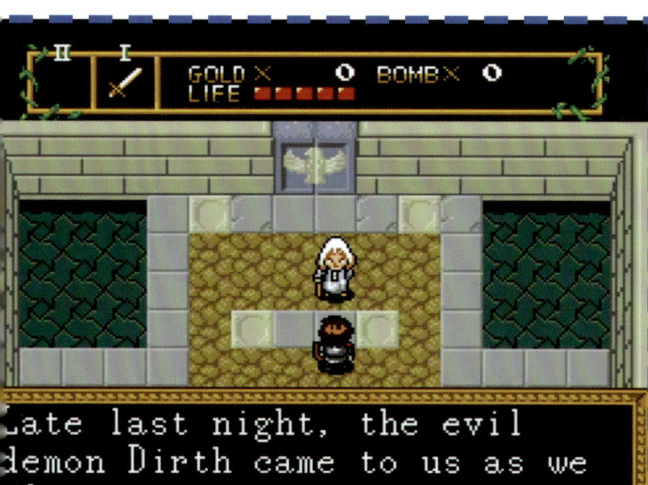

NEUTOPIA

PLATFORM: **PC ENGINE / TURBOGRAFX-16**
DEV: **HUDSON** | PUB: **NEC**
INITIAL RELEASE DATE: **NOV. 1989**

NOTABLE FOR: **RECREATING THE ZELDA FORMULA**

NEITHER NEW NOR UTOPIAN

Perhaps the 8-bit metroidvania boom, which largely evolved on Japanese consoles and computers, was destined to end in 1989 along with Japan's Showa era. The top-down action-RPG began to push aside the side-scrolling platform adventure beginning with 1989's *Willow* for NES. Although, as *Neutopia* demonstrates, it took a little while for developers to come up with a direction for their efforts beyond "cut-rate *Zelda* imitation."

Developed by Hudson for TurboGrafx-16, *Neutopia* adds little to the genre besides slightly nicer graphics. It comes off as a case of Nintendo's competitor reverse-engineering the original *Zelda* to figure out how this whole thing works—a technical exercise, not an attempt to explore new ideas. Perhaps its greatest innovation is its structure. Rather than dropping players into a truly open world, it divides the adventure into four zones based on the elemental treasure stashed there, grants the protagonist magical powers, and generally locks the gameplay progression into a linear sequence.

Those visuals do deserve credit. This was the prettiest of the *Zelda* clones to this point, with a crisp style that would be echoed in Super NES games like *Lagoon* and *Paladin's Quest*. Although far more limited in nature than *Zelda*, Neutopia also has the benefit of being much more direct in its goals and secrets, eschewing the often fruitless searching and fluky luck required to complete older 8-bit titles in favor of clarity and intuitive design.

While it did little to truly innovate within this genre, it did mark a sort of relaunch for a genre that had briefly subsided, and this helped prime the pump for some real advances in the *Zelda*-esque action-RPG space. That includes the third *Zelda* game, a return to this format that would become one of the most structurally influential games of all time—up to and including directly inspiring the definitive entry in the metroidvania genre: *Symphony of the Night*. Would we have had *A Link to the Past* (and therefore *Symphony of the Night*) without *Neutopia*? Well, yeah, probably so. But even *Ys*, arguably the pinnacle of the top-down *Hydlide*-alikes, had seemingly gone side-scrolling by this point. So, it's meaningful to see this soft reboot for a form of gameplay that, for a while, seemed to be in danger of vanishing entirely. *M*

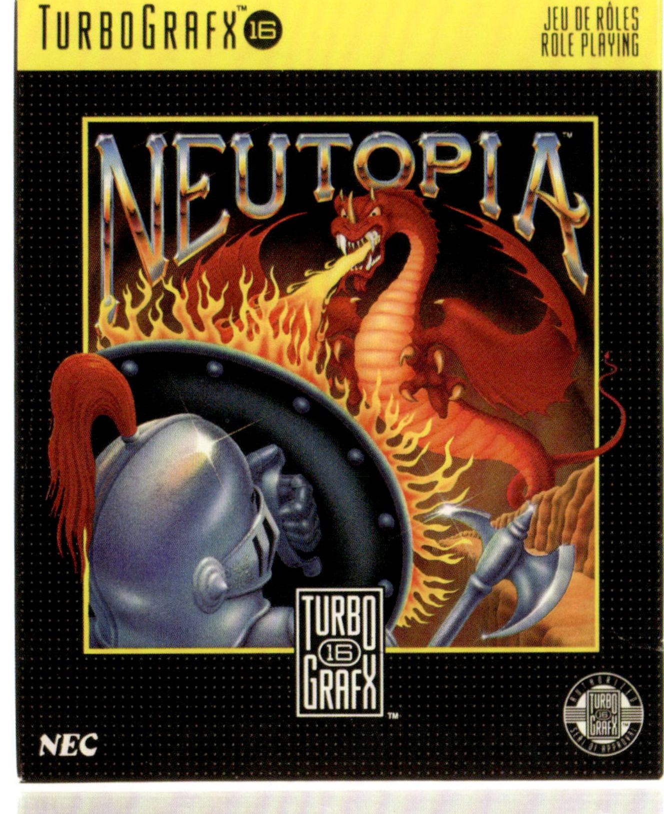

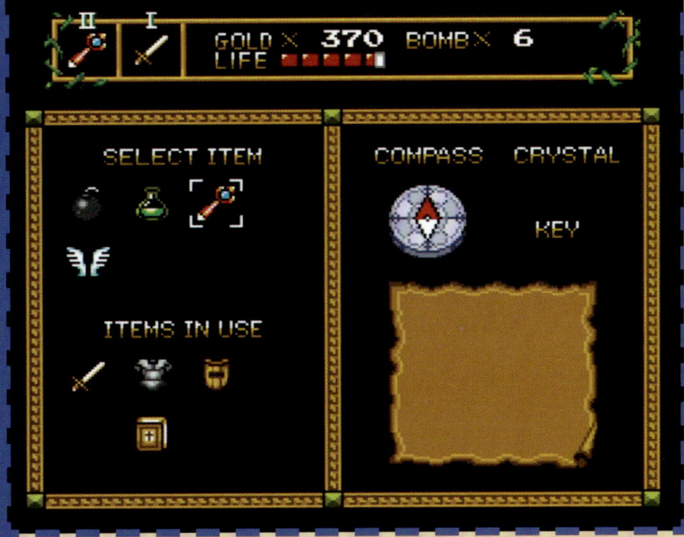

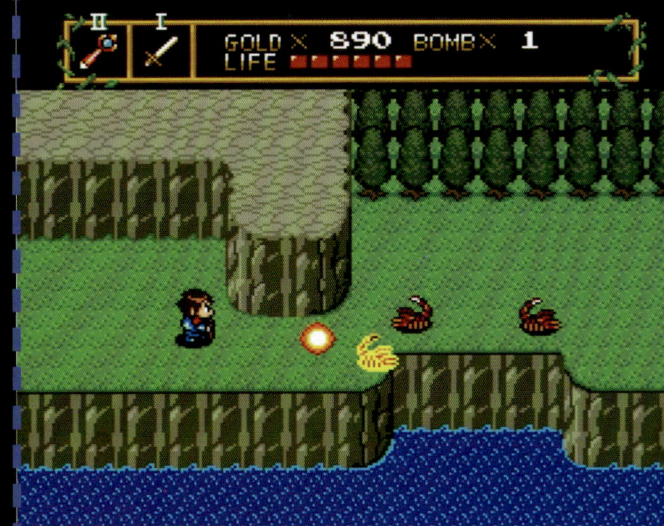

METROIDVANIA TIMELINE 1990

The 1980s came to an end with a startling development: a year without a single game release in the metroidvania mold. The closest anyone came to publishing an exploratory platform-action role-playing adventure came in the form of Capcom's *Gargoyle's Quest* for Game Boy, which consisted of a series of self-contained and generally linear dungeons dotted across the landscape of a top- down, RPG-style world map. Close, but not exactly a format that represents the metroidvania's platonic ideal.

The action-RPG trend that had dominated the NES and Famicom just a couple of years ago had turned out, by all appearances, to be nothing more than a flash in the pan. A fad. A passing flirtation with big ideas that publishers had then abandoned in pursuit of a sure hit. And yet...

As with so many seeming fads, the metroidvania hadn't been forsaken. It had simply shifted in nature. There was plenty of metroidvania spirit to be found in the games of 1990, but it felt as though the genre had been flung into a centrifuge to spin out its individual components. Platform action games were content to be pure platform action games, while action-RPGs reverted wholly to the classic *Legend of Zelda*–mode.

Those barriers and distinctions weren't as resolute as they first appeared, though. *Super Mario World*, which inaugurated Nintendo's powerful, new 16-bit Super NES console, appeared at the end of the year to hint at the shape of things to come in the decade ahead. A crisp action game spanning dozens of standalone stages, *Super Mario World* also contained secrets and alternate routes across its open-ended, interconnected, ever-evolving world. Despite lacking a single role-playing element, it nevertheless invited exploration and retained persistent changes.

The metroidvania hadn't died; it was simply biding its time to return in a more expansive, nuanced, and subtle form. The 1990s would see the genre reach true maturation. It just needed to take a brief side excursion in order to get there. But isn't that the entire point of a metroidvania? M

TIMELINE OF EVENTS

January

A Boy and His Blob
A puzzle-oriented adventure from the creator of *Pitfall!*, *A Boy and His Blob* contains tons of charm and interesting gameplay ideas, but it feels small and underbaked next to its predecessors.

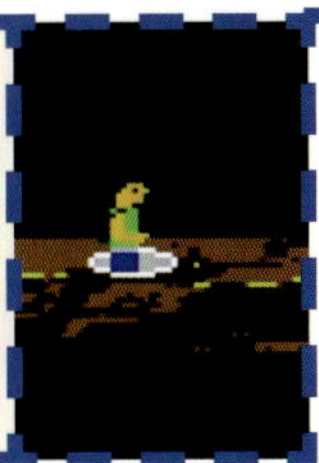

March

Snake's Revenge
A *Metal Gear* sequel created specifically for the U.S. market, *Snake's Revenge* played down stealth and nonlinearity in favor of focusing on more straightforward action and combat.

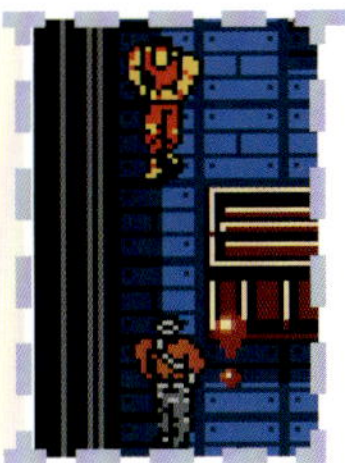

April

Crystalis
A fast-paced action-RPG in the *Ys* style, *Crystalis* worked around an elemental combat system that made gear and stat gains less valuable than simply grasping elemental affinities.

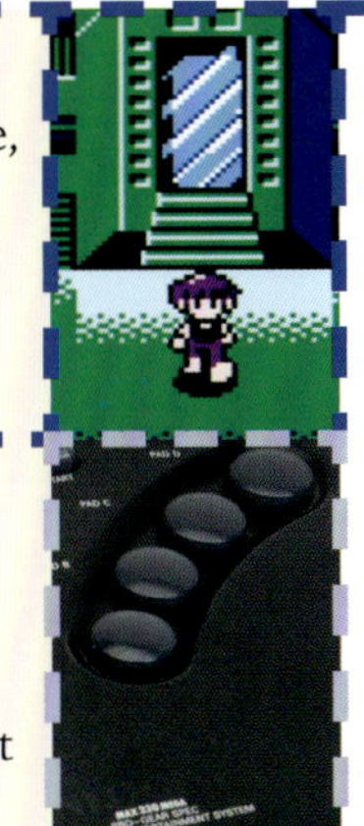

Neo Geo AES
SNK entered the console space by bringing its powerful, flexible MVS hardware home. This pricey console raised the bar for audio and visuals but was limited by its arcade orientation.

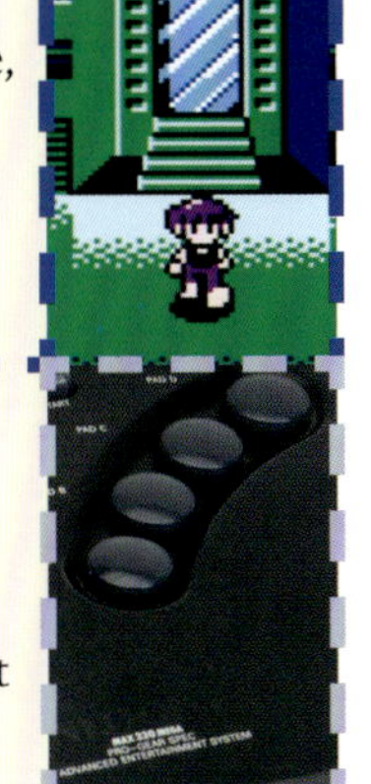

May

Gargoyle's Quest
For its first portable release, Capcom adapted its hit arcade platform shooter *Ghosts 'N Goblins* into an RPG-inspired adventure centered around the red demon that had vexed so many fans.

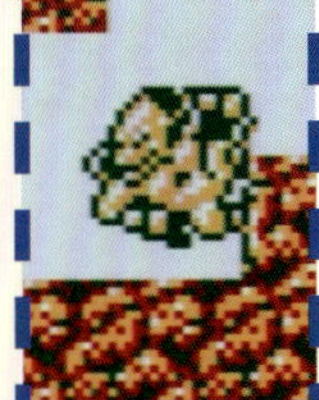

July

Metal Gear 2
By contrast to Snake's Revenge, this proper Metal Gear sequel builds on everything good about the original, delivering perhaps the most sophisticated 8-bit action game of all time.

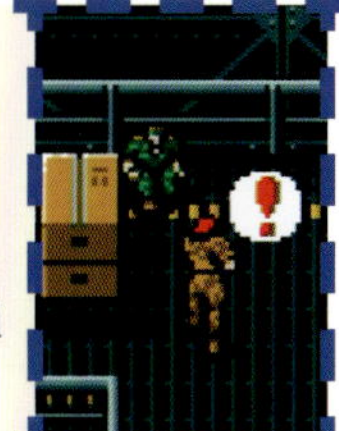

October

The Secret of Monkey Island
LucasArts took the menu-driven graphical adventure style of *Portopia* to the pinnacle of its form with this gorgeous adventure that always treated the player fairly and with respect.

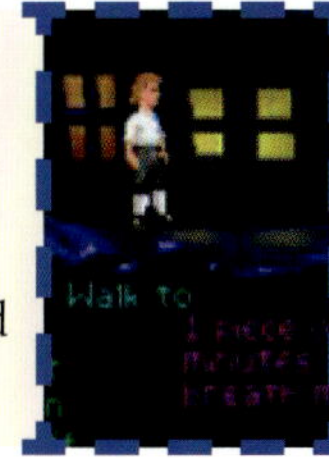

November

Super Famicom
The advent of a next-gen Nintendo console meant that most Japanese developers would begin focusing their most innovative efforts in the 16-bit space—including metroidvania games.

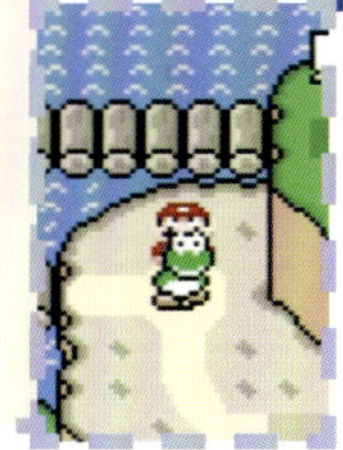

December

Game Gear
Landing at a comfortable midpoint between Lynx's power and Game Boy's software support, the Game Gear was essentially a miniaturized Master System and hosted tons of great games.

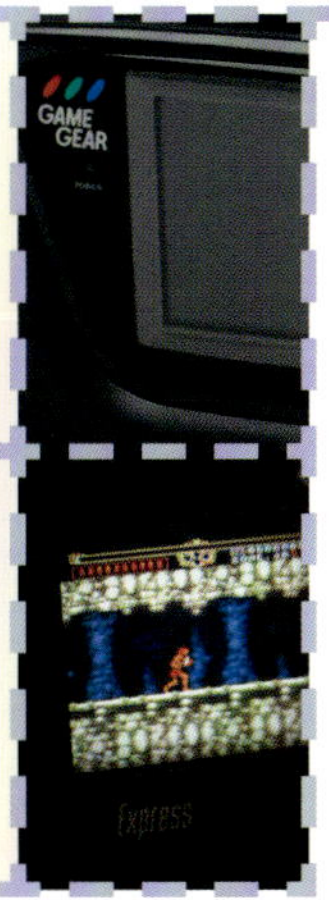

TurboExpress
Meanwhile, NEC scaled down its TurboGrafx-16 hardware into portable form, allowing owners to take their HuCard games on the go—though of course CD-ROM fans were out of luck.

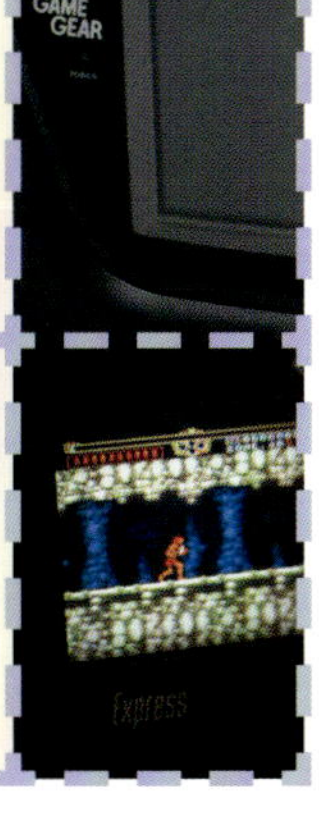

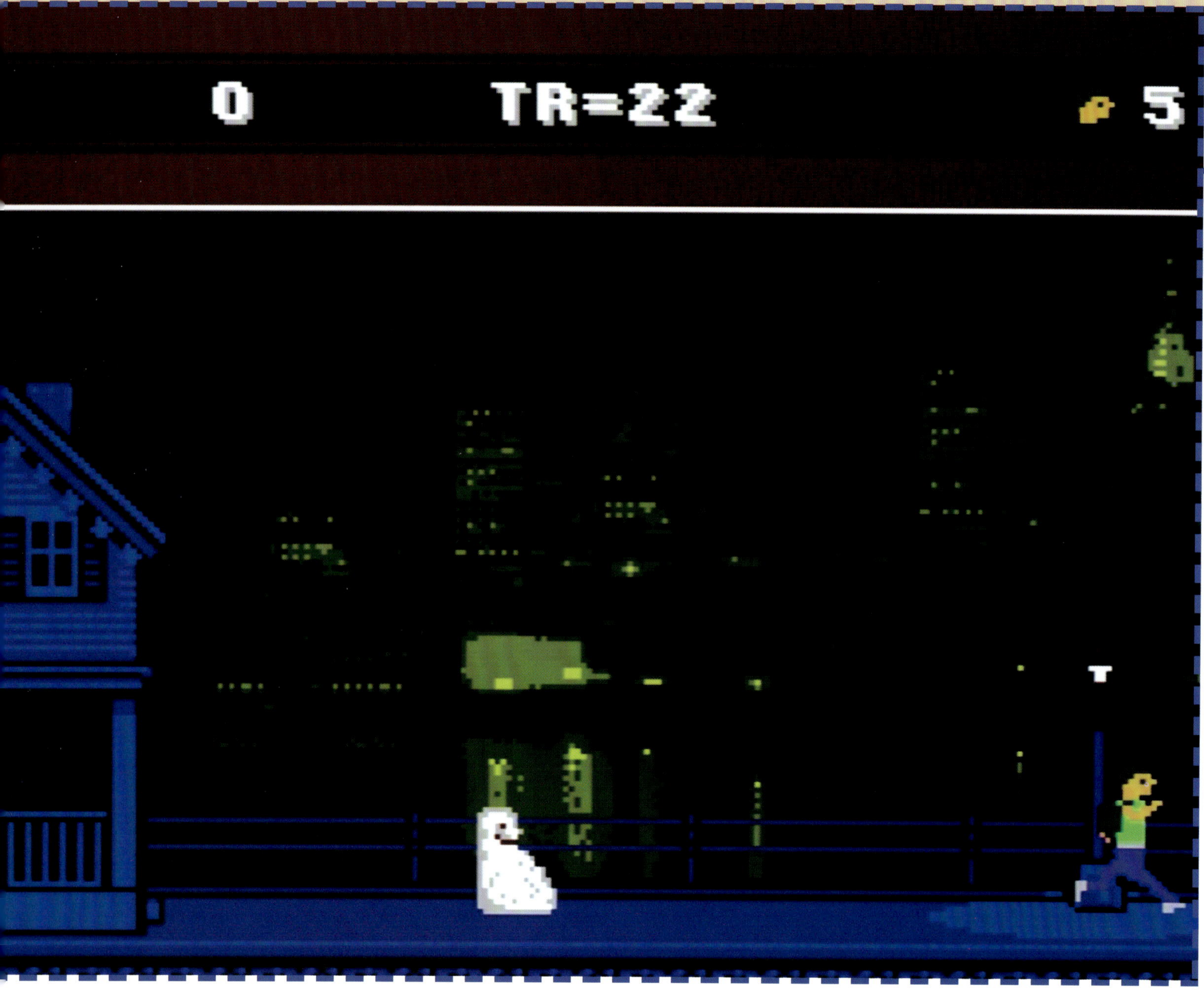

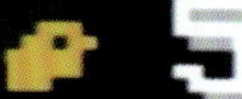

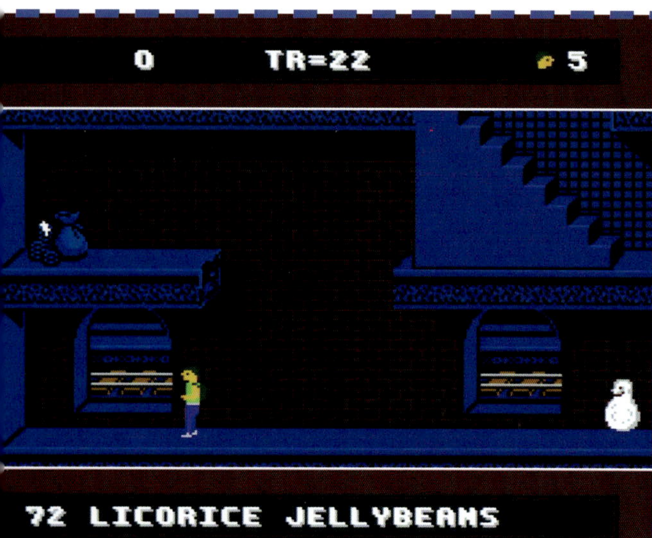

A BOY AND HIS BLOB

PLATFORM: **NES / FAMICOM**
DEV: **IMAGINEERING** | PUB: **ABSOLUTE ENTERTAINMENT**
INITIAL RELEASE DATE: **JAN. 1990**

NOTABLE FOR: *ADDING A PUZZLE DYNAMIC TO PITFALL II*

PITFALLEN

The surge of exploratory platform action games that emerged from Japanese studios throughout the late 1980s slowed to a trickle as the '90s began. This isn't to say that they disappeared, necessarily, but simply that the ones that carried the trend forward suddenly had to do a lot of heavy lifting. I'm not sure that *A Boy and His Blob* (or rather, *David Crane's A Boy and His Blob: Trouble on Blobolonia,* to be formal) pulls off that heavy lifting as well as you might hope. It's an interesting game, but also a messy one that suffers from frustrating, archaic design choices.

The game certainly offers a compelling hook for canny metroidvania-loving observers right there on the box. It promises a return to form for the master of the format after a half-decade absence: David Crane, the creator of *Pitfall!* and *Pitfall II*. This game was built on the tenets of game design he had established way back on the Atari 2600. Exciting stuff!

With *Pitfall!*, Crane had created the first proper action platformer to take place in an open-ended world built around complex interconnections. With its sequel, he opened things up even more by building on the *y*-axis as well as the *x*, removing the time limit, and doing away with the concept of lives entirely. With *Pitfall II*, he effectively created a game that anyone could finish but only a truly skilled player could complete perfectly. When the console market imploded in America, Crane moved his development efforts from the Atari 2600 to home computers. Soon after, he moved himself from Activision to Absolute Entertainment. And, with *A Boy and His Blob*, Crane and his team at Absolute designed their first NES release from the ground up.

As a programmer and designer, Crane had become a legend for his ability to coax unparalleled performance from the 2600's creaky hardware and to cajole the Commodore 64 to do unprecedented things. One could be forgiven for assuming that he would achieve similar miracles on the NES. After all, look at what British studio Rare Ltd. had accomplished on the NES after making the leap from the ZX Spectrum, where they had commanded a sort of savant reputation akin to Crane's. Alas, no. *A Boy and His Blob* does push the *Pitfall!* concept into new territory, but it does so haltingly. It doesn't even properly belong under the

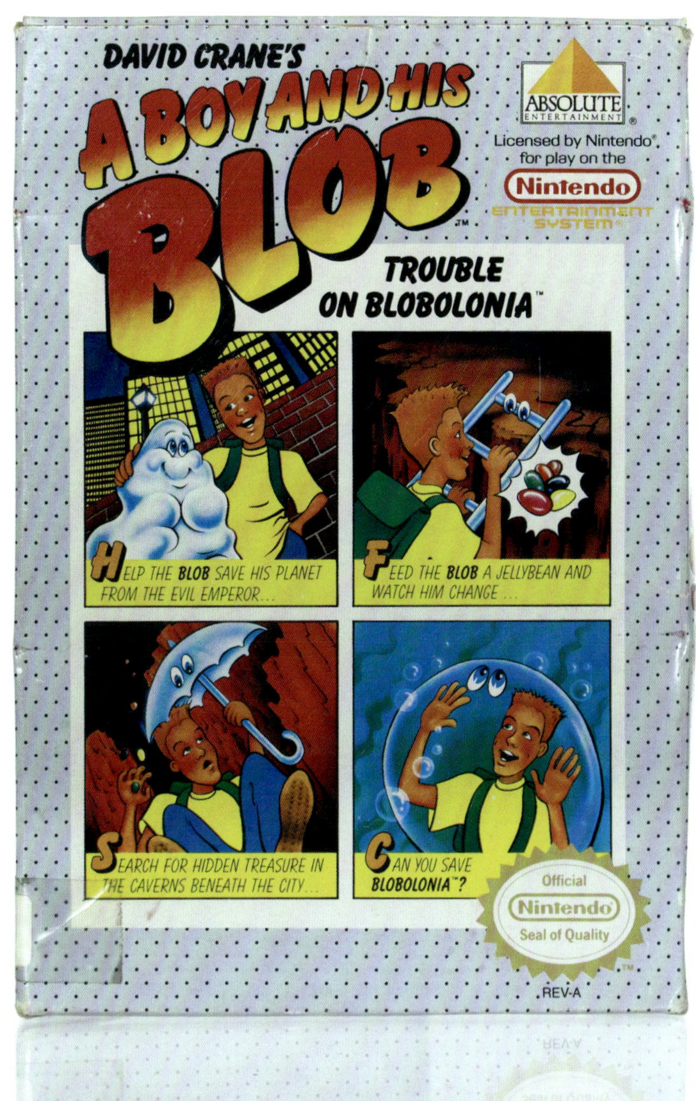

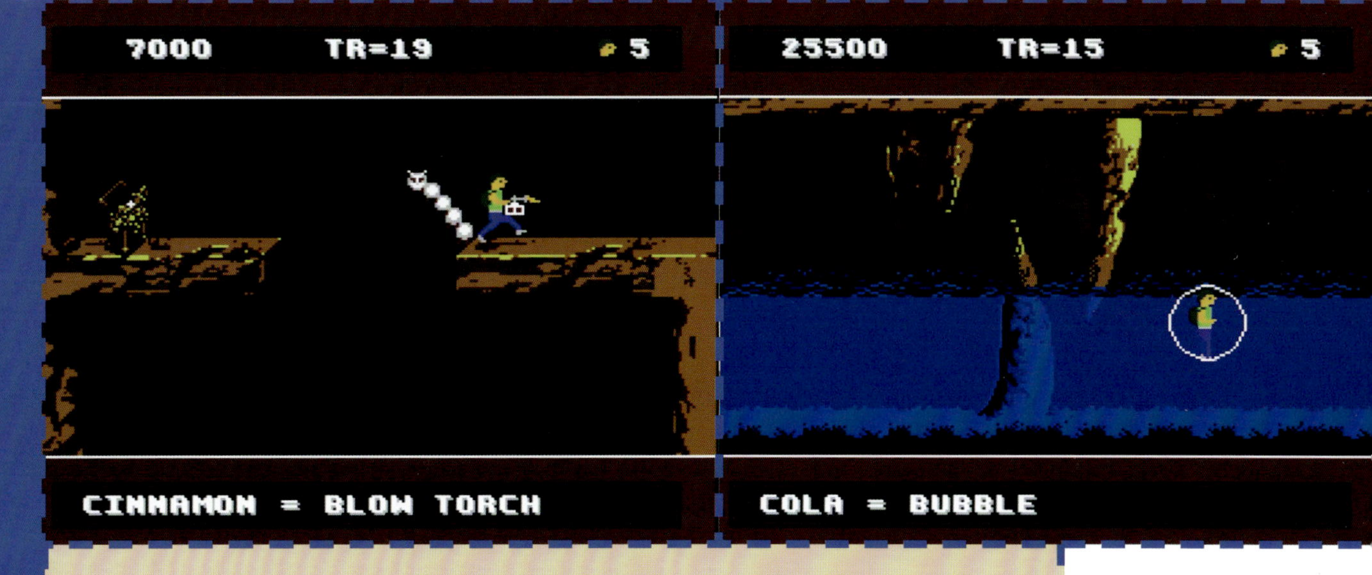

metroidvania header, because you don't gain new powers or abilities during the game—or rather, the handful of new abilities that you do acquire amount to a mandatory key to unlock the back half of the adventure. On top of that, it's entirely possible to screw up so badly by overlooking modest details or misusing your limited resources that you soft-lock the game into an unwinnable state. Meanwhile, the process of completing the game amounts to a series of trial-and-error experiments that would have felt a lot less frustrating if *A Boy and His Blob* had retained *Pitfall II*'s infinite lives mechanic.

Despite these failings, *A Boy and His Blob* does some interesting things with the genre, introducing an element of puzzle-solving that would normally be reserved for single-screen PC action games into an open-ended multidirectional adventure. The overall effect feels akin to playing something like early computer and NES puzzle-action games like *Solomon's Key* or *Flappy*. The difference here is that, rather than each screen consisting of an entire stage, every screen is part of a larger, interconnected world. Rather than needing to solve multiple puzzles or perform several actions in succession to clear a screen, as in classic puzzle platformers, you generally need to resolve a single situation. This could amount to slipping past a deadly creature, making a dangerous leap, or maneuvering around a hazard that could disadvantage you in some way. At the same time, many screens contain no apparent threats or challenges, existing as dead ends or as throughways that connect one area to another. The game shines when you encounter puzzles that require you to work your way across multiple screens. Maybe you need to acquire an inaccessible item by using a tool to leap from below, or perhaps you need to slip past a stubborn monster by performing cartoonish actions that defy real-world physics.

> **DESPITE ITS FAILINGS,** *A BOY AND HIS BLOB* DOES SOME INTERESTING THINGS WITH THE GENRE, INTRODUCING AN ELEMENT OF PUZZLE-SOLVING THAT WOULD NORMALLY HAVE BEEN RESERVED FOR SINGLE-SCREEN PC ACTION GAMES INTO A MORE OPEN-ENDED MULTI-SCREEN ADVENTURE FORMAT.

A Boy and His Blob unfurls its action-oriented puzzles across an extensive subterranean space that spans multiple screens on both axes before moving players to a more linear finale. Unusually, it arms players with nearly all the solutions they need to complete the adventure from the outset in the form of a bag of jellybeans. These beans themselves do nothing on their own. But toss one to the player's computer-controlled companion character—the eponymous Blob, a lumpy white critter that tags along wherever the Boy goes—and interesting things begin to happen. The Blob loves candy, despite suffering what appears to be a severe allergic reaction to it. When the Blob eats a jellybean, its body shifts into a different shape, which varies depending on the flavor of the candy. The Blob's transformations largely have a "dad joke" element of punniness about them—an apple jellybean turns the Blob into a working tire jack (that is, "applejack") while a tangerine bean turns him into a trampoline (because of the words' assonance). While these puns made localization and cultural adaptation as difficult for the translators as the baseball puzzle in *Zork* and the monkey wrench pun in *The Secret of Monkey Island*, the groaners fit the cartoon logic of the whole thing.

Not only is the Blob an indestructible goofball that squashes, deforms, and transforms, it also has powers taken straight from *Looney Tunes* cartoons. A punch-flavored jellybean, for example, creates a hole—a hole punch, you see—which basically turns the Blob into the absence of something: a temporary hole that you can place on floors to allow the Boy to drop through to the level below. You need to bend logic a bit at times to survive *A Boy and His Blob*, but when you bypass a seemingly impossible hazard, or in fact skip it altogether, by decrypting the joke book logic behind a Blob power's interaction with the world, it makes you feel pretty clever.

Unfortunately, these powers also feed into the game's worst design instinct: the need for trial-and-error experimentation. Some solutions are a little too esoteric, meaning that unless you use a strategy guide, you'll be forced to try things that will unavoidably

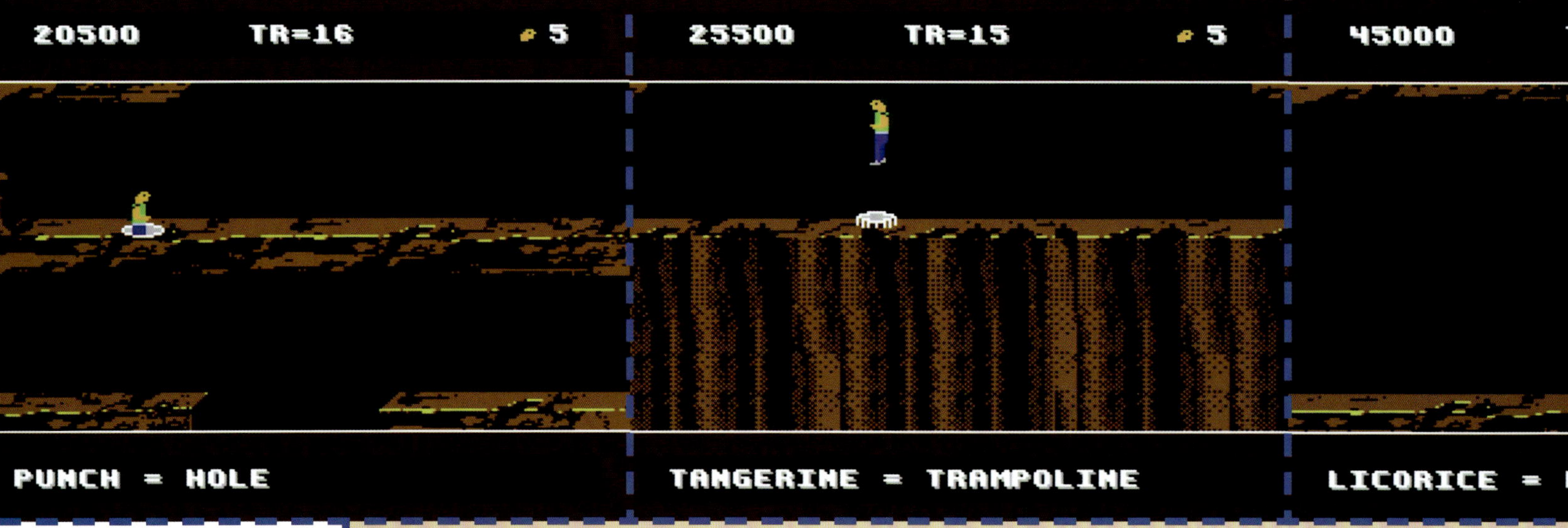

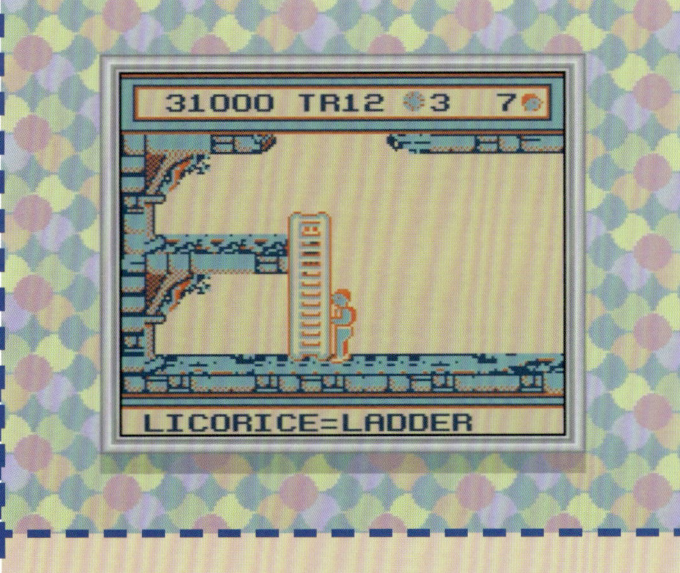

THIS COLUMN: A BOY AND HIS BLOB SAW A GAME BOY SEQUEL AND A "REMAKE" FOR WII, BUT BOTH LACKED THE ORIGINAL'S SCALE.

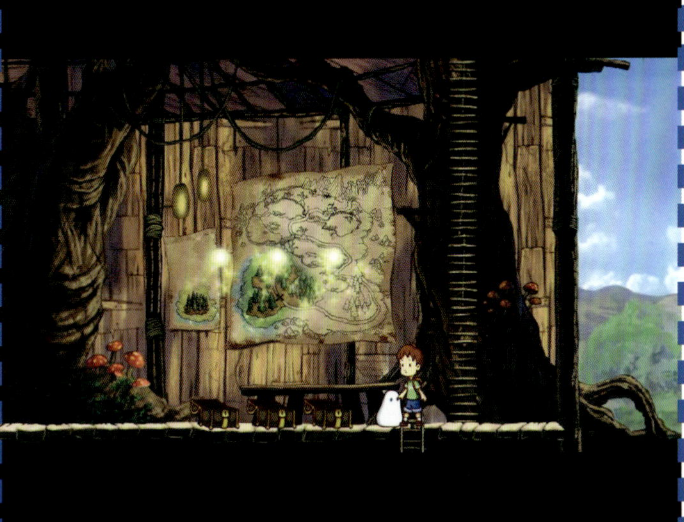

kill you while looking for the correct approach. The awkward hit detection between the Boy and hazards around him adds to the difficulty. This happens as early as the game's first real puzzle. Once you dash from the Boy's home and venture underground, you quickly encounter a dead end. Although you can see inaccessible spaces below you, which suggests that there's more to the subway tunnels than you can actually access on your own, you'll quickly discover that your only means of progress is to create a hole in the lowest level of the subway floor and drop into the caverns below. That's a fine introduction to the game's cartoon logic…but the layout of the caverns beneath the subway means that you have better than even odds of unwittingly deploying a punch jellybean over a space with a ceiling so high that your fall will immediately kill you.

A lot of the game plays out like this, and *A Boy and His Blob* derives most of its overall playtime from the way it deliberately kills you and forces you to restart the adventure from scratch. It's a short game, but it effectively requires you to solve each puzzle you encounter the hard way, run out of lives, and replay the next game while moving through the required steps by rote. Worse, while you can't travel to the Blob's homeworld and complete the game until you collect a special bag of jellybeans hidden in the underground caverns, you also need to collect additional items to make use of the unique transformation unlocked by the supplemental beans. Without access to the full transformation, you can't safely pass through the fields of Blobolonia and the infinite array of falling (sigh) cherry bombs. However, there's no way to know that you need to make this extra stop en route to the other planet. So, unless you go out of your way to collect vitamins at the pharmacy several screens beyond the subway entrance, you'll end up stuck helplessly, unable to move along to the game's final sequence.

Granted, you can complete *A Boy and His Blob* with all treasures collected in about fifteen minutes if you know what you're doing. But the prospect of ending up in this dead end lends to the underbaked feeling of the game. *A Boy and His Blob* has lots of clever moments, and exploring by solving devious puzzles has enormous appeal. But, ultimately, it doesn't have enough of those moments. Whether due to memory constraints or time and budget limitations, *A Boy and His Blob* feels much smaller than *Pitfall!* and *Pitfall II* WayForward Technologies would fix the scale issue 20 years later with is lovely remake for Nintendo Wii, but that came at the expense of this version's freedom of exploration and the sense of being lost in a vast, interconnected, underground world. In the end, *A Boy and His Blob* feels like a tentative foray into a puzzle-focused format for the metroidvania genre that never came to fruition. M

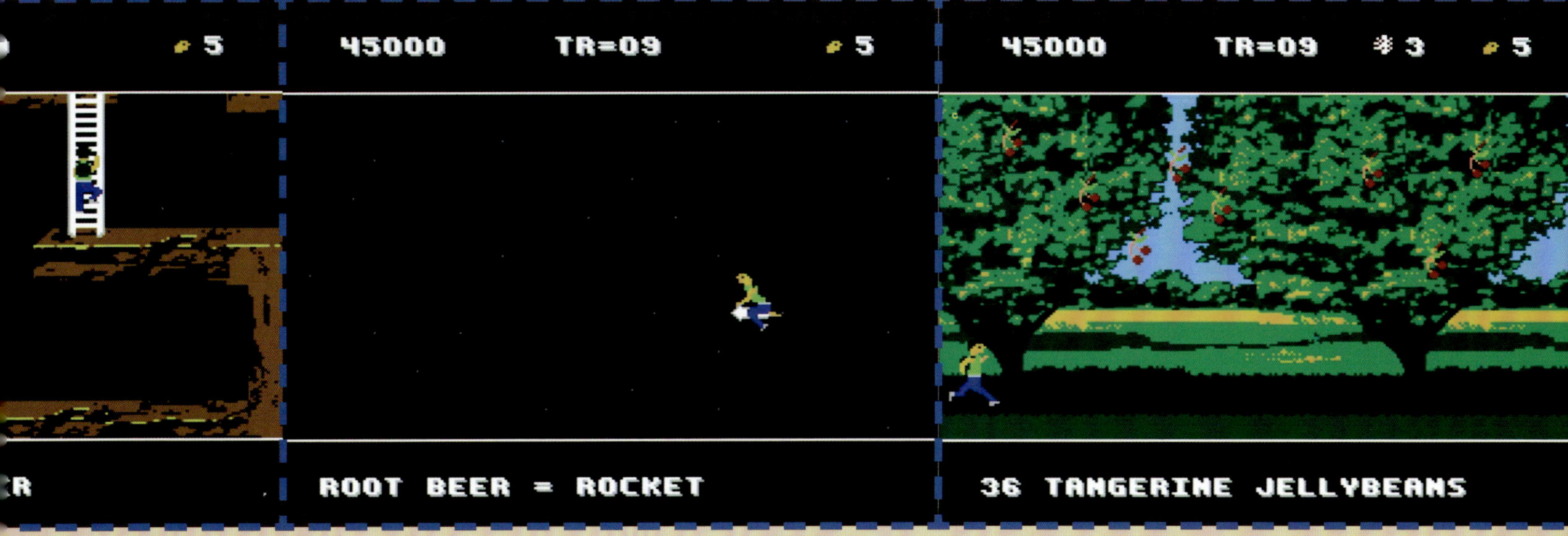

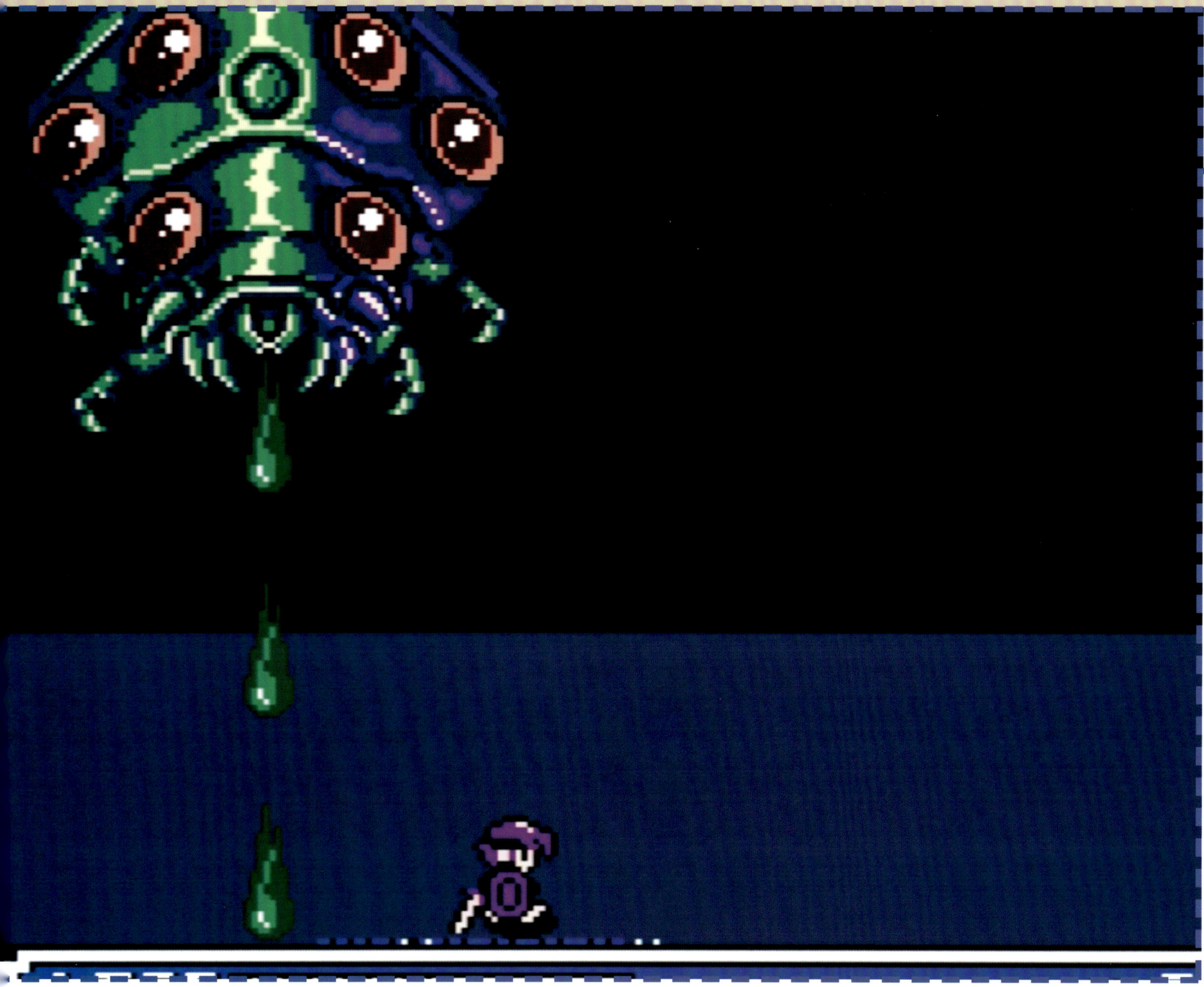

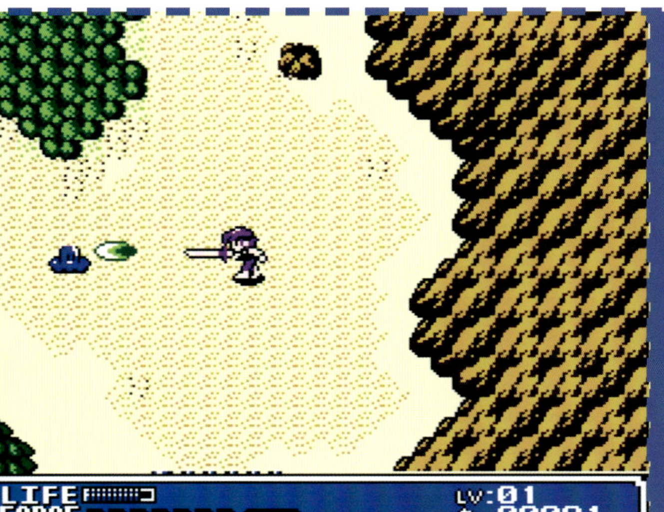

CRYSTALIS

PLATFORM: **FAMICOM / NES**
DEV: **SNK** | PUB: **SNK**
INITIAL RELEASE DATE: **APRIL 1990**

NOTABLE FOR: **UPDATING THE YS FORMULA FOR THE '90S**

ELEMENTALLY, MY DEAR WATSON

Crystalis by SNK pushed the boundaries of action-RPG design much further than anything that had come before. It truly feels like an RPG that happens to involve a lot of action, and it established the tone for the genre in the years to come. A big part of what makes *Crystalis* stand out has to do with the source of its inspiration. Whereas *Neutopia* and *Willow* largely took their design cues from *The Legend of Zelda*, *Crystalis* looked instead toward the work of Nihon Falcom to create a damn good *Ys*-alike.

The irony that SNK crafted this great evolution of the original *Ys* games as Falcom fumbled around with an attempt to bring the *Ys* sensibility into a *Zelda II* or *Romancia* framework cannot be overstated. But make no mistake; *Crystalis* is not a rigid, literal take on *Ys* (or *Hydlide*) the way pure derivatives like *Lagoon*, *Makai Hakkenden Shada*, or the *Xak* series would be. Yes, *Crystalis* unquestionably borrows the *Ys* framework, all the way down to its grid-based equipment and inventory system, and it admirably captures the breezy speed of vintage *Ys* in motion, but at the same time it moves away from simple bump combat.

The nameless protagonist of *Crystalis* dashes swiftly in eight directions, swings and thrusts his sword, and can even use magic and projectile attacks. Swords serve as the crux of *Crystalis*'s gameplay, including its core progression and world-gating. The hero's level has far less impact on the moment-to-moment gameplay than in *Ys*. Jumping up an experience level provides a modest improvement to your stats and endurance caps, but it doesn't cause you to leap immediately from overwhelmed to overpowered the way it does for Adol Christin. Rather, *Crystalis* adopts a strategy similar to one in *Willow* and uses your skill level as a metric for your sword skills. It's a less elegant approach overall, admittedly; whereas reaching a new level allowed *Willow* to wield a blade more capably in terms of his actual speed in action, it's all invisible boundaries and limitations here.

The hero of *Crystalis* simply can't damage certain enemies until his experience level reaches an arbitrary threshold. You also need to be at specific power levels to pass a handful of narrative barriers,

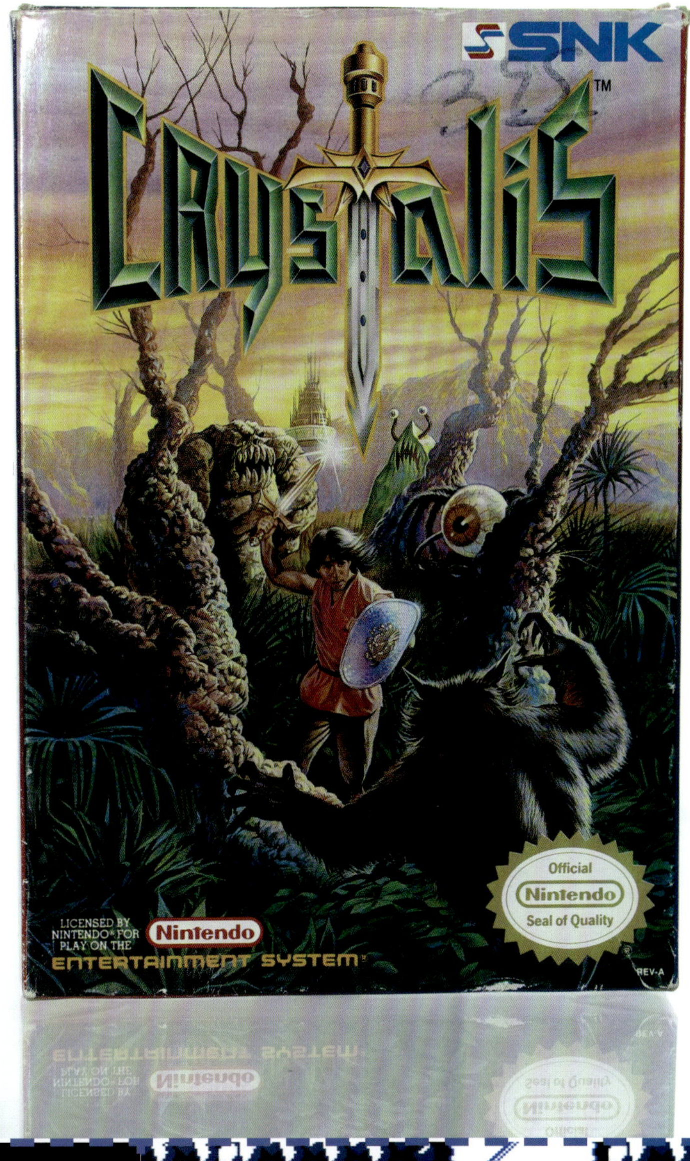

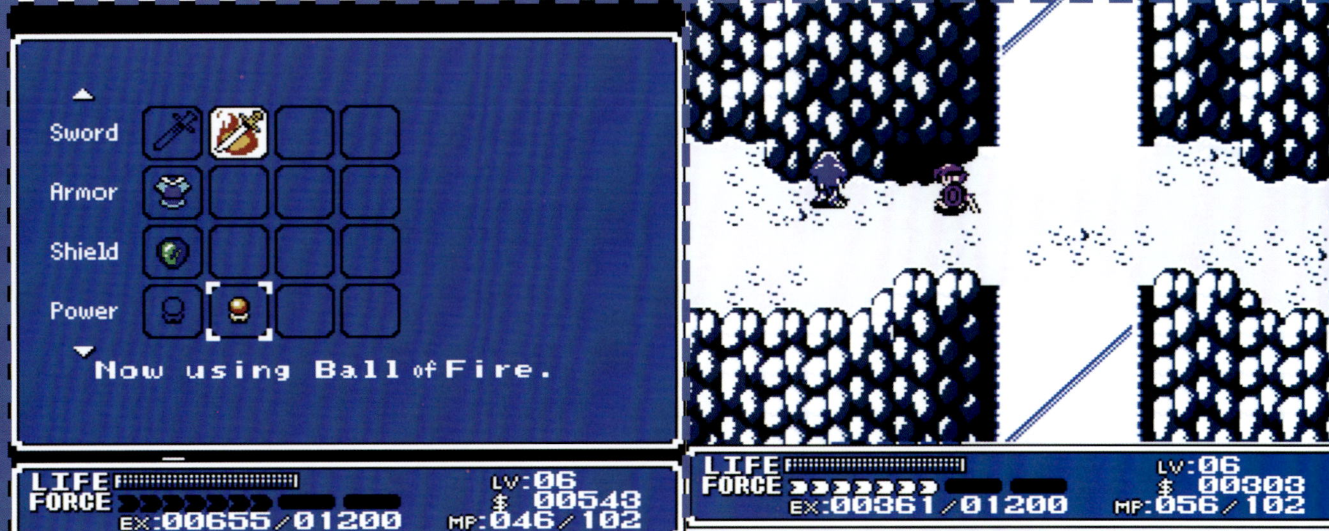

like the show of force against the apprentice outside the forest. Until you've cleared these mandatory stat requirements, you simply can't deal damage to enemies—your attacks will result in nothing more than a metallic tink that denotes uselessness. This results in a game that involves an awful lot of grinding for experi- ence—a component of the *Ys* game loop that *Crystalis* regrettably chose to carry forward.

Raw stats alone won't give you the power to defeat many enemies, though. The elemental nature of the swords you wield also factors in: fire, water, wind, and thunder. During the adventure, players acquire four different swords. These blades don't fall under traditional categories such as rapier, claymore, broadsword, etc.; rather, each one has an elemental affinity. At a basic level, each sword offers approximately equal attack strength to the others. To attack effectively, you need to use a sword whose elemental nature suits the current situation. Each element hits hard against specific monsters and bosses, while being largely ineffectual against others. The Sword of Thunder delivers devastating damage to water-aligned enemies, whereas the Sword of Fire barely affects them. The elements also allow you to break barriers that divide up the world: The Sword of Wind can shatter rocks, while the Sword of Fire can melt away sheets of ice, and so forth.

This approach sounds fairly rote by present-day standards, thanks to decades of other games that have relied on similar puzzle systems and elements. The *Final Fantasy* series (which debuted in Japan in 1987) made elemental magic a fundamental component of its gameplay as its heroes undertook a quest to recover and restore four elemental crystals. However, *Crystalis* is actually the first time an elemental system like this served as a core mechanic in an action-RPG; even *Hydlide* and *Ys* didn't make elemental affinity so central to their gameplay. Near the end of the game, the four swords ultimately merge into the final weapon—the eponymous omni-elemental blade Crystalis—which is the only power capable of felling the final boss.

RAW STATS ALONE

WON'T GIVE YOU THE POWER TO DEFEAT CERTAIN FOES. THE ELEMENTAL NATURE OF THE SWORDS YOU WIELD ALSO FACTORS IN: FIRE, WATER, WIND, AND THUNDER. RATHER THAN OFFER VARYING ATTACK POWER, YOUR FOUR SWORDS HIT THE ELEMENTAL WEAK POINTS OF THE MONSTERS YOU FACE.

Until you manage to reforge the weapons into their combined form, however, you need to rely on the specific capabilities of the swords you collect to allow you to overcome the threats you find along the way. Rather than replacing your blades with more powerful weapons, you instead acquire supplemental accessories that enhance each sword through three levels of force above the default. These bracelets and bands boost the strength of a specific blade, and they also allow you to fire more powerful projectile attacks by holding down the sword button to charge and release your sword's energy. It's a solid system, but it does come with a downside. Due to the limited interface control options inherent to the NES hardware, you have to spend a lot of time fishing around in the system menus. Every time you want to trade out your weapon for one of a different element, you need to jump into the menu and select that sword. Worse, because each enhancement accessory works specifically with a single weapon, you also need to juggle those in or- der to maintain your sword attack power as well.

It's an elegant system dogged by an inelegant interface, one rich with potential and fraught with inconvenience. Squaresoft would more or less lift *Crystalis*'s weapon concept wholesale a few years later for their Super NES action-RPG *Secret of Mana*—a fair cop, given that game's relationship to *Final Fantasy*—while streamlining the upgrade system and introducing a revolutionary overlay-style menu mechanic to reduce the amount of time players lost to fumbling around a separate menu screen. (Of course, *Secret of Mana* also ended up suffering from its own grind-related mechanical shortcomings, but that's a story for the next volume.)

At the time of its debut, *Crystalis* gave fans a preview of several iterative innovations that the action-RPG would experience over the course of the exciting 16-bit era that had just begun to take proper focus in Japan during 1990. In fact, it was a game so good that Nintendo themselves would remake it, clumsily, for the Game Boy Color a decade later: the true testament of quality.

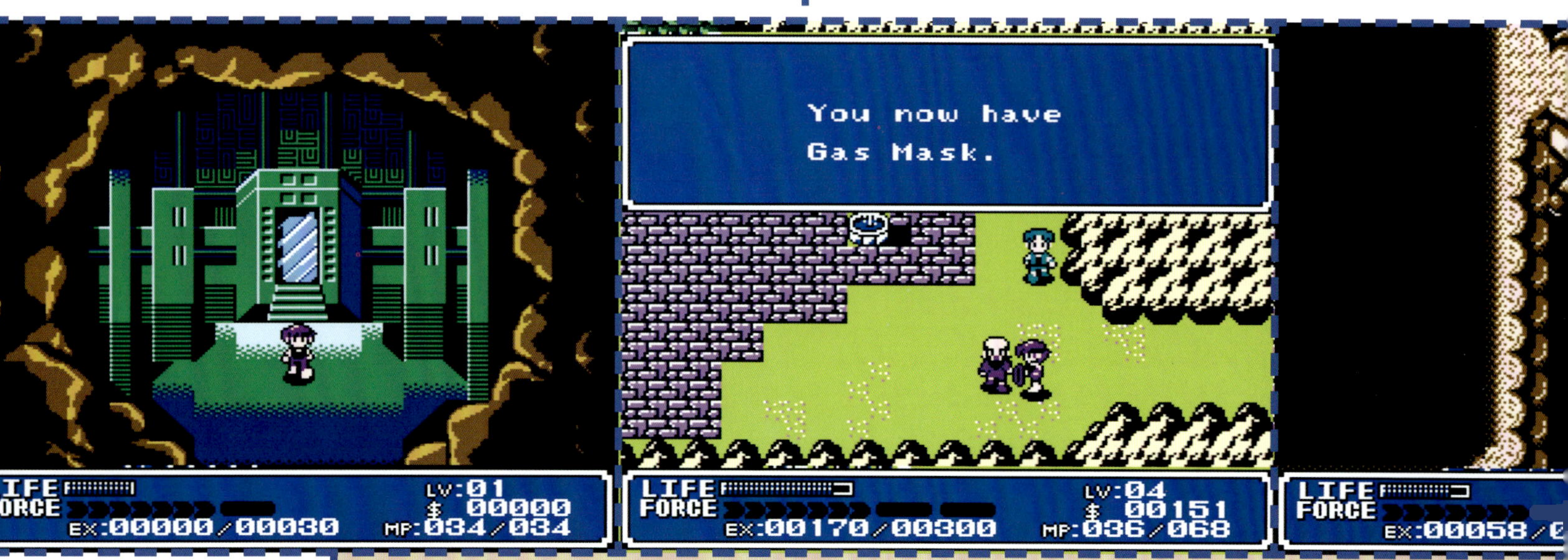

SUPER MARIO WORLD

Another *Mario* game? Yes, this book wouldn't be complete without a look at one final descendant of *Donkey Kong*, which shipped in Japan alongside the 16-bit Super Famicom in November 1990. After *Super Mario Bros. 3* more or less proclaimed the demise of metroidvania evolution on 8-bit consoles by demonstrating the appeal of a well-de- signed platform action game with no persistence and no aspirations of role-playing elements, *Super Mario World* presents a peace offering. Despite consisting of several dozen linear, standalone action stages, Mario's first 16-bit adventure took place in (as the title indicates) a world. Completing stages in *Super Mario World* doesn't simply move our hero another step closer to his goal of rescuing the princess once again; it also opens new paths throughout the world.

Mario's progress here unfolds visually through a world map, which expands on the simple board game–like level selection spaces of *Super Mario Bros. 3* to become a single, interconnected realm that shifts and transforms over the course of the quest. Complete a stage and multiple paths may open as a bridge collapses or a cliff crumbles, with the built-in save battery recording Mario's impact on the world permanently across play sessions. Completing certain tasks effects lasting changes within the levels you play, creating new blocks that act as platforms, barriers, or power-up opportunities. And on top of that, many levels contain multiple exits, inviting you to replay those stages in an exploratory mindset.

It's not a proper metroidvania, mind you. Mario himself never grows in capabilities beyond whatever power-ups he manages to snag along the way, and those powers vanish immediately if Mario dies or takes damage from an enemy. Much of his progress—and uncovering most secrets—depends not on his own innate powers but rather on the assistance of his trusty dinosaur pal Yoshi, whose additional skills expand Mario's moves, especially when used with the temporary power-ups you collect. Still, despite its fundamental lack of character growth and its subdivided world, *Super Mario World* incorporates a proper quest-like structure to its otherwise pure action. This format would become the template for action games half a decade later as 3D platformers further blurred the boundary between the concepts of action and adventure.

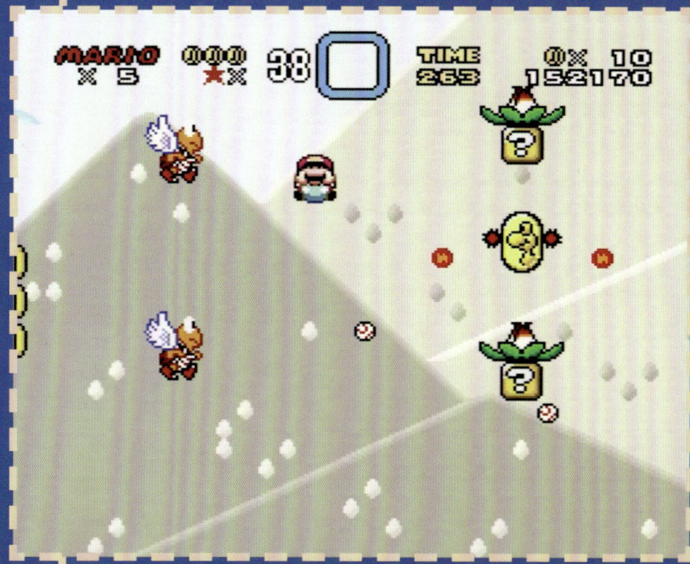

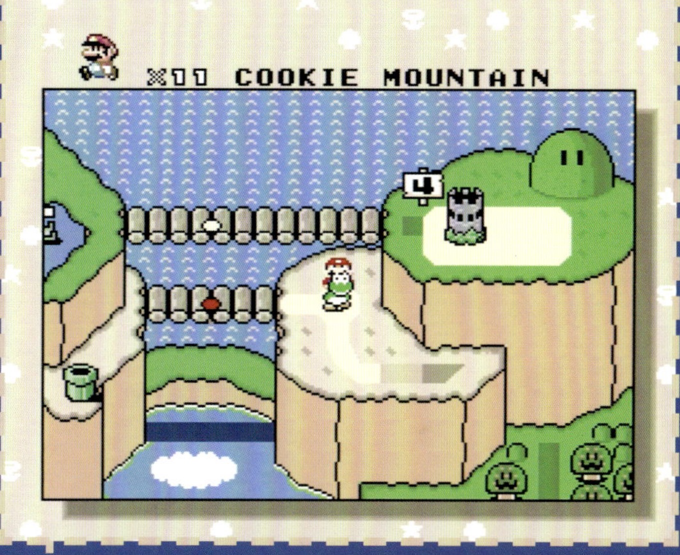

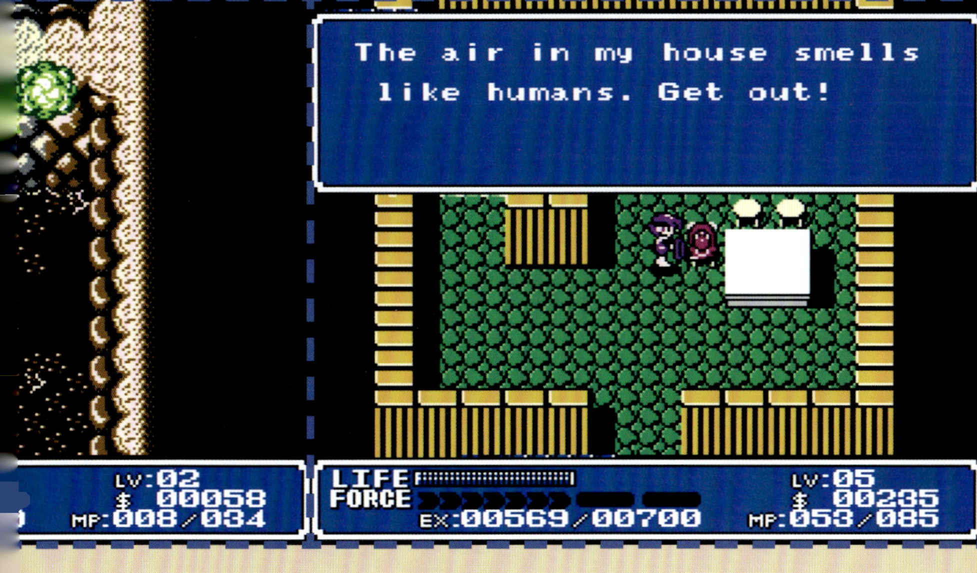

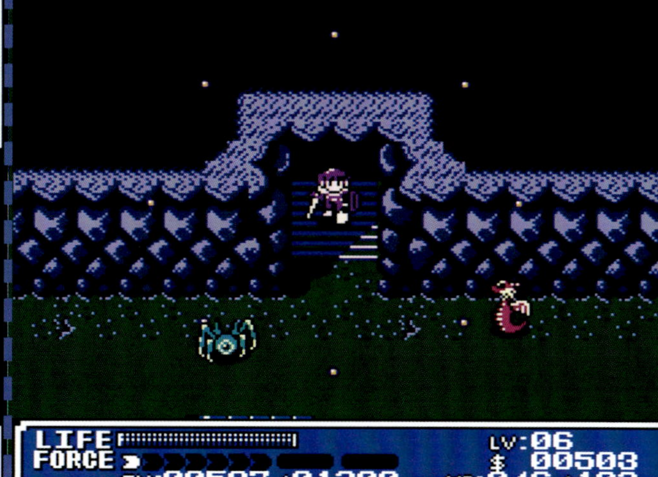

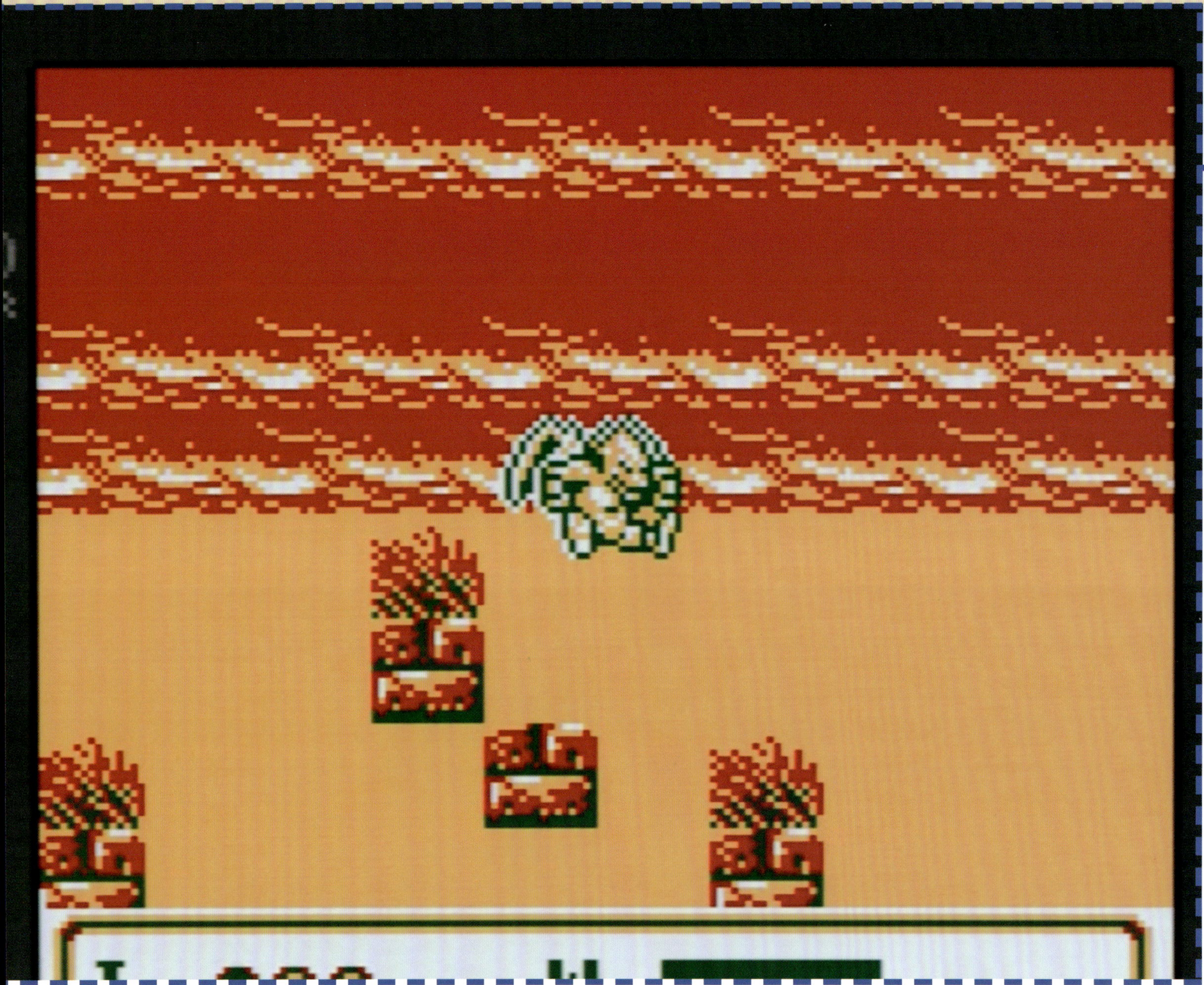

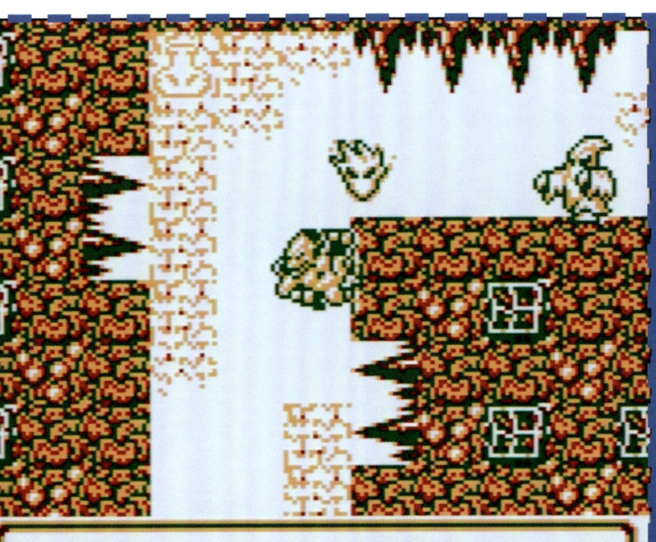

© Capcom

GARGOYLE'S QUEST

PLATFORM: **GAME BOY**
DEV: **CAPCOM** | PUB: **CAPCOM**
INITIAL RELEASE DATE: **MAY 1990**

DEMONSTRABLE PROGRESS

Ghosts 'N Goblins meets *Metroid* and *'Vania*? Well, not quite, but you can kind of see how Capcom's development team was angling for something along those lines with *Gargoyle's Quest*. An unlikely creation on multiple levels, *Gargoyle's Quest* demonstrates Capcom in peak form for the 8-bit era. The company made its debut in portable gaming on the Game Boy, having springboarded there by leaping off the shoulders of its cash cow, *Ghosts 'N Goblins*. Capcom could have simply published a direct conversion of its *Ghosts 'N Goblins* series to the Game Boy. At time, it was Capcom's single most successful franchise, challenged only by an ascendant *Mega Man*. Plenty of competing publishers and developers had taken a similar approach when initially foraying into the handheld space, as with Konami's *Castlevania: The Adventure* and Capcom's own *DuckTales*. But those efforts ended up being unpleasant to play compared to the console and arcade games that inspired them, even if they did boast nice graphics and audio. Still, they proved that, technically speaking, faithful ports from the NES to the Game Boy could exist. Thankfully, cooler heads prevailed and Capcom recognized that *Ghosts 'N Goblins*—a game about fast action, tiny projectiles, and split-second responses—would have made for a terrible experience on a tiny, monochromatic, passive-matrix LCD screen with poor visibility and severe display lag.

Thus, it turned out that the creators of *Ghosts 'N Goblins* didn't hate their players after all, despite their game's notoriously cruel difficulty level. Rather than subjecting the world to the most miserable version of their game imaginable, they instead went back to the drawing board and rebuilt the series in the form of a slow, methodical action-RPG better suited to Game Boy's limitations. Fortunately, they didn't have work from scratch. Back during the initial Famicom boom, Capcom's home team had cheated a bit on their assignment to convert *Pirate Ship Higemaru* from coin-op to console and came up with *Higemaru: Makaijima*, a crossover between *Higemaru* and *Ghosts 'N Goblins* that reimagined both of its component games into a sort of composite *Zelda*-clone.

Gargoyle's Quest builds on that precedent, dropping the *Higemaru* elements while embracing the aesthetics and monsters of

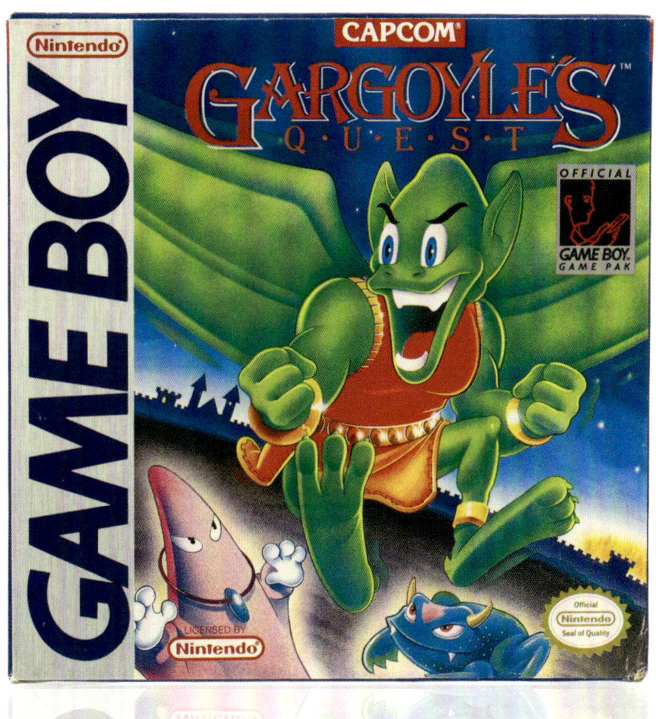

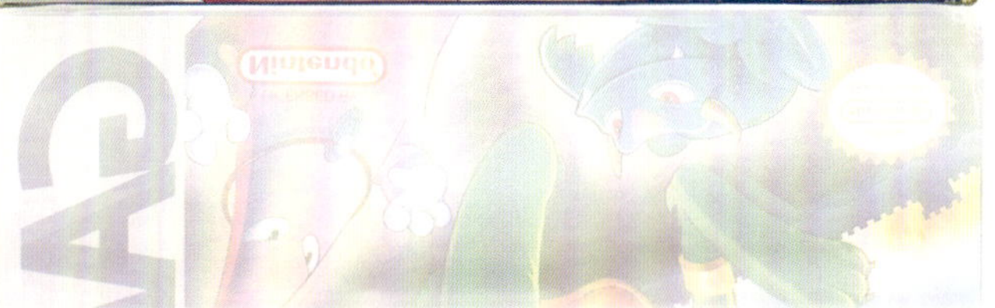

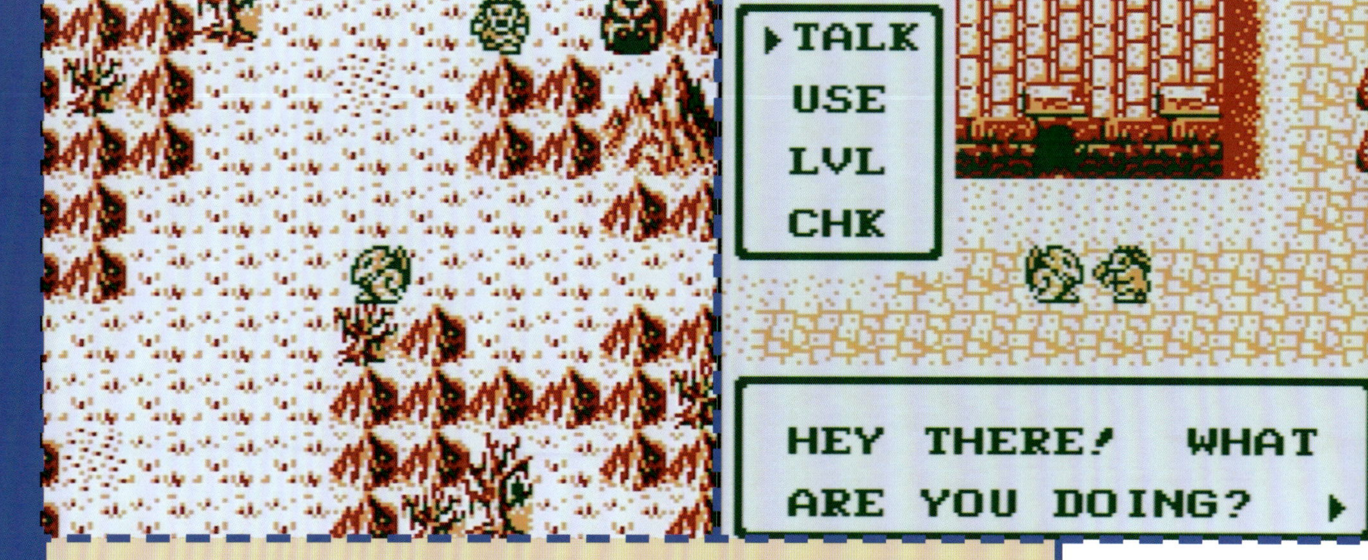

Ghosts 'N Goblins. It maintains that series' trademark side-scrolling format for the bulk of its action while limiting the top-down components to world navigation and NPC interactions. And it dares to place players in the role of the series' most reviled monster, the dreaded Red Arremer that represents the original *Ghosts 'N Goblins*'s infamous first sticking point. Here, though, rather than trying to outwit, outmaneuver, and outfight an Arremer, you play *as* an Arremer, a knight of the satanic realm named Firebrand.

Of course, a video game like this would be no fun without any sort of friction or challenge, so *Gargoyle's Quest* poses a question that no sensible person had ever thought to ask: What kinds of foes could be so dire that they represent a threat to one of the deadliest and most horrible monsters in the video game pantheon? The answer turns out to be "a great many," because just about every creature you encounter can wreck Firebrand if you're not careful. At least at first, anyway.

Firebrand does not begin this adventure as the deadly, Game Over–dealing force of hell fans knew from arcades and the NES. On the contrary, he's a sluggish little guy who commands pitiful attack power and range, can barely jump, and whose flight abilities limit him to hovering for a couple of seconds before plunging to the ground. Shocking as it may be to see the dread nemesis of *Ghosts 'N Goblins* protagonist Arthur reduced to an even weaker state than Arthur himself, it works. Specifically, it works within the context of a Game Boy action game. Firebrand's limited mobility and reduced speed give players more time to spot and react to threats despite the restrictive screen dimensions of the platform.

It neatly answers a question that no one had the opportunity to ask to this point: How do you make metroidvania design work on a portable system? The Game Boy was barely a year old, and developers working on the system had little time to get a handle on the logistics of reworking well-established genres like shooting and sports into portable form. Now, here's *Gargoyle's Quest*, tackling the complexities of nonlinear action driven by narrative and character growth on a platform where everyone else struggled to make simple, straightforward formats work without feeling overly compromised. It's a bold, ambitious effort, and it surprisingly works.

CAPCOM CREATED

A BRILLIANT PORTABLE ACTION-RPG IN *GARGOYLE'S QUEST* BY STREAMLINING AND SIMPLIFYING THE GENRE TO WORK BETTER WITHIN THE CONFINES OF THE GAME BOY, THEN OBSCURING ITS LINEARITY TO GIVE A CONVINCING ILLUSION OF PLAYER AGENCY AS YOU EXPLORE THE TINY WORLD.

Capcom succeeded by turning to a savvy solution here, one that would become a defining trait of portable adventures until the Nintendo Switch shattered the barrier between portable and console gaming nearly thirty years later: streamlining and simplifying the genre. *Gargoyle's Quest* looks like a free-roaming adventure thanks to its top-down RPG framing, but in truth it really offers only a single path through the story. Each major phase of the adventure boils down to gathering clues and tips from NPCs, then venturing through a string of random encounters in order to complete a dungeon where you defeat a boss and collect a power that enables you to advance to the next sequence.

To its credit, *Gargoyle's Quest* does an excellent job of obscuring this linearity to create an illusion of player agency. You can wander off the main path just enough to create the sensation of poking at the edges of the world and venturing into spaces you're not meant to go yet. And, as Firebrand grows in power, the action doubles back into earlier areas long enough to give you the opportunity to flex your new abilities and enhanced strength in a way that reinforces that it's not your imagination—you really *are* that much more powerful now. By organizing the quest into a journey of easily digested pieces, Capcom creates a perfect handheld structure for a relatively long-term adventure. In a system defined by quick, pick-up-and-play sessions, the introduction of dungeons that only take ten or fifteen minutes to complete works perfectly. It's challenging enough that you won't always finish each dungeon on your first attempt, but the compact encounter spaces mean that if you need to shut down your Game Boy midway through, you'll lose little progress. And you can easily return to the nearest town to save as

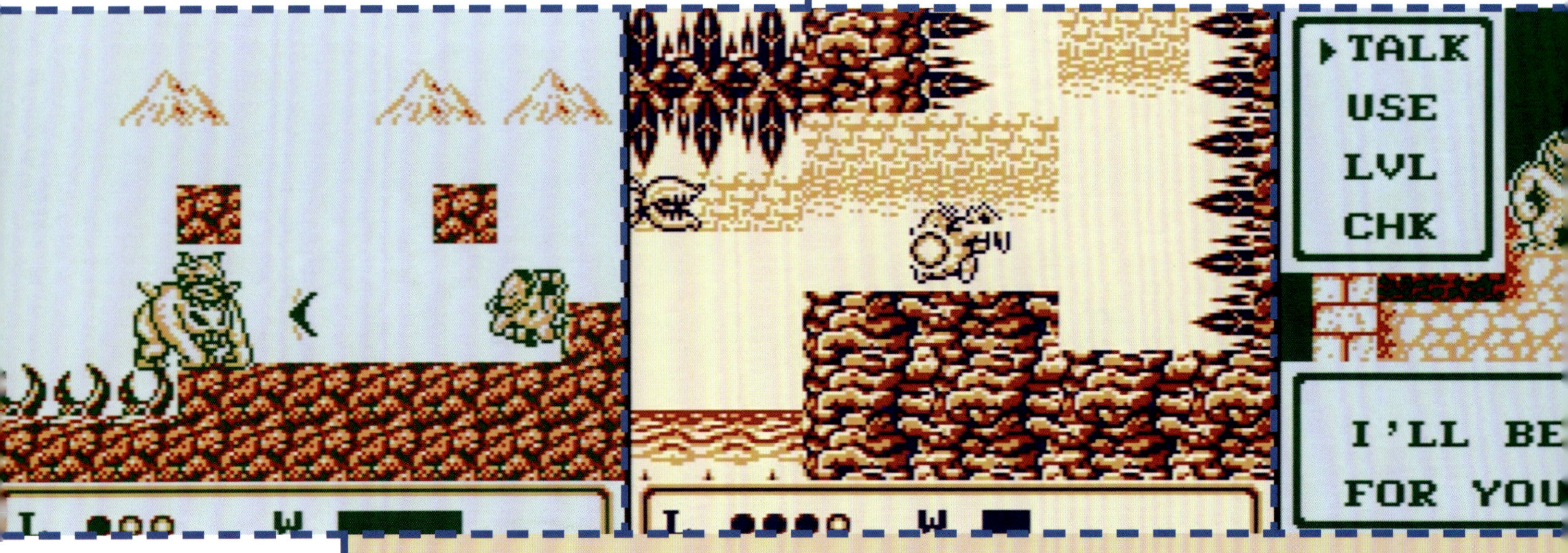

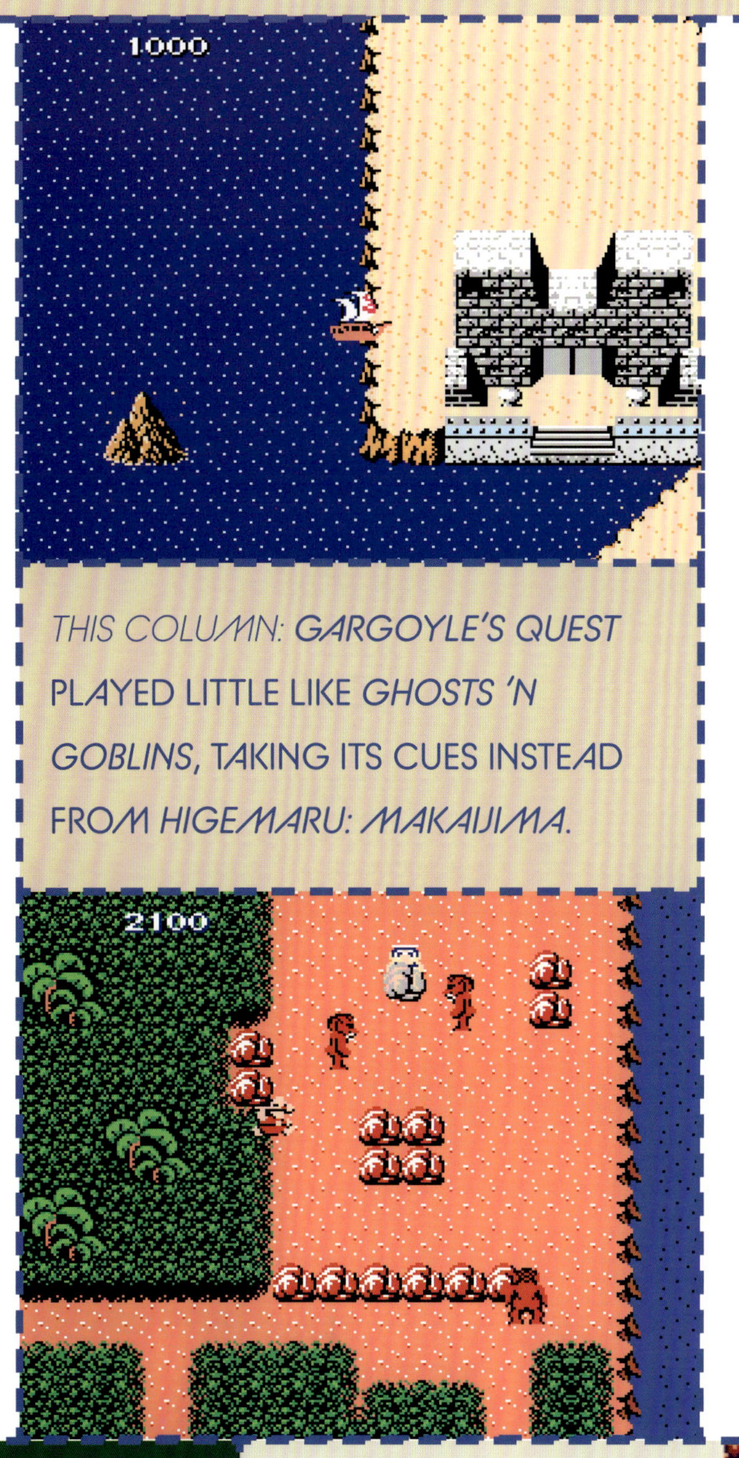

THIS COLUMN: GARGOYLE'S QUEST PLAYED LITTLE LIKE *GHOSTS 'N GOBLINS*, TAKING ITS CUES INSTEAD FROM *HIGEMARU: MAKAIJIMA*.

needed. On top of that, *Gargoyle's Quest* doesn't contain an experience or stat system per se, so you don't need to record your progress until you hit a major milestone an acquire a new ability, weapon, or life upgrade. Again, this means that if you find a play session interrupted and have to shut down your Game Boy before completing a dungeon, you don't lose anything by not being able to save on the spot.

Despite its simplified design, *Gargoyle's Quest* is anything but simplistic. As Firebrand's abilities grow, he gains skills that stand out as unique even today. Firebrand augments his flight powers with the ability to cling to surfaces—giving him a more precise and nuanced version of Strider Hiryu's triangle jump. This power factors into his skill enhancements and gives players reason not to simply treat the latest of their protagonist's attack upgrades as the de facto combat option. Notably, one of the attacks he acquires toward the middle of the game creates a temporary safe membrane over spike-lined walls, allowing you to cling to surfaces that would normally cause injury. This ability is never duplicated, and spiked walls continue to appear throughout the quest, so you'll often want to "downgrade" the attack Firebrand has equipped to achieve better mobility in hazardous spaces.

All these factors combine to create a game that barely plays like the other entries in its parent franchise, yet which feels wholly faithful to its predecessors. *Gargoyle's Quest* demands the same precise control and willingness to endure repeated failure as *Ghosts 'N Goblins*, yet it never pushes too hard against the limitations of its portable platform. In that sense, it really does feel like a kindred spir- it to *Higemaru: Makaijima*. Where that game sought to discover the optimal form for a Famicom adventure, *Gargoyle's Quest* tests the boundaries of another new gaming format. It's a stunning success in that regard, and, again, the examples Capcom established here would become standards for future portable metroidvanias.

Look at the likes of *Metroid II* and *Metroid Fusion*, the portable exploratory *Castlevania* titles, or even landmark works in kindred genres like *The Legend of Zelda: Link's Awakening*. Each of those games would take a different approach than their console kin, downsizing their worlds, breaking their quests into easily digestible chunks, and giving the player clearer guidance—a model established here in an offshoot of a series known for pure, nerve-jangling, arcade action.

Even if it doesn't entirely exemplify the traits we think of as "metroidvania," *Gargoyle's Quest* proved the platform action-RPG can work on a handheld system despite the decreased power and graphical output of portable devices compared to consoles, computers, and arcade cabinets. And, while brief by modern standards, it's still compelling even today—the ultimate sign of a great game. *M*

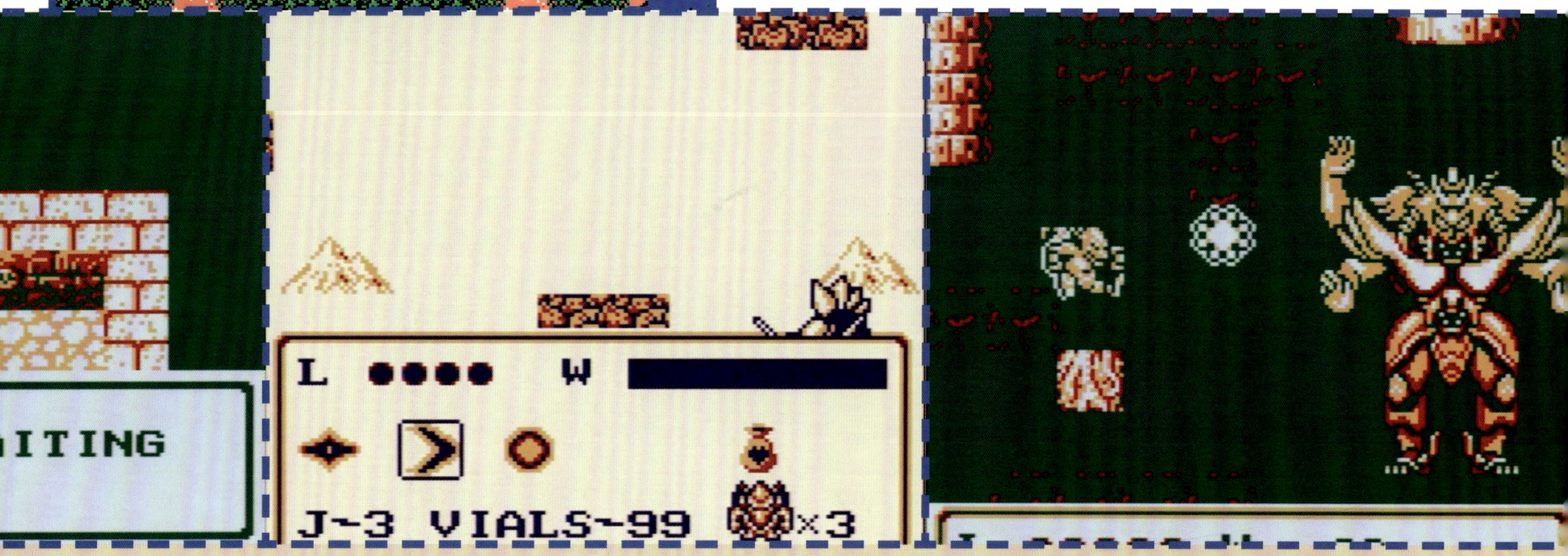

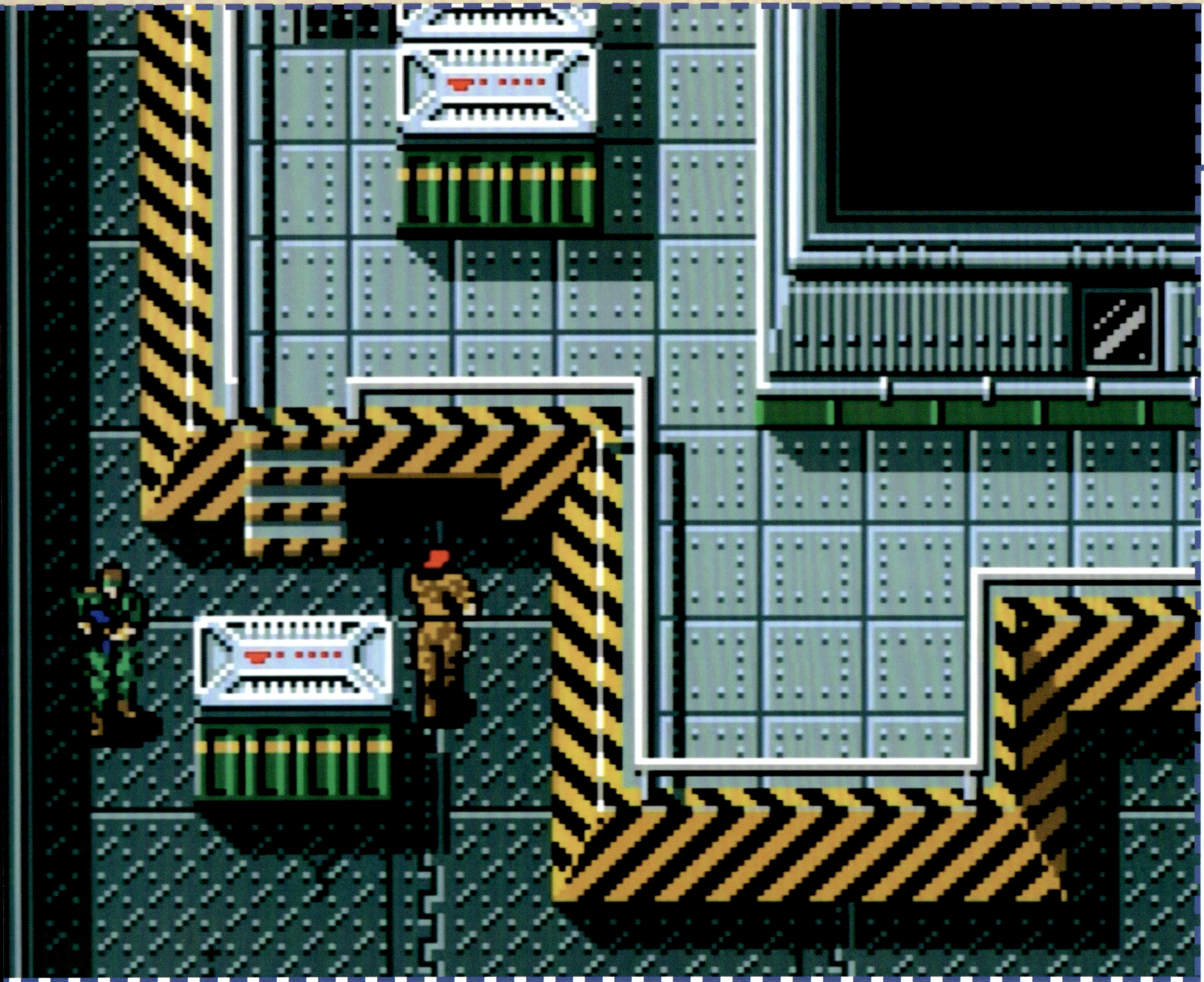

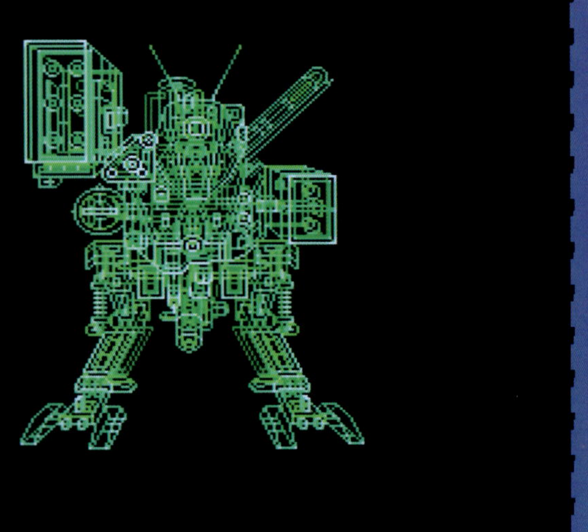

METAL GEAR 2
SOLID SNAKE

PLATFORM: **MSX2**
DEV: **KONAMI** | PUB: **KONAMI**
INITIAL RELEASE DATE: **JULY 1990**

NOTABLE FOR: **PERFECTING THE ACTION-RPG**

INTRUSIVE THOUGHTS

As the 1980s rolled into the 1990s, the evolution of action-RPGs reached what arguably represents the pinnacle of the format—a transcendent work—on 8-bit platforms: *Metal Gear 2: Solid Snake* for MSX2. This was the second of two games that putatively counted as "Metal Gear 2," arriving in the wake of *Snake's Revenge* for the NES. This confusion resulted from the success of *Metal Gear* in the West. Sales of the rearranged American NES port eclipsed the performance of the original on the MSX (and the Famicom release of the NES port). This inspired Konami to create a samizdat follow-up for the American market called *Snake's Revenge*. While not terrible, this effort didn't capture the vibe of the original game, lacking its thoughtful, stealth-forward level design and enemy placement. Players instead found themselves funneled into an action-oriented play style, further reinforced by the introduction of side-view action sequences—yet another case of a top-down adventure series following in the footsteps of *Zelda II*.

That Konami saw fit to create a *Metal Gear* successor (not to mention the questionable fidelity of that effort) inspired *Metal Gear* lead designer Hideo Kojima to stump for a proper sequel for the MSX2, a platform that Konami had supported heavily throughout its long life. The company agreed, and Kojima delivered a work that improved on his previous creation in nearly every respect. *Metal Gear 2* carries forward all the key features of the previous game, including its overall action-RPG vibe: that is, *Zelda* with rocket launchers. However, this sequel adopts a more linear structure, providing players with greater guidance by way of radio conversations. While protagonist Solid Snake made extensive use of his transceiver in the first adventure, the messages largely dealt with gameplay tips. What little story the game contained also unfolded via radio, but calling the plot slight would be an understatement; its entire script would fit on a single page.

Narrative plays a vastly larger role in the game this time, with a massively expanded script that gives Snake's radio contacts a larger, more active role in the adventure. At one point, one ally is even abducted, launching a sub-quest in which you need to seek out and rescue her. *Metal Gear 2* also introduces in-world NPCs

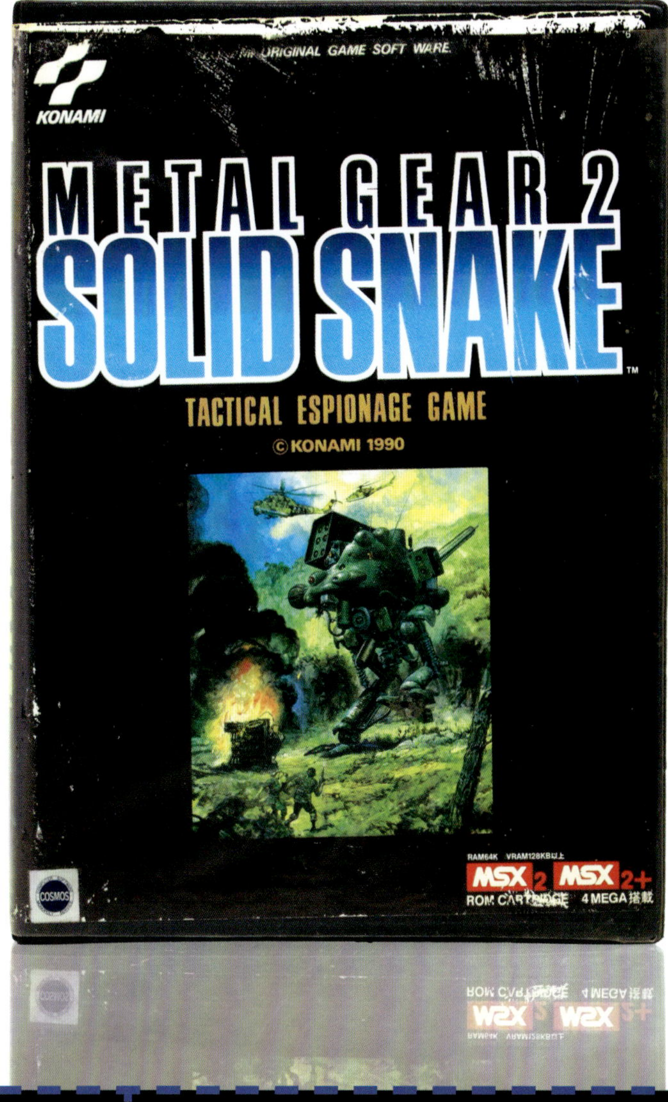

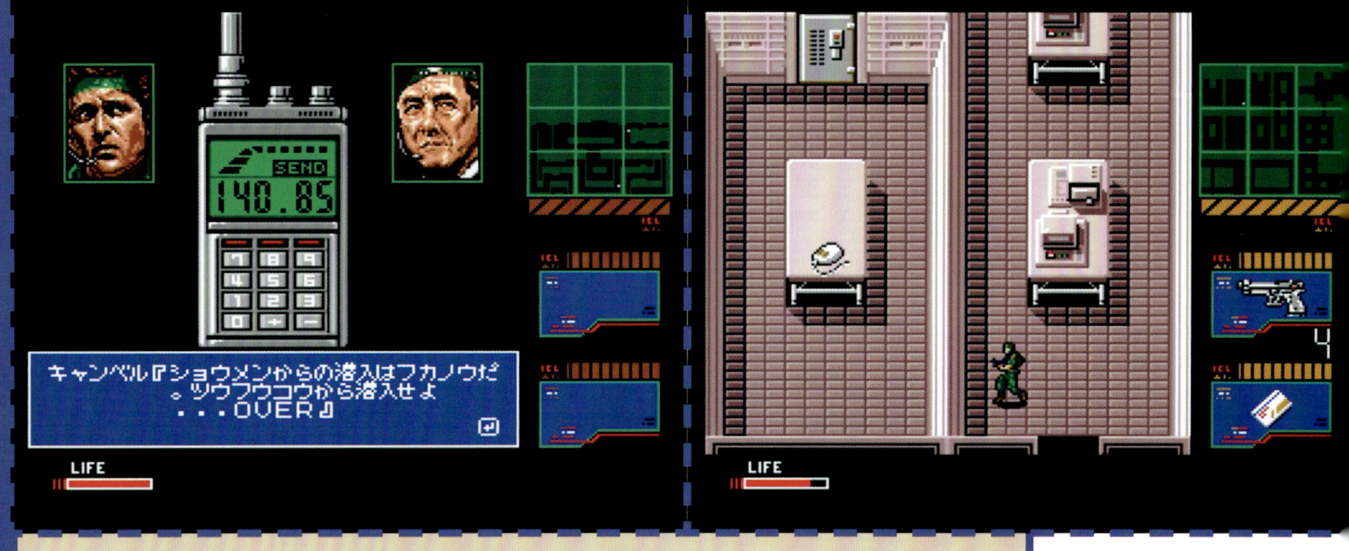

besides allies and enemy soldiers, largely in the form of children who inexplicably wander the corridors of the military fortress that Snake infiltrates. Inexplicable, at least, until the plot comes into focus and we see perhaps the first instance of Kojima as a writer attempting to grapple with geopolitics—an early example of video games channeling the sort of commentary (damning warfare through war fiction) that defined anime megahit *Mobile Suit Gundam*. It also introduces Kojima's love of meta-text, with an MSX cartridge manufactured by Konami playing a significant role in the plot.

Mechanically, *Metal Gear*'s heavy emphasis on stealth and silent combat carries forward here, along with Snake's dual-menu inventory system that divides weapons and gear into separate categories. But everything that returns from the original incorporates new features to add greater depth. For example, stealth once again revolves around enemy line of sight and hearing, but more elements of the environment create noise that can give away your position: loose flooring, sand, and more. Snake can minimize the sounds he creates by making use of his newly added ability to crawl, which causes him to move at a more deliberate pace and balances out his weight to avoid triggering noisy floors. Crawling has other benefits, too. For instance, going in low and slow over a minefield allows you to safely deactivate the mines and add them to your inventory. More importantly, crawling allows you to slip through narrow spaces, which opens up new stealth and exploration options. Crawling under a vehicle or into a vent lets you avoid being spotted in more elegant ways than playing hide-and-seek around corners.

Slipping into those narrow spaces allows you to take paths that wouldn't have existed otherwise. It allows you to move "outside" of the game space, infiltrating the enemy installation through service corridors, vents, and crawlspaces. The idea of coaxing players to break the boundaries of visible level design had been in play since at least 1985, when *Super Mario Bros.* rewarded those who asked, "What happens if I jump over the top of the screen?" by giving them warp zones. *Metal Gear 2* requires the player to exploit this sort of logic—something that *Metroid Fusion* (and, in a non-metroidvania example, *Portal*) would do to great effect more than a decade later.

The concept of what constitutes "active play space" itself takes a level up in *Metal Gear 2* thanks to the addition of a critical new game mechanic: the radar system. Presented as a small green box in the upper-right corner, the radar effectively replaces the first game's cumbersome binocular mechanic. *Metal Gear*'s binoculars allowed players to peek ahead one screen in any cardinal direction to get a sense of geography and enemy locations beyond their immediate location, but it came at the cost of forcing the player to fumble

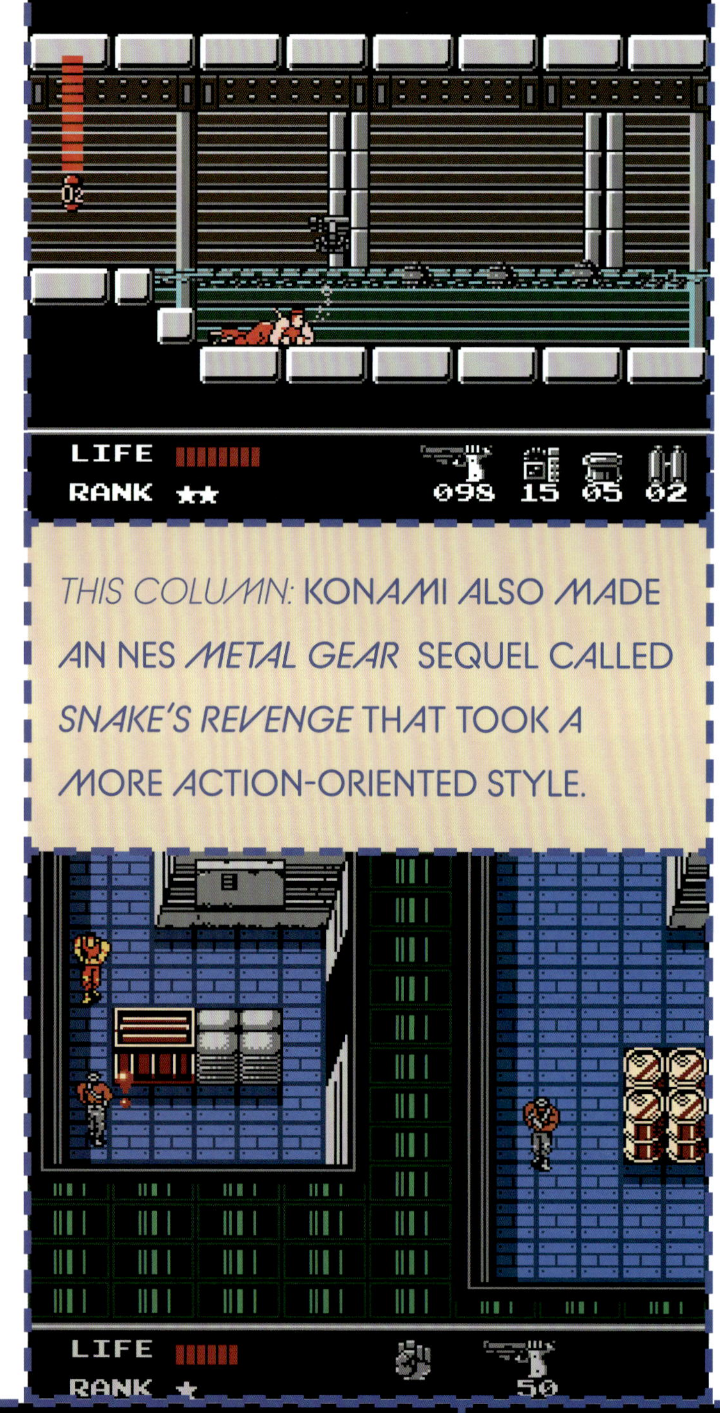

THIS COLUMN: KONAMI ALSO MADE AN NES *METAL GEAR* SEQUEL CALLED *SNAKE'S REVENGE* THAT TOOK A MORE ACTION-ORIENTED STYLE.

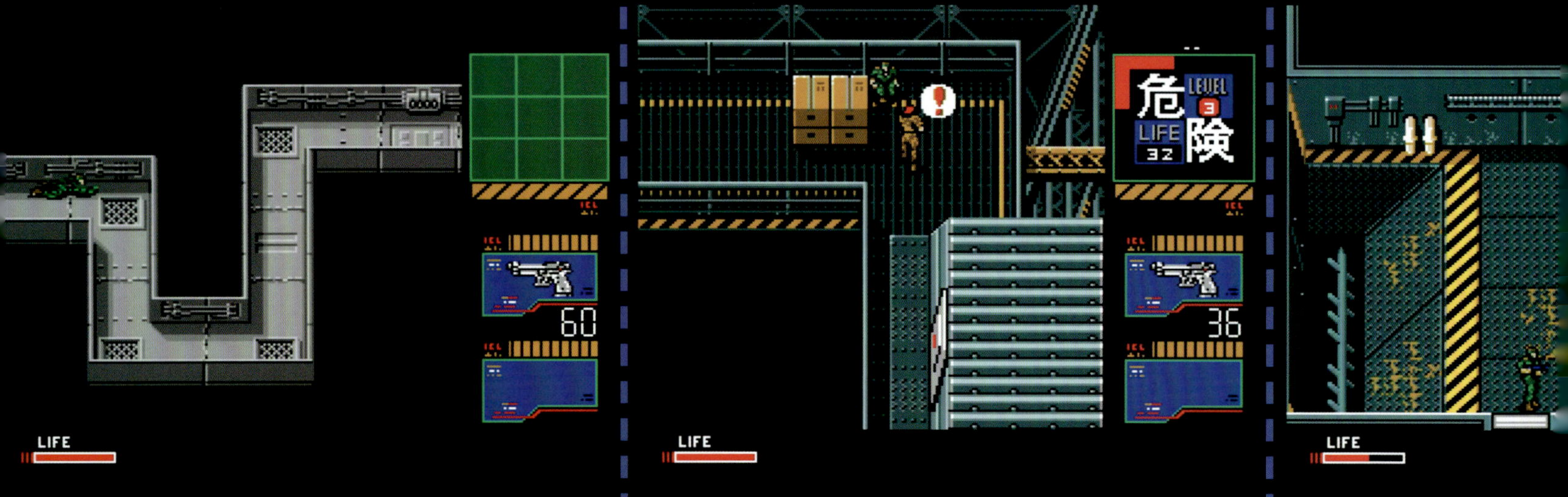

through menus and rendering the action inert while the binoculars remained in play. The radar offers the same benefits, but it does so seamlessly; it presents players with an abstraction of surrounding rooms on a 3×3 grid and simultaneously tracks Snake's position and the movement of enemies as small dots.

Although *Metal Gear 2* operates on the same screen-by-screen level design and movement as the original game—a concession to the MSX2's meager scrolling capabilities—the addition of the radar indicator means that the actual active space at any given moment spans nine screens. Enemies can move freely between spaces, and Snake's actions (such as creating noise and killing guards) maintain an element of persistence lacking in *Metal Gear*. Kill a guard and cross the edge transition back and forth into that screen again and the dead foe no longer respawns but instead remains out of action. Play Zanzibar Land's rousing patriotic anthem when you enter a room and soldiers on adjacent screens will stand at attention. Stumble into a guard's line of sight and the alert phase spans an entire zone, not just a single screen, and all enemies in that space will pass through multiple alert phases as they spread out and search for Snake. Although the original *Metal Gear* operated like this to a certain degree, it always felt inconsistent and arbitrary; here, these phases obey more predictable rules.

> THE ADDITION OF A RADAR INDICATOR TO THE *METAL GEAR* SANDBOX MEANS THAT THE ACTUAL ACTIVE PLAY SPACE AT ANY GIVEN MOMENT EXTENDS BEYOND THE PLAYER'S CURRENT SCREEN IN ALL DIRECTIONS, FORCING YOU TO PAY ATTENTION TO THREATS ACROSS NINE SCREENS AT ONCE.

All this results in a game world that feels larger and less video-game-like than that of *Metal Gear*. And the radar's electronic nature leaves the door open for interesting gameplay twists; you'll occasionally find your radar taken out of action due to interference or the loss of your inventory, forcing you to rely on direct visual observation and stealth rather than by charting the current situation on the radar monitor. This consideration for gameplay systems and the workings of the world runs throughout *Metal Gear 2*. It manifests in small ways, like the need to wait for elevators to arrive at your current floor, unlike in the previous game. You can't simply duck into an elevator at any time to escape the heat of an enemy patrol. Instead, you need to consider the timing of patrol movements versus an elevator's arrival time when planning your ascent. Similarly, the oxygen mask now has limited oxygen, creating a new consideration when in gas-flooded areas. Even things like language matter; the Czech scientist Dr. Marv doesn't speak English, and the need to translate his remarks sends you off on yet another side quest.

Overall, *Metal Gear 2* feels more puzzle-like than its predecessor, though it also has a more guided, linear structure. It's difficult to call *Metal Gear 2* an action-RPG despite its roots in the genre. Given its fairly rigid narrative progression, lack of character experience, and absence of an economy, it shares little in common with what the genre had evolved to become by 1990—games like *Crystalis* or *Ys III*. Which is not a knock on the game by any means. On the contrary, it's a masterpiece, with a design so good that Konami and Kojima would be remake it almost verbatim three times with *Metal Gear Solid* (1998, PlayStation), the other *Metal Gear Solid* (2000, Game Boy Color), and *Metal Gear Solid 2* (2001, PlayStation 2). But, just as the action-RPG had diverged from the metroidvania over time, *Metal Gear 2* diverges from the action-RPG to become the template for a genre that would become fairly dominant in the late '90s. That is, a narrative-driven action game that offers players a moderate amount of freedom to explore and investigate in each moment-to-moment scenario but whose overall structure and flow kept things moving along a well-defined journey according to the developers' story setup.

That makes *Metal Gear 2* a kindred spirit to the likes of *Gargoyle's Quest* or even the linear Japanese console RPGs taking form around the same time. Menu-based commands and party mechanics aside, is there really that much dividing narrative-driven adventures like *Metal Gear 2* and *Final Fantasy IV*? So I suppose you could say this is an action-RPG—just in terms that barely resemble where the genre began a decade earlier. That's evolution. *M*

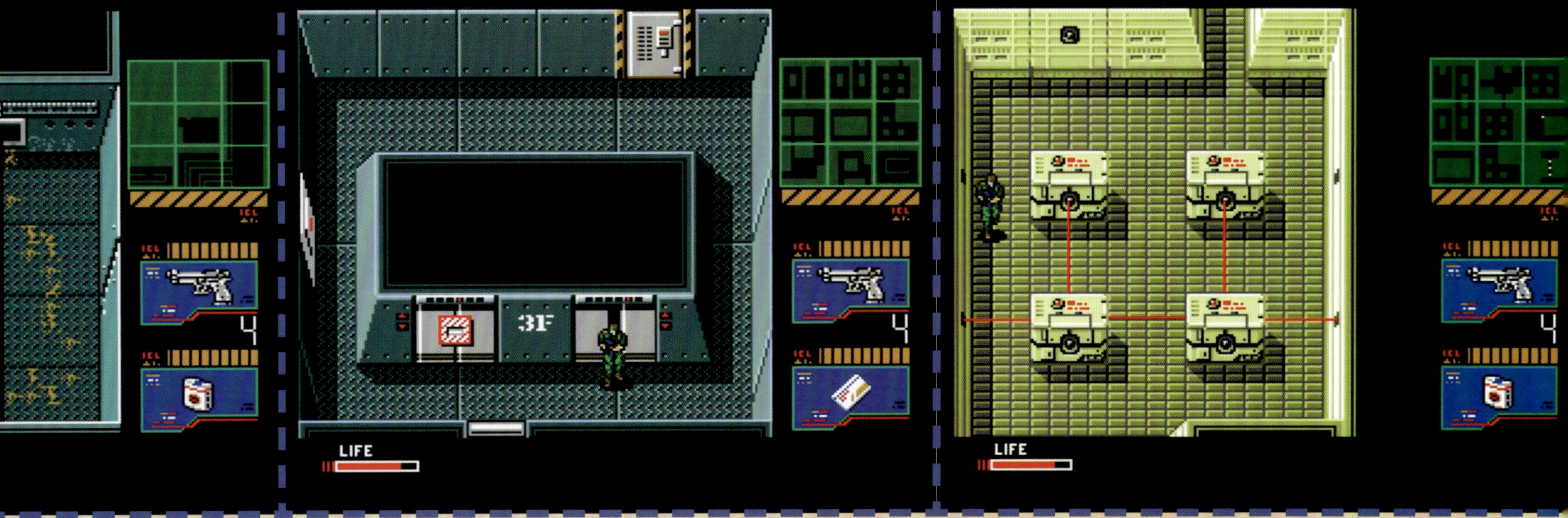

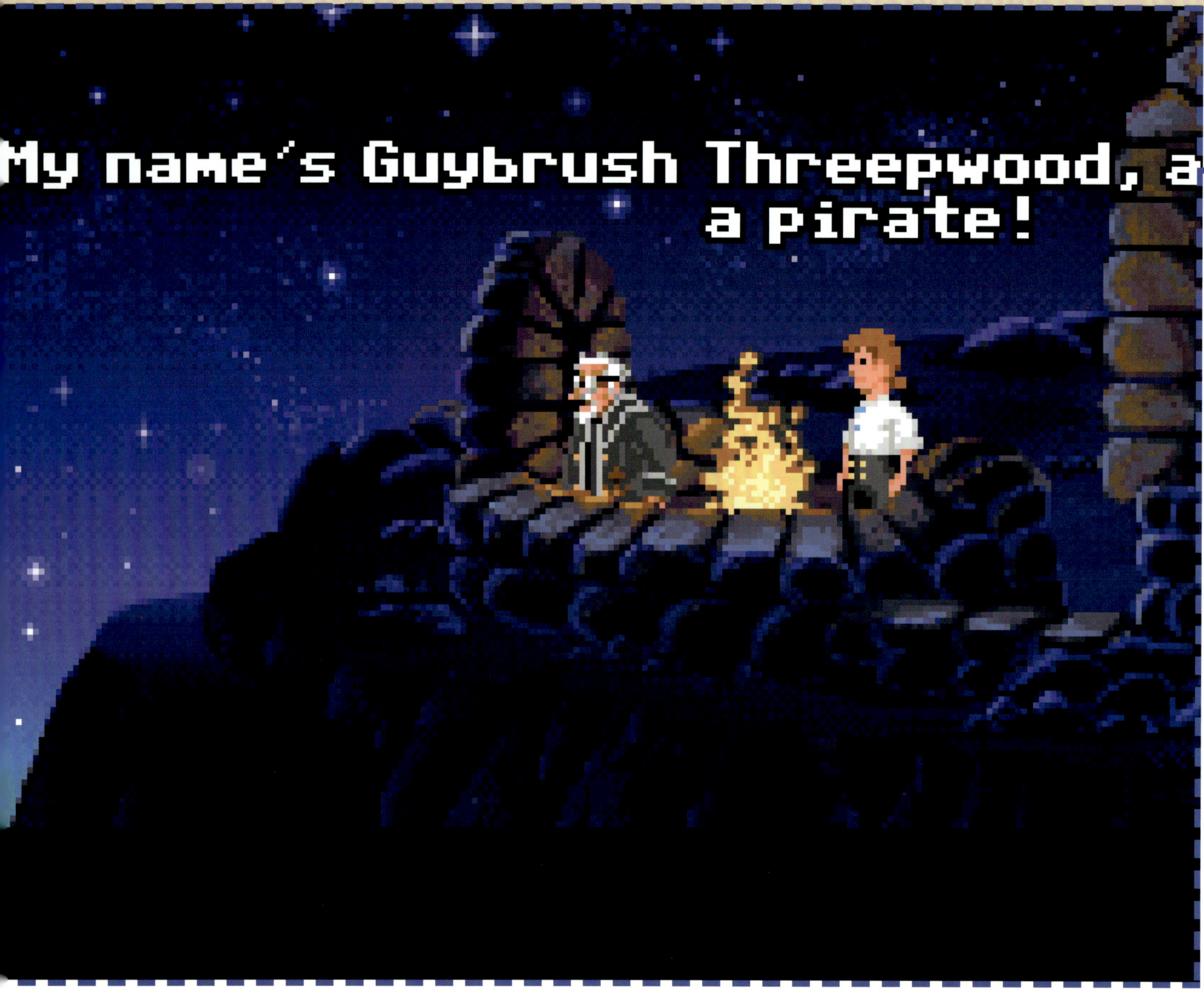

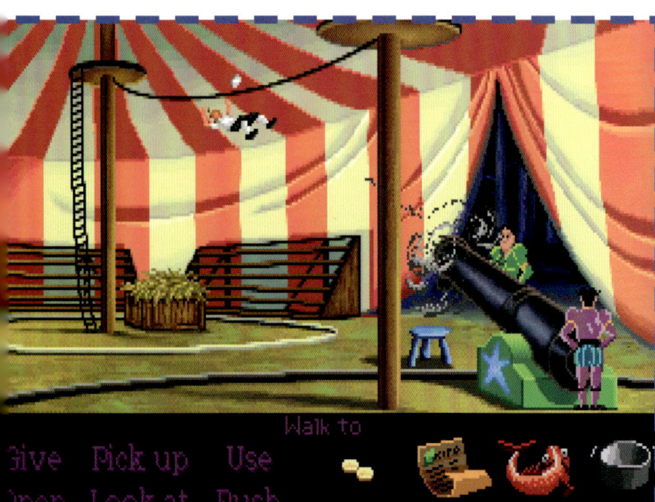

THE SECRET OF MONKEY ISLAND

PLATFORM: **PC / VARIOUS**
DEV: **LUCASFILM GAMES** | PUB: **LUCASFILM GAMES**
INITIAL RELEASE DATE: **OCT. 1990**

IN THE END, IT'S ALL MONKEY BUSINESS

Wither the classic adventure genre at the end of the 1980s? RPGs (and thus action-RPGs and metroidvanias) owe much to games like *Zork*, *Mystery House*, and *Portopia Renzoku Satsujin Jiken*, but these genres went their separate ways quite early on. Text adventures all but vanished as computers evolved sufficient processing power to display nice graphics. Graphical adventures evolved in a sort of feedback loop, growing ever larger, prettier, and more opaque—with one key exception.

Lucasfilm Games, a side venture of the studio responsible for *Star Wars* and *Indiana Jones*, evolved the menu-driven style of *Portopia* with their quirky 1987 adventure *Maniac Mansion*. They shifted away from the cryptic solutions of games like *King's Quest* in favor of outcomes that rewarded players with a sense of humor and a willingness to try doing goofy things. *Maniac Mansion* greatly reduced the bloodthirsty nature of these games, with few instant-kill surprises (and those that remained followed logically from the player's actions, e.g., draining a makeshift nuclear reactor of water) and forcing players to really have to *work* to lose the game.

The Lucas adventure team quite literally built on that work with *The Secret of Monkey Island*, the first of many classics developed with the SCUMM engine (a.k.a. the Script Creation Utility for Maniac Mansion). *Monkey Island* did more than draw upon its predecessor's technology; it carried forward the fundamental fairness of its design. Aside from a few pun-based solutions that didn't translate effectively into other languages, *Monkey Island* presented players with a well-reasoned adventure packed with intricate puzzles that demanded lateral thinking and a sharp wit while avoiding the dead ends, sudden character fatalities, and pure-luck solutions that plagued the adventure genre throughout the 1980s. It placed its emphasis on sharp writing and a fundamental sense of trust that the player could find the keys and answers to explore its compact, interconnected world on their own.

While adventure gaming had thoroughly diverged from metroidvanias and action-RPGs by this point, *The Secret of Monkey Island* proved that these games still shared a key quality in common: Enticing and rewarding player curiosity.

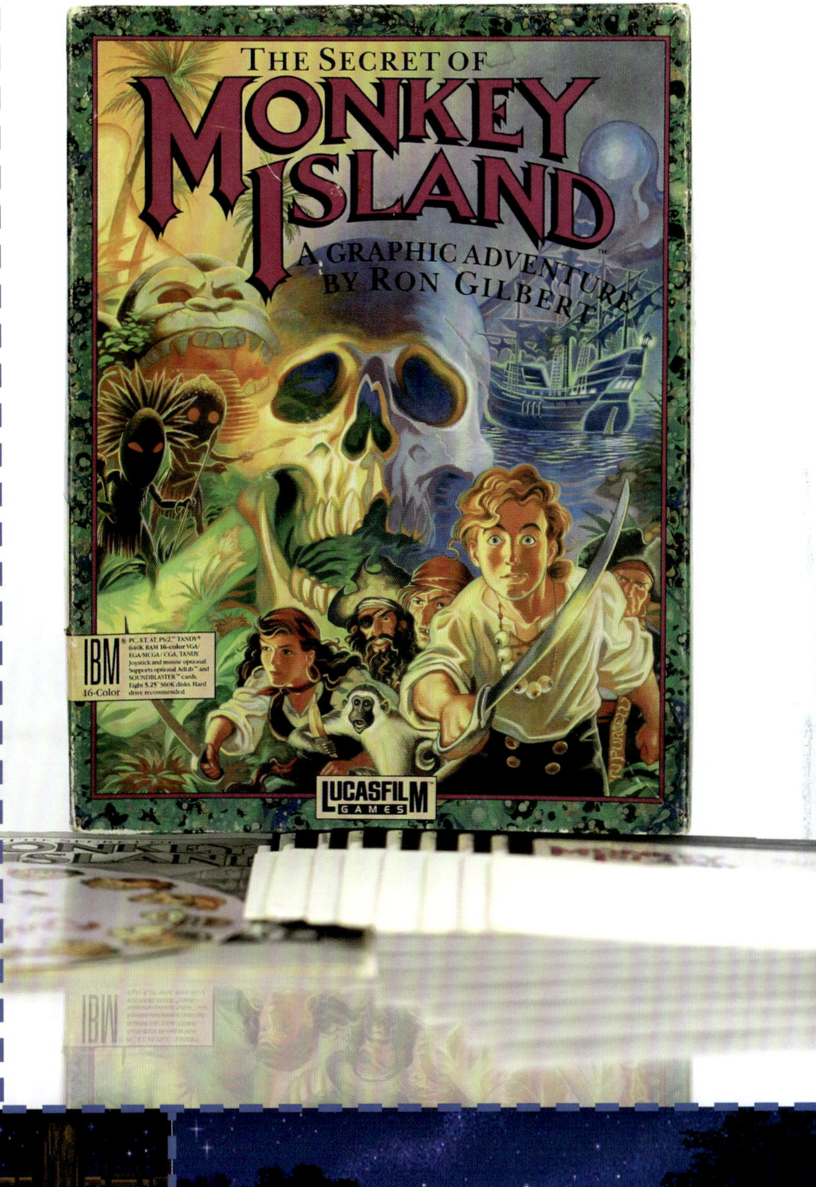

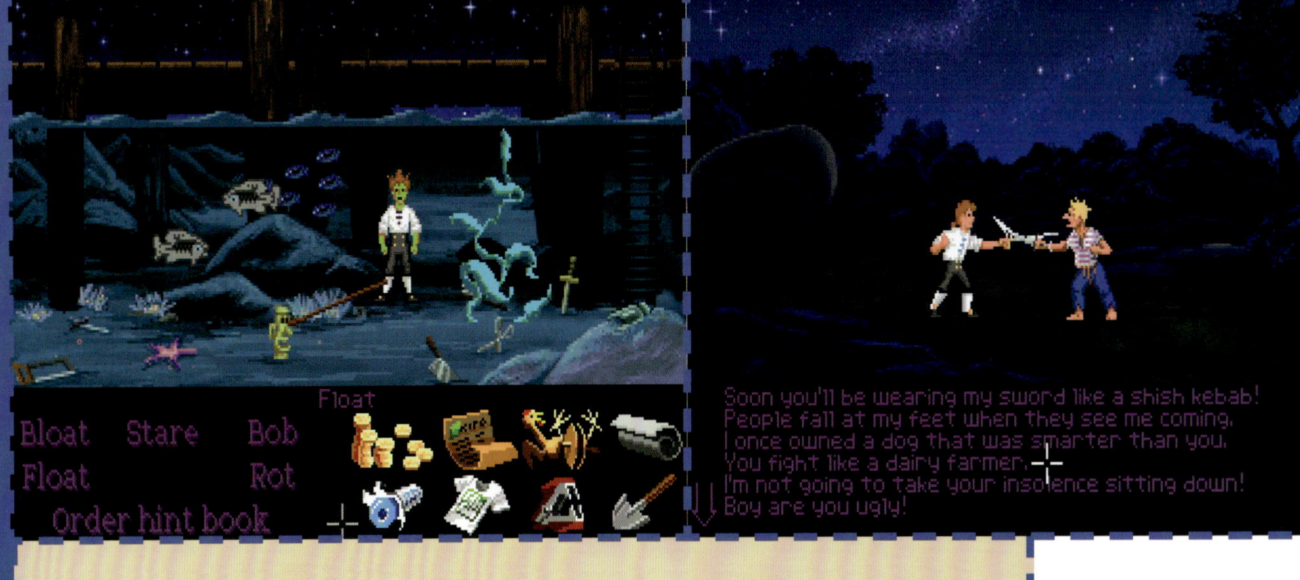

GLOSSARY OF TERMS

Action-RPG: A game that combines role-playing dynamics with the more direct, skill-and reflex-oriented approach of coin-operated arcade games. For example, where Namco's *Pac-Man* was strictly an action game, the same company's *Tower of Druaga* counts as an action-RPG because it takes the *Pac-Man* maze-chase format and incorporates elements like swords and sorcery and the potential for permanent character growth.

Note that this can be a somewhat contentious term; while I've used it to denote games that involve direct control over character action with role-playing mechanics lurking beneath the surface, gamers who cut their teeth on PC software in the 1990s usually have games like Blizzard Entertainment's *Diablo* in mind when they say "action-RPG." To these players, titles like *Diablo* feel fundamentally abstract and hands-off due to their minimal use of menus in favor of streamlined commands, and in which combat plays out in the same view as exploration. It's a subtle distinction, but one that makes some people very angry!

Arcade: A social or commercial space in which video game enthusiasts gather to play coin-operated amusements. The pay-to-play mechanisms of an arcade game generally result in a streamlined style of play and the need for high skill. Metroidvania games could be said to result from applying an arcade-focused mindset to role-playing adventures.

Automap: An automatically generated map of player progression through a game. Early exploratory games such as *Wizardry* and *Zork* expected players to chart their movements with pen-and-paper, but eventually the likes of *The Legend of Zelda* and *The Guardian Legend* normalized the presence of in-game charts that tracked the hero's movements. These have since become a fixture of the medium.

Character Growth: Not in the literary sense. In video games, this refers to the expansion of skills possessed by a player's onscreen avatar. In arcade games, character growth usually appears in a temporary form, such as Mario's hammer in *Donkey Kong* or *Pac-Man*'s energizers. A key component of metroidvania games is the idea that a character's growth has an element of permanence, so that once acquired that power remains a part of the player's skill set for the remainder of the adventure. For example, Samus's High Jump Boots in *Metroid* or the more durable armor the hero purchases in *Faxanadu*. Once acquired, these items remain a feature of the gameplay (unless they are improved on even further by later upgrades).

Console: A computer device designed to plug into a television, usually with minimal need for fine-tuning but also offering more limited capabilities, input options, and upgrade potential than a proper personal computer.

Experience: A component of character growth in many action-RPGs and metroidvanias, drawn from role-playing games. Experience commodifies and codifies the concept of skill improvement, assigning a numeric value to player tasks. Defeat a monster and your hero gains a certain number of experience points; defeat a more powerful monster and they'll gain even more experience. At a certain point, they'll have gained sufficient experience to increase their skill level. It therefore behooves players to seek experience gain through actions that increase it (typically but not always via combat) and to work toward tasks that result in greater experience gain. In most cases, the more experience an action generates, the more difficult or dangerous it is to perform, introducing a calculation of risk versus reward.

Gating: A game design practice that creates temporary barriers to player progression based on various factors. The idea is that these barriers function like a gate, presenting an obstruction only until the player manages to acquire the key to unlocking that barrier. Keys can be literal keys, as in *Faxanadu* where players need to collect or purchase single-use keys themed after the royalty of a card deck (jack, queen, king, ace) or figurative ones, as in *Metroid* where Samus Aran uses weapons to open paths. Other forms of gating include:

Skill gating: A barrier that requires the player to perform specific advanced actions to advance. Boss enemies in video games often function as skill gates, as they demand deft action and reflexes compared to the moment-to-moment action that surrounds them.

Level gating: The use of experience points and player levels for limiting progression. Although typically frowned upon as a design practice, this often manifests subtly in role-play- ing games. For example, *Willow* for the NES allowed its protagonist to equip any weapon in his inventory, but he could only wield each sword clumsily until achieving a certain skill level. Likewise, many RPGs only allow mages to learn various magic skills once they possess a certain amount of wisdom.

Story gating: Blocking away areas of the game until players have achieved a specific story objective. For example, Link can't cross a bridge in *Zelda II* until he speaks to specific villagers who will activate the bridge for him. Story gates often appear with other forms of gating as part of interconnected quests.

Genre: A grouping to describe the style and design of a video game. Metroidvania games could be regarded as their own genre, or possibly as a subset of games in the action and role-playing genres (a.k.a. action-RPGs).

Level: Generally speaking, a concrete interpretation of a game character's current abilities and powers. When a player raises up a level, they typically gain tangible benefits from their success: Greater strength, endurance, or speed, for example.

Metroidvania: A portmanteau of the names "Metroid" + "Castlevania" (which themselves are portmanteaus of "metro" + "android" and "castle" + "Transylvania"), this term—and the foundation of this entire book—loosely describes a video game whose design centers around a certain degree of player freedom and empowerment. Unlike traditional arcade-style games that revolve around scores or reaching the end of a level, metroidvania games generally contain an open-ended map for players to traverse and present more narrative-style objectives than simply earning points (e.g., defeat a monster or recover an item). The term metroidvania came about to describe 1997's *Symphony of the Night,* a game in the *Castlevania* series which seemingly took its cues from Nintendo's *Metroid* games...though it later turned out that Symphony looked primarily to *The Legend of Zelda: A Link to the Past* for inspiration.

PC: A personal computer. Used here to describe any computing platform not designed specifically for use as a television-based console.

Platform: The device on which a game runs. Although game consoles and computers have always operated around similar microchips, the specifics of a given platform—e.g., the keyboard input of a computer or color limitations of a console) do much to shape a game's design ethos.

Platformer: Not to be confused with "platform." Often called "side-scrollers," even though early platformers lacked scrolling. This is a genre of game that involves leaping and climbing surfaces of varying heights. Codified by *Donkey Kong*, which required protagonist Mario to traverse girders and elevators by way of carefully timed jumps. Metroidvania games apply action-RPG concepts to this genre, resulting in arcade-style games with RPG-inspired depth and substance.

RPG: Role-playing games, which is to say, story- and statistic-driven works derived from pen-and-paper tabletop adventure systems like *Dungeons & Dragons*. Metroidvania games could also be said to result from applying an RPG mindset to action games.

Top-Down: Along with side-scrollers/platformers, this is the most common and popular format for action games. Top-down games present the action through an overhead perspective, allowing players a wider range of movement while (usually) minimizing the importance of precise jumping. Exploratory adventures in this style are typically referred to as action-RPGs rather than metroidvanias, as the latter commonly denotes a side-on perspective and emphasis on a certain degree of platforming acrobatics.

ON GAME STRUCTURE

When people talk about game design, they generally refer to moment-to-moment play considerations. How do the controls and play mechanics feel? How well is the difficulty balanced? Are the puzzles fair? Is the narrative coherent? However, when it comes to the metroidvania format, effective game design is more of a big-picture consideration. The minute particulars of the action still count for a lot, of course, but even more important than that is the way the overall adventure flows—that is, the game's structure.

When video games first entered the world, they consisted of play spaces that fit into a single screen. Everything you could see at a glance was everything the game had on offer, so you didn't need to worry about keeping anything in mind beyond the visible onscreen objects. But video games quick- ly grew more complicated. Colossal Cave Adventure and Zork used text to guide players through a world of words that they had to visualize—and, ideally, to map. Defender and Rally-X allowed players to dash around spaces far larger than a single screen, incorporating their own maps into the onscreen display so that players could keep tabs on the aggressive enemies that could move around beyond the boundaries of the active screen. Role-playing games challenged players to chart the layout of dungeons and the geography of the worlds that contained them. The Legend of Zelda allowed players to roam across a sprawling map and make permanent changes to the geogra- phy by burning away trees and bombing open rock walls.

As you've seen throughout this book, these early games ultimately evolved into the metroidvania. The genre couldn't exist until game developers had refined the way their virtual worlds fit together and how the player traversed those spaces. The following pages chart the evolution of structure through several of the games featured earlier in this book as a sort of companion to help readers visualize how these adventures fit together without actually playing them.

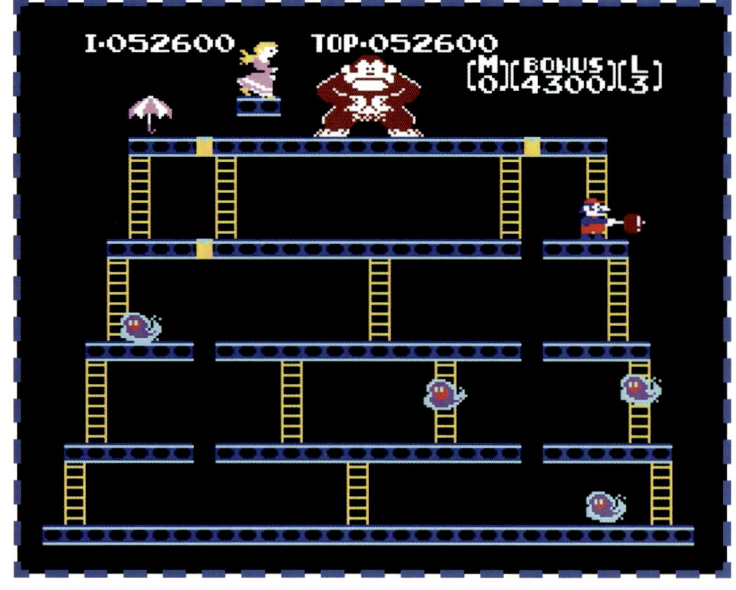

Donkey Kong
Single-Screen Linear

An archetypal arcade-action game, *Donkey Kong* consisted of a sequence of standalone single-screen spaces. Players enjoyed a fair amount of freedom to move around within each screen, but ultimately *Donkey Kong* involved strictly linear progression. It only warrants discussion in the history of metroidvania games due to its role in perfecting the mechanisms of player character movement in action games.

See Also: *Kangaroo, Chack'n Pop, Bubble Bobble.*

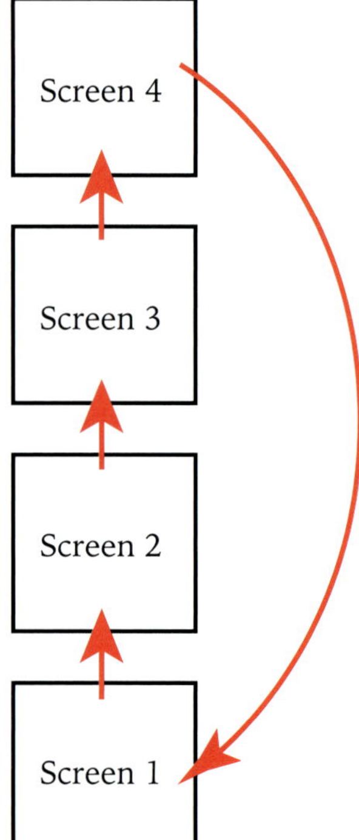

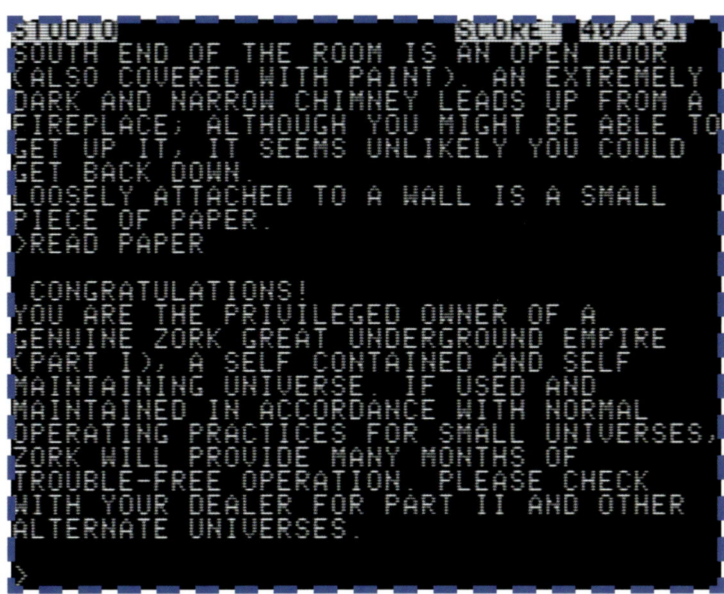

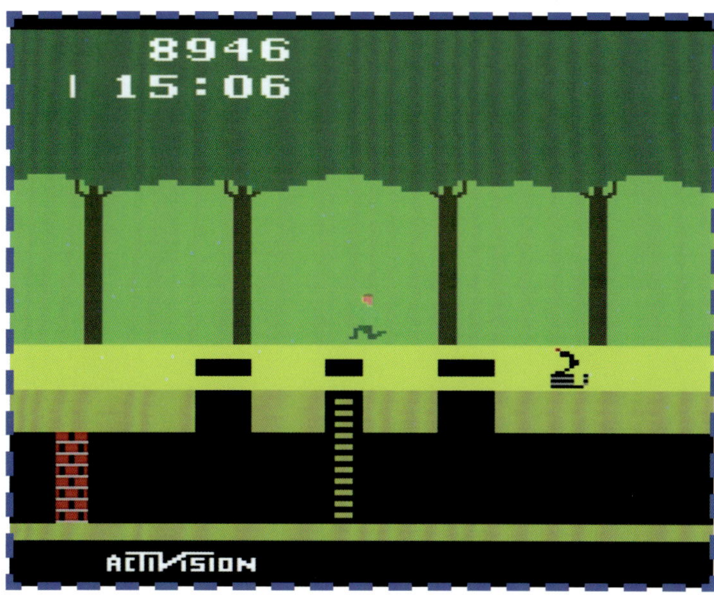

Zork

Node-based Interconnected

In stark contrast to *Donkey Kong*, *Zork* lacked any action whatsoever, playing out entirely through text. However, its world design offered near-total freedom of traversal, consisting of self-contained "rooms" interlocked through a labyrinthine series of connections. While the game used puzzles and keys to lock forward progress along certain paths, for the most part, *Zork* allowed players to travel within the world at their leisure, collecting items and observing details to piece together puzzle solutions and locate the key treasures.

See Also: *Colossal Cave Adventure*, *Shadowgate*

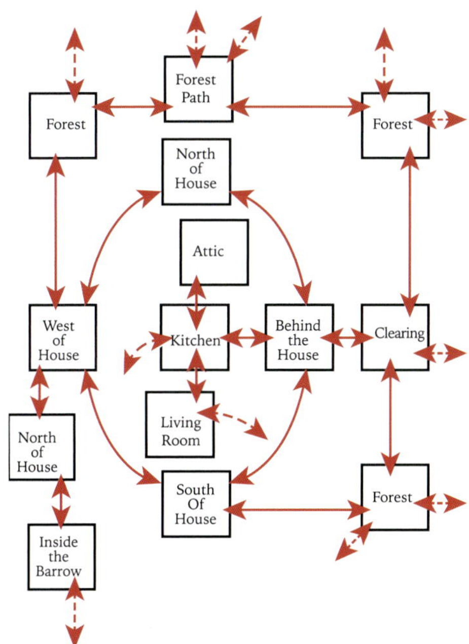

Pitfall!

Single-Screen Linear Interconnected

Building on the run-and-jump design of *Donkey Kong*, *Pitfall!* largely did away with that game's vertical elements in favor of a sort of Möbius strip: hundreds of individual screens linked one to the other on either side. A player could run the length of every screen and eventually loop back to the first. The only remaining vertical element added a touch of complexity to the design. Tunnels beneath the ground connected side to side every third screen, meaning that running off the screen to the right via tunnel would cause you to skip over two of the screens you'd see when running above ground. Players could use this as a shortcut to bypass stretches of jungle that were empty of treasure, but needed to take care they didn't shortcut their way past a crucial item in the process.

See Also: *H.E.R.O.*

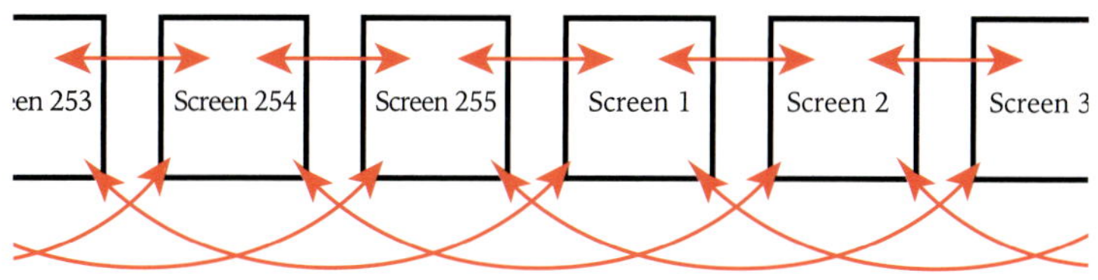

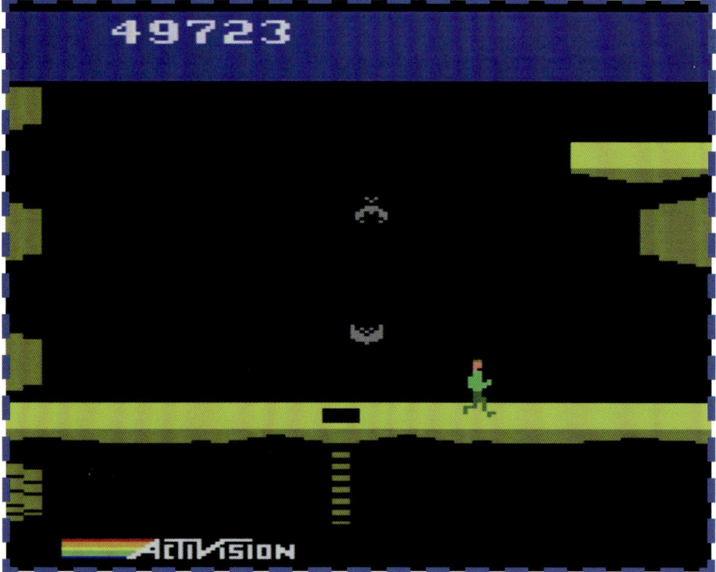

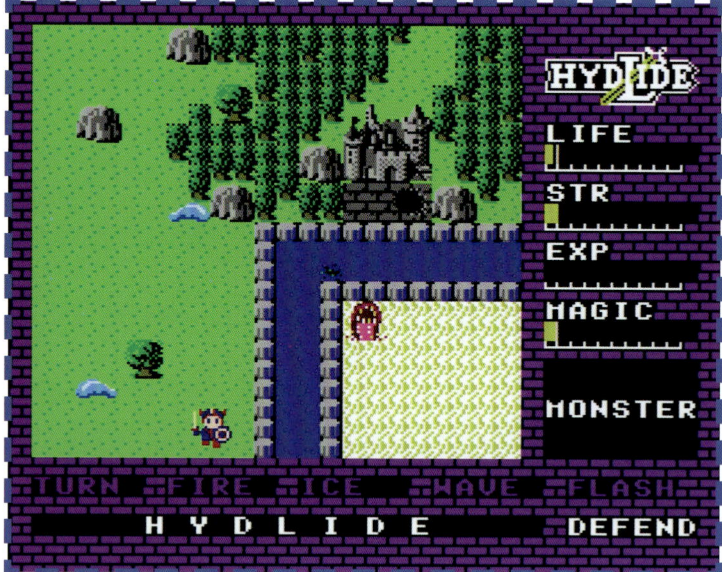

Pitfall II: Lost Caverns

Single-Screen Nonlinear Interconnected

Pitfall II did away with its predecessor's infinite loop, focusing most of its play time into a highly vertical underground space with hard boundaries along the world's perimeter. The caverns below the jungle's surface consisted of hundreds of individual, interconnected screens, which collectively created a sprawling platform maze. While theoretically possible to move freely through the underground, reaching certain areas demanded a certain degree of puzzle-solving and tool use: a *Zork*-mentality married to *Donkey Kong*–mechanics.

See Also: *Deadly Towers, Montezuma's Revenge, La-Mulana*

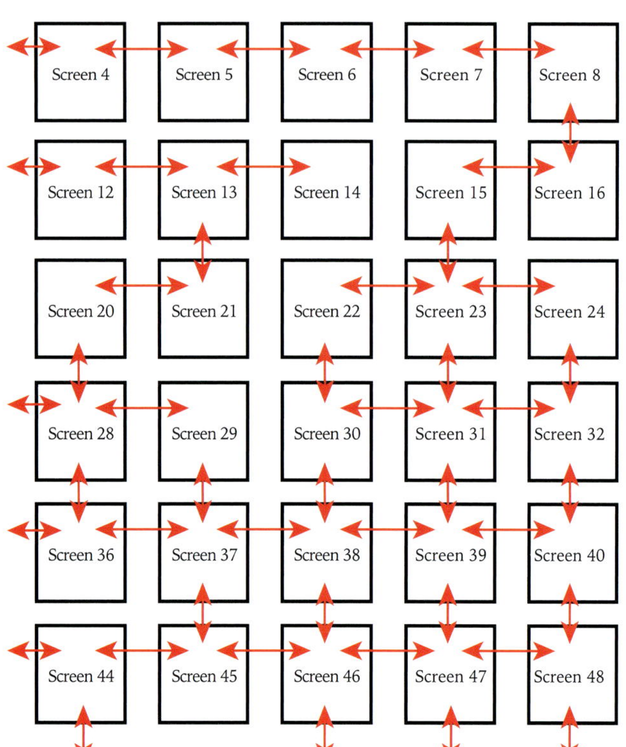

Hydlide

Open World with Sub-Zones

Another game consisting of interconnected standalone screens, *Hydlide* shifted its perspective to an overhead viewpoint reminiscent of a paper map, which helped cement the emphasis on visual geography that *Zork* could only hint at through text. With a world spanning a mere 5×5 grid of screens, *Hydlide* didn't offer much ground to explore. But within that limited space (which, like *Pitfall!*, looped infinitely on all axes), *Hydlide* contained a number of interior spaces below ground, akin to *Pitfall!*'s tunnels. These included castle interiors, dungeons, and even subterranean passages that allowed players to reach otherwise inaccessible spaces.

See Also: *Blaster Master, The Legend of Zelda, The Guardian Legend*

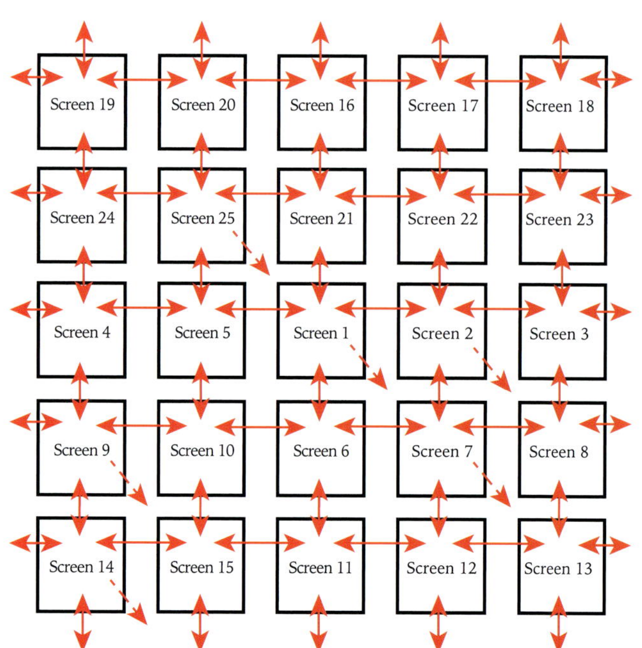

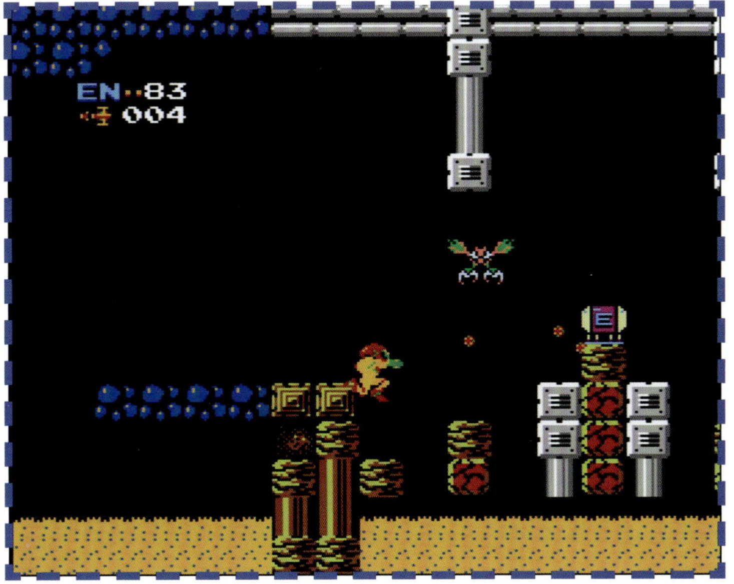

Metroid

Scrolling Zone-Based Open World

Breaking away from the single-screen format by building on the motion scroll tech of games like *Pac-Land* and *Super Mario Bros.*, *Metroid* dropped players into a fully open labyrinth of spaces divided by doors. Player progression was largely gated by barriers that could be broken open with the weapons and tools collected during gameplay. Bombs opened hidden passages, missiles broke open shielded doors, and the High Jump Boots allowed the heroine to reach elevated ground. With its freedom of movement and emphasis on player empowerment, *Metroid* became the standard that exploratory action games would copy in the years to come.

See Also: *Wonder Boy III*, *Faxanadu*

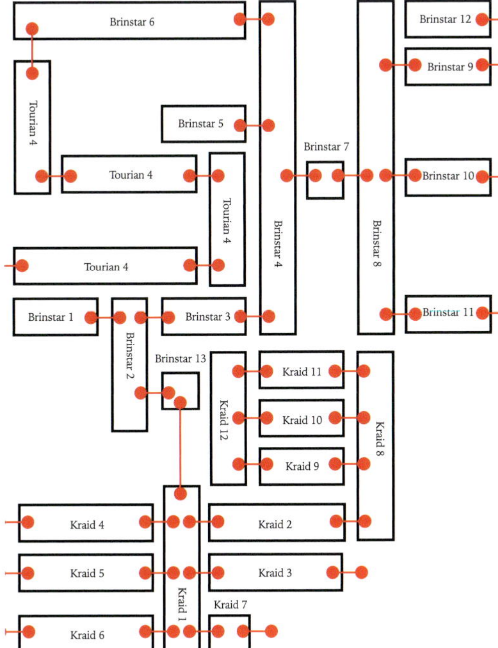

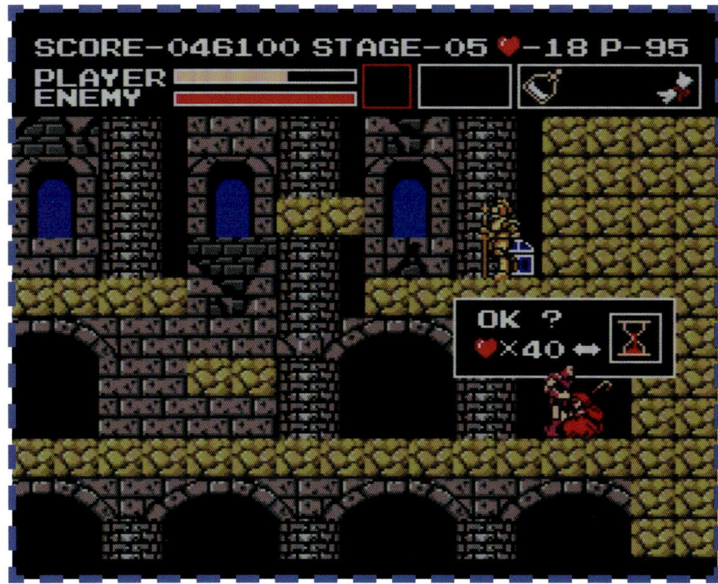

Vampire Killer

Single-Screen Linear Interconnected

Establishing a midpoint between *Pitfall!* and *Pitfall II*, *Vampire Killer* contained a dozen and a half self-contained levels con- sisting of standalone interconnected screens that often looped infinitely on one axis or another. Finding the key to the current level's exit would cause the player to advance permanently to another level, where they would enjoy free movement within that stage while lacking the ability to backtrack to earlier levels. This format was largely supplanted once gaming hardware included the ability to scroll background graphics as a universal standard, meaning that the single-screen layout style became an unnecessary technological relic.

See Also: *Guardic*

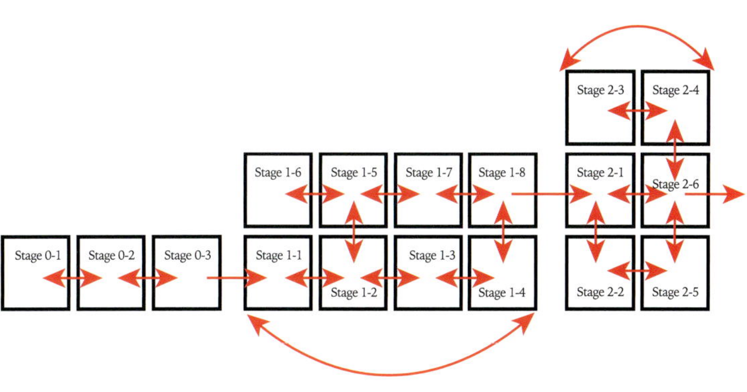

INDEX OF PLATFORMS

Mainframe & Mini Computers

Key Works:
Zork

Computing began on mainframe systems, which tended to be communal devices shared by a number of programmers who queued for precious time on these massive, expensive machines. These large-format computing machines were roughly the size of a home appliance (minicomputer) or as large as several rooms (mainframes). The earliest video games, including *Zork*, began their lives on mainframes, which makes their existence all the more remarkable. Because mainframe access time tended to be in such high demand with so few computers existing in the world, programmers often had to sneak in time to work on frivolous projects that weren't of pressing concern to the academic community.

Arcade Machines

Key Works:
Venture, Donkey Kong, The Tower of Druaga, Dragon Buster

Generally speaking, these are self-contained game systems housed in wood-and-metal cabinets and designed to be installed in public spaces where they can be operated by players in return for a small fee.

Atari 2600

Key Works:
Adventure, Pitfall!, Pitfall II: Lost Caverns

The first truly successful game console, the Atari 2600 featured limited graphics, primitive sound, and rudimentary control options. ...Yet none of this stopped determined programmers and designers from harnessing its meager capabilities for the sake of advancing the state of action game design from simple Pong clones to expansive adventures set in surprisingly immense worlds.

American Microcomputers

Key Works:
Mystery House, Wizardry, Impossible Mission, Below the Root, Shadowgate, Montezuma's Revenge

Beginning in the late 1970s, companies across the US helped transform the computer from a complex, expensive device found almost exclusively in universities and government-run complexes into a compact, affordable format suited for the average home. These computer makers ranged from plucky grassroots organizations (Apple Computer) to members of the existing business technology establishment (IBM). Although home microcomputers lacked the power and potential of room-filling mainframes and appliance-sized minicomputers, they presented users and programmers alike with a blank canvas that begged for creative exploitation. This prompt naturally led to the creation of video games, which made use of the flexible interface options and persistent memory contained on floppy diskettes and tape drives to expand the scope and complexity of games beyond anything that arcade and console software of the era could match.

Japanese Microcomputers

Key Works:
Dragon Slayer, Hydlide, Ys, Portopia Renzoku Satsujin Jiken, Xanadu

Trailing the advent of American computers by several years, Japanese PCs stood apart from overseas offerings in large part due to the visual complexity of the written Japanese language. The dense kanji and subtle kana shapes that comprise Japanese writing demanded more granular visual resolution than what was required to depict the Roman letter forms in the West. And where your find improved graphical resolution, you find more beautiful games. Japanese PC games quickly became known for their exquisite visual detail, where artful design balanced out a lack of color depth.

European microcomputers

Key Works:
Jet Set Willy, Exile, Knight Lore

In contrast to computers from Japan and the US, the machines that originated in Europe generally offered unimpressive graphical capabilities and diminished processing power. But they proved popular all the same, because manufacturers priced them accordingly. The impressive reach that resulted from this budget-friendly approach turned Europe into an incubator for technical and design innovation, as determined programmers learned to squeeze every last drop of performance out of this low-end computer hardware.

MSX / MSX2

Key Works:
Vampire Killer, Metal Gear, Legacy of the Wizard

Although the concept of a console that could expand into a full computer by way of peripheral attachments had quite a bit of traction in the early 1980s, the MSX was something different: a computer with the mindset of a console. Then again, the entire concept of the MSX itself was something out of the ordinary. Rather than belonging to or being manufactured by a single corporation, the MSX instead described a platform standard that any company could produce. This helped make the MSX one of the most popular and varied computers of the era, as its hardware releases varied from basic low-cost models to the powerful Sony-made HitBits featuring premium components and high-end storage options.

Family Computer / Nintendo Entertainment System / Disk System

Key Works:
The Legend of Zelda, Zelda II, Rygar, Castlevania II, Metroid, Blaster Master, Crystalis

Arguably the single most important gaming device of the 1980s, the NES was the first console to become a major hit on mul- tiple continents—it dominated Japan and the US throughout much of the decade. Its incredible reach and record-breaking sales figures made the NES an incredibly popular platform not only for consumers but for developers and publishers as well. With so many creators throwing their best ideas at the system, so as to stand out at retail, it was inevitable that the resulting games would grow ever more complex and in- teresting. But the true ace up the NES's sleeve was its ability to evolve at a hardware level; Nintendo's engineering team future-proofed the console by building hooks into the system that would allow it to accept external upgrades, both through peripherals and by way of extra processors built into cartridges. The introduction of the Famicom Disk System helped push console software to levels of complexity previously only seen on computers. It wasn't long before long cartridges began shipping with sophisticated supplemental chips that allowed the NES and Famicom to surpass the capabilities of the Disk System without needing the peripheral. By the time Nintendo retired the console, most games shipped on cartridges with many times more processing power and RAM than the basic hardware, and those games boasted visuals and designs that took full advantage of those capabilities.

SG-1000 / Mark III / Master System

Key Works:
Zillion, Wonder Boy III: The Dragon's Trap

The same day that Nintendo launched the Famicom in Japan, Sega shipped its SG-1000 console—effectively a ColecoVision clone. While grossly underpowered compared to Nintendo's system, that changed in 1985 when Sega launched the Mark III, which added a hefty graphics chip to the SG-1000 framework. The Mark III became the Master System in the West. Although it ultimately saw less success than the NES, Sega's support for the console—not to mention the creative and technical ambition of the company's internal development teams and partners—meant that the Master System played host to a number of cutting-edge games that added complexity and even persistence to the arcade experiences Sega fans loved.

PC Engine / TurboGrafx-16

Key Works:
Neutopia

An impressive console that saw several alternate hardware formats over the course of its lifetime (including a CD-ROM add-on and two different portable iterations), the PC Engine gave Famicom a run for its money in certain circles. The console didn't fare nearly as well in the West, where it arrived more or less day-and-date with the more capable Sega Genesis. Still, its CD-ROM expansion guaranteed that even the anemic US lineup contained some ambitious offerings that moved the needle on game design.

Game Boy

Key Works:
Gargoyle's Quest

While not the world's first portable console, Nintendo's Game Boy arrived at the perfect combination of price and capabilities. It couldn't do a lot compared to more impressive competitors like the Atari Lynx and Sega Game Gear, but the Game Boy was half their price...and it cost far less to run thanks to its battery-efficient power requirements. Game Boy's massive reach (it was the single bestselling gaming platform of the twentieth century!), along with the natural evolution of an NES-to-Game-Boy software pipeline, meant that the handheld saw some truly revolutionary releases during its lengthy lifetime. And the best of them, as seen with early RPGs like *The Final Fantasy Legend* and *Gargoyle's Quest*, demonstrated a concerted effort by their creators to truly rethink what it meant to present a large-scale adventure on a system designed for quick-fix play sessions on the go.

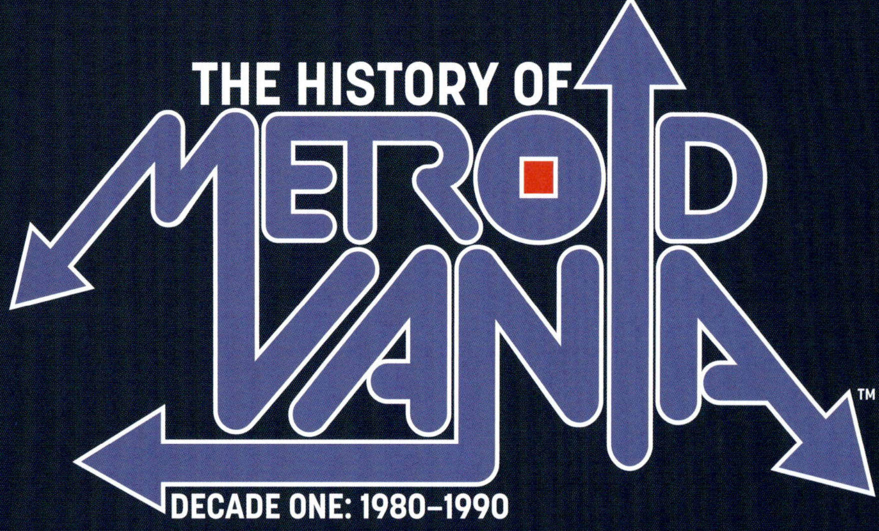

Special thanks:
All Patreon supporters, Jared Petty, Catherine Nguyen, Josh Fairhurst, Patrick Thorpe, Tim Wiesch, Jeremy Pack, Christa Lee, Analogue Co., iFixRetro, MiSTer Add-Ons, and Auston Stewart.

Copy edits by Rachel Lapidow

Some screenshots appearing in this book are courtesy of VG Museum (VGMuseum.com) and HG101 (HardcoreGaming101.net).

The History of Metroidvania is based on the YouTube video series Metroidvania Chronicles / Metroidvania Works. Text in this volume was adapted from video scripts, and game screenshots were taken from footage captured for those videos and upscaled to 720p resolution through an XRGB-Mini Framemeister unit. All images that have been sourced online rather than photographed or captured by the author are credited to the source through captions.

All packaging and product photography, as well as the offscreen CRT photography seen in page borders, was shot digitally with a Canon EOS Rebel T3i or iPhone 12 Pro Max camera.

The History of Metroidvania will return in:
Decade Two: 1991–2000

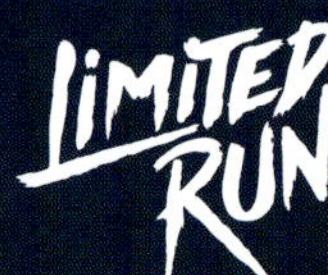

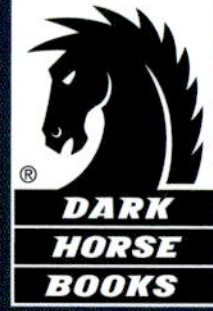